C000220986

MOTOCOURSE™

THE WORLD'S LEADING GRAND PRIX & SUPERBIKE ANNUAL

icon

PUBLISHING LIMITED

They have a MISSION

Alex Salvini
ENDURO RIDER

Takahisa
Fujinami
TRIAL
RIDER

Greg Hancock
SPEEDWAY
RIDER

Randy de Puniet
MotoGP TEST RIDER

You can make it POSSIBLE!

BE CONSIDERATE
TO OTHER SPECTATORS
TO ENSURE EVERYONE
CAN ENJOY THE EVENT.

PREVENT LITTERING
AND POLLUTION OF OUR
NATURAL ENVIRONMENT
DURING THE EVENT.

CONSIDER
YOUR OWN SAFETY
AND THAT OF OTHERS
AT ALL TIMES.

Marc Márquez
MotoGP RIDER

FIM ENVIRONMENTAL
AMBASSADOR

THE FIM ENVIRONMENTAL
AMBASSADORS
are a group of men and women
representing different disciplines
and different cultures who fully
support the FIM's commitment
to environmental values.
They have lent their voices
to the Ride Green campaign
and use their high profile as athletes
to inspire the sports community
to respect the natural environment,
act responsibly
and practise sustainable sport.

Join the conversation,
#FIMridegreen

CONTENTS

MOTOCOURSE 2016–2017

is published by:
Icon Publishing Limited
Regent Lodge
4 Hanley Road
Malvern
Worcestershire
WR14 4PQ
United Kingdom

Tel: +44 (0)1684 564511

Email: info@motocourse.com
Website: www.motocourse.com

Printed in Italy by
L.E.G.O. S.p.A.
Viale dell'Industria, 2,
I-36100 Vicenza
Email: info@legogroup.com

ISBN: 978-1910584-23-1

DISTRIBUTORS

Gardners Books
1 Whittle Drive, Eastbourne,
East Sussex, BN23 6QH
Tel: +44 (0)1323 521555
email: sales@gardners.com

Bertram Books
1 Broadland Business Park, Norwich,
Norfolk, NR7 0WF
Tel: +44 (0)871 803 6709
email: books@bertrams.com

Chaters Wholesale Ltd
25/26 Murrell Green Business Park,
Hook, Hampshire, RG27 9GR
Telephone: +44 (0)1256 765443
Fax: +44 (0)1256 769900
email: books@chaters.co.uk

NORTH AMERICA
Quayside Distribution Services
400 First Avenue North, Suite 300,
Minneapolis, MN 55401, USA
Telephone: (612) 344 8100
Fax: (612) 344 8691

Dust jacket: In a thrilling season, Honda's Marc Marquez scored his third MotoGP championship victory.

Title page: Once again, Jonathan Rea dominated proceedings in the World Superbike Championship on his Kawasaki Ninja.
Photos: Gold & Goose

Acknowledgements

The Editor and staff of MOTOCOURSE wish to thank the following for their assistance in compiling the 2016–2017 edition: Matt Birt, Majo Botella, Alex Briggs, Mufaddal Choonia, Peter Clifford, Steve Day, Federica de Zottis, William Favero, Nick Harris, Isabelle Lariviere, Harry Lloyd, Mat Oxley, Elisa Pavan, David Pato, Ignacio Sagnier, Jon Seidel, Julian Thomas, Mike Trimby, Michel Turco, Frine Vellila, Ken Vreeke, Mike Webb, Günther Wiesinger and Rupert Williamson; as well as many others, including riders and technicians. A special thanks to Marlboro and Honda hospitality staff, and to colleagues and friends for a stream of well-meant advice.

Photographs published in MOTOCOURSE 2016–2017 have been contributed by:
Chief photographers: Gold & Goose.
Other photographs contributed by: BMW Press Club, Whit Bazemore, Gavan Caldwell, Clive Challinor, Dave Collister, Ducati Corse, Bernd Fischer, Honda America, MotoAmerica – Brian J. Nelson, John Morris-Mpix, Movistar Yamaha, Dave Purves, Repsol Honda, Neil Spalding, Mark Walters.

publisher
STEVE SMALL
steve.small@iconpublishinglimited.com

commercial director
BRYN WILLIAMS
bryn.williams@iconpublishinglimited.com

editor
MICHAEL SCOTT

text editor
IAN PENBERTHY

results and statistics
PETER McLAREN

chief photographers
GOLD & GOOSE
David Goldman
Gareth Harford
Brian J. Nelson
David 'Chippy' Wood
www.goldandgoose.com
tel +44 (0)20 8444 2448

MotoGP circuit illustrations
ADRIAN DEAN
f1artwork@blueyonder.co.uk

www.motocourse.com

FOREWORD by MARC MARQUEZ

THIS title was really, really difficult. The start of the year was the most difficult part, maybe the most difficult in my career, because the bike was hard to ride. We had a hill to climb, and we had to find a way. I remember saying to Honda's engineers, "I believe in you, so I will change my mentality for the early races, but in the second part of the season, I need your help."

This help arrived. They did a really great job, working with the new electronics and the overall balance of the bike. Before too long, I had a bike I could ride in the way I like to ride.

An early lead in the championship was important. It made it easier to accept second at tracks where we were not so strong. Then I made a mistake at Le Mans, trying to push past the limit. That helped me to calm down, and to go for good points rather than trying to win when it wasn't possible.

I was waiting for Aragon – it was my time to win again, and I started to open my lead again.

I have to thank Honda for their work. They never gave up, and the championship is our reward.

I also have to thank my team. Their friendly support was as important as their own hard work. They helped to relax, and to focus clearly.

Last year, I paid an expensive price to learn that consistency is important.

This year, I crashed many times in practice, because I was using practice to find the limit. Then in the races, I could pull back from the limit and make sure of getting maximum points without taking too many risks.

It is my third time to write the Foreword to this book, which has for so many years been such an important monument to the glamour, excitement and fun of grand prix racing. MOTOCOURSE keeps the memories alive.

I will do everything to make sure it is not the last time.

 # 93

EVERYONE'S A WINNER...

IF surprise is pleasure, and the unexpected is fulfilling, then 2016 was a very special season of motorbike racing.

Record numbers of grand prix winners in two out of three classes, a return of British riders to the top step, the revival of Ducati and Suzuki, and bright prospects for newcomers Aprilia and KTM.

There was more of the same in World Superbikes, settling in under Dorna's regime; at the Isle of Man TT – where the 133mph average was smashed; in the USA – where the title in the reviving domestic programme went to the last lap of the last race. And on three wheels, where sidecar passenger Kirsi Kainulainen became the first woman to win a full FIM World Championship title.

MOTOCOURSE covers it all.

The success of the grand prix season was helped by several factors, including tactical opportunities offered by returned Michelin's wider range of tyres, and some of very erratic weather. The main credit must go to Dorna's oft-derided dumb-down programme, aimed at limiting the technology, cutting the costs, and bringing the factory teams back within reach of the independent entrants.

It clearly bore fruit in 2016, and promises a good crop for the foreseeable future.

The loss is to cutting-edge technological development. The gain is for the lesser riders, and legions of excited fans. And for the profitable business of racing.

MOTOCOURSE, for a 41st time, followed the progress in every detail, and watched as Marc Marquez showed that even on a level playing field an outstanding player will stand out. Among this book's comprehensive coverage, the following pages remark also on the emergence of another potential racing giant, with a profile of Maverick Vinales.

At the post-season test, mounted on his new Yamaha, the Spaniard was faster than everybody.

The dust has settled now, and the smoke from Valencia's post-race fireworks has cleared.

The view remains enticing.

MICHAEL SCOTT

Richmond, November, 2016

Inset: The first woman to win an open FIM World Championship – sidecar passenger Kirsi Kainulainen with driver Pekka Paivarinta.
Photo: Mark Walters

Main: Nine to the dozen. There were a record nine different MotoGP race winners in 2016.
Photos: Gold & Goose

FIM WORLD CHAMPIONSHIP 2016
TOP TEN RIDERS
THE EDITOR'S CHOICE

Rider Portraits by Gold & Goose

1 MARC MARQUEZ

IF variety and adaptability are the marks of a truly great rider (if there was ever any doubt), Marquez proved the point over and again during 2016.

His crash rate was still higher than average, but there was an important difference. They happened when he was seeking the limits in qualifying, not in races.

He had changed one of his defining traits. In earlier years, he would risk everything to try to win. In 2016 he thought more about finishing, and adding up the points. He could see a bigger picture.

Added to his already astonishing gifts of speed, control and persistence, this made a devastating combination.

It was all the more impressive because this year's factory Repsol Honda RCV, with reversed crank rotation and unified software, missed several targets. The bike had lost its way, with trouble most particularly in acceleration.

From the start, Marquez was still able to make the most of it.

Whether his more thoughtful approach stemmed from Rossi's extraordinary personal attack at the end of 2015 or whether it was simply down to intelligence and the passage of time made no difference.

The youngest ever champion had found maturity. And he was still just 23.

2 VALENTINO ROSSI

IF Marquez is astonishingly young, the opposite serves for Rossi. At an age when most riders have already perforce given way to the tide of youth, the great man from Tavullia was smilingly doing the opposite.

While he was often not quite as fast as younger team-mate Lorenzo, there was no perceptible loss of motivation, nor of self-belief. Tactics, race-craft and perseverance can compensate for mere speed, in the right circumstances.

Two major misfortunes – a race crash in Texas and an engine blow-up at Mugello – meant that Rossi was unable to repeat his 2015 challenge for overall victory, and his season became a battle with Lorenzo.

At the same time, in spite of a handshake in parc ferme in Catalunya, his rivalry with Marquez remained a strong motivation. Experience and skill combine for the multi-champion to use anything and everything to boost his chances.

He clearly enjoyed it, and continued to radiate an infectious love of grand prix racing that does as much to make him so universally popular as his quick wit, charming personality and well-oiled publicity machine.

Nothing lasts for ever. Another universal truth that Rossi continued to defy in 2016.

3 MAVERICK VINALES

FROM his earliest days as a 125 maverick Vinales was marked down as a major future talent. The comingman of the smaller classes has now well and truly arrived. His second year in the premier class did everything to fulfil even the most optimistic early prognostications.

His first victory, a Silverstone masterclass, might have come earlier were he not riding a Suzuki that was itself still climbing the learning curve. As it was, he did not so much prove the GSX-RR's progress as flatter it, and drive it forward. At the same time stretching his more experienced team-mate Aleix Espargaro close to breaking point.

Vinales seldom crashed, but was aggressive when he needed to be. His only weakness, losing pace later in some early races, was more to do with the bike than the rider, and he had largely overcome that by year's end.

At the age of 21, Vinales is already an impressively mature and thoughtful rider. The offer to join Rossi at Yamaha put him through some agonies, but the eventual acceptance was the only thing that made sense.

For 2017, still gaining strength, he will be in a position to pose a serious challenge to Marquez. A quality that can be ascribed to very few.

4 CAL CRUTCHLOW

THE first part of the season was a bruising experience for Britain's first GP winner in 35 years. In his sixth year in GP racing. Crutchlow crashed in four of the first five races. That he remounted on two of those occasions (in Argentina only to crash again) speaks volumes about his courage and determination.

Perhaps a bit too much of both, for the cause of his frequent trips to the gravel traps was trying too hard on a not-quite-factory Honda that not only he was finding extremely difficult to ride at competitive speeds.

His efforts gained great credibility with HRC, and by the time he did finally win a race at a damp Brno he was already filling an important test and development role. He can take much credit for the RCV's improvement through the year.

His second win in Australia was as big a landmark: on a dry track, and under pressure from Rossi.

Crutchlow is a popular figure among his fellow riders, with a sharp sense of humour and a big heart. Popular also with the press, for he is not afraid to speak his mind.

He was one big beneficiary of the levelling out of machinery in 2016; and he proved that he deserved the benefits.

5 JORGE LORENZO

WHEN the level is so high and the margins so small, anyone can go through a bad patch. The surprise with Lorenzo is how often it happened and how long it lasted.

His performance in several wet races – notably at Assen and the Sachsenring – were truly dismal for a man of his talents, but he also faltered from time to time in the dry.

If nothing else, it showed how important confidence and momentum can be, even to the most blatantly talented sportsmen.

On his day, Jorge was still able to show the metronomic perfection that meant his lap times would over-shadowed those of team-mate Rossi, and that carried him to such a convincing third premier-class title in 2016. He claimed pole at Losail, Le Mans, Misano and Valencia. The last three at record speed, and three times carried them through to race wins.

No-one could think for a moment that Lorenzo had forgotten how to race a motorcycle, nor that he does not remain a rider of the highest calibre.

He is a character of still depths, and perhaps he needs another challenge to regain his security and self-belief. He has chosen one, with his move to Ducati in 2017.

6 ANDREA DOVIZIOSO

'DESMO DOVI' redeemed what had seemed a patchy season in Malaysia, with a clear win over Rossi that showed all his depth. Reliable, careful, well-measured and persistent. Also accurate, with a depth of understanding of the capabilities of a still difficult Desmosedici, and the ability to get a steady 99 percent out of it, from the first lap to the last.

The lacklustre perception was not really fair. His results were blighted by awful luck – as when he was blundered down by other riders from potential podium finishes two races in a row, in Argentina and Texas.

Team-mate Iannone, one of his assailants, was often faster. But his propensity for crashing, often simply because he was over-riding the Ducati, made that achievement of less overall value than Dovi's dogged precision. In spite of Iannone's demoralising Austria defeat of his team-mate, thanks to a bold tyre choice.

Now in his 15th GP season and a race winner in all three classes, the former 125 World Champion is better at amassing solid points than winning races: the gap between his first MotoGP win in Britain in 2009 and his second, seven years and 96 days later, fell seven days short of the longest ever (by Phil Read). Another second place for the Italian, to add to those this year at Qatar, Austria and Japan.

7 BRAD BINDER

IT may seem overblown to put a mere Moto3 rider this high up the list. But South Africa's first World Champion since Jon Ekerold in 1980 achieved his success with consistent wins and top placings in the closest and most competitive class in the world. And with four races to spare, to boot.

Binder retained his equanimity while all about were losing theirs. The whole year was a performance of great maturity for a rider who turned 21 more than half-way through.

There was another sharp contrast with his mainly Spanish and nowadays once again also Italian rivals. While they have the benefit of carefully structured and professionally monitored training and talent-spotting regimes, Binder had to do it from far away, and (given the steadfast support of his family) more or less alone.

His biggest stroke of luck was to be hired by the Red Bull-backed team run by Aki Ajo, whose professionalism also led Zarco to his two successive Moto2 titles.

In 2017, Binder will take the Frenchman's place in Moto2. The second test of the depth of his talent will begin.

8 DANI PEDROSA

PEDROSA had more trouble than the other Honda riders in adapting to the new electronics and more particularly the new Michelin tyres. Although only eight kilogrammes lighter than team-mate Marquez, it clearly put him well onto the wrong side of the physics.

The year was looking like a disaster, with very occasional high points, until it got warm enough and the tyre choice soft enough for a convincing ride through from sixth to first at Misano. If not for that, he would have spoiled a 15-year record with at least one win every year.

It has always been easy to under-rate Dani. Many even expressed surprise at his forceful overtaking at that race, forgetting that it is some years since he shrugged off his reputation as a shrinking violet.

Many were also surprised that HRC retained the 31-year-old's services for two more years alongside Marquez. This view however is to forget his reliable strengths, when set against a list of other riders who are available.

Dani's championship chances may have been overtaken by brighter, younger talent. But his abilities remain consistently admirable. And, as he has learned how to express his human side more clearly, so too many other aspects.

9 JOHANN ZARCO

THE Frenchman made history in 2016, the first double Moto2 champion, with the first successful title defence. But his season was not the steady march of perfection achieved in 2015, and there were several races where he was out of step.

His headlong barge into erstwhile rival Sam Lowes at Silverstone was just one, and he deserved the punishment that put him out of the points.

On his good days, as before, Zarco was a cut above the rest: not only the fastest, but also the most intelligent. He had a knack of saving his tyres and his best speed for the end of races.

But there were bad days too. At several races he found himself mired at the far end of the points, and his strengths were left in abeyance along with his professorial reputation.

By the time the flyaways came around, he was under serious threat from Rins. Injuries to the Spaniard played in Zarco's favour – but to his performance in the crucial Malaysian round was to his greater credit.

He took pole by a record two seconds, and once again stamped his authority on a difficult race, to take the crown in the style of a true champion. MotoGP in 2017 will be his next big test.

10 ANDREA IANNONE

SELF-STYLED as "The Maniac", Iannone did little to contradict this assessment when he took himself and his team-mate out of a guaranteed Ducati podium in only the second round.

Several more crashes would follow, including that at round 13 at Misano that took the 27-year-old out of that and the next three races with spinal injuries.

As well, however, Iannone won a well-thought-out race in Austria, taking Ducati back to the top for the first time since Stoner in 2010, and also claimed his first pole position, among four front-row starts.

There is an old racing maxim: that it easier for a fast rider to learn how to stop crashing than for a slower to learn how to go fast. Iannone surely clings to the hope offered by this.

If he could only find consistency and shake off his crash-happy reputation, the established regular winners would need to watch themselves. That remained true even when he didn't find it.

It remains to be seen with his move to Suzuki in 2017 whether a less aggressive motorcycle will make a more stable platform for his obvious gifts than the super-powerful but relatively clumsy Ducati.

A NEW GOLDEN AGE?

New tyres, new rules and new penalties marked Dorna's 25th year of motorcycle grand prix racing. Record-breaking on-track action was a fitting reward, as MICHAEL SCOTT explains...

Above: Marquez explores the limits.
Photo: Repsol Honda

Right: Michelin demanded 17-inch front wheels to make development relevant to the road.
Photo: Gold & Goose

THE 2016 season marked the end of an era of transition. It also showed a considerable overlap with the next era, with a new five-year contract period beginning in 2017. And it laid on a year of superlatively good racing, with an unprecedented number of different winners. Anyone seeking good omens didn't have far to look, and many went so far as to hail the start of a new Golden Age.

The previous five years had seen major changes, including the unloved and mercifully short-lived production-based CRT bikes, and the stepped introduction of control electronics. The forthcoming five introduce a new financial package, which includes more stringent cost control measures and bigger payouts, further favouring independent teams; and the advent of a formal closed shop for participating factories.

It seemed that the good things of 2016 would be guaranteed to continue. At least there was every reason to hope so.

TECHNICALLY SPEAKING

The two biggest factors for 2016 were not the refining of the finances and control of costs, but technical: tyres and one-size-fits-all electronics. Each in its own way had a major influence.

Bridgestone became sole tyre supplier in 2009, but already at the end of 2014, they had tired of this exclusive role, although they agreed to stay on for one more year to allow a replacement to step forward. They had earned much respect, with a few deviations (notably the crash-prone, hard-to-warm tyres of 2012). But they were only beating themselves, and celebrations of a mounting total of wins, passing 100 back in 2012, rang a little hollow.

It was for these reasons that Michelin had pulled out of the original control-tyre proposals in 2008. Since then, in a changing landscape of world racing on four as well as two wheels, the French company had had a change of heart. In the past, racing had been an important development tool, where they had pioneered radial-ply tyres and also developed mixed compounds, all transferred to road use within two years, according to technical director Nicolas Goubert, a familiar face in the paddock, even after seven years away.

To this end, one condition for return had been a switch from 16.5-inch to 17-inch wheels, to match the current generation of street bikes. "If that had not been put in the rules, I don't think we would have come," said Goubert. The company wanted to develop tyre technology "for everyday use."

But changes to the performance were much more profound than just that. Put simply, the biggest difference was that where Bridgestone's front tyre had been stellar in performance, allowing very hard braking and giving riders good feedback and plenty of warning, Michelin's better performer was the rear tyre. The front, already significantly revised after testing problems during 2015, was by comparison the weak

Left: Michelin Man. The vastly experienced Nicolas Goubert returned to oversee development of the new-generation tyres.

Below: Featherweight Dani Pedrosa found himself hunting for grip throughout the year.

Photos: Gold & Goose

link, extending braking zones and – with riders complaining of it giving no warning before letting go – leading to a distinct prevalence of front-end low-side crashes, all year long. These might have had the benefit of being less injurious than high-siders, but at year's end Rossi was one of many who said, "There were too many crashes, and Michelin need to improve the front."

Nor was the rear beyond criticism, for example when, after spectacular failures pre-season and in Argentina involving Ducati riders Baz and Redding, Michelin abandoned the earlier tyre in favour of a harder construction. While the safety aspect of this move was beyond doubt, in that there were no more disintegrations, riders of other machines were dismayed to have to take a step back in grip and response in favour of the apparently clumsier (and certainly more powerful) Ducatis.

There was another aspect that disadvantaged smoother riders: the Michelins needed to be pushed hard to bring them up to temperature, and they lacked the edge grip that smoother riders rely upon to achieve high mid-corner speed. These aspects worked in particular against lightweight Pedrosa and silky-smooth defending champion Lorenzo, and spoiled their seasons.

Michelin worked hard, however, and offered a much bigger range of tyres at most races, including the return of intermediates for semi-dry conditions. This led to an interesting vari-

Above: Follow my leader. Brad Binder heads a trail of riders during practice at Catalunya.

Top right: Taking up the last available manufacturer slot on the MotoGP grid, KTM made their debut in Valencia.

Above right: Success breeds success – LCR was one of the Independent Teams thriving under the new regulations.
Photos: Gold & Goose

Right: Ducati's wings grew all year. They'll be banned in 2017.
Photo: Bernd Fischer

ety of choices from different riders and for different machines, and added an interesting layer of extra tactics, as well as a welcome element of unpredictability to the results.

On balance, Michelin's first year was an impressive comeback, and they will try to make use of the room for improvement. "For next year," said Goubert, "we will change the front profile – that is going to be the next big step for us."

Electronics are an even more complex topic than tyres. Their simplification, "back about five years", according to Yamaha's Jorge Lorenzo, had equally complex consequences.

These were different depending on each team's starting point. For independent teams moving from 2015's much more basic control software, they were a definite step forward. The common factor was that riders and electronics engineers still had to get to grips with getting the best out of them.

As a rule, this would favour the better-financed teams, but this was not the case for HRC, who had to make a bigger step than most, having stubbornly stuck with their in-house software in 2015, when the stock Magneti Marelli hardware became compulsory. By the time of the flyaway rounds, however, they were up to speed.

The change did favour Suzuki, however, who had been forced to abandon their longstanding use of Mitsubishi electronics. They found an immediate improvement, even when still at an early stage of the learning curve. Their success, boosted by Vinales's Silverstone win and three other podium finishes, did mean that in 2017 they will no longer be eligible for the concessions to lesser teams. Like Honda, Yamaha and latterly Ducati, they will be subject to the engine-development freeze from the start of the season, and will no longer benefit from free testing with full-time riders.

Aprilia will still be in the category with these freedoms, and so too KTM, on their debut.

The arrival of these two new factories is a good indicator of the overall health of the series, and in KTM's case, of the overall health of the Austrian company's sales figures – now Europe's largest motorcycle manufacturer, and still growing, according to chief executive Stefan Pierer at the launch of the KTM RC16 V4 at the Red Bull Ring.

It is a return to the premier class, after KTM had pulled out midway through an ill-fated and under-funded attempt in 2005, in league with Team Roberts. The decision to return dates to 2014, after the company had been turned down as engine supplier for Moto2. According to Dorna CEO Carmelo Ezpeleta, "It was not difficult to convince them to join MotoGP instead." KTM will join Moto2 as well in 2017, giving them representation in all three classes, and providing a useful ladder for future stars already in the training system in the all-KTM Red Bull Rookies Cup.

MONEY MATTERS

The new financial package, announced in 2015, was signed and sealed at Assen between Dorna and IRTA, the conditions already known. These included a closed shop for existing teams plus KTM; a minimum of two and maximum of four bikes available to customer teams alongside two factory entries; customer bikes price-capped at 2.2 million euros per year (including running spares, but not crash damage); and more than 30 per cent extra payment to teams. The last was up to two million euros, over and above existing freight allowances. At the same time, freight allowances for the smaller classes were also increased.

While Moto2 was praised for the success of cost limita-

tion, the class awaited news of a replacement engine, with the CBR600 sanction ending in 2018. At year's end, Dorna's Ezpeleta promised an imminent decision.

Moto3, with rival factories head to head, remained a cost concern, however, in spite of restrictive regulations. A new rule for 2017 changed the system, with manufacturers obliged to lease engines and gearboxes "under a rental agreement", rather than teams having to buy them. Each manufacturer must also be ready to supply machines and spare parts for up to 14 riders; and must supply a minimum of six riders as a condition of being approved for the class.

WINGS AND THINGS

Wings were a hot topic, and a bone of contention, especially for Ducati. Controversy started right at the beginning of the season amid safety concerns, with fears not only that wings could inflict injury in crashes (Pedrosa described them as "some sort of knives"), but also that the turbulence in the wake of the Ducatis in particular made slipstream-overtakes more difficult and actually tossed bikes around to the point of causing tank-slappers.

In Moto2, wings had been banned from the outset; Moto3 was allowed to continue for the rest of the season with their very limited devices, and for MotoGP the MSMA was invited to table a proposal for future aerodynamic regulations. Alas, they could not agree, and since all MSMA decisions must be unanimous and none was forthcoming, the GP Commission made up their own minds – with a complete ban on wings and a season-long freeze on fairing design.

The rift between the manufacturers was plain to see at a special press conference at Brno, where Ducati's Dall'Igna deplored the decision. The safety grounds were specious, he said, pointing out that in almost two years and many crashes (especially for Iannone), there had not been a single injury. And the cost grounds were equally irrelevant, since aerodynamic development and wind-tunnel work would still be as important as ever, and in fact now more difficult.

The ban was a loss to the motorcycle industry as a whole,

Above: Like a well-oiled machine, TV interviews get under way after qualifying at the Sachsenring.

Opposite page, from top: The FIM's Vito Ippolito was a frequent GP presence; Rossi remained the star of the show; Marquez used both his head and his talent to prevail again.

Right: Crutchlow's win in Brno was manna from heaven for Dorna's Carmelo Ezpeleta.

Far right: IRTA's Mike Trimby, the sport's unsung hero.
Photos: Gold & Goose

he continued. "For manufacturers, the most important thing is knowledge. If you cannot develop the knowledge, that is a huge problem."

Other decisions from the GP Commission included making rider airbags compulsory for all in 2017; and that in flag-to-flag bike-change races, pit crews (a maximum of four per rider) must wear crash helmets. This was in response to a collision in Argentina, where Alvaro Bautista had knocked over one of his mechanics. An extra detail was "to avoid the possibility of accidental engagement of a gear during the machine change, the mechanic holding the replacement machine may hold in the clutch lever. However, actual selection of the gear can only be made by the rider." Break this rule, and it would "result in automatic disqualification."

TIGHTENING THE REGS

A new level of governance was introduced, making for quicker and clearer penalty decisions, in response to the post-race penalty for Rossi after the infamous tangle with Marquez at Sepang in 2015. This had been the responsibility of the usual Race Direction committee, and the delay was understandable, given that there was a race going on that required direction, and they did not have any spare time to examine the evidence until it was over.

For the 2017 season, an extra panel of stewards would be introduced, with two FIM appointees assisting race director Mike Webb. According to the statement, "Race Direction will continue to be primarily responsible for the efficient and safe running of events. However, the competence of Race Direction concerning the application of sanctions and penalties will be limited to those offences that can be considered as being indisputable matters of fact. These would include such offences as pit-lane speeding, passing under yellow flags, etc.

"All other issues requiring further analysis of actions, including any incidences of dangerous riding, will be reviewed by the Stewards who will exclusively be responsible for issuing any sanctions and penalties on those matters."

The thorny issue of Moto3 riders loitering on track in qualifying, waiting for a tow, needed more attention after 2015's imposition of grid penalties proved ineffective. The new rules were introduced quite suddenly, on Friday evening at the Japanese GP, in line with Webb's threats the previous year to revise regulations as required.

The criterion was taking more than 110 per cent of one's best lap time for any of the track sections, and it would accumulate throughout the weekend, rather than being confined to one session. Three such transgressions at an event would lose the rider 12, rather than the previous three grid

places. One more: back of the grid plus two penalty points; another would earn a pit-lane start and four points. And a sixth offence at the same event would mean disqualification. From now on, the queues will have to form in the pit lane rather than more dangerously out on the track, where champion Binder humorously observed that he would have a gang of riders following him so closely that "if I went into the gravel, they'd follow me in."

Another pronouncement was in the form of a gag. A clause was put into the regulations that "Teams and Riders must not make statements or issue press releases that are considered to be irresponsible and hence damaging to the Championship."

Stricter rules had been applied to many aspects of racing, which may be taken as a sign of maturity.

HAND IN HAND

In its 25th anniversary year, Dorna had learned a lot, not least how to achieve co-operation – not (or not only) by blustering and bullying, but also by collaboration with its partners, the FIM and more particularly IRTA, arguably the greatest influence on GP racing.

The teams' association was already five years old when Dorna came on the scene in 1992, and it had been working (for a time hand in hand with Formula 1's Bernie Ecclestone) on rationalising motorcycle GP racing as a coherent business and sporting entity. This had covered matters ranging from rider safety to fairer financing and unified TV rights, and included also the introduction of permanent passes, the development of on-bike cameras and eventually the use of electronic timing.

Dorna was able to continue development in all these areas, and IRTA President Herve Poncharal paid warm tribute at the Assen press conference, where the new five-year deal was confirmed: "Dorna has improved everything, including the quality of the circuits, ground-breaking TV coverage, and has never compromised on safety. Only recently were there more safe circuits than place for them on the calendar.

"Finally," the Tech 3 team principal continued, "Dorna recognised that investment in the health of [independent] teams was vitally important."

Amid all the mutual congratulation, IRTA founder member and longstanding secretary general Mike Trimby sat silently by, claiming none of the credit. But if one man is responsible for starting the revolution from the bad old days, and keeping it going until today, it is Trimby.

TOP GUN MAVERICK

Named after a 'Top Gun' fighter pilot, Maverick Vinales took himself and Suzuki to the winner's circle. In 2017, he joins Valentino Rossi at Yamaha – as team-mate or nemesis? NEIL MORRISON investigates…

"YOU realise you've achieved one of your dreams," began Maverick Vinales, the next rider touted to join motorcycle racing's elite. "It feels perfect." Five days on from his maiden MotoGP triumph at Silverstone, the 21-year-old had just been asked to describe his feelings. Yet what followed was indicative of the make-up of the man Yamaha had entrusted to replace the highly decorated Jorge Lorenzo, who was departing for Ducati.

"But today I was feeling really good with my riding style. Also the bike was incredible." Second free practice at Misano – the scene of this interview – had only just finished. And he went on, the rider from Figueres in Catalunya glowing when talking at speed, detailing tyre feedback and the riding style adjustments of that afternoon. That cold, dreary afternoon at Silverstone was not mentioned again.

The exchange was intuitive. For the sport's latest young gun with the Hollywood name did not appear interested in dwelling on past achievements. Be it after a ride that had confirmed his supreme ability in Australia a year before, or after a debut top-class podium in France seven months later, it had become commonplace to hear Vinales forcefully state the need for the team to keep working, to maintain focus.

Often vapid platitudes, but his insistence to only look forward was notable for a rider so young. "He always wants more, more and more. He's never 100 per cent happy," said

ex-team boss Pablo Nieto. Those continual demands had acted as a rallying cry for Suzuki's returning MotoGP project, developing around him.

There was reason why the Hamamatsu factory had tried so hard to retain his services for two years beyond 2016. In April, Suzuki team boss Davide Brivio had suggested that Vinales could become an icon of the brand. "Someone like a Kevin Schwantz or a Barry Sheene. But he has to stay." Ultimately, the temptation to learn alongside Valentino Rossi, in a team that had clinched seven of the previous 13 premier-class titles, was too great. It was little wonder that Rossi – only half jokingly – had said, "I'm very worried for next year," as he dismounted the Silverstone podium.

And worry he might, as a second season in MotoGP had allowed Vinales to hone and harness a veritable skill set. An ability to front Suzuki's charge from wide-eyed returnees at the close of 2014 to regular podium contenders just under two years later demonstrated that there was character in abundance. "He's strong," said one-time race boss Ricard Jove. "He believes in himself 110 per cent and he never has doubts." Scoring top-six finishes in all but one dry race throughout 2016 underlined the brawn, and added maturity to boot. And the impression gained from speaking to Vinales was that this was very much only the beginning.

"Every year, I become more strong, more intelligent," he

said, eyes alight. "I know more what the bike wants. I feel incredible in my physical condition. I feel already I have many, many years more in the MotoGP world but I'm just 21. Valentino is 37, so I have a long career ahead."

A tinge of doubt over the young Spaniard's suitability for the Yamaha seat persisted before a protracted signing. Admittedly, his career stats cowered in the shadow cast by a series of broken records racked up by current champion and childhood rival Marc Marquez. One world title and 17 grand prix wins – just five of those outside the junior category – did not shout about an other-worldly talent, capable of challenging the current elite.

But consider Jose Manuel Cazeaux – Maverick's crew chief at Suzuki during his two MotoGP years – recalling that autumnal day outside Valencia when the then 19-year-old climbed aboard a MotoGP machine for the first time: "When a rider takes off his helmet, you can understand how much margin he has: if he's doing it naturally or forcing it too much. The way he was controlling the throttle from the first time on a MotoGP bike, the way he adapted to the carbon brakes so quick, we knew that he was special. For us, it was like an obligation to find the way to give him a bike that allows him to win."

Glance at Vinales's career and you quickly pick up on an innate ability to learn. And learn fast. Here is a rider who had won just his fourth grand prix, a thrilling duel with Nico Terol – six years his elder – in the 125cc event at Le Mans in 2011. A rider who had romped to a debut Moto3 win in Qatar a year later. And one who had made the Moto2 field look decidedly average in just his second showing in the intermediate class.

And while it took longer to find his feet on the MotoGP rung of the ladder, consider his adaptation to Michelin's control 17-inch front tyre – new for 2016. Five crashes in the entire season – two of those in Argentina – point to a thinking rider operating the controls. Only Rossi's fall tally was lower. Tellingly, Vinales crashed less using the French rubber than the Bridgestone, a unique feat in the entire field.

"When I come to one new bike, I have the quality to adapt fast," he said. "When I did the first test with the KTM in Moto3 at Almeria [at the end of 2012], I was already one second faster than with the Honda. That was the first day! It was the same when I went to Jerez for the first time to try the Moto2 bike. I was like 1.5s faster than Luis [Salom, Moto2 teammate]. It means I can find the limits quite fast."

In part, it was this talent that had carried Vinales through the junior ranks of the Catalan championships. A native of Figueres, an hour and a half up the coast from Barcelona and surrealist Salvador Dali's hometown, the young Maverick steered clear of the canvas, instead applying his own broad strokes to the tarmac of the local minibike tracks dotted across the province.

Vinales was fast, too. A bike-mad family was only happy to oblige his talents. "All my family were always riding at the weekend with the motocross or the minibikes," he said. "We were all just enjoying it at first. Then I could see that I was going quite fast compared to the other riders, and I was doing some different categories."

From a family with gypsy origins who had made money from fishing the nearby Mediterranean coast, Vinales's father, An-

Above: **Breakthrough moment at Silverstone as Vinales leads the pack on his way to a dominant victory.**

Centre left: **Baby-face. Maverick in his Moto3 years.**

Centre far left: **Maverick on a 125 in 2011. He is the only rider to win races in 125, Moto3, Moto2 and MotoGP.**

Bottom left: **Heading for the Moto3 title at Valencia in 2013.**
Photos: Gold & Goose

Opening spread: **Speed with style. Vinales on the Suzuki.**
Photo: Bernd Fischer

Above: He won races and was rookie of the year in Moto2 in 2014.
Photo: Gold & Goose

gel, was in a position to provide the tools that allowed his son's early ability to flourish.

While the dusty dirt tracks of Southern California were once the nurturing grounds for grand prix's top crop, in recent years the ragged, arid contours of the Catalan scenery have played host to a selection of the current MotoGP grid's formative years. It was there that Vinales had first set eyes on another prodigious talent, making a similar impression on those around him: Marc Marquez. Two years his elder, the current world champion often raced – and only occasionally beat – his younger countryman. It's not a stretch to suggest that Marquez's own trail-blazing progress through the grand prix hierarchy – always one class ahead until 2015 – had acted as the carrot dangling before Vinales's eyes.

"Honestly, more than a target, it was like, 'Oh, he can do that. So I can also do that.' When you have some great riders that you grew up together … sure you make the level more high. Also it helps your expectations to develop faster, to develop your qualities."

At home on a 50cc bike, then a 70cc, Vinales's forward trajectory really gained momentum aboard a 125cc, and he emerged victorious in the local championship in both 2007 and '08. A step up to the national CEV championship was inevitable. "It was there that I started to believe I could be in the world championship," he said. Having established himself the following year, winning the fiercely contested series in 2010 guaranteed a full-time world championship seat a year later.

Backed by American tabloid celebrity Paris Hilton, Vinales automatically stood out aboard the pink-tinged Blusens Aprilia 125. Soon his own name was in the headlines, that first taste of victor's champagne in just his fourth appearance marking him for greatness. Three more followed before the end of the year, leading members of the Spanish press to suggest that a run toward the 2012 crown – the inaugural Moto3 series –

was but a formality. But not everything goes to plan.

That particular season would come to be defined by a no-show when claiming the title was still a possibility, albeit a small one. Having won five of the first nine races, Vinales soon found his FTR Honda to be little match for Sandro Cortese's KTM. By Sepang, he'd had enough. Flying home sealed his title defeat. "We could have won that title, but he was too much of a rebel," said Jove, Vinales's team manager that year. "There were people behind him trying to make confusion, even Honda. His father was talking with people without telling me. His father was his reference then, so he trusted him."

Paternal relations soon ceased, leaving Vinales operating within a small circle of trust. Even now, he only counts on girlfriend and women's motocross champion Kiara Fontanesi and assistant Alex Salas as trusted associates. Jove again: "He's a difficult guy. He had a very difficult childhood. He has no relationship with his mother because his parents separated. It was difficult. So he's timid and he doesn't trust anyone." For Maverick, it was a valuable lesson. "Apart from losing money at that time, I lost second in the championship," he said. "The best way to do it would be different."

Lessons learnt, a switch to KTM machinery and the Laglisse team was just what was needed for 2013. There were early signs of that relentless consistency throughout that campaign, the furthest he finished from the race winner all year clocking in at just 1.055s. Yet wins weren't freely forthcoming, like the year before. Too often, he lost out in last-lap duels. "I was not good enough," he admitted frankly.

Still, Vinales was granted a stay of execution at the penultimate race when championship contenders Luis Salom and Alex Rins crashed out. Each of the three men went to the last race knowing that a win would be enough for the title. "I remember Pit [Beirer, KTM's technical director] promised me

SUZUKI: MOVING FORWARD

"THE fact that Suzuki decided in a difficult economic situation to come back shows very clearly how important it is to be in MotoGP," said new team boss Davide Brivio at Valencia in 2014, the factory's first race appearance since its three-year absence from the top class.

Suzuki had returned with an in-line four-cylinder engine that bore a resemblance to its road bikes. The early GSX-RR could boast of a sweet-handling chassis. In its rider line-up of Aleix Espargaro and Maverick Vinales, the factory had a proven top-six rider, along with a precocious talent to drive development forward. And that development was swift.

Riders were hamstrung by a horsepower shortage and the lack of a seamless-shift gearbox throughout 2015. That was rectified in a bold, pro-active winter in Hamamatsu, and holding on to Vinales's services was the principle aim.

At once, a new engine solved top-speed woes, while the new transmission also helped a lot. Add that to the technicians' rapid understanding of the workings of the new Magneti Marelli software, and the 2016 GSX-RR was arguably the factory's best machine since 2000, the last time one of its riders had won a title.

"We made a big progress, especially during last winter," Brivio told MOTOCOURSE. "The bike, chassis-wise, was already good from the beginning. But we were missing something in engine performance on the long straights on some circuits like Qatar, Austin, even Assen or some circuits where there is hard acceleration.

"This year, we recover a lot, so we can defend, we can attack at the braking, and this made a big difference."

a really good bike. It was like the fastest one. I was so strong and could battle a lot. I didn't feel strong like I did in Valencia in the other races. I was controlling it there, whereas in the other races I was at the limit."

Showing an icy coolness at the final race that hadn't been evident in the duels before, Vinales remained unflustered when Rins passed at the final corner, to drag his countryman by the line for a first world title. Laglisse team boss Nieto said, "After 2012, we knew he needed more support, like a family. We worked like this and it helped him." Also a small detail on the eve of the championship bow settled any nerves. "On Saturday, I went to the box and put 'P1 World Champion' on the pit board," said Nieto. "I said to him, 'This can happen.' Also, one mechanic took a mattress to the garage and slept next to the bike. When Maverick saw this, it was extra motivation."

Any thoughts that luck had been the principle factor behind that triumph were quickly dispelled in Moto2. Four wins and a further five podiums showed Suzuki that Vinales was primed for a shot at the big time. Still, a factory that had been absent from MotoGP for three seasons was no guarantee of success. "The fact that it's a factory convinced me. When I talked with Suzuki, they transmit confidence in me. Sure, it was a risk. With a new bike, you don't know how it's going to go. But in the first run I did, I thought, 'What an incredible bike!'"

There were the usual teething pains at the start of 2015. After all, the GSX-RR was still in its infancy. An engine that was severely short on top speed and a lack of a seamless-shift gearbox had it lagging behind its rivals. And given Vinales's inexperience, results were patchy. But by Brno, he was getting the hang of it. Then, at Phillip Island, came the breakthrough – a sixth, just six seconds behind the race winner – that fuelled his self-belief even further. "There I was riding most of the race with the leading group. I knew with my riding style I could have the same level as the top guys. The only problem was finding

Above: **Face of the future? Vinales was fastest at Valencia tests, in his first ride on a Yamaha.**

Top, centre: **Yamaha's Jarvis with Maverick at the official announcement of his recruitment for 2017.**

Above left: **Maverick's girlfriend Klara Fontanesi is a womens' motocross champion.**

Top right: **Suzuki made tremendous strides in their second year back.**
Photos: Gold & Goose

the correct set-ups. From there, everything went well."

In fact, pre-season went very well. Strides with a new engine and a seamless gearbox, coupled with a switch to Michelin tyres and spec electronics software, pushed Suzuki and Vinales toward the top six and, occasionally, the podium. So much so that Yamaha came calling in April, when Lorenzo's move away had been confirmed. The decision wasn't easy. "The most difficult of my life," he said at Le Mans.

A move to take his current crew to Yamaha failed. "I tried to bring all my team, but they are really excited for this plan with Suzuki. The teamwork made me feel, 'What do I do?' Ultimately, the temptation to work and learn alongside Rossi was too great. "He's so talented and has had so much success. He must have one way of working that is really good. Trying to learn that will be one key to trying to be really strong in the future."

And now the summit isn't far off. So it begs the question: what kind of threat can Vinales pose at Yamaha? Dealing with a team built around Rossi's continuing genius will provide the greatest obstacle. Ex-boss Sito Pons is sure it's a challenge Maverick will duly accept. "He'll push until he becomes number one," said Pons. "Inside, he will not sleep until he goes all the time in front of Valentino."

There's also that small matter of the familiar Marquez threat. From local minimoto tracks, a rivalry taken all the way to the highest stage. "When you're a kid growing up and you see you can fight in the best category, best level, with the best bikes, this is amazing," said Vinales. "In the future, I see myself fighting with Marc." Brivio agreed: "I'm sure he will be fighting for the championship for the next ten years." Those thinking that Marquez's third premier-class crown signalled the beginning of a Doohan-esque era of dominance might well be premature. For his fellow Catalan won't be going away anytime soon.

HALF-CENTURY HONDA

Fifty years ago, Honda dominated the smaller grand prix classes. Then they decided to take on the big boys. MAT OXLEY tells the story of the bike that nearly did it...

IN the 1960s, Soichiro Honda's relationship with world championship racing had several dimensions. Some were obvious: marketing – to establish his fledgling brand on the world stage; and engineering – to develop roadgoing techniques and machines in the heat of competition.

There was more to it than that. It was 'Pops' Honda's belief that success in racing would develop the pride and the spirit of the company that bore his name. And it was his pledge, after a belittling first visit to the Isle of Man, stronghold of the European and especially British motorcycle industries, that he would return to win the race.

That promise was made in 1954, and he faced a steep learning curve. It took five years for the first Hondas to race in the TT, but only two more years for the first world championship wins. With high-revving, multi-cylinder, four-valve engines, Honda held the high ground in the smaller classes. Or at least most of the high ground. They faced ever-improving two-strokes from Suzuki and Yamaha, and the series was expanded in 1962 to add 50cc lightweights to the existing 125, 250 and 350 stalwarts.

There was a bigger prize, however. The premier class – 500cc, and dominated by the red Italian MV Agustas. At the same time, Honda wanted a publicity boost for its first large-capacity roadster, the CB450 'black bomber'.

For 1966, along with enhanced efforts in the smaller categories, the goal was simple: total domination of all five classes and the return to the factory's pre-eminence of recent years.

The RC181 was the bike made to do it.

Honda's rider line-up was strong and included legend Mike Hailwood, as well as the ever-faithful Jim Redman. Under the aegis of racing chief Michihiko Aika, plans were laid to share out the spoils.

Redman would go for his first 500 crown with back-up from Hailwood, who in turn would concentrate on the 250/6 and 350/4, with Redman in support. Luigi Taveri and Ralph Bryans would stick to what they knew best – riding the miniature five-cylinder 125 and the 50cc twin.

Considering its fabulously complex stablemates and pre-season rumours of a V8 motor, Honda's first ever 500 racer turned out to be a relatively straightforward machine. The RC181 boasted just four cylinders and typical Honda engine architecture: in-line cylinders with gear-driven cams operating four-valve heads. Its first incarnation gave Redman and Hailwood 85 horsepower at 12,500rpm, for a top speed of almost 170mph.

A shortage of horsepower was never the RC181's problem. While Redman was used to the lively characteristics of Honda GP racers, Hailwood found the 500 frightening from the outset – something that would never change. He'd been used to the heavy, but stable MVs, and the new Honda twitched and wobbled like crazy. Honda favoured a rearward weight balance on their GP racers, which was fine for smaller models, but the 500's extra power created a major imbalance under acceleration, when the front end went light, causing instability and understeer.

"It wasn't just the usual matter of trying to win with the RC181," Hailwood wrote later. "It was trying to stay on the thing. It really was the most frightening experience." Taveri also found the 500 terrifying when he gave the bike a brief test ride. "It was enormous," he said. "And it jumped from side to side."

Despite the 181's handling ills, Redman began his and Honda's 500 career in style, easily beating Agostini at superfast Hockenheimring. Badly outgunned, MV unleashed an overbored version of its lightweight 350 triple for the following Dutch GP, where Redman rode an inspired race to defeat the Italian once again. It seemed that Redman was on course to fulfilling his dream of conquering the 500 class before slipping into retirement, even though Ago's 420cc three was at least as fast as the Honda.

Then they came to Spa, in the watery Ardennes, where thunder and lightning crashed around as they started the 500 race. Determined to play it cool in the appalling conditions, Redman followed Hailwood's and Ago's rear wheels. Third would do fine. But blinded by a fog of spray, he moved out of their slipstream to see where he was going. "I pulled over to the other side of the road and there was a lake of water. The bike aquaplaned and down I went at over 250km/h." He heard the crack as his left forearm snapped and he thought he'd broken a leg, too, after kicking his flailing Honda clear. In fact, the wrist was his only serious injury. Six weeks later, he tried to ride at the Ulster GP, but his arm was too weak, so he withdrew from the event, announcing his retirement shortly afterwards.

After Spa, Honda threw all of its weight behind Hailwood, now faced with the Herculean task of fronting the factory's hopes in all three classes – 250, 350 and 500. He was cruising the two smaller categories, having won every round of both championships by the time the responsibility for the 500 title was dropped upon his shoulders.

In contrast to Redman's early successes, Hailwood had yet to score a championship point with the RC181. In Germany, his machine had been requisitioned by Redman after the Rhodesian's bike had broken in practice; at Assen, he had crashed while leading, when the RC181's erratic gearbox hit a false neutral; at Spa, he had been robbed of success by more gearbox problems. So when the circus moved to the Sachsenring for the fourth of the year's nine rounds, he had zero points; Agostini had 20.

Neither would score in East Germany. Hailwood's Honda suffered a broken crankshaft, while Agostini crashed at high speed, just 10km from the finish. Hailwood won at Brno the following weekend, well ahead of a still-bruised and chastened Ago. He also took the 250 and 350 laurels that day, wrapping up the 250 championship and putting one hand on the 350 crown.

A fortnight later, the action moved to Imatra in Finland, where Hailwood walked the 250 and 350 classes, and jousted with Agostini on the 500, only to outbrake himself in the wet. He finished a distant second. At the Ulster GP, he was unable to compete in all three classes, since the three races exceeded the maximum distance in a day specified by FIM rules, so he skipped the 250 and beat the MV in both bigger

Top right: **Hailwood on the 500. He came close to winning Honda's first premier-class title after "doing the work of three men".**
Photo: Günter Geyler

Left: **Built to beat the MV Agusta, Honda's 500cc RC181 was fast but wayward.**
Photo: American Honda

Above: Successful stablemate to the 500, Honda's six-cylinder 250/350 was an intricate master-piece.

Photo: American Honda

classes, clinching the 350 title in the process.

After a short boat ride to the Isle of Man (the 1966 TT was delayed for three months by a seamen's strike), Hailwood won the 250 by over five minutes and then trounced Ago on the 500. But this event took it out of the overstretched Briton. The RC181 was a bucking, wobbling beast on the Mountain circuit, and his two-minute victory belied his efforts. He had "a million hairy slides" during the race, and suggested that it had been easier to do a 104mph lap on the 250 than a 103mph lap on the 500. In fact, he got around at 107mph on the RC181.

There was just one round remaining – the Nations GP at Monza in Italy, and a victory would mean Hailwood could clinch the title. He took pole position, 0.8 of a second ahead of Ago, and made a perfect start while the MV was swallowed by the midfield pack. Cheered on by the deafeningly partisan Monza crowd, Ago quickly chased down the Honda, and the pair repeatedly battered the lap record as they jostled for position. Then the RC181 broke an exhaust valve. A despondent Hailwood pushed in, to be greeted by a standing ovation, while Ago lapped the rest of the field, twice. This was the first of the Italian's 15 world championships, and he would hold on to the 500 crown for the next six years.

The MV/Honda rivalry was at a peak now: racing's glamorous old guard, the plaything of a rich and ageing aristocrat, versus the commercially-driven new breed from the East. And yet despite the intense competition that raged on the racetrack and in the R&D shops, the two teams enjoyed a relationship of mutual respect that verged on friendliness.

"We exchanged presents sometimes," remembered Aika. "MV would give us Italian wine, and we would give them dried seaweed from Japan."

Hailwood may have failed to win the riders' title that Honda most wanted, but with Redman's wins included, the RC181 took the manufacturers' title. Honda won that also in the four other classes, and riders' crowns in 125, 250 and 350.

"That season was our golden era, even though we only

had a few staff in the team," recalled Aika. "We had a maximum of 12 staff at the Isle of Man, and that included engine designers, chassis designer and all the mechanics. We had no drivers or helpers. We did everything ourselves, looking after 30 machines, six for each class."

The enormous effort involved in contesting all five world championships, as well as F1 (since 1964), was taking a toll on Honda, both in personnel and financially. Then came the shock announcement: Honda would withdraw from 50s and 125s – fast becoming two-stroke territory – to concentrate its efforts on the three larger categories and F1.

The rationalisation resulted in Aika being packed off to Europe with just a handful of staff for the 1967 campaign. And the team wasn't just short of mechanics. While streamlining its GP presence, Honda also failed to replace Redman, leaving Hailwood to attack the 250, 350 and 500 series almost alone, with Ralph Bryans doing his best to offer 250 and 350 support on year-old bikes.

But even for the most gifted rider in history, the triple crown would prove too steep a mountain to climb. Hailwood complained often during the year. "I have to do the work of three riders," he told friends mid-season. "I feel I'm being squeezed like a lemon."

Despite the lack of manpower, Honda worked through the winter to give Hailwood three motorcycles that were capable of winning their respective titles. The six-cylinder 250 had a new chassis and a modified engine with a shorter stroke, which allowed it to rev to 19,000rpm for more peak power; a bored-out 297.06cc version was prepared for the 350 class.

The 500 was also improved, growing 10cc to 499cc, for even more power. Of course, speed wasn't a problem; handling was still the worry, and Hailwood's withering criticisms gained him permission to do his own chassis work in collaboration with British engineer Colin Lyster. The idea was to use European expertise to cure the RC181's woes, though Honda insisted he use the original chassis once the world championship started.

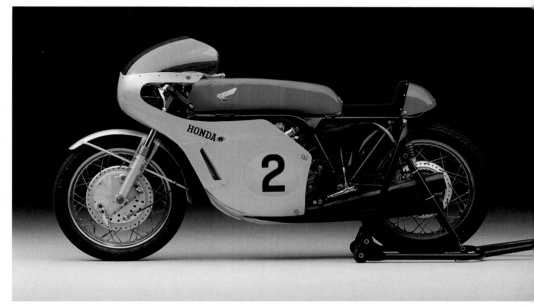

The first 500 race was at Hockenheim, a week after the Spanish round for smaller classes at Montjuich, where a puncture for Hailwood had handed 250 victory to Phil Read's V4 Yamaha.

Hailwood had a troubled start to his attempt on the triple crown. He thrashed Agostini in the 350 race, but suffered bike problems in both the 250 and 500 events, the RC181 breaking its crank while well ahead of Ago's MV.

The next outing for the premier class was at the Isle of Man TT, where Hailwood took clear 250 and 350 wins, then engaged in one of his greatest duels with Agostini in the 500s. The 1967 Senior TT is widely considered the best ever. Both men took their turns out front, Hailwood struggling with a loose twistgrip, Ago gaining the upper hand before retiring with a broken drive chain. The lap record established by Hailwood that day stood for nine years. "Afterwards," Agostini said, "Mike said to me, 'That was your race.'"

Hailwood repeated the hat trick at Assen eight days later, but was outpaced at Spa the following weekend. Around the ultra-fast road circuit, Ago's MV easily outhandled the RC181. Stunned by the MV's improved pace, Honda flew an uprated 181 to the next race at the Sachsenring. The new bike featured a lighter motor with magnesium crankcases and a stiffer frame. But gearbox gremlins struck again, leaving Ago to lap the entire field and take the 500 championship lead.

Hailwood won the 350 class, and again at the next round at Brno, securing that title. This relieved some of the pressure that had been piled upon the Briton and allowed him to pour all his energies into the other classes. Further improvements to the new 500 helped him defeat Ago at Brno.

At Imatra, Hailwood crashed out of the big class, but a double victory followed at the Ulster GP to move him into the 250 points lead and close the gap on Agostini. The triple crown was still a possibility.

Once again, Monza was the turning point. Hailwood had worked a winning lead over the MV when his gearbox began to play up again. He limped home, Agostini passing him with

one lap to go; the Monza crowd erupted with joy. That just about did it. Now Ago needed only a couple of points from the final 500 round. The Monza nightmare was completed by another 250 engine failure, Read's Yamaha winning the race to retake the series lead with two rounds remaining. Aika counts the day as the most miserable of his career. "That was the worst moment. We lost the race and the title because the transmission broke due to a mechanic's mistake. The gearbox had been misassembled."

Hailwood replied with another double win in Canada. Now he was level on points with 250 rival Read, but the main title had been lost. Agostini finished second, and the crown was once more his and MV's.

Hailwood took the 250 crown on a count-back of race wins, having tied on points with Read. It was the great man's ninth world championship, but he was still dismayed. The 500 was his only true goal, and he was still unhappy with the RC181. He insisted that he test Honda's 1968 models before agreeing to a contract for the following season. But other events would nullify all plans.

Firstly, new restrictive regulations, designed to bring costs under control to avoid GP racing bankrupting itself, would be introduced for 1969. A limit on the number of cylinders and gears would outlaw all but one of Honda's GP machines. Only the RC181 500 complied with the new regulations.

Secondly, Honda had a change of heart. With a push into the car market and the F1 project swallowing up cash and resources, and motorcycle engineers engaged in developing the ground-breaking four-cylinder CB750 street bike, something had to give.

In February, 1968, Hailwood and Bryans received telegrams summoning them to Japan. Both men presumed that they were travelling east for pre-season shakedown tests, but on arrival in Tokyo, they were told the stunning news: Honda were quitting all grand prix competition with immediate effect. The revelation came as a terrible shock to Hailwood, and it was the end of his GP career. And the end of the road for RC181.

Above and above left: Honda RC181 at rest. Power was plentiful, but a rearward weight bias made it a handful on the move.

Top right: Honda's stable of complexity. New rules and a change in company policy would soon make them all obsolete..

Photos: Photo: American Honda

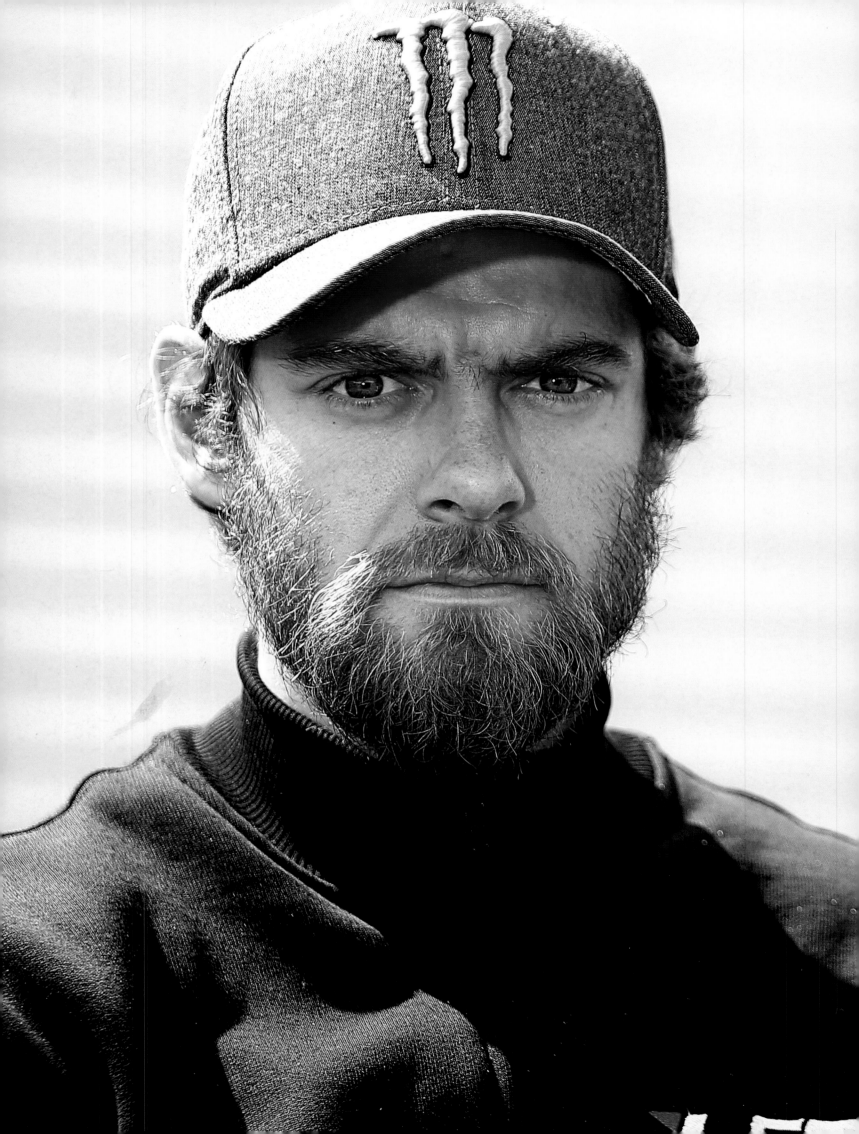

TOUGHING IT OUT

Seen as inheritor of the late, great Barry Sheene's mantle, Briton Cal Crutchlow is driven by an overwhelming determination to succeed, despite the odds. MICHAEL SCOTT examines the career of this gritty, tenacious racer…

Main photo: Sent from Coventry. Crutchlow stepped out of long shadow of Sheene, ending a long drought for Britain.
Photo: Gold & Goose

Right: The thousand-yard stare. Trademark total commitment from the double GP winner.
Photo: Whit Bazemore Photography

"TOUGH, blunt, funny … and very fast, Cal Crutchlow is Britain's best motorcycle grand prix racer since the legendary Barry Sheene in the 1970s."

I wrote those words in 2013. In 2016, the 31-year-old underlined them, in bold type, with two classic race wins in both wet and dry.

In between, the former World Supersport 600 champion and Superbike race winner had a mainly difficult interlude with Ducati, cut short after one of two projected years, and then an up-and-down 2015 with the LCR Honda team, which included a podium. It was all a bit 'almost there', interrupted by too many crashes and illuminated by his trademark determination.

The start of 2016 was more of the same, when it came to crashes – four in the first five races. A lesser man might have been discouraged. Cal (named after US racing legend Cal Rayborn) rationalised it differently.

"I crashed in the first one in Qatar, but it was not my fault. It was the electronics: I had to jump off the bike. The second was in Argentina: I hit the patch of water, and so did five others. The third, I was pushing too hard. So I took confidence: I believed only one of them was a real mistake, as such.

"Crashing is part of racing a motorcycle. I know I am a crasher. I have always crashed motorcycles. But in the end, it depends how you get back up. If you are crashing all the time and doing a shit job, then that's the way it is. I crash and I still make good results, so in the end, who cares? I don't.

"If you race motorcycles, you know the risks. I don't want to get hurt and I don't want to hurt anybody … I've had my fair share of injuries. I'm … not *always* injured, but my body doesn't feel great from years of racing, and crashing. And years of training. But it doesn't stop me coming back."

Crutchlow was born and raised in Coventry in 1985, and his early ambition was to become a professional footballer. Pre-teenage years, "I played for Coventry. I was lucky: I was a centre-forward, so I scored goals." But at the age of 12, a knee injury put paid to that, and motorcycle racing benefited.

Cal believes it is in the blood: "Racers are born, not made. If you look at everybody who's in racing, it's weird how it works. My dad used to race … Haslam, Johnny Rea, the Lavertys; and lots more in MotoGP: Rossi, Lorenzo's dad used to be involved in racing. What makes you want to race a motorbike? It's a thing you grow up with."

Cal won the UK Junior Challenge in 1999 and the Aprilia RS125 Challenge two years later. He started winning on big bikes soon after – British Supersport champion in 2006, and a challenger in BSB for the next two years. Then it was the world stage: winning the World Supersport title at his first attempt in 2009, a race winner in Superbikes the following year.

And then into MotoGP, and it was a sobering introduction, compared with Superbikes.

Halfway through 2011, he told me, "I used to sit and watch Aoyama last year and think 'He's a nobber. I'll smoke him.' All the Superbike riders did. Then I came to the first test in Valencia, jumped on the bike and followed Aoyama. After three laps, I couldn't even see him. Then I woke up, realised this isn't as easy as I thought it was going to be.

"The adaption to the bike is a really, really big thing, because the chassis and the tyres are so much different. But the riders are at another level. Like, beyond belief."

Riding the satellite Yamaha for the Tech 3 (latterly Monster) team, his best result in year one was a fourth, but during that season and the next he had many epic battles with team-mate Andrea Dovizioso.

His first podiums – two third places – came in 2012; but perhaps the most stunning ride was at home at Silverstone, where he had crashed in practice, suffering a fractured and dislocated left ankle. Courage screwed to the sticking point, he managed to demonstrate to medical staff that he was fit to race, and forced through from the back of the grid to sixth.

Fifth in the championship in 2013, with four more podiums, Cal's hopes of a move to the factory Yamaha team were denied, and he switched to Ducati for 2014, back with old team-mate Dovizioso. It was a difficult bike and a difficult year, and

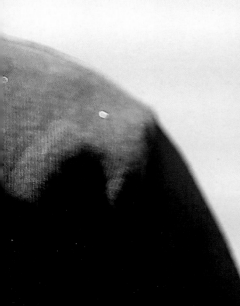

after one top-three finish, Cal and Ducati agreed to abandon their two-year contract. Instead, he joined Lucio Cecchinello's LCR Honda team for 2015. He would have a satellite-factory bike; team-mate Jack Miller an 'Open' version. With one more podium, he was eighth overall. And he signed on for another year before the season was half done.

Determination is Cal's trademark, reflected in a piercing stare, and his own assessment that his greatest strength is "probably determination. To do well, to succeed. If there's something wrong with the bike or with you, to just ride through it. Sometimes that ain't the best thing, but if something goes wrong in the race, it's a good thing. You've just got to get on with it.

"I have an attitude that I like to prove people wrong. Can be a bad way to look at motorcycle racing sometimes, but it's the way that I am: my competitive nature."

Another clear demonstration came at Sepang. Cal had crashed in the morning, sustaining fractures to his left hand, and he had to go through Q1, where he was fastest. At the start of Q2, he fell again. He picked the bike up, right handlebar bent down so "the brake lever was pointing at the ground", and the front brake dragging, which stopped the wheel every time he did a wheelie. Nothing daunted, he pressed on, qualifying fifth. "It was a bit dangerous, but I couldn't start from 12th," he said. Sadly, he crashed again in the race, suffering further foot injuries and concussion. Two weeks later, he was back on the charge at Valencia.

His second season with LCR had started with one crash after another. It was after the summer break that things came good, with his Brno win a major landmark.

The difference from the previous year, he thought, was "probably continuity with the Honda and with the team. The start of the year was difficult for all Honda riders. We were struggling and not doing so well. Honestly speaking, we've not changed so much on the bike at all. It's just Honda riders have decided that is what we've got, and you have to ride it.

"Marc was riding in a different way, to make the champion-

ship. I don't think anybody else could have been on that bike and done it. It's impossible to ride how he rides. If you follow Dani, or look at Dani's data, it's … if you want to learn something from it, you can learn. But with Marc, it's just the way he does things. He's completely different from everybody else. There's nobody riding like him. You can see the difference on TV; we can see it on the data. But to do it … it's difficult.

"Some of the things he does … we call him 'the cat', because he always lands on his feet."

His worst day of the season, he said at Valencia, was not one of the falls, but a sub-standard result at round four in Jerez. "It's a track I like, but with the rear tyre problem, I could hardly ride the bike. I finished 12th."

And the best was not his second win in Australia, where he proved he could win in the dry as well as the wet, but the earlier victory at Brno, "because it was my first. And in Australia, I felt like I was floating. After five laps of the race, when Marc was in front of me, before he crashed, I believed I could have caught him anyway. And I believed I could have won the race – so it was like I expected it myself."

For some, his Brno victory was largely because of a successful gamble on tyres, choosing the hard option for both front and rear. Famously, he said afterwards, that riders who had played it safer with a soft front were "wimps". He does not agree.

"I don't think people have won this year necessarily because of choice of tyres. Everyone can make the choice. It's if you can get them to work. Sometimes people choose the same tyre as me and they are way behind me; others are way ahead of me. It's still down to the rider a lot. Michelin have done a good job: 24 different riders, different bikes, different styles, different weights. You make one tyre for all. It's not easy."

LCR's experienced crew chief Christophe 'Beefy' Bourgignon analyses Cal's 2016 season bit by bit: "Us and Honda were a bit late with development of the Magneti Marelli electronics.

"We had the same bike, basically, the whole season. After Brno, we used a different chassis, which was not so good in

acceleration and braking, but had a bit more rear grip. But the chassis was not the key.

"Through the season, we got a little more understanding of the electronics, so we had better performance and wheelie control. Then wings – all the little things. The rest was Cal. When he reaches the top guys, he seems able to take a step. I've often seen in a race, from looking at the data, that he gets a lot smoother on the throttle and the brakes."

Real Life, Part Two came to Crutchlow when his wife Lucy gave birth to their daughter, Willow, on 2nd August. Typically, he disputed that a child tends to dull the competitive edge.

"The myth is that you suddenly lose a second a lap. I've effing *gained* a second, so I think it's worked the opposite way.

"I was always quite hard on myself, and intense, racing-wise. In the week, in training, even at races, I was relaxed, but also intense. In my day-to day-life, I was intense, hard on myself. Training, as I always do, still now. Now I have to change nappies, have to give her milk. Maybe she's calmed me down a lot. I've had good results since she was born."

So what next, for the long-awaited heir to Barry Sheene? He has one more year on contract to the LCR team. But after that, "I don't know. See how it pans out.

"I don't have to race any more. Financially. But nor does half this paddock.

"I love my sport still, I love racing a motorcycle. I don't like the travelling. I'm over that now. It's starting to wear off a bit.

"I could easily go and sit on the beach for the rest of my life with my wife, and I want to watch my daughter grow up. Don't want to drag her round the paddock forever. I already feel guilty dragging her round now, at three months old. I don't want to miss out on things I could do.

"It depends. See how I feel next year. See what deal I do. Two years, or what. We'll see. The day I wake up and decide I don't want to race any more, I won't race.

"But at the moment, I'm happy. My family are fine."

"TRY AND CATCH THE WIND"

The 2016 season was a time of frenzied aerodynamic development, with wings sprouting race by race. In 2017, they will be gone. NEIL SPALDING looks at how they came, what they did, and what will happen when they are clipped...

Above: Double wings for Dovizioso's Ducati at Motegi in 2016.

Right: Austrian GP winner Iannone ran with only one pair of wings on his Ducati, whereas team-mate Dovizioso ran two.

Photos: Gold & Goose

DURING 2016, Ducati in particular pushed the limits of the rules on aerodynamic assistance. Other factories followed suit, but to a much lesser degree. Now, following much debate on safety, the wings have been banned for 2017.

The rules on bodywork, and thence aerodynamics, had been applied, with just a few tweaks, since the late 1950s. They were a response to the all-enveloping 'dustbin' fairings pioneered by NSU and Moto-Guzzi in GP racing in 1954 and 1955. These wind tunnel-developed fairings covered the front wheel and engine completely, and were carefully shaped to be affected as little as possible by side winds.

In the way of imitative racing fashions, many others joined them on the grid, with less well-designed and engineered fairings. These latter fairings were condemned for being too sensitive to crosswinds, as well as for being poorly mounted. The dustbin was considered dangerous.

Among accusations of dirty dealing and sharp practice, new rules were introduced by the FIM to ensure that front wheels remained uncovered. The factories that had developed efficient streamlining – advanced aerodynamics had kept the lower-powered Moto Guzzi singles competitive for years – blamed those factories without access to wind tunnels for the changes. They had come at a sensitive time: street bike sales were under attack from a new generation of cheap cars, and within a few years many factories withdrew from racing, citing rising costs and reduced sales.

Those 'new' FIM rules established the 'look' of race and sporting motorcycles that survives to this day: front wheel and suspension out in the wind, the rider exposed from the side along with at least half of the rear wheel. It has become fashion. It is how bikes are *meant* to look.

The last two years of aerodynamic development have been all about using up some excess power to allow you to use more excess power. Since the advent of the 1000cc engines, opening up the number to seven engines a year and allowing 22 litres of fuel to power them, MotoGP has had more power than it can use. Past aerodynamic development was aimed at making the fairing slippery, while ensuring minimal drag from the radiator and its ducts. All the new work has been dedicated to the art of going fast.

Sticking a wing on a fairing inevitably will cause more drag, but it may well bring other benefits. If you have power to spare, it's not such a great cost. Motorcycle race bikes have to be a certain height off the ground, so they don't scrape everything on the track in corners. The rider has to be perched quite high on top of the bike for the same reason. Their combined centre of gravity is quite high, but the result-

ing aerodynamic 'centre of pressure' is even higher.

The effect is that once things are moving at anything like 200mph, the bike wants to wheelie; all the more so as power increases. Ducati took the view that straight-line speed would help them a lot, especially while Michelin sorted out their tyres. So their bike was as powerful as possible, as low as possible, as long as possible and bedecked with enough wings to make sure that they could go as fast as possible.

So how did we get here?

Over the last 60 years, there had been minor modifications to the rules. Slightly longer front fairings are now allowed, but little has changed and little has been tried, until the last two years. The leader of the revolution has been Ducati, determined to beat the Japanese, and equally determined to do it in a different way.

Ever since arriving in 2003, Ducati have employed fairing designs optimised for straight-line speeds. All through their 990 years, they used a big-nosed fairing, initially with slab sides for minimal drag, then with large radiator exhaust ducts to improve cooling. The test fairings were even longer, but at the last moment the nose was shortened. The one we all saw race had a small Aston Martin-radiator-shaped air intake, a gift from the British-based designers charged with the last-minute nose job.

At Casey Stoner's request, to reduce side area and improve agility, the subsequent 800s had smaller fairings, but they weren't used all the time. The reason was cooling: the short fairing didn't allow the use of the carefully sculpted inner fairing that routed as much air as possible through the radiator. That meant that on hot days, the old big fairing had to come out again. There was an effort to improve the 'short' fairing, however. Small winglets were fitted at the bottom of the radiator exhaust duct in an attempt to create a vortex to help increase radiator airflow.

But as soon as Stoner left, the big aero fairing was back: Rossi's first rides were with a big new 'straight-line' fairing. These were dropped in short order, by the second day of testing. Rossi and his pragmatic crew chief, Jerry Burgess, weren't having anything on the bike that reduced the rider's ability to flick it on to its side entering corners.

Historically, to hold their bikes down at top speed, the major Japanese factories have used front cowlings with the number plate area moulded at different angles. This allows them to change the trade-off between downforce and drag. For years, that was the limit of the technology. Then came the new 1000cc bikes.

Initially these were power restricted by bore size, number of engines and fuel consumption. But the worst of those restrictions have now been lifted; now, the top teams can use 22 litres of fuel rather than the old 20, and seven engines a year rather than five. That has allowed more revs and more power.

We know that Ducati calculates gearing for 18,000rpm. That's an amazing 29 metres-per-second mean piston speed, and over 10,000g of piston acceleration. These numbers are very near the absolute limits of current racing piston-engine technology.

The power is unprecedented, making wheelies during acceleration and top speed a real issue. One simple solution would be to limit speed by employing electronics to cut the power to hold the bike at the optimum pre-wheelie point. But the aim is to go faster, and the need is to hold the front down, lower the centre of gravity and make the bike longer. Some of these strategies can severely limit the bike's performance elsewhere on track, and balancing that trade-off is the main trick.

Ducati had spent the previous two years doing all of those things. The bike was longer and lower, and it had more aerodynamic aids than the rest; it was the logical outcome of a contrary race strategy. Designing a bike that uses a different strategy to one's competitors is not easy, but it means that on certain circuits and under certain conditions, it will have the advantage.

Ducati have a history of being contrary. In 2005, realising that the then Michelins were built for the Honda and Yamaha style of machine, they decided to go with Bridgestone. That meant going through the pain of a tyre company developing its tyres around their chassis, but it also meant that when Michelin had a problem, there was a chance that Ducati and Bridgestone would not. Michelin's method of operation had freshly developed tyres delivered to the circuit every Sunday morning, tyres tailored to the track and the weather. Bridgestone couldn't compete with that; but as soon as the series raced outside Europe, Michelin couldn't get the tyres delivered overnight, and Bridgestone had the advantage. Ducati duly won in Japan and Malaysia. Daring to be different had begun to pay dividends.

Ducati were clearly hoping that the same philosophy would hold true with aerodynamics. It worked at the Red Bull Ring, a circuit that is a rather simplistic series of straights, and theoretically it should have worked again in Motegi, but it was always a riskier strategy than the Bridgestone gamble. With the rule changes for 2017 banning aerodynamic devices and specifying only one fairing design change during the year, Ducati will need to think again and make some major changes.

Above: Early days, with small winglets amidships as Dovizioso and Iannone sandwich Lorenzo at Losail in 2015.

Far left and left: Ducati's wings at Misano were low; at the same meeting, Rossi's Yamaha wore them high and further forward, to achieve a different effect.

Below left: By the latter part of 2015, Ducati's wings had grown in size and complexity.

Right: Dovizioso at Brno in 2016. By now, wing shapes and surface treatment were highly sophisticated.

Below right: Honda came late to the fashion, but at Misano in 2016 Marquez ran wings similar to Yamaha's – the ultimate compliment.

Photos: Gold & Goose

How Ducati got to where they are

The recent phase of rapid aerodynamic development started in early 2015. The new 'Dall'Igna' Desmosedici finally had the right weight distribution and could be set up to corner really well, but the changes that allowed this also brought some instability. The solution, slightly improbably, was a set of wings mounted halfway up the fairing. These seemed to settle the bike on the brakes.

The wings remained for the first race in Qatar. Small hand-guard extensions were added to fairings so that they complied with the 'no wider than the fairing' rule, and Ducati had two bikes on the podium. The new machine clearly turned and handled well.

Gradually, the wings were developed. First came new 'winglets' (small fences on the ends of the wings); then there was a 'double-decker' version. By Misano, additional wings were on the nose. Ducati's development direction was moving towards maximising straight-line speed, while retaining as much cornering ability as possible. By the middle of the year, Dovisioso, famously a rider who doesn't like much weight on the front wheel, started to complain that his bike wouldn't hold a line through corners. The combination of cornering grip and acceleration aerodynamics clearly wasn't an easy balance to maintain.

Tactically, Ducati were looking to out-accelerate their opponents and get in their way at the next corner entry; it had become a usable strategy because finally they had made more power than they could otherwise employ. The drag cost of the wings was high, but with eased fuel limits they could afford it; they were repaid with harder acceleration and higher top speeds.

By Misano, Yamaha had decided that they could improve their performance with some wings of their own. On Rossi's bike, the downforce generated didn't require any revision to the suspension settings, but the rider liked the 'feel'. The Yamaha didn't have the excess of power enjoyed by the Ducati, so the wings were used sparingly at first. Lorenzo quickly followed and soon became a convert.

For 2016, Yamaha's wings became larger, and Ducati became really serious. Their first wings had been low down on the sides of the fairing, in front of the rider's knees, and appeared to have a distinct droop, effectively an inverted dihedral. In an aircraft, dihedral adds stability in roll; on a motorcycle, with the wings inverted, negative dihedral has the same effect, only upside down.

The logic was sound. For effective handling, a racing motorcycle is designed to pitch forward and back, as well as from side to side, so it sits quite high. A wing adds two major forces, downforce and drag. Ducati mounted the wings as low as they could, so that the drag didn't add height to the overall centre of pressure.

A low-mounted wing can lead to a ground-clearance issue, while the fairing width limits the wing area. Wings at 90 degrees to the fairing flanks provide downforce through the centreline of the bike. That's fine when it is travelling in a straight line, but it isn't so good when the bike is leaned over. Negative-dihedral wings mean that when the bike is leaned over, the upper wing, almost level, continues to provide downforce, while the lower wing is less effective. That same low position means that the rider's knee is right behind the lower wing when the bike is leaned over, helping to stall the airflow.

Winglets and double-decker wings enhanced performance, but low-level mounting was elegant, and effective in terms of minimising drag and lowering the centre of pressure. However, it was not the most effective solution in this environment with a massive excess of power.

What if you were prepared to take a higher drag 'hit' to use more of that power? The higher a wing is mounted, the more it raises the centre of pressure, while since in a wheelie the bike rotates around its rear contact patch, the further forward the wings, the greater their mechanical advantage about that point.

So greater downforce is required, leading to greater drag.

Above: Yamaha wings were more anti-wheelie than pro-top speed.

Above right: Ducati used different configurations for different circuits. These had been designed for the fast straight at Catalunya.

Above centre right: Fairing top sections were widened to make Ducati's plethora legal.

Right: Lorenzo shows how some 'droop' makes the upper wing more effective than the lower at full lean.

Below right: Aprilia's wings were extravagantly scooped.

Bottom right: Honda started off small: this on Marquez's bike at round one of 2016.

Top far right: Top right: Mahindra deployed small wings at pre-season tests. They were later banned in Moto3, by mutual consent.

Photos: Gold & Goose

But at least all of that effort is being placed at the point where it will have the most effect. As 2016 progressed, the Ducatis used their old side-fairing wings less and their ever-larger front wings more.

Ducati were not simply fitting additional wings, however. They were setting them up differently for each rider and track. Gigi Dall'Igna admitted that Ducati's race-simulation software was being employed to choose the best set-up for each track.

Looking closely at the front of each bike, you could see that Dovisioso used less aggressive wing settings than Iannone; the wings were higher at the front, so were mounted 'flatter'. Dovi is famous for not liking much weight on the front, so perhaps that doesn't come as much of a surprise. But at the Catalunya test, and at several races thereafter, Ducati tried asymmetric settings on the front wings, one side higher than the other. That suggests an attempt to increase downforce from the upper wing in long corners in a particular direction.

How the others tried to catch up

It is noticeable that wings have been used by different factories in different ways. With Ducati, employers of the biggest and most aggressive wings, there was a clear move to maximise straight-line downforce, to raise acceleration rates and top speed. Honda tried limited and small deflectors down on the front of the fairing, strictly within the spirit and the letter of the rules. Occasionally, and many suspected to make a point, more adventurous designs were tried.

Aprilia built two versions of a very conventional upside-down wing, narrow and broad, both with winglets on the end. They adopted the more European view of the rulebook and added two 'fairing extenders' in front of the rider's hands to legitimise their wing widths. Suzuki came late to the party, adding a series of small deflectors on the leading edges of their fairing flanks. Later in the year, they too adopted the 'extended hand guard' option and made the highest of their three deflectors a little wider.

By comparison, the Yamaha wings were very sophisticated, and seemed to be optimised to help corner-exit performance, used more as a low-speed wheelie control device than to improve top speed. The shape acted as a deflector under braking and when the forks were compressed, but morphed into a wing as the nose of the bike rose and its aerofoil section took over. Honda paid Yamaha the ultimate compliment by copying this design for Marc Marquez in the latter half of the 2016 season.

The Yamaha wing was held on by six pop rivets, which gives an idea of how little actual force it was transmitting. Reports still mention very small, if any, changes to suspension settings when the wings were used. It is most likely that the Yamahas, and Marquez, were using the wings to add a little front tyre grip and 'rider feel' coming out of corners. That's where the Michelin front tyre design was at its weakest. Just maybe, for most of the grid, a better front Michelin would have meant that there was no need for wings.

For Ducati, however, losing wings will be a much bigger step. We know the bike is capable of turning, and turning quickly; that's why the factory first started their winged experiment. But the settings that Ducati dialled into their chassis meant that it sat low – good for acceleration and top speed, but that also meant it struggled to change direction without massive rider effort. At Silverstone, a long circuit with several short straights and a lot of twisty bits in between, the riders were completely exhausted towards the end of the race. Iannone couldn't hang on and crashed; Dovisioso finished the race suffering from a bad attack of arm-pump. New rules to limit aerodynamic 'add ons' will hurt Ducati in the short term, but may save them from a strategy that seems to have limited long-term effectiveness.

The new rules

The 2017 rules attempt to ban any form of aerodynamic competition:

'Devices or shapes protruding from the fairing or body-work and not integrated in the body streamlining (e.g. wings, fins, bulges, etc.) that may provide an aerodynamic effect (e.g. providing downforce, disrupting aerodynamic wake, etc.) are not allowed.

The Technical Director will be the sole judge of whether a device or fairing design falls into the above definition'

It's a brave attempt to put the genie back into the bottle. Until the last two years, most fairing designs looked relatively simple. But when you take into account the difficulties of routing stable air around fork legs, through radiators and back out of the side of the bike, and the need for minimal air resistance when rolling the bike on to its side, you have to concede that they are actually very sophisticated. For years, factories have had several front cowls, each with a different angle on the number-plate area, all to change the downforce depending on the circuit.

Initially, the rule appeared to allow a basic 'body streamlining', but with no restriction on the number of different fairing designs, you just know someone would have a new fairing for each round. Once this point had sunk home, there came a clarification: only one revision to the fairing design would be allowed every year. That's effectively a design freeze.

Moto2 and Moto3 have already had a year with a ban on advanced aerodynamics. It was supposed to stop major spending on aero, but it didn't stop teams from trying, for instance, multiple versions of their front mudguards to change the balance between cooling and top speed. The latest rule seems to prevent such changes and means that the old system of changing front cowls is no longer allowed.

The rule has the effect of making the initial fairing design very important, and means that the effectiveness of each factory's wheelie control is the final arbiter of top speed. From the organisers' point of view, it saves costs and reduces top speeds, and while both are worthy aims, that reduces the attractiveness of the competition. Indeed, from a technical viewpoint, it closes off one of the last areas where the engineers had some real freedom.

Faster with more power... or faster with less?

MotoGP has spent two years holding the fronts of the motorcycles down to be able to go a bit faster before turning over backwards. Given the importance of reducing emissions and improving energy efficiency, this technology has little real-world relevance.

There is a good argument that MotoGP bikes should be more 'special' than anything on the road, but applying front-end downforce at ultra-high speeds is a potentially very expensive and rather pointless way to achieve that.

There is another good argument that we should be using racing to make progress to improve road bikes.

New rules for 2017 outlaw all but the most basic of fairings. But once there was another way, a way that made racing bikes special while also improving their efficiency.

In the early 1950s, there was no thought of 250-plus bhp, and there weren't that many fairings either, until mid-1953. Then a minor change in the regulations on mudguards led to a series of bikes being fitted with 'porpoise like' beaks on small fairings.

Within a few months, these had evolved into 'dustbin' fairings, which fully enclosed the front wheel. There were experiments, too, with big fairings fitted to the rear of bikes, but these were discontinued quite quickly because of stability issues.

At a time when a top-level GP machine was lucky to go beyond 40bhp, full aerodynamic streamlining made a massive difference to performance. In tests on a street bike, noted technical journalist Vic Willoughby compared the performance of a fully streamlined street 350 with a naked version. At the, admittedly slow, speed of 60mph, fuel consumption improved from 55mpg to 74mpg. Top speed increased from 65 to 72mph, and coast-down from 60 to a standstill went from 388 yards to 500. At racing speeds, this sort of efficiency improvement made a big difference to lap times.

Although NSU arguably made a bigger initial impression, Moto-Guzzi went on to be the kings of motorcycle aerodynamics. Having a wind tunnel at their factory on the shores of Lake Como helped, and it kept them in the game for a bit longer. Their 1956 single-cylinder 350 developed just 35bhp, but could top 135mph. The fairing was so slippery that uprated brakes were required.

In the Moto2 and Moto3 classes, streamlining and aerodynamic modifications were banned for 2016, with development being restricted to different shapes and sizes of mudguards to balance cooling and speed. Just think how different it would be if the smaller classes were allowed to use a little more aerodynamic assistance, even if there were a year-by-year design freeze.

Fashion dictates that fairings exposing the front wheel are considered normal, and the bikes use the performance that such designs allow. Less fairing usually means less top speed, but more manoeuvrability. But why not get a little more performance out of the smaller bikes just by allowing them to be a little more slippery – even by only allowing a rider's arms or the front wheel to be covered?

Motorcycling on public roads faces many threats, from accident statistics and self-driving cars to current poor emissions and fuel consumption. Apart from the Bonneville Speed Trials, the only competition where slippery aerodynamics are encouraged is Craig Vetter's Fuel Economy Challenge, where street bikes ridden at normal speeds achieve close to 200mpg.

It would require a little funding, but MotoGP isn't broke. Let's remove just a few of the racing restrictions in the smaller classes and give better straight-line aerodynamics and the improved efficiency that goes with them a bit more 'race appeal'. Then maybe road bike fashions will follow, and fast road motorcycles might again use less fuel than the most economical of cars.

UNNATURAL SELECTION

The 2016 season was a year of many changes: a new tyre supplier still very much in the development phase; new more basic control electronics; and more fuel and engines for the established factory teams. More power, less sophistication and several moving targets ensured that 2016 was not boring. Nine different race winners says it all: not quite random selection – there was too much skill involved for that. But it became almost impossible to predict winners and losers among all the new variables.

APRILIA RS-GP

APRILIA started the year testing 2015's Superbike-based machine at the Sepang opener, because the all-new machine wasn't ready. Nevertheless, it was a valuable test, as their old electronics could be accurately compared to the new Dorna control electronics. Life became a lot more complicated when the new bike arrived just a few weeks before the start of the season.

With a new engine, initially not making a lot more power than the old one, in a new chassis with new tyres and new electronics, it would have been easy to head off in the wrong direction. The bike was tried with many different settings and soon showed that it was capable of more than its predecessor.

Over the course of the year, there were at least three engine upgrades, each a step up. At Qatar, the bikes were 12–15km/h slower than the fastest opposition; by Catalunya, it was obvious that something was improving; and by the Austrian round, power levels had picked right up.

The 2016 full-race engine had pneumatic valve springs and a seamless-shift gearbox, and it had escaped from the layout of the road-going RSVR. That bike's 65-degree Vee makes for a short street engine, but means that it is very tall, and the throttle system has to sit up even higher, as it is too big to fit in the narrow angle between the cylinders. Aprilia did not confirm the race engine's new Vee angle, but everything pointed to it being 75 degrees. As a result, the cylinder heads were lower, but more importantly, the throttle bodies could be situated in the middle of the Vee, making the overall package much lower.

The engine unit was slightly longer, so to compensate, the gearbox shafts were rearranged to make it shorter, reducing the size of the overall package. In keeping with the rest of the field, the gearbox had its own separate oil supply.

Chassis and swing-arms were uprated as the year progressed. The first chassis was replaced quite quickly with a stiffer version, and by mid-season a new separate front engine mount design had appeared. It was far better at separating lateral flex from torsional and braking rigidity, and was considered a great improvement during corner entry.

DUCATI DESMOSEDICI GP16

DUCATI had had a year with their new smaller V4 engine and its new chassis. It hadn't won a race, but it had improved all year. Initially, they had focused on handling until finally they had a bike that would turn on the control Bridgestones, but the wings that helped provide a bit more braking stability seemed to take over development.

Dovizioso's first ride in 2015 had him running over the inside curbs as the bike changed direction so quickly. By mid-season, however, that trait was gone and there was talk of the bike not holding a line. Wings were added through the year; the bike became lower and longer, and the power increased steadily.

Ducati had looked hard at Michelin's initial options – massive rear grip and a so-so front. If they could maximise the drive from the tyre out of the corners, and carry that speed as deep into the corners at the far end of every straight, they would have the path to the podium they craved.

The bike that arrived at Sepang appeared to have been built for exactly that scenario. The chassis had been redesigned with an open loop at the back; the lower shock mount was stronger and the engine now held the top mount. It looked long and low. The game was a continuation of that played in 2015: to attempt to balance the front downforce needed to increase acceleration and top speed with the push that made it difficult to roll through corners.

Clearly there was a price to pay for the power of the engine, too. To make the power, it revved higher than any other on the track, but that carried its own cost: it was difficult to smooth out initial throttle response, so the riders often used thumb brakes to help calm the bike during corner exit. Wings were added throughout the year, always in an attempt to add to the forces holding the front of the bike down. Ducati top speeds were consistently the highest; only occasionally did another rider get close.

Unlike the other manufacturers, Ducati didn't revert to an earlier design when Michelin brought their improved front at the start of the year. They did resurrect a test bike that had the 'new' front section and a rear section that looked like the 2015 bike for one test at Phillip Island, but it didn't return. Michelin's early tyres worked well for Ducati, but there were issues that led to harder-construction tyres being adopted from Austin onwards. They didn't provide quite the same off-corner drive, but Ducati continued their 'downforce strategy' to try to maximise the rear grip that was there.

New chassis were tried part way through the year, with reinforced headstocks designed to stabilise both braking and improve full-lean grip. Dovi liked them, but Iannone continued with the first version. The wings became bigger and ever more complicated. It all paid off in Austria at the Red Bull Ring and again at Sepang in the wet. As the year went on, Ducati learned to reduce the load transfer on to the front tyre by lowering the swing-arm pivot.

HONDA RC213V

HONDA started the year in considerable disarray, most of it a direct consequence of a difficult 2015. The initial bikes at Sepang were simply the 2015 machines with the new software… and a new engine spec. The Japanese manufacturer had resisted the temptation to work on previous versions of the control software and therefore had to start from scratch at Valencia.

The problem was this: Honda understood that they would not be able to continue to use their ultra-lightweight, forward-rotating-crankshaft design, as this required very advanced and fast software for accurate throttle control. That level of software wasn't going to be available in 2016, but then you had to ask, just how heavy did the crankshaft have to be so that it could easily be controlled by the new software?

Crankshafts take some time to make, so the design decisions probably had to be made straight after the first test at Sepang, and as Honda are one of the top factories whose engine designs were frozen, whatever design they went with would have to stay. They decided that the only way to maintain the right levels of agility was to redesign the engine to allow the crankshaft to rotate backwards. However, that brought a whole bunch of new issues.

Having the crank turn backwards reduces the sum total of the gyroscopic forces and their desire to continue in a straight line. Thus, on a bike so equipped, turn-in requires less effort initially, but then the machine will fall over into the corner slightly more slowly, and all things being equal will want to oversteer slightly less, compared to a bike with a forward-rotating crankshaft.

Right: Casey Stoner tested a fully-instrumented 2015 Ducati at Sepang, and set fastest time.

Far right: Aprilia shows tyre temperature sensors at the Austrian GP.

Below right: Iannone's 2016 Desmosedici at the first test – yet to be painted.

Below far right: Honda started the season on the back foot.

Below: Marquez found a way to ride around the reverse-crank RCV's weaknesses.

Photos: Gold & Goose

There is also crankshaft torque reaction to consider. A forward-rotating crank will enhance a tendency to wheelie on acceleration while upright, but might help hold a line when leaned over. By contrast, the reverse-rotating crank will help keep the front of the bike down as it accelerates while vertical, but encourage it to run wide while leaned over. These torque reactions are very small, but can be enough to turn an understeering bike into an oversteering one.

Honda went for the safe option, spinning the crank backwards and making it relatively heavy to ensure good throttle control. In retrospect, it was too heavy – enough to limit acceleration, and delivering all the reverse-rotation attributes in spades. For a rider like Marquez, there was a massive difference in the way the bike worked and felt. Worse, once the first race had started, Honda couldn't change the design of their bike.

The first chassis were the same as for 2015, but with 15mm added to the swing-arm. That loaded up the front tyre a little more, and given the Michelins' relative dearth of front tyre grip, things had to change. Honda's command of the software would improve – people were under severe pressure to make it so – but now the chassis engineers were going to have to fix their bike's engine problem, again. Through this early period, the bike was an understeering, slow-accelerating disappointment, yet somehow Marquez kept getting to the podium.

It took until Catalunya before the new chassis parts started arriving. There was a new chassis concept for Pedrosa to try. He tested it back to back in practice, and it was so promising that he raced with it and made the podium. It was faster, but he hated the way it felt. In the test on the Monday, Marquez also tried it, and also rejected it.

The frame was almost completely new. It had the same swing-arm and engine, and needed the same wheelbase, so there were major constraints, but everything else had changed. The main beams were thinner, half the section of the standard units, and the route those main beams followed between the swing-arm pivot and the headstock was much straighter. It was a major rebalancing of the bike to suit the latest Michelin tyres, with less lateral strength so that it put less pressure on the tyres when leaned over combined

Above: Suzuki riders chose different chassis solutions in 2016.

Facing page, from top: Like Yamaha, Suzuki mounted the new control electronics under the seat; Lorenzo's M1 shows the webbed engine mounts that improved braking stiffness; Yamaha test bike – chassis with rear-mounted fuel tank was rejected.

Right: Espargaro's Tech 3 Yamaha at Silverstone. The hand-me-down 2015 chassis was a blessing, also chosen by the factory riders.

Photos: Gold & Goose

with straighter beams in an attempt to retain as much rigidity as possible.

Although difficult to measure, I suspect that it had a lowered swing-arm pivot point, too. Under acceleration, that would mean that the swing-arm would not lift the rear with as much force, and less load would be thrown forwards, again helping to reduce unnecessary stress on the Michelins' weak point, the front tyre. The most likely reason for Dani and Mark's rejection was the flexibility of the main frame: to a long-term Honda rider, it would have felt loose and flexy. Over the next few races, Pedrosa used a halfway-house design: it looked like the original, but the main beams followed a slightly straighter path to the headstock. The main beam had the original section, but I suspect it was made of thinner material and/or had a different design treatment near its welds to reduce rigidity.

Marquez received versions of his preferred 2014 chassis modified to lower the swing-arm pivot shortly thereafter. The initial new-concept chassis found a home a couple of races later in the LCR garage. Crutchlow used it for the rest of the year; his broad spread of experience would have allowed him to deal with its likely flexier feel (quite possibly Yamaha-like) far better than the Repsol team's dedicated Honda riders, and clearly it was quite effective.

By the end of the year, the Honda was the bike to have, the one that worked the tyres the best.

SUZUKI GSX-RR

SUZUKI won their first race in years at Silverstone. The track is long, but twisty, and it suited the Suzuki's sweet handling to perfection.

The bike had been slowly, but carefully developed over a few years, and it featured an in-line four with a reverse-rotating cross-plane crank, just like the Yamaha. Indeed, one way of looking at the Suzuki is to ask what Yamaha would do if given a clean sheet of paper and asked to reinvent their own bike.

The chassis looked very spindly, but the only part seen in public was the rear section. Racing chassis have become very sophisticated: it is extremely difficult to create a structure that will resist braking forces, handle acceleration and

twist, yet still flex laterally enough to help with suspension and therefore grip at today's ultra-high lean angles. Suzuki had developed a first. They had tried to split the reinforcement usually designed in to maximise braking rigidity from the main frame's ability to flex laterally, enhancing both aspects at the same time.

The headstock area of the Suzuki was massive, extending away from the beam above the top of the radiator. This sideways extension, which best resembled the head of a hammerhead shark, then stopped with flat ends, provided a lot of resistance to twisting loads. The flat ends were bolted to two simple flat carbon fibre blades, which acted as the front engine mounts. These dropped down to a conventional position in front of the crankshaft, where they were bolted to the engine. The carbon strut is 70mm wide, but only about 5mm thick, and it was kept 'hidden' in plain sight since the bike was launched, as it was the separate section of 'fairing' at the front of the radiator exhaust duct.

The slenderness of the carbon strut meant that it was very stiff under braking forces and as flexible as you could want laterally. There was an added benefit, as the thin strut allowed easy routing of radiator exhaust air out through the side of the bike. This restriction on cooling had been a problem with the across-the-frame fours since the inception of MotoGP.

Suzuki learned from the initial Michelin tests that there was likely to be a massive increase in off-corner acceleration in 2016; they duly arrived at the Sepang test with a new chassis and swing-arm set-up for more rigidity, the better to deal with that grip. Michelin brought an improved front tyre to the same test. As a result, the balance of grip moved forward and there was less need for such an extreme rearward strength bias. Maverick went straight back to the 2015 version; Aleix persevered.

The balance of grip changed again at Austin; Michelin's harder-construction 'emergency' rear tyres actually created a balance between front and rear grip that was familiar. Suzuki built a new frame that took the 2015 design and reconfigured its rigidity to suit the Michelins. By Silverstone, both riders were using this variant.

Suzuki found the new control software very much to their liking; an indication of their level in the open software

pecking order was that they regarded the control software as an upgrade. For Honda and Yamaha, it was a significant step back. Suzuki's results in 2016 were sufficient to lose them their testing and engine-freeze concessions for 2017. Progress had been made; now it gets really difficult.

YAMAHA YZR-MI

YAMAHA had a strange year. The initial Michelin tyre allocation wasn't really to their liking, but the new front that arrived for the Sepang tests allowed them to complete the first half of the year on their 2015 chassis with only small adjustments. Except for one major point, the new software was well understood early in the season and should have been well within Yamaha's control; but Marquez's skill on what initially was a very poor Honda stopped them from pressing their advantage.

Until Catalunya, the Yamahas were either up at the front or not there at all. Yamaha's riders could win races; their bikes were good, but they were on the limit in trying to set them up. Rossi's Austin crash cost him dear, while the Mugello engine breakage didn't help either, but it has to be said that his use of pre-traction-control skills to win on Michelin's 'Flintstone specials' at Jerez was stellar.

Lorenzo had his problems, too, after being 'attacked from the rear' at Catalunya. But as the year went on, the other factories did a better job of using the tyres. The Yamahas, which for over a decade had lived and died by their edge grip, were clearly more sensitive to low tyre and track temperatures than the Hondas, and were simply outperformed as Marquez brilliantly rode around many of his own bike's problems.

Yamaha build a brilliant chassis. Everything on their bikes, including the engine character, is dedicated to working the tyres to perfection and developing maximum grip. But Michelin followed an erratic path as they developed their tyre offering 'on the hoof', and it became apparent that the Yamaha edge-grip strategy needed a little more stability in tyre characteristics to allow them to tailor their machine precisely to the tyres' needs. If Michelin continue to improve, that should be easier in 2017.

Modified chassis were tested at Catalunya, Lorenzo liking the new unit and staying with it. Rossi waited for a second version to arrive later in the year. Both types had plates welded to the top of the front section of the main beams. This made the chassis more rigid under braking and, by raising the point where the chassis twisted, allowed it to be more flexible down at the tyre contact patch at extreme lean angles. New swing-arms came, too. They were stiffer in torsion, but were only used occasionally.

Two engines were lost at Mugello in an unfortunate combination of circumstances. Lorenzo's went in warm-up, so no great damage was done to his title hopes, but Rossi's blew when he was up for a potential win. Mugello has a very-high-speed straight, and the Yamahas were right up against their rev limits. There was a small bump on the fastest part of the straight, enough to allow a jump in engine speed, and Yamaha's rev-limit strategy wasn't up to the job of controlling the resulting surge in rpm.

Approaching the rev limit, all components are under maximum stress. When the rev limiter cuts fuel or ignition, the pressure comes off. It matters then how you reintroduce the sparks or fuel. Too hard a reintroduction creates a massive load spike throughout the engine. It is normal to cut revs at the main limit, then to reintroduce sparks or fuel at a slightly lower point, say 200rpm less.

Yamaha had set up the new software in a way that simply didn't reintroduce power smoothly enough. Then the bump at max power and revs set off a series of off-load to on-load cycles that proved too much for the top end of each motor. The reaction was swift and effective: Yamaha flew several top engine men from Japan to their Italian base and destruction tested several strategies on the dyno. They solved the problem, but by then the damage had been done.

TECHNICAL ESSAY
THAT OLD BLACK MAGIC
KEVIN CAMERON examines the central role played by tyres in motorcycle racing and development...

Above: **The return of the fat man. Michelin took over from Bridgestone in 2016 after seven years away.**

Right: **Fatigue stress after hard work – a worn Michelin at Brno.**

Photos: Gold & Goose

COMPARE any film of motorcycle racing from the 1950s or '60s with one from today and the difference is staggering: corner lean angle has increased tremendously, implying a corresponding increase in corner speed. This is the most visible proof of increased tyre grip. Less visible is the increased ability of modern tyres to handle combined braking and cornering, and acceleration and cornering. The greater the tyre grip, the sooner the rider can begin accelerating, raising the average speed on the next straight. In 2008, Yamaha's trackside instrumentation revealed that Casey Stoner was applying enough throttle at the corner apex to trigger his traction control system. Spin at the apex. At maximum lean angle.

Yet our eyes always go to engines, chassis, brakes and suspension – objects about which visual analysis can instantly tell us something. When Honda or Ducati move an important chassis or swing-arm weld, photographer Neil Spalding is there with his camera to show us 'before' and 'after' pictures, and speculate as to the reason for the change. When a manufacturer alters its exhaust system, we see it at once. When an engine's firing order or intervals are altered, we hear it.

But nothing – not even mass spectrometer analysis applied to rubber samples – tells us what the tyre manufacturer

has done. In 2002, we could see the mould segment lines on Michelins, alerting those interested to the arrival of that company's C3M automated manufacturing system. But the black rubber itself and the unseen fabric structure within are uncommunicative.

The fundamental problem of tyres is heat. To do its job, a tyre must flex as it flattens upon entering the footprint against the pavement, and unflex as it leaves, performing this cycle 23 times per second at 100mph. Rubber is elastic, but not perfectly so. Deform an element of rubber with 100 units of energy and you get back maybe 90 units when the rubber relaxes. The difference becomes heat. Vulcanisation, or curing, transforms putty-like 'green' rubber into a tough elastic solid, but sufficient heat can undo that process, causing rubber gradually to lose its properties. Therefore the generation and management of heat in tyres are fundamental to their design.

The first effect of excessive temperature is loss of peak properties, which riders used to call "going off", though a drop in grip is now called a "step". More dangerous is *blistering*, whereby components of the tread volatilise, producing pox-like eruptions on the tread surface. Riders feel this as abnormal vibration. Worst of all is *chunking*, whereby heat failure of the tread-to-carcase adhesive system allows chunks of tread to

detach from the tyre, as occurred to front rain tyres at Brno in 2016.

To make sense of tyres and what they do, we must identify and describe their basic parts. Tyres flex more than just about any other engineering device, so it's essential that their parts be elastic. Foremost among these is the inflation air contained within the tyre, for its job is to press the flexible fabric carcase and the tread rubber on its outer surface against the pavement to form the tyre footprint, or contact patch. To get a rough idea of the size of this footprint, divide the load carried by the tyre by its inflation pressure. Because the tyre's carcase has some stiffness of its own, the actual footprint area is always less than this ideal.

The tyre's beads are the parts that are pressed outward against the wheel rim's flanges by inflation air, sealing the air in without need for an inner tube. Because inflation pressure produces large forces that tend to lift the tyre off the rim, each bead contains a strong *bead-wire bundle*, consisting of several turns of high-tensile steel wire.

Secured to the bead-wire bundles by folding over are the body ply or plies. In early days, tyre fabric was woven like the cloth in a shirt, but as the tyre flexed in rolling, the interwoven threads sawed each other apart. Tyre plies, therefore, are now made as 'cord fabric', consisting only of unidirectional fibres, sandwiched between two thin layers of rubber.

Two basic tyre constructions exist – the older *bias* (or cross-ply) system, in which alternating plies have their cord angled (biased) right and left of the tyre's centreline, and *radial*, in which one or two plies start from the bead-wire bundles in a radial direction and cross the tyre centreline at 90 degrees.

Bias-ply tyres were universal in motorcycle racing before 1984, and some touring bikes still use them today. 'Scissoring' of the angled plies against each other, by shearing the thin rubber that separates them, generates heat. As two-stroke horsepower shot up in 1981, this heating spelled the end for the racing bias tyre. At the 1982 Belgian 500 GP, Kenny Roberts led easily, but his rear tyre came apart, and Franco Uncini's front tyre chunked.

Radial-ply construction, which eliminates ply scissoring, was introduced by Michelin for motorcycle tyres in 1984 (radial construction for car tyres began in 1948).

Inflation air is retained by a thin *inner liner* of low-gas-permeability butyl rubber, which is applied to the inside surface of the tyre carcase.

Applied atop the carcase plies are one or more *belt plies*. Before 1973, such belts did not exist, but very high speeds at Daytona caused centrifugal radial growth, increasing tyre flex and heating. Dunlop contained this growth by adding bias tread belts in their Racing 200 tyre, which on Giacomo

Agostini's Yamaha won the Daytona 200 in 1974. That same year, Goodyear made slicks the only choice for dry tracks.

A pure radial-ply tyre is unstable, so practical motorcycle radials have under-tread belts to stiffen the tread laterally. Sidewall stiffness can be modified with chafer plies. Each tyre maker has its proprietary belt structure, which may consist of low-angle bias plies, a zero-angle (wound-on) belt, or a combination of these features.

The tread is applied over the tread belt. Rubber generates grip by three basic mechanisms.

The first is mechanical interlock, as the soft rubber fills the texture of the pavement to a degree, locking the two together.

The second is molecular adhesion – through so-called 'short-range forces', rubber is attracted to other surfaces. It is this part of grip that is destroyed by the presence of water or (as at Qatar) fine dust.

The third mechanism is hysteresis – rubber's internal friction. If we think of a pavement asperity (a small projection from the surface) that comes into contact with the tyre as a ship ploughing through a sea of rubber, we see that drag produced as the asperity pushes rubber aside at its 'bow' (the grip generated by the tyre) is partly recovered if the material promptly closes behind it. This gives some push to the passing asperity, which translates as drag to the tyre. By slowing the rubber's closing, this drag is reduced and grip effectively increased. This is the job of hysteresis. High-hysteresis rubber (advertisers called it "cling" or "road-hug" rubber) was first adopted on motorcycle tyres in the early 1960s.

Rubber loses flexibility at lower temperatures. At the *glass transition temperature* of a given compound, it becomes a rigid solid that can be machined just like metal. Compounds giving high grip on the track tend to have high glass transition temperatures, limiting their grip at ambient temperature.

This wasn't a problem in the classic racing era, when the flexing of rib or block water drainage patterns in the tread generated heat that warmed up tyres quickly. Slicks were much slower to warm because their uninterrupted tread was self-bracing. Initially, there were many falls on cold slicks, so today tyre warmers preheat tyres to 80°C. Even so, a race tyre needs two to three laps to reach full grip. Despite the danger of low grip, top riders will push hard to get their tyres up to working temperature.

The ideal tread compound would combine softness, which allows the rubber to take a full 'print' of the pavement's texture, with enough tensile strength to transmit that grip to the rest of the tyre. The result is always a compromise. A soft qualifying tyre gives high grip, but only until its flexure causes it to overheat. A 'Q' tyre lasts through one warm-up lap, then one qualifying lap (the rider hopes!) before it dramatically loses grip. A race tyre sacrifices some grip to be able to go race distance. Much of race practice is devoted to discovering which available tyres offer the best compromise.

In the wet, rain tyres with soft tread compound and tread grooves for water drainage are used. If the rain abates, a dry line may begin to appear here and there on the track, causing overheating and grip loss. The right tyre choices in mixed conditions are often a matter of luck.

Michelin dominated the 1990s, often by its practice of gathering data from Friday and Saturday practice, then making special tyres overnight for Sunday and flying or driving them to the circuit. Manual assembly of tyres continued in this era, but by the turn of the century, Michelin were ready to introduce their C3M automated assembly system. C3M's concentricity allowed rubber thickness, and therefore temperature, to be reduced. Race tyres made this way brought substantial drops in lap time.

Mandated improvements in automobile fuel economy forced tyre makers to find ways to reduce tyre rolling resistance. Research showed that rubber hysteresis – so valuable in generating wet grip – could be retained at the high stick/slip frequencies of rubber traction (up to 2000 cycles per second), but greatly reduced at tyre rotation frequency (5–15 per second). Particularly at Bridgestone in Japan, this research

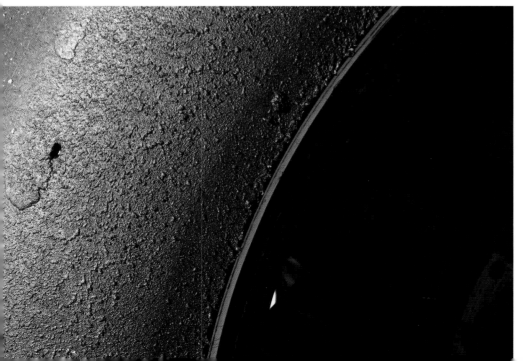

Above: Classic Marquez: elbow skimming the ground as he leans his Honda close to horizontal.
Photo: Repsol Honda

Top right: Rossi's more traditional style in 2005 on the Yamaha.

Above right: Feeding the power on at maximum lean, Stoner lays down his Bridgestone-shod Ducati in his title-winning year.

Right: Fresh Michelins show their asymmetric construction.
Photos: Gold & Goose

developed novel chemical means of broadening the compromise between softness and tensile strength. A big contrast with the past is that rubber chemistry now allows tyres to behave stably even after 'the step', such that fastest race laps are often set near the end of an event.

In the late 1990s, Bridgestone supplied tyres for the smaller racing classes, then fielded a test team to develop tyres for 500s. By 2003, their tyres worked well in cool conditions and they were becoming a force. Michelin had focused on making the ideal tyre for specific conditions, while Bridgestone, far from the races, had to develop a wider operating range. By 2005, Ducati, seeking more leverage on tyre development, switched from Michelin to Bridgestone.

In this period, there were two contrasting riding styles. Valentino Rossi, riding a high-corner-speed style, needed a stiff tyre carcase capable of handling high cornering force without buckling. Riders like Colin Edwards, Kenny Roberts Jr and Dani Pedrosa, who employed a more dirt-track or Superbike-derived point-and-shoot corner style, wanted a soft carcase that could spread out a footprint of maximum area to deliver traction for hard acceleration off the turn. Asked what happened if he tried the soft carcase, Rossi said, "The bike jumps sideways."

Note that I link big footprint to high grip. Some will object that grip should be independent of footprint area because Amonton's Law (1699) says that the friction force between two surfaces depends only on the load pressing them together. Any solid surface, no matter how polished, consists at molecular scale of irregular peaks and valleys. Under light pressure, the only actual contact between the two is peak-to-peak. Double that pressure and the peaks deform in *linear* proportion to load, doubling the area of true contact and doubling the friction between the two. This is the basis of Amonton's Law.

But the deformation of rubber under stress is not linear. Initially, rubber is quite soft, but it stiffens as the load on it is increased. This means that you get more area of contact from the first unit of load than you get from the second, and so on. Illustrating this is Honda's request to Michelin at the end of 2005 for greater footprint area to give their riders traction for faster acceleration. Yamaha, whose riders employ a corner-speed style, had less need for such traction. Michelin produced a low-pressure rear tyre said to require only 0.9–1.1 bar inflation, continuing the trend of the 1990s toward larger footprint. Because each team has its own design philosophy, such changes in tyre design cannot 'lift all boats' equally. With each change in tyre characteristics, the teams have to scramble to adapt.

In 2007, Casey Stoner was world champion on the Ducati 800 and Bridgestone tyres. Michelin's overnight delivery system was ended by new rules requiring all tyres to be available at the beginning of race weekends. Without overnight manufacture, Michelin missed the mark badly a few times and top riders began switching to Bridgestone. For 2009, MotoGP became a spec-tyre series with Bridgestone as sole supplier.

Riders were amazed at the Bridgestone front, saying, "You can just keep on loading it up and it doesn't let go." This was a huge difference from the past, when continuing to load the front on corner entry just made the front tyre let go. Lean angles became truly fantastic, with the old knee-down style replaced by Marc Marquez's way – the rider's whole body offset to the inside of the bike in corners, knee drawn up to the chest for clearance and the inside elbow on the track.

To keep the footprint flat on the pavement while generating such forces, the Bridgestone carcase had to be extremely stiff. Suspension functions that had previously been handled by tyre

flex were passed on to the chassis, which had to be made more flexible laterally.

Race tyres are designed for the riders who can win the championship, not for mid-pack. Top riders work their tyres harder than anyone else, creating a situation in which those riding outdated styles (such as being reflexively unable to make themselves turn the throttle at full lean) may be unable to get tyre temperature. Such riders have no option but to leave the series, but in several cases their skills have given them second careers in World Superbike, where tyres are less specialised.

Bridgestone were succeeded by Michelin as spec-tyre supplier in 2016. As might have been expected, despite testing beforehand, they needed a number of races to correct early shortcomings in front grip (there were many falls from losing the front in pre-season testing) and durability (tread separation in South America). The Michelin approach to MotoGP appeared to employ less stiffness in favour of a larger footprint, but it was a difficult year for the teams, as they had to adapt to Michelins while also learning to use the control software.

Michelin moved forward rapidly. While in early races riders noted that fronts lacked grip, giving "a closing feeling", changes by the time of Brno practice caused Jorge Lorenzo to say, "At this moment with the Michelins, I am really comfortable. For the first time, I could brake even later than with the Bridgestones. At this track, I feel really, truly confident with the front."

Michelin's Nicholas Goubert said that it was Michelin's intention to maintain a close relationship between MotoGP tyre design and its production tyres, as the only justification for the heavy expense of developing racing tyres is to create technologies usable in the marketplace.

A verbal commitment to that old adage: racing improves the breed.

TEAM-BY-TEAM

2016 MOTOGP REVIEW

Teams and Riders

MATTHEW BIRT

Bike Specifications

NEIL SPALDING

MOVISTAR YAMAHA MOTOGP

TEAM STAFF

Masahiko NAKAJIMA: President, Yamaha Motor Racing
Kouichi TSUJI: MotoGP Group Leader
Lin JARVIS: Managing Director, Yamaha Motor Racing
Massimo MEREGALLI: Team Director
Kouji TSUYA: Yamaha M1 Project Leader
Wilco ZEELENBERG: Rider Performance Analyst (Lorenzo)
Luca CADALORA: Rider Performance Analyst (Rossi)
William FAVERO: Communications Manager
Matteo VITELLO: Sponsorship Strategies
Alen BOLLINI/Alberto GOMEZ: Press Officers
Mark CANELA:Team Coordinator
Takehiro SUZUKI: Parts Coordinator
Matteo VITELLO: Sponsorship Strategies Development
Raffaella PASQUINO: Marketing Coordinator

JORGE LORENZO PIT CREW

Ramon FORCADA: Crew Chief
Davide MARELLI: Data Engineer
Yoichi NAKAYAMA: Yamaha Engineer
Mechanics: Javier ULLATE, Jurij PELLEGRINI,
Ian GILPIN, Juan Llansa HERNANDEZ

VALENTINO ROSSI PIT CREW

Silvano GALBUSERA: Crew Chief
Hiroya ATSUMI: Yamaha Engineer
Matteo FLAMIGNI: Data Technician
Mechanics: Alex BRIGGS, Bernard ANSIAU,
Brent STEPHENS

JORGE LORENZO
Born: 4 May, 1987 – Palma de Mallorca, Spain

GP Starts: 250 (156 MotoGP, 48 250cc, 46 125cc)
GP Wins: 65 (44 MotoGP, 17 250cc, 4 125cc)
World Championships: 5 (3 MotoGP, 2 250cc)

VALENTINO ROSSI
Born: 16 February, 1979 – Urbino, Italy

GP Starts: 348 (288 MotoGP/500cc, 30 250cc, 30 125cc)
GP Wins: 114 (88 MotoGP/500cc, 14 250cc, 12 125cc)
World Championships: 9 (6 MotoGP, 1 500cc, 1 250cc, 1 125cc)

HOW could it all have gone so horribly wrong?

That question would top the agenda in Yamaha's post-season post mortem, after a spectacular slide over the course of the year.

Victory in five of the opening seven races had suggested that Yamaha was in a strong position for a second successive triple crown of rider, team and constructor titles. But ultimately the season turned into a nightmare, with bitter Honda rival Marquez winning a third MotoGP crown with three races to spare.

Lorenzo and Rossi's alarming slump was hard to predict and even harder to fathom after the blister-ing start. The new era of Michelin tyres and unified software started as a romp by Lorenzo at Losail, where the Spaniard took pole, fastest lap and the win in the seventh clean sweep of his MotoGP career.

At Le Mans, he blitzed Rossi by 10.6 seconds to cruise to an emphatic second win, by his biggest ever dry-race margin.

Then the reigning world champion won a nail-biting last-lap thriller against Marquez in Mugello to seize control in the standings.

After that, Lorenzo suffered a losing streak that nobody saw coming. He was particularly out of sorts in

YAMAHA YZR-M1

Engine: 1000cc transverse in-line 4; reverse-rotating cross-plane crankshaft, DOHC, 4 valves per cylinder, pneumatic valve return system
Power: Around 270bhp, revs up to 17,000rpm

Ancillaries: Magneti Marelli electronics, NGK sparking plugs, full electronic ride-by-wire • *Lubrication:* Yamalube

Transmission: Gear primary drive, multi-plate dry slipper clutch, six-speed seamless-shift cassette-style gearbox, DID chain

Suspension: Front, Ohlins TRVSP25-8 48mm 'through-rod' forks; Rear, Ohlins TRSP44-12 'through-rod' shock with linkage • *Wheels:* 17in MFR • *Tyres:* Michelin

Brakes: Brembo 340mm carbon-carbon front; Yamaha steel rear

KATSUYUKI NAKASUGA

Born: 9 August, 1981 – Shizuoka, Japan

GP Starts: 10 (7 MotoGP/500cc, 3 250cc)

Rossi's ritual - 21 seasons and counting

cold and wet conditions and didn't win for the next 11 races. A pole-to-flag victory in Valencia meant he eventually ended nine years with Yamaha on a high. Rossi's bid to clinch an elusive tenth world title never recovered momentum after he lost 50 points in three races at CotA, Mugello and Assen.

He'd looked well set to dispense with Lorenzo's challenge at Mugello until a rowdy home crowd was stunned into silence by a spectacular and terminal engine blow-up for the Italian, on a day when Yamaha's normally bulletproof reliability took a pounding.

Lorenzo had blown a motor on the last lap of morning warm-up. Had he done one lap less, Yamaha would have faced the embarrassment of both Lorenzo and Rossi retiring with engine failure. It was Rossi's first technical non-finish since Valencia in 2007, and even tougher to swallow in front of his adoring public, as Lorenzo went on to claim Yamaha's 100th win in the four-stroke era.

Rossi rebounded superbly to take a dominant second win of the season at Catalunya, but that would prove his last, as the evergreen 37-year-old went ten races in a row without adding to his tally of 114 victories.

A crash out of the lead at a wet Assen all but killed off Rossi's challenge prior to the summer sojourn. It was his third DNF in eight rounds.

Yamaha's challenge now started to seriously unravel. Rossi's crash and Lorenzo's inability to cope with cold and wet conditions on his way to a lucky and distant tenth in the Netherlands were followed by more turmoil in Germany.

Lorenzo had to go into Q1 for the first time since the revised qualifying format had been introduced in 2013, and when he finished 15th and Rossi eighth in a flag-to-flag encounter, it was the first time Yamaha's factory team had missed the podium in successive races in nine years.

Rossi and Lorenzo's faltering challenge suffered a final and fatal blow in front of Yamaha's top brass at the Twin Ring Motegi. Both fell out of second place in a futile pursuit of a rampant Marquez. The pair had never both failed to finish a race while together in Yamaha's official factory team; Rossi's fourth DNF of the year made it his worst finishing record since his debut 250cc championship in 1998!

And it was the first time since the Phillip Island race in 2011 that the Yamaha works team had failed to score any points in a MotoGP race.

Talking of Phillip Island, yet more trouble was lurking. Lorenzo's 12th on the grid was his worst qualifying effort since the 2013 Dutch TT. It was even darker for Rossi, who started 15th, his worst qualifying spot since 2011, on the unruly Ducati.

Yamaha's senior management remained intact, with Masahiko Nakajima serving as President of Yamaha Motor Racing. MD Lin Jarvis was very much the public

Ramon Forcada

Silvano Galbusera

Lorenzo and crew after his win in Losail

Massimo Meregali

Lin Jarvis

face of Yamaha; while technical responsibility fell on the shoulders of Kouichi Tsuji and M1 project leader Kouji Tsuya.

Massimo Meregalli was team director, while Lorenzo's crew was headed by Ramon Forcada, with the rider since he had joined Yamaha in 2008. Wilco Zeelenberg was rider performance analyst, but he was a permanent fixture in Lorenzo's camp. Having a riding coach has become something of a fashion in MotoGP, and Rossi jumped on the bandwagon when former 125cc and 250cc World Champion Luca Cadalora was added to his pit crew.

Otherwise, Rossi's crew was unchanged, with Silvano Galbusera in his third year as chief engineer, and the familiar faces of data engineer Matteo Flamigni, and mechanics Alex Briggs, Brent Stephens, Gary Coleman and Bernard Ansiau.

Yamaha's 2016 season may have started well on track, but it was a mixed beginning behind the scenes.

The hangover from the bitter ending to 2015 still poisoned the air in Qatar when Rossi and Lorenzo clashed over their future dealings.

With both out of contract and both expected to feature significantly in a protracted silly season, Rossi saw no reason to hold out. Yamaha were desperate to keep their talisman, and he had no intention of retiring. Negotiations were painless and swift, and his new two-year deal was announced on Saturday evening, ahead of the opening round.

This seemed to irk Lorenzo, who had also been made a two-year pre-season offer. Seeking a new stimulus and perhaps understandably wanting to step out from Rossi's considerable shadow, Lorenzo quit to join Ducati in a deal announced in April.

His move to the Bologna factory will reunite him with Gigi Dall'Igna, who masterminded his success at Derbi in 125s and then his double 250cc triumph for Aprilia in 2006 and 2007.

REPSOL HONDA TEAM

TEAM STAFF

Shuhei NAKAMOTO: HRC Executive Vice President
Livio SUPPO: Team Principal
Takeo YOKOYAMA: Technical Director

MARC MARQUEZ PIT CREW

Santi HERNANDEZ: Race Engineer
Carlo LUZZI: Fuel Injection Engineer
Teruaki MATSUBARA: HRC Engineer
Gerold BUCHER: Data Engineer
Carlos LINAN: Chief Mechanic
Mechanics
Roberto CLERICI
Jordi CASTELLA
Javier ORTIZ
Kochi UJINO

DANI PEDROSA PIT CREW

Ramon AURIN: Race Engineer
Jose Manuel ALLENDE: Fuel Injection Engineer
Yukihide AKITSU: HRC Engineer
Daniel PETZOLD: Data Engineer
Masashi OGO: Chief Mechanic
Mechanics
Emanuel BUCHNER
Pedro CALVET
John EYRE
Denis PAZZAGLINI

DANI PEDROSA
Born: 29 September, 1985 – Sabadell, Spain
GP Starts: 259 (181 MotoGP, 32 250cc, 46 125cc)
GP Wins: 53 (29 MotoGP, 15 250cc, 8 125cc)
World Championships: 3 (2 250cc, 1 125cc)

MARC MARQUEZ
Born: 17 February, 1993 – Cervera, Spain
GP Starts: 150 (72 MotoGP, 32 Moto2, 46 125cc)
GP Wins: 55 (29 MotoGP, 16 Moto2, 10 125cc)
World Championships: 5 (3 MotoGP, 1 Moto2, 1 125cc)

MARC MARQUEZ made a tough 2015 loss, at the hands of Yamaha and Jorge Lorenzo, look nothing more than a blip with a robust retaliation in 2016, continuing his relentless charge to legendary status.

The Spaniard had surrendered his chance of a third successive premier-class crown in 2015 with a series of unforced errors. He wasn't going to make the same mistake twice, and a more measured and calmer strategy paid off handsomely, even if it was a demanding personal journey to banish his natural instinct to go for the jugular on every lap.

He took full responsibility for his failure of the previous year and didn't meddle with a team that had a

proven winning pedigree.

Santi Hernandez continued as crew chief, and Emilio Alzamora was ever-present, in a dual role of manager and mentor.

Honda's senior management figures all remained for one last hurrah.

HRC Executive Vice President Shuhei Nakamoto had been at the helm since 2009, but 2016 would be his last year, as he reached retirement age.

Livio Suppo had joined HRC in 2010 and continued as team principal, a role he had held since 2013.

Development of the RC213V was once again the responsibility of Takeo Yokoyama, technical director

HONDA RC213V – Repsol

Engine: 1000cc 90-degree V4, reverse-rotating 360-degree crank, pneumatic valve return system • **Power:** More than 270bhp, revs up to 17,500rpm
Ancillaries: Magneti Marelli electronics and ride-by-wire throttle and fuel-injection system with torque sensor, NGK sparking plugs • **Lubrication:** Repsol
Transmission: Gear primary drive, multi-plate dry slipper clutch, six-speed seamless-shift cassette-type gearbox, RK chain
Suspension: Front, Ohlins TRVSP25-8 48mm 'through-rod' forks; Rear, TRSP44-12 'through-rod' shock with linkage
Wheels: 17in front and rear: OZ Racing (Marquez); Marchesini (Pedrosa) • **Tyres:** Michelin
Brakes: Brembo 320 or 340mm carbon-carbon front; Yutaka 218mm steel rear

HIROSHI AOYAMA
Born: 25 October, 1981 – Chiba, Japan

GP Starts: 174 (70 MotoGP, 104 250cc)
GP Wins: 9 250cc
World Championships: 1 250cc

NICKY HAYDEN
Born: 30 July, 1981 – Owensboro, Kentucky, USA

GP Starts: 218
GP Wins: 3 MotoGP
World Championships: 1 MotoGP

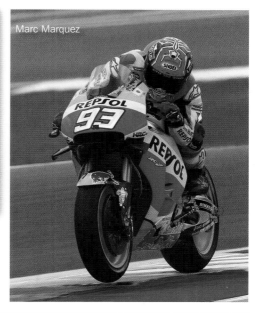

Marc Marquez

since 2013, having previously worked as track engineer to Dani Pedrosa from 2010.

Marquez understood immediately in a troublesome pre-season that he would have to defend early on, with Honda struggling initially to make a quick adjustment to the new unified software. A powerful, but overly aggressive motor spoiled acceleration, and while Honda caught up, Marquez opted to collect precious points rather than high-risk wins.

He did win in Argentina in a mandatory two-part race, and steamrollered the field for a fourth season in a row at CotA in Texas, but he had to wait another six races before he won again. He prevailed for a seventh successive year at the Sachsenring, after a bold, but brilliant switch to slicks on a damp track.

There followed another streak of five winless races, and when he arrived at Motorland Aragon in late September, he was in the worst run of form in his premier-class career, with four races outside the top two.

Then he dominated at Aragon for a 54th career win – only Agostini, Rossi, Nieto, Hailwood and Lorenzo had more. And Marquez is only 23!

Title victory at Motegi seemed impossible, but the 2016 championship was richly unpredictable. In just another chapter in a story that sometimes felt like fiction, Marquez won the race and was crowned champion after both Rossi and Lorenzo crashed out.

If Marquez had reluctantly ridden within himself so far, the shackles were off for the final three races. He could throw caution to the wind, and his first DNF of the season came at the next race, when he fell out of a comfortable lead in Australia for the second time in three years. He crashed out of podium contention again in Malaysia before concluding the season with a close second behind Lorenzo in Valencia.

Marquez never hinted at leaving Honda, despite a brief approach from Ducati, and signed a new two-year deal, announced on the eve of his home round at Catalunya.

If 2016 was a familiar tale of success for Marquez, it was a familiar saga of underachievement and injury for team-mate Dani Pedrosa.

It was his 11th season in the world-famous Repsol Honda livery, and after a stunning end to 2015, when he won two of the last four races, Pedrosa was tipped by many as a serious title threat. His challenge never materialised, however, and he scored just two podium finishes in the first 12 races – his worst run since his 125 rookie year of 2001.

When he qualified eighth on the grid at Misano, there seemed little to suggest that he would play a starring role in a milestone race in MotoGP. Yet he created history by becoming the eighth different winner in eight races, while preserving his proud record of winning in each of his 11 premier-class seasons in MotoGP – a feat matched only by Rossi and Agostini.

Honda's title celebrations in Motegi

Livio Suppo

Shuhei Nakamoto

As so often in the past for Pedrosa, a career highlight was quickly followed by adversity. This time, the spectacular fall from grace came in FP2 of the Japanese Grand Prix at the Twin Ring Motegi. A vicious off-throttle cold-tyre high-side can give any rider sleepless nights, but Pedrosa was left with a broken right collarbone and facing the prospect of yet more major corrective surgery.

He was out until the final round in Valencia, but his immediate replacement in Japan was an easy pick for Honda. Former 250cc world champion and current HRC test rider Hiroshi Aoyama was already on site, and he finished 15th. He also stood in for Pedrosa in Malaysia.

Pedrosa's Phillip Island substitute was a universally popular decision, Nicky Hayden being called up to race in Repsol Honda livery for the first time since 2008. He was locked in a frantic six-rider fight for seventh when he fell out after contact with Jack Mill-

er, whom ironically he had replaced at Aragon.

Pedrosa's late injury woes came on the back of yet more unrest on his side of the HRC garage. His crew had undergone massive upheaval at the end of 2014, when he axed Christophe Leonce and Mark Barnett, which then led to the departure of long serving crew chief Mike Leitner, since a key figure in the development of the KTM RC16.

Data engineer Ramon Aurin took over, but his two-year stint ended in 2016. He would be replaced by Giacomo Guidotti, from Pramac.

Two other crew members – mechanic John Eyre and data engineer Daniel Petzold – left of their own accord at year's end, with Eyre moving to work with Bradley Smith at KTM.

One man going nowhere is Pedrosa himself. He was linked to a shock Yamaha move, while they sweated on an answer from Vinales, but he signed for two more years with HRC in mid-May.

DUCATI TEAM

TEAM STAFF

Luigi DALL'IGNA: Ducati Corse General Manager
Paolo CIABATTI: Ducati Corse Sports Director
Davide TARDOZZI: Team Manager
Riccardo SAVIN: Vehicle Dynamics Engineer
Fabiano STERLACCHINI: Track Technical Coordinator
Gabriele CONTI: Software and Strategies Manager
Massimo BARTOLINI: Track Engineer
Michele MUZZI: Data Analyst
Francesco RAPISARDA: Communications Director
Julian THOMAS: Press Manager
Paola BRAIATO: Adminstration and Logistics
Mauro GRASSILLI: Sponsorship Manager
Silvio SANGALLI: Crew Coordinator
Davide BARALDINI: Warehouse & Components

ANDREA DOVIZIOSO PIT CREW

Alberto GIRIBUOLA: Track Engineer
Dario MASSARIN: Electronics Engineer
Michele PERUGINI: Chief Mechanic
Mechanics: Enrico SAMPERI, Fabio ROVELLI,
Mark ELDER, Massimo TOGNACCI
Peter BERGVALL: Ohlins Suspension Technician

ANDREA IANNONE PIT CREW

Marco RIGAMONTI: Track Engineer
Tommaso PAGANO: Electronics Engineer
Marco VENTURA: Chief Mechanic
Mechanics: Ivan BRANDI, Michele BUBBOLINI,
Giuliano POLETTI, Lorenzo CANESTRARI,
Giacomo MASSAROTTO: Ohlins Suspension Engineer

ANDREA DOVIZIOSO
Born: 23 March, 1986 – Forlimpopoli, Forli, Italy
GP Starts: 258 (160 MotoGP, 49 250cc, 49 125cc)
GP Wins: 11 (2 MotoGP, 4 250cc, 5 125cc)
World Championships: 1 125cc

ANDREA IANNONE
Born: 9 August, 1989 – Vasto, Italy
GP Starts: 193 (65 MotoGP, 51 Moto2, 77 125cc)
GP Wins: 13 (1 MotoGP, 8 Moto2, 4 125cc)

DUCATI entered 2016 with renewed vigour and optimistic of finally ending its six-year victory drought.

They had missed the target of at least one win in a resurgent 2015 season, but the shoots of recovery were sufficient to suggest that Ducati could pose its biggest threat to Honda and Yamaha's domination since it was last victorious with Casey Stoner in 2010.

There was mounting pressure on Ducati Corse General Manager Gigi Dall'Igna to consign the dark days of the Rossi disaster of 2011 and 2012, and the senior management upheaval of 2013 to distant memory. But all the ingredients certainly seemed to be in place for the Bologna factory to return to winning ways.

Dall'Igna was in his third season at the helm of Ducati's effort, with familiar faces in Paolo Ciabatti operating as sports director and Davide Tardozzi as team manager. Dall'Igna was also surrounded by a wealth of technical talent and expertise, and was hoping that continuity would breed success.

Senior technical roles again went to Riccardo Savin, who continued as vehicle dynamics engineer, and Fabiano Sterlacchini as track technical co-ordinator. The software and strategies role was filled by Gabriele

DUCATI Desmosedici GP16

Engine: 1000cc 90-degree V4, reverse-rotating 180-degree crank, DOHC, 4-valves per cylinder, desmodromic valve gear, variable-length inlet tracts
Power: Around 280bhp, revs up to 18,500rpm

Ancillaries: Magneti Marelli electronics, NGK sparking plugs, full electronic ride-by-wire • *Lubrication:* Shell Advance

Transmission: Gear primary drive, Xtrac six-speed seamless-shift cassette-type gearbox

Suspension: Front, Ohlins TRVSP25-8 48mm 'through-rod' forks; Rear, Ohlins TRSP44-12 'through-rod' shock with linkage

Wheels: 17in Marchesini • *Tyres:* Michelin • *Brakes:* Brembo, 320 and 340mm carbon-carbon front; 200mm steel rear

MICHELE PIRRO
Born: 5 July, 1986 – San Giovanni Rotondo, Italy

GP Starts: 93 (46 MotoGP, 18 Moto2, 29 125cc)

GP Wins: 1 Moto2

HECTOR BARBERA
Born: 2 November, 1986 – Dos Aguas, Spain

GP Starts: 243 (121 MotoGP, 75 250cc, 47 125cc)

GP Wins: 10 (4 250cc, 6 125cc)

Iannone takes victory in Austria

Victory for Dovi and Ducati in Malaysia

Conti once more, while Massimo Bartolini acted as track engineer.

Armed with another year of data and information, Dall'Igna rolled out the 2016-spec Desmosedici GP contender, convinced it could finally put Ducati back on the top step of the podium.

Andrea Dovizioso and Andrea Iannone were both in their fourth years at Ducati, and after they had shared eight podium finishes between them in 2015, it was expected that the improved Desmosedici GP would be the final piece of the jigsaw to help them emerge from the shadow of Stoner.

Stoner himself would play a pivotal role in Ducati's campaign, after his shock decision to quit Honda and return to the Borgo Panigale brand in a test rider and ambassadorial role.

The season started in hugely promising fashion, with many believing that had Iannone not crashed out of second, he might have won the floodlit inaugural race in Qatar. He had fluffed his lines, and controversy and blown opportunities became a constant theme of what would prove to be his swan-song year at Ducati.

A kamikaze move at the penultimate corner in Argentina, which cost team-mate Dovizioso a nailed-on third, attracted criticism and consternation from all quarters. With his aggressive and wild riding style still under microscopic scrutiny when the paddock convened at Catalunya, he slammed the self-destruct button for the second time in six races.

His inexcusable wiping out of Lorenzo prompted some calls for a one-race ban, but Race Direction felt a suitable deterrent would be a back-of-the-grid start at the next race in Assen.

Having crashed out of second in Qatar, he repeated that feat when pursuing Marc Marquez at Le Mans, and surrendered further potential podiums at Silverstone and Sepang with unforced errors; but when he stayed upright, Iannone proved he could be devastatingly fast.

Again working closely with crew chief Marco Rigamonti, Iannone was on the podium in Austin and Mugello, before he put all the bad press behind him with a performance that assured him of his place in Ducati folklore. Always his own man, in Austria he stuck to the courage of his convictions to race a medium-compound rear tyre against the advice of Michelin. It proved a tactical masterstroke, sparking celebrations almost as wild as his riding after Ducati's first win in six years, over a demoralised and deflated Dovizioso.

It was Iannone's first premier-class win and Ducati's first 1-2 since Stoner headed Capirossi at Phillip Island in 2007. It was also the first time Italian riders on Italian machinery had taken the top two places since MV Agusta team-mates Giacomo Agostini and Alberto Pagani in Finland in 1972.

Iannone had long been confirmed to move to Ecstar Suzuki, taking Rigamonti with him, when his final season at Ducati was badly disrupted by a serious back injury at Misano, causing him to miss the next four races.

Pirro took his place at Misano and Aragon, and Barbera in Japan and Australia.

Ducati's fairy-tale didn't end in Austria.

Dovizioso seemed destined to be reflecting on another year of what might have been, after he finished second in Qatar, Austria and Japan. He'd led four races at the height of the summer in Assen, Sachsenring, Red Bull Ring and Brno, but a combination of crashes and tyre issues meant that he had won none of them.

After replacing crew chief Cristian Pupulin, at his side since he had joined Ducati in 2013, with Alberto Giribuola, Dovizioso's personal winless run was even longer than Ducati's – back to the British Grand Prix at Donington Park in 2009: a total of 2,653 days when the popular Italian lined up on pole at Sepang.

A typically measured ride on a drying track ensured that Dovizioso created history as the ninth different winner in a MotoGP season of unprecedented variety. It was the first time Ducati had had two different winners in the same year since the halcyon days of Stoner and Capirossi in 2007.

The win took some of the heat off Dovizioso, who had faced criticism when Ducati extended his contract for 2017 and 2018, just ahead of his home race in Mugello.

Ducati had made a tentative approach to test the loyalty of Marquez to HRC, before completing a successful chase of Jorge Lorenzo, in a deal rumoured to be worth a whopping 25 million euros over two years.

Then it was then a straight choice between the two Andreas for the second ride, and many felt that Ducati had opted for the safer, not faster, choice.

Time will tell.

Gigi Dall'Igna

TEAM SUZUKI ECSTAR

TEAM STAFF

Satoru TERADA: Team Director

Davide BRIVIO: Team Manager

Ken KAWAUCHI: Technical Manager

Sadayuki TSUJIMURA: Engine Management Engineer

Atsushi KAWASAKI: Chassis Engineer

Yuta SHIMBUKURO: Engine Management Engineer

Russell JORDAN: Parts Manager

Roberto BRIVIO & Mitia DOTTA: Coordinators

Federico TONDELLI: Press Office & Social Media Manager

Hatsumi TSUKAMOTO: Marketing Relations and Operations

ALEIX ESPARGARO PIT CREW

Tom O'KANE: Crew Chief:

Claudio RAINATO: Data Engineer

Mechanics: Raymond HUGHES, Tsutomu MATSUGANO, Jacques ROCA

Fernando Mendez PICON (Helper)

MAVERICK VINALES PIT CREW

Jose Manuel CAZEAUX: Crew Chief

Elvio DEGANELLO: Data Engineer

Mechanics: Davide MANFREDI, Massimo MIRANO

Marco Rosa GASTALDO

Paco NOQUEIRA (Helper)

ALEIX ESPARGARO

Born: 30 July, 1989 – Granollers, Spain

GP Starts: 196 (112 MotoGP, 61 Moto2/250cc, 23 125cc)

MAVERICK VINALES

Born: 12 January, 1995 – Figueres, Spain

GP Starts: 103 (36 MotoGP, 18 Moto2, 49 Moto3/125cc)

GP Wins: 17 (1 MotoGP, 4 Moto2, 12 Moto3/125cc)

World Championships: 1 Moto3

Photos: Gold & Goose

IF there were an award for most improved factory in 2016, surely it would be declared a 'no contest' in favour of Suzuki.

The Hamamatsu factory's return from a three-year, self-imposed exile in 2015 was impressive without ever being spectacular. Three top-six finishes for Maverick Vinales and Aleix Espargaro hardly suggested that Suzuki would be capable of upsetting the established elite in MotoGP on a regular basis in 2016. Yet the record books will show that Suzuki roared back to prominence with a vengeance, thanks to a radical upgrade in the performance of the GSX-RR.

Team director Satoru Terada and technical manager Ken Kawauchi must take enormous credit for implementing such a performance overhaul. All of Suzuki's key weak points were eradicated by a combination of clever engineering and a massive overhaul of the technical regulations for 2016.

The previous year's GSX-RR had been a work of art, with a chassis so compliant and user-friendly that the bike could be turned on a sixpence. But the absence of crucial horsepower left it badly exposed on fast tracks, while a lack of acceleration on corner exit negated any advantage gained on the brakes and mid-corner.

SUZUKI GSX-RR

Engine: 1000cc transverse in-line 4, reverse-rotating 90-degree cross-plane crankshaft, DOHC, 4 valves per cylinder, pneumatic valve return system

Power: Approximately 265bhp, revs to approximately 17,000rpm

Ancillaries: Magneti Marelli electronics, NGK sparking plugs, full electronic ride-by-wire • *Lubrication:* Ecstar

Transmission: Gear primary drive, multi-plate dry slipper clutch, six-speed constant-mesh seamless-shift cassette-style gearbox, RK chain

Suspension: Front, Ohlins TRVSP25-8 48mm 'through-rod' forks; Rear, Ohlins TRSP44-12 'through-rod' shock with linkage • *Wheels:* 17in MFR • *Tyres:* Michelin

Brakes: Brembo 340mm carbon-carbon front; steel rear

Aleix Espargaro leads Vinales in the Japanese GP

Maverick's first MotoGP victory

Photos: Gold & Goose

The team celebrate their victory at Silverstone

Maverick Vinales

The absence of a seamless-shift gearbox, now effectively compulsory for MotoGP, also handicapped Vinales and Espargaro.

The 2016 GSX-RR took a quantum leap forward in engine performance, while a faultless seamless-shift gearbox moved the package even closer to Honda, Yamaha and Ducati. At first it was for up-shifts only, until the start of the European season.

The switch to control software for all, however, also played an essential role in Suzuki's success. It stopped the rapid rate at which rivals were improving their bespoke electronic strategies. With less manpower and budget, and a steely determination to persist with Mitsubishi electronics until it quit MotoGP at the end of 2011, Suzuki always had been the poor relation in the electronics department. Now the playing field was level.

And so it proved. Vinales was on the front row of the grid at the season opener in Qatar. But after tumbling out of a top-three place in Argentina, he had to wait until Le Mans to take his first MotoGP podium, Suzuki's first since 2008.

By then, speculation was rife that Vinales was poised to pen a lucrative two-year deal to join boyhood idol Rossi in Yamaha's factory squad. to take the place of departing fellow-Spaniard Lorenzo.

The Spaniard was torn between the move and remaining loyal to Suzuki, who, thanks to the vision and renowned talent-spotting skills of team manager Davide Brivio, had gambled on taking him out of Moto2 after just one season.

The alluring alternative option was a once-in-a-lifetime chance, however, and the answer came just 11 days after his breakthrough podium: Yamaha announced that he'd accepted the sizeable task of replacing Ducati-bound Jorge Lorenzo.

Vinales would have to wait a further seven races to rediscover his podium form, but when he did, it was in unforgettable circumstances for Suzuki, as he dominated at Silverstone for the factory's first victory since Chris Vermeulen had triumphed in the rain at Le Mans in 2007. Their last dry win had been with Kenny Roberts Junior at Motegi in 2000. Vinales, meanwhile, became the first rider in history to win 125cc, Moto3, Moto2 and MotoGP races.

That maiden win triggered a stunning run of form from the former Moto3 world champion, who didn't finish outside of the top six in the final six races and and even threatened Lorenzo's third overall until the latter's Valencia win.

His success came at a price, however. His fourth podium in Australia meant that Suzuki would have to sacrifice their technical concessions for 2017, no longer having access to nine engines and unlimited testing, nor exempt from the engine development freeze.

Vinales worked again with crew chief Jose Manuel Cazeaux, but he was unable to take him to Yamaha, who favoured the vast experience of Lorenzo's crew chief, Ramon Forcada.

Espargaro's crew was also unchanged from an encouraging 2015 campaign, with Tom O'Kane's calm approach and encyclopaedic knowledge proving key assets again.

Three top-six finishes in the opening five races suggested that Espargaro would pose the same podium threat as Vinales, but his best result was a fourth in Japan, after he had recovered from a dreadful summer run of just two point-scoring finishes in seven races.

That fourth in Japan, behind Vinales, was still a landmark for Suzuki, the first time since Vermeulen and John Hopkins had been second and third at Misano in 2007 that the Japanese marque had enjoyed a double top-four finish.

Espargaro's place on a GSX-RR had always looked vulnerable, even when confirmation came about the exit of Vinales. On the same day, Suzuki pulled off its own coup by signing Andrea Iannone. Then they went in search of a top Moto2 talent to nurture alongside his undoubted, if wayward, talent.

Johann Zarco was a strong candidate, given that he had signed an option with Suzuki. He tested a GSX-RR in Japan and was planning on competing in the Suzuka 8 Hours for Suzuki when it became clear that he was not the first choice.

Instead, it was Zarco's main Moto2 title threat, Alex Rins, who grabbed the second seat. Rins had been earmarked to join the Monster Yamaha Tech 3 Team, but Suzuki pounced, able to fulfil his demands for a full factory bike.

Suzuki's deal for Rins was confirmed in the build-up to the Dutch TT at Assen. Out in the cold and bewildered at his treatment by Suzuki, Espargaro publicly criticised the factory on more than one occasion before unveiling his own 2017 move to Aprilia. Only a delayed flight prevented his plan of announcing the move in fanfare fashion at the Dutch TT press conference.

MONSTER YAMAHA TECH 3

TEAM STAFF

Hervé PONCHARAL: Team Manager

Gérard VALLEE: Team Coordinator

Laurence COTTIN: Team Assistant

Fabien ROPERS: Parts Manager

Thomas RUBANTEL: Fuel/Tyres

Milena KOERNER/William MOODY: Press & Communications

BRADLEY SMITH PIT CREW

Guy COULON: Crew Chief

Maxime DUPONCHEL: Telemetry

Mechanics

Steve BLACKBURN, Jerôme PONCHARAL

Josian RUSTIQUE

POL ESPARGARO PIT CREW

Nicolas GOYON: Crew Chief

Mechanics

Eric LABORIE, David LIEBERT, Xavier QUIEXALOS

Maxime REYSZ: Telemetry

POL ESPARGARO
Born: 10 June, 1991 – Granollers, Spain
GP Starts: 175 (53 MotoGP, 51 Moto2, 71 125cc)
GP Wins: 10 Moto2; 5 125cc
World Championships: 1 Moto2

BRADLEY SMITH
Born: 28 November, 1990 – Oxford, England
GP Starts: 182 (69 MotoGP, 33 Moto2, 80 125cc)
GP Wins: 3 125cc

IF 2016 was the year of the underdog and the Independent Teams' opportunity in MotoGP to grab a rare share of the limelight, then nobody told the Monster Yamaha Tech 3 squad.

While rival independents were plundering the podium with shock wins and other eye-catching finishes, the best non-factory outfit in recent premier-class history missed out on their chance to seize a slice of the glory.

For the first time since its struggles on a Dunlop-shod 800cc Yamaha in 2007, no rider from Herve Poncharal's French-based team made it on to the podium. The closest the squad got to preserving that proud recent record came in a weather-disrupted Dutch TT at Assen, where Pol Espargaro fought Scott Redding for the podium before running out of steam by the end.

Espargaro's fourth-place finish in the Netherlands equalled his best ever MotoGP finish, but his third season in the premier class failed to yield any significant improvement in performance. The Spaniard finished inside the top six in six other races and at one stage seemed destined to cruise to the top Independent Team rider prize, until he was blown away

YAMAHA YZR-M1 – Tech 3

Engine: 1000cc transverse in-line 4, reverse-rotating cross-plane crankshaft, DOHC, 4 valves per cylinder, pneumatic valve return system

Power: Approximately 270bhp, revs to approximately 17,000rpm

Ancillaries: Magneti Marelli electronics, NGK sparking plugs, full electronic ride-by-wire • *Lubrication:* Motul

Transmission: Gear primary drive, multi-plate dry slipper clutch, six-speed constant-mesh floating-dog-ring cassette-style gearbox, RK chain

Suspension: Front, Ohlins TRSP25 48mm forks; Rear, Ohlins TRSP44 shock with linkage

Wheels: 17in MFR • *Tyres:* Michelin *Brakes:* Brembo 340mm carbon-carbon front; Yamaha steel rear

ALEX LOWES
Born: 14 September, 1990 – Lincoln, England
GP Starts: 3 (2 MotoGP, 1 125cc)

Espargaro's fourth at Assen was the team's best result of the season

by former Monster Yamaha Tech 3 star Crutchlow's dramatic transformation after Germany.

Espargaro again worked with crew chief Nicolas Goyon, who was closely supported by data engineer Maxime Reysz, schooled and readied for MotoGP in Tech 3 Racing's Moto2 project.

Espargaro was contracted directly to Yamaha and effectively leased back to the Tech 3 team, which bore the famous Monster livery for an eighth year in a row. He had made no secret of his desire to graduate to Yamaha's factory team, but that door was slammed shut when Maverick Vinales was signed up.

Like so many in the paddock, Espargaro aspired to a plum factory ride and he completed the new KTM line-up in a deal he announced on the eve of his home race at the Circuit de Barcelona-Catalunya in early June. He will take mechanic Xavi Queixalos with him. Queixalos had moved into Tech 3 with Espargaro in 2014, after they had worked together the previous season en route to winning the Moto2 crown.

The rapidly expanding KTM factory had completed a second successful raid on Tech 3 in the space of three months.

With almost every rider out of contract in 2016, the paddock was full of anticipation in advance of an open rider market that was expected to fill gossip columns well into the new season. The lights hadn't even gone on to start the new season under the Losail International Circuit floodlights in Qatar when Bradley Smith blinked first.

Thanks to his enhanced reputation after a strong 2015 and keen to avoid being part of the crazy rumour mill, he had quickly negotiated a deal with KTM to ride the new RC16 machine.

It had already become apparent that Poncharal and Yamaha were pondering a shake-up of the Tech 3 line-up for 2017. Poncharal said at the first winter test in Sepang that there was only a remote chance of Smith and Espargaro retaining their seats for 2017, and at least one would be sacrificed, if not both.

Poncharal and Yamaha have worked together since 2000, but of late Tech 3 has willingly positioned itself as a 'junior team', with a prime role of unearthing and developing young talent for the official team.

Smith proved astute in sorting out his future so rapidly, because his KTM switch was a rare highlight in a difficult fourth season at Tech 3. Working again with crew chief and Tech 3 co-founder Guy Coulon, he struggled to adjust to the Michelin tyres, and he made the top ten in only four of the first 11 rounds, including a season's best seventh at Mugello. This confirmed a dip in form, as he'd taken ten top-six finishes in 2015.

A tough season was further complicated by a se-rious injury to his right knee, suffered in a practice crash for the Oschersleben 8 Hours endurance race, and he missed three rounds before a heroic return in Japan after only a seven-week lay-off, to end the season with point scoring finishes in the final four races.

His vacant YZR-M1 went to Briton Alex Lowes, who was fast-tracked in after winning a second successive Suzuka 8 Hours for Yamaha. The Pata Yamaha World Superbike rider gave a good account of himself, with 13th on his Silverstone debut and an excellent 14th place on the grid before he fell out of contention at Misano. His adventure ended painfully when he withdrew from the Motorland Aragon round, after "one of the biggest crashes of my career".

Rins was favoured for 2017, with a factory contract, but a learner role, and Yamaha and Poncharal had initiated contact at the end of 2015, but the Spaniard made it clear that he would accept only a full factory ride

Poncharal instead signed German Moto2 rider Jonas Folger, confirmed at Le Mans; and the 2017 line-up was completed at Germany, when Johann Zarco finally inked a MotoGP deal.

Zarco will work with Coulon, and Folger will team up with Goyon in an unchanged crew-chief line-up for a team with two class rookie riders.

Tech3 garage at Silverstone

Bradley Smith

Hervé Poncharal

Photos: Gold & Goose

OCTO PRAMAC YAKHNICH

TEAM STAFF

Paolo CAMPINOTI: Team Principal
Giacomo GUIDOTTI: Team Manager
Felix RODRIGUEZ: Team Coordinator
Federico CAPELLI: Press Officer
Jacopo MENGHETTI: Marketing & sponsorship
Alex GHINI: Hospitality & PR
Federico CAPELLI: Press Officer
Luciano BONCI: Warehouse & spare parts

DANILO PETRUCCI PIT CREW

Daniele ROMAGNOLI: Crew Chief
Cristian BATTAGLIA: Electronic Engineer
Alberto GIRIBUOLA: Technical Coordinator
Federico PECCI: Chief Mechanic
Mechanics: Fabrizio MALAGUTI, Edoardo CIFERRI
Morris GRAZZI (Tyres & Fuel)

SCOTT REDDING PIT CREW

Giacomo GUIDOTTI: Crew Chief
Nicola MANNA: Chief Mechanic
Mario FRIGIERO: Data Engineer
Mechanics: David GALACHO, Pedro RIVERA
Francesco GALINDO
Marco POLASTRI (Tyres & Fuel)

DANILO PETRUCCI

Born: 24 October, 1990 – Terni, Italy

GP Starts: 82 MotoGP

SCOTT REDDING

Born: 4 January, 1993 – Quedgeley, England

GP Starts: 153 (54 MotoGP, 66 Moto2 33 125cc)

GP Wins: 4 (3 Moto2, 1 125cc)

THE Italian-based Pramac squad started the year optimistic that it could celebrate its fifth MotoGP season with a better return than the single podium of 2015. So when it concluded the 2016 world championship with just one rostrum again, it appeared that Ducati's established leading Independent Team had experienced a season of underachievement.

The senior management remained unchanged, with Paolo Campinoti fulfilling the role of team principal, while team affairs were again placed in the safe hands of Francesco Guidotti,

Octo, one of the world's biggest suppliers of insurance telematics technology, remained as title sponsor for a first full season, having taken over in the early part of 2015.

It was again early in the year when the team expanded in name after a deal was signed with Russian-based Yakhnich Motorsport. The collaboration was said to actively involve the Russian Motorcycle Federation and was aimed at the "further development of motorsport in Russia". The involvement with Yakhnich, which is best known for winning the 2013 World Supersport title with British rider Sam Lowes, led to the team being rebranded as Octo Pramac Yakhnich.

Danilo Petrucci had been a revelation in his first season at Pramac in 2015, and with the team having been upgraded to that year's factory Desmosedici GP15, confidence was booming that the Italian would continue to flourish.

Petrucci was paired again with crew chief Daniele

DUCATI Desmosedici GP15 – Pramac

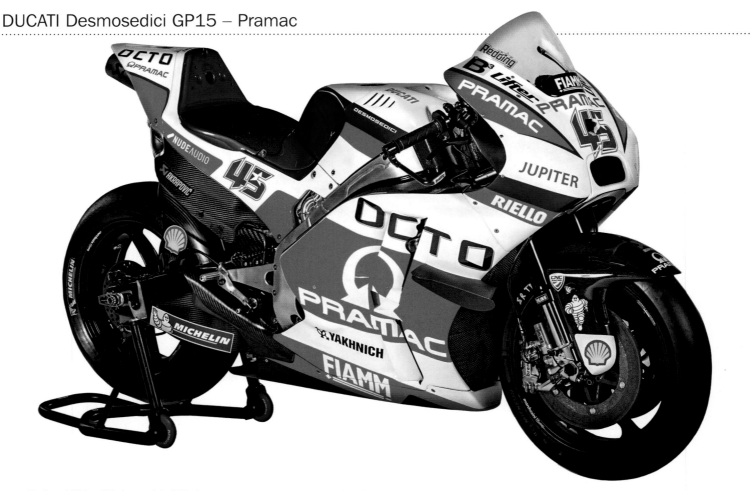

Engine: 1000cc 90-degree L4, 360-degree reverse-rotating crankshaft, DOHC, 4 valves per cylinder, desmodromic valve gear, variable-length inlet system
Power: Around 270bhp, revs to 18,000rpm

Ancillaries: Magneti Marelli electronics, NGK sparking plugs, full electronic ride-by-wire • *Lubrication:* Shell

Transmission: Xtrac six-speed seamless-shift cassette-type gearbox

Suspension: Front, Ohlins TRSP25 48mm forks; Rear, Ohlins TRSP44 shock with linkage

Wheels: 17in Marchesini • *Tyres:* Michelin • *Brakes:* Brembo 340mm carbon-carbon front; 200mm steel rear

MICHELE PIRRO
Born: 5 July, 1986 – San Giovanni Rotondo, Italy
GP Starts: 93 (46 MotoGP, 18 Moto2, 29 125cc)
GP Wins: 1 Moto2

Scott Redding scored a podium in the Dutch TT at Assen

Danilo Petrucci leads Ducati's Michele Pirro in Austria

Paulo Campinoti

Giacomo Guidotti

Romagnoli, who had previously worked with Colin Edwards and Cal Crutchlow during spells with Yamaha's factory team and then Monster Yamaha Tech 3. His entire crew remained the same, with Cristian Battaglia a key member as data engineer, while Alberto Giribuola was Ducati's eyes and ears in the garage as technical co-ordinator.

However, Petrucci suffered a pre-season nightmare during the second official test at Phillip Island. A fast crash through Turn Eight left him with a badly broken right hand, the second, third and fourth metacarpals being smashed to pieces.

He bravely tried to ride in the season opener in Qatar, but withdrew after FP3, one fracture having re-opened from the stress of riding. He wasn't seen again until round five at Le Mans, and while he was undertaking a lengthy recuperation, Ducati test rider Michele Pirro took his ride in Argentina, Austin and Jerez, scoring a best of eighth at CotA.

Petrucci's return was impressive, and he scored three successive top-ten finishes, including an equal season-best seventh in France. There were wasted opportunities to add to his 2015 podium, however, as when he crashed out of the lead in wet conditions in Germany. At the season's conclusion, he was without a top-six finish since the Sepang round in Malaysia in 2015, but there was a huge consolation prize ahead

of the 2017 campaign.

Initially it was assumed that Ducati would maintain its policy of supplying Pramac with year-old factory machinery for the following season, which would have meant Petrucci and team-mate Scott Redding racing hand-me-down 2016 Desmosedicis. It transpired, however, that Ducati would be able to offer one 2017 bike, and they devised a unique in-team competition to determine who would secure the coveted seat.

The competition ran for eight races, from Brno to Valencia, and it was simply decided on who had scored the most points after each had been allowed to drop one of their worst results. The stakes were high, and there was no doubt that Ducati's decision ramped up the pressure and tension within Pramac. That tension was never more evident than on the first lap at Motorland Aragon, where Petrucci barged Redding off the track, and received a ride-through penalty for his trouble.

As a gesture of goodwill to Redding, he was allowed to claim the points for the position he was in at the time of the collision. Even so, the last laugh went to Petrucci, who landed the GP17 by a comfortable margin, and was also one place ahead overall.

Redding inherited the entire squad left behind by Yonny Hernandez as he attempted to rebound from an atrocious experience on a Honda RC213V in 2015.

Giacomo Guidotti was his crew chief, Nicola Manna chief mechanic and Mario Frigiero data engineer.

Redding's first top-six came in Austin, after a mechanical failure had robbed him of a similar result at the previous round in Argentina. He didn't score another point in the next four rounds, further technical gremlins having ruled him out at Le Mans and Mugello. He followed up a career-first MotoGP front row in Assen by splashing his way to a brilliant third, and in similar tricky conditions in Sachsenring and Brno, he narrowly missed the podium.

However, just two top-ten finishes in those crucial final eight races cost Redding his opportunity to snare the GP17.

It was a tough end to the year for the British rider, who not only lost the battle for the latest-spec Desmosedici, but also crew chief Guidotti, who was given the golden opportunity to join Dani Pedrosa as crew chief in the Repsol Honda squad. That happened at Misano, and it took until Phillip Island to confirm Christian Pupulin as his replacement.

Pupulin was well known to Pramac and Redding, having worked as a Ducati Corse engineer in the team. His most recent engagement had been as Andrea Dovizioso's crew chief between 2013 and 2015, and he had been on the Bologna factory's racing staff since its MotoGP debut back in 2003.

APRILIA RACING TEAM GRESINI

TEAM STAFF

Romano ALBESIANO: Aprilia Racing Manager
Fausto GRESINI: Team Manager
Marco BERTOLATTI: Vehicle Engineer
Massimo MENEGHINI: Spare Parts
Paolo BONORA: Electric and Electronic Manager
Dario RAIMONDI: Sports Manager
Paolo PEZZINI: Press Manager

STEFAN BRADL PIT CREW

Diego GUBELLINI: Race Engineer
Marcius ESCHENBACHER: Electronic Engineer
Guido FONTANA: Data Recorder
Craig CUMMINGS: Suspension
Mechanics
Andrea BONASOLI: Crew Chief, Carlo TOCCAFONDI,
Federico VICINO, Jerome GALLAND
Eddy BOSI: Tyres and Fuel

ALVARO BAUTISTA PIT CREW

Giulio NAVA: Race Engineer
Sander DONKERS: Electronic Engineer
Loris CONTE: Data Recording
Oscar BOLZONELLA: Suspension
Mechanics
Ivano MANCURTI: Crew Chief, Alberto PRESUTTI,
Maurizio VISANI, Roberto MARINONI
Gianpiero CANETTI: Tyres and Fuel

ALVARO BAUTISTA

Born: 21 November, 1984 – Talavera de la Reina, Spain

GP Starts: 238 (122 MotoGP, 49 250cc, 67 125cc)

GP Wins: 16 (8 250cc, 8 125cc)
World Championships: 1 125cc

STEFAN BRADL

Born: 29 November, 1989 – Augsberg, Germany

GP Starts: 173 (86 MotoGP, 33 Moto2, 54 125cc)

GP Wins: 7 (5 Moto2, 2 125cc)
World Championships: 1 Moto2

APRILIA'S second season back in the cut-throat world of MotoGP competition was geared more towards steady progress than headline-grabbing results. A complicated return to the top level of motorcycle racing in 2015, for the first time in 11 years, meant that it would have been foolish to expect more than small incremental steps to help transform the RS-GP contender into a competitive force.

Nobody was more realistic about that than racing manager Romano Albesiano, who mapped out a consistent challenge for the top ten in the second half of the season, ahead of a top-six assault in 2017.

Once again, the Noale factory squad was badged Aprilia Racing Team Gresini, the result of a four-year partnership with former 125cc World Champion Fausto Gresini that began in 2015.

Gresini was master of the day-to-day running of the team, but all strategic and policy decisions, like rider selection and machine development, had to be signed off by Albesiano. He was still trying to step out from the overpowering shadow of influential predecessor Gigi Dall'Igna.

The 2015 version of the RS-GP was effectively a souped-up RSV4 superbike, which was used as a 'lab'

APRILIA RS-GP

Engine: 1000cc 75-degree V4, reverse-rotating 180-degree crankshaft, DOHC, 4 valves per cylinder, pneumatic valve return system
Power: Approximately 260bhp, revs to 17,500rpm

Ancillaries: Magneti Marelli electronics, NGK sparking plugs, full electronic ride-by-wire • *Lubrication:* Shell Advance

Transmission: Gear primary drive, Zeroshift six-speed seamless-shift cassette-type gearbox

Suspension: Front, Ohlins TRVSP25-8 48mm 'through-rod' forks; Rear, Ohlins TRSP44-12 'through-rod' shock with linkage • *Wheels:* 17in Marchesini

Tyres: Michelin • *Brakes:* Brembo, 320 or 340mm carbon-carbon front; 200mm steel rear

Stefan Bradl

Romano Albesiano with riders Alvaro Bautista and Stefan Bradl

Fausto Gresini

bike in advance of a full-blown prototype 1000cc RS-GP machine being rolled out for 2016.

As in the previous season, Aprilia threw new parts at the RS-GP like confetti at a wedding. There were five frames, to improve rear grip and understeer issues, and countless engine modifications to bolster top speed and acceleration. This constant tweaking began to reap rewards in the final third of the season, when Alvaro Bautista and Stefan Bradl often made good on Albesiano's top-ten target.

Albesiano was supported again by sport manager Dario Raimondi and engineering and aerodynamic specialist Marco Bertolatti.

Bautista was back for a second season, working again with crew chief Giulio Nava, previously data engineer with Casey Stoner at Repsol Honda.

Former Moto2 World Champion Bradl returned for his first full season at Aprilia, having impressed in the second half of 2015 when he had replaced the less-than-average Marco Melandri from Indianapolis onwards. The German's crew chief was Diego Gubellini.

The experienced line-up wasted no time in making an impression. Round two, at the Termas de Rio Hondo track in Argentina, might have been a chaotic crash fest, but incredibly Bradl's seventh and Bautista's tenth place marked Aprilia's first double top-ten finish since Noriyuki Haga and Colin Edwards at Donington Park's British Grand Prix in 2003.

The new season was only seven races old when the two riders had already amassed 37 points between them, one more than Aprilia had mustered in the entire 2015 campaign.

Spaniard Bautista took profit from the improvements that appeared from Misano onwards, claiming six top-ten finishes in the last seven races. That included equalling Aprilia's best ever seventh place in Japan and Malaysia, which went a little way to make up for the late heartache of Assen. There he had been on course to score Aprilia's first ever top-six when he crashed out on the last lap.

Bradl matched Bautista's seventh in Argentina and registered five other top-ten finishes, and the pair mounted a regular challenge for Q2 towards the end of the season. In the bizarre rain-hit Phillip Island qualifying, Bradl's eighth was Aprilia's best since Edwards had been seventh at Valencia in 2003 on the wild three-cylinder RS 'Cube'.

Aprilia's top-six quest in 2017 will be undertaken by an all-new line-up.

Bautista and Bradl had gone into 2016 knowing that if they wanted to stay on strength, they would be fighting it out for just one vacancy. The other seat had been set in stone in September, 2015, when Briton Sam Lowes had been announced as an Aprilia MotoGP rider following a single-season stint in Gresini's Moto2 squad. The former World Supersport champion ran a handful of tests on the RS-GP machine.

The door was firmly slammed shut in the faces of both incumbents at the end of June, when it was confirmed that Aleix Espargaro would be team-mate to Lowes.

Bradl briefly flirted with Avintia Ducati, but in the summer break confirmed that he would replace Michael van der Mark in the Ten Kate Honda World Superbike squad for 2017.

Bautista's switch to the Aspar Ducati squad was confirmed a short time afterwards.

Alvaro Bautista leads Stefan Bradl in Argentina

Bradl, sporting Aprilia's final-race all-red livery.

Photos: Gold & Goose

LCR HONDA

TEAM STAFF

Lucio CECCHINELLO: CEO
Martine FELLONI: Administration & Legal
Oscar HARO: Public Relations
Elisa PAVAN: Press Officer
Elena CECCHINELLO: Hospitality
Sergio PARENTI: Workshop

CAL CRUTCHLOW PIT CREW

Christophe BOURGIGNON: Chief Engineer
Mechanics
Joan CASAS, Xavier CASANOVAS, Chris RICHARDSON
Ugo GELMI (Tyres)
Marco BARBIANI: Telemetry

CAL CRUTCHLOW
Born: 29 October, 1985 – Coventry, England
GP Starts: 105 MotoGP,
GP Wins: 2 MotoGP,
World Championships: 1 World Supersport

Lucio Cecchinello

THE 2016 MotoGP World Championship was a milestone and memorable year, both on and off the track, for Lucio Cecchinello's LCR Honda squad.

This was Cecchinello's tenth MotoGP season since he had joined the premier class in 2006 with the raw and precocious talent of Casey Stoner. It was the 20th year since he had founded his successful and much admired LCR project in 1996. And it was the 30th anniversary of the hugely respected Italian's involvement in motorcycle racing, which had begun humbly as a 17-year-old mechanic in the Italian NS 125 Trophy

The anniversary celebrations coincided with an unforgettable year for the LCR Honda squad, which made a huge contribution to records smashed in a landmark season.

British rider Cal Crutchlow was retained, after it transpired that Cecchinello's status as a two-rider effort in 2015, unfortunately, had been a short and not so sweet experience. He was forced to revert to just a single entry for 2016, after the unsavoury demise of his 2015 sponsors, London-based foreign exchange trading company CWM and its extrovert owner Anthony Constantinou.

Cecchinello returned to a successful sponsorship formula for the new season, with four backers securing title sponsor rights at selected races throughout the season.

HONDA RC213V – LCR

Engine: 1000cc 90-degree V4, reverse-rotating 360-degree crankshaft, pneumatic valve return system **Power:** More than 270bhp, revs to 17,500rpm

Ancillaries: Magneti Marelli electronics, ride-by-wire throttle and fuel injection system, Denso sparking plugs **Lubrication:** Castrol

Transmission: Gear primary drive, multi-plate dry slipper clutch, six-speed seamless-shift cassette-style gearbox, DID chain

Suspension: Front, Ohlins TRVSP25-8 48mm 'through-rod' forks • Rear, TRSP44-12 'through-rod' shock with linkage

Wheels: 17in OZ Racing **Tyres:** Michelin

Brakes: Nissin/Brembo 320 or 340mm carbon-carbon front; HRC 218mm steel rear

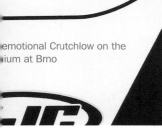

PRIX
REPUBLIKY

emotional Crutchlow on the
ium at Brno

Crutchlow wheelies to victory at Phillip Island

The team celebrate their victory in Australia

Hunting down Rossi at Brno to record his first MotoGP win

Crutchlow ran the majority of the races in the livery of motorcycle accessories brand Givi, a loyal and long-term LCR backer, which had stepped in during the latter stages of 2015 to fill the void left by the sudden departure of CWM. Leading motorcycle component producer Rizoma was the predominant backer in Austin and Catalunya, while Custom Spa, an Italian-based hardware and software supplier, took the role at Mugello. Crutchlow was also back in the famous and distinctive Castrol livery for his 100th GP at Misano, and at Sepang, in a season when he would end a long losing streak for once-dominant British riders.

Crutchlow's crew was largely unchanged, with LCR stalwart Christophe Bourguignon again operating as his crew chief. The only significant switch in personnel occurred when Marco Barbiani replaced Brian Harden in charge of data recording, after the latter's exit to join KTM's ambitious new RC16 project.

In the first half of the season, Crutchlow's form suggested little of the huge impact he would have in a stellar second half. He scored just 20 points in the first eight races and was languishing in 18th overall when the series landed in Germany.

A second place on a drying track in a flag-to-flag encounter there was quickly followed by a golden run, not only for Crutchlow, but also for British motorcycle sport. He brilliantly conquered tricky drying conditions at Brno, coming from outside the top ten to take a victory that ended Britain's 35-year wait since Barry Sheene had won in Sweden in 1981. It was the first British win in 532 races, while the last Briton to have won on a Honda had been Mike Hailwood in 1967.

Crutchlow also became the 17th rider to win in MotoGP and World Superbikes, but his record-breaking exploits were only just beginning.

At the next race in front of his home crowd at Silverstone, he was the first British rider on a home pole since Sheene in 1977. And when he brilliantly fought off Rossi and Marquez to finish runner-up behind Vinales, he was the first home rider on the podium since Jeremy McWilliams had been third in Donington Park's 500cc encounter in 2000.

Then, with a stunning victory at Phillip Island, he joined an exclusive club, whose members included Leslie Graham, Geoff Duke, John Surtees, Hailwood, Phil Read and Sheene, as British riders who had won more than one premier-class race in a season.

In the year of the underdog, it was the first dry MotoGP race win by an Independent Team rider since Toni Elias in 2006 at Estoril. These were just some of the records he broke.

At the Dutch TT at Assen, Crutchlow confirmed that he will remain with LCR Honda for a third season in 2017. The declaration ended speculation that Cecchinello had been eyeing a shock switch to run a Suzuki satellite team for reigning Moto2 World Champion Johann Zarco.

AVINTIA RACING

TEAM STAFF

Raul ROMERO: Team Owner
Antonio MARTIN: General Manager
Augustin ESCOBAR: Team Manager
Marc VIDAL: Team Coordinator (Logistics)
David DE GEA: Team Coordinator
Jose MAROTO: Press Manager

HECTOR BARBERA PIT CREW

Jarno POLASTRI: Chief Mechanic
Renato PENNACCHIO: Data Engineer
Mechanics
Simone FALCINI, Jesus MORENO, Jordi PRADES,
Gaspar CELDRAN

LORIS BAZ PIT CREW

Alessandro TOGNELLI: Chief Mechanic
Alessandro DAMIA: Data Engineer
Mechanics
Toni MIR, Rafael LOPEZ, Jose MA ROJAS,
Luis MARTINEZ

HECTOR BARBERA

Born: 2 November, 1986 – Dos Aguas, Spain

GP Starts: 243 (121 MotoGP, 75 250cc, 47 125cc)
GP Wins: 10 (4 250cc, 6 125cc)

LORIS BAZ

Born: 1 February, 1993 – Sallanches, France

GP Starts: 31 (31 MotoGP)

FOR a barometer of the success of the implementation of MotoGP's major 2016 technical revolution, you need look no further than the Spanish-based Avintia Racing squad.

The rule changes were aimed specifically at helping Independent Teams compete against the mega-money factories. Avintia provided indisputable evidence that this move was a resounding success, particularly when you analyse the fortunes of Spanish rider Hector Barbera.

Riding Ducati's old, but still competitive, 2014-spec GP14.2, Barbera was once again paired with crew chief Jarno Polastri, and between them they made an instant impact in MotoGP's brave new era.

It was not until round six at Mugello that Barbera missed the top ten for the first time, and his rising stock was confirmed at Germany's Sachsenring, where he scored only the second front-row start of his premier-class career.

In the wet conditions of Brno and Sepang, Barbera and team-mate Loris Baz were able to demonstrate the impact of the ban on the sophisticated bespoke electronics hitherto the exclusive domain of factory teams. Baz was fourth at Brno, and Barbera fifth, the first time since 2012 that a non-factory team had two riders finish in the top five (Crutchlow and Dovizioso for Monster Yamaha). They repeated the feat at a soaking Sepang, where the places were reversed,

DUCATI Desmosedici GP14.2 – Avintia

Engine: 1000cc 90-degree L4, 360-degree reverse-rotating crankshaft, DOHC, 4 valves per cylinder, desmodromic valve gear, variable-length inlet system
Power: Around 270bhp, revs to 18,000rpm

Ancillaries: Magneti Marelli electronics, NGK sparking plugs, full electronic ride-by-wire • *Lubrication:* Shell

Transmission: Xtrac six-speed seamless-shift cassette-type gearbox

Suspension: Front, Ohlins TRSP25 48mm forks; Rear, Ohlins TRSP44 shock with linkage

Wheels: 17in Marchesini • *Tyres:* Michelin • *Brakes:* Brembo 340mm carbon-carbon front; 200mm steel rear

MICHELE PIRRO
Born: 5 July, 1986 – San Giovanni Rotondo, Italy
GP Starts: 93 (46 MotoGP, 18 Moto2, 29 125cc)
GP Wins: 1 Moto2

JAVIER FORES
Born: 16 September, 1985 – Llombas, Spain
GP Starts: 12 (1 MotoGP, 10 Moto2, 1 125cc)

MIKE JONES
Born: 25 February, 1994 – Brisbane, Australia
GP Starts: 2 (2 MotoGP)

Javier Fores

Michele Pirro

Mike Jones

Barbera taking a career-best fourth.

The final rankings gave a convincing measure of Barbera's rapid progress. He had joined the class in 2010, but 2016 yielded his best ever points tally, putting him in the overall top ten for the first time in his premier-class career.

His efforts were appreciated by senior Ducati management, and when Iannone was absent injured for Japan and Australia, and usual stand-in Michele Pirro was unavailable, Barbera was called up to move to the factory team. The temporary transfer emphasised the close relationship that Avintia Racing management, led by team owner Raul Romero, general manager Antonio Martin and team manager Augustin Escobar, had forged with Ducati since their relationship had begun in 2015.

It was a canny move to give Barbera a head start for 2017, for he will ride a 2016-spec Desmosedici for Avintia in the new season (his fourth with the team, confirmed on race day in Austria). But the transition to the latest model was not easy, and this was only the second time all year he finished out of the points.

It was also confirmed in Austria that Frenchman Baz would remain for a third GP season, his second with Avintia, after a 2016 campaign blighted by injury. He will be allocated a GP15 Ducati. He had been sweating on his future, with Avintia pursuing Bradl before the German opted to move to World Superbikes.

Having joined Avintia from the defunct Forward Yamaha squad, Baz teamed up with crew chief Alessandro Tognelli. Their relationship would be brief, however; Tognelli will move to the Aspar team in 2017 with Bautista.

Baz hadn't threatened the top ten in the opening five races when he suffered multiple injuries to his right foot in a first-turn crash at Mugello. That had been instigated by Bautista, and it also collected luckless Aussie Jack Miller.

Replaced by Ducati test rider Michele Pirro at Catalunya and Assen, Baz claimed an outstanding fourth on his Brno return. He was still working his way back to full fitness, however, when more disaster and pain struck on the opening lap of Silverstone's British Grand Prix, following a high-speed collision with Pol Espargaro.

A career-best fourth for Hector Barbera in Malaysia

Initial checks appeared to show that the Frenchman had escaped any significant injury, but additional assessments in Switzerland confirmed a lower fracture in his right tibia and new fracture in his right foot. He was out of the next round at Misano, his GP14.2 seat going to former European Superstock Champion and current World Superbike campaigner Xavi Fores. It was a baptism of fire for the 30-year-old Spaniard, who was forced to retire with arm-pump.

The game of musical chairs at Avintia Racing wasn't finished. Barbera's secondment to the factory squad for Japan and Australia triggered an 11th-hour call to 2015 Australian Superbike Champion Mike Jones. The 22-year-old was riding for a domestic Ducati team co-owned by ex-World Superbike Champion and MotoGP winner Troy Bayliss, and he acquitted himself brilliantly – a commendable 18th in Japan. Then he scored a solitary point with a gutsy ride to 15th in front of his home crowd at Phillip Island.

Loris Baz heads to fourth place in Brno

PULL & BEAR ASPAR TEAM

TEAM STAFF

Jorge MARTINEZ: Team Manager
Gino BORSOI: Sporting Director
Maria Jose BOTELLA: Media & Logistics
Vicente VILA: Media Officer
Roger MARCACCINI: Co-Ordinator
Jose Maria IBANEZ: General Manager

YONNY HERNANDEZ PIT CREW

Francesco CARCHEDI: Chief Mechanic
Erkki Juhanni SIUKOLA: Data engineer
Mechanics
Bruno LEONI, Salvador FRANCO, Daniel VILLAR,
Oscar GRAU

EUGENE LAVERTY PIT CREW

Miguel Angel GALLEGO: Chief Mechanic
Davide TAGLIATESTA: Data Engineer
Phil MARRON: Chief Engineer
Mechanics
Antonio HABA, Adrian VILA, Salvador MORALEDA

EUGENE LAVERTY

Born: 3 June, 1986 – Ballymena, Northern Ireland

GP Starts: 66 (36 MotoGP, 29 250cc, 1 125cc)

YONNY HERNANDEZ

Born: 25 July, 1988 – Medelin, Colombia

GP Starts: 118 (87 MotoGP, 31 Moto2)

THE Valencia-based Aspar squad followed a familiar path in 2016 in an attempt to bounce back from an uninspiring recent performance in the obsolete Open category.

A bastion of the smaller classes for the majority of a history that stretched back to 1992, Spanish racing icon Jorge Martinez had moved into MotoGP in 2010, having agreed a two-year collaboration with Ducati. More recent stints with Aprilia's ART machine in the defunct CRT class, and latterly with Honda's uncompetitive production RCV1000R and RC213V-S in the Open class convinced Martinez to renew his Ducati ties for 2016.

The Italian factory could only lease two-year-old GP14.2-spec Desmosedicis, but with unified software for all, Martinez felt it was the best chance to galvanise the team's fortunes. He would be completely vindicated, predominantly thanks to some outstanding performances from Irish rider Eugene Laverty, who pulled off more than one giant-killing act in his second season with the team. Martinez, who continued in his role as a very high-profile team manager, had not seen a top-six since Barbera at Jerez in 2011.

Laverty scored the team's best ever MotoGP result in a crash-strewn Argentine GP, where he survived a race of attrition to finish fourth. He scored more points in South America alone than in his entire 2015 campaign, and he was inside the top ten at Jerez and

DUCATI Desmosedici GP14.2 – Aspar

Engine: 1000cc 90-degree L4, 360-degree reverse-rotating crankshaft, DOHC, 4 valves per cylinder, desmodromic valve gear, variable-length inlet system
Power: Around 270bhp, revs to 18,000rpm
Ancillaries: Magneti Marelli electronics, NGK sparking plugs, full electronic ride-by-wire • *Lubrication:* Shell
Transmission: Xtrac six-speed seamless-shift cassette-type gearbox
Suspension: Front, Ohlins TRSP25 48mm forks; Rear, Ohlins TRSP44 shock with linkage
Wheels: 17in Marchesini • *Tyres:* Michelin • *Brakes:* Brembo 340mm carbon-carbon front; 200mm steel rear

Jorge Martinez

Yonny Hernandez

Assen, and returned to the top six at rain-hit Brno.

In tandem with Aspar Moto3 rider Pecco Bagnaia's history-making success for Indian brand Mahindra, Laverty's form was crucial in convincing associate sponsor Pull & Bear, the Spanish clothing and accessories retailer, to become the naming rights backer for all of Aspar's racing activities, from the Sachsenring onwards.

In 2016, Laverty was reunited with former World Superbike crew chief Phil Marron, who happens to be his brother-in-law. Marron had been his mechanic in 2015, but had taken over chief engineer duties with Miguel Angel Gallego, reverting to chief mechanic.

The Irishman had an outstanding season, and would have scored points in the opening 14 races had Danilo Petrucci not knocked him off at the Red Bull Ring's final turn. His one and only DNF came in Japan, and an undoubted highlight was a superb charge to second place at Silverstone before the red flags came out on lap one.

His performance meant that Martinez and longserving sporting director Gino Borsoi had every intention of retaining his services for 2017, and he was keen to remain. The big stumbling block took the form of a split of machinery in the Aspar garage for 2017.

Ducati made it clear that it could supply a two-yearold GP15 for one rider and a 2016-spec Desmosedici for the other. When signing Alvaro Bautista at Brno, Aspar agreed that the Spaniard would be allocated the latest version. This loyalty was understandable, for Bautista had won the 2006 125cc World Championship for Aspar, plus eight 250cc races for the team between 2007 and 2009.

That decision prompted Laverty to quit MotoGP. Being on inferior machinery to his team-mate was more than he could swallow. After talks with several prominent World Superbike teams, he joined the Britishbased Milwaukee squad, running factory-supported Aprilia RSV4s for 2017. This move was confirmed just five days after news broke of Bautista's signing.

His departure appeared to give current team-mate Yonny Hernandez a career lifeline, before that was scuppered late on by a signing that appeared motivated more by financial than sporting reasons.

Karel Abraham's MotoGP career had come to an end at the end of 2015, after a five-year spell. The Czech rider had embarked on a woeful year on a BMW S1000RR in the Milwaukee squad, but out of the blue, rumours surfaced that he would join Aspar in late September. Rumour became fact between the Japan and Australia flyaway races.

Ultimately, Hernandez paid for a frustrating and disappointing season that ended without a single topten finish.

The Colombian collaborated with crew chief Francesco Carchedi, and there were two well-known figures in his support team: chief mechanic Bruno Leoni (ex-Ducati and Honda) and data technician Erkki Siukola, who has Suzuki and Yamaha's factory teams on his CV.

Hernandez had his 15 minutes of fame in a deluge at Assen when he led for eight laps before crashing out of the lead. In 2017, he will move back to Moto2 for the first time since 2011, with the Spanish-based AGR Team.

Fourth – and top independent in Argentina

Eugene Laverty

ESTRELLA GALICIA 0,0 MARC VDS

TEAM STAFF

Marc VAN DER STRATEN: Team President
Michael BARTHOLEMY: Team Principal:
Marina ROSSI: Team Coordinator
Patrick KRAMER: Logistics Coordinator
Stefan PREIN: Rider Coach
Mike WATT: Öhlins Technician
Ian WHEELER: Marketing & Communications Manager

TITO RABAT PIT CREW

Chris PIKE: Chief Mechanic
Francesco FAVA: Fuel Injection Engineer
Andrew: GRIFFITH: Data Engineer
Mark LLOYD: Gearbox Mechanic
Mechanics
Craig BURTON, Matt LLOYD, Christian AUSSEMS
Ignacio LORENZANA: Tyres and Fuel

JACK MILLER PIT CREW

Cristian GABBARINI: Chief Mechanic
Riccardo SANCASSANI: Fuel Inhection
Kazuhiko YAMANO: Gearbox Mechanic
Mechanics
Daniele GRELLI, Filippo BRUNETTI, Michele ANDREINI
Olivier BOUTRON: Tyres and Spare Parts

JACK MILLER

Born: 18 January, 1995 – Townsville, Queensland, Australia
GP Starts: 86 (31 MotoGP, 55 Moto3/125cc)
GP Wins: 7 (1 MotoGP, 6 Moto3)

TITO RABAT

Born: 25 May, 1989 – Barcelona, Spain
GP Starts: 176 (17 MotoGP, 55, 68 Moto2, 76 125cc)
GP Wins: 13 (13 Moto2)

NO other team on the 2016 MotoGP grid experienced the contrasting fortunes and emotions that motorcycle racing can deliver more than the Estrella Galicia 0,0 Marc VDS squad.

The highs were surprising and startling, with Jack Miller becoming only the 12th Australian rider to win in premier-class history when he brilliantly mastered treacherous conditions at the Dutch TT at Assen to take a famous victory.

The lows, however, highlighted what a brutally unforgiving arena MotoGP can be. Miller spent a large part of the season riding injured, while rookie teammate Tito Rabat found the transition from Moto2 a chastening experience.

It was the high-profile Belgian-based team's sec-

ond season in MotoGP, having run a single-rider entry in 2015 with Scott Redding. With LCR unable to finance a two-rider effort to keep Miller alongside Cal Crutchlow in 2016, and in an arrangement beneficial to both, Honda and Marc VDS cut a deal to lease two factory RC213Vs.

Since the team was bankrolled by multi-millionaire Marc van der Straten, with support from Spanish brewery giant Estrella Galicia, there was never any doubt about its financial credibility.

Miller was set for the second year of HRC's bold and risky three-year experiment that had fast-tracked the Aussie straight from Moto3 into MotoGP, and the Japanese factory needed to find him a new seat.

Team principal Michael Bartholemy was also a big

HONDA RC213V – Marc VDS

Engine: 1000cc 90-degree V4, 360-degree reverse-rotating crankshaft, pneumatic valve return system • **Power:** More than 270bhp, revs to 17,500rpm

Ancillaries: Magneti Marelli electronics and ride-by-wire throttle and fuel injection system, NGK sparking plugs • **Lubrication:** Elf

Transmission: Gear primary drive, multi-plate dry slipper clutch, six-speed seamless-shift constant-mesh cassette-style gearbox, RK chain

Suspension: Front, Ohlins TRVSP25-8 48mm 'through-rod' forks; Rear, Ohlins TRSP44-12 'through-rod' shock with linkage

Wheels: 17in OZ Racing • **Tyres:** Michelin

Brakes: Brembo 320 or 340mm carbon-carbon; HRC 218mm steel rear

NICKY HAYDEN

Born: 30 July, 1981 – Owensboro, Kentucky, USA

GP Starts: 218
GP Wins: 3 MotoGP
World Championships: 1 MotoGP

Miller eases away from Marquez on his way to victory at Assen

Tito Rabat

Assen 2016

First MotoGP win for the Jackass

Marc Van Der Straten

Cristian Gabbarini

Michael Bartholemy

admirer of Miller, having recognised his skills when he was in Moto3 in 2014, so much so that he thought he had signed him to the team's Moto2 squad for 2015. Then Miller had inked his unprecedented three-year MotoGP deal with Honda. Despite the ensuing bitter fallout, Bartholemy wasn't about to miss out on another chance to employ the talented rider.

Miller brought all of his LCR crew, including the respected Cristian Gabbarini, technical mastermind behind Casey Stoner's titles at Ducati in 2007 and Honda in 2011.

The Australian's season got off to the worst possible start when he suffered a motocross training crash in Spain just a day before his 21st birthday, breaking his right tibia and fibula. As a result, he missed the opening Sepang test. It was the start of an injury-hit campaign, and eventually he missed five races.

He aggravated his leg injury in an FP4 crash in Austin and had to withdraw. Heading to Assen, he had scored just eight points in the opening seven rounds, before his win there was one of the shocks of a remarkable season. He was the first Independent Team winner since Toni Elias in Estoril in 2006, and the first

in history to win in both Moto3 and MotoGP.

There followed another impressive ride to seventh in variable conditions in Germany, before his fortunes plummeted in Austria. He'd only just regained full fitness when his body took another battering in a high-speed warm-up crash, which left him with a fractured right wrist and T6 vertebra. He missed Austria and Brno, before bravely riding to 16th at Silverstone.

Then he withdrew on race-day morning at Misano, the constant stress on his right hand having slowed the healing process. He was forced out of the Motorland Aragon race, too, which opened the door for immensely popular Nicky Hayden to make a shock return to MotoGP.

Hayden had been on standby to ride Miller's Honda RC213V at Silverstone. He finished 15th at Aragon, in a return that hammered home the significance of 2016 being the first premier-class season since 1975 with no American on the full-time entry list.

However, Miller did at least end a tough year strongly, with top-ten finishes in Australia and Malaysia.

Miller's mid-season turmoil coincided with a major

blow: at year's end, crew chief Gabbarini would return to Ducati for the first time since 2010, having been headhunted for the role of Jorge Lorenzo's crew chief. Filling the vacancy will be Ramon Aurin, axed by Dani Pedrosa from the Repsol Honda squad.

Rabat's MotoGP bow proved a humbling experience as he struggled to make any major impression on Honda's notoriously wild RC213V. At times, it was uncomfortable to watch the former Moto2 world champion look so lost and bemused. At one stage, he was crashing so often that he was in danger of running out of leathers. The low point came at Mugello, where he fractured his left collarbone in an FP3 fall. He never qualified higher than 18th and scored only two top-ten finishes, in Argentina and Brno.

Rabat was paired with crew chief Chris Pike, his previous technician, Pete Benson, having remained in the VDS Moto2 team to pass on his wealth of experience to rising Italian Franco Morbidelli.

Pike quit at the end of 2016 to head up Honda's World Endurance effort, so for 2017, long-serving Gresini employee Diego Gubellini, with Stefan Bradl in Aprilia, was drafted in.

2016 TEAMS AND RIDERS

By PETER McLAREN

JOHANN ZARCO will move to MotoGP as the first rider to successfully defend a Moto2 title and the first Frenchman to win more than a single grand prix world championship. But if Zarco though it would be easier second time around, he was in for an unpleasant surprise.

Three of his rivals exchanged the points lead before Zarco finally reached the front. However, mistakes and missed opportunities by all the title favourites allowed the rider, who had been fifth in the standings after Brno, to mount a late title challenge.

Meanwhile, a tragic accident for Luis Salom cast a dark shadow over the season.

Kalex would win every race, the German chassis manufacturer filling 24 of the 30 start-of-season places. The remaining rides were divided between three chassis brands, which became two by the middle of the season.

Teams had been migrating to Kalex for several years, creating something of a self-fulfilling prophesy: as more top teams and riders switched to Kalex, the more Kalex would dominate the results, in turn fuelling demand from those not yet using the frame. The chances of a non-Kalex victory were largely extinguished when Sam Lowes switched from Speed Up as part of his future Aprilia/Gresini MotoGP deal.

With engines, tyres and electronics already identical, the biggest technical variable at the front of the field became suspension rather than chassis. WP and Ohlins battled for supremacy, while further back Tech 3 ran KYB.

Fortunately, given the mechanical monotony, a multi-rider fight for the title kept fans entertained throughout the season.

Chassis competition will receive a much-needed boost in 2017. Triple Moto2 constructors' champion Suter, which had withdrawn after a sparse 2015 line-up, is to make an official return. The biggest news, however, is a new KTM Moto2 chassis, meaning that the multiple Moto3 champions will be active in all three grand prix classes.

Tito Rabat was the only Moto2 rider to join MotoGP for 2016. Mika Kallio (KTM MotoGP test rider) and Randy Krummenacher (WorldSSP) were other familiar names to leave the class, but the rest of 2015's top 20 were back on the grid in Qatar.

Every reigning Moto3 champion has moved up to the 600cc category, and Danny Kent was no exception, the Englishman taking a second bite at the Moto2 apple. Seven rookies also joined the class, led by Kent's new team-mate and former title rival, Miguel Oliveira.

The 30 full-time riders (the same number as in 2016) comprised nine Spaniards, six Italians, four Swiss, three Germans, two Britons and one representative each from Malaysia, Portugal, France, Thailand, Japan and Belgium. Seven of those countries would celebrate a race win, the most variety of any grand prix class. At 18, Valentino Rossi's half-brother, Luca Marini, was the youngest on the grid, while countryman Mattia Pasini was the oldest at 30.

Rule changes during the season included a preemptive ban on aerodynamic devices (such as wings), plus the addition of a second brand of approved quickshifter "to reduce the incidence of missed gears".

There will be new faces at the front of Moto2 in 2017, with Zarco (Tech 3), Alex Rins (Suzuki), Sam Lowes (Aprilia) and Jonas Folger (Tech 3) all confirmed as stepping up to MotoGP.

KALEX

With 24 full-time entries, for Kalex, it must have seemed as though it was supporting a single-chassis championship. A casual glance at the podium in 2016 would have reinforced such a view, with almost every race ending with a Kalex top three.

Two new Kalex entries were needed for the return of the (Leopard-backed) Kiefer team, while the loss of a bike each at JiR and Italtrans was countered by an extra rider at both Dynavolt and AGR.

Remaining with Ajo Motorsport on the Kalex-WP package, reigning champion **Johann Zarco** (25) appeared difficult to dislodge. Just as in 2015, however, he began the year on the back foot in Qatar.

The good news for Zarco was that fellow favourites Rins and Lowes were also caught up in a flood of jump-start penalties. Although soon back to winning ways, seesawing fortunes meant that Johann would not lead the standings until round eight. That was in the middle of four wins in five races, as the Frenchman loaded pressure on his less-experienced rivals, only to weaken at the most unlikely of moments, when main challenger Rins was struck by injury, before a back-flipping return to form.

Away from Moto2, Zarco made his MotoGP debut during a private test for Suzuki. But the factory was already leaning towards Rins, and instead he signed for his 'home' team, Tech 3 Yamaha. Twenty-seventeen will be his ninth season in grands prix, having spent three years in 125cc and five in Moto2. Ajo Motorsport will be defending titles in both classes for the first time.

After gaining two victories and title runner-up in his rookie Moto2 season, few doubted that **Alex Rins** (20) would win more races for the Sito Pons-run Paginas Amarillas HP 40 team in 2016. The question, however, was whether he had what it took to claim the title.

Rins's supporters saw an obvious comparison with Maverick Vinales, the former Pons Moto2 rider who would win for Suzuki in MotoGP. Others were less convinced. The doubters were silenced, though, when he swept into the title lead as the first double race winner of the season, only for momentum to swing towards Zarco.

Former Moto3 runner-up Rins would prove his mettle with some brave rides after suffering a broken collarbone in training. He had clawed to within one point of Zarco by the start of the flyaway races.

Having resisted offers of satellite MotoGP rides, Rins will replace Vinales at Suzuki in 2017.

Edgar Pons (20), son of former champion Sito and younger brother of fellow Moto2 racer Axel, was drafted in as a rookie team-mate to Rins. He had won 2015's CEV Moto2 European championship and had made eight grand prix starts, the majority in place of Kallio at Italtrans. His early season was disrupted by illness, however, and he was forced to miss Argentina, Austin and Jerez due to dizziness and weakness caused by hepatitis A. He would return to score his first world championship points.

Sam Lowes (25) was the only rider to start the Moto2 season having already secured a MotoGP seat for 2017. The former Speed Up rider had signed a multi-year deal with Aprilia, for the first year of which he would remain in Moto2, but switch to Gresini, Aprilia's MotoGP partner. That meant the 2013 World Supersport champion, a debut grand prix winner in

JOHANN ZARCO

SAM LOWES

JONAS FOLGER

2015, would get the chance to challenge Zarco and Rins on the same Kalex chassis (albeit fitted with Ohlins, rather than WP, suspension).

The fired-up Englishman would be the first of the favourites to hold the world championship lead, returning to the top of the standings at Mugello. But a spate of no-scores – including a dramatic second fall in the Austrian race, due to handlebar damage in the first – plus a controversial clash with Zarco at Silverstone would leave his title dream in tatters.

The Dynavolt Intact GP team, built around Moto3 champion **Sandro Cortese** (26) for his graduation to Moto2 in 2013, added a second machine for countryman **Jonas Folger** (22) to campaign in 2016.

Folger had enjoyed a breakthrough 2015, celebrating two wins with AGR to surpass Cortese as Germany's top Moto2 rider. He was already being watched by the Tech 3 Yamaha team, and some strong early performances paved the way for a MotoGP deal – after which, his form promptly plummeted. He would bounce back with a victory later in the season.

Photos: Gold & Goose

Cortese's early season was marred by DNFs, and he was forced out of Le Mans by a knee injury, but the German would stand on the rostrum later in the year. He will continue with the team in 2017, while Folger's place will be taken by Marcel Schrotter.

The CarXpert/Garage Plus Interwetten team began the season with an unchanged line-up of **Thomas Luthi** (29), **Dominique Aegerter** (25) and **Robin Mulhauser** (24). It wouldn't end that way.

Aegerter's five ever-improving seasons on a Suter had culminated in a debut grand prix victory in 2014, but the progression had come to an abrupt halt when Interwetten joined the Kalex club in 2015. He continued to look uncomfortable in 2016.

Rumours abounded that Interwetten would sign up for the return of Suter in 2017, but it seems Aegerter wasn't convinced and he accepted a rival Suter offer from Leopard Racing. Interwetten promptly responded by dropping him for the remaining four rounds, hiring instead 16-year-old Spaniard Iker Lecuona, who had replaced Aegerter when a shoulder injury in

a motocross accident had forced him to miss Silverstone and Misano.

The premature exit, combined with an early fall at the Suzuka 8 Hours, meant 2016 would be a year to forget for Aegerter.

By contrast, Luthi began the season with a victory and was called up by KTM to test its MotoGP machine in June. The Swiss rider later escaped injury when his Moto2 bike was spectacularly launched over the fence on Saturday morning at Brno, only to be knocked unconscious by an afternoon high-side. That forced him out of the race, but he would make a triumphant return at Silverstone, setting up a late charge for the championship that would include his first back-to-back wins. He also surpassed Rabat for all-time Moto2 podiums. Luthi is set to be joined by Lecuona and Raffin in 2017.

Having scored a single point in 2015, Mulhauser would marginally increase his tally in 2016.

Franco Morbidelli (21) was brought in to fill Tito Rabat's shoes at Estrella Galicia 0,0 Marc VDS. The

results don't show it, but the Italian came within 0.047s of winning on his debut for the Belgian team. His efforts were erased from the record books, however, by a post-race jump-start penalty. Thereafter, he would prove a safe pair of hands, scoring regular podiums en route to his best grand prix season – although a debut victory would be snatched away by a fraction of a second at Phillip Island.

Team-mate **Alex Marquez** (19) would also earn a 2017 contract extension, despite spending the first half of the season sampling the texture of the gravel traps. Marc's younger brother weathered the storm, however, and silenced his critics with a first podium. A collision with an out-of-fuel Simon at Phillip Island ruled him out of the Australian race.

Takaaki Nakagami (24) seemed to be living off past glories at the start of the year, with only one rostrum visit since 2013. But he and Taddy Okada's team would take a victory in 2016 (the first by a Japanese rider since Yuki Takahashi in 2010) plus multiple podiums, which put his career firmly back on track.

Photos: Gold & Goose

Ratthapark Wilairot (27) took over from Azlan Shah on the second IDEMITSU Honda Team Asia machine. It would be the Thai rider's first full grand prix campaign since 2012, but unfortunately for the World Supersport race winner, points would remain rare commodities.

Hafizh Syahrin (21) would continue his steady upward trajectory during his third grand prix season. All three have been spent with his home Petronas Raceline Malaysia team. As his nickname 'Pescao' ('Little Fish') suggests, Syahrin is always one to watch in the wet.

Forward Racing's MotoGP project may have closed its doors at the end of 2015, following the tax-related turmoil, but the Moto2 team continued and – while Simone Corsi sought pastures new – teenage star **Lorenzo Baldassarri** (19) was back to try to build on a debut rostrum.

Baldassarri's determination couldn't be faulted; he tried to race in Qatar, despite having dislocated *both* shoulders in practice. Doctors thought otherwise, however. He would suffer another dislocation at the Sachsenring, but the pain would be worth the gain when he won in front of his home fans, also becoming the first Italian to win in Moto2 since Andrea Iannone.

Team-mate to 'Balda' was rookie **Luca Marini** (18), Valentino Rossi's half-brother being the youngest and least experienced rider on the grid. He coped well with the inevitable pressure, however, and scored regular points, including a top-six and fastest lap.

Both Baldassarri and Marini re-signed with Forward during the summer break.

After two seasons at Tech 3, **Marcel Schrotter** (23) threw in the towel for a return to the proven Kalex package, joining AGR. While he wouldn't repeat his 2014 season on the French chassis, he would claim his best Moto2 race finish, finally matching the 2009 Valencia 125cc fifth place that had kick-started his grand prix career.

Schrotter had taken over from Jonas Folger, while **Axel Pons** (24) was starting his third season at the team – and what would be his best world championship campaign so far.

Pons will join RW Racing in 2017, when Yonny Hernandez will return from MotoGP to ride for AGR. The team is also planning a Moto3 project.

The Italtrans Racing Team cut back to a single entry in 2016, hiring veteran **Mattia Pasini** (30), who had raced in 125cc, 250cc, Moto2 and MotoGP during the previous 11 years. The Italian – who has both the front brake and clutch lever fitted to the left handlebar, due to arm injuries received early in his career, narrowly missed out on a first rostrum since 2009.

Italtrans will return to a two-rider line-up for 2017, having signed Andrea Locatelli alongside Pasini.

Moto2 world champions with Stefan Bradl in 2011, Kiefer returned to the intermediate class on the back of 2015's Moto3 title victory by **Danny Kent** (22). The Englishman's former Red Bull KTM rival **Miguel Oliveira** (21) completed a promising Leopard Rac-

ing line-up, but it would be a disappointing season for both.

Kent had endured a miserable rookie Moto2 season at Tech 3 in 2013, prompting a return to Moto3, where ultimately he had become Britain's first grand prix champion since Barry Sheene.

Sticking with the same team and riding the proven Kalex-WP package might have mitigated the risk of a 2013 repeat, but the result would be only marginally better. Kent missed the German race due to rib injuries received in a karting accident, while Portuguese rookie Oliveira was ruled out of Aragon and beyond after being hit by Morbidelli just minutes into opening practice.

The Italian was penalised, but it would be little consolation to Oliveira, who was left nursing a broken collarbone. During his recovery, he was replaced by Italian Alessandro Nocco.

While Kent will continue at Kiefer in 2017, he will have a new bike (Suter), crew chief and team-mate, in the form of Dominique Aegerter. Dental student Oliveira will head back to the Ajo team, where he had achieved his greatest success, riding the new KTM Moto2 chassis alongside Brad Binder.

Former Moto3 title runner-up **Luis Salom** (24) switched from Pons to SAG for 2016, gaining instant success by riding from 17th to second in the penalty-littered Qatar race. But tragedy struck when the Spaniard lost control during practice for the Catalunya event and followed his motorcycle into the air-fence.

JULIAN SIMON

LUIS SALOM

XAVIER SIMEON

TETSUTA NAGASHIMA

REMY GARDNER

ANTHONY WEST

XAVI VIERGE

DANNY KENT

ISAAC VINALES

SIMONE CORSI

At the time of his death, Salom remained the most successful Moto3 rider in history, with nine wins.

With SAG electing not to sign another rider, Salom's team-mate, **Jesko Raffin** (19), rode alone for the rest of the year. During his second season in grands prix, he would score his first points, battle for pole at Phillip Island and ultimately sign for CarXpert.

SAG is due to run Isaac Vinales and Tetsuta Nagashima in the new season.

Tasca Racing Scuderia Moto2 switched its entry from Tech 3 to Kalex, initially hiring **Alessandro Tonucci** (22) in place of Louis Rossi. Tonucci lasted six pointless races before being replaced by **Remy Gardner** (18), son of 1987 World Champion Wayne Gardner, who broke the top 15 on his first attempt.

Gardner had been forced to step back from grands prix after a frustrating season on a CIP Mahindra in Moto3, but he continued the momentum from his impressive Moto2 debut by claiming his first victory in the FIM CEV Repsol European Moto2 Championship. The Australian was confirmed as a permanent Tasca Moto2 rider from Assen and later named at Tech 3 for 2017, when Tasca will run Xavier Simeon.

Wild-card **Ramdam Rosli** (20) added to the Kalex points scorers in Malaysia with a fine tenth place.

SPEED UP

Speed Up kept the same team format for 2016, running one machine itself while also supporting QMMF.

With star rider Sam Lowes having switched to Gresini, Speed Up Racing signed **Simone Corsi** (28) to carry on its victory hopes. The Italian veteran, who had made his grand prix debut in 2002, would be by far the most successful non-Kalex rider. But he would also infuriate his rivals with some cut-throat moves, resulting in a ride-through penalty at Brno.

Speed Up is set to run a second official rider in 2017, but not any customer teams.

With Mika Kallio having opted for KTM test-riding duties, the Qatar-backed QMMF Racing Team picked up 2015 race winner **Xavier Simeon** (26) from Gresini to partner the continuing **Julian Simon** (28). The latter was ruled out of the Jerez race after hitting his head in warm-up, while he injured his foot in a pre-Sachsenring training accident, before claiming an emotional first podium since 2012. Simon's luck would change once again, however, with a back injury at Sepang.

QMMF is absent from the 2017 entry list, when Simeon will join Tasca and Simon retire from racing.

TECH 3

With established riders unwilling to consider anything but a Kalex – despite the bait of being associated with a MotoGP team – Tech 3 Racing kept 2015 stand-in **Xavi Vierge** (18) for a full season, adding Moto3's **Isaac Vinales** (22) for an all-rookie line-up.

Continuing with their own chassis design – which had taken podiums in the opening seasons of Moto2,

including one victory – the team, founded in 1989, took a further step away from the masses with its choice of suspension. Having flirted with KYB in 2015, Tech 3 made the full-time switch from Ohlins, while news of Vierge trying a CEV-spec Kalex in a late-summer test raised eyebrows. Poncharal insisted that the test was to settle any doubts in the mind of the rider, while gathering useful data for KYB.

Vierge, who will ride alongside Gardner in 2017, would score the most points and seal the Rookie of the Year title. Vinales matched his compatriot by breaking into the top ten.

SUTER

Despite scrapping its official Moto2 project, a Suter chassis was present for the opening six rounds, courtesy of the JPMoto Malaysia team.

Efren Vazquez (29) began the season, but suffered a broken ankle in Austin and wouldn't be seen at the team again. Daytona 200 winner Danny Eslick put police problems to one side by stepping in for Le Mans, with Ricky Cardus making what would be the team's final appearance of the season at Mugello.

Nevertheless, a Suter chassis would go on to claim world championship points in the hands of former Moto2 race winner Anthony West, competing as a wild-card at Brno.

Kiefer and Dynavolt Intact will form Suter's comeback effort for 2017.

2016 TEAMS AND RIDERS

By PETER McLAREN

BRAD BINDER began the 2016 season without a grand prix win. He made good on that shortfall from last on the grid, becoming South Africa's first world champion since 1980 with four races to spare.

Binder's peerless form also returned KTM to the top of the Moto3 riders' championship after back-to-back titles for Honda, while debut victories for Mahindra and Peugeot meant that all four manufacturers would feature on the top step of the podium.

In fact, the Peugeot was a rebadged Mahindra, and it arrived on the grid just as KTM called time on a similar scheme with Husqvarna. The result was that the 33 full-time grid places were divided almost equally between KTM, Honda and Mahindra/Peugeot.

Technical rules for the 250cc four-strokes remained stable, with open engine and chassis competition ring-fenced by strict limits on in-season updates and equality of supply from each constructor to its teams. Minimum weight (rider and bike) increased from 149 to 152kg.

While cost – especially relative to the Moto2 class – remained a concern, there was no doubting the quality of racing in Moto3. The class replicated the constant stream of different winners seen in the MotoGP class. Of the nine riders to win a race (a tally only seen once before, in 2003), six celebrated their first grand prix victory.

In a year when newcomers filled almost a third of the grid, two of the race winners were also rookies. One of them was Khairul Idham Pawi, Malaysia's first ever grand prix winner. Malaysia was one of 12 countries represented in the junior class, with past fears concerning the next generation of Italian talent being laid to rest by a total of 11 competitors – almost twice the number of those from Spain.

France began with three riders, with South Africa (or more accurately the Binder brothers), Czech Republic and Japan matching Malaysia on two. Belgium, Germany, Netherlands, Argentina and Great Britain each had a single competitor.

Race Direction made progress in the ongoing battle to thwart riders from cruising on track, in search of someone quicker to follow in qualifying. But there were some notable exceptions and numerous grid penalties – leading to a harsher range of punishments from Motegi. There was also nothing Race Direction could do about riders waiting until a faster rider was leaving the pits, then tucking in behind them as they rode down the pit lane.

On the technical front, while Moto2 winglets had been banned before the season began, experiments by Mahindra meant that initially the aerodynamic devices were allowed in Moto3 until the end of the season. By mid-May, however, the manufacturers unanimously agreed to make the wing ban effective immediately.

Moto3's control ECU system was thrown into the spotlight during the pre-season, when KTM accused Honda of exceeding the rev limit (13,500rpm) by 100rpm during 2015. Technical Director Danny Aldridge investigated the claims: "We have established that there is nothing unusual or unexpected about how the rev limiter works and that the cut point is consistent on all engines. Nevertheless, moderate and temporary overshoots of the defined rev limit were identified."

He concluded, "There is no desire to reduce the point at which the limiter cuts power just to avoid data showing minimal overshoots. It may therefore be necessary to modify regulations to take account of inevitable overshoots."

In 2017, there will be a significant change in the spirit of the Moto3 regulations, with engines and gearboxes provided "under a rental agreement with ownership retained by the manufacturer" rather than sold to the teams. Each manufacturer must also be prepared to supply machines and spare parts for up to 14 riders if requested (two more than in 2016) and a minimum of six riders as a condition of entry.

KTM

KTM's 13 machines on the start-of-season grid might have been just one fewer than in 2015 (counting the Husqvarnas), but there were some significant changes in team formation.

The most obvious was the arrival of reigning champion Leopard, which switched its three machines from Honda, while Valentino Rossi's VR46 team added a third bike to its ranks. By contrast, the factory Red Bull KTM Ajo squad cut back to two entries, as did RBA, while the Laglisse Husqvarnas briefly morphed into a single KTM. Drive M7 SIC switched both its riders to Honda.

The Red Bull KTM Ajo squad placed rookie **Bo Bendsneyder** (17 years old at the beginning of season) alongside class 'veteran' **Brad Binder** (20). The South African is one of the few riders – including Romano Fenati, Niccolo Antonelli and Jakub Kornfeil – to have been a full-time Moto3 competitor since the championship replaced 125cc in 2012, steering Kalex KTM (RW Racing) and Mahindra (Ambrogio) machinery before joining Ajo in 2015.

Binder would take over the title lead at round two and never look back, his sensational last-to-first Jerez victory being the first grand prix win for a South African in 35 years. Such racecraft would be repeated when he headed the closest top-five finish in grand prix history at Mugello.

Described as quiet and humble by those who work with him, Binder still managed a smile when the swarms of tow-seeking riders reached farcical levels in qualifying: "They even followed me when I ran into the gravel!" quipped the rider from Krugersdorp, outside Johannesburg.

Binder's title was the fourth in the junior grand prix category for Finnish team owner Aki Ajo, but the first since Sandro Cortese during the inaugural 2012 Moto3 season.

Binder and Miguel Oliveira were announced as joining the new KTM Moto2 project just after the summer break. Rumours suggest that Binder may also have some form of KTM MotoGP option for 2019.

After the disappointment of Ajo predecessor Karel Hanika, all eyes were on Bendsneyder to defend the honour of the Red Bull Rookies Cup, which Hanika had won in 2013 and Bendsneyder in 2015. Fortunately, the young Dutchman would prove a safe and steadily improving pair of hands, climbing the podium and leading a race. He will stay for 2017.

SKY Racing Team VR46 retained **Romano Fenati** (20) and **Andrea Migno** (20), while adding a third machine for exciting young talent **Nicolo Bulega** (16), winner of the 2015 FIM CEV Moto3 Junior World Championship.

Fenati, a VR46 rider since the team's formation in 2014, began his fifth grand prix campaign with the clear objective of winning the Moto3 crown. Despite six previous race wins and 15 podiums, inconsistency had always been his Achilles heel – leaving him no higher than fourth in the standings – but few could have foreseen the meltdown that was to come.

The Italian would end a near year-long win drought in Austin, but results were up and down again, not helped by factors outside his control, such as a broken chain at Mugello. Then came a shock statement from the VR46 team on Saturday night at the Red Bull Ring:

"Following repeated behaviour not in line with the disciplinary rules of the Team – the rider Romano Fenati has been suspended."

No further details were given regarding the behaviour that had prompted such drastic action, and the team rejected lurid rumours of a physical confrontation with the management. To put the decision into perspective, however, Fenati was third in the world championship and due to spearhead a new VR46 Moto2 project in 2017.

The split was confirmed as permanent a few days later, with **Lorenzo dalla Porta** (19) being parachuted into the team from Silverstone. He had been due to continue at Laglisse for what would have been a first full grand prix season in 2016, but the team's financial problems meant that instead he returned with them to the CEV.

In addition to his CEV commitments, dalla Porta would be called up in place of the injured Philipp Oettl

BRAD BINDER

JOAN MIR

FABIO QUARTARARO

ROMANO FENATI

BO BENDSNEYDER

NICOLO BULEGA

GABRIEL RODRIGO

ANDREA MIGNO

JUANFRAN GUEVARA

LORENZO DALLA PORTA

ANDREA LOCATELLI

RAUL FERNANDEZ

MARIA HERRERA

PHILIPP OETTL

(Schedl GP KTM) at Mugello, where he led a lap. Then he took the place of Jorge Navarro (Estrella Galicia Honda) at Assen.

Dalla Porta's performances in both championships ensured that he had been signed already by Aspar Mahindra for the 2017 season when the VR46 stand-in call arrived.

Fenati would sit out the rest of the season, ahead of a fresh start with Ongetta Rivacold in 2017. Mahindra star Francesco Bagnaia – dropped by VR46 after the 2014 season – was rehired for the team's Moto2 project.

Compensating for the Fenati chaos was emerging star Bulega, whose on-track form and off-track appearance soon prompted comparisons with a young Valentino Rossi.

Unlike The Doctor, however, Bulega would not celebrate a victory in his rookie season, but did claim a debut pole, podium and fastest race lap as he battled with Mir and Di Giannantonio for top newcomer honours. A less welcome 'first' came in the form of a 300-euro fine for making a derogatory hand gesture in practice at Aragon, following a controversial crackdown on such gestures by the FIM.

Bulega was also the first VR46 rider to be re-signed for 2017, in June, with Migno's new contract being confirmed at Silverstone in September. On paper, Migno could count himself fortunate, having failed to get

near Bulega's points tally, despite double the grand prix experience.

Nevertheless, Migno would celebrate his first world championship podiums in 2016 (and inherit a pole, despite not being fastest in qualifying), while the sportsmanship he displayed when caught up in Bagnaia's accident at Silverstone reflected positively on his character.

KTM's winter claims of rev limit exploitation by Honda, and the inference that it could have made a difference in the six points that had separated Oliveira from world champion Danny Kent, was hardly the warm welcome Leopard might have expected after switching to the Austrian brand.

With Kent having moved up to the Moto2 team, Leopard fielded an all-new Moto3 line-up of **Fabio Quartararo** (16), **Andrea Locatelli** (19) and **Joan Mir** (18).

Quartararo was the star signing, having made the surprise break from Emilio Alzamora and Estrella Galicia 0,0 Honda, where he had claimed two podiums during an injury-interrupted debut grand prix season. But a podium, let alone a first win, would prove out of reach in 2016, prompting the French teenager to make another big career decision and move to Moto2 with Pons in 2017.

It would be Locatelli – riding for his third different team, in his third grand prix season – who handed the

Leopard-Honda project its debut podium. However, Mir, another graduate of the FIM CEV Moto3 series, went one better with a grand prix win and Rookie of the Year title.

Mir will remain at Leopard for 2017, when the team will switch back to Honda, and be joined by Livio Loi.

After the excitement of a shock podium at Indianapolis in 2015, Schedl GP Racing's sole rider, **Philipp Oettl** (19), would overcome a broken wrist at Le Mans to take another forward step in the overall championship standings.

Aleix Espargaro's RBA Racing Team slimmed down to two riders for its second world championship season, pairing **Gabriel Rodrigo** (19) with new signing **Juanfran Guevara** (20). Previously, the latter had been at Aspar Mahindra; he would be riding his fifth different machine in five seasons.

With the Husqvarna branding having been dropped, Laglisse – world champions with Maverick Vinales in 2013 – was provisionally listed as running **Maria Herrera** (19) and dalla Porta in 2016. But financial problems soon put the project in serious doubt. The Laglisse name was present in Qatar only as part of a single KTM entry for Herrera. Then it was dropped entirely after Jerez.

After three seasons in grands prix, former RBA rider Ana Carrasco lost her battle to remain on the grid, leaving Herrera as the only full-time female racer

JORGE NAVARRO

FABIO DI GIANNANTONIO

ENEA BASTIANINI

NICCOLO ANTONELLI

FRANCESCO BAGNAIA

JORGE MARTIN

JULES DANILO

TATSUKI SUZUKI

ARON CANET

JAKUB KORNFEIL

KHAIRUL IDHAM PAWI

ADAM NORRODIN

(Shizuka Okazaki was a wild-card entry at her home round at Motegi). Herrera would beat her rookie-season points tally, despite missing the Sachsenring and Valencia races due to injuries. Raul Fernandez would impress as a stand-in for Herrera at Valencia.

HONDA

Honda had 11 full-time machines in 2016, having lost Leopard and RTG, but gained Drive M7 SIC and a new entry from Honda Team Asia.

After the previous year's Leopard success, HRC's best hope of a third straight Moto3 riders' title rested with Alzamora's Estrella Galicia 0,0 Honda squad. The 2014 champions (with Alex Marquez) retained four-times podium finisher **Jorge Navarro** (19) and signed rookie **Aron Canet** (16) in place of Quartararo.

Former CEV runner-up Navarro laid the basis for a title challenge with a string of early podiums, culminating in a debut victory in Catalunya, but he would break his left tibia and fibula during a training accident less than a week later. Although he would win again, it came during an otherwise miserable run of five non-finishes in six races. He will make a fresh start in Moto2 in 2017, joining Gresini in place of Sam Lowes.

Canet, whose 2015 CEV title hopes had been undone by injury, would prove his raw pace with several front-row starts and a podium, but he was denied the chance to start from pole at Valencia. The Spaniard will remain at the Estrella team in 2017, when he is to be joined by **Enea Bastianini** (18).

Having claimed a first grand prix victory, Bastianini began the new season with real championship aspirations. A Gresini rider (with KTM and then Honda) since his 2014 debut, he would make a slow start to the season, then suffer a right wrist fracture while training prior to Le Mans.

The Italian – whose number 33 is inspired by riding a motorcycle for the first time at 3 years and 3 months – tried to compete in France, but was declared unfit. The setback seemed to do some good, however, as he ended a podium drought upon his return and would be a frequent rostrum visitor thereafter.

Bastianini put himself on course for title runner-up with victory in Japan, only to be injured during McPhee's accident at Phillip Island. Red Bull Rookies Champion Ayumu Sasaki took the absent Bastianiani's place for Sepang, ahead of a full-time grand prix ride for the SIC team in 2017.

Team-mate **Fabio Di Giannantonio** (17), runner-up to Bendsneyder in 2015's Red Bull Rookies series, wouldn't score a point in the opening five rounds, but then he promptly claimed a podium. Further success followed, and not surprisingly the Roman was re-signed by Gresini for 2017, when he will be joined by Jorge Martin.

Tady Okada's Honda Team Asia expanded downwards for the 2016 season, forming a Moto3 team alongside its Moto2 project. Japanese rider **Hiroki Ono** (23) joined from Leopard for his second full season, but rookie **Khairul Idham Pawi** (17) would grab all the headlines.

Pawi, whose career began in scooter racing in his native Malaysia, secured the grand prix seat after claiming sixth overall in the FIM CEV proving ground. A wild-card at the 2015 Aragon round, Pawi would make a forgettable start to 2016 in Qatar. But then he rode as if on rails to a colossal 26-second victory during damp conditions in Argentina.

Pawi is the first Malaysian to win a grand prix and youngest non-European winner, taking the record from a certain Casey Stoner. He would go on to repeat his victory feat, yet he often struggled to score points under normal dry conditions. He will be a class rookie again in 2017, moving straight to Moto2 with Honda Team Asia.

Ono would make sporadic top-six appearances, missing Assen after requiring surgery for a fracture of his left index finger in Catalunya. The Japanese rider would be stripped of a home pole due to a penalty, then lose a first podium under similar circumstances in the race. A concussion in qualifying would prevent him from even starting the Sepang race.

Having put his Gresini woes behind him with a pair of race wins during a breakthrough 2015 season, **Niccolo Antonelli** (20) found his winter preparations dogged by collarbone injuries. The bone had not healed completely by Qatar, when he also had to battle sickness, but he emerged with a shock victory.

The Italian would have little to celebrate thereafter,

DARRYN BINDER

JOHN McPHEE

LIVIO LOI

STEFANO MANZI

ALBERT ARENAS

MARCOS RAMIREZ

LORENZO PETRARCA

STEFANO VALTULINI

HIROKI ONO

Bagnaia's reward for a second win would be the chance to ride Aspar's Ducati MotoGP machine at the Valencia test, before starting a new chapter in his career with the VR46 Moto2 team.

Despite requiring an operation for hand injuries in Catalunya, team-mate **Jorge Martin** (18) would also claim a new personal high in the form of a podium, although injuries would rule him out of several races. FIM CEV runner-up and grand prix wild-card Albert Arenas stood in for Martin at Assen and is to join the team full time in 2017.

Arenas would gain further valuable grand prix experience during the second half of the season at the Peugeot team, despite a broken collarbone at Brno, where the race was won by team-mate **John McPhee** (21).

McPhee had used his wet-weather prowess to break into the top seven in Argentina and Germany during an otherwise 'character building' year for the Scotsman, which included the departure of Dirk Heidolf.

Almost six years after his first grand prix start, McPhee would receive his reward for persevering by triumphing in the Czech rain. The rollercoaster would continue, however, with a scary race-stopping accident at Phillip Island, which ruled him out of Sepang and Valencia.

After a year away from grands prix, Malaysian Hafiq Azmi claimed his best yet result while acting as a stand-in for McPhee in front of his home fans at Sepang.

Jakub Kornfeil and rookie Patrik Pulkkinen will form an all-new Peugeot Saxoprint line-up for the 2017 season, with McPhee set to join a new 'GB Team' Honda project.

Alexis Masbou (28) began the year with McPhee. The Frenchman, a winner in 2014 and 2015, failed to score a point, however, and would be dropped during the summer break in favour of Arenas.

Team Italia ran an all-new, all-rookie line-up of **Stefano Valtulini** (19) and **Lorenzo Petrarca** (18). Points proved out of reach for much of the season, and the team, which in its early years had run the likes of Fausto Gresini and Luca Cadalora, was not expected to return in 2017.

The reason? While young Italians were a rarity in 2011, when Team Italia returned to grands prix, the likes of VR46, Gresini and Paolo Simoncelli's new project mean that now there are plenty of home-grown teams eager to support Italian riders.

The CIP outfit, home to Remy Gardner and **Tatsuki Suzuki** (18) in 2015, placed Italian rookie **Fabio Spiranelli** (18) alongside the Japanese rider for 2016. The pair would prompt a circuit scooter ban after falling during the Thursday track familiarisation session at Sepang, the Italian suffering nasty leg and foot injuries that kept him out of the race.

Darryn Binder (18), younger brother of Brad, would score his first points during his second grand prix season at the rebranded Platinum Bay Real Estate team – and get to within metres of joining his brother on the podium. Ajo outcast **Karel Hanika** (20) began the season alongside the South African, but was dropped after Catalunya, having failed to finish in the top 15.

Danny Webb, out of grands prix since 2013, made an unexpected return, but he would last for only two races before also being shown the door. Spaniard **Marcos Ramirez** (18) was next in the hot seat. Platinum Bay will switch to KTMs in 2017.

Stefano Manzi (17) would produce an eye-catching performance as an official Mahindra Racing wild-card at Silverstone, where he fought for a podium from 24th on grid. He is to join the VR46 team in Moto2 for 2017.

however. He missed Germany after an oil spill left him with another collarbone fracture, while he was disqualified from Silverstone when his machine failed to reach the minimum weight. Good news finally arrived in the form of a factory Red Bull KTM contract for 2017.

Jules Danilo (20) continued as team-mate to Antonelli, the Frenchman's third world championship season being by far his best yet.

Drive M7 SIC Racing, born out of the ashes of the 2014 Caterham Moto2 project, switched from KTM to Honda machinery, retaining **Jakub Kornfeil** (22), but making the difficult decision to drop home star Zulfahmi Khairuddin for rookie countryman **Adam Norrodin** (17).

A graduate of the Shell Advance Asia Talent Cup, Norrodin almost instantly proved his worth by getting within two corners of a debut podium in Argentina – and what would have been a dream Malaysian 1-2 behind Pawi. Although he gamely pushed his machine over the line, falls would become a feature of his season.

The experienced Kornfeil would deliver a solid, if largely unspectacular season, his seventh in grands prix, handing the SIC team a 'farewell' present in the form of a home podium at Sepang. Kornfeil will join Peugeot for 2017, his place alongside Norrodin being taken by Red Bull Rookies Champion Ayumu Sasaki.

Having revived his grand prix career with a shock win at Indianapolis, **Livio Loi** (18) would return to put the RW Racing Honda regularly in the points. That's no easy task in Moto3; look at the race results for Mugello and

you'll see Loi classified 16th, despite having crossed the finish line just 2.4s from victory!

Among the Honda teams on the grid in 2017 will be SIC 58 Squadra Corse, run by Marco Simoncelli's father. The squad is stepping up from the CEV.

Mahindra/Peugeot

Mahindra's quest for a historic grand prix victory – which had begun in the former 125cc class in 2011 – became a reality in 2016, when its factory Aspar team and a new Peugeot-branded entry both took to the top step of the rostrum.

The Indian manufacturer retained all of its 2015 teams, although Aspar trimmed down to two entries, while adding the Saxoprint Peugeot project.

While KTM and Honda rolled out evolutions of their proven winning machines, Mahindra had embarked on an ambitious redesign of the MGP3O at its facility in Italy. The scale of the changes contributed to some early gearshift issues, prompting the installation of a revised shift mechanism for Catalunya and a new gearbox from Sachsenring.

Aspar Mahindra Team's star rider, **Francesco Bagnaia** (19), suffered less from the false neutrals and would start his fourth world championship season with a podium in Qatar. More champagne would follow, both before and after the Italian wrote history for Mahindra at Assen.

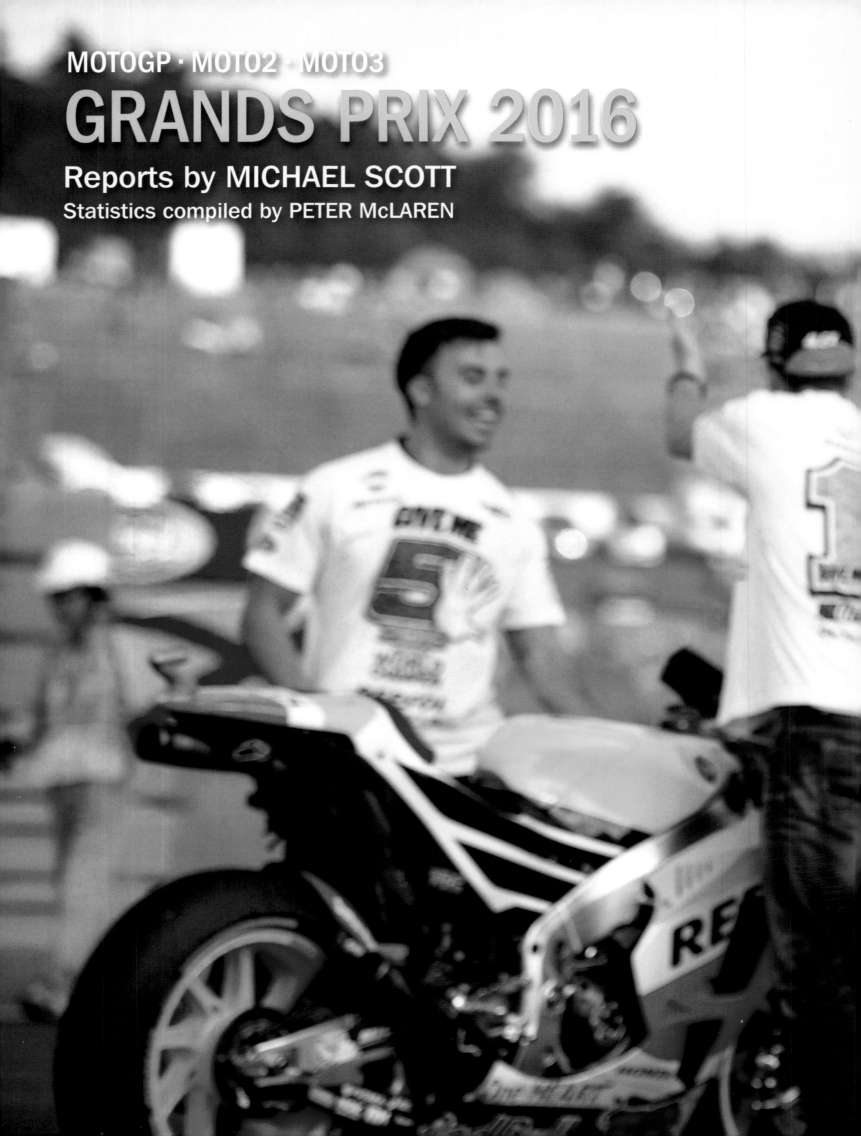

MOTOGP · MOTO2 · MOTO3
GRANDS PRIX 2016
Reports by MICHAEL SCOTT
Statistics compiled by PETER McLAREN

QATAR GRAND PRIX

LOSAIL CIRCUIT

Above: Second for Desmo Dovi augured well for the new Duke.

Top: Lorenzo's superiority was ominous, but would prove short-lived.

Main: Zip it. Lorenzo admonishes the crowd for their jeers.

Photos: Gold & Goose

Above: As easy as 1-2-3. Lorenzo leads Dovi and Marquez.

Top, right and far right: Lorenzo's Yamaha grew a moustache; the Ducatis gained airline livery as wings grabbed the attention.

Above right: Ducatisti: injury victim Petrucci is flanked by the factory Andreas.

Centre right: Bagnaia's Mahindra gained massive speed using 2015's fairing, and made the podium. Next time, all Mahindra riders would have it, too.

Centre far right: A little older and perhaps a little wiser: Michelin's Nicolas Goubert was a familiar face to paddock old-timers.

Below right: All smiles at Yamaha after Rossi's new two-year contract is agreed.

Photos: Gold & Goose

THIS was the first race on a heavily remodelled technical landscape: the biggest changes since the switch to MotoGP four-strokes in 2002. Pre-season tests had been close, but inconclusive, though there was firm evidence that Honda, having made the biggest change in electronics, were having the most trouble adapting.

The effect of the control electronics varied from one group of riders to another. Those accustomed to factory team software found them a step backwards – "five or six years," according to Lorenzo. There was more for the rider to do, requiring more sensitivity with the throttle. But for those up from the Open class, they were a significant step forward. Jack Miller: "The traction control is so much nicer ... you can't feel it, and it doesn't upset the bike. And the wheelie control has more adjustment."

The new Michelin tyres were the biggest factor, affecting everybody, and not all had made the full adjustment yet, especially with the much-changed 2016 front, which had rendered Yamaha's rear-tank 2016 chassis redundant before it had been used; Espargaro and, in a race or two, Vinales would also revert to the 2015 unit.

The tyres weren't worse or better, just different, the riders agreed; and you had to change your approach to suit. Redding, the most spectacular exponent of a renewed ability to spin and slide the rear, was experiencing "quite a lot of skidding under braking. It feels a lot different from the Bridgestones. But it's not bad; it's about understanding it." One side effect was disappointment for photographers, hoping to snap the usual glowing front discs at the end of the straight. They weren't glowing – though Brembo said another factor was a near-universal switch to the larger 340mm discs.

Dovizioso was asked why the Avintia and Aspar satellite riders' GP14.2 was now more competitive than when it had been current, and he named the tyres. "With Bridgestone, there was only one way. With Michelin, there are different ways on different bikes. You can make the lap time with different style and different lines. Though you have to be very smooth and flowing."

This was one explanation of very close times and an interesting reshuffle of riders, which carried over somewhat from the tests. In the big boys' Q2, first to 12th was covered by less than a second. Rossi: "You need to go for every tenth. Qualifying is a casino."

It was different in another way. Dovi again: "With Bridgestone, you had to do it quickly, on the second or third lap. The Michelins need more time to warm." Accordingly, he eschewed the usual mid-qualifying bike change and took a long non-stop run; Smith did the same. They placed sixth and 11th.

If testing had been a little muddled in terms of the usual order, Lorenzo nonetheless had dominated, and he would do so again at Qatar. With Rossi outpaced and Marquez living conspicuously close to the edge, this looked like an ominous sign. The coming races, however, would prove that the one-size-fits-all technical regulations could offer variety also in the results.

Marquez's life of peril reflected an unusual problem for Honda: a lack of top speed – he clocked a best of 342.7km/h over the weekend (equalled by Miller's satellite Honda), which put him ninth fastest behind six Ducatis and two Yamahas. The fastest was Iannone, at 351.2. The reasons were manifold, according to Pedrosa: problems with electronics, the bike itself and throttle response combining to spoil corner exit as well as entry.

Wings were sprouting: Lorenzo favoured two huge soup plates, while the factory Dukes had their flank-wings integrated into the graphics. But with many riders complaining of dangerous turbulence in the wake of the superfast Desmosedicis (staunchly denied by Dovizioso), there were rumblings that they might soon be clipped; while a strange pair of 'anti-drafting' wings on the seat of Aegerter's Moto2 bike were ordered off before practice began because they were the widest part of the motorcycle, against regulations. Race director Mike Webb confirmed that the matter was under consideration: soon afterwards came a diktat banning wings forthwith in the so-far smooth-flanked Moto2, and from 2017 in Moto3, where "some aerodynamic wings are currently being used".

It was Mahindra experimenting in this way, but the immediate outcome was unexpected, after official Aspar Mahindra

rider Bagnaia was given 2015's fairing (they happened to have one with them) and immediately leapt up the qualifying order to fifth. The new bodywork for the substantially revised bike was proving disastrous. A meeting with all the Mahindra teams elicited agreement to make the one bodywork upgrade allowed for the year immediately, before race one – along with the promise that all of them would have the old fairing available for the next race. Bagnaia made the podium.

Pramac Ducati's Danilo Petrucci was back wearing a special prosthetic glove to support the hand he had injured badly in tests in Australia, but he gave up the unequal struggle on the second of three days of practice. The other injury victim was equally brave and also Italian: a whirling trip through the gravel dislocated *both* of Moto2 rider Lorenzo Baldassarri's shoulders. The Forward Racing man returned next day determined to race, but was ruled out by the medics.

The who-goes-where silly season got off to an unprecedented early start on race eve, with the announcement that Rossi had signed for a further two years at Yamaha. That would carry him to 2018 and the age of 39. Details emerged: it had been at Lorenzo's request that contracts were sorted early, explained Yamaha race chief Lin Jarvis. Yamaha had made him "our biggest ever offer". In the interests of equal treatment, Rossi had also been offered a renewal. He'd jumped at it; Lorenzo was stalling, pending an approaching deadline. By now, however, news had leaked that he was also negotiating with Ducati. Before race four, it was confirmed that he would move to the Italian team for the 2017 season.

To round it off, Bradley Smith revealed that he had also struck a deal for 2017 and would be joining the returning KTM squad.

There was an unedifying spectacle before and after the race when rabid Rossi fans booed Marquez and Lorenzo. After his win, Lorenzo repeatedly made the 'zip-it' sign – not to the crowd, but to indicate his own wish to remain silent. "Today I spoke on the track," he explained.

Moto3 team tactics by Red Bull Ajo riders Brad Binder and Rookies Cup champion Bo Bendsneyder in practice cost both three grid positions, under a newly introduced ad hoc punishment system (replacing penalty points) for slow riding. The pair had spent much of practice together, helping each other with slipstreams and for Bendsneyder taking expert tuition in his first time at the track.

Earth Hour 2016 – an international eco-awareness notion whereby all non-essential lights were to be turned off for an hour – passed unobserved during Saturday's MotoGP Q1 and Q2 sessions at the only floodlit track of the year.

MOTOGP RACE – 21 laps

The Ducatis were flying, and Iannone led the first three free practices, before Lorenzo took over in FP4, going on to take the first pole of the season by just over a tenth. Second – Marquez, overcoming the RCV's real or perceived weaknesses with a resumption of his familiar high-risk acrobatics. And third – Vinales, showing that the levelling rules and some committed development had elevated the Suzuki significantly. He essayed the new full seamless-shift gearbox in practice, but it was deemed not yet ready to race.

Rossi was on row three, flanked by the factory Ducatis; Barbera was top non-factory rider in eighth, behind Pedrosa.

An excellent race went further to vindicate the aim of the regulations: closer competition; while a variety of tyre choices underlined new possibilities offered by the Michelins. The top three were all on different tyre combinations (Lorenzo hard front/soft rear; Dovizioso soft/soft; Marquez hard/medium), with Lorenzo making the change from Michelin's recommended harder medium rear on the grid.

In spite of the testing, it was something of a leap into the unknown for all. Some had done race simulations on the new tyres, although sometimes in two runs. But things might be different in the heat of battle.

This time, the Michelins emerged with full credit: a new lap record on the 20th of 21 laps and a race time seven seconds faster than 2015 on Bridgestones.

Lorenzo had leapt away from the start and was still in front as they ran out of the final corner. Then came the Ducati surge: one each side of him, and by the time they reached the first corner again, it was Iannone and Dovizioso ahead of the Yamaha.

Fast starter Pedrosa soon began to lose touch in sixth: not enough pace to stay with the leaders, but enough straight-line speed to frustrate slow starter Vinales, who eventually would abandon the struggle, having used up his tyres.

A leading quintet broke away directly: the Ducatis led Lorenzo and Marquez, who had pushed past Rossi. Then there were four. Dovizioso had taken the lead from his team-mate, who immediately fought back, and an ominous red-on-red battle ensued, ending when the ever-impetuous Iannone ran on to the inside curb on Turn 13 and slid off on lap six.

From then on, the lap chart shows it to be somewhat processional, but the closeness meant otherwise. Time and again, Dovizioso would power away down the straight. Lorenzo spoke afterwards of understanding he would have to overtake early in the lap and take an immediate gap to avoid being swallowed up again.

He timed it for lap nine, executed it with precision and took command, though the others stayed threateningly close, Marquez riding with familiar élan on an obviously more unruly machine, Rossi seesawing somewhat at the back.

Only on lap 19 did Lorenzo show his full hand, increasing the gap to more than a second for the first time, then continuing to stretch it to better than two seconds with that remarkable new record on the penultimate lap. "This was one of the best three races in my career," he said.

Dovizioso and Marquez were to-and-fro over the last four laps, the Italian ahead into the last corner, until Marquez made a desperate late lunge for the apex, only to run wide on the exit, and Dovi powered away once more. Rossi was just a tenth adrift.

A somewhat glum Pedrosa was almost 15 seconds further back; Vinales was sixth, equalling his best finish, but hoping for more power to come.

Four seconds behind, a lively quartet.

Pol Espargaro narrowly fended off team-mate Smith's last-lap attack, both having got ahead of Barbera; Ducati first-timer Redding had lost touch by the finish.

Aleix Espargaro had switched to a 2015 chassis after warm-up and ended up a lone 11th. Then Laverty won out in a sustained battle with Bautista and Jack Miller, the trio all over one another to the end. It was a satisfactory, if not breathtaking, debut for the new Aprilia RS-GP.

Sole rookie Rabat had a low-key weekend, almost half a minute behind, but still earned a point for 15th and last.

Crutchlow was an early and unlucky faller after his electronics went awry. "On the straight, I had traction control, and none in Turn One. I crashed because I closed the throttle and it stayed wide open." Bradl, Baz and Hernandez joined Iannone on the crash list.

MOTO2 RACE – 20 laps

Folger took the first pole of the year by less than a tenth from the newly Kalex-mounted Lowes, with much-fancied Rins completing the front row. Zarco took time to get into fourth, alongside Morbidelli and Cortese. Baldassarri was seventh, but out, which promoted row-three denizens Schrotter, Nakagami and Luthi.

Things went wrong for the ill-favoured production-powered middle class even before the lights went off – triggered, said some riders, by a long delay, then a premature flicker.

All but two of the nine riders occupying the front three rows moved at least slightly, Morbidelli by quite a lot. Then they roared off.

One rider who hadn't moved was Folger, and his timing meant he had a lead of better than a second at the end of the first lap, from Lowes, Luthi, Nakagami, Cortese, Morbidelli and the pack.

The other non-jumper was Luthi, who would win the race after an ultimately quite unnecessary battle with Morbidelli.

Folger was architect of his own downfall, slipping off on the third lap.

For the rest, misfortune came from a rather confused and in some cases badly delayed series of decisions from Race Direction.

Before the first lap was done, Lowes, Rins, Zarco and Schrotter had been given ride-through penalties, Zarco running into the pit lane before completing the lap.

Two minutes later, the same penalty was applied to Nakagami and back-of-the-grid man Robin Mulhauser.

This took the cream out of the front battle, leaving Luthi and Morbidelli – unaccountably unpunished – to fight it out to the end. They swapped several times until Luthi seized the lead finally at the start of the final lap. But by then, very belatedly, Morbidelli had become the latest victim of the red-light rumpus. Cortese (lying fourth on the track) had also been found guilty. It was too late for a ride-through, but the 20-second penalty applied seemed somewhat lenient by comparison.

The penalties to others undoubtedly took the pressure off tenth-fastest qualifier Luthi, but he still won at a faster pace than in 2015. "I saw that other riders had jumped the start, but I knew I hadn't. I knew I had good pace; I just made a

Above: A confused Moto2 race – Luthi (12) and Morbidelli fought up front, but the latter wasn't really there, demoted to seventh for a jump-start.
Photo: Gold & Goose

Above left: Marquez had to settle for third with a Honda that in 2016 lacked speed.
Photo: Repsol Honda Team

Left: Salom's second would be his last taste of success before his tragic accident in Catalunya.

Below left: Piccolo e Grande. Moto3 winner Niccolo Antonelli celebrates with fellow Italian podium finisher Pecco Bagnaia.

Below: Antonelli took his third Moto3 win by a whisker.
Photos: Gold & Goose

small mistake in qualifying. I passed many riders very early, so I was in a brilliant situation."

With Morbidelli docked 20 seconds, second went instead to SAG Kalex rider Luis Salom, through from 18th on the grid in his best ride since 2014. He had passed Cortese and long-time pursuit leader Corsi on the final lap, finishing five-hundredths ahead.

Syahrin held on to fourth after a long battle with Moto3 champion Kent; then Aegerter swiped fifth from the English rider by less than a tenth.

Morbidelli was dropped to seventh, a lucky tenth-of-a-second ahead of Rins, who had served a ride-through. Fellow-victim Lowes was a couple of seconds down in ninth and philosophical: "Things happen in racing," he said, "and at least I got some points."

Rossi's half-brother Luca Marini was tenth in his first GP as a full-time rider; class rookie Oliveira 11th ahead of an off-form Zarco; with Cortese dropped to 15th behind Wilairot and Nakagami.

MOTO3 RACE – 18 laps

The first race of the year started as dusk fell over the desert, and it was a thriller.

Fenati snatched a last-gasp pole from Loi, but the latter led lap one with Brad Binder third. Loi was tenth next time after a tangle in the heavy traffic, and he spent the rest of the race trying to close up on an eight-strong leading group.

Binder made most of the running, with Fenati leading over the line several times and Navarro also prominent at the front of the typically furious gang. Also present, Bagnaia on the only Mahindra with the benefit of 2015's fairing. Slip-streaming on the long straight added to the great variety.

By half-distance, impressive rookie Nicolo Bulega had joined in, after finishing the first lap 12th. He even led briefly with three laps to go, but by then the tough guys were getting going – among them Bastianini and an up-and-down Antonelli, still nursing a pre-season skiing injury, and three times a crasher in practice.

Binder had tried running on to the straight second a few times, but "I was never ahead over the line, so I tried leading out of the last corner instead. I knew I would either win by very little or come second by very little."

It was the latter, after Antonelli had drafted past to win by inches.

Bagnaia was next in a well-ridden podium after qualifying 12th; then came Fenati, Bastianini, Bulega and Navarro, victim of a last-corner nudge from Bulega. The first seven crossed the line in 0.674 of a second; Loi was eighth, another second down.

What a great start.

COMMERCIAL BANK
GRAND PRIX OF QATAR

2016 FIM MotoGP™ WORLD CHAMPIONSHIP

17–20 MARCH, 2016

LOSAIL INTERNATIONAL CIRCUIT
22 laps
Length: 5.380 km. / 3,343 miles
Width: 12m

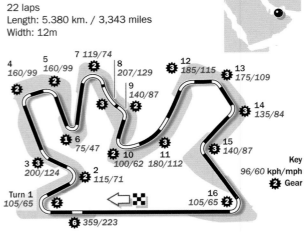

Key
96/60 kph/mph
Gear

MotoGP
RACE DISTANCE: 22 laps, 73.545 miles/118.360km · RACE WEATHER: Dry (air 21°C, humidity 71%, track 23°C)

Pos.	Rider	Nat.	No.	Entrant	Machine	Tyres	Race tyre choice	Laps	Time & speed
1	Jorge Lorenzo	SPA	99	Movistar Yamaha MotoGP	Yamaha YZR-M1	M	F: Hard/R: Soft	22	42m 28.452s
									103.8mph/
									167.1km/h
2	Andrea Dovizioso	ITA	4	Ducati Team	Ducati Desmosedici	M	F: Soft/R: Soft	22	42m 30.471s
3	Marc Marquez	SPA	93	Repsol Honda Team	Honda RC213V	M	F: Hard/R: Medium	22	42m 30.739s
4	Valentino Rossi	ITA	46	Movistar Yamaha MotoGP	Yamaha YZR-M1	M	F: Hard/R: Medium	22	42m 30.839s
5	Dani Pedrosa	SPA	26	Repsol Honda Team	Honda RC213V	M	F: Soft/R: Soft	22	42m 42.535s
6	Maverick Vinales	SPA	25	Team SUZUKI ECSTAR	Suzuki GSX-RR	M	F: Soft/R: Soft	22	42m 43.875s
7	Pol Espargaro	SPA	44	Monster Yamaha Tech 3	Yamaha YZR-M1	M	F: Soft/R: Soft	22	42m 47.081s
8	Bradley Smith	GBR	38	Monster Yamaha Tech 3	Yamaha YZR-M1	M	F: Soft/R: Soft	22	42m 47.104s
9	Hector Barbera	SPA	8	Avintia Racing	Ducati Desmosedici	M	F: Soft/R: Soft	22	42m 49.612s
10	Scott Redding	GBR	45	OCTO Pramac Yakhnich	Ducati Desmosedici	M	F: Soft/R: Soft	22	42m 52.887s
11	Aleix Espargaro	SPA	41	Team SUZUKI ECSTAR	Suzuki GSX-RR	M	F: Soft/R: Soft	22	43m 04.299s
12	Eugene Laverty	IRL	50	Aspar Team MotoGP	Ducati Desmosedici	M	F: Soft/R: Soft	22	43m 10.208s
13	Alvaro Bautista	SPA	19	Aprilia Racing Team Gresini	Aprilia RS-GP	M	F: Soft/R: Soft	22	43m 10.384s
14	Jack Miller	AUS	43	Estrella Galicia 0,0 Marc VDS	Honda RC213V	M	F: Soft/R: Soft	22	43m 10.434s
15	Tito Rabat	SPA	53	Estrella Galicia 0,0 Marc VDS	Honda RC213V	M	F: Soft/R: Soft	22	43m 23.405s
	Stefan Bradl	GER	6	Aprilia Racing Team Gresini	Aprilia RS-GP	M	F: Soft/R: Soft	11	DNF-crash
	Loris Baz	FRA	76	Avintia Racing	Ducati Desmosedici	M	F: Soft/R: Soft	8	DNF-crash
	Cal Crutchlow	GBR	35	LCR Honda	Honda RC213V	M	F: Hard/R: Medium	6	DNF-crash
	Andrea Iannone	ITA	29	Ducati Team	Ducati Desmosedici	M	F: Soft/R: Soft	5	DNF-crash
	Yonny Hernandez	COL	68	Aspar Team MotoGP	Ducati Desmosedici	M	F: Hard/R: Soft	1	DNF-technical
	Danilo Petrucci	ITA	9	OCTO Pramac Yakhnich	Ducati Desmosedici	M	–	–	DNS-injured

Fastest lap: Jorge Lorenzo, on lap 20, 1m 54.927s, 104.7mph/168.5km/h (record).
Previous lap record: Casey Stoner, AUS (Ducati), 1m 55.153s, 104.5mph/168.1km/h (2008).
Event best maximum speed: Andrea Iannone, 218.2mph/351.2km/h (warm up) – new MotoGP record.

Qualifying
Weather: Dry
Air Temp: 21° Track Temp: 21°
Humidity: 60%

1	Lorenzo	1m 54.543s
2	Marquez	1m 54.634s
3	Vinales	1m 54.638s
4	Iannone	1m 54.693s
5	Rossi	1m 54.815s
6	Dovizioso	1m 54.963s
7	Pedrosa	1m 55.078s
8	Barbera	1m 55.165s
9	P. Espargaro	1m 55.302s
10	Crutchlow	1m 55.352s
11	Smith	1m 55.414s
12	Redding	1m 55.508s
13	Hernandez	1m 56.157s
14	Laverty	1m 56.186s
15	A. Espargaro	1m 56.238s
16	Baz	1m 56.375s
17	Bautista	1m 56.595s
18	Miller	1m 56.620s
19	Rabat	1m 57.108s
20	Bradl	1m 57.216s

Fastest race laps

1	Lorenzo	1m 54.927s
2	Dovizioso	1m 55.149s
3	Rossi	1m 55.171s
4	Marquez	1m 55.223s
5	Iannone	1m 55.632s
6	Crutchlow	1m 55.780s
7	Pedrosa	1m 55.918s
8	Vinales	1m 55.942s
9	Smith	1m 55.963s
10	P. Espargaro	1m 55.986s
11	Barbera	1m 55.993s
12	Redding	1m 56.165s
13	A. Espargaro	1m 56.441s
14	Baz	1m 56.562s
15	Bautista	1m 56.739s
16	Laverty	1m 56.841s
17	Miller	1m 56.942s
18	Bradl	1m 56.961s
19	Rabat	1m 57.215s

Grid order	1	2	3	4	5	6	7	8	9	10	11	12	13	14	15	16	17	18	19	20	21	22	
99 LORENZO	29	29	29	29	29	4	4	4	99	99	99	99	99	99	99	99	99	99	99	99	99	99	1
93 MARQUEZ	99	4	4	4	4	99	99	99	4	4	4	4	4	4	4	4	4	4	93	93	4	4	2
25 VINALES	4	99	99	99	99	93	93	93	93	93	93	93	93	93	93	93	93	4	4	93	93	3	
29 IANNONE	46	46	93	93	93	46	46	46	46	46	46	46	46	46	46	46	46	46	46	46	46	46	4
46 ROSSI	93	93	46	46	46	26	26	26	26	26	26	26	26	26	26	26	26	26	26	26	26	26	5
4 DOVIZIOSO	26	26	26	26	26	25	25	25	25	25	25	25	25	25	25	25	25	25	25	25	25	25	6
26 PEDROSA	25	25	25	25	25	35	8	8	8	8	44	44	44	44	44	44	44	44	44	44	44	44	7
8 BARBERA	68	35	35	35	35	8	44	44	44	44	8	8	8	8	8	38	38	38	38	38	38	8	
44 P. ESPARGARO	35	8	8	8	8	38	38	38	38	38	38	38	38	38	38	8	8	8	8	8	8	9	
35 CRUTCHLOW	38	38	38	38	38	44	45	45	45	45	45	45	45	45	45	45	45	45	45	45	45	10	
38 SMITH	44	44	44	44	44	45	41	41	41	41	41	41	41	41	41	41	41	41	41	41	41	11	
45 REDDING	8	45	45	41	45	41	76	76	43	43	50	50	50	43	50	50	50	50	50	50	50	12	
68 HERNANDEZ	45	43	41	45	41	76	43	43	50	50	43	43	43	50	43	43	43	19	43	19	19	13	
50 LAVERTY	43	41	43	43	43	50	50	19	19	19	19	19	19	19	19	19	19	43	19	43	43	14	
41 A. ESPARGARO	41	76	76	76	76	19	19	19	6	6	53	53	53	53	53	53	53	53	53	53	53	15	
76 BAZ	6	50	50	50	50	19	6	6	53	53	53												
19 BAUTISTA	76	53	53	53	53	53	53	53															
43 MILLER	50	19	19	19	19	6																	
53 RABAT	53	6	6	6	6																		
6 BRADL	19																						

Championship Points

1	Lorenzo	25
2	Dovizioso	20
3	Marquez	16
4	Rossi	13
5	Pedrosa	11
6	Vinales	10
7	P. Espargaro	9
8	Smith	8
9	Barbera	7
10	Redding	6
11	A. Espargaro	5
12	Laverty	4
13	Bautista	3
14	Miller	2
15	Rabat	1

Constructor Points

1	Yamaha	25
2	Ducati	20
3	Honda	16
4	Suzuki	10
5	Aprilia	3

Moto2

RACE DISTANCE: 20 laps, 66.860 miles/107.600km · RACE WEATHER: Dry (air 22°C, humidity 68%, track 24°C)

Pos.	Rider	Nat.	No.	Entrant	Machine	Laps	Time & Speed
1	**Thomas Luthi**	SWI	12	Garage Plus Interwetten	Kalex	20	40m 14.293s 99.7mph/ 160.4km/h
2	**Luis Salom**	SPA	39	SAG Team	Kalex	20	40m 23.903s
3	**Simone Corsi**	ITA	24	Speed Up Racing	Speed Up	20	40m 23.958s
4	**Hafizh Syahrin**	MAL	55	Petronas Raceline Malaysia	Kalex	20	40m 27.851s
5	**Dominique Aegerter**	SWI	77	CarXpert Interwetten	Kalex	20	40m 30.357s
6	**Danny Kent**	GBR	52	Leopard Racing	Kalex	20	40m 30.407s
7	**Franco Morbidelli**	ITA	21	Estrella Galicia 0,0 Marc VDS	Kalex	20	40m 34.340s
8	**Alex Rins**	SPA	40	Paginas Amarillas HP 40	Kalex	20	40m 34.463s
9	**Sam Lowes**	GBR	22	Federal Oil Gresini Moto2	Kalex	20	40m 36.312s
10	**Luca Marini**	ITA	10	Forward Team	Kalex	20	40m 38.542s
11	**Miguel Oliveira**	POR	44	Leopard Racing	Kalex	20	40m 38.547s
12	**Johann Zarco**	FRA	5	Ajo Motorsport	Kalex	20	40m 38.863s
13	**Ratthapark Wilairot**	THA	14	IDEMITSU Honda Team Asia	Kalex	20	40m 39.957s
14	**Takaaki Nakagami**	JPN	30	IDEMITSU Honda Team Asia	Kalex	20	40m 41.285s
15	**Sandro Cortese**	GER	11	Dynavolt Intact GP	Kalex	20	40m 44.029s
16	Mattia Pasini	ITA	54	Italtrans Racing Team	Kalex	20	40m 44.697s
17	Marcel Schrotter	GER	23	AGR Team	Kalex	20	40m 52.739s
18	Jesko Raffin	SWI	2	Sports-Millions-EMWE-SAG	Kalex	20	41m 00.656s
19	Isaac Vinales	SPA	32	Tech 3 Racing	Tech 3	20	41m 00.836s
20	Robin Mulhauser	SWI	70	CarXpert Interwetten	Kalex	20	41m 32.616s
21	Alessandro Tonucci	ITA	33	Tasca Racing Scuderia Moto2	Kalex	20	41m 39.295s
22	Efren Vazquez	SPA	8	JPMoto Malaysia	Suter	20	41m 53.865s
	Axel Pons	SPA	49	AGR Team	Kalex	16	DNF
	Xavi Vierge	SPA	97	Tech 3 Racing	Tech 3	15	DNF
	Xavier Simeon	BEL	19	QMMF Racing Team	Speed Up	14	DNF
	Alex Marquez	SPA	73	Estrella Galicia 0,0 Marc VDS	Kalex	6	DNF
	Jonas Folger	GER	94	Dynavolt Intact GP	Kalex	2	DNF
	Julian Simon	SPA	60	QMMF Racing Team	Speed Up	1	DNF
	Edgar Pons	SPA	57	Paginas Amarillas HP 40	Kalex	1	DNF

Fastest lap: Sam Lowes, on lap 20, 1m 59.421s, 100.7mph/162.1km/h (record).
Previous lap record: Johann Zarco, FRA (Kalex), 1m 59.918s, 100.4mph/161.5km/h (2015).
Event best maximum speed: Robin Mulhauser, 178.1mph/286.7km/h (race).

Qualifying
Weather: Dry
Air Temp: 23° **Track Temp:** 23°
Humidity: 37%

1	Folger	1m 59.052s
2	Lowes	1m 59.124s
3	Rins	1m 59.354s
4	Zarco	1m 59.419s
5	Morbidelli	1m 59.509s
6	Cortese	1m 59.627s
7	Baldassarri	1m 59.716s
8	Schrotter	1m 59.759s
9	Nakagami	1m 59.811s
10	Luthi	1m 59.920s
11	Kent	1m 59.956s
12	Pons	1m 59.999s
13	Marquez	2m 00.009s
14	Corsi	2m 00.019s
15	Aegerter	2m 00.159s
16	Syahrin	2m 00.176s
17	Pons	2m 00.188s
18	Salom	2m 00.249s
19	Pasini	2m 00.454s
20	Vierge	2m 00.627s
21	Simeon	2m 00.738s
22	Oliveira	2m 00.757s
23	Wilairot	2m 00.790s
24	Simon	2m 00.816s
25	Raffin	2m 01.130s
26	Marini	2m 01.414s
27	Vinales	2m 01.970s
28	Mulhauser	2m 02.057s
29	Tonucci	2m 03.367s
30	Vazquez	2m 03.604s

Fastest race laps

1	Lowes	1m 59.421s
2	Folger	1m 59.622s
3	Morbidelli	1m 59.710s
4	Zarco	1m 59.794s
5	Rins	1m 59.909s
6	Luthi	1m 59.992s
7	Nakagami	1m 59.997s
8	Marquez	2m 00.094s
9	Cortese	2m 00.112s
10	Salom	2m 00.141s
11	Corsi	2m 00.235s
12	Syahrin	2m 00.301s
13	Kent	2m 00.550s
14	Aegerter	2m 00.686s
15	Pons	2m 00.738s
16	Schrotter	2m 00.749s
17	Simeon	2m 00.766s
18	Oliveira	2m 00.769s
19	Vierge	2m 00.828s
20	Marini	2m 00.834s
21	Wilairot	2m 00.885s
22	Pasini	2m 01.260s
23	Vinales	2m 01.748s
24	Raffin	2m 01.956s
25	Mulhauser	2m 02.011s
26	Tonucci	2m 03.365s
27	Vazquez	2m 04.821s

Championship Points

1	Luthi	25
2	Salom	20
3	Corsi	16
4	Syahrin	13
5	Aegerter	11
6	Kent	10
7	Morbidelli	9
8	Rins	8
9	Lowes	7
10	Marini	6
11	Oliveira	5
12	Zarco	4
13	Wilairot	3
14	Nakagami	2
15	Cortese	1

Constructor Points

1	Kalex	25
2	Speed Up	16

Moto3

RACE DISTANCE: 18 laps, 60.174 miles/96.840km · RACE WEATHER: Dry (air 22°C, humidity 61%, track 29°C)

Pos.	Rider	Nat.	No.	Entrant	Machine	Laps	Time & Speed
1	**Niccolo Antonelli**	ITA	23	Ongetta-Rivacold	Honda	18	38m 12.161s 94.4mph/ 152.0km/h
2	**Brad Binder**	RSA	41	Red Bull KTM Ajo	KTM	18	38m 12.168s
3	**Francesco Bagnaia**	ITA	21	ASPAR Mahindra Team Moto3	Mahindra	18	38m 12.309s
4	**Romano Fenati**	ITA	5	SKY Racing Team VR46	KTM	18	38m 12.596s
5	**Enea Bastianini**	ITA	33	Gresini Racing Moto3	Honda	18	38m 12.767s
6	**Nicolo Bulega**	ITA	8	SKY Racing Team VR46	KTM	18	38m 12.786s
7	**Jorge Navarro**	SPA	9	Estrella Galicia 0,0	Honda	18	38m 12.835s
8	**Livio Loi**	BEL	11	RW Racing GP BV	Honda	18	38m 13.871s
9	**Philipp Oettl**	GER	65	Schedl GP Racing	KTM	18	38m 20.772s
10	**Jakub Kornfeil**	CZE	84	Drive M7 SIC Racing Team	Honda	18	38m 23.108s
11	**Jules Danilo**	FRA	95	Ongetta-Rivacold	Honda	18	38m 24.540s
12	**Joan Mir**	SPA	36	Leopard Racing	KTM	18	38m 24.541s
13	**Fabio Quartararo**	FRA	20	Leopard Racing	KTM	18	38m 24.562s
14	**Bo Bendsneyder**	NED	64	Red Bull KTM Ajo	KTM	18	38m 24.887s
15	**Aron Canet**	SPA	44	Estrella Galicia 0,0	Honda	18	38m 24.945s
16	Maria Herrera	SPA	6	MH6 Laglisse	KTM	18	38m 25.100s
17	Andrea Migno	ITA	16	SKY Racing Team VR46	KTM	18	38m 29.313s
18	Hiroki Ono	JPN	76	Honda Team Asia	Honda	18	38m 29.528s
19	Gabriel Rodrigo	ARG	19	RBA Racing Team	KTM	18	38m 29.612s
20	Adam Norrodin	MAL	7	Drive M7 SIC Racing Team	Honda	18	38m 29.680s
21	Andrea Locatelli	ITA	55	Leopard Racing	KTM	18	38m 29.727s
22	Khairul Idham Pawi	MAL	89	Honda Team Asia	Honda	18	38m 29.769s
23	Darryn Binder	RSA	40	Platinum Bay Real Estate	Mahindra	18	38m 44.100s
24	Alexis Masbou	FRA	10	Peugeot MC Saxoprint	Peugeot	18	38m 44.110s
25	Juanfran Guevara	SPA	58	RBA Racing Team	KTM	18	38m 44.281s
26	Fabio di Giannantonio	ITA	4	Gresini Racing Moto3	Honda	18	38m 44.494s
27	John McPhee	GBR	17	Peugeot MC Saxoprint	Peugeot	18	38m 44.708s
28	Tatsuki Suzuki	JPN	24	CIP-Unicom Starker	Mahindra	18	38m 44.973s
29	Stefano Valtulini	ITA	43	3570 Team Italia	Mahindra	18	38m 46.745s
30	Karel Hanika	CZE	98	Platinum Bay Real Estate	Mahindra	18	39m 11.266s
31	Lorenzo Petrarca	ITA	77	3570 Team Italia	Mahindra	18	39m 11.270s
32	Fabio Spiranelli	ITA	3	CIP-Unicom Starker	Mahindra	18	39m 47.109s
	Jorge Martin	SPA	88	ASPAR Mahindra Team Moto3	Mahindra	17	DNF

Fastest lap: Livio Loi, on lap 8, 2m 6.171s, 95.4mph/153.5km/h.
Lap record: Alexis Masbou, FRA (Honda), 2m 5.862s, 95.6mph/153.8km/h (2014).
Event best maximum speed: Bo Bendsneyder, 149.3mph/240.3km/h (race).

Qualifying
Weather: Dry
Air Temp: 23° **Track Temp:** 25°
Humidity: 35%

1	Fenati	2m 06.131s
2	Loi	2m 06.178s
3	B. Binder	2m 06.245s
4	Quartararo	2m 06.399s
5	Navarro	2m 06.448s
6	Canet	2m 06.462s
7	Antonelli	2m 06.536s
8	Bendsneyder	2m 06.539s
9	Bastianini	2m 06.657s
10	Oettl	2m 06.707s
11	Mir	2m 06.728s
12	Bagnaia	2m 06.733s
13	Bulega	2m 06.786s
14	Martin	2m 06.931s
15	Guevara	2m 06.939s
16	Kornfeil	2m 06.948s
17	Pawi	2m 06.982s
18	Rodrigo	2m 06.983s
19	Migno	2m 07.101s
20	Locatelli	2m 07.170s
21	Masbou	2m 07.209s
22	Danilo	2m 07.220s
23	Hanika	2m 07.359s
24	Herrera	2m 07.371s
25	Suzuki	2m 07.441s
26	D. Binder	2m 07.558s
27	Norrodin	2m 07.582s
28	Di Giannantonio	2m 07.611s
29	Ono	2m 07.801s
30	McPhee	2m 07.847s
31	Valtulini	2m 08.336s
32	Spiranelli	2m 10.229s
33	Petrarca	2m 10.433s

Fastest race laps

1	Loi	2m 06.171s
2	Bulega	2m 06.300s
3	Antonelli	2m 06.309s
4	Guevara	2m 06.349s
5	Oettl	2m 06.360s
6	Navarro	2m 06.400s
7	Fenati	2m 06.409s
8	Herrera	2m 06.426s
9	Bagnaia	2m 06.443s
10	B. Binder	2m 06.454s
11	Danilo	2m 06.471s
12	Quartararo	2m 06.536s
13	Bastianini	2m 06.580s
14	Kornfeil	2m 06.677s
15	Canet	2m 06.720s
16	Rodrigo	2m 06.723s
17	Migno	2m 06.810s
18	Ono	2m 06.828s
19	Bendsneyder	2m 06.847s
20	Pawi	2m 06.860s
21	Locatelli	2m 06.894s
22	Martin	2m 06.905s
23	Norrodin	2m 06.970s
24	Mir	2m 06.982s
25	Masbou	2m 07.390s
26	D. Binder	2m 07.391s
27	Di Giannantonio	2m 07.642s
28	Valtulini	2m 07.738s
29	McPhee	2m 07.755s
30	Suzuki	2m 07.827s
31	Hanika	2m 08.235s
32	Petrarca	2m 09.394s
33	Spiranelli	2m 10.468s

Championship Points

1	Antonelli	25
2	B. Binder	20
3	Bagnaia	16
4	Fenati	13
5	Bastianini	11
6	Bulega	10
7	Navarro	9
8	Loi	8
9	Oettl	7
10	Kornfeil	6
11	Danilo	5
12	Mir	4
13	Quartararo	3
14	Bendsneyder	2
15	Canet	1

Constructor Points

1	Honda	25
2	KTM	20
3	Mahindra	16

ARGENTINE GRAND PRIX

TERMAS DE RIO HONDO CIRCUIT

Inset, top left: Zarco was unstoppable; Lowes (*left*) had to be content with second.

Inset, top right: Top-ranking rank rookie. Malaysian Khairul Idham Pawi took a runaway win.
Photos: Gold & Goose

Inset, above: Marquez took revenge for his 2015 defeat; his team had plenty to celebrate.
Photo: Repsol Honda Team

Main: Under tricky track conditions, Marquez motored away.
Photo: Gold & Goose

Above: Disaster for Ducati. Iannone scuppers a safe podium for the updated Desmosedicis.

Top right: Flanked by Lowes and Marquez, Rossi gazes into the distance at an ill-tempered pre-race press conference.

Above right: Battle scars. Tyre-struck Scott Redding shows off the damage.

Above far right: Ducati's Tardozzi saw his bikes show speed, and his riders show something else.

Centre right: Eugene Laverty (50) took a splendid fourth ahead of Barbera's newer Ducati.

Below right: Proceedings were delayed by fickle race-day weather.

Photos: Gold & Goose

NOTHING is ordinary at the Argentine GP: not getting there, not being there, nor a chance of the event proceeding without several dramas. In 2016, the major drama concerned the Michelin tyres. The strong start in Qatar had gone a long way towards reassuring riders following the disintegration of Loris Baz's rear tyre at top speed during testing at Sepang (Michelin's investigations later blamed a puncture). Now another spectacular rear tyre failure, combined with a fickle change in the race-day weather, set off a flurry of schedule changes, postponements, tyre choice restrictions and ultimately a shortened MotoGP race with a compulsory pit stop halfway through.

The failure struck during FP4, and the victim was (significantly enough) another heavily-built rider on a Ducati – Scott Redding, who was just back on the gas in fifth gear when all hell broke loose as the tyre shed a huge arc of tread. This wiped out rear bodywork and exhausts, and gave the rider a hefty thump in the back; but at least the inner casing remained inflated and he was able to stop safely.

This time, the French investigations laid the blame on three factors. The track was extremely hot – conditions the new-generation tyres had not yet encountered; the track surface and layout particularly punishing; and the rider heavier than most. Put together, said development chief Nicolas Goubert, they tipped the tyre over the edge.

The result was far-reaching, affecting not only this race. Henceforth, the rear tyres would use a harder construction rather than the preferred existing carcase, on safety grounds and to the dismay of those riders whose style or motorcycles weren't afflicting the tyres in the same way. Rossi in particular, who said he was ready to run the full race on the softer of the two rear covers.

Fortuitously, Michelin had brought along enough of the untested harder 'Option' tyre, and by Sunday morning a plan had been hatched: an extended 30-minute warm-up session would give enough familiarity for race distance, this tyre being mandatory.

Then it rained overnight and into race morning. A new plan was required, and for the second time in history a shortened race was scheduled (from 25 to 20 laps) with a compulsory

bike change halfway through, as at Phillip Island in 2013. However, riders could revert to the original tyre allocation. There was at least one prang during the changeover, when Bautista knocked down one of his mechanics, leading to calls for a reduced speed limit.

It was a shambolic run-up to a race of great surprises. Not so much that Marquez won, in spite of continuing difficulties with his new reverse-crank Honda, but in the other two on the podium.

Rossi was second, having been beaten thoroughly after the pit stop not only by Marquez, but also by both Ducatis. Far, far away – almost half a minute – Pedrosa was a surprised and disconsolate third.

Because in a move that ultimately cost him his factory seat, Iannone had knocked Dovizioso down when a trademark over-ambitious lunge on the penultimate corner put the red bikes out of copybook second and third places. Iannone had already added to his crash-happy reputation at the other end of the race, having cannoned into the back of Marquez (who was lucky to stay on board) going into the very first corner, then bouncing off into Pedrosa and pushing him wide.

He was docked three grid places at the following race and given a single penalty point; four races later, he learned that the remaining 2017 place at Ducati would go to Dovizioso instead.

In the meantime, Lorenzo had faded and fallen off; Vinales had sparkled bright – then also fallen off, out of third place; while in Moto3, a rank rookie from Malaysia had galloped away on a treacherous surface to claim an utterly unexpected win. Termas de Rio Hondo is always a place for the extraordinary.

The remotest race of the year picked a high-profile victim to highlight the travel difficulties that faced many. Marquez arrived in the small hours of Thursday after a nightmare 60-hour trip, which had included cancelled and missed connecting flights, and ultimately a mid-air engine failure. But if arriving had been difficult, leaving was even more so, with fog causing the closure of Tucuman airport on Monday. Sundry riders and other GP folk were left killing the hours at the airport. Some troubled souls resorted to flying back to Europe

to be able to turn around and get to Texas in just three-and-a-half days' time.

Perhaps it was not so surprising that tempers seemed a little fraught at the race-eve press conference, where Rossi not merely studiously ignored the adjacent Marquez, but spent the whole time while not actually answering questions chatting ostentatiously to Sam Lowes, on his other side. Then somebody asked the Spaniard whether Rossi was still his idol. Rossi gazed into the distance as Marquez gave his choirboy smile and replied, "Valentino is a reference for all riders in MotoGP, but now I look at him with different eyes."

At Suzuki, anxious to keep hold of the increasingly impressive Vinales, at last the both-ways seamless-shift gearbox was declared ready to race, for both riders; both of whom still preferred the 2015 chassis – something that would last at least for the first half of the season.

Michele Pirro was back as a Ducati part-timer, this time on a Pramac GP15 in place of the injured Petrucci, arriving from tests only in time for the second day of practice. This finally quashed hopes that the other Ducati tester, Casey Stoner, who had ridden at Qatar the day after the race, might make an appearance on the bike.

Younger Moto2 Pons brother Edgar flew home before the race, suffering from hepatitis.

There was a mixture of disappointment tinged with relief at rumours that this would be the last race at this picturesque, characterful, but hard-to-reach venue, with its fine, but under-used circuit. And a concomitant mixture of relief tinged with disappointment with the race-day announcement that a contract had been signed for a further three years.

MOTOGP RACE – 20 laps (flag-to-flag)

Marquez had taken charge of free practice, and he secured pole by an impressive 0.375 of a second, ahead of the two Yamahas. This time, Rossi was the faster, making good on his pledge to adapt better to the current qualifying format.

The Ducatis were alongside fourth-fastest Pedrosa on row two; Vinales led the third.

Aside from a very few dark slicks on a handful of corners, the track was dry and the foreboding weather gradually lifting. Those little stripes, however, particularly one bracketing the apex of the first corner, would prove very crucial for six fallen riders.

Lorenzo led off the line, from Marquez and Rossi, while Iannone caused his first upset right behind. By the end of lap one, Dovizioso's Ducati had given the first demonstration of its exceptional top speed, surging into the lead on the back straight, with Rossi now ahead of Marquez, then the on-form Vinales ahead of Iannone.

Lorenzo had been losing places all lap and now was just ahead of Crutchlow and Aleix Espargaro – who would both promptly fall victim to that slick patch on the first corner, falling independently, but in tandem. Both remounted for an afternoon of catch-up, although Crutchlow would fall again before the end.

On the fourth lap, Rossi got past Dovi and soon began pressing Marquez hard, while the Ducati fell back a couple of seconds, into the hands of Iannone and Vinales.

The last laps of the first half were something of a replay of the previous year: Rossi and Marquez trading places back and forth several times. This time, however, nobody collided and nobody fell off. The battle was to be first into the pits at the end of lap ten, and Marquez won it with aggressive assurance under severe pressure.

All the riders had been practising bike changes, and nobody was better than Marquez. He'd already gained clear air on Rossi at the end of the pit lane, and he set fastest lap on the 12th to underline his superiority.

Rossi's misfortune started at the pit exit: he came out close to Marquez, but with Rabat (yet to pit) between them. He should have been able to slice past; that he couldn't

was symptomatic of a greater malaise: his second bike didn't handle like the first. He had more trouble ahead.

By the time of the pit stops, there had been three other victims of the treacherous surface; the first was local hero Hernandez after just two laps. More significant drama came in an unexpected battle for sixth.

Miller, undaunted by three falls in practice, was on blazing form, and by lap three he was ahead of Lorenzo, only to slide off on the corner before the long straight. But Lorenzo, far from comfortable in the conditions, would last only one more lap, falling (for the second time of the weekend) on that treacherous first corner after running on to the damp slick.

There were more surprises as Marquez pushed steadily clear of Rossi.

Vinales had passed the Ducatis before the pit stops, and now the Suzuki led the trio as they closed on Rossi with five laps to go. Soon the youngster was attacking and Rossi struggling manfully to stay ahead. Then, at the start of lap 18, Vinales became another victim of the first turn.

Now it was Rossi and the Ducatis, and it was clear that they had him beat. On lap 19, Iannone attacked Rossi at the end of the straight, pushing both wide. Craftily, Dovizioso seized the moment and passed the pair of them to start the last lap in second.

He surely would have finished second, if headlong Iannone hadn't tried up the inside into the penultimate corner. He lost the front and slid straight into his team-mate, putting both down and leaving a lucky second to Rossi. Dovi pushed over the line for 13th and understandably was disgusted.

This also favoured third-place Pedrosa, who had been struggling, with no answer to Redding, until the Briton sputtered to a stop by the guardrail with five laps to go.

The attrition brought great rewards to the survivors, with a career-best fourth for Eugene Laverty. He'd been battling with Barbera and Pol Espargaro, but won out when the Spaniards clashed on the last lap.

Bradl was a worthwhile seventh; Smith could count himself lucky with eighth after a very dispirited afternoon. An untried setting on both bikes hadn't worked. He was just two-tenths ahead of Rabat and survived being passed by rival Crutchlow when the latter fell for a second time on the last lap.

Bautista was a lone tenth; then came Aleix Espargaro and Pirro, who had also slipped off and restarted.

MOTO2 RACE – 23 laps

Warm-up was wet, the preceding Moto3 race less so, the skies were very gloomy, and the track still had many damp streaks – black and treacherous. But the race was declared dry and all fitted slicks, with many taking the precaution of two sighting laps to measure conditions.

Lowes, enjoying his switch to Kalex, was on pole; the first 16 riders completed within a second. Zarco and Folger completed row one; Morbidelli was in the middle of row two, between Nakagami and Qatar winner Luthi. Rins was only 11th on row four.

Folger was again fastest away, leading for two laps as everybody tiptoed around. Then it was the turn of Lowes; while Morbidelli had tagged on to make a quarrelsome quartet, taking turns to rescue slides and wobbles.

Approaching half-distance, Lowes seemed to have a bit of breathing space, as Morbidelli and Zarco swapped paint, with Folger seesawing to stay in touch. But Zarco was biding his time, and with ten laps to go he eased past Lowes to lead for the first time. He would never lose it; a slip from Lowes with five laps to go let Morbidelli through to second and gave Zarco a gap he was able to stretch to almost 1.5 seconds over the line.

It was a familiar demonstration from the Frenchman, celebrated with a familiar back-flip off the tyre wall. "I couldn't know if I could be stronger than them, but when it was a little bit more dry, I was more comfortable and able to use my line."

Lowes and Folger completed the podium, the German another second down. It might have been different had Morbidelli not fallen victim to the notorious Turn One damp patch on the penultimate lap, shortly after Lowes had regained second.

Another six seconds away, a puzzlingly off-form Rins had dropped behind the storming Aegerter (from 19th on the grid) and Syahrin. At half-distance, however, he found his pace, repassing both in two laps to set off in hopeless pursuit of the leading quartet.

Aegerter and Syahrin remained locked in combat, one-tenth apart over the line.

Luthi was a disappointed and distant seventh, but at least relieved of pressure from second Dynavolt rider Cortese when the German fell off.

Above: Out of sorts, out of character, and out of the race. Lorenzo was an early victim of a tricky wet patch.

Top: Bradl took a worthwhile seventh on the Aprilia, in a depleted field.

Top right: Zarco took control over Lowes and a fading Folger in Moto2.

Above centre right: Rookie Adam Norrodin's spirited battle for second with Navarro ended in a heartbreaking last-corners crash.

Right: Pawi, another Malaysian rookie, took control in Moto3, with an astonishing debut win. Loi (11) and Binder (41) lead the pursuit on lap one.

Photos: Gold & Goose

Axel Pons was eighth, narrowly ahead of Nakagami and Pasini to complete the top ten, fending off Schrotter. Simeon was the first non-Kalex in 12th; Qatar double dislocation victim Baldassarri was an impressive 13th. Vierge gained his first points, then Salom took the last one, just two-tenths ahead of Kent.

Alex Marquez was the remaining rider to crash – on the second lap.

MOTO3 RACE – 21 laps

The first race of the day was fraught. The rain had stopped and the track was drying, but there were still swirls of moisture, and the threat of more. Almost all came out on wet tyres; all but one had changed to slicks for the start.

The exception was Loi, big winner of such a gamble at Indy in 2015; and sure enough, his RW Honda did surge away from his slick-shod rivals to lead into the first corner.

Amazingly, indeed historically, he wasn't there for long, thanks to a 17-year-old Malaysian in only his third GP. Asia Cup and CEV graduate Khairul Idham Pawi cared nothing for his slick tyres and seized the lead on the first lap; by the end, he had stretched it to 25 yawning seconds.

Conditions had varied through the race; Pawi just got faster and faster, in spite of signals from his Honda Team Asia crew to slow down. "It was easy for me," he said. "I just focused on my lap time."

Loi held an increasingly distant second for six laps, while first-time pole starter Binder played it cool in a pursuit pack that was soon seven-strong.

The first to emerge was another 17-year-old Malaysian rookie, Adam Norrodin. By the time he'd passed Loi, he'd been joined by Navarro, who nipped ahead after a couple of laps.

Norrodin shadowed the more experienced Spaniard and pounced on the final lap. Navarro got him back, and "I knew he would come again, so I made it difficult for him".

Heartbreakingly, Norrodin's final attack on the penultimate corner found a damp patch, and he fell. Picking up the bike, he pushed over the line 11th.

The group behind had been to and fro, but Binder played it best to lead Locatelli by a couple of tenths, with Mir, Ono and McPhee hard up behind.

Top Mahindra Martin had dropped off the back to eighth with gearbox trouble; a battling Kornfeil and Antonelli completed the top ten, footslogger Norrodin less than three-tenths behind over the line.

GRAN PREMIO MOTUL
DE LA REPÚBLICA ARGENTINA

1-3 APRIL, 2016

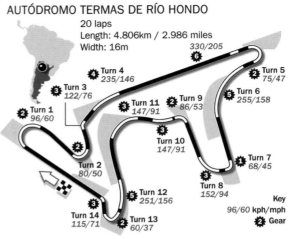

AUTÓDROMO TERMAS DE RÍO HONDO
20 laps
Length: 4.806km / 2.986 miles
Width: 16m

Turn 1 96/60
Turn 2 80/50
Turn 3 122/76
Turn 4 235/146
Turn 5 75/47
Turn 6 255/158
Turn 7 68/45
Turn 8 152/94
Turn 9 86/53
Turn 10 147/91
Turn 11 147/91
Turn 12 251/156
Turn 13 60/37
Turn 14 115/71
330/205

Key
96/60 kph/mph
Gear

MotoGP

RACE DISTANCE: 20 laps, 59.726 miles/96.120km · RACE WEATHER: Dry (air 25°C, humidity 89%, track 30°C)

Pos.	Rider	Nat.	No.	Entrant	Machine	Tyres	Race tyre choice	Laps	Time & speed
1	**Marc Marquez**	SPA	93	Repsol Honda Team	Honda RC213V	M	F: Hard/R: Medium	20	34m 13.628s 104.6mph/ 168.4km/h
2	**Valentino Rossi**	ITA	46	Movistar Yamaha MotoGP	Yamaha YZR-M1	M	F: Hard/R: Medium	20	34m 21.307s
3	**Dani Pedrosa**	SPA	26	Repsol Honda Team	Honda RC213V	M	F: Hard/R: Medium	20	34m 41.728s
4	**Eugene Laverty**	IRL	50	Aspar Team MotoGP	Ducati Desmosedici	M	F: Hard/R: Medium	20	34m 50.170s
5	**Hector Barbera**	SPA	8	Avintia Racing	Ducati Desmosedici	M	F: Hard/R: Medium	20	34m 50.339s
6	**Pol Espargaro**	SPA	44	Monster Yamaha Tech 3	Yamaha YZR-M1	M	F: Hard/R: Medium	20	34m 50.873s
7	**Stefan Bradl**	GER	6	Aprilia Racing Team Gresini	Aprilia RS-GP	M	F: Hard/R: Medium	20	34m 54.981s
8	**Bradley Smith**	GBR	38	Monster Yamaha Tech 3	Yamaha YZR-M1	M	F: Medium/R: Medium	20	35m 04.337s
9	**Tito Rabat**	SPA	53	Estrella Galicia 0,0 Marc VDS	Honda RC213V	M	F: Hard/R: Medium	20	35m 04.611s
10	**Alvaro Bautista**	SPA	19	Aprilia Racing Team Gresini	Aprilia RS-GP	M	F: Hard/R: Medium	20	35m 15.016s
11	**Aleix Espargaro**	SPA	41	Team SUZUKI ECSTAR	Suzuki GSX-RR	M	F: Medium/R: Hard	20	35m 22.496s
12	**Michele Pirro**	ITA	51	OCTO Pramac Yakhnich	Ducati Desmosedici	M	F: Hard/R: Medium	20	35m 32.615s
13	**Andrea Dovizioso**	ITA	4	Ducati Team	Ducati Desmosedici	M	F: Hard/R: Medium	20	35m 47.047s
	Andrea Iannone	ITA	29	Ducati Team	Ducati Desmosedici	M	F: Hard/R: Medium	19	DNF-crash
	Cal Crutchlow	GBR	35	LCR Honda	Honda RC213V	M	F: Hard/R: Medium	19	DNF-crash
	Maverick Vinales	SPA	25	Team SUZUKI ECSTAR	Suzuki GSX-RR	M	F: Medium/R: Medium	17	DNF-crash
	Scott Redding	GBR	45	OCTO Pramac Yakhnich	Ducati Desmosedici	M	F: Hard/R: Medium	15	DNF-technical
	Loris Baz	FRA	76	Avintia Racing	Ducati Desmosedici	M	F: Hard/R: Medium	12	DNF-technical
	Jorge Lorenzo	SPA	99	Movistar Yamaha MotoGP	Yamaha YZR-M1	M	F: Hard/R: Medium	5	DNF-crash
	Jack Miller	AUS	43	Estrella Galicia 0,0 Marc VDS	Honda RC213V	M	F: Hard/R: Medium	3	DNF-crash
	Yonny Hernandez	COL	68	Aspar Team MotoGP	Ducati Desmosedici	M	F: Hard/R: Medium	2	DNF-crash

Fastest lap: Marc Marquez, on lap 12, 1m 40.243s, 107.2mph/172.5km/h.
Lap record: Valentino Rossi, ITA (Yamaha), 1m 39.019s, 108.6mph/174.7km/h (2015).
Event best maximum speed: Andrea Iannone, 205.1mph/330.0km/h (free practice).

Qualifying

Weather: Dry
Air Temp: 31° **Track Temp:** 43°
Humidity: 56%

1	Marquez	1m 39.411s
2	Rossi	1m 39.786s
3	Lorenzo	1m 39.944s
4	Pedrosa	1m 40.011s
5	Dovizioso	1m 40.198s
6	Iannone	1m 40.272s
7	Vinales	1m 40.375s
8	Barbera	1m 40.524s
9	Crutchlow	1m 40.528s
10	P. Espargaro	1m 40.654s
11	A. Espargaro	1m 40.708s
12	Smith	1m 40.893s
13	Baz	1m 40.744s
14	Redding	1m 40.750s
15	Miller	1m 40.881s
16	Bradl	1m 40.897s
17	Laverty	1m 40.990s
18	Pirro	1m 41.116s
19	Rabat	1m 41.157s
20	Bautista	1m 41.611s
21	Hernandez	1m 41.692s

Fastest race laps

1	Marquez	1m 40.243s
2	Iannone	1m 40.342s
3	Dovizioso	1m 40.433s
4	Rossi	1m 40.635s
5	Vinales	1m 40.695s
6	Pirro	1m 41.103s
7	Crutchlow	1m 41.167s
8	Redding	1m 41.414s
9	Barbera	1m 41.535s
10	Pedrosa	1m 41.609s
11	Lorenzo	1m 41.695s
12	P. Espargaro	1m 41.822s
13	Miller	1m 41.898s
14	Bradl	1m 41.951s
15	Laverty	1m 41.988s
16	A. Espargaro	1m 42.087s
17	Smith	1m 42.191s
18	Bautista	1m 42.313s
19	Baz	1m 42.543s
20	Rabat	1m 42.747s
21	Hernandez	1m 43.297s

Championship Points

1	Marquez	41
2	Rossi	33
3	Pedrosa	27
4	Lorenzo	25
5	Dovizioso	23
6	P. Espargaro	19
7	Barbera	18
8	Laverty	17
9	Smith	16
10	Vinales	10
11	A. Espargaro	10
12	Bautista	9
13	Bradl	9
14	Rabat	8
15	Redding	6
16	Pirro	4
17	Miller	2

Constructor Points

1	Yamaha	45
2	Honda	41
3	Ducati	33
4	Suzuki	15
5	Aprilia	12

Grid order		1	2	3	4	5	6	7	8	9	10	11	12	13	14	15	16	17	18	19	20	
93	MARQUEZ	4	4	93	93	93	93	93	93	93	93	93	93	93	93	93	93	93	93	93	93	1
46	ROSSI	46	46	4	46	46	46	46	46	46	46	46	46	46	46	46	46	46	4	46		2
99	LORENZO	93	93	46	4	4	4	4	25	4	4	25	25	25	25	25	25	29	29	26		3
26	PEDROSA	25	25	25	29	25	29	29	29	25	45	4	4	4	4	29	29	29	4	46	50	4
4	DOVIZIOSO	29	29	29	25	25	25	25	4	29	51	29	29	29	29	4	4	4	26	26		5
29	IANNONE	99	99	43	99	99	26	26	26	45	44	53	26	45	45	45	26	26	44	44	44	6
25	VINALES	35	43	99	76	26	76	76	76	51	53	26	45	26	26	26	8	44	8	8	6	7
8	BARBERA	41	44	44	8	76	8	8	8	44	38	45	8	8	8	8	44	8	50	50	38	8
35	CRUTCHLOW	8	8	8	26	8	44	44	45	26	25	8	44	44	44	44	50	50	6	6	53	9
44	P. ESPARGARO	44	76	76	44	44	45	45	44	76	29	44	50	50	50	6	6	38	38	19		10
41	A. ESPARGARO	45	50	50	50	45	19	19	19	8	26	76	6	6	6	38	38	35	35	41		11
38	SMITH	43	26	26	45	19	51	51	51	50	76	50	53	53	53	53	53	53	53	51		12
76	BAZ	50	68	51	19	50	50	50	50	53	8	6	38	38	38	38	35	53	19	19	4	13
45	REDDING	76	51	45	51	6	6	6	6	38	50	38	76	35	35	35	19	19	41	41		
43	MILLER	26	45	19	6	6	53	53	53	6	6	35	35	19	19	41	41	41	51	51		
6	BRADL	68	19	6	38	38	38	38	38	19	19	19	19	41	41	41	51	51				
50	LAVERTY	19	6	38	53	53	35	35	35	35	35	41	41	51	51	51						
51	PIRRO	51	38	53	41	41	41	41	41	41	41	51	51									
53	RABAT	6	53	41	35	35																
19	BAUTISTA	53	41	35																		
68	HERNANDEZ	38	35																			

25 Pit stop

Moto2 — RACE DISTANCE: 23 laps, 68.685 miles/110.538km · RACE WEATHER: Dry (air 24°C, humidity 90%, track 28°C)

Pos.	Rider	Nat.	No.	Entrant	Machine	Laps	Time & Speed
1	**Johann Zarco**	FRA	5	Ajo Motorsport	Kalex	23	40m 57.806s
							100.6mph/
							161.9km/h
2	**Sam Lowes**	GBR	22	Federal Oil Gresini Moto2	Kalex	23	40m 59.153s
3	**Jonas Folger**	GER	94	Dynavolt Intact GP	Kalex	23	41m 00.560s
4	**Alex Rins**	SPA	40	Paginas Amarillas HP 40	Kalex	23	41m 03.907s
5	**Dominique Aegerter**	SWI	77	CarXpert Interwetten	Kalex	23	41m 15.190s
6	**Hafizh Syahrin**	MAL	55	Petronas Raceline Malaysia	Kalex	23	41m 15.290s
7	**Thomas Luthi**	SWI	12	Garage Plus Interwetten	Kalex	23	41m 24.217s
8	**Axel Pons**	SPA	49	AGR Team	Kalex	23	41m 28.822s
9	**Takaaki Nakagami**	JPN	30	IDEMITSU Honda Team Asia	Kalex	23	41m 29.209s
10	**Mattia Pasini**	ITA	54	Italtrans Racing Team	Kalex	23	41m 29.622s
11	**Marcel Schrotter**	GER	23	AGR Team	Kalex	23	41m 30.135s
12	**Xavier Simeon**	BEL	19	QMMF Racing Team	Speed Up	23	41m 38.774s
13	**Lorenzo Baldassarri**	ITA	7	Forward Team	Kalex	23	41m 45.689s
14	**Xavi Vierge**	SPA	97	Tech 3 Racing	Tech 3	23	41m 53.833s
15	**Luis Salom**	SPA	39	SAG Team	Kalex	23	41m 56.084s
16	Danny Kent	GBR	52	Leopard Racing	Kalex	23	41m 56.243s
17	Ratthapark Wilairot	THA	14	IDEMITSU Honda Team Asia	Kalex	23	41m 56.421s
18	Luca Marini	ITA	10	Forward Team	Kalex	23	41m 57.051s
19	Julian Simon	SPA	60	QMMF Racing Team	Speed Up	23	41m 57.341s
20	Simone Corsi	ITA	24	Speed Up Racing	Speed Up	23	41m 57.684s
21	Miguel Oliveira	POR	44	Leopard Racing	Kalex	23	41m 58.212s
22	Robin Mulhauser	SWI	70	CarXpert Interwetten	Kalex	23	42m 07.060s
23	Jesko Raffin	SWI	2	Sports-Millions-EMWE-SAG	Kalex	23	42m 12.631s
24	Isaac Vinales	SPA	32	Tech 3 Racing	Tech 3	23	42m 14.598s
25	Franco Morbidelli	ITA	21	Estrella Galicia 0,0 Marc VDS	Kalex	23	42m 39.336s
26	Efren Vazquez	SPA	8	JPMoto Malaysia	Suter	22	41m 32.249s
27	Alessandro Tonucci	ITA	33	Tasca Racing Scuderia Moto2	Kalex	22	41m 32.511s
	Sandro Cortese	GER	11	Dynavolt Intact GP	Kalex	12	DNF
	Alex Marquez	SPA	73	Estrella Galicia 0,0 Marc VDS	Kalex	1	DNF

Fastest lap: Johann Zarco, on lap 23, 1m 44.345s, 103.0mph/165.8km/h.

Lap record: Jonas Folger, GER (Kalex), 1m 43.001s, 104.3mph/167.9km/h (2015).

Event best maximum speed: Dominique Aegerter, 169.6mph/272.9km/h (free practice).

Qualifying

Weather: Dry
Air Temp: 30° Track Temp: 41°
Humidity: 58%

1	Lowes	1m 43.347s
2	Zarco	1m 43.466s
3	Folger	1m 43.637s
4	Nakagami	1m 43.709s
5	Morbidelli	1m 43.733s
6	Luthi	1m 43.813s
7	Cortese	1m 43.823s
8	Kent	1m 43.858s
9	Baldassarri	1m 43.981s
10	Pons	1m 43.982s
11	Rins	1m 43.989s
12	Syahrin	1m 44.055s
13	Corsi	1m 44.060s
14	Salom	1m 44.104s
15	Marquez	1m 44.154s
16	Schrotter	1m 44.172s
17	Simeon	1m 44.396s
18	Oliveira	1m 44.424s
19	Aegerter	1m 44.443s
20	Pasini	1m 44.523s
21	Wilairot	1m 44.572s
22	Marini	1m 44.603s
23	Vierge	1m 44.703s
24	Simon	1m 44.767s
25	Raffin	1m 45.294s
26	Mulhauser	1m 45.848s
27	Vinales	1m 45.859s
28	Vazquez	1m 46.272s
29	Tonucci	1m 46.554s

Fastest race laps

1	Zarco	1m 44.345s
2	Lowes	1m 44.481s
3	Rins	1m 44.598s
4	Folger	1m 44.724s
5	Morbidelli	1m 44.970s
6	Aegerter	1m 45.437s
7	Schrotter	1m 45.552s
8	Syahrin	1m 45.648s
9	Nakagami	1m 45.695s
10	Pasini	1m 45.762s
11	Simeon	1m 45.867s
12	Pons	1m 46.095s
13	Raffin	1m 46.158s
14	Marini	1m 46.293s
15	Kent	1m 46.331s
16	Luthi	1m 46.366s
17	Wilairot	1m 46.414s
18	Simon	1m 46.480s
19	Corsi	1m 46.616s
20	Cortese	1m 46.662s
21	Salom	1m 46.725s
22	Oliveira	1m 46.848s
23	Baldassarri	1m 46.945s
24	Mulhauser	1m 47.197s
25	Vinales	1m 47.355s
26	Vierge	1m 47.647s
27	Tonucci	1m 48.722s
28	Vazquez	1m 49.741s

Championship Points

1	Luthi	34
2	Zarco	29
3	Lowes	27
4	Syahrin	23
5	Aegerter	22
6	Salom	21
7	Rins	21
8	Corsi	16
9	Folger	16
10	Kent	10
11	Morbidelli	9
12	Nakagami	9
13	Pons	8
14	Marini	6
15	Pasini	6
16	Oliveira	5
17	Schrotter	5
18	Simeon	4
19	Wilairot	3
20	Baldassarri	3
21	Vierge	2
22	Cortese	1

Constructor Points

1	Kalex	50
2	Speed Up	20
3	Tech 3	2

Moto3 — RACE DISTANCE: 21 laps, 62.713 miles/100.926km · RACE WEATHER: Wet (air 23°C, humidity 97%, track 27°C)

Pos.	Rider	Nat.	No.	Entrant	Machine	Laps	Time & Speed
1	**Khairul Idham Pawi**	MAL	89	Honda Team Asia	Honda	21	41m 35.452s
							90.4mph/
							145.5km/h
2	**Jorge Navarro**	SPA	9	Estrella Galicia 0,0	Honda	21	42m 01.622s
3	**Brad Binder**	RSA	41	Red Bull KTM Ajo	KTM	21	42m 05.512s
4	**Andrea Locatelli**	ITA	55	Leopard Racing	KTM	21	42m 05.791s
5	**Joan Mir**	SPA	36	Leopard Racing	KTM	21	42m 05.958s
6	**Hiroki Ono**	JPN	76	Honda Team Asia	Honda	21	42m 06.188s
7	**John McPhee**	GBR	17	Peugeot MC Saxoprint	Peugeot	21	42m 07.945s
8	**Jorge Martin**	SPA	88	ASPAR Mahindra Team Moto3	Mahindra	21	42m 16.048s
9	**Jakub Kornfeil**	CZE	84	Drive M7 SIC Racing Team	Honda	21	42m 21.119s
10	**Niccolo Antonelli**	ITA	23	Ongetta-Rivacold	Honda	21	42m 21.345s
11	**Adam Norrodin**	MAL	7	Drive M7 SIC Racing Team	Honda	21	42m 21.625s
12	**Juanfran Guevara**	SPA	58	RBA Racing Team	KTM	21	42m 26.886s
13	**Fabio Quartararo**	FRA	20	Leopard Racing	KTM	21	42m 33.345s
14	**Maria Herrera**	SPA	6	MH6 Laglisse	KTM	21	42m 41.435s
15	**Philipp Oettl**	GER	65	Schedl GP Racing	KTM	21	42m 43.878s
16	Livio Loi	BEL	11	RW Racing GP BV	Honda	21	42m 45.617s
17	Enea Bastianini	ITA	33	Gresini Racing Moto3	Honda	21	42m 47.116s
18	Nicolo Bulega	ITA	8	SKY Racing Team VR46	KTM	21	42m 47.243s
19	Gabriel Rodrigo	ARG	19	RBA Racing Team	KTM	21	42m 47.603s
20	Romano Fenati	ITA	5	SKY Racing Team VR46	KTM	21	42m 47.722s
21	Alexis Masbou	FRA	10	Peugeot MC Saxoprint	Peugeot	21	42m 47.834s
22	Bo Bendsneyder	NED	64	Red Bull KTM Ajo	KTM	21	42m 47.974s
23	Francesco Bagnaia	ITA	21	ASPAR Mahindra Team Moto3	Mahindra	21	42m 54.336s
24	Karel Hanika	CZE	98	Platinum Bay Real Estate	Mahindra	21	43m 00.567s
25	Fabio di Giannantonio	ITA	4	Gresini Racing Moto3	Honda	21	43m 07.427s
26	Jules Danilo	FRA	95	Ongetta-Rivacold	Honda	21	43m 13.852s
27	Tatsuki Suzuki	JPN	24	CIP-Unicom Starker	Mahindra	21	43m 14.236s
28	Stefano Valtulini	ITA	43	3570 Team Italia	Mahindra	21	43m 14.503s
29	Andrea Migno	ITA	16	SKY Racing Team VR46	KTM	21	43m 19.487s
30	Darryn Binder	RSA	40	Platinum Bay Real Estate	Mahindra	20	41m 43.176s
31	Lorenzo Petrarca	ITA	77	3570 Team Italia	Mahindra	20	41m 43.306s
32	Fabio Spiranelli	ITA	3	CIP-Unicom Starker	Mahindra	20	41m 43.576s
	Aron Canet	SPA	44	Estrella Galicia 0,0	Honda	18	DNF

Fastest lap: Joan Mir, on lap 21, 1m 56.365s, 92.3mph/148.6km/h.

Lap record: Miguel Oliveira, POR (KTM), 1m 48.977s, 98.6mph/158.7km/h (2015).

Event best maximum speed: Juanfran Guevara, 143.1mph/230.3km/h (qualifying).

Qualifying:

Weather: Dry
Air Temp: 30° Track Temp: 44°
Humidity: 59%

1	B. Binder	1m 49.767s
2	Fenati	1m 50.091s
3	Navarro	1m 50.134s
4	Pawi	1m 50.204s
5	Bulega	1m 50.278s
6	Mir	1m 50.342s
7	Bastianini	1m 50.392s
8	Antonelli	1m 50.400s
9	Quartararo	1m 50.428s
10	Loi	1m 50.522s
11	Ono	1m 50.710s
12	Guevara	1m 50.714s
13	Oettl	1m 50.716s
14	Canet	1m 50.733s
15	Kornfeil	1m 50.753s
16	Migno	1m 50.904s
17	Norrodin	1m 50.948s
18	Rodrigo	1m 51.001s
19	Martin	1m 51.024s
20	Locatelli	1m 51.037s
21	Danilo	1m 51.146s
22	Bendsneyder	1m 51.194s
23	Masbou	1m 51.196s
24	Di Giannantonio	1m 51.231s
25	Bagnaia	1m 51.408s
26	Herrera	1m 51.416s
27	Suzuki	1m 51.474s
28	McPhee	1m 51.729s
29	Hanika	1m 52.392s
30	Valtulini	1m 52.737s
31	D. Binder	1m 53.310s
32	Petrarca	1m 53.704s
33	Spiranelli	1m 54.463s

Fastest race laps

1	Mir	1m 56.365s
2	B. Binder	1m 56.942s
3	Ono	1m 57.059s
4	McPhee	1m 57.089s
5	Locatelli	1m 57.108s
6	Bastianini	1m 57.272s
7	Pawi	1m 57.387s
8	Masbou	1m 57.698s
9	Bulega	1m 57.718s
10	Antonelli	1m 57.752s
11	Canet	1m 57.842s
12	Oettl	1m 57.898s
13	Bendsneyder	1m 57.941s
14	Norrodin	1m 57.982s
15	Navarro	1m 58.066s
16	Fenati	1m 58.072s
17	Kornfeil	1m 58.074s
18	Martin	1m 58.257s
19	Bagnaia	1m 58.384s
20	Rodrigo	1m 58.789s
21	Suzuki	1m 58.800s
22	Di Giannantonio	1m 58.920s
23	Danilo	1m 58.999s
24	Guevara	1m 59.192s
25	Quartararo	1m 59.209s
26	Hanika	1m 59.241s
27	Herrera	1m 59.322s
28	Valtulini	1m 59.408s
29	Migno	1m 59.957s
30	Loi	2m 00.432s
31	D. Binder	2m 00.739s
32	Petrarca	2m 01.758s
33	Spiranelli	2m 01.818s

Championship Points

1	B. Binder	36
2	Antonelli	31
3	Navarro	29
4	Pawi	25
5	Bagnaia	16
6	Mir	15
7	Fenati	13
8	Kornfeil	13
9	Locatelli	13
10	Bastianini	11
11	Bulega	10
12	Ono	10
13	McPhee	9
14	Loi	8
15	Oettl	8
16	Martin	8
17	Quartararo	6
18	Danilo	5
19	Norrodin	5
20	Guevara	4
21	Bendsneyder	2
22	Herrera	2
23	Canet	1

Constructor Points

1	Honda	50
2	KTM	36
3	Mahindra	24
4	Peugeot	9

Main: Marquez the Unbeatable ... again. He had won every time he had raced in the US.

Inset: Another 'selfie' for the *Tres Hombres*.

Photos: Repsol Honda Team

FIM WORLD CHAMPIONSHIP · ROUND 3

GRAND PRIX OF THE AMERICAS

CIRCUIT OF THE AMERICAS

Above: Too light for the tyres? Pedrosa battles with his Honda
Photo: Whit Bazemore Photography

Top right: Dovi, down and out for a second race in a row. Pedrosa apologised fulsomely.

Above right: Miller's smack-down ruled him out of the race. Dorna's Dylan Gray gets the low-down.

Right: Scott Redding had a strong ride to sixth; top non-factory rider.
Photos: Gold & Goose

RIDERS seldom, if ever, complain about having too much power. When they do, it is not about their own bikes. True to this form, Rossi fingered the superfast Ducatis for being too powerful for the tyres, for both Baz's and Redding's failures had been on Desmosedicis.

The Yamahas had suffered no problems in testing, nor in both races so far, he said. "I hope the other bikes, especially the Ducati, can fix the problem, because otherwise we all must race with a very hard tyre, and this is not good for the show or for performance. They have to fix the problem," he continued.

Michelin's response to the Argentine problems was impressive. Five days after the race, a whole new generation of rear tyres had been commissioned, constructed and delivered – 500 of them in time for the race in Texas. Project manager Piero Taramasso explained: "The casing is a little bit stronger than before, and the compound a little bit softer." They had also added a third front tyre choice. "After seven years away, we are still experimenting," he added.

In fact, only the softer of the two rear tyres arrived for Friday's practice, with the harder version there on Saturday. The majority agreed that it was the better choice for the race, with the Suzuki pair and both satellite Yamaha riders among the exceptions.

And Dani Pedrosa, whose tyre difficulties were much more acute than anybody's. The smallest and lightest MotoGP rider was already suffering worse than the other Honda riders from the new reverse-crank RC213V's several vicissitudes.

A combination of factors, including harsh throttle response, was robbing the bike of grip and drive out of the corners, but his featherweight 51kg exacerbated the problems because he was finding it difficult to get heat into the rear tyre.

The altered crank direction also changed the character of the bike, according to Marquez. Among other gyroscopic advantages, fully analysed in the previous edition of MOTO-COURSE, this meant that the torque reaction under acceleration tended to pitch the bike forward – helpful in resisting wheelies; conversely, a decelerating crank lightened the front wheel during braking. The double champion covertly acknowledged the change when he explained that on corner entry "you must use more a Yamaha style – go in more wide and prepare the exit." The bike was now slower in changing direction, but more stable, so "you can keep the [corner] speed more".

His performance spoke volumes of his own adaptability, for Marquez again effectively owned CoTA, and he remained dominant in the USA. He has won every one of his last nine races in North America, starting in 2011 and 2012 at Indy in Moto2, then joining MotoGP to add not only the last visit to Laguna Seca, but also the first to Austin. In 2014 and 2015, he won both Indy and Austin, with a full house of pole positions at the Texas track. And again in 2016. Unstoppable.

Suggestions that the Ducati was "too powerful" were born out again when they took the best four top-speed figures. Kink notwithstanding, CoTA has the longest straight on the calendar (1,200m, with Mugello, Qatar and Catalunya at

1,141, 1,068 and 1,047m respectively), but with a first-gear corner at each end not the highest top speed. This is symptomatic of a circuit with many quirks for the riders, and technical challenges for the machines. With 20 corners and the longest lap time (though not longest lap), it is both fascinating and difficult. A number of crashes proved the latter, but left a rather processional race for the survivors.

One victim was Dovizioso, already the unluckiest of 2016 competitors after being knocked out of second by his team-mate the weekend before. Now, after a strong start, he was lying third at the start of lap seven, peeling into the first tight corner, when a deeply remorseful Pedrosa, close behind, lost

control under braking and fell. His skittering Honda hit the Ducati, fortunately behind the rider rather than directly. Once again, Dovi was innocently robbed of a likely podium finish.

The paddock was awash with rumours of Lorenzo's impending switch to Ducati, with a domino effect on almost all other riders, and Rossi preparing the ground for his possible success on the Desmosedici by pointing out that the current machine was "a very different bike from when I switched". Who would he replace? Iannone's indiscretion at Argentina was an important part of it. He was contrite and explained that he hadn't been trying to pass his team-mate, rather to avoid an impending attack by Rossi. Either way, apologies were all very well, but the word from Ducati was bleak, as it was confirmed that contract renewal negotiations with him had been "suspended".

Wings continued to sprout, Ducati again leading the way with several variations during the weekend. Their fairing-nose blades were complemented by a monoplane or biplane on the fairing flanks, with large end-plates in the shape of a twisted teardrop. They worked well enough for satellite rider Scott Redding to be given a set on day two.

Though the Suzukis remained unadorned, and an unconvinced Rossi likewise, Lorenzo's large thrust-forward nose wings had now become a fixture, with smaller versions on the satellite bikes. Honda remained tentative, with small fairing-flank winglets at a much steeper angle of attack; but they added a jutting chin-piece to Marquez's air intake. Complaints of turbulence by following riders were commonplace, while the cost aspects of wind-tunnel development remained an anathema to Dorna's MotoGP philosophy. Could a ban be far away?

The EG-Marc VDS team were not the only ones who had reported a nightmare journey, but perhaps their 68-hour travail from Argentina might have played a part in a costly error by Jack Miller, who was caught out by a cold tyre on an out-lap on Friday. The resultant high-side was spectacular and injurious, not only adding a fracture to his right foot, but exacerbating the plated and still healing lower leg injury. He came back on Saturday morning to cut two seconds off his previous day's best time, but withdrew after three laps of FP4, the pain too severe. "This track is really physical, with a lot of changes of direction," he explained. "The pain just got worse and worse where I had the plates in. Maybe it pulled a screw loose."

MOTOGP RACE – 21 laps

Somebody suggested they should name a CoTA corner after Marc Marquez. Why stop there? Why not name that giddyingly steep 40m swoop up to the tight first corner 'Mount Marquez'? Having become the youngest ever GP winner with his first ascent in 2013, his fourth was as flawless. Again, as once with Doohan and Rossi, this race was about who would come second.

That was Lorenzo, back from a morning warm-up crash and two uncharacteristic lap-one errors to take up an ultimately hopeless pursuit. He'd admitted the day before that he was relying on the "anything can happen" syndrome. "Nobody is unbeatable."

Marquez was. The gap had stretched steadily to eight seconds as they started the last lap. Getting there was an achievement, on a track rendered slippery by not only a MotoAmerica oil spill, but also (a growing concern) Michelin tyres racing on freshly laid Moto2 Dunlop rubber. Rossi was one of a number to fall, his first non-finish in 24 races, during which he had only been off the podium four times.

He'd cooked his clutch off the line and dropped from a second successive front row to sixth on lap two. It was coming back when he fell on the fast second turn. "I didn't feel from the bike I was too fast, but looking at the result, maybe I was."

Compatriots Crutchlow and Smith crashed independently, but in close formation while closing on Redding shortly before half-distance. Both remounted, to finish out of the points; ahead of them, Baz had also slipped off after the start, but he remounted without losing as much time.

Lorenzo was in the middle of the front row; Iannone led the second from Vinales and Crutchlow, times now closing up. Less than a tenth covered Dovi, Pedrosa and Aleix Espargaro (through from Q1) on the third.

Tyre choice was mixed, with Marquez one of nine to gamble on the softer front in the hopes of an early breakaway. "Michelin told me it would be good for 12 or 15 laps, and after that I would have to manage to the situation more." It was as predicted; his lap times had stretched by almost two seconds by the end, "but it was enough."

Lorenzo led into the first corner, only to run wide and drop to fourth. A similar lunge at the next first-gear corner, leading on to the straight, had a similar result. "I was having trouble

stopping with a full tank," he explained, later expounding further. Compared with the Bridgestone, the front Michelin had "not the same confidence. Last year, you could lose the front and recover it. Now you can't. The range of performance is less, and different with a full tank or empty; or with a hard or soft tyre. You have to be aware."

Dovizioso's fast Ducati took over the pursuit down the straight, but he ceded second (now more than two seconds adrift) to Lorenzo on lap five. Pedrosa was poised close behind; just over a lap later, he would make the braking blunder that would cost both of them the race.

This left Iannone to a mercifully undramatic third place, matching Lorenzo's pace some five seconds behind for the later laps.

Again, there was some variation in tyre choice. Aleix Espargaro had joined Marquez among nine riders to choose the softer front; ten riders opted for the softer rear. But Espargaro had soft at both ends, and the early advantage was clear as the Suzuki forced through to fourth on lap one.

He had lost touch with Iannone when Vinales arrived, after finishing lap one tenth. The two Suzukis fought hard for team honours, but Vinales had the harder front tyre, and it paid dividends with a career-best fourth, Espargaro only two seconds adrift.

Redding had a strong if lonely ride to sixth, top non-factory finisher and staying clear of a somewhat distant late-race attack from Pol Espargaro. By the end, the Spaniard was fending off Pramac Ducati substitute Pirro. On his first visit, Pirro had got the better of Barbera.

It was a good day for the all-new Aprilia. Bradl had been tailing the three ahead closely; Bautista was 11th, while a couple of seconds behind, Laverty narrowly fended off improving rookie Rabat. Hernandez was dropping away in 14th; Baz was a distant 15th, then Crutchlow and Smith.

Over the first three flyaways, Marquez was the only one of the top riders to score in every race, extending a handy early lead on points.

MOTO2 RACE – 19 laps

Rins had dominated practice and qualifying, and he went on to do the same in the race. In both cases, however, Lowes ran him close. Often very close.

Zarco was between the pair on the front row, but it was

Above: Suzuki's civil war: Vinales and Espargaro waged a private battle for fourth place.

Above right: Alex Rins celebrates his first win of the season.

Right: Rins was shadowed by Sam Lowes, but the Spaniard was in complete control.
Photos: Gold & Goose

Below right: Romano Fenati won Moto3 by almost seven seconds.
Photo: Whit Bazemore Photography

Below: Sage and superstar: Rossi added former champion Luca Cadalora to his team.
Photo: Gold & Goose

Aegerter who surged forward from the second row to lead into the first corner. By the second, however, both Rins and Zarco were past the Swiss charger.

Rins would never be headed; but a lively Lowes set a new lap record second time around as he surged through from fourth to second and rapidly halved a gap that had grown to more than a second. He was within just over three-tenths on laps six and seven, but would never get closer. Nor much further away, until the 16th of 19 laps, when his challenge was clearly spent.

"I pushed hard at the start, but the last four laps I had no grip from the front," he said, happy enough that second gave him the lead on points, if only narrowly.

Rins's worst moment was when spots of rain fell on the last lap. Aside from that, "I was able to control the race."

The battle for third was lively until the closing stages. Aegerter had taken over from Zarco as Luthi moved past Folger and an at-last-on-form Takaaki Nakagami to challenge.

They shuffled around as Corsi arrived in typically aggressive style, adding to the confusion as Luthi took over third from laps nine to 14.

Now Zarco was feeling more comfortable and ready to push, and the time was right. He took over; just behind him, a desperate Corsi collided with Nakagami, who had just taken fourth, and knocked him off at the difficult first corner.

That gave Zarco breathing space, and he pushed on to secure a podium to follow his Argentina win.

Aegerter won the last-lap scramble from Folger; a couple of seconds behind, Corsi took sixth from Luthi on the last lap.

A well-earned eighth went to Simeon, who had caught and fought through a group to close on and pass his QMMF Speed Up team-mate, Julian Simon, to make it three Speed Up chassis among the dominant Kalexes in the top ten. Simon was seven-tenths behind; Schrotter a similar distance further back in tenth.

Alex Marquez had dropped out of this group for 11th, his first finish of his second Moto2 season; Cortese, Salom, Morbidelli and the remounted Nakagami took the remainder of the points.

A third winner in three races meant the main rivals would go to Europe neck and neck: just four points separated the top four, and Lowes – the only one without a win so far – with a margin of just one point.

MOTO3 RACE – 18 laps

Rain-hit qualifying shuffled the grid, giving Oettl a maiden pole and putting title contender Antonelli down in 30th. But it was second qualifier Navarro who seized the lead from the start, and made a convincing attempt at a runaway – his lead approaching two seconds after just three laps.

By then, Fenati had taken second from Oettl, and he started to hunt down the Honda.

When he got there, Navarro made his pass easy, running wide into the tight Turn One at the start of lap eight. The Spaniard stayed close, until the same error lost him more than a second at two-thirds distance. His challenge was done, the first two places decided. It was the 20-year-old Italian's seventh win.

The field was relatively spread out, and Quartararo had come through, bringing Binder. They had caught Oettl by half-distance, and the Frenchman nipped ahead directly.

Binder dropped a couple of seconds behind, blaming bad front-end chatter; Oettl stayed with the Frenchman, who seemed to have a first rostrum of the year in his pocket when suddenly he slowed, with a gearshift malady. Now Binder closed steadily to snatch third from the German at the end of the straight on the last lap.

Locatelli was the long-time leader and eventual winner of a big battle for fifth; Bastianini was still close.

Antonelli had cut through from the back to join this group and was near the front of it when he fell with two laps left.

Impressive rookie Aron Canet had cannily followed him through, narrowly missed being knocked flying when he crashed and taken a fine seventh, finally outpacing Loi, Danilo, plus Kornfeil and Guevara; eighth to 12th was covered by 0.923 of a second.

Quartararo was 13th, with Bagnaia and Migno taking the final points.

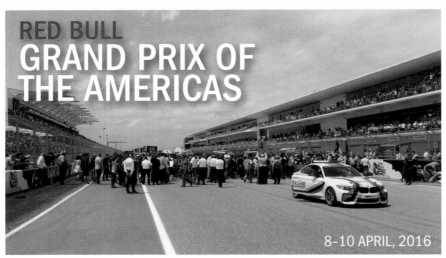

RED BULL
GRAND PRIX OF THE AMERICAS

8–10 APRIL, 2016

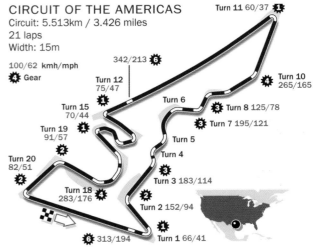

CIRCUIT OF THE AMERICAS
Circuit: 5.513km / 3.426 miles
21 laps
Width: 15m

100/62 kmh/mph — Gear

Turn 11 60/37
Turn 10 265/165
Turn 8 125/78
Turn 7 195/121
Turn 6
Turn 12 75/47
Turn 15 70/44
Turn 19 91/57
Turn 20 82/51
Turn 18 283/176
Turn 5
Turn 4
Turn 3 183/114
Turn 2 152/94
Turn 1 66/41
342/213
313/194

MotoGP

RACE DISTANCE: 21 laps, 71.938 miles/115.773km · **RACE WEATHER:** Dry (air 26°C, humidity 62%, track 34°C)

Pos.	Rider	Nat.	No.	Entrant	Machine	Tyres	Race tyre choice	Laps	Time & speed
1	**Marc Marquez**	SPA	93	Repsol Honda Team	Honda RC213V	M	F: Soft/R: Medium	21	43m 57.945s 98.1mph/157.9km/h
2	**Jorge Lorenzo**	SPA	99	Movistar Yamaha MotoGP	Yamaha YZR-M1	M	F: Medium/R: Medium	21	44m 04.052s
3	**Andrea Iannone**	ITA	29	Ducati Team	Ducati Desmosedici	M	F: Medium/R: Medium	21	44m 08.892s
4	**Maverick Vinales**	SPA	25	Team SUZUKI ECSTAR	Suzuki GSX-RR	M	F: Medium/R: Soft	21	44m 16.367s
5	**Aleix Espargaro**	SPA	41	Team SUZUKI ECSTAR	Suzuki GSX-RR	M	F: Soft/R: Soft	21	44m 18.656s
6	**Scott Redding**	GBR	45	OCTO Pramac Yakhnich	Ducati Desmosedici	M	F: Medium/R: Medium	21	44m 26.906s
7	**Pol Espargaro**	SPA	44	Monster Yamaha Tech 3	Yamaha YZR-M1	M	F: Soft/R: Soft	21	44m 30.057s
8	**Michele Pirro**	ITA	51	OCTO Pramac Yakhnich	Ducati Desmosedici	M	F: Medium/R: Soft	21	44m 30.702s
9	**Hector Barbera**	SPA	8	Avintia Racing	Ducati Desmosedici	M	F: Soft/R: Soft	21	44m 32.537s
10	**Stefan Bradl**	GER	6	Aprilia Racing Team Gresini	Aprilia RS-GP	M	F: Soft/R: Soft	21	44m 38.156s
11	**Alvaro Bautista**	SPA	19	Aprilia Racing Team Gresini	Aprilia RS-GP	M	F: Soft/R: Soft	21	44m 43.368s
12	**Eugene Laverty**	IRL	50	Aspar Team MotoGP	Ducati Desmosedici	M	F: Medium/R: Medium	21	44m 45.072s
13	**Tito Rabat**	SPA	53	Estrella Galicia 0,0 Marc VDS	Honda RC213V	M	F: Soft/R: Soft	21	44m 45.371s
14	**Yonny Hernandez**	COL	68	Aspar Team MotoGP	Ducati Desmosedici	M	F: Soft/R: Medium	21	44m 49.135s
15	**Loris Baz**	FRA	76	Avintia Racing	Ducati Desmosedici	M	F: Soft/R: Soft	21	45m 10.874s
16	Cal Crutchlow	GBR	35	LCR Honda	Honda RC213V	M	F: Medium/R: Soft	21	45m 17.197s
17	Bradley Smith	GBR	38	Monster Yamaha Tech 3	Yamaha YZR-M1	M	F: Medium/R: Soft	21	45m 25.981s
	Dani Pedrosa	SPA	26	Repsol Honda Team	Honda RC213V	M	F: Medium/R: Soft	11	DNF-crash
	Andrea Dovizioso	ITA	4	Ducati Team	Ducati Desmosedici	M	F: Medium/R: Medium	6	DNF-crash
	Valentino Rossi	ITA	46	Movistar Yamaha MotoGP	Yamaha YZR-M1	M	F: Medium/R: Medium	2	DNF-crash
	Jack Miller	AUS	43	Estrella Galicia 0,0 Marc VDS	Honda RC213V	M	–	–	DNS-Injured

Fastest lap: Marc Marquez, on lap 11, 2m 4.682s, 98.9mph/159.1km/h.

Lap record: Marc Marquez, SPA (Honda), 2m 3.575s, 99.8mph/160.6km/h (2014).

Event best maximum speed: Andrea Dovizioso, 214.5mph/345.2km/h (free practice).

Qualifying

Weather: Dry
Air Temp: 22° **Track Temp:** 26°
Humidity: 60%

1	Marquez	2m 03.188s
2	Lorenzo	2m 03.257s
3	Rossi	2m 03.644s
4	Iannone	2m 03.913s
5	Vinales	2m 04.247s
6	Crutchlow	2m 04.265s
7	Dovizioso	2m 04.339s
8	Pedrosa	2m 04.379s
9	A. Espargaro	2m 04.408s
10	Redding	2m 04.485s
11	Smith	2m 04.988s
12	Baz	2m 05.159s
13	P. Espargaro	2m 04.867s
14	Barbera	2m 04.944s
15	Laverty	2m 05.425s
16	Bradl	2m 05.625s
17	Pirro	2m 05.702s
18	Hernandez	2m 06.029s
19	Bautista	2m 06.049s
20	Rabat	2m 06.562s
	Miller	No Time

Fastest race laps

1	Marquez	2m 04.682s
2	Lorenzo	2m 04.908s
3	Pedrosa	2m 04.950s
4	Dovizioso	2m 05.181s
5	Iannone	2m 05.275s
6	Vinales	2m 05.479s
7	A. Espargaro	2m 05.734s
8	Rossi	2m 05.801s
9	Crutchlow	2m 05.910s
10	Redding	2m 06.004s
11	Smith	2m 06.042s
12	Barbera	2m 06.199s
13	P. Espargaro	2m 06.254s
14	Bradl	2m 06.471s
15	Pirro	2m 06.494s
16	Hernandez	2m 06.494s
17	Baz	2m 06.582s
18	Bautista	2m 06.866s
19	Rabat	2m 06.988s
20	Laverty	2m 07.208s

Championship Points

1	Marquez	66
2	Lorenzo	45
3	Rossi	33
4	P. Espargaro	28
5	Pedrosa	27
6	Barbera	25
7	Dovizioso	23
8	Vinales	23
9	Laverty	21
10	A. Espargaro	21
11	Iannone	16
12	Redding	16
13	Smith	16
14	Bradl	15
15	Bautista	14
16	Pirro	12
17	Rabat	11
18	Miller	2
19	Hernandez	2
20	Baz	1

Constructor Points

1	Honda	66
2	Yamaha	65
3	Ducati	49
4	Suzuki	28
5	Aprilia	18

Grid order		1	2	3	4	5	6	7	8	9	10	11	12	13	14	15	16	17	18	19	20	21	
93	MARQUEZ	93	93	93	93	93	93	93	93	93	93	93	93	93	93	93	93	93	93	93	93	93	1
99	LORENZO	4	4	4	4	99	99	99	99	99	99	99	99	99	99	99	99	99	99	99	99	99	2
46	ROSSI	99	99	99	99	4	4	29	29	29	29	29	29	29	29	29	29	29	29	29	29	29	3
25	VINALES	41	41	26	26	26	26	41	41	41	41	25	25	25	25	25	25	25	25	25	25	25	4
35	CRUTCHLOW	26	26	41	41	41	29	25	25	25	25	41	41	41	41	41	41	41	41	41	41	41	5
4	DOVIZIOSO	46	46	29	29	29	41	45	45	45	45	45	45	45	45	45	45	45	45	45	45	45	6
29	IANNONE	29	29	45	45	25	25	35	51	51	44	44	44	44	44	44	44	44	44	44	44	44	7
26	PEDROSA	45	45	25	25	45	45	38	44	44	8	8	8	8	8	51	51	51	51	51	51	51	8
41	A. ESPARGARO	35	25	35	35	35	35	51	8	8	51	51	51	51	51	8	8	8	8	8	8	8	9
45	REDDING	25	35	38	38	38	38	44	6	6	6	6	6	6	6	6	6	6	6	6	6	6	10
38	SMITH	38	38	51	51	51	51	68	68	68	68	68	68	19	19	19	19	19	19	19	19	19	11
76	BAZ	44	51	68	68	68	68	8	19	19	19	19	19	68	68	68	68	50	50	50	50	50	12
44	P. ESPARGARO	76	44	44	44	44	44	6	50	50	50	50	50	50	50	50	68	68	53	53	53	53	13
8	BARBERA	19	68	8	8	8	8	19	53	53	53	53	53	53	53	53	53	53	68	68	68	68	14
50	LAVERTY	51	6	6	6	6	6	50	38	76	76	76	76	76	76	76	76	76	76	76	76	76	15
6	BRADL	68	8	50	50	50	19	53	76	38	38	38	38	38	38	38	35	35	35	35	35	35	
51	PIRRO	6	50	53	53	19	50	76	26	26	26	35	35	35	35	35	38	38	38	38	38		
68	HERNANDEZ	50	53	19	19	53	53	26	35	35	35	26											
19	BAUTISTA	8	19	76	76	76	76																
53	RABAT	53	76																				

26 Pit stop

Moto2 — RACE DISTANCE: 19 laps, 65.087 miles/104.747km · RACE WEATHER: Dry (air 23°C, humidity 73%, track 28°C)

Pos.	Rider	Nat.	No.	Entrant	Machine	Laps	Time & Speed
1	**Alex Rins**	SPA	40	Paginas Amarillas HP 40	Kalex	19	41m 22.174s 94.4mph/ 151.9km/h
2	**Sam Lowes**	GBR	22	Federal Oil Gresini Moto2	Kalex	19	41m 24.265s
3	**Johann Zarco**	FRA	5	Ajo Motorsport	Kalex	19	41m 29.911s
4	**Dominique Aegerter**	SWI	77	CarXpert Interwetten	Kalex	19	41m 30.820s
5	**Jonas Folger**	GER	94	Dynavolt Intact GP	Kalex	19	41m 30.965s
6	**Simone Corsi**	ITA	24	Speed Up Racing	Speed Up	19	41m 33.257s
7	**Thomas Luthi**	SWI	12	Garage Plus Interwetten	Kalex	19	41m 33.452s
8	**Xavier Simeon**	BEL	19	QMMF Racing Team	Speed Up	19	41m 40.107s
9	**Julian Simon**	SPA	60	QMMF Racing Team	Speed Up	19	41m 40.892s
10	**Marcel Schrotter**	GER	23	AGR Team	Kalex	19	41m 41.582s
11	**Alex Marquez**	SPA	73	Estrella Galicia 0,0 Marc VDS	Kalex	19	41m 44.347s
12	**Sandro Cortese**	GER	11	Dynavolt Intact GP	Kalex	19	41m 46.072s
13	**Luis Salom**	SPA	39	SAG Team	Kalex	19	41m 47.569s
14	**Franco Morbidelli**	ITA	21	Estrella Galicia 0,0 Marc VDS	Kalex	19	41m 49.057s
15	**Takaaki Nakagami**	JPN	30	IDEMITSU Honda Team Asia	Kalex	19	41m 49.772s
16	Hafizh Syahrin	MAL	55	Petronas Raceline Malaysia	Kalex	19	41m 51.515s
17	Mattia Pasini	ITA	54	Italtrans Racing Team	Kalex	19	41m 52.371s
18	Isaac Vinales	SPA	32	Tech 3 Racing	Tech 3	19	41m 59.037s
19	Ratthapark Wilairot	THA	14	IDEMITSU Honda Team Asia	Kalex	19	42m 00.557s
20	Xavi Vierge	SPA	97	Tech 3 Racing	Tech 3	19	42m 00.611s
21	Jesko Raffin	SWI	2	Sports-Millions-EMWE-SAG	Kalex	19	42m 07.380s
22	Axel Pons	SPA	49	AGR Team	Kalex	19	42m 09.862s
23	Lorenzo Baldassarri	ITA	7	Forward Team	Kalex	19	42m 16.047s
24	Alessandro Tonucci	ITA	33	Tasca Racing Scuderia Moto2	Kalex	19	42m 33.333s
	Miguel Oliveira	POR	44	Leopard Racing	Kalex	11	DNF
	Danny Kent	GBR	52	Leopard Racing	Kalex	5	DNF
	Robin Mulhauser	SWI	70	CarXpert Interwetten	Kalex	3	DNF
	Luca Marini	ITA	10	Forward Team	Kalex	3	DNF

Fastest lap: Sam Lowes, on lap 2, 2m 9.994s, 94.8mph/152.6km/h (record)
Previous lap record: Maverick Vinales, SPA (Kalex), 2m 10.103s, 94.8mph/152.5km/h (2014).
Event best maximum speed: Alex Rins, 177mph/284.9km/h (free practice).

Qualifying
Weather: Dry
Air Temp: 25° **Track Temp:** 31°
Humidity: 51%

1	Rins	2m 08.850s
2	Zarco	2m 09.066s
3	Lowes	2m 09.100s
4	Aegerter	2m 09.163s
5	Luthi	2m 09.171s
6	Nakagami	2m 09.206s
7	Folger	2m 09.226s
8	Corsi	2m 09.421s
9	Morbidelli	2m 09.910s
10	Cortese	2m 09.940s
11	Simon	2m 09.999s
12	Baldassarri	2m 10.012s
13	Schrotter	2m 10.039s
14	Salom	2m 10.103s
15	Pons	2m 10.236s
16	Kent	2m 10.274s
17	Syahrin	2m 10.292s
18	Simeon	2m 10.299s
19	Pasini	2m 10.375s
20	Oliveira	2m 10.405s
21	Marquez	2m 10.418s
22	Marini	2m 10.453s
23	Vierge	2m 10.705s
24	Wilairot	2m 10.734s
25	Vinales	2m 11.297s
26	Raffin	2m 11.539s
27	Mulhauser	2m 12.202s
28	Tonucci	2m 12.801s
29	Vazquez	2m 12.962s

Fastest race laps

1	Lowes	2m 09.994s
2	Rins	2m 10.050s
3	Nakagami	2m 10.275s
4	Folger	2m 10.300s
5	Aegerter	2m 10.376s
6	Corsi	2m 10.434s
7	Luthi	2m 10.439s
8	Marquez	2m 10.527s
9	Simon	2m 10.618s
10	Oliveira	2m 10.637s
11	Pons	2m 10.669s
12	Simeon	2m 10.687s
13	Zarco	2m 10.732s
14	Cortese	2m 10.960s
15	Schrotter	2m 10.980s
16	Salom	2m 11.040s
17	Pasini	2m 11.238s
18	Baldassarri	2m 11.253s
19	Morbidelli	2m 11.369s
20	Wilairot	2m 11.437s
21	Vierge	2m 11.511s
22	Vinales	2m 11.517s
23	Syahrin	2m 11.561s
24	Marini	2m 11.860s
25	Raffin	2m 11.946s
26	Mulhauser	2m 12.218s
27	Kent	2m 12.686s
28	Tonucci	2m 12.864s

Championship Points

1	Lowes	47
2	Rins	46
3	Zarco	45
4	Luthi	43
5	Aegerter	35
6	Folger	27
7	Corsi	26
8	Salom	24
9	Syahrin	23
10	Simeon	12
11	Morbidelli	11
12	Schrotter	11
13	Kent	10
14	Nakagami	10
15	Pons	8
16	Simon	7
17	Pasini	6
18	Marini	6
19	Oliveira	5
20	Cortese	5
21	Marquez	5
22	Wilairot	3
23	Baldassarri	3
24	Vierge	2

Constructor Points

1	Kalex	75
2	Speed Up	30
3	Tech 3	2

Moto3 — RACE DISTANCE: 18 laps, 61.661 miles/99.234km · RACE WEATHER: Dry (air 23°C, humidity 68%, track 28°C)

Pos.	Rider	Nat.	No.	Entrant	Machine	Laps	Time & Speed
1	**Romano Fenati**	ITA	5	SKY Racing Team VR46	KTM	18	41m 14.868s 89.7mph/ 144.3km/h
2	**Jorge Navarro**	SPA	9	Estrella Galicia 0,0	Honda	18	41m 21.480s
3	**Brad Binder**	RSA	41	Red Bull KTM Ajo	KTM	18	41m 25.403s
4	**Philipp Oettl**	GER	65	Schedl GP Racing	KTM	18	41m 25.843s
5	**Andrea Locatelli**	ITA	55	Leopard Racing	KTM	18	41m 28.713s
6	**Enea Bastianini**	ITA	33	Gresini Racing Moto3	Honda	18	41m 28.991s
7	**Aron Canet**	SPA	44	Estrella Galicia 0,0	Honda	18	41m 31.177s
8	**Livio Loi**	BEL	11	RW Racing GP BV	Honda	18	41m 36.709s
9	**Jules Danilo**	FRA	95	Ongetta-Rivacold	Honda	18	41m 36.872s
10	**Nicolo Bulega**	ITA	8	SKY Racing Team VR46	KTM	18	41m 37.219s
11	**Jakub Kornfeil**	CZE	84	Drive M7 SIC Racing Team	Honda	18	41m 37.582s
12	**Juanfran Guevara**	SPA	58	RBA Racing Team	KTM	18	41m 37.632s
13	**Fabio Quartararo**	FRA	20	Leopard Racing	KTM	18	41m 40.892s
14	**Francesco Bagnaia**	ITA	21	ASPAR Mahindra Team Moto3	Mahindra	18	41m 43.029s
15	**Andrea Migno**	ITA	16	SKY Racing Team VR46	KTM	18	41m 43.127s
16	Alexis Masbou	FRA	10	Peugeot MC Saxoprint	Peugeot	18	41m 54.091s
17	Fabio di Giannantonio	ITA	4	Gresini Racing Moto3	Honda	18	41m 54.216s
18	Gabriel Rodrigo	ARG	19	RBA Racing Team	KTM	18	41m 54.607s
19	Tatsuki Suzuki	JPN	24	CIP-Unicom Starker	Mahindra	18	41m 55.028s
20	Khairul Idham Pawi	MAL	89	Honda Team Asia	Honda	18	42m 02.975s
21	John McPhee	GBR	17	Peugeot MC Saxoprint	Peugeot	18	42m 03.202s
22	Bo Bendsneyder	NED	64	Red Bull KTM Ajo	KTM	18	42m 03.310s
23	Maria Herrera	SPA	6	MH6 Laglisse	KTM	18	42m 30.739s
24	Lorenzo Petrarca	ITA	77	3570 Team Italia	Mahindra	18	42m 30.911s
25	Hiroki Ono	JPN	76	Honda Team Asia	Honda	18	42m 34.309s
26	Fabio Spiranelli	ITA	3	CIP-Unicom Starker	Mahindra	18	43m 00.797s
	Niccolo Antonelli	ITA	23	Ongetta-Rivacold	Honda	16	DNF
	Karel Hanika	CZE	98	Platinum Bay Real Estate	Mahindra	11	DNF
	Stefano Valtulini	ITA	43	3570 Team Italia	Mahindra	9	DNF
	Jorge Martin	SPA	88	ASPAR Mahindra Team Moto3	Mahindra	7	DNF
	Darryn Binder	RSA	40	Platinum Bay Real Estate	Mahindra	5	DNF
	Joan Mir	SPA	36	Leopard Racing	KTM	4	DNF
	Adam Norrodin	MAL	7	Drive M7 SIC Racing Team	Honda	1	DNF

Fastest lap: Romano Fenati, on lap 6, 2m 16.842s, 90.1mph/145.0km/h.
Lap record: Luis Salom, SPA (KTM), 2m 16.345s, 90.4mph/145.5km/h (2013).
Event best maximum speed: Juanfran Guevara, 147.3mph/237.1km/h (free practice).

Qualifying:
Weather: Dry
Air Temp: 21° **Track Temp:** 23°
Humidity: 68%

1	Oettl	2m 18.398s
2	Navarro	2m 18.985s
3	Bastianini	2m 18.996s
4	Kornfeil	2m 19.068s
5	Fenati	2m 19.135s
6	Norrodin	2m 19.469s
7	Locatelli	2m 19.708s
8	Danilo	2m 19.790s
9	Quartararo	2m 20.118s
10	Loi	2m 20.230s
11	Bulega	2m 20.444s
12	B. Binder	2m 20.456s
13	Suzuki	2m 20.499s
14	Guevara	2m 20.649s
15	Masbou	2m 20.773s
16	Ono	2m 21.151s
17	McPhee	2m 21.159s
18	Bagnaia	2m 21.309s
19	Hanika	2m 21.379s
20	Martin	2m 21.486s
21	Migno	2m 21.957s
22	Canet	2m 22.232s
23	Bendsneyder	2m 22.251s
24	Rodrigo	2m 22.687s
25	Petrarca	2m 22.794s
26	D. Binder	2m 23.097s
27	Herrera	2m 23.461s
28	Valtulini	2m 23.495s
29	Mir	2m 23.578s
30	Antonelli	2m 24.379s
31	Di Giannantonio	2m 24.477s
32	Pawi	2m 24.640s
33	Spiranelli	2m 31.357s

Fastest race laps

1	Fenati	2m 16.842s
2	Navarro	2m 16.928s
3	Antonelli	2m 17.059s
4	Oettl	2m 17.310s
5	Quartararo	2m 17.393s
6	Canet	2m 17.405s
7	B. Binder	2m 17.421s
8	Kornfeil	2m 17.434s
9	Danilo	2m 17.470s
10	Guevara	2m 17.485s
11	Bulega	2m 17.502s
12	Locatelli	2m 17.604s
13	Loi	2m 17.659s
14	Bastianini	2m 17.740s
15	Bagnaia	2m 17.786s
16	Migno	2m 18.042s
17	Rodrigo	2m 18.251s
18	Masbou	2m 18.312s
19	Martin	2m 18.393s
20	Suzuki	2m 18.471s
21	Di Giannantonio	2m 18.535s
22	D. Binder	2m 18.621s
23	Pawi	2m 18.624s
24	Ono	2m 18.672s
25	Mir	2m 18.931s
26	McPhee	2m 19.123s
27	Bendsneyder	2m 19.240s
28	Hanika	2m 19.272s
29	Herrera	2m 19.928s
30	Valtulini	2m 20.454s
31	Petrarca	2m 20.650s
32	Spiranelli	2m 21.728s

Championship Points

1	B. Binder	52
2	Navarro	49
3	Fenati	38
4	Antonelli	31
5	Pawi	25
6	Locatelli	24
7	Oettl	21
8	Bastianini	21
9	Bagnaia	18
10	Kornfeil	18
11	Bulega	16
12	Loi	16
13	Mir	15
14	Danilo	12
15	Ono	10
16	Canet	10
17	McPhee	9
18	Quartararo	9
19	Martin	8
20	Guevara	8
21	Norrodin	5
22	Herrera	2
23	Bendsneyder	2
24	Migno	1

Constructor Points

1	Honda	70
2	KTM	61
3	Mahindra	26
4	Peugeot	9

SPANISH GRAND PRIX

JEREZ CIRCUIT

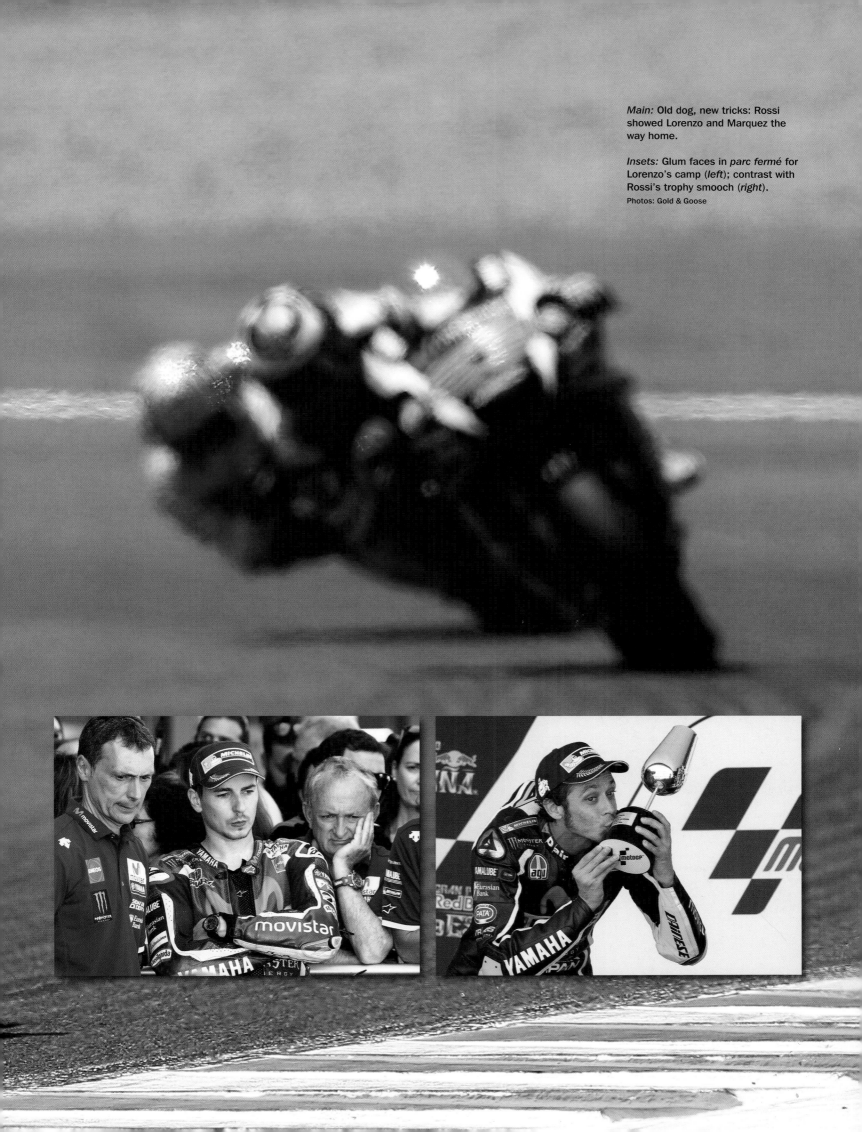

Main: Old dog, new tricks: Rossi showed Lorenzo and Marquez the way home.

Insets: Glum faces in *parc fermé* for Lorenzo's camp (*left*); contrast with Rossi's trophy smooch (*right*).

Photos: Gold & Goose

Above: Eugene Laverty again performed above his pay grade: here he heads Pol Espargaro, Barbera, Crutchlow, Bautista, Bradl, Iannone and the gang in the early stages.

Top right: Aleix Espargaro held the upper hand over Vinales in the Suzuki battle.

Above right: More woe for Dovi as he is forced to retire.

Above far right: Lin Jarvis describes his disco disappointment.
Photos: Gold & Goose

Right: Discretion was the better part of valour for Marquez, showing his new maturity to preserve his points lead.
Photo: Repsol Honda

Below right: Where do we go from here? A mystified Scott Redding finished dead last.
Photos: Gold & Goose

I N 2015, Lorenzo's pole-to-flag victory at Jerez – the start of a four-race purple patch – was described as a master-class. A year later, we were treated to the prowess of an unlikely pupil: mature student Rossi, as he did more or less the same thing.

More than an emphatic rebuttal of any suggestions that, at 37, he was getting a bit past it, it was an astonishing demonstration of how the old warhorse continued to be able to adapt, both in his style and his approach. After losing ground with poor qualifying positions and early race laps in 2015, Rossi had applied himself to improving these aspects. And how.

This was his 62nd pole start, and his 52nd in the premier class – but the first since his one and only of 2015, at Assen. So far in 2016, he hadn't been off the front row of the grid.

Rossi did see the back end of Lorenzo's Yamaha once during this race, as they swung into the Dry Sack hairpin for the second of 27 times. But the Spaniard ran a little wide, and Rossi was straight back in front again.

It was a classic victory, at what has become a classic event – the European season opener, attracting some 200,000 fans over race weekend. This was the 30th year at the Circuito de Velocidad outside the sherry capital of Andalucía.

In some ways, Jerez proved a bit too classic, with a resurface decidedly overdue. Riders complained of a lack of rear grip, especially drive grip, all weekend, and most especially in the race, when track temperature was up by more than ten degrees from qualifying, from 29 to 40 degrees centigrade. Drive was in such short supply that riders were experiencing severe wheelspin even in the upper gears with the bikes upright. Many spoke of having to short-shift through to sixth, and then having to back off the throttle when they got there.

This was due to a combination of factors, including the temperature, and the fact that Moto2 had preceded the race, whereas in practice and qualifying, the Dunlop-shod middle class had always run after the big bikes. For 2016, the electronics were also cruder than in the previous year; while the latest generation of Michelin tyres were of harder construction.

Rossi was not the only top rider to have reinvented him-

self. In 2015, Marquez would not have given up on trying to take second from Lorenzo, and might easily have crashed in the attempt. He did have a couple of stabs at making it up under braking, but just after half-distance decided it was too risky, in line with his own over-winter rethink, and settled for a safe 16 points for third. Post-race, however, he promised, "You will see the old Marc again. It is a big fight inside myself, but the bike is not ready, so I must be quiet."

In the other sense, being quiet was over for Lorenzo, with confirmation shortly before the race that he was to make the big leap to Ducati for 2017 and 2018. He still tried to say as little as possible, beyond, "It was the most important and difficult decision of my career, but 15 races remain [with Yamaha] and my focus is on the present championship." Pressed further, the main reason had been "my motivation", and a need to keep it fresh. "After so many years, to give maximum effort every day … I think I am one of the most professional riders. I felt I needed this new challenge to keep my motivation. It is a risky decision, but a calculated risky decision."

He was cagey on his expectations, beyond stating the obvious: "It will probably be very fast on the straights," adding, "Every year, the evolution of the bike has been forward. This has been a big influence." But he was more forthcoming about ex-Aprilia Ducati Corse chief Dall'Igna, a close ally during his 125 years and his two 250 titles. "I always had a good relationship with Gigi, from 2004 with the Derbi. For me, he has always been a genius as an engineer – very successful in whatever category.

Yamaha Racing's Lin Jarvis was also present at the conference; he raised a smile by describing Lorenzo's defection as "like asking a girl to dance at a disco, and she chooses the bloke next to you." He pledged continued equal support for both Rossi and Lorenzo for the season to come, but admitted that things might change should important developments come along.

More winglets, the latest transparent side-strakes on Rossi's helmet linked to the ducktail on the back. More significantly, he also finally overcame his objection to their "ugly look" on the bike and matched Lorenzo with the biggest pair of anhedral trays in Yamaha's box. "The wings help a little

bit the front contact, so when you open the throttle the front tyre has a little more touch," he said, also noting "a slight advantage in the last fast corners".

The rest, including Aprilia, were catching up, although in some cases not until the first official group tests of the following day, when both Suzuki and Honda had a variation of the triplane theme, with three parallel strakes on each side of the fairing. For the race, the Repsol Hondas had smaller versions of the Yamaha canards. Ducati, meanwhile, reverted to a single-plane lower side wing.

And on Saturday night, the MSMA (manufacturers' association) convened a special meeting to open discussions on possible future aerodynamic regulations. With Ducati vehemently in favour and with eight bikes on the grid, it was not surprising that no agreement was forthcoming.

Michelin confirmed that they intended to stick with the harder-construction rear tyre used at Austin for the rest of the season, to the dismay of the usual suspects, but obviously without much disruption to the prospects of the most prominent among them. But Rossi might at least have been mildly amused by another Michelin disruption: when they lost so many of their tyre fitting staff to an attack of food poisoning on Saturday, which caused FP4 and both qualifying sessions to be delayed.

Brad Binder made history in Moto3 as not only the first South African to win a GP since 350 champion Jon Ekerold in 1981, but also with an epic ride from last on the grid to a clear victory. Only two riders had managed that feat in history: Noboru Ueda in 1997, after pitting for a late tyre change, and Marc Marquez at Valencia in 2012, pushed back by a penalty.

MOTOGP RACE – 27 laps

On the home turf of his self-elected two deadliest rivals, the weekend was all about Valentino, culminating in his 113th career win – one step closer to Agostini's record of 122.

"Last year, I did not qualify so well and I was strong later in the races, but it was too late," he said. There was no such weakness this time: a perfect start, leading into the first corner, and – but for that brief interruption on lap two – all the way to the flag. He was better than a second clear by lap two, set fastest lap of the race next time around (more than a second short of the record), and better than two seconds by lap nine and still pulling.

Lorenzo did cut it back to two seconds again with seven laps to go, but only briefly. The Spaniard later blamed the straight-line wheelspin, opining that otherwise he believed he could have won the race, but he had been unable to open the throttle "more than 80 per cent in any gear".

Given this opportunity for one-upmanship, Rossi promptly put his own maximum opening possibility at only 50 per cent. While again pulling clear. Each was lapping two seconds slower than his best at the end of the race. By then, Lorenzo had chosen caution and was more than four seconds behind as they started the final lap.

Likewise Marquez, who had harried Lorenzo strongly until shortly before half-distance. Thus the first three qualifiers finished in the same order; while Marquez maintained a podium full house and an only slightly smaller points lead.

Dovizioso led the Suzukis on row two and was quick off the line, but dropped back from the start. Instead it was Pedrosa, off the third row past even Marquez and lying third at the end of lap one.

Aleix Espargaro was also ahead of the Ducati, with plenty to prove, his team-mate Vinales having garnered all the attention in the early rounds. The fancied youngster was lying seventh, behind Dovi, after another poor start.

The factory Hondas were the other way around after another lap, with Pedrosa losing ground. He was doing his best to save his tyres, he later explained, while also keeping a very persistent Espargaro at bay. By the end, though, he had gained pace to close to within three seconds of Marquez.

Above: Lowes leads Folger, Rins and Morbidelli as Cortese exits in the background.

Top far right: Brad Binder was dropped from the front row to the back after a team technical infringement.

Above far right: Now he's reached the front. Binder has just passed Bagnaia (21), Navarro (09) and Bulega (8), to claim a historic last-to-first victory.

Above right: Cheerful is as cheerful does. Sam Lowes "really wanted this one".

Right: Thumbs up from a gleeful Binder, who was taking control of the tiddler class.

Photos: Gold & Goose

Fourth was his first time off the Jerez MotoGP rostrum since his debut second place in 2006.

Espargaro held on to an ego-boosting fifth, his second in a row, not only comfortably clear of Vinales, but still close to Pedrosa. Point proved, though it would not necessarily do him much good. Vinales was never able to make up ground lost in the early laps. Not that it would do him much harm.

It might have been different if Dovizioso's bad luck hadn't persisted. His troubles from the start grew worse, and he lost another place to Vinales on lap six, complaining of several big moments. He managed three more difficult laps before cruising back to the pits, complaining of dangerous handling. A cooling pressure problem meant his back tyre was getting sprayed with water.

At that point, he had been losing ground to Laverty, up from the fifth row of the grid and having another impressive race at a track that clearly suited the oldest of the Ducatis. Laverty had got ahead of Pol Espargaro on lap two and gained some breathing space, but as the fuel load lightened the satellite Yamaha rider became more comfortable, and he was back in front before half-distance, now narrowly ahead of a gang of four, with Barbera and Crutchlow tucked in behind Laverty.

By then, Iannone had caught the group, after a difficult weekend so far. He'd qualified only 11th and finished lap one 14th. Now he was gaining positions, picking his way through the group; by lap 17, he had disposed of Espargaro for seventh.

Laverty finished an excellent ninth, narrowly beating the similarly mounted Barbera. Crutchlow had dropped away, mindful that he needed a first finish of the year; he managed to stay ahead of Smith's closing Monster Yamaha.

Baz came through for 13th; Bradl finally got the better of

last points-scorer Yonny Hernandez by a tenth of a second.

Close behind, Michele Pirro (again riding injured Petrucci's Pramac Ducati) stayed a tenth clear of a late attack from returned injury victim Miller. The Australian's team-mate, Tito Rabat, was four seconds down, and a badly out-of-sorts Scott Redding a distant last.

Bautista joined Dovizioso as the only other non-finisher, crashing out on lap six.

MOTO2 RACE – 26 laps

The seemingly ever-cheerful Lowes had plenty to smile about at Jerez. Riding in his usual 'Sideways Sam' style, the former 600 World Supersport champion claimed pole at the last gasp, then turned it into a clear first win of the season to extend his title lead.

He was three-tenths clear of Folger and Cortese, separated by three-hundredths. Morbidelli led the second row from Luthi and Baldassarri; Rins the third from Corsi and Marquez. Zarco's puzzlingly erratic form continued: he qualified 16th, behind class-rookie team-mates Oliveira and Kent.

The race up front was rather austere, especially after three riders crashed out of the top six in the first four laps: including Cortese and the increasingly troubled Marquez.

By then, in fact on only lap two, Lowes had seized the lead from second qualifier Folger, and he stayed there to the end. Folger's pressure was constant until lap 18, when the gap opened to more than a second for the first time. He settled for second, a willing Lowes for first, almost 2.5 seconds clear as he wheelied over the line.

"It was a long race, no doubt," said Lowes. "Track conditions have changed all weekend, and today they changed again. But the bike worked well. I wanted to win this one."

Corsi fell out of third on only the second lap, and thereafter there was only one other overtaking move up front, on the same lap, when home favourite Rins slipped past Franco Morbidelli for his inherited third.

The first four positions were settled: Rins got clear of the Italian, but while he pushed hard to close to within less than 1.5 seconds of Folger before half-distance, thereafter the gap began to stretch again, to more than five seconds at the flag.

Morbidelli gradually fell out of touch, and by around lap 20 he was coming under pressure from Baldassarri. This intensified until the last lap, when his attacker slipped off, remounting to finish out of the points.

A strong start put Oliveira through to sixth; but by half-distance a high-class gang was closing the gap.

This was led by Luthi from compatriot Aegerter, with Zarco, Nakagami and, for a time, Salom close behind.

Oliveira resisted, but finally Luthi's pressure proved too much, and he fell. Zarco consigned Luthi to seventh, and then all were promoted one place by Baldassarri's fall – a potentially important piece of damage limitation for the defender in his quest to become the first back-to-back (indeed the first double) champion in the class.

Luthi had his hands full fending off a resurgent Nakagami on the last lap, with Aegerter out of touch in eighth, and Salom likewise in ninth.

Simeon had a lonely ride to tenth on the top Speed Up; Syahrin managed to regain control of a close trio to take 11th, ahead of Pasini and Vinales. Swiss pair Raffin and Mulhauser took the final points – and career bests in both cases.

Kent was another among several to crash, as was Rossi's half-brother, Luca Marini, who remounted to finish 16th.

MOTO3 RACE – 23 laps

Binder's last-to-first made Moto3 history; rookie Bulega added a footnote, qualifying on pole and seizing a fighting second over the line.

The former's back-row start (he had qualified second) was applied at the last minute, for a technical infringement by his Red Bull Ajo team (using unhomologated software). He battled through the backmarkers, setting fastest lap on the fourth, then surged through a big midfield battle. Before ten laps were done, he was at the front of the gang, in fourth.

Four seconds ahead, Bulega, Bagnaia and Navarro were locked in combat, Navarro making most of the running.

The hunt-down was compelling and remorseless. It took Binder just seven more laps to catch the trio. Four more, and he was in front, and pulling steadily way for a truly memorable career first win.

"I knew I could still do it, even if I started last," he said. "I'd worked hard on used tyres, and I had a good rhythm … though I knew the first few laps'd be hard."

The three-way brawl behind went to the flag, changing constantly. They all piled into the final hairpin almost abreast. Rookie Bulega was toughest and on the inside; Navarro was pushed wide, and Bagnaia slipped into the last podium slot. Second to fourth was covered by less than two-tenths.

Another ten seconds down, a huge brawl was gradually whittled down, with Kornfeil seizing fifth ahead of Mir, Fenati, Bastianini, Danilo, Oettl and Migno, all within 1.1 seconds.

Guevara and Rodrigo had dropped away in 12th and 13th, the last points going to Argentine winner Pawi and Suzuki.

Antonelli and Quartararo were among several crashers, the former after starting from the pit lane, having stalled on the grid.

GRAN PREMIO
RED BULL
DE ESPAÑA

RedBull

22-24 APRIL, 2016

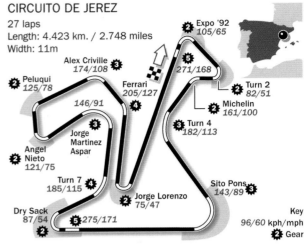

CIRCUITO DE JEREZ
27 laps
Length: 4.423 km. / 2.748 miles
Width: 11m

Expo '92 105/65
Alex Criville 174/108
271/168
Peluqui 125/78
Ferrari 205/127
Turn 2 82/51
146/91
Michelin 161/100
Jorge Martinez Aspar
Turn 4 182/113
Angel Nieto 121/75
Sito Pons 143/89
Turn 7 185/115
Jorge Lorenzo 75/47
Dry Sack 87/54
275/171
Key 96/60 kph/mph
Gear

MotoGP

RACE DISTANCE: 27 laps, 74.205 miles/119.421km · RACE WEATHER: Dry (air 25°C, humidity 37%, track 40°C)

Pos.	Rider	Nat.	No.	Entrant	Machine	Tyres	Race tyre choice	Laps	Time & speed
1	**Valentino Rossi**	ITA	46	Movistar Yamaha MotoGP	Yamaha YZR-M1	M	F: Hard/R: Medium	27	45m 28.834s 97.9mph/ 157.5km/h
2	**Jorge Lorenzo**	SPA	99	Movistar Yamaha MotoGP	Yamaha YZR-M1	M	F: Hard/R: Medium	27	45m 31.220s
3	**Marc Marquez**	SPA	93	Repsol Honda Team	Honda RC213V	M	F: Hard/R: Medium	27	45m 35.921s
4	**Dani Pedrosa**	SPA	26	Repsol Honda Team	Honda RC213V	M	F: Hard/R: Medium	27	45m 39.185s
5	**Aleix Espargaro**	SPA	41	Team SUZUKI ECSTAR	Suzuki GSX-RR	M	F: Hard/R: Medium	27	45m 42.977s
6	**Maverick Vinales**	SPA	25	Team SUZUKI ECSTAR	Suzuki GSX-RR	M	F: Medium/R: Medium	27	45m 45.606s
7	**Andrea Iannone**	ITA	29	Ducati Team	Ducati Desmosedici	M	F: Hard/R: Medium	27	45m 55.111s
8	**Pol Espargaro**	SPA	44	Monster Yamaha Tech 3	Yamaha YZR-M1	M	F: Soft/R: Soft	27	45m 59.584s
9	**Eugene Laverty**	IRL	50	Aspar Team MotoGP	Ducati Desmosedici	M	F: Soft/R: Medium	27	46m 01.159s
10	**Hector Barbera**	SPA	8	Avintia Racing	Ducati Desmosedici	M	F: Soft/R: Soft	27	46m 01.458s
11	**Cal Crutchlow**	GBR	35	LCR Honda	Honda RC213V	M	F: Hard/R: Medium	27	46m 07.331s
12	**Bradley Smith**	GBR	38	Monster Yamaha Tech 3	Yamaha YZR-M1	M	F: Medium/R: Soft	27	46m 08.503s
13	**Loris Baz**	FRA	76	Avintia Racing	Ducati Desmosedici	M	F: Soft/R: Medium	27	46m 14.061s
14	**Stefan Bradl**	GER	6	Aprilia Racing Team Gresini	Aprilia RS-GP	M	F: Hard/R: Medium	27	46m 16.720s
15	**Yonny Hernandez**	COL	68	Aspar Team MotoGP	Ducati Desmosedici	M	F: Hard/R: Medium	27	46m 16.822s
16	Michele Pirro	ITA	51	OCTO Pramac Yakhnich	Ducati Desmosedici	M	F: Soft/R: Medium	27	46m 18.248s
17	Jack Miller	AUS	43	Estrella Galicia 0,0 Marc VDS	Honda RC213V	M	F: Hard/R: Medium	27	46m 18.347s
18	Tito Rabat	SPA	53	Estrella Galicia 0,0 Marc VDS	Honda RC213V	M	F: Medium/R: Medium	27	46m 22.168s
19	Scott Redding	GBR	45	OCTO Pramac Yakhnich	Ducati Desmosedici	M	F: Medium/R: Soft	27	46m 34.389s
	Andrea Dovizioso	ITA	4	Ducati Team	Ducati Desmosedici	M	F: Soft/R: Medium	9	DNF-technical
	Alvaro Bautista	SPA	19	Aprilia Racing Team Gresini	Aprilia RS-GP	M	F: Medium/R: Medium	5	DNF-crash

Fastest lap: Valentino Rossi, on lap 3, 1m 40.090s, 98.8mph/159.0km/h.

Lap record: Jorge Lorenzo, SPA (Yamaha), 1m 38.735s, 100.2mph/161.2km/h (2015).

Event best maximum speed: Andrea Iannone, 183.7mph/295.7km/h (free practice).

Qualifying

Weather: Dry
Air Temp: 24° **Humidity:** 29%
Track Temp: 47°

1	Rossi	1m 38.736s
2	Lorenzo	1m 38.858s
3	Marquez	1m 38.891s
4	Dovizioso	1m 39.580s
5	Vinales	1m 39.581s
6	A. Espargaro	1m 39.588s
7	Pedrosa	1m 39.678s
8	P. Espargaro	1m 39.720s
9	Barbera	1m 39.742s
10	Crutchlow	1m 39.881s
11	Iannone	1m 40.054s
12	Baz	1m 40.184s
13	Bautista	1m 40.239s
14	Smith	1m 40.242s
15	Laverty	1m 40.292s
16	Hernandez	1m 40.335s
17	Redding	1m 40.595s
18	Bradl	1m 40.835s
19	Miller	1m 40.968s
20	Pirro	1m 40.985s
21	Rabat	1m 41.039s

Fastest race laps

1	Rossi	1m 40.090s
2	Marquez	1m 40.317s
3	Lorenzo	1m 40.317s
4	Pedrosa	1m 40.688s
5	A. Espargaro	1m 40.704s
6	Vinales	1m 40.996s
7	Dovizioso	1m 41.025s
8	Iannone	1m 41.079s
9	Laverty	1m 41.162s
10	Crutchlow	1m 41.348s
11	Barbera	1m 41.355s
12	P. Espargaro	1m 41.395s
13	Hernandez	1m 41.646s
14	Bautista	1m 41.648s
15	Smith	1m 41.676s
16	Baz	1m 41.789s
17	Bradl	1m 41.796s
18	Pirro	1m 42.107s
19	Redding	1m 42.187s
20	Rabat	1m 42.231s
21	Miller	1m 42.234s

Championship Points

1	Marquez	82
2	Lorenzo	65
3	Rossi	58
4	Pedrosa	40
5	P. Espargaro	36
6	Vinales	33
7	A. Espargaro	32
8	Barbera	31
9	Laverty	28
10	Iannone	25
11	Dovizioso	23
12	Smith	20
13	Bradl	17
14	Redding	16
15	Bautista	14
16	Pirro	12
17	Rabat	11
18	Crutchlow	5
19	Baz	4
20	Hernandez	3
21	Miller	2

Constructor Points

1	Yamaha	90
2	Honda	82
3	Ducati	58
4	Suzuki	39
5	Aprilia	20

Grid order	1	2	3	4	5	6	7	8	9	10	11	12	13	14	15	16	17	18	19	20	21	22	23	24	25	26	27	
46 ROSSI	46	46	46	46	46	46	46	46	46	46	46	46	46	46	46	46	46	46	46	46	46	46	46	46	46	46	46	1
99 LORENZO	99	99	99	99	99	99	99	99	99	99	99	99	99	99	99	99	99	99	99	99	99	99	99	99	99	99	99	2
93 MARQUEZ	26	93	93	93	93	93	93	93	93	93	93	93	93	93	93	93	93	93	93	93	93	93	93	93	93	93	93	3
4 DOVIZIOSO	93	26	26	26	26	26	26	26	26	26	26	26	26	26	26	26	26	26	26	26	26	26	26	26	26	26	26	4
25 VINALES	41	41	41	41	41	41	41	41	41	41	41	41	41	41	41	41	41	41	41	41	41	41	41	41	41	41	41	5
41 A. ESPARGARO	4	4	4	4	4	25	25	25	25	25	25	25	25	25	25	25	25	25	25	25	25	25	25	25	25	25	25	6
26 PEDROSA	25	25	25	25	25	4	4	4	4	50	50	44	44	44	44	44	44	44	44	44	29	29	29	29	29	29	29	7
44 P. ESPARGARO	44	50	50	50	50	50	50	50	50	44	44	50	50	50	50	50	29	29	29	29	44	44	44	44	44	44		8
8 BARBERA	50	44	44	44	44	44	44	44	44	8	8	8	8	8	8	29	50	50	50	50	50	50	50	50	50	50		9
35 CRUTCHLOW	8	8	8	8	8	8	8	8	8	35	35	35	35	29	29	8	8	8	8	8	8	8	8	8	8	8		10
29 IANNONE	35	19	19	35	35	35	35	35	35	29	29	29	29	35	35	35	35	35	35	35	35	35	35	35	35	35		11
76 BAZ	19	35	35	19	19	6	29	29	29	38	38	38	38	38	38	38	38	38	38	38	38	38	38	38	38	38		12
19 BAUTISTA	6	6	6	6	6	29	38	38	38	68	68	68	76	76	76	76	76	76	76	76	76	76	76	76	76	76		13
38 SMITH	29	29	29	29	29	38	6	6	68	6	6	6	68	68	68	68	68	68	68	68	68	68	6	6	6	6		14
50 LAVERTY	38	68	68	38	38	68	68	68	6	76	76	76	6	6	6	6	6	6	6	6	6	6	68	68	68	68		15
68 HERNANDEZ	68	38	38	68	68	51	51	76	76	51	51	51	51	51	51	51	51	51	51	51	51	51	51	51	51	51		
45 REDDING	51	51	51	51	51	76	76	51	45	45	45	45	45	43	43	43	43	43	43	43	43	43	43	43	43	43		
6 BRADL	45	45	45	45	76	45	45	45	51	43	43	43	43	45	45	45	45	45	45	45	45	45	45	45	45	45		
43 MILLER	43	43	76	76	45	43	43	43	53	53	53	53	53	53	53	53	53	53	53	53	53	53	53	53	53	53		
51 PIRRO	53	76	43	43	43	53	53	53	53																			
53 RABAT	76	53	53	53	53																							

4 Pit stop

Moto2

RACE DISTANCE: 26 laps, 71.456 miles/114.998km · **RACE WEATHER:** Dry (air 22°C, humidity 65%, track 33°C)

Pos.	Rider	Nat.	No.	Entrant	Machine	Laps	Time & Speed
1	**Sam Lowes**	GBR	22	Federal Oil Gresini Moto2	Kalex	26	44m 58.624s
							95.3mph/
							153.4km/h
2	**Jonas Folger**	GER	94	Dynavolt Intact GP	Kalex	26	45m 01.104s
3	**Alex Rins**	SPA	40	Paginas Amarillas HP 40	Kalex	26	45m 06.737s
4	**Franco Morbidelli**	ITA	21	Estrella Galicia 0,0 Marc VDS	Kalex	26	45m 09.283s
5	**Johann Zarco**	FRA	5	Ajo Motorsport	Kalex	26	45m 13.218s
6	**Thomas Luthi**	SWI	12	Garage Plus Interwetten	Kalex	26	45m 14.643s
7	**Takaaki Nakagami**	JPN	30	IDEMITSU Honda Team Asia	Kalex	26	45m 14.976s
8	**Dominique Aegerter**	SWI	77	CarXpert Interwetten	Kalex	26	45m 17.057s
9	**Luis Salom**	SPA	39	SAG Team	Kalex	26	45m 20.126s
10	**Xavier Simeon**	BEL	19	QMMF Racing Team	Speed Up	26	45m 29.924s
11	**Hafizh Syahrin**	MAL	55	Petronas Raceline Malaysia	Kalex	26	45m 34.604s
12	**Mattia Pasini**	ITA	54	Italtrans Racing Team	Kalex	26	45m 35.972s
13	**Isaac Vinales**	SPA	32	Tech 3 Racing	Tech 3	26	45m 36.078s
14	**Jesko Raffin**	SWI	2	Sports-Millions-EMWE-SAG	Kalex	26	45m 47.547s
15	**Robin Mulhauser**	SWI	70	CarXpert Interwetten	Kalex	26	45m 54.456s
16	Luca Marini	ITA	10	Forward Team	Kalex	26	46m 00.419s
17	Lorenzo Baldassarri	ITA	7	Forward Team	Kalex	26	46m 08.089s
18	Federico Fuligni	ITA	42	Team Ciatti	Kalex	26	46m 08.825s
19	Alessandro Tonucci	ITA	33	Tasca Racing Scuderia Moto2	Kalex	26	46m 09.266s
	Miguel Oliveira	POR	44	Leopard Racing	Kalex	20	DNF
	Marcel Schrotter	GER	23	AGR Team	Kalex	11	DNF
	Danny Kent	GBR	52	Leopard Racing	Kalex	5	DNF
	Axel Pons	SPA	49	AGR Team	Kalex	5	DNF
	Sandro Cortese	GER	11	Dynavolt Intact GP	Kalex	4	DNF
	Alex Marquez	SPA	73	Estrella Galicia 0,0 Marc VDS	Kalex	2	DNF
	Simone Corsi	ITA	24	Speed Up Racing	Speed Up	1	DNF
	Ratthapark Wilairot	THA	14	IDEMITSU Honda Team Asia	Kalex	0	DNF
	Xavi Vierge	SPA	97	Tech 3 Racing	Tech 3	0	DNF

Fastest lap: Alex Rins, on lap 3, 1m 42.979s, 96.1mph/154.6km/h.

Lap record: Jonas Folger, GER (Kalex), 1m 42.876s, 96.1mph/154.7km/h (2014).

Event best maximum speed: Takaaki Nakagami, 156.8mph/252.4km/h (race).

Qualifying

Weather: Dry
Air: 24° **Track:** 29°
Humidity: 54%

1	Lowes	1m 42.408s
2	Folger	1m 42.436s
3	Cortese	1m 42.439s
4	Morbidelli	1m 42.480s
5	Luthi	1m 42.535s
6	Baldassarri	1m 42.571s
7	Rins	1m 42.628s
8	Corsi	1m 42.653s
9	Marquez	1m 42.664s
10	Salom	1m 42.772s
11	Marini	1m 42.884s
12	Nakagami	1m 42.906s
13	Schrotter	1m 43.070s
14	Oliveira	1m 43.083s
15	Kent	1m 43.169s
16	Zarco	1m 43.171s
17	Pons	1m 43.207s
18	Aegerter	1m 43.235s
19	Simeon	1m 43.256s
20	Simon	1m 43.342s
21	Wilairot	1m 43.543s
22	Vierge	1m 43.621s
23	Pons	1m 43.770s
24	Syahrin	1m 43.897s
25	Vinales	1m 43.960s
26	Raffin	1m 44.062s
27	Pasini	1m 44.295s
28	Tonucci	1m 44.473s
29	Mulhauser	1m 44.497s
30	Fuligni	1m 44.666s

Fastest race laps

1	Rins	1m 42.979s
2	Folger	1m 43.143s
3	Lowes	1m 43.157s
4	Morbidelli	1m 43.242s
5	Oliveira	1m 43.269s
6	Schrotter	1m 43.399s
7	Baldassarri	1m 43.422s
8	Luthi	1m 43.452s
9	Marquez	1m 43.525s
10	Zarco	1m 43.526s
11	Cortese	1m 43.547s
12	Aegerter	1m 43.592s
13	Salom	1m 43.637s
14	Nakagami	1m 43.661s
15	Marini	1m 43.670s
16	Simeon	1m 43.676s
17	Pons	1m 43.885s
18	Kent	1m 44.074s
19	Mulhauser	1m 44.336s
20	Vinales	1m 44.374s
21	Syahrin	1m 44.523s
22	Raffin	1m 44.542s
23	Pasini	1m 44.596s
24	Tonucci	1m 44.925s
25	Fuligni	1m 45.531s

Championship Points

1	Lowes	72
2	Rins	62
3	Zarco	56
4	Luthi	53
5	Folger	47
6	Aegerter	43
7	Salom	31
8	Syahrin	28
9	Corsi	26
10	Morbidelli	24
11	Nakagami	19
12	Simeon	18
13	Schrotter	11
14	Kent	10
15	Pasini	10
16	Pons	8
17	Simon	7
18	Marini	6
19	Oliveira	5
20	Marquez	5
21	Cortese	5
22	Wilairot	3
23	Baldassarri	3
24	Vinales	3
25	Vierge	2
26	Raffin	2
27	Mulhauser	1

Constructor Points

1	Kalex	100
2	Speed Up	36
3	Tech 3	5

Moto3

RACE DISTANCE: 23 laps, 63.211 miles/101.729km · **RACE WEATHER:** Dry (air 18°C, humidity 86%, track 25°C)

Pos.	Rider	Nat.	No.	Entrant	Machine	Laps	Time & Speed
1	**Brad Binder**	RSA	41	Red Bull KTM Ajo	KTM	23	41m 29.882s
							91.3mph/
							147.0km/h
2	**Nicolo Bulega**	ITA	8	SKY Racing Team VR46	KTM	23	41m 33.218s
3	**Francesco Bagnaia**	ITA	21	ASPAR Mahindra Team Moto3	Mahindra	23	41m 33.323s
4	**Jorge Navarro**	SPA	9	Estrella Galicia 0,0	Honda	23	41m 33.395s
5	**Jakub Kornfeil**	CZE	84	Drive M7 SIC Racing Team	Honda	23	41m 43.610s
6	**Joan Mir**	SPA	36	Leopard Racing	KTM	23	41m 43.815s
7	**Romano Fenati**	ITA	5	SKY Racing Team VR46	KTM	23	41m 43.875s
8	**Enea Bastianini**	ITA	33	Gresini Racing Moto3	Honda	23	41m 43.934s
9	**Jules Danilo**	FRA	95	Ongetta-Rivacold	Honda	23	41m 44.291s
10	**Philipp Oettl**	GER	65	Schedl GP Racing	KTM	23	41m 44.470s
11	**Andrea Migno**	ITA	16	SKY Racing Team VR46	KTM	23	41m 44.756s
12	**Juanfran Guevara**	SPA	58	RBA Racing Team	KTM	23	42m 00.199s
13	**Gabriel Rodrigo**	ARG	19	RBA Racing Team	KTM	23	42m 00.550s
14	**Khairul Idham Pawi**	MAL	89	Honda Team Asia	Honda	23	42m 05.628s
15	**Tatsuki Suzuki**	JPN	24	CIP-Unicom Starker	Mahindra	23	42m 05.665s
16	Adam Norrodin	MAL	7	Drive M7 SIC Racing Team	Honda	23	42m 05.789s
17	Livio Loi	BEL	11	RW Racing GP BV	Honda	23	42m 05.967s
18	Albert Arenas	SPA	12	MRW Mahindra Aspar Team	Mahindra	23	42m 06.189s
19	Maria Herrera	SPA	6	MH6 Laglisse	KTM	23	42m 15.473s
20	Davide Pizzoli	ITA	37	Procercasa - 42 Motorsport	KTM	23	42m 20.650s
21	Bo Bendsneyder	NED	64	Red Bull KTM Ajo	KTM	23	42m 23.677s
22	Enzo Boulom	FRA	99	Procercasa - 42 Motorsport	KTM	23	42m 23.867s
23	Fabio Spiranelli	ITA	3	CIP-Unicom Starker	Mahindra	23	42m 51.908s
	Fabio di Giannantonio	ITA	4	Gresini Racing Moto3	Honda	22	DNF
	Darryn Binder	RSA	40	Platinum Bay Real Estate	Mahindra	16	DNF
	Alexis Masbou	FRA	10	Peugeot MC Saxoprint	Peugeot	16	DNF
	Niccolo Antonelli	ITA	23	Ongetta-Rivacold	Honda	11	DNF
	John McPhee	GBR	17	Peugeot MC Saxoprint	Peugeot	8	DNF
	Fabio Quartararo	FRA	20	Leopard Racing	KTM	6	DNF
	Aron Canet	SPA	44	Estrella Galicia 0,0	Honda	5	DNF
	Karel Hanika	CZE	98	Platinum Bay Real Estate	Mahindra	2	DNF
	Hiroki Ono	JPN	76	Honda Team Asia	Honda	2	DNF
	Andrea Locatelli	ITA	55	Leopard Racing	KTM	2	DNF
	Lorenzo Petrarca	ITA	77	3570 Team Italia	Mahindra	2	DNF
	Jorge Martin	SPA	88	ASPAR Mahindra Team Moto3	Mahindra	0	DNF

Fastest lap: Brad Binder, on lap 4, 1m 46.922s, 92.5mph/148.9km/h.

Lap record: Brad Binder, RSA (KTM), 1m 46.723s, 92.6mph/149.1km/h (2015).

Event best maximum speed: Maria Herrera, 135.4mph/217.9km/h (race).

Qualifying:

Weather: Dry
Air: 21° **Track:** 24°
Humidity: 51%

1	Bulega	1m 46.223s
2	Navarro	1m 46.678s
3	Bagnaia	1m 46.680s
4	Antonelli	1m 46.705s
5	Bastianini	1m 46.827s
6	Mir	1m 46.962s
7	Guevara	1m 46.967s
8	Fenati	1m 47.072s
9	Kornfeil	1m 47.131s
10	Canet	1m 47.154s
11	Quartararo	1m 47.271s
12	Oettl	1m 47.276s
13	Martin	1m 47.281s
14	Danilo	1m 47.325s
15	Arenas	1m 47.361s
16	Migno	1m 47.397s
17	Bendsneyder	1m 47.528s
18	Ono	1m 47.580s
19	Loi	1m 47.618s
20	Suzuki	1m 47.654s
21	Di Giannantonio	1m 47.734s
22	Rodrigo	1m 47.736s
23	Pawi	1m 47.740s
24	McPhee	1m 47.746s
25	Hanika	1m 47.830s
26	Locatelli	1m 47.978s
27	Norrodin	1m 48.025s
28	Pizzoli	1m 48.090s
29	Masbou	1m 48.431s
30	D. Binder	1m 48.499s
31	Petrarca	1m 48.595s
32	Herrera	1m 49.245s
33	Spiranelli	1m 49.580s
34	Boulom	1m 49.821s
	Valtulini	No Time
	B. Binder	DSQ

Fastest race laps

1	B. Binder	1m 46.922s
2	Bulega	1m 47.185s
3	Bagnaia	1m 47.258s
4	Navarro	1m 47.29s
5	Rodrigo	1m 47.461s
6	Oettl	1m 47.521s
7	Mir	1m 47.539s
8	Canet	1m 47.673s
9	Kornfeil	1m 47.678s
10	Guevara	1m 47.731s
11	Fenati	1m 47.754s
12	Migno	1m 47.794s
13	Antonelli	1m 47.805s
14	Danilo	1m 47.808s
15	Bastianini	1m 47.809s
16	Arenas	1m 48.039s
17	D. Binder	1m 48.169s
18	Pawi	1m 48.198s
19	Norrodin	1m 48.321s
20	Suzuki	1m 48.362s
21	Di Giannantonio	1m 48.399s
22	Masbou	1m 48.447s
23	McPhee	1m 48.454s
24	Locatelli	1m 48.506s
25	Hanika	1m 48.511s
26	Bendsneyder	1m 48.527s
27	Loi	1m 48.528s
28	Ono	1m 48.563s
29	Herrera	1m 48.573s
30	Quartararo	1m 48.797s
31	Pizzoli	1m 48.997s
32	Boulom	1m 49.617s
33	Spiranelli	1m 49.721s
34	Petrarca	1m 49.903s

Championship Points

1	B. Binder	77
2	Navarro	62
3	Fenati	47
4	Bulega	36
5	Bagnaia	34
6	Antonelli	31
7	Bastianini	29
8	Kornfeil	29
9	Pawi	27
10	Oettl	27
11	Mir	25
12	Locatelli	24
13	Danilo	19
14	Loi	16
15	Guevara	12
16	Ono	10
17	Canet	10
18	McPhee	9
19	Quartararo	9
20	Martin	8
21	Migno	6
22	Norrodin	5
23	Rodrigo	3
24	Herrera	2
25	Bendsneyder	2
26	Suzuki	1

Constructor Points

1	KTM	86
2	Honda	83
3	Mahindra	42
4	Peugeot	9

Main: By the first chicane, Lorenzo was already turning left while the rest were still turning right. He would keep stretching away.
Photo: Gold & Goose

Inset, left: Lorenzo was top dog once more, beating team-mate Rossi by more than ten seconds.
Photo: Movistar Yamaha

FIM WORLD CHAMPIONSHIP · ROUND 5

FRENCH GRAND PRIX

LE MANS CIRCUIT

Above row (from left): **Fly me to the ground – sundry winglets: Repsol Honda, Aprilia, Ducati and two Yamaha variations.**

Top: **Podium-bound Vinales gave a welcome boost to Suzuki.**

Top right: **Home-fan hopes crashed along with Johann Zarco.**

Above centre right: **Results notwithstanding, these were happy times for Count van der Straten and VDS team chief Michael Bartholemy.**

Right: **Leathers scuffed, Iannone runs down the pit lane after a puzzling qualifying crash.**

Photos: Gold & Goose

THE French GP came at the climax of a long weekend of beautiful weather – rather unexpected at a frequently rainy venue. Oddly though, it made little difference to the frequently high crash rate. The teeth were pulled from a potentially exciting MotoGP race by no fewer than eight crashes; while the partisan crowd was left disappointed when home hero Johann Zarco tumbled out of the Moto2 race.

What was the cause?

It was also French. In the seesaw progress of Michelin's return to top-level racing, the previous race's rear grip problems had been promptly addressed with a new rear construction. Now the fronts were letting go. Victims came from all ranks of rider, the most picturesque being a tandem formation crash by Dovizioso and Marquez at the Museum left-hander. At first, it looked as though there might have been a touch, but in fact they fell in identical ways quite independently, the rearmost Marquez first. Only one of them, Marquez, was able to remount.

That left the way clear for a second successive Yamaha one-two, although in reverse order. Ominously for his rivals, Lorenzo was able to turn in yet another trademark pole-to-chequer run, threatening what had been a championship full of the promise of variety. For him, though, it was a fresh start. With Marquez managing to salvage but three points, it meant that all of the top three had now effectively dropped one race, leaving them more or less equal for a fresh start, "but with me five points ahead".

The crashes reflected the downside of Michelin's catch-up after seven years away. The company again earned kudos for their quick response to the straight-line wheelspin of Jerez and pleased the rear-tyre doubters with yet another revision, amending an earlier plan to stay with the harder rear for the full season. This latest was a step back towards the tyre that had been used earlier, but rejected after Argentina – a sort of halfway house, with the compound unchanged, but the construction a stage softer. This threw the focus on the front, and it was found wanting, with a spate of low-side corner-entry crashes.

Wing development continued. Marquez went tri-plane on the fairing flanks, and Ducati with yet another variation of their top wings: an air-fence halfway along and another smaller angled outer winglet, also fenced. The only bikes without some sort of aerodyne were the four lowlier GP14.2 satellite Ducatis of Laverty, Baz, Barbera and Hernandez, and the junior satellite Hondas of Miller and Rabat.

The criticism also carried on, with Pedrosa (continuing to use only a tiny triangular pair either side of the nose) articulate on the issue of safety. "The rider is very exposed. In the Safety Commission, we are making improvements to the kerbs, to the grass, to the run-off, the air-fence ... Then we put these kinds of knives on the bike," he said. Marquez

had another angle, saying that the wings made overtaking more difficult, "a bit like Formula 1. When you are in the slipstream, you don't have the downforce, so you wheelie more, and it is hard to pass," he explained.

Pramac Ducati rider Danilo Petrucci made a strong return to Le Mans, his injured right hand still bandaged and undergoing frequent medical checks to ensure the stresses of riding were not causing further trouble. Nothing daunted, he managed to get through to Q2, qualified tenth, with identically mounted team-mate Scott Redding 14th, then outraced Barbera for seventh. Impressive.

The usual flurry of rumours was led by one so unexpected that only the most gullible or most sensation-hungry lent it any real weight: that Dani Pedrosa was to switch from his 16-year career-long alliance with Honda – 11 of those years in the factory MotoGP team – to take Lorenzo's place at Yamaha. There was clearly some foundation, with two possible explanations, both of which were to do with bargaining power. On the one hand, it might have come from within Yamaha, intended to put pressure on Vinales to make up his mind. Or it might have come from Pedrosa's camp, to put pressure on Honda. A third possibility was a spark from somebody's imagination, that caught hold in the oxygen-rich atmosphere. Soon afterwards, it would turn out to be so much hooey.

There was one firm announcement: that Jonas Folger had signed to join the Monster Tech 3 satellite Yamaha team. "It is every rider's dream," the German confirmed, as his own bright, but erratic Moto2 form continued.

And one confirmed rumour: that Johann Zarco was to test the Suzuki MotoGP bike in the summer break in Japan, and that he was to race for Suzuki in the forthcoming Suzuka 8 Hours. This was the start of a fresh line of uncertainty.

Meanwhile, hopes that the MotoGP grid would grow from 23 to 24 riders in 2017 were put on hold, because of a shortage of machinery. Dorna had invited applications for one more rider, and although five teams had shown interest, and three of those had been adjudged possible candidates, it all went wrong when simultaneous discussions with the manufacturers showed "a reluctance ... to commit to making additional equipment available, at least for 2017." As a result, it had been "reluctantly decided to postpone a decision to a later season."

There was a feeling of familiarity when Iannone took a tumble on an out-lap during qualifying, but this time his air of surprise was unfeigned. He had been riding slowly, he explained, when a red warning light came on. "I knew it was to do with the water, but I don't know what exactly," he said. The next thing, he was down – sprinting from the last corner back to the pits for his other bike, but too puffed to be able to improve on his lap time. He was already on the front row, third fastest, so that didn't actually matter. A similar leakage on to the back tyre had spoiled team-mate Dovizioso's race at Jerez two weeks before.

MOTOGP RACE – 28 laps

Lorenzo claimed an imperious pole by better than four-tenths; the remaining 11 in Q2 were all within seven-tenths. It was ominous for his rivals. Marquez and Iannone were alongside up front; Pol Espargaro, Dovizioso and Smith on row two, while Rossi headed the third.

The leading Movistar Yamaha rider continued in copybook fashion – a perfect start, a handy gap even before they'd reached the Dunlop bridge. From there, he sailed away serenely for his second win, by better than ten seconds, and a return to the championship lead that he'd lost when he crashed in the second race.

"Everything was almost perfect in the race," he said. "Now in the championship, three riders scored zero or almost zero in one race, so in some way we are starting the championship again ... but with us five points ahead."

The "almost zero" was Marquez, one of eight to crash, and the only one to remount and save three potentially valuable

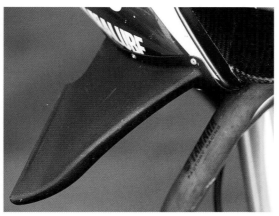

Above: Marquez pilots what's left of his Honda, to last place – but still in the points.

Top right: It was a long-delayed podium return for Moto2 charger Simone Corsi.

Above right: AMA rider Danny Eslick substituted for the injured Vazquez in Moto2.

Above far right: Moto2 winner Rins leads Corsi, Baldassari and the rest.

Right: Binder's second win rewarded perfect tactics, as he held off Fenati (hidden) and team-mates, Canet and Navarro.

Below right: Teenage rookie Aron Canet qualified on the front row, and fought for the win.

Photos: Gold & Goose

points, on a day when steady riding paid dividends. Rossi, however, had to fight from his third-row start through some fierce early laps that preceded a processional finish. Vinales claimed his first podium and also Suzuki's first since their return to MotoGP.

At first, Lorenzo was pursued by the Ducatis, Dovizioso in front, with Pol Espargaro fourth, ahead of older brother Aleix. Rossi was seventh away and up to fifth by lap three; he set fastest lap next time around, almost half a second down on his own record from 2015.

Lorenzo's lead had stretched to a second by the time Iannone had pushed past Dovi, Marquez clearly struggling to stay in touch at a track that emphasised the Honda's weakest point – acceleration.

Iannone lasted just one more lap before he was the first to prove how easy it was to lose the front.

Dovi was still losing ground, Marquez closing, likewise Rossi. He had got ahead of both when they performed their synchronised crash at the second looping U-turn, the left-hander Museum. Metres apart, Marquez in the rear went down a split second before Dovi.

The Ducati rider was mystified, with an increasingly common theme: where the previous Bridgestones had given some warning, and even a good chance of recovering a front slide, the Michelins just folded.

Marquez's explanation was straightforward: "These things can happen when you're at the limit on every lap. I could have been more conservative, but here you can end up far back if you do that. I had to take risks with braking."

By now, Vinales had passed his team-mate and was a lone third, which he would sustain to the finish.

Aleix, in turn, had got clear of brother Pol, while behind him fast-starting team-mate Smith had his hands full with a gradually improving Pedrosa, who was gaining pace and comfort as the fuel burned off. The Repsol Honda rider was ahead of both when Smith fell at the same Museum corner, another to complain of no warning.

By lap 17, Pedrosa had also passed the second Suzuki, but he would finish a disappointedly distant fourth. Nonetheless, he was the top Honda rider at a track where the troublesome new reverse-crank RC213V was at its worst.

Six seconds behind, Pol had got back ahead of his rapidly fading brother for fifth; but there was a big gap behind, so sixth was safe for the Suzuki.

Still five seconds away at the finish, Petrucci finally prevailed over Barbera's older Ducati by two-tenths after a race-long battle.

A long way back, Bautista claimed another top ten, with team-mate Bradl six seconds away in tenth. Eugene Laverty faded to 11th, but was comfortably clear of a very slow Baz in a disappointing home GP. Marquez was a lap down and last, but given the high rate of attrition, he finished 13th.

The crash list was long and implacable, claiming beginners and old hands alike. Among the former group was Miller, who had moved up to 12th from 18th on the grid. Rookie team-mate Tito Rabat also slid off, his first non-finish of the year. And Hernandez, plus the increasingly dismayed Crutchlow, who had gone down at four out of five races so far. Redding stayed upright, but also stopped, for a second time in the season, with a mechanical failure. Warning lights preceded a loss of power for his GP15 Ducati, and once again he needed a lift back to the pits.

MOTO2 RACE – 26 laps

Luthi was on pole, from Rins and rising star Baldassari, but the Italian teenager was penalised after his tyre pressures were found to be below the minimum. That put him back to row three. His place went to veteran compatriot Corsi, continuing his revival after switching to the Speed Up. Zarco now led row two from Morbidelli and Nakagami.

Luthi made a flying start, from Morbidelli and Rins. Folger, starting from row three, crashed out on lap one.

Rins was directly up to second, and on lap seven he pounced on Luthi to take a lead he would never relinquish – a second win that put him at the head of the championship.

Not without pressure, however: "I pushed hard to pass Luthi, because I knew he was fast, but when I was there I got a signal that there were four riders behind me, so I had to keep pushing."

They were the two mentioned, plus Corsi and Baldassarri.

By lap ten, Morbidelli was out of touch, but the front four were still close, Baldassari now past Luthi. The pair were soon battling over third, which allowed Rins and Corsi to get away up front.

It was an austere run from there to the end, Rins only gaining some clear air with four laps to go, to take his second win of the season by 1.8 seconds.

mate Kent, who could manage no better than 19th. Salom completed the top ten, but only narrowly, for Simeon had come charging up in the later laps on the Speed Up to a couple of tenths behind.

Still close, Rossi's half-brother Marini scored points for a second time in 12th, ahead of Aegerter and Schrotter, who had dropped to the back of the gang. The last point went to Xavi Vierge's French-built Tech 3.

American first-timer Danny Eslick, substituting for the injured Efren Vazquez, found it tough in the deep end, finishing last, but still (just) on the same lap as the leader.

MOTO3 RACE – 24 laps

A thriller, as usual, and a second straight win for Binder, achieved with strong speed and perfect last-lap tactics.

The South African had seized the lead on the first lap from pole qualifier Antonelli, and the usual early brawl continued until after half-distance, when four broke away up front – Binder plus Fenati and the Honda pairing of Navarro and rookie team-mate Aron Canet.

Fenati led most often over the line, but Binder was waiting: "I tried to pull away, but I saw today it wouldn't be possible … but I knew if I pushed really hard on the last lap, I could brake a little later and close the lines well enough not to give anyone a chance."

Exactly how it played out, Binder leading the last two laps and a frustrated Fenati finishing 0.099 second adrift.

Canet demonstrated no team orders as he got ahead of Navarro several times. Then he made a desperate lunge into the last pair of corners, only to run wide, which also spoiled any of his team-mate's last hopes of better than third.

The quartet behind had grown to six again by the end, with another rookie, Nicolo Bulega, pipping Quartararo (Leopard KTM), from Migno, Antonelli, Kornfeil and Locatelli. Kornfeil had been with the leaders, before taking to the escape road at high speed.

Loi, in 11th, had escaped from a battle involving Bagnaia, Guevara and Pawi, with Suzuki still close for the last point.

Bastianini was a non-starter, ruled unfit after breaking his wrist testing following the previous round in Spain.

Moto3 racing is close, but the 2016 championship was less so as Binder stretched his lead over Navarro to better than 20 points.

Corsi's second was his first since 2014, also at Le Mans, and also his first podium since that same year.

The battle for third was resolved when Baldassari slipped off; he remounted to finish out of the points. That promoted Morbidelli to fourth, five seconds adrift and under severe pressure at the end.

Not only had Nakagami closed to within less than a second, but also Lowes, just eight-tenths behind after a storming final few laps, in spite of "struggling with the front and to make the bike turn in."

Behind, Zarco had been narrowly leading a huge midfield gang, only for his home crowd to give a collective moan of despair when he crashed on lap 17. He also remounted, but finished second-last.

Seventh ultimately went to an inspired Axel Pons, who had moved steadily through the gang after finishing the first lap in 19th.

His last victim had been Zarco's long-time pursuer, Syahrin. Class rookie Oliveira took a best-so-far ninth, moving ahead on points of erstwhile Moto3 rival and new team-

MONSTER ENERGY
GRAND PRIX DE FRANCE
6–8 MAY, 2016

LE MANS – BUGATTI
28 laps
Length: 4.185 km / 2.600 miles
Width: 13m

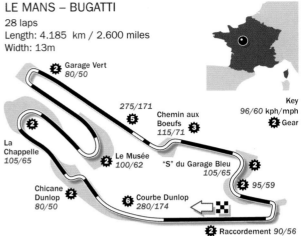

Garage Vert 80/50
275/171
Chemin aux Boeufs 115/71
La Chappelle 105/65
Le Musée 100/62
"S" du Garage Bleu 105/65
95/59
Chicane Dunlop 80/50
Courbe Dunlop 280/174
Raccordement 90/56

Key
96/60 kph/mph
Gear

MotoGP — RACE DISTANCE: 28 laps, 72.812 miles/117.180km · RACE WEATHER: Dry (air 22°C, humidity 40%, track 35°C)

Pos.	Rider	Nat.	No.	Entrant	Machine	Tyres	Race tyre choice	Laps	Time & speed
1	Jorge Lorenzo	SPA	99	Movistar Yamaha MotoGP	Yamaha YZR-M1	M	F: Medium/R: Soft	28	43m 51.290s / 99.6mph/ 160.3km/h
2	Valentino Rossi	ITA	46	Movistar Yamaha MotoGP	Yamaha YZR-M1	M	F: Medium/R: Soft	28	44m 01.944s
3	Maverick Vinales	SPA	25	Team SUZUKI ECSTAR	Suzuki GSX-RR	M	F: Medium/R: Soft	28	44m 05.467s
4	Dani Pedrosa	SPA	26	Repsol Honda Team	Honda RC213V	M	F: Medium/R: Soft	28	44m 10.009s
5	Pol Espargaro	SPA	44	Monster Yamaha Tech 3	Yamaha YZR-M1	M	F: Medium/R: Soft	28	44m 16.221s
6	Aleix Espargaro	SPA	41	Team SUZUKI ECSTAR	Suzuki GSX-RR	M	F: Medium/R: Soft	28	44m 24.211s
7	Danilo Petrucci	ITA	9	OCTO Pramac Yakhnich	Ducati Desmosedici	M	F: Medium/R: Soft	28	44m 29.541s
8	Hector Barbera	SPA	8	Avintia Racing	Ducati Desmosedici	M	F: Medium/R: Soft	28	44m 29.794s
9	Alvaro Bautista	SPA	19	Aprilia Racing Team Gresini	Aprilia RS-GP	M	F: Medium/R: Soft	28	44m 39.826s
10	Stefan Bradl	GER	6	Aprilia Racing Team Gresini	Aprilia RS-GP	M	F: Medium/R: Soft	28	44m 45.792s
11	Eugene Laverty	IRL	50	Aspar Team MotoGP	Ducati Desmosedici	M	F: Medium/R: Soft	28	44m 53.967s
12	Loris Baz	FRA	76	Avintia Racing	Ducati Desmosedici	M	F: Hard/R: Soft	28	44m 58.948s
13	Marc Marquez	SPA	93	Repsol Honda Team	Honda RC213V	M	F: Hard/R: Soft	27	44m 27.515s
	Bradley Smith	GBR	38	Monster Yamaha Tech 3	Yamaha YZR-M1	M	F: Medium/R: Soft	19	DNF-crash
	Jack Miller	AUS	43	Estrella Galicia 0,0 Marc VDS	Honda RC213V	M	F: Medium/R: Soft	17	DNF-crash
	Andrea Dovizioso	ITA	4	Ducati Team	Ducati Desmosedici	M	F: Medium/R: Soft	15	DNF-crash
	Andrea Iannone	ITA	29	Ducati Team	Ducati Desmosedici	M	F: Medium/R: Soft	11	DNF-crash
	Tito Rabat	SPA	53	Estrella Galicia 0,0 Marc VDS	Honda RC213V	M	F: Hard/R: Soft	7	DNF-crash
	Cal Crutchlow	GBR	35	LCR Honda	Honda RC213V	M	F: Hard/R: Soft	6	DNF-crash
	Yonny Hernandez	COL	68	Aspar Team MotoGP	Ducati Desmosedici	M	F: Medium/R: Soft	6	DNF-crash
	Scott Redding	GBR	45	OCTO Pramac Yakhnich	Ducati Desmosedici	M	F: Medium/R: Soft	5	DNF-technical

Fastest lap: Valentino Rossi, on lap 4, 1m 33.293s, 100.3mph/161.4km/h.

Lap record: Valentino Rossi, ITA (Yamaha), 1m 32.879s, 100.8mph/162.2km/h (2015).

Event best maximum speed: Andrea Iannone, 196.5mph/316.3km/h (free practice).

Qualifying

Weather: Dry
Air Temp: 22° **Track Temp:** 35°
Humidity: 44%

1	Lorenzo	1m 31.975s
2	Marquez	1m 32.416s
3	Iannone	1m 32.469s
4	P. Espargaro	1m 32.502s
5	Dovizioso	1m 32.587s
6	Smith	1m 32.820s
7	Rossi	1m 32.829s
8	Vinales	1m 32.933s
9	Crutchlow	1m 32.963s
10	Petrucci	1m 33.102s
11	Pedrosa	1m 33.109s
12	A. Espargaro	1m 33.115s
13	Barbera	1m 33.291s
14	Redding	1m 33.310s
15	Hernandez	1m 33.360s
16	Laverty	1m 33.452s
17	Bradl	1m 34.003s
18	Miller	1m 34.049s
19	Bautista	1m 34.333s
20	Rabat	1m 34.348s
21	Baz	1m 34.455s

Fastest race laps

1	Rossi	1m 33.293s
2	Iannone	1m 33.374s
3	Lorenzo	1m 33.432s
4	Dovizioso	1m 33.520s
5	Marquez	1m 33.576s
6	Vinales	1m 33.803s
7	P. Espargaro	1m 33.917s
8	Pedrosa	1m 33.941s
9	Smith	1m 34.040s
10	A. Espargaro	1m 34.054s
11	Crutchlow	1m 34.135s
12	Redding	1m 34.175s
13	Barbera	1m 34.561s
14	Petrucci	1m 34.720s
15	Bradl	1m 34.770s
16	Miller	1m 34.824s
17	Hernandez	1m 34.833s
18	Bautista	1m 34.903s
19	Laverty	1m 34.971s
20	Rabat	1m 35.283s
21	Baz	1m 35.359s

Championship Points

1	Lorenzo	90
2	Marquez	85
3	Rossi	78
4	Pedrosa	53
5	Vinales	49
6	P. Espargaro	47
7	A. Espargaro	42
8	Barbera	39
9	Laverty	33
10	Iannone	25
11	Dovizioso	23
12	Bradl	23
13	Bautista	21
14	Smith	20
15	Redding	16
16	Pirro	12
17	Rabat	11
18	Petrucci	9
19	Baz	8
20	Crutchlow	5
21	Hernandez	3
22	Miller	2

Constructor Points

1	Yamaha	115
2	Honda	95
3	Ducati	67
4	Suzuki	55
5	Aprilia	27

Grid order	1	2	3	4	5	6	7	8	9	10	11	12	13	14	15	16	17	18	19	20	21	22	23	24	25	26	27	28	
99 LORENZO	99	99	99	99	99	99	99	99	99	99	99	99	99	99	99	99	99	99	99	99	99	99	99	99	99	99	99	99	1
93 MARQUEZ	4	4	4	4	4	29	4	4	4	4	4	4	4	46	46	46	46	46	46	46	46	46	46	46	46	46	46	46	2
29 IANNONE	29	29	29	29	29	4	93	93	93	93	93	93	46	4	4	25	25	25	25	25	25	25	25	25	25	25	25	25	3
44 P. ESPARGARO	93	93	93	93	93	93	46	46	46	46	46	46	93	93	93	41	26	26	26	26	26	26	26	26	26	26	26	26	4
4 DOVIZIOSO	44	44	46	46	46	46	41	25	25	25	25	25	25	25	26	41	41	41	41	44	44	44	44	44	44	44	44	44	5
38 SMITH	41	46	44	41	41	41	25	41	41	41	41	41	41	41	44	44	44	44	44	41	41	41	41	41	41	41	41	41	6
46 ROSSI	46	41	41	25	25	25	44	44	44	44	44	26	26	26	38	38	38	38	9	9	9	9	9	9	9	9	9	9	7
25 VINALES	38	38	25	44	44	44	38	38	38	38	26	44	44	44	9	9	9	9	8	8	8	8	8	8	8	8	8	8	8
35 CRUTCHLOW	25	25	38	38	38	38	26	26	26	26	38	38	38	38	8	8	8	8	19	19	19	19	19	19	19	19	19	19	9
9 PETRUCCI	26	35	35	35	35	35	9	9	9	9	9	9	9	9	43	43	19	19	6	6	6	6	6	6	6	6	6	6	10
26 PEDROSA	35	26	26	26	26	26	50	50	50	50	50	8	8	8	50	50	50	50	50	50	50	50	50	50	50	50	50	50	11
41 A. ESPARGARO	45	45	45	45	45	68	6	6	6	8	8	50	50	43	19	19	6	6	76	76	76	76	76	76	76	76	76		12
8 BARBERA	68	68	68	68	68	9	8	8	8	43	43	43	43	43	50	6	6	76	76	93	93	93	93	93	93	93	93		13
45 REDDING	9	9	9	9	9	50	43	43	43	6	19	19	19	19	76	76	93	93											
68 HERNANDEZ	50	50	50	50	50	6	76	19	19	19	6	6	6	6	93	93													
50 LAVERTY	76	76	6	6	6	43	53	76	76	76	76	76	76	76															
6 BRADL	6	6	76	76	43	8	19	29	29	29	29																		
43 MILLER	43	43	43	43	8	76	29																						
19 BAUTISTA	53	53	53	8	76	53																							
53 RABAT	19	8	8	53	53	19																							
76 BAZ	8	19	19	19	19																								

29 Pit stop   93 Lapped rider

Moto2

RACE DISTANCE: 26 laps, 67.611 miles/108.810km · RACE WEATHER: Dry (air 21°C, humidity 39%, track 27°C)

Pos.	Rider	Nat.	No.	Entrant	Machine	Laps	Time & Speed
1	**Alex Rins**	SPA	40	Paginas Amarillas HP 40	Kalex	26	42m 27.312s 95.5mph/ 153.7km/h
2	**Simone Corsi**	ITA	24	Speed Up Racing	Speed Up	26	42m 29.114s
3	**Thomas Luthi**	SWI	12	Garage Plus Interwetten	Kalex	26	42m 31.920s
4	**Franco Morbidelli**	ITA	21	Estrella Galicia 0,0 Marc VDS	Kalex	26	42m 36.460s
5	**Takaaki Nakagami**	JPN	30	IDEMITSU Honda Team Asia	Kalex	26	42m 37.140s
6	**Sam Lowes**	GBR	22	Federal Oil Gresini Moto2	Kalex	26	42m 37.938s
7	**Axel Pons**	SPA	49	AGR Team	Kalex	26	42m 52.789s
8	**Hafizh Syahrin**	MAL	55	Petronas Raceline Malaysia	Kalex	26	42m 53.273s
9	**Miguel Oliveira**	POR	44	Leopard Racing	Kalex	26	42m 56.793s
10	**Luis Salom**	SPA	39	SAG Team	Kalex	26	42m 56.680s
11	**Xavier Simeon**	BEL	19	QMMF Racing Team	Speed Up	26	42m 56.885s
12	**Luca Marini**	ITA	10	Forward Team	Kalex	26	42m 57.085s
13	**Dominique Aegerter**	SWI	77	CarXpert Interwetten	Kalex	26	42m 57.495s
14	**Marcel Schrotter**	GER	23	AGR Team	Kalex	26	42m 57.556s
15	**Xavi Vierge**	SPA	97	Tech 3 Racing	Tech 3	26	43m 03.850s
16	Mattia Pasini	ITA	54	Italtrans Racing Team	Kalex	26	43m 05.914s
17	Lorenzo Baldassarri	ITA	7	Forward Team	Kalex	26	43m 12.223s
18	Robin Mulhauser	SWI	70	CarXpert Interwetten	Kalex	26	43m 12.609s
19	Danny Kent	GBR	52	Leopard Racing	Kalex	26	43m 13.067s
20	Isaac Vinales	SPA	32	Tech 3 Racing	Tech 3	26	43m 17.590s
21	Ratthapark Wilairot	THA	14	IDEMITSU Honda Team Asia	Kalex	26	43m 23.085s
22	Alessandro Tonucci	ITA	33	Tasca Racing Scuderia Moto2	Kalex	26	43m 29.102s
23	Jesko Raffin	SWI	2	Sports-Millions-EMWE-SAG	Kalex	26	43m 29.513s
24	Johann Zarco	FRA	5	Ajo Motorsport	Kalex	26	43m 29.796s
25	Danny Eslick	USA	69	JPMoto Malaysia	Suter	26	44m 06.814s
	Alex Marquez	SPA	73	Estrella Galicia 0,0 Marc VDS	Kalex	13	DNF
	Julian Simon	SPA	60	QMMF Racing Team	Speed Up	7	DNF
	Jonas Folger	GER	94	Dynavolt Intact GP	Kalex	1	DNF

Fastest lap: Alex Rins, on lap 4, 1m 37.297s, 96.2mph/154.8km/h.

Lap record: Thomas Luthi, SWI (Kalex), 1m 37.281s, 96.2mph/154.8km/h (2015).

Event best maximum speed: Marcel Schrotter, 162mph/260.7km/h (free practice).

Qualifying

Weather: Dry **Air Temp:** 22° **Track Temp:** 35° **Humidity:** 45%

1	Luthi	1m 36.847s
2	Rins	1m 36.899s
3	Corsi	1m 37.168s
4	Zarco	1m 37.180s
5	Morbidelli	1m 37.239s
6	Nakagami	1m 37.324s
7	Baldassarri	1m 37.335s
8	Folger	1m 37.359s
9	Lowes	1m 37.396s
10	Marini	1m 37.438s
11	Pons	1m 37.496s
12	Schrotter	1m 37.631s
13	Aegerter	1m 37.700s
14	Oliveira	1m 37.764s
15	Simon	1m 37.812s
16	Marquez	1m 37.942s
17	Syahrin	1m 37.994s
18	Salom	1m 38.003s
19	Pasini	1m 38.030s
20	Simeon	1m 38.091s
21	Kent	1m 38.281s
22	Vierge	1m 38.326s
23	Vinales	1m 38.550s
24	Wilairot	1m 38.748s
25	Mulhauser	1m 38.855s
26	Tonucci	1m 39.370s
27	Raffin	1m 39.873s
28	Eslick	1m 40.404s

Fastest race laps

1	Rins	1m 37.297s
2	Baldassarri	1m 37.401s
3	Corsi	1m 37.408s
4	Luthi	1m 37.442s
5	Morbidelli	1m 37.466s
6	Lowes	1m 37.509s
7	Nakagami	1m 37.650s
8	Oliveira	1m 38.001s
9	Pons	1m 38.054s
10	Zarco	1m 38.056s
11	Marquez	1m 38.081s
12	Marini	1m 38.095s
13	Syahrin	1m 38.110s
14	Simeon	1m 38.128s
15	Simon	1m 38.205s
16	Aegerter	1m 38.239s
17	Schrotter	1m 38.260s
18	Salom	1m 38.300s
19	Pasini	1m 38.461s
20	Vierge	1m 38.473s
21	Mulhauser	1m 38.679s
22	Kent	1m 38.793s
23	Vinales	1m 38.864s
24	Wilairot	1m 38.983s
25	Raffin	1m 39.298s
26	Tonucci	1m 39.356s
27	Eslick	1m 40.150s

Championship Points

1	Rins	87
2	Lowes	82
3	Luthi	69
4	Zarco	56
5	Folger	47
6	Corsi	46
7	Aegerter	46
8	Salom	37
9	Morbidelli	37
10	Syahrin	36
11	Nakagami	30
12	Simeon	23
13	Pons	17
14	Schrotter	13
15	Oliveira	12
16	Kent	10
17	Pasini	10
18	Marini	10
19	Simon	7
20	Marquez	5
21	Cortese	5
22	Baldassarri	3
23	Wilairot	3
24	Vinales	3
25	Vierge	3
26	Raffin	2
27	Mulhauser	1

Constructor Points

1	Kalex	125
2	Speed Up	56
3	Tech 3	6

Moto3

RACE DISTANCE: 24 laps, 62.411 miles/100.440km · RACE WEATHER: Dry (air 19°C, humidity 44%, track 21°C)

Pos.	Rider	Nat.	No.	Entrant	Machine	Laps	Time & Speed
1	**Brad Binder**	RSA	41	Red Bull KTM Ajo	KTM	24	41m 31.041s 90.2mph/ 145.1km/h
2	**Romano Fenati**	ITA	5	SKY Racing Team VR46	KTM	24	41m 31.140s
3	**Jorge Navarro**	SPA	9	Estrella Galicia 0,0	Honda	24	41m 31.428s
4	**Aron Canet**	SPA	44	Estrella Galicia 0,0	Honda	24	41m 32.395s
5	**Nicolo Bulega**	ITA	8	SKY Racing Team VR46	KTM	24	41m 38.188s
6	**Fabio Quartararo**	FRA	20	Leopard Racing	KTM	24	41m 38.657s
7	**Andrea Migno**	ITA	16	SKY Racing Team VR46	KTM	24	41m 39.057s
8	**Niccolo Antonelli**	ITA	23	Ongetta-Rivacold	Honda	24	41m 39.498s
9	**Jakub Kornfeil**	CZE	84	Drive M7 SIC Racing Team	Honda	24	41m 40.891s
10	**Andrea Locatelli**	ITA	55	Leopard Racing	KTM	24	41m 40.967s
11	**Livio Loi**	BEL	11	RW Racing GP BV	Honda	24	41m 43.334s
12	**Francesco Bagnaia**	ITA	21	ASPAR Mahindra Team Moto3	Mahindra	24	41m 44.779s
13	**Juanfran Guevara**	SPA	58	RBA Racing Team	KTM	24	41m 44.552s
14	**Khairul Idham Pawi**	MAL	89	Honda Team Asia	Honda	24	41m 44.948s
15	**Tatsuki Suzuki**	JPN	24	CIP-Unicom Starker	Mahindra	24	41m 45.423s
16	Bo Bendsneyder	NED	64	Red Bull KTM Ajo	KTM	24	41m 51.956s
17	Fabio di Giannantonio	ITA	4	Gresini Racing Moto3	Honda	24	41m 52.270s
18	Jorge Martin	SPA	88	ASPAR Mahindra Team Moto3	Mahindra	24	41m 55.132s
19	Alexis Masbou	FRA	10	Peugeot MC Saxoprint	Peugeot	24	42m 09.823s
20	John McPhee	GBR	17	Peugeot MC Saxoprint	Peugeot	24	42m 09.893s
21	Maria Herrera	SPA	6	MH6 Team	KTM	24	42m 10.027s
22	Stefano Valtulini	ITA	43	3570 Team Italia	Mahindra	24	42m 25.591s
23	Fabio Spiranelli	ITA	3	CIP-Unicom Starker	Mahindra	24	42m 34.567s
24	Lorenzo Petrarca	ITA	77	3570 Team Italia	Mahindra	24	42m 34.634s
25	Joan Mir	SPA	36	Leopard Racing	KTM	24	42m 36.532s
	Gabriel Rodrigo	ARG	19	RBA Racing Team	KTM	23	DNF
	Enzo Boulom	FRA	99	Procercasa - 42 Motorsport	KTM	16	DNF
	Hiroki Ono	JPN	76	Honda Team Asia	Honda	15	DNF
	Darryn Binder	RSA	40	Platinum Bay Real Estate	Mahindra	10	DNF
	Philipp Oettl	GER	65	Schedl GP Racing	KTM	3	DNF
	Jules Danilo	FRA	95	Ongetta-Rivacold	Honda	2	DNF
	Adam Norrodin	MAL	7	Drive M7 SIC Racing Team	Honda	0	DNF
	Karel Hanika	CZE	98	Platinum Bay Real Estate	Mahindra	0	DNF

Fastest lap: Aron Canet, on lap 11, 1m 42.923s, 90.9mph/146.3km/h.

Lap record: Enea Bastianini, ITA (Honda), 1m 42.525s, 91.3mph/146.9km/h (2015).

Event best maximum speed: Jakub Kornfeil, 138mph/222.1km/h (qualifying).

Qualifying

Weather: Dry **Air Temp:** 21° **Track Temp:** 25° **Humidity:** 44%

1	Antonelli	1m 42.756s
2	B. Binder	1m 42.823s
3	Canet	1m 42.825s
4	Navarro	1m 42.842s
5	Fenati	1m 42.865s
6	Bulega	1m 42.888s
7	Guevara	1m 43.084s
8	Quartararo	1m 43.092s
9	Pawi	1m 43.106s
10	Di Giannantonio	1m 43.198s
11	Kornfeil	1m 43.214s
12	Loi	1m 43.224s
13	Suzuki	1m 43.275s
14	Locatelli	1m 43.330s
15	Masbou	1m 43.353s
16	Ono	1m 43.376s
17	Migno	1m 43.448s
18	Oettl	1m 43.458s
19	Bagnaia	1m 43.496s
20	Rodrigo	1m 43.643s
21	Bendsneyder	1m 43.687s
22	D. Binder	1m 43.725s
23	Martin	1m 43.732s
24	Mir	1m 43.766s
25	McPhee	1m 43.767s
26	Hanika	1m 43.807s
27	Danilo	1m 44.056s
28	Valtulini	1m 44.211s
29	Boulom	1m 44.314s
30	Herrera	1m 44.378s
31	Norrodin	1m 45.207s
32	Petrarca	1m 45.526s
33	Spiranelli	1m 45.603s

Fastest race laps

1	Canet	1m 42.923s
2	Quartararo	1m 42.960s
3	B. Binder	1m 43.064s
4	Fenati	1m 43.081s
5	Migno	1m 43.129s
6	Navarro	1m 43.188s
7	Antonelli	1m 43.229s
8	Bulega	1m 43.263s
9	Guevara	1m 43.264s
10	Kornfeil	1m 43.268s
11	Martin	1m 43.341s
12	Bagnaia	1m 43.342s
13	Mir	1m 43.431s
14	Suzuki	1m 43.437s
15	Locatelli	1m 43.444s
16	Pawi	1m 43.478s
17	Di Giannantonio	1m 43.494s
18	Loi	1m 43.503s
19	Ono	1m 43.742s
20	D. Binder	1m 43.755s
21	McPhee	1m 43.758s
22	Rodrigo	1m 43.796s
23	Bendsneyder	1m 43.808s
24	Masbou	1m 43.869s
25	Herrera	1m 43.898s
26	Oettl	1m 44.337s
27	Valtulini	1m 44.530s
28	Boulom	1m 44.536s
29	Spiranelli	1m 45.179s
30	Petrarca	1m 45.345s

Championship Points

1	B. Binder	102
2	Navarro	78
3	Fenati	67
4	Bulega	47
5	Antonelli	39
6	Bagnaia	38
7	Kornfeil	36
8	Locatelli	30
9	Pawi	29
10	Bastianini	29
11	Oettl	27
12	Mir	25
13	Canet	23
14	Loi	21
15	Quartararo	19
16	Danilo	19
17	Migno	15
18	Guevara	15
19	Ono	10
20	McPhee	9
21	Martin	8
22	Norrodin	5
23	Rodrigo	3
24	Herrera	2
25	Bendsneyder	2
26	Suzuki	2

Constructor Points

1	KTM	111
2	Honda	99
3	Mahindra	46
4	Peugeot	9

Win number three for Lorenzo. Aside from his Argentine crash, he had been second everywhere else. He was looking unstoppable, but appearances were deceptive.
Photo: Gold & Goose

ITALIAN GRAND PRIX

MUGELLO CIRCUIT

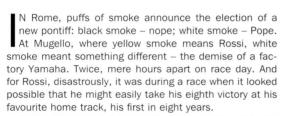

I N Rome, puffs of smoke announce the election of a new pontiff: black smoke – nope; white smoke – Pope. At Mugello, where yellow smoke means Rossi, white smoke meant something different – the demise of a factory Yamaha. Twice, mere hours apart on race day. And for Rossi, disastrously, it was during a race when it looked possible that he might easily take his eighth victory at his favourite home track, his first in eight years.

Engine blow-ups are not unknown nowadays, but rare enough to occasion some surprise; and two in one day all the more so. What was disastrous for Rossi was also embarrassing for Yamaha, who within two weeks had issued the usual, but this time plausible, "electrical fault" explanation. Electronic, to be more precise: unfamiliarity with 2016's control software had led to an error in Yamaha's application of the rev limiter. What worked in 2015 did not a year later; and when the bikes made their small, but always spectacular little jump at top speed and full throttle at the end of the straight, both engines – Lorenzo's in morning warm-up and Rossi's after eight of 23 laps in the race – had gone over the limit. Resultant derangement of the valves had the same result in each case: terminal top-end failure. Whether the valves had touched pistons or tangled with one another was not clear, but it made no difference to the result.

There was a record crowd, but some went home early. No Rossi, no point. They missed one of the most thrilling finishes, as Lorenzo seized the narrowest of victories from the jaws of defeat, leaving a valiant Marquez little left to say but "I told you so." Though he did add, "Today, I lost the race in the last 50 metres. That has never happened before in my career." He could have asked for no clearer proof of his frequent complaints of how his Honda lacked acceleration.

Nor could Lorenzo have asked for better luck than that his engine blow-up came in the morning, rather than in the race.

The weekend had begun with a flurry of announcements, all but ending the earliest ever silly season after the first third of the calendar.

The first, on Monday, was that Pedrosa had signed for a further two years with the factory Repsol Honda team, taking his tenure to 13 years.

No surprise, wacky rumours notwithstanding. A little more, if only for the early timing, when Ducati announced the next day that they would retain Dovizioso until 2018, alongside Jorge Lorenzo. But certainly more than a frisson on Thursday, with two statements from Suzuki and one from Yamaha.

Suzuki announced that they had secured the services of Ducati reject Iannone, also for two years. Their other statement mirrored Yamaha's. Vinales (who said the call to Suzuki manager Davide Brivio had been "the most difficult of my life") was to replace Lorenzo as Rossi's team-mate for the next two years. This fulfilled the expectations of all, as well as the desire for sponsor Movistar to retain a Spaniard in the team.

Only one major rider remained to be settled, but Marquez's two-year renewal with Repsol Honda was barely a week away. Lesser riders remained in limbo, most especially Aleix Espargaro, who gave the first comments about his disappointment that Suzuki were not treating him with the affection and respect he thought he deserved.

Speed records tumbled, six Ducatis on top, and Iannone's factory bike at 354.9km/h, smashing his own 351.2 MotoGP record from the opening round in Qatar. Surprisingly, Vinales's Suzuki was seventh, at 347.7. Pedrosa's top Honda was only tenth, at 346.9km/h, marginally slower than Pol Espargaro's top Yamaha. Lorenzo's best was only 341.6. Aprilia had a new engine, and Bradl clocked a best of 338.7 in the race.

And slowing down again? Brembo's annual "last of the late brakers" data came from the first corner, where riders shed around 160km/h in just 318 metres over 5.6 seconds – from 351 to 91km/h. The winner was Rossi, braking later than Marquez, Iannone, Vinales and Lorenzo. But all were braking earlier than in 2015, the consequence of Michelin's softer front tyre compared with Bridgestone's.

Thursday was rainy, and Friday's first free practice damp, giving a first chance to try Michelin's new intermediate tyres. Very few did so; most stayed indoors for the session, while Rossi used the time to make eight practice starts, trying different master cylinders – he had cooked his clutch in Texas, with costly consequences.

The weather cleared promptly, as predicted by a humorous Petrucci at the pre-event conference, who said the plates and screws in his throttle hand had given him "a weather forecast station". He also told the press that during his long absence he had missed everybody, "even the journalists. It's like … what is your favourite nightmare?"

Dorna's was the possibility that death threats to Lorenzo and Marquez from Rossi fans on social media should actually be taken seriously. Accordingly, they provided bodyguards for the pair, with Lorenzo saying, "There are a lot of fans here and you never know how they will react. If I don't need [bodyguards], okay. But if needed, they are ready to do their work." Marquez was more sanguine. His reception had been entirely positive, "asking for pictures and signatures. I already said to Dorna that I don't need bodyguards. I want to feel normal. I think we are in a sport where it will not happen."

Rabat missed the race after a heavy crash on his out-lap in FP3 left him with a badly broken left collarbone; rising Moto3 rider Oettl was already absent, having fractured his wrist at Le Mans, and had been replaced by Italian frequent sub Lorenzo dalla Porta. But Bastianini was back and going well after missing Le Mans.

Rossi remained the centre of attention, and his traditional special helmet for Mugello celebrated his relationship with the track: a striking yellow, with a simple punning legend: 'MUGIALLO' in bold capitals on the chin-piece. 'Giallo' is Italian for yellow.

By then, he had already claimed his first pole in almost a year, and been rewarded with the usual Tissot watch – presented by Italian actress and TV presenter Eleonora Pedron. He made sure to give the blonde an extra cuddle for the cameras. Pedron is the ex-wife of Max Biaggi.

Above: Last-lap frenzy. Lorenzo and Marquez were even closer over the line, but the other way around.

Top left: A Plasmon baby-biscuit poster was photoshopped to pour scorn on public enemies Marquez and Lorenzo. It was better-natured than death threats on social media.

Above far left: A delicious moment for Rossi as he receives his Tissot pole watch from Biaggi's ex-wife, Eleonora Pedron. Iannone shares the joke.

Above left: Another Mugello special helmet for The Doctor.

Centre far left: Rabat was down and out.

Centre left: Plucky Petrucci's injured hand acted as a reliable weather forecaster.

Left: A bad start wrecked Iannone's chance of victory. He set fastest lap and finished third.

Photos: Gold & Goose

MOTOGP RACE – 23 laps

Rossi's first pole since Assen in 2015 came after a to-and-fro play with 2017 team-mate Vinales; Lorenzo complained that it was "like schoolmates copying one another's work". Rossi admitted that the Suzuki's slipstream had helped, denying the Suzuki rider his first pole by less than a tenth. Times were close in spite of the long lap. With Iannone third, the front row was covered by 0.103 second; Lorenzo was 0.378 off pole, on row two, between Marquez and Aleix Espargaro; and all 12 in Q2 were covered by less than one second.

Lorenzo seized the lead into the first corner, from Rossi and fast starter Aleix Espargaro; then Marquez and Smith.

Front-row men Vinales and Iannone both got away badly. The Suzuki rider, who finished the first lap 11th, had plenty to do. Iannone blamed a clutch problem; he finished lap one eighth and the second lap 11th. Team-mate Dovizioso, by contrast, had passed Smith for fifth by the end of lap one, from 13th on the grid – he had failed to make Q2, troubled all weekend by the recurrence of an old neck injury.

Three riders didn't make it past the first corner: Miller, Bautista and Baz, the last named suffering foot injuries that required major reconstructive surgery.

The Yamahas soon put a small gap on a determined Marquez, who was soon joined by Dovizioso as Espargaro dropped back. Rossi was pushing and probing, mainly into the first corner, getting ahead, but running wide at the start of lap two. Lorenzo was steadfast under this constant pressure. Anyway, there was still time for a more determined attack later in the race.

Until Rossi's bike slowed, then expired in a white cloud on the ninth lap. "It's a great shame," he said. "I was feeling comfortable, and I think I could have fought for victory."

Marquez was pushing hard, up to within a tenth on lap 15. But again Lorenzo seemed impregnable, and he drew marginally clear once more.

But it wasn't over, and in the last two laps Marquez was attacking, pushing past repeatedly, only for Lorenzo to get him back promptly. After the race, both said that they had been prepared to settle for second, but it didn't show, with at least one strong contact knocking Marquez's elbow slider off at top speed on the straight. It was only in the final yards that the matter was settled, after a thrilling final lap.

Lorenzo fended him off into Turn One; Marquez pushed past three corners later. It looked like he had done it, even after Lorenzo got ahead at the final chicane, for Marquez seized the lead back into the last corner and came out of it three or four bike lengths ahead.

Only for the Yamaha to accelerate alongside and marginally ahead over the line

And the rest? Shortly before one-third distance, Pedrosa, in his 250th GP start, was picking up pace as the fuel burned off, passing Espargaro's Suzuki. At the same time, Dovizioso had closed on Marquez and was once briefly ahead. But the fastest on the track was his team-mate, Iannone, who charged through the midfield. As Dovi lost touch with Marquez, Iannone was past Pedrosa, and the pair were closing fast on the Ducati.

With six laps to go, the trio were closely engaged. Iannone got ahead, Dovi fought back – and then ran wide into the first corner. The fight was over, with Iannone now third, Pedrosa tailing him over the line by less than two-tenths.

Iannone set fastest lap of the race on the last lap, disappointed that his bad start had robbed him of the chance to fight for the win.

Dovi held on to fifth, explaining after the race that as well as a stiff neck, arm-pump had spoiled his pace. Vinales was up to sixth, still a couple of seconds adrift, but clear of top satellite rider Smith, seventh his best of the year so far.

Petrucci took eighth off Espargaro with four laps to go. Ducati wild-card Pirro was a solid tenth; Crutchlow a cautious 11th, determined to get a decent finish after a nightmare season so far.

Barbera was a lone 12th; Laverty eventually prevailed over Bradl's Aprilia after a long battle for 13th; Pol Espargaro took the last point, after falling for a third time of the weekend and remounting. He was four seconds ahead of Hernandez, who received a ride-through penalty for a jump start.

Redding joined Rossi on the retirement list. He had been up to seventh in the early laps before pitting with yet another technical problem.

Lorenzo's third win, his second in a row, was Yamaha's 100th in the MotoGP class, compared with 116 for Honda. It extended his lead over Marquez to ten points, while Rossi's second no-score dropped him 37 behind.

MOTO2 RACE – 10 laps (shortened)

Sam Lowes took his third pole of the year, from Nakagami and front-row first-timer Baldassarri, who had lost the position at the previous round. Axel Pons led row two from Schrotter and Zarco; Luthi the third from Corsi and Rins; Marini impressively headed the fourth.

The race went badly, twice.

It had started fine, Lowes disputing the lead with Luthi. Then, on lap four, Xavier Vierge crashed at speed, and while he was okay, his Tech 3 bike speared into the air-fence, which deflated. Red flag, and results taken back to lap three to determine grid positions for a restart.

At that point, Luthi was second, then Nakagami, Baldassarri, Rins and Pons. This would determine the grid positions. Marini was already out, having become tangled with a falling Marquez. The latter had remounted, so was able to join the restart; likewise Folger, who had pitted with a quick-shifter problem.

An 11-lap race was scheduled, down by ten laps.

New-for-2016 quick-restart rules dictated that riders had to leave the pit lane within 60 seconds of opening. Not all managed it, some blaming poor information from officials. So as they lined up again in revised order, several riders were ordered to go to the pit lane. No easy operation, and the rest sat there, engines and tempers becoming hotter as time ticked away.

Eventually the process was stopped, riders returned to the pits, and yet another restart – this time ten laps – was scheduled, with even more errant riders now put to the back as they lined up again, this time for delaying the restart.

Among those punished were Nakagami, Rins, Corsi, Simon, Edgar Pons and Simeon.

Now it was a sprint, and quite exciting.

Luthi led into the first corner, but Baldassarri was ahead by the end, with Syahrin, Zarco, Schrotter, Lowes and Axel Pons in hot pursuit.

Luthi would lead once more on lap three; Zarco would drop to fourth. But before half-distance, he was second, behind Baldassarri, and the pair scrapped it out to the finish, changing places with increasing frequency until the flag, with Zarco ahead for a second win of the year by just three-hundredths.

Lowes had chosen the harder tyre and suffered as a result, scrapping for fourth behind Luthi with the persistent Syahrin.

On the final lap, Lowes got ahead of both of them with a daring swoop into the fast Arrabbiata section. Luthi was fourth, then Syahrin and Pons.

The pursuit group saw plenty of variety, with Rins moving steadily forward within it for an impressive seventh, passing Morbidelli on the last lap. Nakagami had followed through for ninth, with Aegerter hanging on to complete the top ten.

The final points went to Cortese, Corsi, Oliveira, Kent and Folger, after his lucky restart; Marquez was a second out of the points in 16th.

Simeon had crashed out on the sighting lap, then also Pasini and Salom.

Third was good enough for Lowes to regain the title lead, by just two points.

MOTO3 RACE – 20 laps

Binder walked away from a fast crash in free practice, and fortunately avoided the same in a trademark close Mugello tiddler race. He took a third straight win, outfoxing a lead group reduced from 15 to five only by a last-corner crash. Those five were all over the line within less than a tenth of a second.

The South African's win was all the sweeter because his main title rivals scored no points. Pole starter Fenati had frequently led, but his chain broke after nine thrilling laps. Navarro crashed in one of many collisions in a pack that swung into the corners four or five abreast.

Positions shuffled corner by corner. Argentine GP winner Pawi led briefly, team-mate Ono twice over the line; Migno once, and team-mate Bulega at least once out over the hillsides. More frequently, Quartararo was up front, after coming through from 18th on the grid.

At half-distance, first to 23rd was covered by some three seconds, and the first 11 were within one second. It was still anybody's race, and would remain so.

Only on the final lap, when rookies Pawi and Canet crashed out, Canet on the last corner, were five clear front-runners left to battle to the line.

Binder had led on to the final straight, and he stayed ahead by less than four-hundredths. Rookie Fabio Di Giannantonio took second by inches from Bagnaia's Mahindra, Antonelli and Quartararo virtually alongside. Antonelli had also come through, having started 21st after a crash in qualifying.

A second away, Ono narrowly shaded Mir; Bulega, Guevara and Migno completed the top ten, the remaining points going to Danilo, Bastianini (back from injury), Rodrigo, Martin and sub dalla Porta.

GRAN PREMIO D'ITALIA TIM
20–22 MAY, 2016

AUTODROMO INTERNAZIONALE DEL MUGELLO
23 laps
Length: 5.245 km / 3,259 miles
Width: 14m

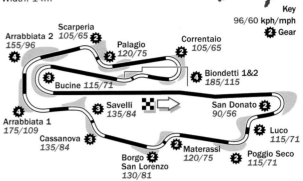

Key
96/60 kph/mph
Gear

Corners:
- Arrabbiata 2 — 155/96
- Scarperia — 105/65
- Palagio — 120/75
- Correntaio — 105/65
- Biondetti 1&2 — 185/115
- Bucine — 115/71
- Savelli — 135/84
- San Donato — 90/56
- Luco — 115/71
- Arrabbiata 1 — 175/109
- Cassanova — 135/84
- Borgo San Lorenzo — 130/81
- Materassi — 120/75
- Poggio Seco — 115/71

MotoGP

RACE DISTANCE: 23 laps, 74.959 miles/120.635km · RACE WEATHER: Dry (air 26°C, humidity 40%, track 48°C)

Pos.	Rider	Nat.	No.	Entrant	Machine	Tyres	Race tyre choice	Laps	Time & speed
1	Jorge Lorenzo	SPA	99	Movistar Yamaha MotoGP	Yamaha YZR-M1	M	F: Hard/R: Soft	23	41m 36.535s 108.1mph/173.9km/h
2	Marc Marquez	SPA	93	Repsol Honda Team	Honda RC213V	M	F: Medium/R: Soft	23	41m 36.554s
3	Andrea Iannone	ITA	29	Ducati Team	Ducati Desmosedici	M	F: Hard/R: Soft	23	41m 41.277s
4	Dani Pedrosa	SPA	26	Repsol Honda Team	Honda RC213V	M	F: Hard/R: Soft	23	41m 41.445s
5	Andrea Dovizioso	ITA	4	Ducati Team	Ducati Desmosedici	M	F: Hard/R: Soft	23	41m 42.791s
6	Maverick Vinales	SPA	25	Team SUZUKI ECSTAR	Suzuki GSX-RR	M	F: Hard/R: Soft	23	41m 45.205s
7	Bradley Smith	GBR	38	Monster Yamaha Tech 3	Yamaha YZR-M1	M	F: Hard/R: Soft	23	41m 49.875s
8	Danilo Petrucci	ITA	9	OCTO Pramac Yakhnich	Ducati Desmosedici	M	F: Hard/R: Soft	23	41m 51.133s
9	Aleix Espargaro	SPA	41	Team SUZUKI ECSTAR	Suzuki GSX-RR	M	F: Hard/R: Soft	23	41m 55.178s
10	Michele Pirro	ITA	51	Ducati Team	Ducati Desmosedici	M	F: Hard/R: Soft	23	41m 58.833s
11	Cal Crutchlow	GBR	35	LCR Honda	Honda RC213V	M	F: Medium/R: Soft	23	42m 04.471s
12	Hector Barbera	SPA	8	Avintia Racing	Ducati Desmosedici	M	F: Hard/R: Soft	23	42m 12.247s
13	Eugene Laverty	IRL	50	Aspar Team MotoGP	Ducati Desmosedici	M	F: Hard/R: Soft	22	42m 14.567s
14	Stefan Bradl	GER	6	Aprilia Racing Team Gresini	Aprilia RS-GP	M	F: Hard/R: Soft	19	42m 16.629s
15	Pol Espargaro	SPA	44	Monster Yamaha Tech 3	Yamaha YZR-M1	M	F: Hard/R: Soft	17	42m 36.346s
16	Yonny Hernandez	COL	68	Aspar Team MotoGP	Ducati Desmosedici	M	F: Medium/R: Soft	15	42m 40.932s
	Valentino Rossi	ITA	46	Movistar Yamaha MotoGP	Yamaha YZR-M1	M	F: Hard/R: Soft	8	DNF-technical
	Scott Redding	GBR	45	OCTO Pramac Yakhnich	Ducati Desmosedici	M	F: Hard/R: Soft	8	DNF-technical
	Jack Miller	AUS	43	Estrella Galicia 0,0 Marc VDS	Honda RC213V	M	F: Hard/R: Soft	0	DNF-crash
	Alvaro Bautista	SPA	19	Aprilia Racing Team Gresini	Aprilia RS-GP	M	F: Hard/R: Soft	0	DNF-crash
	Loris Baz	FRA	76	Avintia Racing	Ducati Desmosedici	M	F: Hard/R: Soft	0	DNF-crash
	Tito Rabat	SPA	53	Estrella Galicia 0,0 Marc VDS	Honda RC213V	M	–	–	DNS-Injured

Fastest lap: Andrea Iannone, on lap 23, 1m 47.687s, 108.9mph/175.3km/h.
Lap record: Marc Marquez, SPA (Honda), 1m 47.639s, 109.0mph/175.4km/h (2013).
Event best maximum speed: Andrea Iannone, 220.5mph/354.9km/h (race) – new MotoGP record.

Qualifying

Weather: Dry
Air Temp: 27° Track Temp: 47°
Humidity: 36%

1	Rossi	1m 46.504s
2	Vinales	1m 46.598s
3	Iannone	1m 46.607s
4	Marquez	1m 46.759s
5	Lorenzo	1m 46.882s
6	A. Espargaro	1m 47.186s
7	Pedrosa	1m 47.218s
8	Smith	1m 47.247s
9	Petrucci	1m 47.261s
10	Redding	1m 47.359s
11	Pirro	1m 47.361s
12	Hernandez	1m 47.436s
13	Dovizioso	1m 47.089s
14	P. Espargaro	1m 47.159s
15	Barbera	1m 47.555s
16	Crutchlow	1m 47.659s
17	Miller	1m 47.830s
18	Laverty	1m 48.111s
19	Bautista	1m 48.372s
20	Bradl	1m 48.646s
21	Baz	1m 48.991s
	Rabat	No Time

Fastest race laps

1	Iannone	1m 47.687s
2	Pedrosa	1m 47.734s
3	Marquez	1m 47.871s
4	Lorenzo	1m 47.961s
5	Dovizioso	1m 47.997s
6	Rossi	1m 48.092s
7	Vinales	1m 48.147s
8	P. Espargaro	1m 48.357s
9	Smith	1m 48.371s
10	Petrucci	1m 48.428s
11	A. Espargaro	1m 48.571s
12	Redding	1m 48.581s
13	Crutchlow	1m 48.623s
14	Pirro	1m 48.746s
15	Barbera	1m 48.873s
16	Hernandez	1m 49.159s
17	Bradl	1m 49.248s
18	Laverty	1m 49.260s

Championship Points

1	Lorenzo	115
2	Marquez	105
3	Rossi	78
4	Pedrosa	66
5	Vinales	59
6	A. Espargaro	49
7	P. Espargaro	48
8	Barbera	43
9	Iannone	41
10	Laverty	36
11	Dovizioso	34
12	Smith	29
13	Bradl	25
14	Bautista	21
15	Pirro	18
16	Petrucci	17
17	Redding	16
18	Rabat	11
19	Crutchlow	10
20	Baz	8
21	Hernandez	3
22	Miller	2

Constructor Points

	Constructor	Points
1	Yamaha	140
2	Honda	115
3	Ducati	83
4	Suzuki	65
5	Aprilia	29

Lap chart

Grid order	1	2	3	4	5	6	7	8	9	10	11	12	13	14	15	16	17	18	19	20	21	22	23	Pos
46 ROSSI	99	99	99	99	99	99	99	99	99	99	99	99	99	99	99	99	99	99	99	99	99	99	99	1
25 VINALES	46	46	46	46	46	46	46	46	93	93	93	93	93	93	93	93	93	93	93	93	93	93	93	2
29 IANNONE	41	41	93	93	93	93	93	93	4	4	4	4	4	4	4	4	29	29	29	29	29	29	29	3
93 MARQUEZ	93	93	41	41	4	4	4	4	26	29	29	29	29	29	29	29	4	4	26	26	26	26	26	4
99 LORENZO	4	4	4	4	41	41	26	26	29	26	26	26	26	26	26	26	26	26	4	4	4	4	4	5
41 A. ESPARGARO	38	26	26	26	26	26	41	41	41	25	25	25	25	25	25	25	25	25	25	25	25	25	25	6
26 PEDROSA	26	38	45	45	45	25	29	29	25	41	41	41	41	41	38	38	38	38	38	38	38	38	38	7
38 SMITH	29	45	25	25	25	45	25	25	38	38	38	38	38	38	41	41	41	41	41	9	9	9	9	8
9 PETRUCCI	45	9	38	29	29	29	45	38	9	9	9	9	9	9	9	9	9	9	41	41	41	41	41	9
45 REDDING	9	25	29	38	38	38	38	45	51	51	51	51	51	51	51	51	51	51	51	51	51	51	51	10
51 PIRRO	25	29	9	9	9	9	9	9	35	35	35	35	35	35	35	35	35	35	35	35	35	35	35	11
68 HERNANDEZ	51	51	51	51	51	51	44	44	6	8	8	8	8	8	8	8	8	8	8	8	8	8	8	12
4 DOVIZIOSO	6	68	68	68	44	44	51	51	8	6	6	6	6	6	6	6	50	50	50	50	50	50	50	13
44 P. ESPARGARO	68	6	44	44	68	35	35	35	50	50	50	50	50	50	50	6	6	6	6	6	6	6	6	14
8 BARBERA	44	35	6	6	6	6	6	6	44	68	68	68	68	68	68	68	44	44	44	44	44	44	44	15
35 CRUTCHLOW	35	44	35	35	35	8	8	8	68	44	44	44	44	44	44	44	68	68	68	68	68	68	68	16
43 MILLER	50	50	50	50	50	8	50	50																
50 LAVERTY	8	8	8	8	8	68	68																	
19 BAUTISTA																								
6 BRADL																								
76 BAZ																								

45 Pit stop   68 Ride-through penalty

Moto2

RACE DISTANCE: 10 laps, 32.591 miles/52.450km · RACE WEATHER: Dry (air 26°C, humidity 41%, track 46°C)

Pos.	Rider	Nat.	No.	Entrant	Machine	Laps	Time & Speed
1	**Johann Zarco**	FRA	5	Ajo Motorsport	Kalex	10	18m 59.391s
							103.0mph/
							165.7km/h
2	**Lorenzo Baldassari**	ITA	7	Forward Team	Kalex	10	18m 59.421s
3	**Sam Lowes**	GBR	22	Federal Oil Gresini Moto2	Kalex	10	19m 00.487s
4	**Thomas Luthi**	SWI	12	Garage Plus Interwetten	Kalex	10	19m 00.606s
5	**Hafizh Syahrin**	MAL	55	Petronas Raceline Malaysia	Kalex	10	19m 01.044s
6	**Axel Pons**	SPA	49	AGR Team	Kalex	10	19m 01.501s
7	**Alex Rins**	SPA	40	Paginas Amarillas HP 40	Kalex	10	19m 05.040s
8	**Franco Morbidelli**	ITA	21	Estrella Galicia, 0,0 Marc VDS	Kalex	10	19m 05.640s
9	**Takaaki Nakagami**	JPN	30	IDEMITSU Honda Team Asia	Kalex	10	19m 05.671s
10	**Dominique Aegerter**	SWI	77	CarXpert Interwetten	Kalex	10	19m 05.713s
11	**Sandro Cortese**	GER	11	Dynavolt Intact GP	Kalex	10	19m 06.111s
12	**Simone Corsi**	ITA	24	Speed Up Racing	Speed Up	10	19m 07.050s
13	**Miguel Oliveira**	POR	44	Leopard Racing	Kalex	10	19m 07.109s
14	**Danny Kent**	GBR	52	Leopard Racing	Kalex	10	19m 07.136s
15	**Jonas Folger**	GER	94	Dynavolt Intact GP	Kalex	10	19m 07.437s
16	Alex Marquez	SPA	73	Estrella Galicia 0,0 Marc VDS	Kalex	10	19m 08.691s
17	Julian Simon	SPA	60	QMMF Racing Team	Speed Up	10	19m 09.801s
18	Marcel Schrotter	GER	23	AGR Team	Kalex	10	19m 10.976s
19	Ricard Cardus	SPA	88	JPMoto Malaysia	Suter	10	19m 11.045s
20	Federico Fulgni	ITA	42	Team Ciatti	Kalex	10	19m 14.130s
21	Robin Mulhauser	SWI	70	CarXpert Interwetten	Kalex	10	19m 14.480s
22	Ratthapark Wilairot	THA	14	IDEMITSU Honda Team Asia	Kalex	10	19m 14.489s
23	Edgar Pons	SPA	57	Paginas Amarillas HP 40	Kalex	10	19m 20.403s
24	Isaac Vinales	SPA	32	Tech 3	Tech 3	10	19m 21.125s
25	Alessandro Tonucci	ITA	33	Tasca Racing Scuderia Moto2	Kalex	10	19m 29.396s
26	Jesko Raffin	SWI	2	Sports-Millions-EMWE-SAG	Kalex	10	19m 49.814s
	Luis Salom	SPA	39	SAG Team	Kalex	8	DNF
	Mattia Pasini	ITA	0	Italtrans Racing Team	Kalex	1	DNF
	Xavier Simeon	BEL	0	QMMF Racing Team	Seed Up	0	DNS
	Luca Marini	ITA	0	Forward Team	Kalex	0	DNS
	Xavi Vierge	SPA	0	Tech 3 Racing	Tech 3	0	DNS

Fastest lap: Thomas Luthi, on lap 3, 1m 52.718s, 104.1mph/167.5km/h. (race part 1).

Lap record: Tito Rabat, SPA (Kalex), 1m 52.530s, 104.2mph/167.7km/h (2015).

Event best maximum speed: Luis Salom, 180.6mph/290.6km/h (race).

Qualifying

Weather: Dry
Air Temp: 26° **Track Temp:** 47°
Humidity: 38%

1	Lowes	1m 51.965s
2	Nakagami	1m 52.012s
3	Baldassarri	1m 52.088s
4	Pons	1m 52.091s
5	Schrotter	1m 52.134s
6	Zarco	1m 52.198s
7	Luthi	1m 52.265s
8	Corsi	1m 52.321s
9	Rins	1m 52.321s
10	Marini	1m 52.330s
11	Cortese	1m 52.343s
12	Aegerter	1m 52.361s
13	Morbidelli	1m 52.394s
14	Marquez	1m 52.399s
15	Syahrin	1m 52.466s
16	Salom	1m 52.624s
17	Folger	1m 52.652s
18	Kent	1m 52.694s
19	Simeon	1m 52.743s
20	Simon	1m 52.754s
21	Oliveira	1m 53.170s
22	Pasini	1m 53.238s
23	Wilairot	1m 53.318s
24	Mulhauser	1m 53.623s
25	Cardus	1m 53.778s
26	Vinales	1m 53.806s
27	Pons	1m 53.881s
28	Fulgni	1m 53.949s
29	Vierge	1m 54.288s
30	Tonucci	1m 54.832s
31	Raffin	1m 55.197s

Fastest race laps

1	Lowes	1m 52.756s
2	Zarco	1m 52.813s
3	Syahrin	1m 52.835s
4	Corsi	1m 52.899s
5	Luthi	1m 52.931s
6	Folger	1m 52.957s
7	Aegerter	1m 52.985s
8	Nakagami	1m 53.042s
9	Pons	1m 53.048s
10	Baldassarri	1m 53.063s
11	Rins	1m 53.133s
12	Salom	1m 53.170s
13	Oliveira	1m 53.331s
14	Morbidelli	1m 53.457s
15	Kent	1m 53.497s
16	Simon	1m 53.509s
17	Cortese	1m 53.514s
18	Marquez	1m 53.556s
19	Wilairot	1m 53.744s
20	Mulhauser	1m 53.796s
21	Cardus	1m 53.903s
22	Fulgni	1m 54.005s
23	Schrotter	1m 54.167s
24	Pons	1m 54.717s
25	Vinales	1m 54.759s
26	Tonucci	1m 55.594s
27	Raffin	1m 56.461s

Championship Points

1	Lowes	98
2	Rins	96
3	Luthi	82
4	Zarco	81
5	Aegerter	52
6	Corsi	50
7	Folger	48
8	Syahrin	47
9	Morbidelli	45
10	Salom	37
11	Nakagami	37
12	Pons	27
13	Baldassarri	23
14	Simeon	23
15	Oliveira	15
16	Schrotter	13
17	Kent	12
18	Pasini	10
19	Marini	10
20	Cortese	10
21	Simon	7
22	Marquez	5
23	Wilairot	3
24	Vinales	3
25	Vierge	3
26	Raffin	2
27	Mulhauser	1

Constructor Points

1	Kalex	150
2	Speed Up	60
3	Tech 3	6

Moto3

RACE DISTANCE: 20 laps, 65.182 miles/104.900km · RACE WEATHER: Dry (air 25°C, humidity 41%, track 39°C)

Pos.	Rider	Nat.	No.	Entrant	Machine	Laps	Time & Speed
1	**Brad Binder**	RSA	41	Red Bull KTM Ajo	KTM	20	39m 49.382s
							98.2mph/
							158.0km/h
2	**Fabio di Giannantonio**	ITA	4	Gresini Racing Moto3	Honda	20	39m 49.420s
3	**Francesco Bagnaia**	ITA	21	ASPAR Mahindra Team Moto3	Mahindra	20	39m 49.451s
4	**Niccolo Antonelli**	ITA	23	Ongetta-Rivacold	Honda	20	39m 49.457s
5	**Fabio Quartararo**	FRA	20	Leopard Racing	KTM	20	39m 49.459s
6	**Hiroki Ono**	JPN	76	Honda Team Asia	Honda	20	39m 50.419s
7	**Joan Mir**	SPA	36	Leopard Racing	KTM	20	39m 50.914s
8	**Nicolo Bulega**	ITA	8	SKY Racing Team VR46	KTM	20	39m 50.920s
9	**Juanfran Guevara**	SPA	58	RBA Racing Team	KTM	20	39m 50.949s
10	**Andrea Migno**	ITA	16	SKY Racing Team VR46	KTM	20	39m 51.144s
11	**Jules Danilo**	FRA	95	Ongetta-Rivacold	Honda	20	39m 51.173s
12	**Enea Bastianini**	ITA	33	Gresini Racing Moto3	Honda	20	39m 51.174s
13	**Gabriel Rodrigo**	ARG	19	RBA Racing Team	KTM	20	39m 51.315s
14	**Jorge Martin**	SPA	88	ASPAR Mahindra Team Moto3	Mahindra	20	39m 51.393s
15	**Lorenzo dalla Porta**	ITA	48	Schedl GP Racing	KTM	20	39m 51.423s
16	Livio Loi	BEL	11	RW Racing GP BV	Honda	20	39m 51.773s
17	Jakub Kornfeil	CZE	84	Drive M7 SIC Racing Team	Honda	20	39m 51.816s
18	Bo Bendsneyder	NED	64	Red Bull KTM Ajo	KTM	20	39m 51.959s
19	Tatsuki Suzuki	JPN	24	CIP-Unicom Starker	Mahindra	20	39m 52.157s
20	Karel Hanika	CZE	98	Platinum Bay Real Estate	Mahindra	20	39m 53.671s
21	Maria Herrera	SPA	6	MH6 Team	KTM	20	39m 54.298s
22	Adam Norrodin	MAL	7	Drive M7 SIC Racing Team	Honda	20	40m 24.036s
23	John McPhee	GBR	17	Peugeot MC Saxoprint	Peugeot	20	40m 24.074s
24	Stefano Valtulini	ITA	43	3570 Team Italia	Mahindra	20	40m 24.121s
25	Lorenzo Petrarca	ITA	77	3570 Team Italia	Mahindra	20	40m 32.010s
	Aron Canet	SPA	44	Estrella Galicia 0,0	Honda	19	DNF
	Khairul Idham Pawi	MAL	89	Honda Team Asia	Honda	19	DNF
	Fabio Spiranelli	ITA	3	CIP-Unicom Starker	Mahindra	19	DNF
	Andrea Locatelli	ITA	55	Leopard Racing	KTM	13	DNF
	Jorge Navarro	SPA	9	Estrella Galicia 0,0	Honda	11	DNF
	Romano Fenati	ITA	5	SKY Racing Team VR46	KTM	9	DNF
	Darryn Binder	RSA	40	Platinum Bay Real Estate	Mahindra	7	DNF
	Alexis Masbou	FRA	10	Peugeot MC Saxoprint	Peugeot	3	DNF

Fastest lap: Juanfran Guevara, on lap 3, 1m 58.009s, 99.4mph/160.0km/h.

Lap record: Brad Binder, RSA (KTM), 1m 57.318s, 100.0mph/160.9km/h (2015).

Event best maximum speed: Nicolo Bulega, 151.6mph/244.0km/h (race).

Qualifying

Weather: Dry
Air Temp: 25° **Track Temp:** 43°
Humidity: 40%

1	Fenati	1m 57.289s
2	Migno	1m 57.586s
3	Pawi	1m 57.605s
4	B. Binder	1m 57.661s
5	Navarro	1m 57.956s
6	Bastianini	1m 57.994s
7	Bulega	1m 58.013s
8	Bagnaia	1m 58.049s
9	Canet	1m 58.123s
10	Mir	1m 58.151s
11	Ono	1m 58.152s
12	Di Giannantonio	1m 58.228s
13	Bendsneyder	1m 58.305s
14	Dalla Porta	1m 58.343s
15	Martin	1m 58.344s
16	Kornfeil	1m 58.375s
17	Locatelli	1m 58.426s
18	Quartararo	1m 58.486s
19	Hanika	1m 58.494s
20	Suzuki	1m 58.520s
21	Rodrigo	1m 58.577s
22	Antonelli	1m 58.606s
23	Loi	1m 58.676s
24	D. Binder	1m 58.745s
25	Danilo	1m 58.763s
26	Guevara	1m 58.767s
27	Masbou	1m 58.931s
28	McPhee	1m 59.041s
29	Herrera	1m 59.260s
30	Valtulini	1m 59.448s
31	Norrodin	1m 59.453s
32	Spiranelli	2m 00.482s
33	Petrarca	2m 00.570s

Fastest race laps

1	Guevara	1m 58.009s
2	Pawi	1m 58.122s
3	Rodrigo	1m 58.161s
4	Fenati	1m 58.171s
5	Antonelli	1m 58.180s
6	Quartararo	1m 58.183s
7	Canet	1m 58.276s
8	Martin	1m 58.284s
9	Mir	1m 58.288s
10	Di Giannantonio	1m 58.289s
11	Bulega	1m 58.307s
12	Dalla Porta	1m 58.308s
13	Bastianini	1m 58.323s
14	Bendsneyder	1m 58.327s
15	D. Binder	1m 58.332s
16	Suzuki	1m 58.360s
17	Danilo	1m 58.368s
18	Kornfeil	1m 58.396s
19	Navarro	1m 58.400s
20	Loi	1m 58.410s
21	B. Binder	1m 58.412s
22	Bagnaia	1m 58.417s
23	Ono	1m 58.439s
24	Herrera	1m 58.459s
25	Hanika	1m 58.492s
26	Migno	1m 58.515s
27	Norrodin	1m 59.277s
28	Spiranelli	1m 59.406s
29	Locatelli	1m 59.468s
30	Valtulini	1m 59.572s
31	McPhee	1m 59.577s
32	Masbou	1m 59.729s
33	Petrarca	2m 00.248s

Championship Points

1	B. Binder	127
2	Navarro	78
3	Fenati	67
4	Bulega	55
5	Bagnaia	54
6	Antonelli	52
7	Kornfeil	36
8	Mir	34
9	Bastianini	33
10	Locatelli	30
11	Quartararo	30
12	Pawi	29
13	Oettl	27
14	Danilo	24
15	Canet	23
16	Guevara	22
17	Migno	21
18	Loi	21
19	Di Giannantonio	20
20	Ono	20
21	Martin	10
22	McPhee	9
23	Rodrigo	6
24	Norrodin	5
25	Bendsneyder	2
26	Herrera	2
27	Suzuki	2
28	Dalla Porta	1

Constructor Points

1	KTM	136
2	Honda	119
3	Mahindra	62
4	Peugeot	9

CATALUNYA GRAND PRIX

CATALUNYA CIRCUIT

Above: A contact sport? Crash-happy Iannone and victim Lorenzo had different views.

Top right: Patched up and plated, Tito Rabat was declared fit to ride.

Above centre right: Spain's first premier-class champion Alex Criville (left) was inducted to the MotoGP Hall of Fame.

Above right: The GP Safety Commission of riders and officials at the scene of Salom's catastrophe. The track was revised for the race.

Right: Jack Miller and Hector Barbera had their positions reversed after a last-lap tussle.

Below right: Black shirts on a sombre podium: Marquez, Rossi and Pedrosa paid tribute to Salom.

Opening spread: Marquez was no match for old master Rossi. In the 21st season of an amazing career, he claimed win number 114.

Photos: Gold & Goose

IT goes without saying that racing in the shadow of sudden death is difficult. What once was common in racing nowadays is so rare and so shocking. According to both riders and Dorna, the meeting was close to cancellation. Only a track alteration and the sanction of the victim's family allowed it to go ahead.

Salom's Friday afternoon crash was analysed in depth. The telemetry showed that he had braked "seven or eight metres" later than on previous laps, and that the front wheel had tucked under. Investigator Lluis Lleonart Gomez – a telemetry expert appointed by the rider's family – speculated that he may have been looking behind, missed his braking point and been a little off line.

A far from unusual minor rider error, but with freakishly severe consequences. Salom's fall had been part and parcel of racing. The place where it happened and the manner in which it happened were simply the worst possible luck. Turn 12 is a right-hander taken at some 140km/h, with the run-off area restricted by grandstands. Previous discussion at the Safety Commission, Marquez confirmed, had been satisfied with the provision of an air-fence. But instead of a full gravel trap, the outside of the corner had a paved run-off area, an increasingly common provision, mainly in the interests of F1. It is an unusual place for a bike crash. Salom's trajectory carried him at barely reduced speed across the asphalt. His bike struck the air-fence and bounced back just as he arrived to hit it headfirst. He suffered immediate cardiac arrest, and despite the promptest medical attention he was declared dead an hour later.

While the machine and tyres were exonerated, the circuit was not. Turn 12 had to have its teeth pulled. Fortunately, the slightly different F1 layout offered a solution: a tighter Turn Ten at the end of the back straight and a chicane before the front straight slowed both entry and exit at the corner, introducing hard braking and providing two more first-gear corners to add to Turn Five. The new Turn Ten had earlier been tested and rejected by MotoGP riders, for it spoiled the rhythm of the final section. For now, it was a stopgap solution – but likely to become permanent.

Agreement was reached at the usual Friday Safety Commission meeting, unusually well attended – by Marquez, Iannone, Pol and Aleix Espargaro, Miller, Smith, Bautista,

Dovizioso, Crutchlow and Rabat, and after a visit to the site of the crash.

Neither of the Yamaha factory riders was there, and later Lorenzo complained that all riders and teams should have been consulted, and that the slower version of Turn Ten was an unnecessary change. His view was understandable: the Yamaha was favoured by fast corners, and the new layout played against it. Less so his protestations that he had not joined the forum because "Usually, the meeting is in the Dorna office at 5.30, but this time it was at the corner." Marquez quickly contradicted him: "We were in the Dorna office from 5.30 until 6.15."

Feelings were running high at the post-qualifying press conference, and Moto2 pole qualifier Zarco took explosive offence at one question, which concerned apparent contradictions between various statements. "That is a really shit question," was the angry Frenchman's instant response. "You are trying to make a problem, but you are the problem. You should shut up." Although badly framed, the question was legitimate, and Marquez quickly leapt in to calm the troubled waters.

Track staff worked late into the night, painting new kerbs and adjusting barriers; the revised layout effectively made a new circuit, with a section that riders would have to learn from scratch. Accordingly, all Saturday morning's Free Practice sessions were extended by 15 minutes, to make a full hour for MotoGP and Moto2, and 55 minutes for Moto3.

Finding braking points and lines was well within the grasp of world championship-level riders, but the matter of re-gearing and revising suspension settings meant hard work also for the pit crews. One unexpected result, explained KTM technical chief Tom Jojic, had been that with a new first-gear corner before the front straight, they had expected top speeds to be lower. "They turned out to be higher, so we got that wrong."

Pedrosa explained the anomaly. Though the approach to the last corner was slower, it was on a more favourable wider line, and instead of slowing through the bend, "you are accelerating all the way".

Two more contracts were confirmed on race eve at Catalunya. One was expected: Marquez would stay for two more years with Repsol Honda. The second had two aspects: first-

ly that Pol Espargaro would be leaving Yamaha after three patchy seasons with the satellite team, confounding earlier expectations that he was bound for the factory team. Then, on Thursday evening, a beaming Pol confirmed that he was going to join long-time team-mate Smith at the new factory KTM team.

Rabat was declared fit to ride on race eve, and his freshly repaired collarbone (plated and with eight screws) survived a heavy crash on the first day of practice. Moto3's Oettl was also back after missing Mugello, but Loris Baz was absent, his place in the Avintia team having been taken by Ducati test rider Michele Pirro, the third team he had raced for during the season.

Spain's first 500-class champion Alex Criville, winner of 15 500cc GPs, was appointed the 24th MotoGP Legend when he was formally inducted into the Hall of Fame at the circuit closest to his home. "I never wanted to be a racer when I was young. I just enjoyed riding bikes," the ever-modest Spaniard said.

MOTOGP RACE – 25 laps

Evergreen and ever amazing at 37, Rossi claimed career win number 114 in the full fighting style of a master. It put him just eight races short of equalling Agostini's record of 122 wins. More importantly, as it became Lorenzo's turn for a luckless zero points, it put him right back in the title chase.

A crowd of almost 100,000 had joined in a minute of silence before racing began. By the time of MotoGP, blazing heat and an already slippery surface made the race a test of tyre endurance, with all but four riders choosing the harder rear – team-mates Smith and Pol Espargaro, Rabat and, at the last moment on the grid, Pedrosa.

Marquez and Pedrosa flanked Lorenzo on the front row; Rossi qualified seventh, behind Barbera. Lorenzo led away, while Rossi made only an average start. But by the seventh lap, he had fought through to dispossess his team-mate.

Marquez followed him past, and ran him ragged to the finish, getting ahead with two laps to go. Then he ran wide after a determined, but unsuccessful last-lap attack, and the Honda rider cruised home 2.65 seconds adrift.

"For me, it was the perfect Sunday," said Rossi, fastest in morning warm-up. "The key was this morning, when we modified the bike to make it better in the slow section, and I knew I could be fast. I tried to pull away. This strategy worked for all the other riders except Marc.

"Race weekend is always difficult," he continued. "But after what happened, it was much harder to focus. This was the best way to remember Salom, homage to him. It's not much, but it's all a rider can do." Rostrum finishers all donned black T-shirts in a tribute to their fallen comrade; while Rossi and Marquez shook hands in parc fermé, seemingly bringing to an end at least the overt enmity that began late in 2015.

Second was also a relief to Marquez, after the altered track removed some of the rhythm at a second successive circuit that suited the Yamahas, allowing the Spaniard to extend his title lead again: "Now we come to some circuits that I like better."

Lorenzo was already in trouble in the race, his hard tyres graining, and it looked as though he would be lucky to finish sixth. He wouldn't get the chance, as crash-happy Iannone put both of them down in the gravel and himself back in the doghouse. The last time the Italian had collided with the rider in front of him had been in Argentina, where he cost Ducati team-mate Dovizioso a safe second place. Now a similar over-ambitious lunge at the end of the back straight did for Jorge.

He denied any mistake, saying, "Lorenzo was very slow at that point." Race Direction saw it differently, and Iannone would start the next race from the back of the grid and receive two penalty points. "I accept the punishment, but I will not change my style," he said.

Lorenzo was livid, refusing what appeared to be an apology. "It's unbelievable he should make this mistake. Instead of saying sorry, he asked me if I had an engine failure or something. I thought it was his fault."

By then, both Pedrosa and Vinales had outpaced the fading Yamaha rider. Pedrosa had lost touch with the leading pair while fighting off several headstrong attacks "in the wrong place" from Vinales, but he made the podium again.

With Vinales a secure, but ultimately distant fourth, the Lorenzo/Iannone crash left fifth to Pol Espargaro, equalling his best of the year so far, after prevailing in an early battle with Dovizioso.

An at-last-on-form Crutchlow also caught, fought and, with ten laps remaining, finally passed Dovizioso, who suspected a faulty rear tyre for a disappointing race. The factory Ducati rider had fallen back into the hands of Petrucci and Barbera, though by the finish he had got clear again. Bautista, on the clearly improving Aprilia, had also caught up from miles behind, passing Petrucci for eighth on the final lap; Barbera now out of touch.

Miller had a strong ride, passing first Redding, who was suffering tyre problems, and then a fading Hernandez, only to lose a late-race battle with Bautista. The Australian crossed the line 11th, but was promoted to his first top-ten finish when Barbera was docked a place for exceeding track limits.

Bradl was five seconds behind in 12th, the remaining points going to Laverty, Rabat and Pirro.

Aleix Espargaro retired, complaining of a ruined tyre; likewise Smith, with an electronic glitch that destroyed his engine braking.

MOTO2 RACE – 23 laps

Defending champion Zarco took an emotional pole ahead of Rins, dedicating it to Salom, a rival since their earliest days in the Red Bull Rookies Cup.

But it was third qualifier Luthi who led into the first corner, from Nakagami, up from row two.

The early sorting out provided much of the excitement from the front-runners, with Rins having seized the lead by the end of the lap, while Zarco had also passed Luthi next time around.

The pair soon pulled clear, Zarco shadowing his Spanish rival faithfully, able to study his lines and assess his strengths and weaknesses. "Johann was thinking more than me, and he had a different gearbox from me," said Rins, who had the consolation of taking over the title lead.

As so often before, the Frenchman was biding his time, and at the start of lap 17 he pounced on the way into the first corner, and that was the end of that.

"I stayed behind Rins and I saw I was faster than him except in the last sector, and I needed to get ahead on the faster part," he said, also dedicating his win to Salom.

Rins hung on for a couple of laps, but it was a hopeless struggle, and with three laps to go he settled for second, eventually four seconds adrift.

He was still safe from a fierce battle for the last rostrum position. Luthi had appeared set to take the place, while Marquez led the chase, until he crashed out once again shortly before half-distance.

Hafizh Syahrin had been with him from the early laps, with Lowes in close pursuit; but now Nakagami – who had faded in the early laps – had picked up pace again and joined battle with the Malaysian.

The pair left Lowes trailing and with eight laps to go had caught Luthi for a strong three-way fight. By the end of it, Nakagami had escaped, while the other two were changing places until the last lap, with Syahrin claiming fourth.

Lowes was a couple of seconds adrift in sixth; Folger picked his way steadily through from 12th on lap one to a clear seventh.

A four-bike battle in his wake had closed on Axel Pons, and on the last lap class rookie Oliveira passed the Spaniard for eighth, best so far and second top ten of the year.

Second AGR rider Schrotter had dropped out of touch by the finish, likewise Morbidelli, who just managed to shade veteran Pasini.

Julian Simon was 13th on the QMMF Speed Up, the first non-Kalex; Baldassarri an impressive 14th. He'd been put off the track by headlong crasher Corsi on lap three and had come through from last.

Remy Gardner, son of 1987 500 champion Wayne, took the last point in his first Moto2 race, defeating Isaac Vinales after a long fight. Gardner was substituting for the out-of-favour Alessandro Tonucci and was waiting to hear if he could keep the ride.

Aegerter was among eight non-finishers, having been forced to pull out of a strong top-ten place with an extraordinary rear wheel collapse.

MOTO3 RACE – 22 laps

Could Binder break an 11-race run whereby the pole starter had not won a Moto3 race? No, as it turned out, through little fault of his own.

In a typical action-packed maelstrom, there was still an eight-strong lead pack at half-distance, with the usual suspects and some unexpected fast chargers swapping back and forth.

Binder led the first lap and several others, with Fenati also taking to the front several times. Rookie Pawi also headed one early lap and was in the mix until he crashed out with two laps to go, as did another erstwhile front-runner, Rodrigo.

The lion's share went to Navarro, in spite of a lap-eight error that dropped him to fifth. Eventually he was able to escape to take his first win by half a second – but it might have been different, because a couple of laps before Rodrigo crashed, he clipped Binder's back wheel, knocking him to eighth with four laps to go.

A couple of days later, Navarro ruined his season, breaking his leg badly in a training crash.

In a ride reminiscent of Jerez, Binder started the last lap fifth, but he had forged his way through to second at the end.

The surviving gang members were still close, first to sixth over the line in just over 1.5 seconds.

Bastianini's third was his first podium of the year; then came Fenati and rookies Bulega and Canet.

Quartararo led the next group from team-mate Mir and Di Giannantonio, with Kornfeil still close in tenth.

A high rate of attrition helped Brad Binder's younger brother, Darryn, to his first points, 12th on the top Mahindra after Bagnaia was knocked down from the leading group by Guevara (who went on to finish 13th) and Martin crashed, injuring his right hand. In all, there were 16 crashers, including Antonelli.

Above: In front of packed grandstands, the MotoGP family gathered to remember a fallen son.

Top right: Moto3 young guns Bulega and Canet battle it out for fifth.

Above right: Close as paint, Syahrin (55) and Marquez trade blows, before the latter crashed out.

Right: Johann Zarco took control once more in Moto2.

Below right: Another sombre podium for Rins, Zarco and Nakagami.

Below: Winner Jorge Navarro leads Bastianini, Fenati, Rodrigo and Brad Binder in a typical Moto3 maelstrom.
Photos: Gold & Goose

LUIS SALOM 1991–2016

LUIS SALOM (24), who had ridden competitively from the age of eight, was typical of the current generation of Spanish riders – dedicated and determined. But compared to some more privileged compatriots, he had had to fight to gain high-level support.

He was a unique character, with an often sombre mien, and openly emotional in victory and defeat. This was reflected in the strength of the emotion he left behind him.

Salom had been born in Palma de Mallorca on 7th August, 1991, and he moved rapidly through the junior ranks of Spanish racing. A single race winner in 2007's new Red Bull Rookies Cup, he finished runner-up in 2008, just four points adrift of American JD Beach.

His first GP appearance, in 2009, was as a 125 wild-card at Jerez, for the same SAG team he rejoined in 2016. For the last ten rounds, he rode for the Jack & Jones team, with a best of sixth at Donington Park.

After a chequered 2010, he switched from Lambretta to Aprilia, with a best of fifth at Estoril among nine top-ten finishes. Salom was 12th that year, eighth the next, and in 2012 in the new Moto3, riding a Kalex-KTM, he finished a distant second overall to Sandro Cortese, having claimed his first win at Indianapolis and added one more at Aragon.

His combative style earned him a place in the factory-backed Red Bull KTM team for 2013. He won seven races in his best season, but his bad luck struck again. He was leading the championship until the last round at Valencia, in spite of scoring zero points, when he was knocked flying at the previous race at Motegi.

Fighting for the lead in the final showdown, he slipped off, but remounted to score just two points, while Maverick Vinales narrowly defeated Alex Rins for the crown.

Salom moved to Moto2 in 2014. He made the podium twice in his first year, but struggled more in 2015, although he still took eight top-ten finishes. In 2016, back with the SAG team, he finished an emotional second in the first round at Qatar, but again battled to find consistency, with a best of ninth among four more finishes in the points.

Among many messages of condolence, one from his former Red Bull Moto3 team, Ajo Motorsport, ended simply: "Rest in peace, 'Mexicano', we will never forget you." One of the most apposite was from Cal Crutchlow: "Our sport is the best sport in the world, but it can be so very cruel sometimes."

Luis would have loved the motorcycle racing on Sunday. It was a feast, with three magnificent victories immediately dedicated to his memory.

GRAN PREMI MONSTER ENERGY DE CATALUNYA

3-5 JUNE, 2016

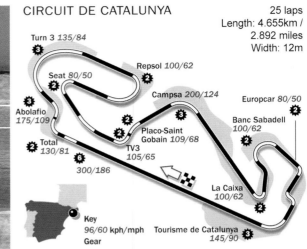

CIRCUIT DE CATALUNYA

25 laps
Length: 4.655km / 2.892 miles
Width: 12m

Turn 3 135/84
Repsol 100/62
Seat 80/50
Campsa 200/124
Europcar 80/50
Abolafio 175/109
Banc Sabadell 100/62
Placo-Saint Gobain 109/68
Total 130/81
TV3 105/65
300/186
La Caixa 100/62
Key 96/60 kph/mph Gear
Tourisme de Catalunya 145/90

MotoGP

RACE DISTANCE: 25 laps, 72.312 miles/116.375km · RACE WEATHER: Dry (air 27°C, humidity 44%, track 48°C)

Pos.	Rider	Nat.	No.	Entrant	Machine	Tyres	Race tyre choice	Laps	Time & speed
1	Valentino Rossi	ITA	46	Movistar Yamaha MotoGP	Yamaha YZR-M1	M	F: Hard/R: Hard	25	44m 37.589s 97.2mph/ 156.4km/h
2	Marc Marquez	SPA	93	Repsol Honda Team	Honda RC213V	M	F: Hard/R: Hard	25	44m 40.241s
3	Dani Pedrosa	SPA	26	Repsol Honda Team	Honda RC213V	M	F: Hard/R: Medium	25	44m 43.902s
4	Maverick Vinales	SPA	25	Team SUZUKI ECSTAR	Suzuki GSX-RR	M	F: Hard/R: Hard	25	45m 01.977s
5	Pol Espargaro	SPA	44	Monster Yamaha Tech 3	Yamaha YZR-M1	M	F: Medium/R: Medium	25	45m 07.135s
6	Cal Crutchlow	GBR	35	LCR Honda	Honda RC213V	M	F: Hard/R: Hard	25	45m 13.833s
7	Andrea Dovizioso	ITA	4	Ducati Team	Ducati Desmosedici	M	F: Hard/R: Hard	25	45m 19.053s
8	Alvaro Bautista	SPA	19	Aprilia Racing Team Gresini	Aprilia RS-GP	M	F: Hard/R: Hard	25	45m 20.564s
9	Danilo Petrucci	ITA	9	OCTO Pramac Yakhnich	Ducati Desmosedici	M	F: Hard/R: Hard	25	45m 22.926s
10	Jack Miller	AUS	43	Estrella Galicia 0,0 Marc VDS	Honda RC213V	M	F: Hard/R: Hard	25	45m 27.103s
11	Hector Barbera	SPA	8	Avintia Racing	Ducati Desmosedici	M	F: Hard/R: Hard	25	45m 24.258s
12	Stefan Bradl	GER	6	Aprilia Racing Team Gresini	Aprilia RS-GP	M	F: Hard/R: Hard	25	45m 32.722s
13	Eugene Laverty	IRL	50	Aspar Team MotoGP	Ducati Desmosedici	M	F: Hard/R: Hard	25	45m 35.563s
14	Tito Rabat	SPA	53	Estrella Galicia 0,0 Marc VDS	Honda RC213V	M	F: Hard/R: Medium	25	45m 37.730s
15	Michele Pirro	ITA	51	Avintia Racing	Ducati Desmosedici	M	F: Hard/R: Hard	25	45m 38.018s
16	Scott Redding	GBR	45	OCTO Pramac Yakhnich	Ducati Desmosedici	M	F: Hard/R: Hard	25	45m 45.858s
17	Yonny Hernandez	COL	68	Aspar Team MotoGP	Ducati Desmosedici	M	F: Hard/R: Hard	24	44m 56.487s
	Aleix Espargaro	SPA	41	Team SUZUKI ECSTAR	Suzuki GSX-RR	M	F: Hard/R: Hard	18	DNF-technical
	Jorge Lorenzo	SPA	99	Movistar Yamaha MotoGP	Yamaha YZR-M1	M	F: Hard/R: Hard	16	DNF-crash
	Andrea Iannone	ITA	29	Ducati Team	Ducati Desmosedici	M	F: Hard/R: Hard	16	DNF-crash
	Bradley Smith	GBR	38	Monster Yamaha Tech 3	Yamaha YZR-M1	M	F: Medium/R: Medium	6	DNF-technical

Fastest lap: Maverick Vinales, on lap 5, 1m 45.971s, 98.2mph/158.1km/h (record).

Previous lap record: New circuit layout.

Event best maximum speed: Andrea Iannone, 215.7mph/347.2km/h (free practice).

Qualifying

Weather: Dry
Air Temp: 25° Track Temp: 41°
Humidity: 46%

1	Marquez	1m 43.589s
2	Lorenzo	1m 44.056s
3	Pedrosa	1m 44.307s
4	Barbera	1m 44.322s
5	Rossi	1m 44.324s
6	Vinales	1m 44.329s
7	Crutchlow	1m 44.366s
8	Iannone	1m 44.458s
9	Petrucci	1m 44.911s
10	Dovizioso	1m 45.029s
11	Redding	1m 45.030s
12	P. Espargaro	1m 45.218s
13	A. Espargaro	1m 44.914s
14	Smith	1m 45.197s
15	Pirro	1m 45.538s
16	Hernandez	1m 45.690s
17	Laverty	1m 45.885s
18	Bradl	1m 45.892s
19	Miller	1m 45.942s
20	Rabat	1m 46.205s
21	Bautista	1m 46.463s

Fastest race laps

1	Vinales	1m 45.971s
2	Marquez	1m 46.040s
3	Rossi	1m 46.102s
4	Pedrosa	1m 46.308s
5	Lorenzo	1m 46.438s
6	Iannone	1m 46.796s
7	Crutchlow	1m 46.842s
8	P. Espargaro	1m 46.858s
9	A. Espargaro	1m 46.873s
10	Barbera	1m 46.909s
11	Dovizioso	1m 47.025s
12	Hernandez	1m 47.128s
13	Petrucci	1m 47.385s
14	Miller	1m 47.478s
15	Redding	1m 47.527s
16	Bautista	1m 47.685s
17	Rabat	1m 47.750s
18	Pirro	1m 47.910s
19	Laverty	1m 47.944s
20	Bradl	1m 48.008s
21	Smith	1m 48.080s

Championship Points

1	Marquez	125
2	Lorenzo	115
3	Rossi	103
4	Pedrosa	82
5	Vinales	72
6	P. Espargaro	59
7	A. Espargaro	49
8	Barbera	48
9	Dovizioso	43
10	Iannone	41
11	Laverty	39
12	Smith	29
13	Bradl	29
14	Bautista	29
15	Petrucci	24
16	Crutchlow	20
17	Pirro	19
18	Redding	16
19	Rabat	13
20	Miller	8
21	Baz	8
22	Hernandez	3

Constructor Points

1	Yamaha	165
2	Honda	135
3	Ducati	92
4	Suzuki	78
5	Aprilia	37

Grid order	1	2	3	4	5	6	7	8	9	10	11	12	13	14	15	16	17	18	19	20	21	22	23	24	25	
93 MARQUEZ	99	99	99	99	99	99	46	46	46	46	46	46	46	46	46	46	46	46	46	46	46	93	46	46	46	1
99 LORENZO	93	93	93	93	93	46	93	93	93	93	93	93	93	93	93	93	93	93	93	93	93	46	93	93	93	2
26 PEDROSA	26	26	46	46	46	93	99	99	26	26	26	26	26	26	26	26	26	26	26	26	26	26	26	26	26	3
8 BARBERA	29	46	26	26	26	26	26	26	99	99	99	25	25	25	25	25	25	25	25	25	25	25	25	25	25	4
46 ROSSI	25	25	25	25	25	25	25	25	25	25	25	99	99	99	99	99	44	44	44	44	44	44	44	44	44	5
25 VINALES	46	29	29	29	29	29	29	29	29	29	29	29	29	29	29	35	35	35	35	35	35	35	35	35	35	6
35 CRUTCHLOW	4	4	44	44	44	44	44	44	44	44	44	44	44	44	44	4	4	4	4	4	4	4	4	4	4	7
29 IANNONE	44	44	4	4	4	4	4	4	4	4	4	4	35	35	35	35	9	9	9	9	9	9	9	19		8
9 PETRUCCI	8	9	35	35	35	35	35	35	35	35	35	35	4	4	4	4	8	8	8	8	8	8	19	9		9
4 DOVIZIOSO	9	35	8	8	8	8	8	8	8	8	8	8	9	9	9	9	43	43	19	19	19	19	8	8		10
45 REDDING	35	8	9	41	41	41	9	9	9	9	9	9	8	8	8	8	41	19	43	43	43	43	43	43		11
44 P. ESPARGARO	41	41	41	9	9	9	41	41	41	41	41	41	41	41	41	41	19	45	6	6	6	6	6	6		12
41 A. ESPARGARO	50	68	68	68	68	68	68	68	68	68	68	43	43	43	43	43	45	6	53	53	53	50	50	50		13
38 SMITH	6	45	45	45	45	45	45	45	43	43	43	68	45	45	45	19	6	53	45	45	50	51	51	53		14
51 PIRRO	45	50	50	43	43	43	43	43	45	45	45	19	19	19	19	6	53	50	45	45	53	53	51	51		15
68 HERNANDEZ	68	43	43	50	50	50	50	50	50	50	50	19	68	6	6	6	50	51	51	51	51	45	45	45		
50 LAVERTY	43	6	6	6	6	6	6	6	19	19	50	6	6	68	68	53	51	41	68	68	68	68	68	68		
6 BRADL	19	51	51	51	51	51	51	51	51	6	6	6	50	50	50	50	68	68								
43 MILLER	38	19	19	19	19	19	19	19	19	51	51	51	51	51	53	51										
53 RABAT	51	53	38	38	38	53	53	53	53	53	53	53	53	51	68											
19 BAUTISTA	53	38	53	53	53	38																				

38 Pit stop   68 Lapped rider

Moto2 — RACE DISTANCE: 23 laps, 66.527 miles/107.065km · RACE WEATHER: Dry (air 25°C, humidity 50%, track 42°C)

Pos.	Rider	Nat.	No.	Entrant	Machine	Laps	Time & Speed
1	**Johann Zarco**	FRA	5	Ajo Motorsport	Kalex	23	42m 31.347s 93.8mph/151.0km/h
2	**Alex Rins**	SPA	40	Paginas Amarillas HP 40	Kalex	23	42m 35.527s
3	**Takaaki Nakagami**	JPN	30	IDEMITSU Honda Team Asia	Kalex	23	42m 40.660s
4	**Hafizh Syahrin**	MAL	55	Petronas Raceline Malaysia	Kalex	23	42m 42.124s
5	**Thomas Luthi**	SWI	12	Garage Plus Interwetten	Kalex	23	42m 42.308s
6	**Sam Lowes**	GBR	22	Federal Oil Gresini Moto2	Kalex	23	42m 44.347s
7	**Jonas Folger**	GER	94	Dynavolt Intact GP	Kalex	23	42m 48.393s
8	**Miguel Oliveira**	POR	44	Leopard Racing	Kalex	23	42m 51.984s
9	**Axel Pons**	SPA	49	AGR Team	Kalex	23	42m 51.993s
10	**Marcel Schrotter**	GER	23	AGR Team	Kalex	23	42m 54.510s
11	**Franco Morbidelli**	ITA	21	Estrella Galicia 0,0 Marc VDS	Kalex	23	42m 59.492s
12	**Mattia Pasini**	ITA	54	Italtrans Racing Team	Kalex	23	42m 59.695s
13	**Julian Simon**	SPA	60	QMMF Racing Team	Speed Up	23	43m 05.829s
14	**Lorenzo Baldassarri**	ITA	7	Forward Team	Kalex	23	43m 08.914s
15	**Remy Gardner**	AUS	87	Tasca Racing Scuderia Moto2	Kalex	23	43m 14.345s
16	Isaac Vinales	SPA	32	Tech 3 Racing	Tech 3	23	43m 15.979s
17	Edgar Pons	SPA	57	Paginas Amarillas HP 40	Kalex	23	43m 19.883s
18	Alex Marquez	SPA	73	Estrella Galicia 0,0 Marc VDS	Kalex	23	43m 22.393s
19	Ramdan Rosli	MAL	93	Petronas AHM Malaysia	Kalex	23	43m 53.813s
20	Xavi Vierge	SPA	97	Tech 3 Racing	Tech 3	23	43m 56.809s
21	Robin Mulhauser	SWI	70	CarXpert Interwetten	Kalex	22	43m 08.578s
	Ratthapark Wilairot	THA	14	IDEMITSU Honda Team Asia	Kalex	15	DNF
	Dominique Aegerter	SWI	77	CarXpert Interwetten	Kalex	14	DNF
	Luca Marini	ITA	10	Forward Team	Kalex	14	DNF
	Danny Kent	GBR	52	Leopard Racing	Kalex	10	DNF
	Sandro Cortese	GER	11	Dynavolt Intact GP	Kalex	5	DNF
	Simone Corsi	ITA	24	Speed Up Racing	Speed Up	2	DNF
	Xavier Simeon	BEL	19	QMMF Racing Team	Speed Up	1	DNF

Fastest lap: Johann Zarco, on lap 2, 1m 49.968s, 94.6mph/152.3km/h (record).
Previous lap record: New circuit layout.
Event best maximum speed: Marcel Schrotter, 177.2mph/285.1km/h (race).

Qualifying
Weather: Dry · Air Temp: 25° · Track Temp: 40° · Humidity: 41%

1	Zarco	1m 49.179s
2	Rins	1m 49.214s
3	Luthi	1m 49.472s
4	Nakagami	1m 49.606s
5	Lowes	1m 49.619s
6	Pons	1m 49.661s
7	Marquez	1m 49.712s
8	Baldassarri	1m 49.753s
9	Schrotter	1m 49.949s
10	Cortese	1m 49.980s
11	Corsi	1m 50.066s
12	Folger	1m 50.072s
13	Syahrin	1m 50.152s
14	Aegerter	1m 50.196s
15	Oliveira	1m 50.430s
16	Simeon	1m 50.479s
17	Simon	1m 50.493s
18	Morbidelli	1m 50.628s
19	Pasini	1m 50.658s
20	Marini	1m 50.868s
21	Kent	1m 50.902s
22	Vierge	1m 51.229s
23	Wilairot	1m 51.235s
24	Gardner	1m 51.241s
25	Pons	1m 51.739s
26	Mulhauser	1m 51.847s
27	Vinales	1m 51.853s
28	Rosli	1m 52.159s

Fastest race laps

1	Zarco	1m 49.968s
2	Rins	1m 50.074s
3	Luthi	1m 50.161s
4	Lowes	1m 50.235s
5	Marquez	1m 50.318s
6	Nakagami	1m 50.464s
7	Morbidelli	1m 50.477s
8	Syahrin	1m 50.543s
9	Folger	1m 50.573s
10	Pons	1m 50.642s
11	Oliveira	1m 50.764s
12	Marini	1m 50.784s
13	Aegerter	1m 50.789s
14	Schrotter	1m 50.799s
15	Baldassarri	1m 50.858s
16	Simon	1m 50.865s
17	Corsi	1m 50.906s
18	Pasini	1m 50.937s
19	Vinales	1m 51.047s
20	Cortese	1m 51.288s
21	Gardner	1m 51.334s
22	Vierge	1m 51.535s
23	Pons	1m 51.715s
24	Wilairot	1m 51.839s
25	Mulhauser	1m 51.990s
26	Kent	1m 52.459s
27	Rosli	1m 52.564s

Championship Points

Pos	Rider	Points
1	Rins	116
2	Lowes	108
3	Zarco	106
4	Luthi	93
5	Syahrin	60
6	Folger	57
7	Nakagami	53
8	Aegerter	52
9	Corsi	50
10	Morbidelli	50
11	Salom	37
12	Pons	34
13	Baldassarri	25
14	Oliveira	23
15	Simeon	23
16	Schrotter	19
17	Pasini	14
18	Kent	12
19	Simon	10
20	Marini	10
21	Cortese	10
22	Marquez	5
23	Vinales	3
24	Wilairot	3
25	Vierge	3
26	Raffin	2
27	Mulhauser	1
28	Gardner	1

Constructor Points

Pos	Constructor	Points
1	Kalex	175
2	Speed Up	63
3	Tech 3	6

Moto3 — RACE DISTANCE: 22 laps, 63.635 miles/102.410km · RACE WEATHER: Dry (air 23°C, humidity 53%, track 34°C)

Pos.	Rider	Nat.	No.	Entrant	Machine	Laps	Time & Speed
1	**Jorge Navarro**	SPA	9	Estrella Galicia 0,0	Honda	22	42m 18.228s 90.2mph/145.2km/h
2	**Brad Binder**	RSA	41	Red Bull KTM Ajo	KTM	22	42m 18.792s
3	**Enea Bastianini**	ITA	33	Gresini Racing Moto3	Honda	22	42m 19.045s
4	**Romano Fenati**	ITA	5	SKY Racing Team VR46	KTM	22	42m 19.153s
5	**Nicolo Bulega**	ITA	8	SKY Racing Team VR46	KTM	22	42m 19.759s
6	**Aron Canet**	SPA	44	Estrella Galicia 0,0	Honda	22	42m 19.809s
7	**Fabio Quartararo**	FRA	20	Leopard Racing	KTM	22	42m 31.833s
8	**Joan Mir**	SPA	36	Leopard Racing	KTM	22	42m 31.900s
9	**Fabio di Giannantonio**	ITA	4	Gresini Racing Moto3	Honda	22	42m 31.981s
10	**Jakub Kornfeil**	CZE	84	Drive M7 SIC Racing Team	Honda	22	42m 33.042s
11	**Bo Bendsneyder**	NED	64	Red Bull KTM Ajo	KTM	22	42m 33.068s
12	**Darryn Binder**	RSA	40	Platinum Bay Real Estate	Mahindra	22	42m 48.088s
13	**Juanfran Guevara**	SPA	58	RBA Racing Team	KTM	22	42m 50.234s
14	**Tatsuki Suzuki**	JPN	24	CIP-Unicom Starker	Mahindra	22	42m 51.533s
15	**John McPhee**	GBR	17	Peugeot MC Saxoprint	Peugeot	22	42m 51.994s
16	Livio Loi	BEL	11	RW Racing GP BV	Honda	22	42m 53.214s
17	Philipp Oettl	GER	65	Schedl GP Racing	KTM	22	42m 54.612s
18	Andrea Migno	ITA	16	SKY Racing Team VR46	KTM	22	42m 59.959s
19	Andrea Locatelli	ITA	55	Leopard Racing	KTM	22	43m 01.213s
20	Niccolo Antonelli	ITA	23	Ongetta-Rivacold	Honda	22	43m 17.263s
21	Fabio Spiranelli	ITA	3	CIP-Unicom Starker	Mahindra	22	43m 47.941s
22	Lorenzo Petrarca	ITA	77	3570 Team Italia	Mahindra	22	43m 48.868s
	Karel Hanika	CZE	98	Platinum Bay Real Estate	Mahindra	21	DNF
	Davide Pizzoli	ITA	37	Procercasa - 42 Motorsport	KTM	21	DNF
	Gabriel Rodrigo	ARG	19	RBA Racing Team	KTM	20	DNF
	Khairul Idham Pawi	MAL	89	Honda Team Asia	Honda	19	DNF
	Jorge Martin	SPA	88	ASPAR Mahindra Team Moto3	Mahindra	16	DNF
	Albert Arenas	SPA	12	MRW Mahindra Aspar Team	Mahindra	13	DNF
	Francesco Bagnaia	ITA	21	ASPAR Mahindra Team Moto3	Mahindra	5	DNF
	Adam Norrodin	MAL	7	Drive M7 SIC Racing Team	Honda	5	DNF
	Hiroki Ono	JPN	76	Honda Team Asia	Honda	3	DNF
	Jules Danilo	FRA	95	Ongetta-Rivacold	Honda	3	DNF
	Maria Herrera	SPA	6	MH6 Team	KTM	2	DNF
	Stefano Valtulini	ITA	43	3570 Team Italia	Mahindra	2	DNF
	Alexis Masbou	FRA	10	Peugeot MC Saxoprint	Peugeot	0	DNF

Fastest lap: Romano Fenati, on lap 8, 1m 54.145s, 91.2mph/146.8km/h (record).
Previous lap record: New circuit layout.
Event best maximum speed: Romano Fenati, 151.1mph/243.1km/h (race).

Qualifying:
Weather: Dry · Air Temp: 27° · Track Temp: 43° · Humidity: 42%

1	B. Binder	1m 54.024s
2	Antonelli	1m 54.078s
3	Navarro	1m 54.112s
4	Bulega	1m 54.131s
5	Bastianini	1m 54.167s
6	Pawi	1m 54.392s
7	Bagnaia	1m 54.439s
8	Danilo	1m 54.472s
9	Canet	1m 54.603s
10	Fenati	1m 54.718s
11	Ono	1m 54.726s
12	Quartararo	1m 54.737s
13	Di Giannantonio	1m 54.799s
14	Bendsneyder	1m 54.830s
15	Migno	1m 54.857s
16	Kornfeil	1m 54.881s
17	Arenas	1m 54.888s
18	Mir	1m 54.957s
19	Rodrigo	1m 55.152s
20	Loi	1m 55.173s
21	Guevara	1m 55.183s
22	Martin	1m 55.197s
23	Locatelli	1m 55.225s
24	Suzuki	1m 55.518s
25	Norrodin	1m 55.576s
26	McPhee	1m 55.720s
27	Herrera	1m 55.814s
28	Oettl	1m 55.995s
29	Pizzoli	1m 56.089s
30	D. Binder	1m 56.102s
31	Hanika	1m 56.219s
32	Valtulini	1m 56.362s
33	Masbou	1m 56.492s
34	Petrarca	1m 57.230s
35	Spiranelli	1m 57.868s

Fastest race laps

1	Fenati	1m 54.145s
2	Rodrigo	1m 54.148s
3	Navarro	1m 54.204s
4	B. Binder	1m 54.301s
5	Canet	1m 54.483s
6	Pawi	1m 54.554s
7	Migno	1m 54.563s
8	Bastianini	1m 54.584s
9	Kornfeil	1m 54.611s
10	Bulega	1m 54.619s
11	Martin	1m 54.766s
12	Quartararo	1m 54.830s
13	Antonelli	1m 54.860s
14	Di Giannantonio	1m 54.878s
15	Guevara	1m 54.999s
16	Bendsneyder	1m 55.004s
17	D. Binder	1m 55.078s
18	Mir	1m 55.155s
19	Ono	1m 55.264s
20	Bagnaia	1m 55.356s
21	Arenas	1m 55.420s
22	Danilo	1m 55.459s
23	Locatelli	1m 55.675s
24	McPhee	1m 55.721s
25	Oettl	1m 55.733s
26	Pizzoli	1m 55.782s
27	Suzuki	1m 55.827s
28	Loi	1m 55.932s
29	Hanika	1m 55.990s
30	Herrera	1m 56.224s
31	Spiranelli	1m 57.873s
32	Petrarca	1m 57.968s
33	Norrodin	2m 04.785s

Championship Points

Pos	Rider	Points
1	B. Binder	147
2	Navarro	103
3	Fenati	80
4	Bulega	66
5	Bagnaia	54
6	Antonelli	52
7	Bastianini	49
8	Mir	42
9	Kornfeil	42
10	Quartararo	39
11	Canet	33
12	Locatelli	30
13	Pawi	29
14	Di Giannantonio	27
15	Oettl	27
16	Guevara	25
17	Danilo	24
18	Migno	21
19	Loi	21
20	Ono	20
21	McPhee	10
22	Martin	10
23	Bendsneyder	7
24	Rodrigo	6
25	Norrodin	5
26	D. Binder	4
27	Suzuki	4
28	Herrera	2
29	Dalla Porta	1

Constructor Points

Pos	Constructor	Points
1	KTM	156
2	Honda	144
3	Mahindra	66
4	Peugeot	10

Main: Dreamtime for the latest Australian winner: Miller passed Marquez.

Inset, right: Miller crushed the opposition, and then his Red Bull can as well.

Inset, far right: Wet-weather star Scott Redding claimed his second MotoGP podium.
Photos: Gold & Goose

Inset, below right: Marquez used his head, and then pointed it out.
Photo: Repsol Honda Team

Inset, below: The pillion-ride of shame after Rossi crashed out of the lead.
Photos: Gold & Goose

FIM WORLD CHAMPIONSHIP · ROUND 8

DUTCH TT

ASSEN CIRCUIT

THE last time a non-factory rider had won a grand prix had been ten years before – at Estoril in Portugal in 2006, where Toni Elias had shaded Rossi by two-thousandths. It happened again at Assen, seeming to give justification to Dorna's drive to clip the wings of the works bikes.

Or was it just the weather?

Either way, Jack Miller was a hugely popular first-time winner, and his hard-earned maiden victory showed not only clear ability, but also courage, and the skill to survive when the big names of MotoGP signally failed to do so, one way or another.

All except one, who even had the presence of mind to accept second place when only a year before he would have likely found that impossible. The reward for Marquez was 20 points, while Rossi got zero and a mystifyingly slow Lorenzo only six. If the championship had a fulcrum, this was probably it.

A tradition going back to long before the foundation of the world championship was shattered at the northernmost circuit on the calendar. Racing had taken place at Assen on Saturday since 1925. Now, in the same drive for modernisation that had emasculated the classic circuit in 2006, the management had stepped into line with the rest of racing, with the television expectations of the rest of the world, and with the marketing advantage of two weekend days on which to sell tickets. This was the first ever Dutch TT to take place on Sunday.

Another small change was to the often crucial final chicane. Where in 2015 Rossi had beaten Marquez with a motocrossing ride across gravel, now there was a paved surface. The opportunities for surprise outcomes remained.

One aspect resisted modernisation: the notoriously fickle weather of the Drenthe flatlands. After a balmy Friday, the first rain arrived at lunchtime on Saturday. Race morning was dry, but the skies loomed. Moto3 escaped; Moto2 was cut short by rain. MotoGP, last race of the day, paid the biggest price, when a drying track was engulfed by a cloudburst and the race was red-flagged. A 12-lap restart demonstrated just how easily the mighty could become the fallen.

Marquez had already been through a busy Saturday, with two notable YouTube moments – the first in free practice, with an almighty save after locking the front under braking for the first corner, triggered (he thought) by a bump. The Honda tied itself in knots in a cloud of tyre smoke. Surely he was down? The tankslapper was violent enough to trigger the airbags in his leathers, and after running on straight, he was seen flapping his arms to deflate them again. It was, he admitted, "a little bit scary. I lost confidence there."

Then came qualifying, on a tricky damp surface. He was on his out-lap, not pushing, when he was tipped off the low side. The bike was still sliding as he regained his feet and sprinted off the track to commandeer a photographer's scooter to race back to his pit. The photographer gave him the nod, but he said later, "I would have gone anyway, even if he'd said no." His haste was not matched by his team's readiness. His second bike was set for dry weather, and he had to wait patiently as they hastily changed brakes, tyres, suspension and so on. With five minutes left, he secured a second-row slot. Had he not set a time, he would have had to start from the back.

Wing play continued at Assen, but a GP Commission meeting on Saturday decreed that it would be for the last time. For 2017, MotoGP would follow the smaller classes, with aerodynamic aids banned. The decision came in the absence of any counter-proposal from the MSMA manufacturers' association, whose members were deeply divided on the issue – Ducati vigorously campaigning for freedom to develop in the interests of motorcycling at large, the Japanese dragging their feet.

The paddock was abuzz with contract talk, at all levels.

Most important for the fans, 100,000 on race day, was the renewal of the circuit's contract for another ten years, until 2026.

Most significant for racing was the renewal for another five years of the agreement between Dorna and the teams' association, IRTA, which would take their co-operation to 30 years, which (the heads of both organisations agreed) had been entirely fruitful, although Dorna's Ezpeleta allowed that the start had been "not easy". Not only had the commercial side been developed, but also the sporting rules and most importantly safety – an aspect of which IRTA chief Herve Poncharal said, "Dorna has never compromised."

And the riders. First off, the announcement that Alex Rins would join Iannone at Suzuki, finally confirming Aleix Espargaro's oft-expressed dismay that his two years of effort would

Left: Thumbs-up from Dovi for his season's first pole.

Below left: Young man in a hurry: Marquez returns to the pits on a purloined scooter.

Far left: At the first start, Scott Redding leads Rossi, Dovizioso and the pack into the first corner.

Below left: Lorenzo, sporting bruises and abrasions, had a race to forget.

Photos: Gold & Goose

not be rewarded. He would be moving to Aprilia, however, an announcement also planned for Assen, but deferred due to flight delays.

With the other Aprilia seat already taken by Sam Lowes, former world champions Bautista and Bradl were left in the air. The former, it was later confirmed, would move to the Aspar Ducati squad; while Bradl's thoughts of a return to Moto2 would soon be overtaken when he signed for Honda's World Superbike squad.

There was more. Zarco's flirtation with Suzuki was also brought to an end. He had tested the GSX-RR MotoGP bike in the break and had been scheduled to race for Suzuki in the forthcoming Suzuka 8 Hours. That was now cancelled, and shortly it was announced that he would be joining Folger at Tech 3 Yamaha.

And more. Crutchlow would be staying with LCR Honda for 2017 with an option for 2018. In Moto2, Remy Gardner was back for another race with Tasca, replacing Tonucci; while Briton Danny Webb had returned to Moto3 after two years, replacing another underperformer – Karel Hanika – on the Platinum Bay Mahindra. Webb's previous race, in sharp contrast, had been on a BMW Superbike at the Isle of Man TT.

MOTOGP RACE – 12 laps (restarted)

Dovizioso claimed his first pole of the year on the wet track, with Rossi second and Redding third, first time on the front row. Marquez, Crutchlow and Hernandez were behind; Lorenzo on row four in 11th. Pedrosa, 16th, didn't even make Q1.

The race, scheduled for 26 laps, started on time and had one unexpected hero – Colombian satellite Ducati rider Hernandez – who took the lead as the big stars tiptoed around on a drying circuit.

Sadly, Hernandez would fall. After remounting and swapping to his spare bike, he fell again, by which time renewed heavy rain had become a cloudburst, and the red flags came out, the track awash with standing water.

That was on the 15th lap, short of the two-thirds distance required for a full race. Results were taken from lap 14 and a new 12-lap race scheduled.

At that point, Dovizioso was narrowly leading Petrucci and Rossi, with Petrucci taking the lead on lap 15, but in vain.

They occupied the new front row. Redding led the second from Marquez and Pedrosa, through from 16th.

Miller had also had a strong first race, in the middle of row three, between Crutchlow and Pol Espargaro.

Hernandez was already out, and not eligible for the restart. Pirro, again taking the place of Baz on the Avintia Ducati, had just pitted, but was allowed to start from the back.

Iannone was luckier still. Having started from the back row of the grid after his Catalunyan penalty, he had forced through to fifth on lap 13 before also falling. But he'd remounted, finished lap 14 17th and therefore could restart in a better position than in the first race.

Lorenzo was suffering badly, having dropped to 19th, with only Pirro behind him.

The rain had stopped and the track was drenched, but drying when they got under way again, all riders now on the softer rear wet Michelin option, and many of them in sprint mode, with just 12 laps to go.

There had been many crashes, caused by losing the front on the wet track, the day before. They continued in the race.

The first to go, on lap one, was Pedrosa. A little further around, also Crutchlow. On lap two, Dovizioso crashed out of second; while earlier contender Petrucci sputtered to a stop, his engine dead. Next time around, Smith and Aleix Espargaro fell.

Most sensationally, also on lap three and out of the lead – Rossi, who lost the front on the entry to Mandeveen, the first of the classic double rights at the far end of the track. He tried to restart, but to no avail. A catastrophe after his win at the previous race.

Marquez was a close spectator, with Miller by now on his

Above: Hero to zero: Yonny Hernandez stormed off in the lead, only to crash out.

Left: Not waving, but drowning – MotoGP riders splash to the pits after the race was red-flagged.

Photos: Gold & Goose

back wheel. The Australian observed at once that Marquez "calmed down – obviously thinking of the bigger picture." It was time for him to take his chance; he slipped past into the chicane at the end of the next lap and immediately started to draw clear.

Some way behind, Pol Espargaro had quickly recovered from a first-corner run-off and had got ahead of a cautious Redding. The Briton stalked him; then, with three laps to go, he pounced. "My bike was sliding a lot, but by now I had the feeling," he said. "I took the risk." It put him on the podium for the second time in his career.

A long way back, Iannone had been holding fifth, but at the end he was coming under threat from Bautista and Barbera. He survived after Bautista slipped off on the last lap; Barbera was sixth.

The ever reliable Laverty came through to take seventh from a fading Bradl. A couple of seconds behind, Vinales was ninth, two seconds clear of a deeply dispirited Lorenzo, whose longstanding apprehension about wet weather at Assen had born bitter fruit.

Rabat fell and remounted to finish a very distant 11th, but still clear of Pedrosa, who had also restarted. Likewise Smith, three laps down and plumb last, but still 13th and in the points.

Pirro had also crashed out of the second race.

Miller's victory put him in a select group of Australian GP winners. It also vindicated his move direct from Moto3, as he underlined in an emotional *parc fermé* interview. A lot of people, he recalled, had put him down and said "this project wouldn't work. I just hope I showed them they're wrong. I can ride a bike. I'm not an idiot. Thanks to Honda for taking this risk on me."

Marquez's third consecutive second place gave him a comforting lead of 24 points over Lorenzo, with Rossi's challenge badly dented.

MOTO2 RACE – 21 laps (shortened from 24)

The sun was shining at the start of Moto2, but it didn't last. The rain held off long enough, however, for more than two-thirds distance to be run and a completed race to be declared when there were still officially three laps to go.

Luthi was on pole, from Zarco and Aegerter. The Swiss

rider led into the first corner and for the first three laps, with Aegerter and second-row starters Lowes, Morbidelli and Nakagami jockeying for position behind him; Zarco was in close attendance.

They stayed close as Morbidelli took to the front from laps four to nine, but all the while Nakagami was moving forward.

It took him a couple of goes to get ahead, but on lap ten he was able to make it stick, and immediately he started to open up a gap – a second by lap 12, and up to three seconds just two laps later.

From then on, he was in control, for his long awaited first win, and the first by a Japanese rider since Yuki Takahashi won in Catalunya in 2010.

The battle became a little stretched behind him; Aegerter had already dropped out of contention. Morbidelli gave way to Zarco on lap 14, the pair of them gaining a little gap on Baldassarri, through from eighth on lap one and now engaged with Lowes.

Luthi had run into grip problems and dropped behind both of them, and now was coming under pressure from a below-par erstwhile points leader Rins, in turn being harried by Speed Up rider Corsi.

By lap 19, Zarco was alone in second and gradually closing up again on the leader. With five laps to go, there was a slender chance he could have caught him – but they didn't get that far.

Morbidelli was a lone third; Lowes was attacking Baldassarri – but a couple of major moments demonstrated that conditions were becoming tricky. It was starting to rain.

Luthi paid the price, crashing out on lap 19. On the 22nd, the red flags came out, and results were taken back one lap.

At that point, Nakagami was still better than two seconds clear, while Lowes had finally managed to get ahead of Baldassarri for fourth.

Rins narrowly clung to fifth from Corsi. Another five seconds down, Alex Marquez defeated Aegerter, Folger, Simeon and Cortese in a big battle for eighth. It was former Moto3 champion Cortese's best showing so far in a difficult second year in Moto2.

Schrotter had dropped off the back of this, but he saved 13th from Moto3 champion Kent, with the last point going to his Leopard team-mate, Oliveira.

Axel Pons and Luca Marini were the only other crashers;

Above: Moto3's top six almost dead-heated. Bagnaia (in white) heads (*from left*) Migno, Fenati, Antonelli, Di Giannantonio and Danilo.

Left: Luthi dropped back in Moto2, then crashed out.

Above far left: Takaaki Nakagami: the first Japanese winner since 2010.

Bottom left: Aron Canet cartwheels to destruction as Bendsneyder and Danilo watch.

Top left: Bagnaia's first win was also the first for an Indian constructor. He celebrates on the shoulders of team boss 'Aspar' Martinez.

Left: Nakagami pulls clear for a commanding first Moto2 win.

Photos: Gold & Goose

Gardner finished out of the points in 20th; Malaysian bright hope Hafizh Syahrin retired.

Second was enough to give defending champion Zarco the championship lead – equal on 126 points with Rins, but with three wins to the Spaniard's two, with Lowes just five points down.

MOTO3 RACE – 22 laps

Pecco Bagnaia made history by inches at Assen, in all sorts of ways. He won the first ever Dutch TT on a Sunday, his own first GP and the first for Mahindra. Furthermore, it was the first ever for an Indian constructor.

The first race of the day got away with it weather-wise, with a typical Moto3 maelstrom: a huge front pack continually changing places. At half-distance, by which time four members had already crashed, the top 13 were still covered by just over 1.6 seconds. The absentees included free practice superstar Canet, who had crashed at the start of qualifying to deny himself a classic debut pole. He was with the top gang when he fell, taking out Guevara. By then, Rodrigo and Quartararo had also crashed together.

Fenati led nine times over the line, and team-mates Migno and Bulega (once) took their turns. Another one-lap rookie leader was Di Giannantonio.

The Mahindra was there all the time, and Bagnaia took the honour six times in the race, and crucially for a seventh on the last lap.

It was by the narrowest of margins, for Migno had led into and out of the chicane. But Bagnaia was in front anyway, and then his rival was docked a further place for exceeding track limits on the last lap, ceding second to Di Giannantonio.

The top three were within 0.039 of a second; the top six inside 0.161; with Fenati fourth, then team-mates Antonelli and Danilo.

The race was almost a disaster for Binder, in the top three at every race so far. He was in the lead group when a slip after being pushed off line in the fast Ramshoek left-hander sent him careening perilously across the wet grass at high speed. Amazingly, he collected it, and finished 12th.

Pole starter Bastianini joined a long crash list with four laps to go.

The top ten, still all close, was completed by Bulega, Mir, home hero Bendsneyder and fellow rookie dalla Porta, substituting for absent/injured Navarro.

MOTUL
TT ASSEN

24–26 JUNE, 2016

TT ASSEN
22 laps
Length: 4.542km / 2.822 miles
Width: 10-14m

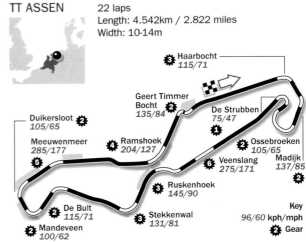

Haarbocht 115/71
Geert Timmer Bocht 135/84
De Strubben 75/47
Duikersloot 105/65
Meeuwenmeer 285/177
Ramshoek 204/127
Ossebroeken 105/65
Veenslang 275/171
Madijk 137/85
Ruskenhoek 145/90
De Bult 115/71
Stekkenwal 131/81
Mandeveen 100/62

Key
96/60 kph/mph
Gear

MotoGP
RACE DISTANCE: 12 laps, 33.867 miles/54.504km · RACE WEATHER: Wet (air 15°C, humidity 93%, track 19°C)

Pos.	Rider	Nat.	No.	Entrant	Machine	Tyres	Race tyre choice	Laps	Time & speed
1	Jack Miller	AUS	43	Estrella Galicia 0,0 Marc VDS	Honda RC213V	M	F: Soft Wet/R: Soft Wet	12	22m 17.447s 91.2mph/ 146.7km/h
2	Marc Marquez	SPA	93	Repsol Honda Team	Honda RC213V	M	F: Soft Wet/R: Soft Wet	12	22m 19.438s
3	Scott Redding	GBR	45	OCTO Pramac Yakhnich	Ducati Desmosedici	M	F: Soft Wet/R: Soft Wet	12	22m 23.353s
4	Pol Espargaro	SPA	44	Monster Yamaha Tech 3	Yamaha YZR-M1	M	F: Soft Wet/R: Soft Wet	12	22m 27.259s
5	Andrea Iannone	ITA	29	Ducati Team	Ducati Desmosedici	M	F: Soft Wet/R: Soft Wet	12	22m 35.282s
6	Hector Barbera	SPA	8	Avintia Racing	Ducati Desmosedici	M	F: Soft Wet/R: Soft Wet	12	22m 36.139s
7	Eugene Laverty	IRL	50	Aspar Team MotoGP	Ducati Desmosedici	M	F: Soft Wet/R: Soft Wet	12	22m 40.052s
8	Stefan Bradl	GER	6	Aprilia Racing Team Gresini	Aprilia RS-GP	M	F: Soft Wet/R: Soft Wet	12	22m 41.050s
9	Maverick Vinales	SPA	25	Team SUZUKI ECSTAR	Suzuki GSX-RR	M	F: Soft Wet/R: Soft Wet	12	22m 43.595s
10	Jorge Lorenzo	SPA	99	Movistar Yamaha MotoGP	Yamaha YZR-M1	M	F: Soft Wet/R: Soft Wet	12	22m 45.051s
11	Tito Rabat	SPA	53	Estrella Galicia 0,0 Marc VDS	Honda RC213V	M	F: Soft Wet/R: Soft Wet	12	23m 39.277s
12	Dani Pedrosa	SPA	26	Repsol Honda Team	Honda RC213V	M	F: Soft Wet/R: Soft Wet	12	24m 11.816s
13	Bradley Smith	GBR	38	Monster Yamaha Tech 3	Yamaha YZR-M1	M	F: Soft Wet/R: Soft Wet	9	23m 34.917s
	Alvaro Bautista	SPA	19	Aprilia Racing Team Gresini	Aprilia RS-GP	M	F: Soft Wet/R: Soft Wet	11	DNF-crash
	Michele Pirro	ITA	51	Avintia Racing	Ducati Desmosedici	M	F: Soft Wet/R: Soft Wet	5	DNF-crash
	Valentino Rossi	ITA	46	Movistar Yamaha MotoGP	Yamaha YZR-M1	M	F: Soft Wet/R: Soft Wet	2	DNF-crash
	Aleix Espargaro	SPA	41	Team SUZUKI ECSTAR	Suzuki GSX-RR	M	F: Soft Wet/R: Soft Wet	2	DNF-crash
	Andrea Dovizioso	ITA	4	Ducati Team	Ducati Desmosedici	M	F: Soft Wet/R: Soft Wet	1	DNF-crash
	Danilo Petrucci	ITA	9	OCTO Pramac Yakhnich	Ducati Desmosedici	M	F: Soft Wet/R: Soft Wet	1	DNF-technical
	Cal Crutchlow	GBR	35	LCR Honda	Honda RC213V	M	F: Soft Wet/R: Soft Wet	0	DNF-crash
	Yonny Hernandez	COL	68	Aspar Team MotoGP	Ducati Desmosedici	M	F: Soft Wet/R: Soft Wet	0	DNS

Fastest lap: Danilo Petrucci, on lap 8, 1m 48.339s, 93.760mph/150.9km/h (race part 1)
Lap record: Marc Marquez, SPA (Honda), 1m 33.617s, 108.5mph/174.6km/h (2015).
Event best maximum speed: Andrea Iannone, 197mph/317.1km/h (free practice).

Qualifying
Weather: Wet
Air Temp: 17° **Track Temp:** 21°
Humidity: 87%

1	Dovizioso	1m 45.246s
2	Rossi	1m 45.961s
3	Redding	1m 46.312s
4	Marquez	1m 46.430s
5	Crutchlow	1m 46.568s
6	Hernandez	1m 46.828s
7	P. Espargaro	1m 46.997s
8	A. Espargaro	1m 47.118s
9	Iannone	1m 47.567s
10	Petrucci	1m 47.601s
11	Lorenzo	1m 47.897s
12	Vinales	1m 48.415s
13	Barbera	1m 48.830s
14	Smith	1m 48.909s
15	Bautista	1m 49.163s
16	Pedrosa	1m 49.364s
17	Laverty	1m 49.678s
18	Bradl	1m 49.685s
19	Miller	1m 49.775s
20	Rabat	1m 49.779s
21	Pirro	1m 50.204s

Fastest race laps

1	Rossi	1m 49.485s
2	Redding	1m 49.866s
3	Miller	1m 50.296s
4	Marquez	1m 50.399s
5	Laverty	1m 50.716s
6	P. Espargaro	1m 50.998s
7	Vinales	1m 51.304s
8	Barbera	1m 51.393s
9	Iannone	1m 51.511s
10	Bautista	1m 51.599s
11	Lorenzo	1m 51.643s
12	Bradl	1m 51.899s
13	Pirro	1m 52.007s
14	A. Espargaro	1m 52.019s
15	Rabat	1m 52.353s
16	Pedrosa	1m 53.662s
17	Smith	2m 12.775s

Championship Points

1	Marquez	145
2	Lorenzo	121
3	Rossi	103
4	Pedrosa	86
5	Vinales	79
6	P. Espargaro	72
7	Barbera	58
8	Iannone	52
9	A. Espargaro	49
10	Laverty	48
11	Dovizioso	43
12	Bradl	37
13	Miller	33
14	Redding	32
15	Smith	32
16	Bautista	29
17	Petrucci	24
18	Crutchlow	20
19	Pirro	19
20	Rabat	18
21	Baz	8
22	Hernandez	3

Constructor Points

1	Yamaha	178
2	Honda	160
3	Ducati	108
4	Suzuki	85
5	Aprilia	45

Grid order		1	2	3	4	5	6	7	8	9	10	11	12	
4	DOVIZIOSO	46	46	93	43	43	43	43	43	43	43	43	43	1
9	PETRUCCI	4	93	43	93	93	93	93	93	93	93	93	93	2
46	ROSSI	93	43	44	44	44	44	44	44	44	44	45	45	3
45	REDDING	43	44	45	45	45	45	45	45	45	45	44	44	4
93	MARQUEZ	9	45	19	29	29	29	29	29	29	29	29	29	5
26	PEDROSA	44	19	53	19	19	19	19	19	19	19	19	8	6
35	CRUTCHLOW	38	53	29	53	6	6	8	8	8	8	8	50	7
43	MILLER	45	50	6	6	8	8	6	6	6	6	50	6	8
44	P. ESPARGARO	53	29	50	8	50	50	50	50	50	50	6	25	9
19	BAUTISTA	50	6	8	50	51	25	25	25	25	25	99		10
6	BRADL	19	99	99	99	25	99	99	99	99	99	53		11
38	SMITH	29	8	51	51	99	53	53	53	53	53	26		12
25	VINALES	6	51	25	25	53	26	26	26	26	26			13
53	RABAT	99	25	26	26	26	38	38	38	38				
41	A. ESPARGARO	8	41	38	38	38								
8	BARBERA	51	26											
29	IANNONE	25	38											
50	LAVERTY	41												
99	LORENZO	26												
51	PIRRO													

38 Pit stop   38 Lapped rider

Moto2

RACE DISTANCE: 21 laps, 59.268 miles/95.382km · **RACE WEATHER:** Dry (air 20°C, humidity 61%, track 23°C)

Pos.	Rider	Nat.	No.	Entrant	Machine	Laps	Time & Speed
1	Takaaki Nakagami	JPN	30	IDEMITSU Honda Team Asia	Kalex	21	34m 33.948s / 102.8mph/ 165.5km/h
2	Johann Zarco	FRA	5	Ajo Motorsport	Kalex	21	34m 36.383s
3	Franco Morbidelli	ITA	21	Estrella Galicia 0,0 Marc VDS	Kalex	21	34m 39.618s
4	Sam Lowes	GBR	22	Federal Oil Gresini Moto2	Kalex	21	34m 41.017s
5	Lorenzo Baldassarri	ITA	7	Forward Team	Kalex	21	34m 41.831s
6	Alex Rins	SPA	40	Paginas Amarillas HP 40	Kalex	21	34m 43.163s
7	Simone Corsi	ITA	24	Speed Up Racing	Speed Up	21	34m 43.430s
8	Alex Marquez	SPA	73	Estrella Galicia 0,0 Marc VDS	Kalex	21	34m 48.952s
9	Dominique Aegerter	SWI	77	CarXpert Interwetten	Kalex	21	34m 49.175s
10	Jonas Folger	GER	94	Dynavolt Intact GP	Kalex	21	34m 49.352s
11	Xavier Simeon	BEL	19	QMMF Racing Team	Speed Up	21	34m 50.322s
12	Sandro Cortese	GER	11	Dynavolt Intact GP	Kalex	21	34m 50.515s
13	Marcel Schrotter	GER	23	AGR Team	Kalex	21	34m 58.718s
14	Danny Kent	GBR	52	Leopard Racing	Kalex	21	34m 58.965s
15	Miguel Oliveira	POR	44	Leopard Racing	Kalex	21	34m 59.490s
16	Julian Simon	SPA	60	QMMF Racing Team	Speed Up	21	34m 59.677s
17	Xavi Vierge	SPA	97	Tech 3 Racing	Tech 3	21	35m 08.063s
18	Jesko Raffin	SWI	2	Sports-Millions-EMWE-SAG	Kalex	21	35m 08.128s
19	Mattia Pasini	ITA	54	Italtrans Racing Team	Kalex	21	35m 08.712s
20	Remy Gardner	AUS	87	Tasca Racing Scuderia Moto2	Kalex	21	35m 15.386s
21	Isaac Vinales	SPA	32	Tech 3 Racing	Tech 3	21	35m 16.006s
22	Robin Mulhauser	SWI	70	CarXpert Interwetten	Kalex	21	35m 22.631s
23	Edgar Pons	SPA	57	Paginas Amarillas HP 40	Kalex	21	35m 30.044s
	Thomas Luthi	SWI	12	Garage Plus Interwetten	Kalex	18	DNF
	Luca Marini	ITA	10	Forward Team	Kalex	17	DNF
	Hafizh Syahrin	MAL	55	Petronas Raceline Malaysia	Kalex	14	DNF
	Axel Pons	SPA	49	AGR Team	Kalex	4	DNF

Fastest lap: Takaaki Nakagami, on lap 13, 1m 38.055s, 103.6mph/166.7km/h.
Lap record: Tito Rabat, SPA (Kalex), 1m 37.449s, 104.2mph/167.7km/h (2015).
Event best maximum speed: Sandro Cortese, 160.1mph/257.6km/h (free practice).

Qualifying

Weather: Dry
Air Temp: 18° **Track Temp:** 22°
Humidity: 85%

1	Luthi	1m 37.954s
2	Zarco	1m 38.402s
3	Aegerter	1m 38.449s
4	Lowes	1m 38.494s
5	Morbidelli	1m 38.544s
6	Nakagami	1m 38.615s
7	Cortese	1m 38.631s
8	Rins	1m 38.873s
9	Folger	1m 39.076s
10	Baldassarri	1m 39.259s
11	Oliveira	1m 39.294s
12	Pasini	1m 39.322s
13	Marquez	1m 39.337s
14	Simeon	1m 39.432s
15	Simon	1m 39.513s
16	Corsi	1m 39.555s
17	Schrotter	1m 39.647s
18	Kent	1m 39.663s
19	Pons	1m 39.778s
20	Syahrin	1m 39.840s
21	Marini	1m 40.545s
22	Mulhauser	1m 40.933s
23	Raffin	1m 40.935s
24	Vinales	1m 41.119s
25	Vierge	1m 41.898s
26	Gardner	1m 42.629s
27	Pons	1m 44.229s

Fastest race laps

1	Nakagami	1m 38.055s
2	Baldassarri	1m 38.163s
3	Morbidelli	1m 38.163s
4	Rins	1m 38.171s
5	Zarco	1m 38.181s
6	Luthi	1m 38.281s
7	Lowes	1m 38.327s
8	Corsi	1m 38.410s
9	Aegerter	1m 38.448s
10	Cortese	1m 38.462s
11	Folger	1m 38.545s
12	Marquez	1m 38.621s
13	Simon	1m 38.625s
14	Kent	1m 38.635s
15	Simeon	1m 38.841s
16	Oliveira	1m 38.856s
17	Schrotter	1m 38.876s
18	Marini	1m 38.892s
19	Syahrin	1m 39.031s
20	Vierge	1m 39.039s
21	Pasini	1m 39.149s
22	Raffin	1m 39.218s
23	Vinales	1m 39.435s
24	Pons	1m 39.540s
25	Gardner	1m 39.574s
26	Mulhauser	1m 39.613s
27	Pons	1m 39.746s

Championship Points

1	Zarco	126
2	Rins	126
3	Lowes	121
4	Luthi	93
5	Nakagami	78
6	Morbidelli	66
7	Folger	63
8	Syahrin	60
9	Corsi	59
10	Aegerter	59
11	Salom	37
12	Baldassarri	36
13	Pons	34
14	Simeon	28
15	Oliveira	24
16	Schrotter	22
17	Kent	14
18	Pasini	14
19	Cortese	14
20	Marquez	13
21	Simon	10
22	Marini	10
23	Vinales	3
24	Wilairot	3
25	Vierge	3
26	Raffin	2
27	Mulhauser	1
28	Gardner	1

Constructor Points

		Points
1	Kalex	200
2	Speed Up	72
3	Tech 3	6

Moto3

RACE DISTANCE: 22 laps, 62.090 miles/99.924km · **RACE WEATHER:** Dry (air 18°C, humidity 67%, track 28°C)

Pos.	Rider	Nat.	No.	Entrant	Machine	Laps	Time & Speed
1	Francesco Bagnaia	ITA	21	ASPAR Mahindra Team Moto3	Mahindra	22	38m 11.535s / 97.5mph/ 156.9km/h
2	Fabio di Giannantonio	ITA	4	Gresini Racing Moto3	Honda	22	38m 11.574s
3	Andrea Migno	ITA	16	SKY Racing Team VR46	KTM	22	38m 11.553s
4	Romano Fenati	ITA	5	SKY Racing Team VR46	KTM	22	38m 11.619s
5	Niccolo Antonelli	ITA	23	Ongetta-Rivacold	Honda	22	38m 11.671s
6	Jules Danilo	FRA	95	Ongetta-Rivacold	Honda	22	38m 11.696s
7	Nicolo Bulega	ITA	8	SKY Racing Team VR46	KTM	22	38m 12.361s
8	Joan Mir	SPA	36	Leopard Racing	KTM	22	38m 12.374s
9	Bo Bendsneyder	NED	64	Red Bull KTM Ajo	KTM	22	38m 12.558s
10	Lorenzo dalla Porta	ITA	48	Estrella Galicia 0,0	Honda	22	38m 12.521s
11	Philipp Oettl	GER	65	Schedl GP Racing	KTM	22	38m 12.688s
12	Brad Binder	RSA	41	Red Bull KTM Ajo	KTM	22	38m 23.704s
13	Jakub Kornfeil	CZE	84	Drive M7 SIC Racing Team	Honda	22	38m 27.176s
14	Maria Herrera	SPA	6	MH6 Team	KTM	22	38m 30.053s
15	Livio Loi	BEL	11	RW Racing GP BV	Honda	22	38m 30.084s
16	John McPhee	GBR	17	Peugeot MC Saxoprint	Peugeot	22	38m 30.137s
17	Darryn Binder	RSA	40	Platinum Bay Real Estate	Mahindra	22	38m 48.454s
18	Stefano Valtulini	ITA	43	3570 Team Italia	Mahindra	22	38m 53.097s
19	Adam Norrodin	MAL	7	Drive M7 SIC Racing Team	Honda	22	38m 53.182s
20	Lorenzo Petrarca	ITA	77	3570 Team Italia	Mahindra	22	39m 06.174s
21	Fabio Spiranelli	ITA	3	CIP-Unicom Starker	Mahindra	22	39m 06.830s
22	Danny Webb	GBR	22	Platinum Bay Real Estate	Mahindra	22	39m 15.806s
	Enea Bastianini	ITA	33	Gresini Racing Moto3	Honda	18	DNF
	Andrea Locatelli	ITA	55	Leopard Racing	KTM	18	DNF
	Alexis Masbou	FRA	10	Peugeot MC Saxoprint	Peugeot	12	DNF
	Tatsuki Suzuki	JPN	24	CIP-Unicom Starker	Mahindra	12	DNF
	Juanfran Guevara	SPA	58	RBA Racing Team	KTM	7	DNF
	Aron Canet	SPA	44	Estrella Galicia 0,0	Honda	6	DNF
	Gabriel Rodrigo	ARG	19	RBA Racing Team	KTM	1	DNF
	Fabio Quartararo	FRA	20	Leopard Racing	KTM	1	DNF
	Khairul Idham Pawi	MAL	89	Honda Team Asia	Honda	1	DNF
	Albert Arenas	SPA	12	ASPAR Mahindra Team Moto3	Mahindra	0	DNF

Fastest lap: Aron Canet, on lap 3, 1m 42.778s, 98.8mph/159.0km/h.
Lap record: Jorge Navarro, SPA (Honda), 1m 42.135s, 99.4mph/160.0km/h (2015).
Event best maximum speed: Brad Binder, 137mph/220.4km/h (qualifying).

Qualifying

Weather: Dry
Air Temp: 18° **Track Temp:** 24°
Humidity: 77%

1	Bastianini	1m 42.463s
2	Migno	1m 42.516s
3	Bulega	1m 42.529s
4	Fenati	1m 42.582s
5	B. Binder	1m 42.599s
6	Guevara	1m 42.644s
7	Bendsneyder	1m 42.655s
8	Quartararo	1m 42.703s
9	Di Giannantonio	1m 42.724s
10	Bagnaia	1m 42.746s
11	Rodrigo	1m 42.792s
12	Dalla Porta	1m 42.887s
13	Antonelli	1m 42.911s
14	Danilo	1m 42.959s
15	Oettl	1m 42.968s
16	Canet	1m 43.214s
17	Locatelli	1m 43.235s
18	Mir	1m 43.368s
19	Loi	1m 43.399s
20	D. Binder	1m 43.407s
21	McPhee	1m 43.515s
22	Herrera	1m 43.641s
23	Masbou	1m 43.647s
24	Pawi	1m 43.692s
25	Kornfeil	1m 43.692s
26	Suzuki	1m 43.754s
27	Arenas	1m 43.873s
28	Valtulini	1m 44.699s
29	Norrodin	1m 45.024s
30	Spiranelli	1m 45.149s
31	Petrarca	1m 45.153s
32	Webb	1m 45.225s

Fastest race laps

1	Canet	1m 42.778s
2	Di Giannantonio	1m 43.018s
3	Migno	1m 43.097s
4	Danilo	1m 43.125s
5	Oettl	1m 43.158s
6	Mir	1m 43.192s
7	Bagnaia	1m 43.202s
8	Bastianini	1m 43.204s
9	Antonelli	1m 43.216s
10	B. Binder	1m 43.236s
11	Bulega	1m 43.297s
12	Bendsneyder	1m 43.298s
13	Dalla Porta	1m 43.315s
14	Fenati	1m 43.326s
15	Guevara	1m 43.438s
16	Kornfeil	1m 43.582s
17	Suzuki	1m 43.606s
18	McPhee	1m 43.612s
19	Masbou	1m 43.750s
20	Herrera	1m 43.909s
21	Loi	1m 43.917s
22	D. Binder	1m 43.943s
23	Valtulini	1m 44.052s
24	Norrodin	1m 44.290s
25	Locatelli	1m 44.622s
26	Petrarca	1m 45.224s
27	Webb	1m 45.454s
28	Spiranelli	1m 45.525s

Championship Points

1	B. Binder	151
2	Navarro	103
3	Fenati	93
4	Bagnaia	79
5	Bulega	75
6	Antonelli	63
7	Mir	50
8	Bastianini	49
9	Di Giannantonio	47
10	Kornfeil	45
11	Quartararo	39
12	Migno	37
13	Danilo	34
14	Canet	33
15	Oettl	32
16	Locatelli	30
17	Pawi	29
18	Guevara	25
19	Loi	22
20	Ono	20
21	Bendsneyder	14
22	McPhee	10
23	Martin	10
24	Dalla Porta	7
25	Rodrigo	6
26	Norrodin	5
27	D. Binder	4
28	Herrera	4
29	Suzuki	4

Constructor Points

		Points
1	KTM	172
2	Honda	164
3	Mahindra	91
4	Peugeot	10

FIM WORLD CHAMPIONSHIP · ROUND 9
GERMAN GRAND PRIX
SACHSENRING

Above: After his early bike change, Marquez finds the drying line.
Photo: Repsol Honda

Centre, from left: Rossi grins as Marquez dabs his grazed chin after his Sunday morning fall; Lorenzo crashed three times in practice and finished a dispirited 15th; Barbera's place on the front row was the surprise of qualifying.

Below right: Remy Gardner was confirmed as a regular rider for Tasca Racing.

Bottom, right: Stefan Bradl's warm-up crash put him out of the race.

Below far right: Crutchlow, Rossi and Dovizioso were late to change bikes, and Rossi's crew chose intermediates. Dovi checks his own rear slick.

Opening spread: Finger and flag – Honda's Marquez celebrates his audacious victory.

Photos: Gold & Goose

THE matter of so-called 'ship-to-shore' communications has simmered for some decades in motorcycle grand prix racing – ever since Team Roberts essayed some rather unsuccessful experiments in the late 1980s. It came back into sharp focus at the Sachsenring, in a race where the hero of a record crowd of 93,000 ruined his chances by failing to respond to a vitally important message from his pit crew.

Valentino Rossi was locked in a close four-way battle, his bike shod with soft wet tyres on a rapidly drying track, his attention fixed on his immediate companions. At the tiny German circuit, pit signals come on the shortest of straights where the riders are extremely busy recovering from the previous corner and preparing for the next.

The ignored signals, given with increasing desperation over three laps, left his Yamaha pit crew shrugging with growing exasperation as he powered past each time. Then, when eventually he did pit after 24 of the 30 laps, they sent him out on Michelin's all-new intermediate tyres front and rear. That was their mistake.

Meanwhile, on full slicks, because "for my team, intermediates don't exist", Marquez was scything through from 14th on lap 18 to first, circulating six or more seconds faster than

the rest to take a seventh successive win on the postage-stamp circuit. That doubled his points lead over a once-again bafflingly slow Lorenzo, who managed just one point.

Even after this demonstration of the advantage of clear communication, the mood remained against the use of radio. Too much like F1, opined Marquez, as if uttering an obscenity.

The point being that in MotoGP, the rider decides his own fate. The Honda rider's decision had proved a tactical masterstroke. Or a massive stroke of luck. In fact, he hadn't been the first to go on to slicks: a couple of laps earlier, Loris Baz had switched to a bike with an intermediate front and a slick rear – only to pit directly, having found it unrideable.

Marquez's gamble, in the nature of gambles, might easily have gone in the other direction, leaving him looking like the silly one. As it was, he had run off in the earlier, wetter part of the race, narrowly saving the day with a rock-spitting gallop through the gravel at Turn Eight, where he had fallen heavily in morning warm-up. "I went into motocross mode, but there was too much traction control," he said later. His early laps on slicks had been fraught, balancing precariously on a narrow dry line, while the others were running off it, looking for damp patches to keep their tyres cool.

In the end, he'd guessed the weather correctly. And taken a fine reward.

Lorenzo's weekend could hardly have been more different. He crashed three times in practice, equalling his tally for the whole of 2015. "It's not normal," he admitted, blaming an attempt at a different setting so that "we lost our way".

In the wake of the atrocity in Nice, where a lorry driver on a personal *fatwah* had ploughed into shorefront revellers, race day began under brooding skies with another seemingly regular minute's silence. The fine weather of practice had turned wet and nasty.

Michelin were ready for it, though, having rushed in an extra allocation of extra-soft wet front tyres on Friday, in response to Assen's many crashes. They had already prepared for the notoriously daunting over-the-brow right-hand Turn 11, following seven left-handers, with their first asymmetric front of the year. It differed from Bridgestone's in that the soft compound ran over the crown of the tyre as well as the right shoulder. It was a hit, but all the same there were a number of fallers at that corner, including Lorenzo.

It was a different bend, however, that meant no home GP, for a second year in a row, for Stefan Bradl, who suffered concussion after crashing in a wet warm-up. Thus he was unable to take advantage of Aprilia's latest engine development, with improved mid-range.

A spate of accidents in Moto3 qualifying also brought out the red flags. It was caused by an oil leak from Danny Webb's Mahindra, which claimed Fenati, Martin, Di Giannantonio and luckless Qatar winner Antonelli, who was out of the race with a broken left collarbone. Webb's unwitting leakage ran from the fourth corner to the seventh, where finally he also fell. (Danny Kent was out of Moto2 for a different reason: a big bang in a go-kart race in the preceding week had left him with painfully broken ribs.)

The weekend had its share of announcements: one being the formalisation of MotoGP's closed shop, as the seven premier-class private teams and Dorna signed up to an agreement of exclusivity.

Then came a further five-year contract for the continuation of the German GP. But where? The Nürburgring and the Lausitzring were touted as possible venues, until the local government finally agreed to the financial requirements in the coming weeks. It would stay at the Sachsenring – a circuit that everyone agrees is really too tight for MotoGP racing. Not that the actual racing is any the worse for it. Finland, Ezpeleta announced at the same time, would also be joining the calendar in 2018, at the Kymiring circuit, already under construction.

Zarco's future was confirmed as well. He had signed to join Yamaha's satellite Tech 3 squad, making a double-rookie line-up with Jonas Folger.

There was more rider movement in Moto2, where Remy Gardner's race-by-race sojourn with the Tasca team became permanent. Before that happened, however, he'd taken part in a national race at the little circuit outside Chemnitz, which put the 18-year-old in breach of the rules. A token 20-minute ban from the first free practice was the result.

Mahindra Moto3 riders had been suffering all season with erratic gear-shifting, unexpected downshifts and a box full of false neutrals. The solution was a complete redesign, which had been tested successfully by Peugeot MGP30 rider John McPhee at a CEV race at Catalunya the week after the GP there. Now it was available to all seven Mahindras and two Peugeots, and it was described colourfully by Mahindra Racing CEO Mufaddal Choonia: "The old gearbox sometimes had a mind of its own. We've taken out the mind. Now it's just a gearbox."

MOTOGP RACE – 30 laps

The halfway GP of the season was much a race of two halves. One was wet, the other wasn't.

Practice and qualifying were dry; Marquez was on pole from Barbera and Rossi; Petrucci led row two from Pol Espargaro and Vinales. The factory Ducatis were either side of row three; Pedrosa led the fourth from the downcast Lorenzo, who had been obliged to come through from Q1.

It started streaming wet, with most riders choosing Michelin's new extra-soft front tyre, rushed in when conditions on Friday proved colder than expected. Not all took the seemingly obvious decision – there were six exceptions, most notably Crutchlow, Petrucci, Redding and Assen winner Miller. Rabat and Bautista did the same.

This bolder decision proved better as the track started to dry, but it took a few laps to become clear.

The first had been led by Rossi from Dovizioso, with Petrucci already moving past Marquez into third.

Dovi took over on lap three; but then frequent wet hero Petrucci charged past and held on convincingly until lap 11, when he slipped off.

Dovi and Rossi were still with him, but things had changed a lot in their wake. Marquez had succumbed to Jack Miller – again showing wet speed and confidence – on lap six, and three laps later also to Barbera. He had more trouble ahead, narrowly surviving a high-speed run-off into the gravel at Turn 8, which left Pedrosa, Iannone and Redding disputing fifth.

Above: Crutchlow had slicks front and rear; Dovi had an inter front. They took them to the podium.

Top right: Zarco and Folger battled for victory in Moto2. They would be Tech3 team-mates in 2017.

Above right: Folger and Simon enjoy Zarco's back flip on the podium.

Right: Andrea Locatelli scored a career-best second in Moto3.

Below right: Rookie rainmaster Pawi survived this and other moments to take a second runaway Moto3 win.

Photos: Gold & Goose

Petrucci remounted and pitted for a bike change – not least because his crashed bike was on fire between his feet. Soon afterwards he retired.

He was the first to change bikes (discounting early crasher Hernandez). Next came Baz, on to a rear slick, only to pit again after one scary lap.

Then the still-fading Marquez. His timing and brave choice of slicks while other bikes were being prepared with intermediates proved inspired.

He pitted on lap 17, dropping from eighth to a distant 14th. He was now more than 38 seconds behind new leader Dovizioso, who was concentrating so hard on managing his lead over a growing pursuit pack – Rossi, Barbera, Crutchlow and Miller – that (he said later) he did not have time to think about stopping himself for a bike change. He was one of many to regret the delay.

Marquez very soon began making up time hand over fist. By lap 22, he was sixth, still 20 seconds shy, but lapping seven seconds faster than the leader. And none of them had stopped yet.

Next time around, all of them eventually did call in, except for a brave Miller, now in the lead, but he had no answer when Marquez came blazing past on lap 25.

The Spaniard was almost 20 seconds clear as he started the last lap, and he was able to cruise over the line waving triumphantly and still win by almost ten seconds.

The battle for second was a thriller. Some chose slicks, some intermediates, and it did make the difference in the final sprint.

Redding, on inters front and rear, had inherited second after Miller finally pitted, but as the laps counted down, Dovizioso (inter front, slick rear) was closing fast. Crutchlow, however, on full slicks, was closing even faster.

The LCR Honda was past the factory Ducati with three laps to go, ahead of Redding next time around, and he was second – his first podium since the beginning of 2015. If he'd changed earlier, he opined, he could have won. Why did he not do so? "I was following Rossi and Dovi, and I thought they had enough experience to make the right choice. But they made the wrong choice," he said.

There was more heartbreak for Redding when Dovi consigned him to fourth on the final lap.

The order behind was confused, different riders taking different amounts of time to adapt to the tyre changes, with Rossi just one of the losers in the game.

Iannone was fifth, four seconds ahead of Pedrosa; Miller was seventh, having repassed a struggling Rossi (on intermediates) and Barbera. Bautista was tenth, the ever-steadfast Laverty following. Vinales struggled to 12th; next came Smith and Aleix Espargaro.

And only then Lorenzo, whose late change to intermediates had caused him to go backwards even faster than the similarly shod Rossi.

Rabat, Baz and Hernandez trailed in one or more laps behind; Pol Espargaro had joined Petrucci on the crash list.

And Marquez could go on holiday with a very comforting 48-point lead.

MOTO2 RACE – 29 laps

Fresh from his first win, Nakagami was on pole from title rivals Zarco and Rins; third contender Lowes languished in tenth. He was about to start a barren spell that would severely dent his title challenge.

The race started streaming wet; Zarco led into the first corner, but Nakagami, full of confidence, had taken over by the end of the lap. He held on for the next six, Rins and an inspired Folger in pursuit.

Meanwhile, Zarco dropped behind Schrotter, until the German crashed out on lap five; then he had his hands full ahead of EG-VDS team-mates Morbidelli and Marquez.

But it would be a race of many crashes. On lap seven, Nakagami slipped off, then two laps later also Lowes, after pushing through to sixth. Both remounted, Lowes only to fall again later on.

Rins inherited the lead from Nakagami, only to have a near-spill himself, giving way to Folger for laps eight and nine before taking over and stretching a convincing gap shortly before half-distance.

Now Zarco had picked up his pace and was second, narrowly ahead of Folger and the EG team-mates, with Marquez's challenge ending on lap 15 after he had moved past Folger into fourth. He also remounted, but fell again.

It seemed that the strongest of the leaders was Morbidelli,

for after he had taken over on lap 17, he had soon gained a gap of better than 1.6 seconds, while Rins – battling with a fogged visor – was holding off Zarco, Folger a couple of seconds adrift.

But Morbidelli also was destined for the gravel, to remount and then fall again.

By now, Zarco had got ahead of Rins once more, and the Spaniard would drop behind Folger as well before he also fell on lap 26.

It was not over yet, for Folger had been saving his tyres and mounted a last-ditch attack on the final lap. He actually got ahead into the last corner, but Zarco's exit was better, and he claimed his fourth win of the year by six-hundredths of a second.

A long way back, Julian Simon got the reward of third for staying on board after a lonely afternoon, having worked his way past (among others) fourth-placed Pasini during the early stages.

Close behind, Lorenzo Baldassarri had a remarkable recovery, finally passing sixth-placed Forward Kalex team-mate Luca Marini (the rookie also impressively steadfast). Baldassarri had crashed in morning warm-up and dislocated his shoulder, a repeat of the injury that had put him out of the first round in Qatar.

Syahrin, Raffin, Vinales and Aegerter completed the top ten; Nakagami came through for 11th, ahead of Remy Gardner. With only 15 finishers, there were points for all, including double faller Sandro Cortese, two laps adrift.

Xavier Simeon also crashed twice, the second time terminally, but he did set fastest lap. Other notable crashers were Luthi and Corsi; joined by Oliveira, Vierge, Wilairot and Axel Pons.

With his main rivals zero-pointing, Zarco seized half-time control of the championship.

MOTO3 RACE – 27 laps

Bastianini was on pole for a second successive race, with Locatelli and rookie Aron Canet alongside. Binder was on the far end of row two, one down on title rival Navarro, making an impressive return from injury.

Then the weather came, and handed the advantage to a rookie on the middle of the seventh row of the grid.

Bastianini led away, then second-row starter Bo Bendsneyder took a lap up front.

But Honda Team Asia's Khairul Idham Pawi, wet winner in Argentina, was charging from 20th on the grid, and on lap four he led for the first time, and all the way to the end. His strongest challenge came from team-mate Hiroki Ono, until the Japanese rider fell. He remounted only to fall again.

As in Argentina, Pawi (17) took no notice of pit signals suggesting he should slow down, coming very close to falling several times as he kept on pulling out, better than ten seconds clear by half-distance. Eventually, he took his second career win by 11 seconds.

In his wake, Locatelli was embroiled with Bastianini and rain-man McPhee. Then, as Locatelli drew away for a safe second, Kornfeil was closing, while Di Giannantonio was not far adrift.

The main title men were close behind, a prudent Binder, mindful of giving away only one point, finally ceded to Navarro's persistence. The Spaniard kept on pushing, and with three laps to go he mounted a fierce, but flawed challenge on Di Giannantonio and Kornfeil.

This last reshuffle spaced them out, with Kornfeil safe in third, then Di Giannantonio, and McPhee fighting back to take sixth ahead of Navarro.

Binder was less than three seconds adrift; then Danilo led Bagnaia's Mahindra over the line, making up the top ten.

Binder's points lead over Navarro was a comfortable 47, leaving Bagnaia and non-scoring Fenati and Bulega scrapping over third. Fenati was an off-colour 18th; Bulega was one of eight to crash out.

GOPRO MOTORRAD
GRAND PRIX DEUTSCHLAND
15–17 JULY, 2016

SACHSENRING GP CIRCUIT
30 laps
Length: 3.671 km / 3,259 miles
Width: 12m

Castrol Omega 90/56
Karthallen 155/96
Sternquell 170/106
Turn 8 145/90
Coca Cola Kurve 75/47
Turn 5 115/71
Queckenburg Kurve 100/62
Turn 9 185/115
Sachsen Kurve 115/71
Turn 10 155/96
Turn 11 275/171

Key
96/60 kph/mph
Gear

MotoGP

RACE DISTANCE: 30 laps, 68.432 miles / 110.130km · RACE WEATHER: Wet (air 21°C, humidity 86%, track 24°C)

Pos.	Rider	Nat.	No.	Entrant	Machine	Tyres	Race tyre choice*	Laps	Time & speed
1	**Marc Marquez**	SPA	93	Repsol Honda Team	Honda RC213V	M	F: S-Soft Wet/R: Soft Wet	30	47m 03.239s 87.2mph/ 140.4km/h
2	**Cal Crutchlow**	GBR	35	LCR Honda	Honda RC213V	M	F: Soft Wet/R: Soft Wet	30	47m 13.096s
3	**Andrea Dovizioso**	ITA	4	Ducati Team	Ducati Desmosedici	M	F: S-Soft Wet/R: Soft Wet	30	47m 14.852s
4	**Scott Redding**	GBR	45	OCTO Pramac Yakhnich	Ducati Desmosedici	M	F: Soft Wet/R: Soft Wet	30	47m 15.231s
5	**Andrea Iannone**	ITA	29	Ducati Team	Ducati Desmosedici	M	F: S-Soft Wet/R: Soft Wet	30	47m 25.994s
6	**Dani Pedrosa**	SPA	26	Repsol Honda Team	Honda RC213V	M	F: S-Soft Wet/R: Soft Wet	30	47m 29.159s
7	**Jack Miller**	AUS	43	Estrella Galicia 0,0 Marc VDS	Honda RC213V	M	F: S-Soft Wet/R: Soft Wet	30	47m 29.282s
8	**Valentino Rossi**	ITA	46	Movistar Yamaha MotoGP	Yamaha YZR-M1	M	F: S-Soft Wet/R: Soft Wet	30	47m 29.688s
9	**Hector Barbera**	SPA	8	Avintia Racing	Ducati Desmosedici	M	F: S-Soft Wet/R: Soft Wet	30	47m 29.853s
10	**Alvaro Bautista**	SPA	19	Aprilia Racing Team Gresini	Aprilia RS-GP	M	F: Soft Wet/R: Soft Wet	30	47m 34.513s
11	**Eugene Laverty**	IRL	50	Pull & Bear Aspar Team	Ducati Desmosedici	M	F: S-Soft Wet/R: Soft Wet	30	47m 44.447s
12	**Maverick Vinales**	SPA	25	Team SUZUKI ECSTAR	Suzuki GSX-RR	M	F: S-Soft Wet/R: Soft Wet	30	47m 45.397s
13	**Bradley Smith**	GBR	38	Monster Yamaha Tech 3	Yamaha YZR-M1	M	F: S-Soft Wet/R: Soft Wet	30	48m 06.368s
14	**Aleix Espargaro**	SPA	41	Team SUZUKI ECSTAR	Suzuki GSX-RR	M	F: S-Soft Wet/R: Soft Wet	30	48m 09.330s
15	**Jorge Lorenzo**	SPA	99	Movistar Yamaha MotoGP	Yamaha YZR-M1	M	F: S-Soft Wet/R: Soft Wet	30	48m 20.933s
16	**Tito Rabat**	SPA	53	Estrella Galicia 0,0 Marc VDS	Honda RC213V	M	F: S-Soft Wet/R: Soft Wet	29	47m 49.257s
17	Loris Baz	FRA	76	Avintia Racing	Ducati Desmosedici	M	F: S-Soft Wet/R: Soft Wet	28	48m 01.949s
18	Yonny Hernandez	COL	68	Pull & Bear Aspar Team	Ducati Desmosedici	M	F: S-Soft Wet/R: Soft Wet	27	47m 30.750s
	Pol Espargaro	SPA	44	Monster Yamaha Tech 3	Yamaha YZR-M1	M	F: S-Soft Wet/R: Soft Wet	17	DNF-crash
	Danilo Petrucci	ITA	9	OCTO Pramac Yakhnich	Ducati Desmosedici	M	F: Soft Wet/R: Soft Wet	12	DNF-crash
	Stefan Bradl	GER	6	Aprilia Racing Team Gresini	Aprilia RS-GP	M	–	–	DNS-injured

*at start of race.

Fastest lap: Cal Crutchlow, on lap 30, 1m 25.019s, 96.6mph/155.4km/h.

Lap record: Marc Marquez, SPA (Honda), 1m 21.530s, 100.7mph/162.0km/h (2015).

Event best maximum speed: Andrea Iannone, 184.6mph/297.1km/h (free practice).

Qualifying

Weather: Dry
Air Temp: 23° **Track Temp:** 40°
Humidity: 37%

1	Marquez	1m 21.160s
2	Barbera	1m 21.572s
3	Rossi	1m 21.666s
4	Petrucci	1m 21.666s
5	P. Espargaro	1m 21.738s
6	Vinales	1m 21.784s
7	Dovizioso	1m 21.858s
8	A. Espargaro	1m 21.883s
9	Iannone	1m 21.890s
10	Pedrosa	1m 21.892s
11	Lorenzo	1m 22.088s
12	Hernandez	1m 22.346s
13	Crutchlow	1m 21.783s
14	Smith	1m 21.994s
15	Redding	1m 22.236s
16	Miller	1m 22.382s
17	Bradl	1m 22.493s
18	Laverty	1m 22.567s
19	Bautista	1m 22.670s
20	Baz	1m 22.860s
21	Rabat	1m 23.075s

Fastest race laps

1	Crutchlow	1m 25.019s
2	Dovizioso	1m 25.446s
3	Miller	1m 26.510s
4	Iannone	1m 26.713s
5	Marquez	1m 26.750s
6	Barbera	1m 26.760s
7	Vinales	1m 26.821s
8	Redding	1m 26.882s
9	Smith	1m 26.893s
10	Rossi	1m 27.022s
11	Pedrosa	1m 27.190s
12	Laverty	1m 28.187s
13	Bautista	1m 28.208s
14	Rabat	1m 28.212s
15	A. Espargaro	1m 28.361s
16	Lorenzo	1m 29.176s
17	Baz	1m 29.954s
18	Hernandez	1m 31.793s
19	Petrucci	1m 33.865s
20	P. Espargaro	1m 34.988s

Championship Points

1	Marquez	170
2	Lorenzo	122
3	Rossi	111
4	Pedrosa	96
5	Vinales	83
6	P. Espargaro	72
7	Barbera	65
8	Iannone	63
9	Dovizioso	59
10	Laverty	53
11	A. Espargaro	51
12	Redding	45
13	Miller	42
14	Crutchlow	40
15	Bradl	37
16	Smith	35
17	Bautista	35
18	Petrucci	24
19	Pirro	19
20	Rabat	18
21	Baz	8
22	Hernandez	3

Grid Order	1	2	3	4	5	6	7	8	9	10	11	12	13	14	15	16	17	18	19	20	21	22	23	24	25	26	27	28	29	30	
93 MARQUEZ	46	46	4	9	9	9	9	9	9	9	4	4	4	4	4	4	4	4	4	4	4	4	43	43	93	93	93	93	93	93	1
8 BARBERA	4	4	9	4	4	4	4	4	4	46	46	46	46	8	8	8	46	46	46	46	46	4	93	43	45	45	45	45	35		2
46 ROSSI	93	93	46	46	46	46	46	46	46	46	43	8	8	8	46	46	46	8	8	8	8	35	46	45	45	4	4	35	35	4	3
9 PETRUCCI	9	9	93	93	93	43	43	43	43	43	8	43	43	43	43	43	43	35	35	35	35	8	35	4	4	35	35	4	4	45	4
44 P. ESPARGARO	8	8	43	43	43	93	93	93	8	8	26	26	26	26	35	35	35	43	43	43	43	43	8	35	35	29	29	29	29		5
25 VINALES	43	43	8	8	8	8	8	8	93	93	35	35	35	35	26	26	26	26	26	26	26	93	93	8	46	26	26	26	26	26	6
4 DOVIZIOSO	29	29	29	29	29	29	29	29	26	26	4	45	45	45	45	45	45	45	19	19	99	45	46	8	43	46	46	46	43		7
41 A. ESPARGARO	44	44	26	26	26	26	26	29	29	35	29	29	93	93	93	19	19	19	19	25	93	99	99	26	26	8	8	8	46		8
29 IANNONE	26	26	44	44	44	44	45	45	45	45	93	93	19	19	19	19	93	25	25	99	25	26	26	19	29	8	43	43	43	8	9
26 PEDROSA	25	99	99	99	45	45	44	44	35	29	19	19	44	44	44	44	50	50	41	99	19	19	29	19	19	19	19	19	19		10
99 LORENZO	99	25	19	45	19	19	35	35	44	19	44	44	29	25	25	25	25	99	99	93	45	29	29	99	50	50	50	50	50		11
68 HERNANDEZ	41	41	41	19	35	19	19	19	44	25	25	25	50	50	50	50	41	41	45	41	50	50	25	25	25	25	25	25			12
35 CRUTCHLOW	35	35	45	35	99	99	99	99	99	41	41	41	41	41	41	99	53	93	29	29	25	25	25	41	41	41	41	38	38		13
38 SMITH	38	19	25	41	41	41	41	41	25	50	50	50	99	99	99	41	93	53	50	50	41	41	99	38	38	38	41	41			14
45 REDDING	19	45	35	25	25	25	25	25	99	99	99	99	53	53	53	38	38	38	38	38	38	38	38	38	99	99	99	99	99	99	15
43 MILLER	50	76	76	76	76	76	50	50	50	53	76	38	38	38	38	53	53	53	53	53	53	53	53	53	53						
50 LAVERTY	45	53	53	50	50	50	50	76	53	76	53	53	38	29	29	29	68	68	76	76	76	76	76	76	76	76					
19 BAUTISTA	68	50	50	53	53	53	53	53	76	38	38	38	29	76	68	68	76	68	68	68	68	68	68	68							
76 BAZ	76	38	38	38	38	38	38	38	38	9	9	68	68	68	76	76															
53 RABAT	53	68	68	68	68	68	68	68	68	68																					

68 Pit stop   68 Lapped rider

Constructor Points

1	Yamaha	186
2	Honda	185
3	Ducati	124
4	Suzuki	89
5	Aprilia	51

Moto2

RACE DISTANCE: 29 laps, 66.151 miles/106.459km · RACE WEATHER: Wet (air 18°C, humidity 100%, track 19°C)

Pos.	Rider	Nat.	No.	Entrant	Machine	Laps	Time & Speed
1	Johann Zarco	FRA	5	Ajo Motorsport	Kalex	29	47m 18.646s / 83.9mph / 135.0km/h
2	Jonas Folger	GER	94	Dynavolt Intact GP	Kalex	29	47m 18.705s
3	Julian Simon	SPA	60	QMMF Racing Team	Speed Up	29	47m 39.079s
4	Mattia Pasini	ITA	54	Italtrans Racing Team	Kalex	29	47m 49.101s
5	Lorenzo Baldassarri	ITA	7	Forward Team	Kalex	29	47m 50.417s
6	Luca Marini	ITA	10	Forward Team	Kalex	29	47m 52.847s
7	Hafizh Syahrin	MAL	55	Petronas Raceline Malaysia	Kalex	29	48m 00.588s
8	Jesko Raffin	SWI	2	Sports-Millions-EMWE-SAG	Kalex	29	48m 06.601s
9	Isaac Vinales	SPA	32	Tech 3 Racing	Tech 3	29	48m 08.405s
10	Dominique Aegerter	SWI	77	CarXpert Interwetten	Kalex	29	48m 09.693s
11	Takaaki Nakagami	JPN	30	IDEMITSU Honda Team Asia	Kalex	29	48m 24.032s
12	Remy Gardner	AUS	87	Tasca Racing Scuderia Moto2	Kalex	29	48m 32.511s
13	Robin Mulhauser	SWI	70	CarXpert Interwetten	Kalex	29	48m 38.191s
14	Edgar Pons	SPA	57	Paginas Amarillas HP 40	Kalex	29	48m 49.148s
15	Sandro Cortese	GER	11	Dynavolt Intact GP	Kalex	27	48m 52.260s
	Alex Rins	SPA	40	Paginas Amarillas HP 40	Kalex	26	DNF
	Franco Morbidelli	ITA	21	Estrella Galicia 0,0 Marc VDS	Kalex	26	DNF
	Sam Lowes	GBR	22	Federal Oil Gresini Moto2	Kalex	25	DNF
	Alex Marquez	SPA	73	Estrella Galicia 0,0 Marc VDS	Kalex	24	DNF
	Xavier Simeon	BEL	19	QMMF Racing Team	Speed Up	22	DNF
	Thomas Luthi	SWI	12	Garage Plus Interwetten	Kalex	17	DNF
	Axel Pons	SPA	49	AGR Team	Kalex	10	DNF
	Ratthapark Wilairot	THA	14	IDEMITSU Honda Team Asia	Kalex	8	DNF
	Simone Corsi	ITA	24	Speed Up Racing	Speed Up	5	DNF
	Xavi Vierge	SPA	97	Tech 3 Racing	Tech 3	5	DNF
	Marcel Schrotter	GER	23	AGR Team	Kalex	4	DNF
	Miguel Oliveira	POR	44	Leopard Racing	Kalex	3	DNF

Fastest lap: Xavier Simeon, on lap 20, 1m 36.619s, 84.9mph/136.7km/h.

Lap record: Franco Morbidelli, ITA (Kalex), 1m 24.538s, 97.1mph/156.3km/h (2015).

Event best maximum speed: Sandro Cortese, 155.3mph/250.0km/h (qualifying).

Qualifying

Weather: Dry
Air Temp: 24° **Track Temp:** 38°
Humidity: 38%

1	Nakagami	1m 24.274s
2	Zarco	1m 24.514s
3	Rins	1m 24.641s
4	Corsi	1m 24.680s
5	Morbidelli	1m 24.731s
6	Cortese	1m 24.754s
7	Baldassarri	1m 24.845s
8	Marquez	1m 24.942s
9	Schrotter	1m 24.964s
10	Lowes	1m 24.976s
11	Syahrin	1m 25.004s
12	Luthi	1m 25.030s
13	Folger	1m 25.053s
14	Pons	1m 25.056s
15	Marini	1m 25.089s
16	Oliveira	1m 25.173s
17	Simon	1m 25.182s
18	Simeon	1m 25.236s
19	Raffin	1m 25.412s
20	Pasini	1m 25.481s
21	Gardner	1m 25.871s
22	Vierge	1m 25.876s
23	Aegerter	1m 25.945s
24	Vinales	1m 26.101s
25	Wilairot	1m 26.143s
26	Mulhauser	1m 26.378s
27	Pons	1m 26.707s

Fastest race laps

1	Simeon	1m 36.619s
2	Simon	1m 36.750s
3	Rins	1m 36.861s
4	Morbidelli	1m 36.959s
5	Folger	1m 36.969s
6	Cortese	1m 37.082s
7	Zarco	1m 37.090s
8	Marquez	1m 37.225s
9	Pasini	1m 37.594s
10	Luthi	1m 37.671s
11	Nakagami	1m 37.677s
12	Lowes	1m 37.766s
13	Corsi	1m 37.790s
14	Marini	1m 37.842s
15	Baldassarri	1m 37.859s
16	Schrotter	1m 38.093s
17	Syahrin	1m 38.210s
18	Raffin	1m 38.410s
19	Vinales	1m 38.595s
20	Aegerter	1m 38.649s
21	Vierge	1m 38.709s
22	Gardner	1m 39.198s
23	Pons	1m 39.256s
24	Pons	1m 39.263s
25	Mulhauser	1m 39.525s
26	Oliveira	1m 40.240s
27	Wilairot	1m 40.360s

Championship Points

1	Zarco	151
2	Rins	126
3	Lowes	121
4	Luthi	93
5	Nakagami	83
6	Folger	83
7	Syahrin	69
8	Morbidelli	66
9	Aegerter	65
10	Corsi	59
11	Baldassarri	47
12	Salom	37
13	Pons	34
14	Simeon	28
15	Pasini	27
16	Simon	26
17	Oliveira	24
18	Schrotter	22
19	Marini	20
20	Cortese	15
21	Kent	14
22	Marquez	13
23	Raffin	10
24	Vinales	10
25	Gardner	5
26	Mulhauser	4
27	Wilairot	3
28	Vierge	3
29	Pons	2

Constructor Points

1	Kalex	225
2	Speed Up	88
3	Tech 3	13

Moto3

RACE DISTANCE: 27 laps, 61.588 miles/99.117km · RACE WEATHER: Wet (air 17°C, humidity 100%, track 18°C)

Pos.	Rider	Nat.	No.	Entrant	Machine	Laps	Time & Speed
1	Khairul Idham Pawi	MAL	89	Honda Team Asia	Honda	27	47m 07.763s / 78.4mph / 126.1km/h
2	Andrea Locatelli	ITA	55	Leopard Racing	KTM	27	47m 18.894s
3	Enea Bastianini	ITA	33	Gresini Racing Moto3	Honda	27	47m 21.122s
4	Jakub Kornfeil	CZE	84	Drive M7 SIC Racing Team	Honda	27	47m 26.304s
5	Fabio di Giannantonio	ITA	4	Gresini Racing Moto3	Honda	27	47m 28.383s
6	John McPhee	GBR	17	Peugeot MC Saxoprint	Peugeot	27	47m 28.461s
7	Jorge Navarro	SPA	9	Estrella Galicia 0,0	Honda	27	47m 28.673s
8	Brad Binder	RSA	41	Red Bull KTM Ajo	KTM	27	47m 31.096s
9	Jules Danilo	FRA	95	Ongetta-Rivacold	Honda	27	47m 38.081s
10	Francesco Bagnaia	ITA	21	Pull & Bear ASPAR Mahindra Team	Mahindra	27	47m 38.858s
11	Tatsuki Suzuki	JPN	24	CIP-Unicom Starker	Mahindra	27	47m 45.451s
12	Bo Bendsneyder	NED	64	Red Bull KTM Ajo	KTM	27	47m 52.768s
13	Gabriel Rodrigo	ARG	19	RBA Racing Team	KTM	27	47m 55.556s
14	Livio Loi	BEL	11	RW Racing GP BV	Honda	27	47m 55.836s
15	Aron Canet	SPA	44	Estrella Galicia 0,0	Honda	27	48m 04.684s
16	Alexis Masbou	FRA	10	Peugeot MC Saxoprint	Peugeot	27	48m 18.550s
17	Philipp Oettl	GER	65	Schedl GP Racing	KTM	27	48m 21.636s
18	Romano Fenati	ITA	5	SKY Racing Team VR46	KTM	27	48m 22.576s
19	Maximillian Kappler	GER	97	KRM-RZT	KTM	27	48m 22.966s
20	Stefano Valtulini	ITA	43	3570 Team Italia	Mahindra	27	48m 23.197s
21	Tim Georgi	GER	27	Freudenberg Racing Team	KTM	27	48m 31.669s
22	Danny Webb	GBR	22	Platinum Bay Real Estate	Mahindra	27	48m 46.311s
23	Fabio Quartararo	FRA	20	Leopard Racing	KTM	26	47m 13.887s
	Nicolo Bulega	ITA	8	SKY Racing Team VR46	KTM	14	DNF
	Adam Norrodin	MAL	7	Drive M7 SIC Racing Team	Honda	12	DNF
	Hiroki Ono	JPN	76	Honda Team Asia	Honda	11	DNF
	Jorge Martin	SPA	88	Pull & Bear ASPAR Mahindra Team	Mahindra	10	DNF
	Andrea Migno	ITA	16	SKY Racing Team VR46	KTM	10	DNF
	Darryn Binder	RSA	40	Platinum Bay Real Estate	Mahindra	8	DNF
	Juanfran Guevara	SPA	58	RBA Racing Team	KTM	8	DNF
	Lorenzo Petrarca	ITA	77	3570 Team Italia	Mahindra	7	DNF
	Joan Mir	SPA	36	Leopard Racing	KTM	0	DNF

Fastest lap: Khairul Idham Pawi, on lap 5, 1m 42.544s, 80.0mph/128.8km/h.

Lap record: Brad Binder, RSA (Mahindra), 1m 26.877s, 94.5mph/152.1km/h (2014).

Event best maximum speed: Gabriel Rodrigo, 131.7mph/212.0km/h (free practice).

Qualifying

Weather: Dry
Air Temp: 21° **Track Temp:** 34°
Humidity: 45%

1	Bastianini	1m 27.129s
2	Locatelli	1m 27.448s
3	Canet	1m 27.501s
4	Bendsneyder	1m 27.522s
5	Navarro	1m 27.538s
6	B. Binder	1m 27.566s
7	Danilo	1m 27.639s
8	McPhee	1m 27.739s
9	Ono	1m 27.819s
10	Martin	1m 27.875s
11	Bagnaia	1m 27.939s
12	Quartararo	1m 27.990s
13	Guevara	1m 28.017s
14	Rodrigo	1m 28.022s
15	Kornfeil	1m 28.219s
16	Loi	1m 28.317s
17	Fenati	1m 28.323s
18	Mir	1m 28.360s
19	Oettl	1m 28.390s
20	Pawi	1m 28.397s
21	Bulega	1m 28.402s
22	Di Giannantonio	1m 28.424s
23	Suzuki	1m 28.469s
24	Masbou	1m 28.492s
25	Herrera	1m 28.492s
26	Norrodin	1m 28.698s
27	Valtulini	1m 28.780s
28	Kappler	1m 28.955s
29	Antonelli	1m 28.973s
30	Migno	1m 29.343s
31	D. Binder	1m 29.412s
32	Petrarca	1m 29.619s
33	Georgi	1m 30.265s
34	Spiranelli	1m 30.526s
35	Webb	No Time

Fastest race laps

1	Pawi	1m 42.544s
2	Locatelli	1m 42.680s
3	Bastianini	1m 42.812s
4	Ono	1m 42.961s
5	D. Binder	1m 43.392s
6	Oettl	1m 43.681s
7	Bendsneyder	1m 43.828s
8	McPhee	1m 43.837s
9	Bagnaia	1m 43.893s
10	Danilo	1m 43.965s
11	Kornfeil	1m 44.027s
12	Norrodin	1m 44.069s
13	Navarro	1m 44.146s
14	Suzuki	1m 44.169s
15	Bulega	1m 44.258s
16	Di Giannantonio	1m 44.312s
17	B. Binder	1m 44.451s
18	Loi	1m 44.487s
19	Martin	1m 44.837s
20	Rodrigo	1m 45.000s
21	Guevara	1m 45.132s
22	Georgi	1m 45.205s
23	Kappler	1m 45.270s
24	Masbou	1m 45.328s
25	Fenati	1m 45.632s
26	Valtulini	1m 45.661s
27	Migno	1m 45.832s
28	Canet	1m 45.901s
29	Webb	1m 45.991s
30	Petrarca	1m 46.171s
31	Quartararo	1m 47.896s

Championship Points

1	B. Binder	159
2	Navarro	112
3	Fenati	93
4	Bagnaia	85
5	Bulega	75
6	Bastianini	65
7	Antonelli	63
8	Di Giannantonio	58
9	Kornfeil	58
10	Pawi	54
11	Locatelli	50
12	Mir	50
13	Danilo	41
14	Quartararo	39
15	Migno	37
16	Canet	34
17	Oettl	32
18	Guevara	25
19	Loi	24
20	Ono	20
21	McPhee	20
22	Bendsneyder	18
23	Martin	10
24	Suzuki	9
25	Rodrigo	9
26	Dalla Porta	7
27	Norrodin	5
28	D. Binder	4
29	Herrera	4

Constructor Points

1	KTM	192
2	Honda	189
3	Mahindra	97
4	Peugeot	20

AUSTRIAN GRAND PRIX

RED BULL RING

Above: Jack Miller's catastrophic high-side in warm-up put him out of this and several other races.

Centre, from top: Bad boy Fenati's bike stayed covered up; Marquez crashes and dislocates his shoulder; Marquez and Honda mock up in the welcome centre.

Right: Mika Kallio and Alex Hoffmann showed the Red Bull KTM 2017 MotoGP bike to enthusastic home support.

Far right: The impressive press room was just part of the circuit's extensively revamped facilities.

Below far right: Geoff Duke oversaw the Walk of Legends – even the tunnel under the track received the five-star treatment.

Opening spread: Made for Ducati? Rossi, Lorenzo, Marquez and Vinales chased Iannone and Dovizioso in vain.

Photos: Gold & Goose

THE Red Bull Ring in the Alpine foothills took just two practice sessions to oust Phillip Island as the fastest track on the calendar, on a cold day with limited grip. Next day, pole qualifier Iannone's Ducati set the best average of the weekend, at 186.9km/h, just over 116mph. Lorenzo's best lap of the Australian circuit stood at 182.1km/h.

After almost 20 years away, MotoGP returned to an unchanged circuit layout, but to vastly improved facilities, Red Bull's millions having been lavished in almost every conceivable area. There was one other big change, demonstrating different modern standards. In 1997, when Mick Doohan's best lap had been only 8mph slower, nobody said anything about danger. Now it was a major topic, with riders hoping that some more millions would be spent on introducing gravel traps and moving the barriers back.

Dovizioso set that fast Friday average, and he said afterwards that he had felt every km/h of it, "especially because the guardrail is very close on the straights. The maximum speed is not so high here, but you are on full throttle, and with our bike when you are on full throttle, the speed goes up very quick and you can feel it. But it's nice."

Jack Miller had a graphic description: "I had a sore jaw here after the tests, from gritting my teeth the whole way round. I only do that wide open, at more than 300km/h."

With small run-off areas paved for F1, and sinuous straights containing several 'vertical corners', there were chances for unusual accidents. Crutchlow: "Some places you are wheeling with the rear wheel doing 300km/h and the front doing 40. When it touches down, it's easy for it to lock up." That happened to Bradl, whose Aprilia slid for hundreds of metres, though he was lucky not to hit anything. Likewise Pedrosa, who locked the front under braking. While he slid to a safe stop, his bike vaulted the air-fence and landed atop the tyre wall beyond, bringing out the red flag while it was recovered.

While Rossi and others fingered the right kink, Turn Eight – very fast, the barriers worryingly adjacent – another danger spot was modified on race eve. This was the last corner, Turn Ten, where a few pots of paint reduced the exit width from 13 to 10m, slowing mid-corner and exit speed, and giving officials an extra task in watching for those who ran over the red. Practice lap times would be cancelled, and frequently were, while race transgressions would be judged individually on the circumstances.

The fast layout played much to the Ducatis, with the most power and the best wheelie control, which was partly (thought Dovi) down to their better engine management. And the winglets, with yet another variation, comprising double air dams and kinked main planes. As if this was not enough to provoke envy, Michelin had brought another harder rear tyre to cope with the speed. Another sop, thought the others, to the Italian marque.

It meant the rest, especially the wheelie-prone Hondas, had to take more risks in the corners. Doubtless this contributed to a potential FP3 disaster for Marquez, who lost control under braking at the top of the hill. He could have saved it, but unfortunately team-mate Pedrosa was already cutting across in front of him. Narrowly avoiding collision, Marquez fell in the gravel and dislocated his shoulder. Once again, his legendary bounce-back meant the errant joint was popped back into place, and that afternoon he was able to qualify fifth.

Miller was less fortunate, suffering a morning warm-up crash that left him with hairline fractures to his back and right wrist, and (it would transpire) to his right hand. He was out of this and the next race, and again two races after that when the lingering injuries continued to play up. Aleix Espargaro also suffered painful hand injuries in a practice fall, but was able to race, if not to finish.

KTM launched their 2017 MotoGP RC16-V4 in a good-natured press-room ceremony and with Kallio riding a demo

lap on race day. Although designed by the same ex-F1 engineer as the ill-fated 2005 attempt with Team Roberts, Kurt Trieb, this was a very different matter, said CEO Stefan Pierer. That had been the most powerful engine of the 990 era, but hampered by primitive electronics and a lack of finance and development. KTM pulled out before the end of the season.

Already dominant in Moto3 and with a Moto2 project planned for 2017, the Austrian company was much stronger, now the biggest bike manufacturer in Europe, and the commitment likewise.

The bike's V4 engine was largely conventional, but it sported unique (KTM-owned) White Power suspension and a heretical orange-painted tubular-steel frame, mainly because of familiarity with the material, said technical director Sebastian Risse. "You have to know the advantages and disadvantages, and then use them," he said.

After running within half a second of the private Hondas at tests, KTM was "ready to race now," said motor sport director Pit Beirer. "We have two crews and strong engines that don't break. We have tested on all kinds of tracks, with big and small riders. We are not dramatically far away."

The year's newcomers were Aprilia, and both riders and the Gresini team received a roasting from the Italian factory high-ups in a written statement after a misfortunate race in which both jumped the start. Bradl was most unlucky, thinking that the red light on his dash signalled an engine fault rather than a ride-through penalty. He pitted, only to be sent out again to serve the ride-through next time around. Piaggio Group MD Roberto Colaninno said, "We cannot accept … that human error keeps us from demonstrating our true value." Aprilia racing manager Romano Albesiano added, "I am the first to be furious. We can't accept that our potential is squandered because our riders are distracted at the start, and because of trivial mistakes on our part in managing the messages on the dashboard."

News that Casey Stoner's respected crew chief at Ducati and Honda, Cristian Gabarrini, would be returning to the Italian marque with Lorenzo in 2017 gave the Spanish rider something to relieve his current doldrums, though it would leave Miller bereft of an important mentor.

There was a Moto3 meltdown in Rossi's SKY VR46 team, when volatile race winner Romano Fenati threw one tantrum too many and was suspended on Saturday night, and sacked soon afterwards. Various accounts emerged, but trouble had been brewing all season. Fenati did not fit in well with Rossi's entourage, declining to join the group practice sessions at the Tavullia riding ranch, and not seeing eye to eye with the team, especially 'sporting manager' and Valentino's bosom buddy 'Uccio' Salucci. Until then, the 20-year-old had been a serious candidate for second overall, and possibly (given a hiccup from Binder) the title itself.

MOTOGP RACE – 28 laps

The deceptively simple track layout put huge emphasis on acceleration and braking. It was made for Ducati. The only question – which Ducati? Iannone answered that with a daring on-the-grid switch to the softer tyre, and a race of careful tactics quite at odds with his reputation. He was the only leading rider on the soft front, and nobody else chose the soft rear. The switch was against his team's advice. "It was a difficult decision, and a strong decision. But I believed in myself," he said later.

It was not only his first win, but also the first for Ducati for six years, and their previous winner, Casey Stoner, was in the pits to savour the moment.

Only second-placed Dovizioso was not as ecstatic. He'd led his team-mate for a chunk of the 28 laps, but was beaten by almost a full second when Iannone's gamble paid off.

Rossi had made an impressive bid for pole in a furious qualifying session, only to be shaded by Iannone at the last, with Dovizioso third. Lorenzo led row two from Marquez and

Above: A kiss for his Desmosedici: Gigi Dall'Igna had made a winner.

Above right: Iannone's soft-tyre gamble lasted just long enough to take the victory.
Photos: Gold & Goose

Top: It was only a question of which Ducati would win.
Photo: Bernd Fischer

Above right: The victorious Ducati squad celebrates after enduring a six-year drought.

Right: Johann Zarco leads Morbidelli and Luthi to strengthen his grip on the title lead.

Below right: Rookie's delight: Mir celebrates his first win; Binder, Quartararo (20) and Oettl (65) share the moment.
Photos: Gold & Goose

Vinales. Crutchlow, through from Q1, was seventh; Laverty was also through for his first time after leading Q1, and he qualified a career-best 11th, ahead of a troubled Pedrosa.

The first few laps were also furious. Iannone and Dovi led away, Rossi in hot pursuit as Marquez made a lunge into the slow first corner, running wide and pushing Lorenzo way out across the paved run-off.

Rossi seized the lead in the final corner, much to the appreciation of the 95,000-strong crowd. But Iannone had taken him back by Turn Three, while Lorenzo sneaked into second in the confusion. Dovizioso would get ahead of Rossi as well. And next time around, also Marquez, after Rossi ran very wide due to a braking error going into Turn Three at the top of the hill.

Dovi had regained second from Lorenzo by lap six, and from then it was all about the Ducatis. After another three laps, the older rider took over up front. Now it was a game of tactics. Iannone was riding carefully in second. "It was very important not to spin and slide," he explained. "And I used less fuel for the first half of the race. After I switched maps, the bike pushed harder."

The Yamahas stayed close and even looked threatening until just before two-thirds-distance, the point at which the Ducati riders stopped nursing their tyres and conserving fuel. In this way, the pair were a second ahead of the Yamahas by lap 20, and they stretched it further over the closing laps. It was on the 21st that Iannone outbraked Dovi, and from then on he was in control.

It was the same for Lorenzo, controlling his team-mate in a strong comeback after two bad races. Valentino pushed and probed, but could never get ahead.

Marquez, almost ten seconds off Rossi by the end, spent most of the race successfully fending off Vinales, leaving his compatriot frustrated again, although still less than two seconds down.

"After how yesterday went, I'm happy," said Marquez. Fifth was "the best possible outcome, and we've only lost five points compared with Lorenzo. With our difficulties, my objective was to think of the championship."

Pedrosa had to be happy with seventh, a major improvement on his 12th-placed qualifying and comfortably clear of any pursuers.

There had been some variety in the battle for eighth, led for half the race by Laverty's Aspar Ducati. Then he was displaced by compatriots Redding and Smith, and fell back into the clutches of Aleix Espargaro, until the Suzuki rider retired, in too much pain from a broken finger.

Worse was to come for the very consistent Irish rider. He had regained 11th from Petrucci on the last lap and seemed set to preserve his perfect points record. Petrucci made a last-corner lunge and knocked him off, receiving a penalty of three grid positions at the next race. Laverty remounted, but was out of the points.

Redding managed to stay four-tenths ahead of Smith; some way back, Pol Espargaro had got clear of Petrucci and Ducati wild-card Pirro. The still-injured Baz was a lone 13th, after Rabat had dropped away with sliding tyres.

Five riders had their chances wrecked by jump-starts. Of them, Crutchlow was the best finisher, in 15th. Hernandez, Bautista and Bradl also served ride-through penalties. The fifth was Barbera, who failed to heed the instruction. He was black-flagged and disqualified, spoiling his own perfect points record. Now only Marquez had scored at every round.

MOTO2 RACE – 25 laps

Zarco was on pole for only the second time in 2016, from Morbidelli and Luthi, with main title rivals Lowes and Rins seventh and ninth.

Lowes would not be a factor – he slipped off on lap four and then crashed terminally with 16 laps to go; Rins seemed to have ruled himself out of the front group, running wide on lap one and finishing it a relatively distant seventh.

Zarco got a poor start, braked late for the tight first corner and also ran wide, leaving Morbidelli to escape, chased by team-mate Marquez and Marcel Schrotter.

Marquez would drop back, and after seven laps he was sixth, out of touch with the lead group. Schrotter was now

second, ahead of Luthi and Zarco, with Rins a couple of seconds down in fifth.

As so often, Zarco was biding his time. "It was hot and I was having some trouble with the brakes, but I knew I could be better when the tyres went down," he said.

Quite so, and shortly before half-distance he started to pick up places – first Luthi, then Schrotter, so that by lap 16 he had closed almost a second's gap to Morbidelli and was ready to pounce.

"I thought I could do it," said Morbidelli, "but when Johann came past, he was so fast I couldn't stay with him."

Thus the defending champion forged clear to take his fifth win of the season, his fourth in the previous five races, by better than three seconds. His hopes of becoming the first Moto2 champion to defend his title were growing race by race as again he extended his points lead.

Luthi tried to follow him past Morbidelli and did get ahead on lap 18, but he couldn't escape. At the same time, Rins was closing on the fading Schrotter and was soon ahead, working on closing a gap of 1.5 seconds.

He was still over a second behind as they started the last lap, "but I pushed over the limit". Meanwhile, Morbidelli was roughing up Luthi, slowing their pace.

It all came down to the last two corners: Morbidelli regained second on the penultimate, then Rins pushed past Luthi on the final one. The trio was covered by four-tenths, and Luthi was off the rostrum.

Schrotter was just over a second adrift for a career-best fifth; Marquez managed to fend off a late attack by Nakagami for sixth, significantly his best of a dire second season in which he had crashed out of half of the first ten rounds.

Baldassarri finally came out on top after a long battle with Axel Pons and Aegerter, with the last named having dropped away by the finish. Cortese, Kent, Pasini, Oliveira and Simon wrapped up the rest of the points.

Johan Folger was an early crasher, rejoining in last; Corsi also crashed out.

MOTO3 RACE – 23 laps

Binder dominated free practice, but complained of being blocked on his fast qualifying lap, which handed a first pole to Joan Mir, one of a crop of bright rookies. Bastianini completed the front row.

They finished a typically frantic race in exactly the same order, after plenty more banging and shoving during the closing laps.

The three of them had done most of the leading, and Binder most of that, but it was typically full of shuffling, and both Quartararo and Oettl took turns.

The lead group was still ten-strong as they approached half-distance, but thereafter the five of them broke clear, fighting to the finish.

Binder looked the strongest, but the track's hard braking offered opportunities for crazy late braking, and in the end he just lost out to the Spanish teenager.

Quartararo was fourth and Oettl fifth, all being covered by six-tenths.

While senior Mahindra rider Bagnaia had started strongly, but then dropped back, his younger team-mate, Martin, pushed through to sixth and held on to the end. He was very narrowly ahead of rookie Bendsneyder, with another, Di Giannantonio, just off the back; they were two-thousandths ahead of a third, Bulega, and Livio Loi, who had come through impressively in the wake of Navarro (EG Honda). Bagnaia was inches behind Loi in 11th.

And Navarro? The erstwhile title challenger had qualified a lowly 17th and pushed through to within reach of the lead group, only to crash out, so that Binder again increased his points lead, now 67 clear of the Spaniard.

Guevara, Locatelli, Herrera and Ono took the rest of the points; returned injury victim Antonelli was 18th.

NEROGIARDINI MOTORRAD GRAND PRIX VON ÖSTERREICH

12-14 AUGUST, 2016

RED BULL RING, SPIELBERG
Circuit: 4.318km / 2.683 miles
28 laps

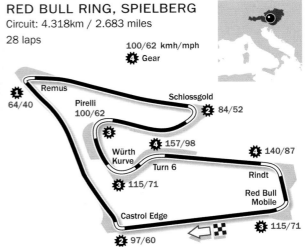

MotoGP — RACE DISTANCE: 28 laps, 75.126 miles/120.904km · RACE WEATHER: Dry (air 27°C, humidity 38%, track 46°C)

Pos.	Rider	Nat.	No.	Entrant	Machine	Tyres	Race tyre choice	Laps	Time & speed
1	**Andrea Iannone**	ITA	29	Ducati Team	Ducati Desmosedici	M	F: Soft/R: Medium	28	39m 46.255s 113.3mph/ 182.4km/h
2	**Andrea Dovizioso**	ITA	4	Ducati Team	Ducati Desmosedici	M	F: Medium/R: Hard	28	39m 47.193s
3	**Jorge Lorenzo**	SPA	99	Movistar Yamaha MotoGP	Yamaha YZR-M1	M	F: Medium/R: Hard	28	39m 49.644s
4	**Valentino Rossi**	ITA	46	Movistar Yamaha MotoGP	Yamaha YZR-M1	M	F: Medium/R: Hard	28	39m 50.070s
5	**Marc Marquez**	SPA	93	Repsol Honda Team	Honda RC213V	M	F: Medium/R: Hard	28	39m 58.068s
6	**Maverick Vinales**	SPA	25	Team SUZUKI ECSTAR	Suzuki GSX-RR	M	F: Medium/R: Hard	28	40m 00.596s
7	**Dani Pedrosa**	SPA	26	Repsol Honda Team	Honda RC213V	M	F: Medium/R: Hard	28	40m 03.318s
8	**Scott Redding**	GBR	45	OCTO Pramac Yakhnich	Ducati Desmosedici	M	F: Medium/R: Hard	28	40m 15.692s
9	**Bradley Smith**	GBR	38	Monster Yamaha Tech 3	Yamaha YZR-M1	M	F: Soft/R: Hard	28	40m 16.040s
10	**Pol Espargaro**	SPA	44	Monster Yamaha Tech 3	Yamaha YZR-M1	M	F: Medium/R: Hard	28	40m 23.349s
11	**Danilo Petrucci**	ITA	9	OCTO Pramac Yakhnich	Ducati Desmosedici	M	F: Medium/R: Hard	28	40m 26.020s
12	**Michele Pirro**	ITA	51	Ducati Team	Ducati Desmosedici	M	F: Medium/R: Hard	28	40m 26.021s
13	**Loris Baz**	FRA	76	Avintia Racing	Ducati Desmosedici	M	F: Medium/R: Hard	28	40m 30.539s
14	**Tito Rabat**	SPA	53	Estrella Galicia 0,0 Marc VDS	Honda RC213V	M	F: Medium/R: Hard	28	40m 31.259s
15	**Cal Crutchlow**	GBR	35	LCR Honda	Honda RC213V	M	F: Medium/R: Hard	28	40m 49.501s
16	Alvaro Bautista	SPA	19	Aprilia Racing Team Gresini	Aprilia RS-GP	M	F: Medium/R: Hard	28	40m 58.703s
17	Yonny Hernandez	COL	68	Pull & Bear Aspar Team	Ducati Desmosedici	M	F: Soft/R: Hard	28	41m 00.772s
18	Eugene Laverty	IRL	50	Pull & Bear Aspar Team	Ducati Desmosedici	M	F: Soft/R: Hard	28	41m 22.765s
19	Stefan Bradl	GER	6	Aprilia Racing Team Gresini	Aprilia RS-GP	M	F: Medium/R: Hard	27	40m 53.077s
	Aleix Espargaro	SPA	41	Team SUZUKI ECSTAR	Suzuki GSX-RR	M	F: Medium/R: Hard	24	DNF-injured
	Hector Barbera	SPA	8	Avintia Racing	Ducati Desmosedici	M	F: Medium/R: Hard	–	DSQ
	Jack Miller	AUS	43	Estrella Galicia 0,0 Marc VDS	Honda RC213V	M	–	–	DNS-injured

Fastest lap: Andrea Iannone, on lap 24, 1m 24.561s, 114.2mph/183.8km/h (record).

Previous lap record: New circuit.

Event best maximum speed: Andrea Dovizioso, 194.5mph/313.0km/h (race).

Qualifying
Weather: Dry
Air Temp: 24° **Track Temp:** 37°
Humidity: 48%

1	Iannone	1m 23.142s
2	Rossi	1m 23.289s
3	Dovizioso	1m 23.298s
4	Lorenzo	1m 23.361s
5	Marquez	1m 23.475s
6	Vinales	1m 23.584s
7	Crutchlow	1m 23.597s
8	Redding	1m 23.777s
9	A. Espargaro	1m 23.813s
10	Barbera	1m 23.822s
11	Laverty	1m 24.218s
12	Pedrosa	1m 24.263s
13	Petrucci	1m 24.123s
14	Smith	1m 24.126s
15	P. Espargaro	1m 24.265s
16	Hernandez	1m 24.472s
17	Pirro	1m 24.593s
18	Rabat	1m 24.665s
19	Bautista	1m 24.673s
20	Miller	1m 24.852s
21	Bradl	1m 24.895s
22	Baz	1m 25.192s

Fastest race laps

1	Iannone	1m 24.561s
2	Dovizioso	1m 24.686s
3	Lorenzo	1m 24.786s
4	Rossi	1m 24.854s
5	Vinales	1m 25.073s
6	Marquez	1m 25.117s
7	Pedrosa	1m 25.206s
8	Bautista	1m 25.342s
9	Barbera	1m 25.368s
10	Crutchlow	1m 25.479s
11	Redding	1m 25.508s
12	Smith	1m 25.521s
13	A. Espargaro	1m 25.580s
14	Laverty	1m 25.651s
15	Hernandez	1m 25.809s
16	Pirro	1m 25.859s
17	Petrucci	1m 25.875s
18	P. Espargaro	1m 25.878s
19	Bradl	1m 25.934s
20	Rabat	1m 25.969s
21	Baz	1m 26.024s

Championship Points

1	Marquez	181
2	Lorenzo	138
3	Rossi	124
4	Pedrosa	105
5	Vinales	93
6	Iannone	88
7	Dovizioso	79
8	P. Espargaro	78
9	Barbera	65
10	Redding	53
11	Laverty	53
12	A. Espargaro	51
13	Miller	42
14	Smith	42
15	Crutchlow	41
16	Bradl	37
17	Bautista	35
18	Petrucci	29
19	Pirro	23
20	Rabat	20
21	Baz	11
22	Hernandez	3

Lap chart

Grid order	1	2	3	4	5	6	7	8	9	10	11	12	13	14	15	16	17	18	19	20	21	22	23	24	25	26	27	28
29 IANNONE	46	29	29	29	29	29	29	29	29	4	4	4	4	4	4	4	4	4	4	29	29	29	29	29	29	29	29	1
46 ROSSI	29	99	99	99	99	4	4	4	4	29	29	29	29	29	29	29	29	29	29	4	4	4	4	4	4	4	4	2
4 DOVIZIOSO	4	46	4	4	4	99	99	99	99	99	99	99	99	99	99	99	99	99	99	99	99	99	99	99	99	99	99	3
99 LORENZO	99	4	46	93	93	46	46	46	46	46	46	46	46	46	46	46	46	46	46	46	46	46	46	46	46	46	46	4
93 MARQUEZ	93	93	93	46	46	93	93	93	93	93	93	93	93	93	93	93	93	93	93	93	93	93	93	93	93	93	93	5
25 VINALES	25	25	25	25	25	25	25	25	25	25	25	25	25	25	25	25	25	25	25	25	25	25	25	25	25	25	25	6
35 CRUTCHLOW	8	8	8	41	8	8	8	8	8	8	8	8	26	26	26	26	26	26	26	26	26	26	26	26	26	26	26	7
45 REDDING	41	41	41	8	50	50	50	50	26	26	26	26	50	50	50	50	45	45	45	45	45	45	45	45	45	45	45	8
41 A. ESPARGARO	26	26	26	26	26	26	26	26	50	50	50	50	45	45	45	45	38	38	38	38	38	38	38	38	38	38	38	9
8 BARBERA	45	50	50	50	45	45	45	45	45	45	45	45	38	38	38	38	50	50	50	50	50	50	44	44	44	44	44	10
50 LAVERTY	38	45	45	45	41	41	41	38	38	38	38	38	41	41	41	41	41	41	41	41	41	44	50	50	50	9	9	11
26 PEDROSA	50	38	38	38	38	38	38	41	41	41	41	41	9	9	44	44	44	44	44	44	41	9	9	9	50	51	12
9 PETRUCCI	44	9	9	9	9	9	9	44	44	44	9	44	44	9	9	9	9	9	9	9	9	51	51	51	51	76	13
38 SMITH	9	44	35	35	35	44	44	9	9	9	44	9	51	51	51	51	51	51	51	51	51	53	53	53	53	53	14
44 P. ESPARGARO	35	35	44	44	44	53	53	53	51	51	51	51	53	53	53	53	53	53	53	53	53	76	76	76	76	35	15
68 HERNANDEZ	19	19	19	68	53	51	51	51	53	53	53	53	76	76	76	76	76	76	76	76	76	35	35	35	35	19		
51 PIRRO	68	68	68	53	51	76	76	76	76	76	76	76	35	35	35	35	35	35	35	35	35	68	68	68	19	68		
53 RABAT	51	53	53	19	76	35	35	35	35	35	35	35	68	68	68	68	68	68	68	68	68	19	19	19	68	50		
19 BAUTISTA	6	51	51	51	68	68	68	68	68	68	68	68	19	19	19	19	19	19	19	19	19	41	6	6	6			
6 BRADL	53	6	76	76	6	19	19	19	19	19	19	19	6	6	6	6	6	6	6	6	6							
76 BAZ	76	76	6	6	19	6	6	6	6	6	6	6																

6 Pit stop   6 Lapped rider   68 Ride-through penalty

Constructor Points

1	Yamaha	202
2	Honda	196
3	Ducati	149
4	Suzuki	99
5	Aprilia	51

Moto2 — RACE DISTANCE: 25 laps, 67.077 miles/107.950km · RACE WEATHER: Dry (air 26°C, humidity 50%, track 40°C)

Pos.	Rider	Nat.	No.	Entrant	Machine	Laps	Time & Speed
1	**Johann Zarco**	FRA	5	Ajo Motorsport	Kalex	25	37m 34.180s / 107.1mph / 172.3km/h
2	**Franco Morbidelli**	ITA	21	Estrella Galicia 0,0 Marc VDS	Kalex	25	37m 37.238s
3	**Alex Rins**	SPA	40	Paginas Amarillas HP 40	Kalex	25	37m 37.556s
4	**Thomas Luthi**	SWI	12	Garage Plus Interwetten	Kalex	25	37m 37.647s
5	**Marcel Schrotter**	GER	23	AGR Team	Kalex	25	37m 38.920s
6	**Alex Marquez**	SPA	73	Estrella Galicia 0,0 Marc VDS	Kalex	25	37m 43.596s
7	**Takaaki Nakagami**	JPN	30	IDEMITSU Honda Team Asia	Kalex	25	37m 44.358s
8	**Lorenzo Baldassarri**	ITA	7	Forward Team	Kalex	25	37m 46.131s
9	**Axel Pons**	SPA	49	AGR Team	Kalex	25	37m 46.981s
10	**Dominique Aegerter**	SWI	77	CarXpert Interwetten	Kalex	25	37m 48.157s
11	**Sandro Cortese**	GER	11	Dynavolt Intact GP	Kalex	25	37m 52.226s
12	**Danny Kent**	GBR	52	Leopard Racing	Kalex	25	37m 52.464s
13	**Mattia Pasini**	ITA	54	Italtrans Racing Team	Kalex	25	37m 52.604s
14	**Miguel Oliveira**	POR	44	Leopard Racing	Kalex	25	37m 53.010s
15	**Julian Simon**	SPA	60	QMMF Racing Team	Speed Up	25	37m 54.202s
16	Xavi Vierge	SPA	97	Tech 3 Racing	Tech 3	25	38m 03.065s
17	Luca Marini	ITA	10	Forward Team	Kalex	25	38m 03.150s
18	Isaac Vinales	SPA	32	Tech 3 Racing	Tech 3	25	38m 03.212s
19	Remy Gardner	AUS	87	Tasca Racing Scuderia Moto2	Kalex	25	38m 03.295s
20	Edgar Pons	SPA	57	Paginas Amarillas HP 40	Kalex	25	38m 03.604s
21	Hafizh Syahrin	MAL	55	Petronas Raceline Malaysia	Kalex	25	38m 04.157s
22	Ratthapark Wilairot	THA	14	IDEMITSU Honda Team Asia	Kalex	25	38m 12.115s
23	Xavier Simeon	BEL	19	QMMF Racing Team	Speed Up	25	38m 17.456s
24	Jesko Raffin	SWI	2	Sports-Millions-EMWE-SAG	Kalex	25	38m 18.386s
25	Robin Mulhauser	SWI	70	CarXpert Interwetten	Kalex	25	38m 23.015s
26	Jonas Folger	GER	94	Dynavolt Intact GP	Kalex	25	38m 46.328s
	Simone Corsi	ITA	24	Speed Up Racing	Speed Up	12	DNF
	Sam Lowes	GBR	22	Federal Oil Gresini Moto2	Kalex	9	DNF

Fastest lap: Johann Zarco, on lap 8, 1m 29.497s, 107.9mph/173.6km/h (record).
Previous lap record: New circuit.
Event best maximum speed: Thomas Luthi, 161.1mph/259.2km/h (warm up).

Qualifying

Weather: Dry
Air Temp: 24°   **Track Temp:** 39°
Humidity: 46%

1	Zarco	1m 29.255s
2	Morbidelli	1m 29.367s
3	Luthi	1m 29.480s
4	Schrotter	1m 29.645s
5	Marquez	1m 29.702s
6	Pons	1m 29.702s
7	Lowes	1m 29.714s
8	Nakagami	1m 29.728s
9	Rins	1m 29.752s
10	Folger	1m 29.844s
11	Aegerter	1m 29.861s
12	Baldassarri	1m 29.926s
13	Cortese	1m 29.978s
14	Pons	1m 30.031s
15	Kent	1m 30.129s
16	Syahrin	1m 30.264s
17	Pasini	1m 30.305s
18	Oliveira	1m 30.308s
19	Marini	1m 30.332s
20	Simon	1m 30.400s
21	Wilairot	1m 30.438s
22	Corsi	1m 30.622s
23	Gardner	1m 30.743s
24	Simeon	1m 30.762s
25	Vinales	1m 30.775s
26	Raffin	1m 30.870s
27	Vierge	1m 30.878s
28	Mulhauser	1m 30.884s

Fastest race laps

1	Zarco	1m 29.497s
2	Luthi	1m 29.591s
3	Rins	1m 29.660s
4	Morbidelli	1m 29.717s
5	Schrotter	1m 29.743s
6	Pons	1m 29.761s
7	Kent	1m 29.880s
8	Nakagami	1m 29.882s
9	Simon	1m 29.900s
10	Marquez	1m 29.981s
11	Baldassarri	1m 29.992s
12	Folger	1m 30.060s
13	Syahrin	1m 30.092s
14	Oliveira	1m 30.140s
15	Cortese	1m 30.142s
16	Aegerter	1m 30.147s
17	Pasini	1m 30.148s
18	Corsi	1m 30.365s
19	Marini	1m 30.480s
20	Vinales	1m 30.493s
21	Gardner	1m 30.536s
22	Vierge	1m 30.567s
23	Pons	1m 30.595s
24	Wilairot	1m 30.841s
25	Lowes	1m 30.901s
26	Mulhauser	1m 30.955s
27	Raffin	1m 30.987s
28	Simeon	1m 31.137s

Championship Points

1	Zarco	176
2	Rins	142
3	Lowes	121
4	Luthi	106
5	Nakagami	92
6	Morbidelli	86
7	Folger	83
8	Aegerter	71
9	Syahrin	69
10	Corsi	59
11	Baldassarri	55
12	Pons	41
13	Salom	37
14	Schrotter	33
15	Pasini	30
16	Simeon	28
17	Simon	27
18	Oliveira	26
19	Marquez	23
20	Marini	20
21	Cortese	20
22	Kent	18
23	Raffin	10
24	Vinales	10
25	Gardner	5
26	Mulhauser	4
27	Wilairot	3
28	Vierge	3
29	Pons	2

Constructor Points

1	Kalex	250
2	Speed Up	89
3	Tech 3	13

Moto3 — RACE DISTANCE: 23 laps, 61.711 miles/99.314km · RACE WEATHER: Dry (air 24°C, humidity 55%, track 35°C)

Pos.	Rider	Nat.	No.	Entrant	Machine	Laps	Time & Speed
1	**Joan Mir**	SPA	36	Leopard Racing	KTM	23	37m 23.325s / 99.0mph / 159.3km/h
2	**Brad Binder**	RSA	41	Red Bull KTM Ajo	KTM	23	37m 23.604s
3	**Enea Bastianini**	ITA	33	Gresini Racing Moto3	Honda	23	37m 23.756s
4	**Fabio Quartararo**	FRA	20	Leopard Racing	KTM	23	37m 23.764s
5	**Philipp Oettl**	GER	65	Schedl GP Racing	KTM	23	37m 23.925s
6	**Jorge Martin**	SPA	88	Pull & Bear ASPAR Mahindra Team	Mahindra	23	37m 27.459s
7	**Bo Bendsneyder**	NED	64	Red Bull KTM Ajo	KTM	23	37m 27.486s
8	**Fabio Di Giannantonio**	ITA	4	Gresini Racing Moto3	Honda	23	37m 28.295s
9	**Nicolo Bulega**	ITA	8	SKY Racing Team VR46	KTM	23	37m 28.297s
10	**Livio Loi**	BEL	11	RW Racing GP BV	Honda	23	37m 28.587s
11	**Francesco Bagnaia**	ITA	21	Pull & Bear ASPAR Mahindra Team	Mahindra	23	37m 28.740s
12	**Juanfran Guevara**	SPA	58	RBA Racing Team	KTM	23	37m 29.196s
13	**Andrea Locatelli**	ITA	55	Leopard Racing	KTM	23	37m 29.230s
14	**Maria Herrera**	SPA	6	MH6 Team	KTM	23	37m 36.100s
15	**Hiroki Ono**	JPN	76	Honda Team Asia	Honda	23	37m 36.164s
16	Jules Danilo	FRA	95	Ongetta-Rivacold	Honda	23	37m 36.267s
17	Darryn Binder	RSA	40	Platinum Bay Real Estate	Mahindra	23	37m 37.415s
18	Niccolo Antonelli	ITA	23	Ongetta-Rivacold	Honda	23	37m 37.731s
19	Jakub Kornfeil	CZE	83	Drive M7 SIC Racing Team	Honda	23	37m 37.842s
20	Stefano Manzi	ITA	62	Mahindra Racing	Mahindra	23	37m 37.870s
21	Aron Canet	SPA	44	Estrella Galicia 0,0	Honda	23	37m 37.988s
22	Albert Arenas	SPA	12	Peugeot MC Saxoprint	Peugeot	23	37m 40.457s
23	Adam Norrodin	MAL	7	Drive M7 SIC Racing Team	Honda	23	37m 40.768s
24	John McPhee	GBR	17	Peugeot MC Saxoprint	Peugeot	23	37m 51.631s
25	Andrea Migno	ITA	16	SKY Racing Team VR46	KTM	23	37m 51.730s
26	Marcos Ramirez	SPA	42	Platinum Bay Real Estate	Mahindra	23	38m 03.538s
27	Khairul Idham Pawi	MAL	89	Honda Team Asia	Honda	23	38m 03.846s
28	Stefano Valtulini	ITA	43	3570 Team Italia	Mahindra	23	38m 27.365s
29	Fabio Spiranelli	ITA	3	CIP-Unicom Starker	Mahindra	23	38m 27.383s
30	Lorenzo Petrarca	ITA	77	3570 Team Italia	Mahindra	23	38m 27.838s
	Jorge Navarro	SPA	9	Estrella Galicia 0,0	Honda	18	DNF
	Gabriel Rodrigo	ARG	19	RBA Racing Team	KTM	14	DNF
	Marco Bezzecchi	ITA	53	Mahindra Racing	Mahindra	5	DNF
	Tatsuki Suzuki	JPN	24	CIP-Unicom Starker	Mahindra	5	DNF
	Romano Fenati	ITA	5	SKY Racing Team VR46	KTM	-	DNS

Fastest lap: Philipp Oettl, on lap 15, 1m 36.557s, 100.0mph/160.9km/h (record).
Previous lap record: New circuit.
Event best maximum speed: Hiroki Ono, 136.1mph/219.1km/h (free practice).

Qualifying

Weather: Dry
Air Temp: 22°   **Track Temp:** 25°
Humidity: 55%

1	Mir	1m 36.228s
2	B. Binder	1m 36.335s
3	Bastianini	1m 36.600s
4	Canet	1m 36.661s
5	Quartararo	1m 36.693s
6	Bagnaia	1m 36.843s
7	Bulega	1m 36.919s
8	Oettl	1m 36.929s
9	Di Giannantonio	1m 36.950s
10	Bendsneyder	1m 36.965s
11	Fenati	1m 36.993s
12	Danilo	1m 37.159s
13	Antonelli	1m 37.203s
14	Martin	1m 37.209s
15	Guevara	1m 37.217s
16	Locatelli	1m 37.224s
17	D. Binder	1m 37.233s
18	Navarro	1m 37.237s
19	Rodrigo	1m 37.252s
20	Bezzecchi	1m 37.280s
21	Migno	1m 37.308s
22	Loi	1m 37.462s
23	Manzi	1m 37.538s
24	Arenas	1m 37.589s
25	Kornfeil	1m 37.619s
26	Ono	1m 37.644s
27	Norrodin	1m 37.808s
28	Pawi	1m 37.812s
29	McPhee	1m 37.874s
30	Valtulini	1m 38.075s
31	Herrera	1m 38.250s
32	Ramirez	1m 38.347s
33	Suzuki	1m 38.395s
34	Spiranelli	1m 38.455s
35	Petrarca	1m 39.331s

Fastest race laps

1	Oettl	1m 36.557s
2	Bastianini	1m 36.650s
3	Quartararo	1m 36.810s
4	Navarro	1m 36.811s
5	B. Binder	1m 36.813s
6	Rodrigo	1m 36.848s
7	Loi	1m 36.899s
8	Di Giannantonio	1m 36.900s
9	Martin	1m 36.930s
10	Bendsneyder	1m 36.952s
11	Mir	1m 36.955s
12	Bulega	1m 36.982s
13	Herrera	1m 36.989s
14	Guevara	1m 36.997s
15	Bagnaia	1m 37.030s
16	Locatelli	1m 37.060s
17	Danilo	1m 37.098s
18	Ono	1m 37.121s
19	Kornfeil	1m 37.154s
20	D. Binder	1m 37.183s
21	Manzi	1m 37.210s
22	Antonelli	1m 37.211s
23	Canet	1m 37.334s
24	Arenas	1m 37.359s
25	Norrodin	1m 37.432s
26	Migno	1m 37.680s
27	Bezzecchi	1m 37.822s
28	Suzuki	1m 37.926s
29	McPhee	1m 37.984s
30	Pawi	1m 38.096s
31	Ramirez	1m 38.136s
32	Valtulini	1m 38.342s
33	Spiranelli	1m 39.470s
34	Petrarca	1m 39.516s

Championship Points

1	B. Binder	179
2	Navarro	112
3	Fenati	93
4	Bagnaia	90
5	Bulega	82
6	Bastianini	81
7	Mir	75
8	Di Giannantonio	66
9	Antonelli	63
10	Kornfeil	58
11	Pawi	54
12	Locatelli	53
13	Quartararo	52
14	Oettl	43
15	Danilo	41
16	Migno	37
17	Canet	34
18	Loi	30
19	Guevara	29
20	Bendsneyder	27
21	Ono	21
22	McPhee	20
23	Martin	20
24	Suzuki	9
25	Rodrigo	9
26	Dalla Porta	7
27	Herrera	6
28	Norrodin	5
29	D. Binder	4

Constructor Points

1	KTM	217
2	Honda	205
3	Mahindra	107
4	Peugeot	20

CZECH REPUBLIC GRAND PRIX

BRNO CIRCUIT

Above: Just cruising – Crutchlow cuts inside Barbera and Redding on his way to the front.

Above right, from top: Rain-master Ant West came from the back to head Zarco; it was the opposite for Lorenzo, a dispirited 17th; wings notwithstanding, Dovi was grounded by tyre trouble.

Right: Marquez chases down Barbera to rescue a podium place.

Below right: Loris Baz, chased here by Vinales, took a splendid fourth.

Opening spread: Wimps don't win. Crutchlow, with ecstatic LCR team owner Lucio Cecchinello, heads Rossi and Marquez to the rostrum, the first English winner since Barry Sheene in 1981.

Photos: Gold & Goose

A PO-FACED reader's letter to the hallowed US weekly *Cycle News* criticised first-time GP winner Cal Crutchlow for his choice of words to describe his gamble on the hard front tyre. The other riders, not brave enough to take that chance, were "wimps". Surely, thought the writer, having risked their lives and tried their hardest, they deserved more respect.

This posed an interesting question on what we are to think, for example, of yet another dire wet-weather performance from Lorenzo. On what we are to think of racing in general. Is it just a question of talent? Should all riders be on identical tyres, motorcycles, gearing? Would it be better if the element of educated guesswork (or, if you will, gambling) were removed? Just a matter of how well each rider operated the controls?

If so, why is Moto2 reliably the dullest of the three grand prix classes?

Or is it better when the individual responses to changing conditions produce a series of surprise results, including three surprise winners?

MOTOCOURSE is firmly in the latter camp, and so too legions of flag-waving British fans, who celebrated not only Crutchlow's emphatic victory, but also that of John McPhee in Moto3, plus a podium in Moto2 for Sam Lowes.

It was a combination of the weather – astonishingly the first rainy MotoGP race at Brno since the new circuit opened in 1987 – and the nature of Michelin's choice of available tyres. As for Iannone the weekend before, the fact that different tyres work for different bikes and riding styles introduced a variable that helped to make what some were already calling a new Golden Age. Crutchlow was not only the second independent-team rider to win in 2016, but also the sixth different winner in six races. A trend that would continue.

Race eve was 20 years to the day since Rossi won his first GP, in the 125 class, at Brno. Now 37, he had won another 113 races in 340 starts (not counting Brno), along with nine championships, all but two in the premier class. His two-year Ducati hiatus apart, he had won races every year, and come within an ace of the title in 2015. In 2016, he admitted,

results had been harder to come by. "It's the opposite of last year – good in qualifying and practice, with more times on the front row, but more problems in the race."

Marquez continued his perfect points score, but was still living dangerously, with yet another sensational save preceding a record-breaking pole position. As at Brno tests in 2014, he seemed long since to have crashed at the top of the hill when he miraculously regained control. "The slide this time was very long, but the angle of the bike was 67.5 degrees," he said. "In 2014, it was more than 68 degrees."

Asked if he could have managed the same feat, Rossi spoke with amusement. "It is something he does a lot." He survives "because of his position on the bike, and because of his talent. I don't know if I could do it. But I ride a bit slower, so I don't lose the front."

Dorna arranged the now regular Brno press briefing from the four major manufacturers (Aprilia was left out), where arguments about winglets already won or lost in the MSMA surfaced again. The three Japanese manufacturers were lukewarm at best, with HRC's Nakamoto rather surprisingly complaining about the cost. When he had been with Honda's F1 team, wind-tunnel development had accounted for a significant part of the budget, he said.

Ducati's Dall'Igna, however, was impassioned and deplored 2017's prohibition. "Frankly, I don't understand why we banned winglets." Safety had been top of the list, but "we have been using winglets since the beginning of last season, and we have had many crashes in that year-and-a-half. In that time, wings had neither caused any crashes nor inflicted any injuries."

Most infuriating was the loss of an opportunity for research on the increasingly important matter of motorcycle aerodynamics. Winglets could have a production application, he said, while aerodynamics would remain important without the winglets, and the research costs would not be affected.

"For manufacturers, the most important thing is knowledge. If you cannot develop the knowledge, that is a huge problem," he said. In terms of cost and safety, the MSMA (manufacturers' association) had tried to reach a reasonable

agreement. "But if 'reasonable' means wings of very limited length, I think it is better to have no wings," he said.

Jack Miller missed the race, much to his chagrin when Sunday turned out rainy. He'd been passed fit by medical staff, but HRC and his EG-VDS team took the opposite view, given his spinal fracture. Moto2's Tom Luthi was also an absentee, after a heavy fall in qualifying left him concussed.

Old campaigner and GP winner Anthony West made a GP return as a wild-card in Moto2, and the weather worked for him. He forged through into the top ten and beat Zarco, after qualifying 29th and last on the Montaze Broz Racing Team's four-year-old Suter. "The rain was a big help. It's always nice to turn up as a wild-card – old bike, new team – and get a good result," he said.

Another 2017 saddle was settled, with Aprilia reject Alvaro Bautista returning to his long-ago Aspar team, where he was promised a factory Ducati. This was to the dismay of current teamster Eugene Laverty, after a solid season of strong results on an old GP14. With only one factory bike for the team, he would again be offered another hand-me-down; soon afterwards, he confirmed that he would rather return to World Superbikes, where he could expect to be fully competitive.

From Superbikes, Sam Lowes's identical twin brother, Alex, was on hand, for a first MotoGP ride in tests the day after the race – a reward for his Suzuka 8 Hours victory with Pol Espargaro. Though a dirty track cut his opportunities short, it would prove to be a timely first outing – he would be back on the Monster Yamaha in earnest at the next race.

MOTOGP RACE – 22 laps

Marquez claimed a stunning pole, smashing the outright track record in spite of having to slice past both Rossi and Pol Espargaro in the final corners. He displaced an erstwhile confident Lorenzo, equalling his (and Rossi's) tally of 63 poles, in a much shorter career.

Iannone completed row one; Rossi was on the far end of row two, behind Aleix Espargaro and Barbera. Pedrosa had endured Q1 for a second time in the season (Assen the other), but this time he got through to Q2 to place ninth.

The weather turned overnight, drenching 82,000 fans and setting the scene for Crutchlow to become the first Briton to win in the premier class since Barry Sheene in Sweden in 1981.

It actually stopped raining an hour before the main race, but the track stayed sodden, and with no previous wet-race experience here, nobody knew how quickly it would dry.

All started on wet tyres, with spare bikes warming up in case of a swap to slicks.

Crutchlow was already on the grid when he decided to fit the harder rear. So too Rossi, Lorenzo, Rabat and Baz. More crucial was Crutchlow's opinion that "if you fit the hard rear, you should fit the hard front as well. I didn't know what the others were doing, but if they didn't do that ... they were wimps." Only Baz made the same choice, and he was rewarded with fourth, significantly his career best.

Crutchlow finished lap one 15th, while the factory Yamahas were clearly in trouble, Lorenzo tenth and dropping like a stone; Rossi 13th and doing the same. "Riders were passing me inside and outside, and I was feeling desperate," he said.

Had it rained again, soft tyres would have paid off. As it was, they stayed in control for the first half of the race.

Dovi, in his 250th GP start, took over the lead on lap two; on the fourth, Iannone moved ahead. By then, Redding had joined them, and Marquez was a couple of seconds behind, nursing his tyres.

Barbera was also moving through and soon joined the leaders. Dovi had dropped behind Redding, biding his time – until suddenly he slowed on lap ten and cruised to the pits, his front tyre disintegrating. Another non-finish for the luckless Ducati rider.

By now, however, the hard tyres were up to temperature and paying big dividends.

Crutchlow, setting fastest lap on the ninth, had been gaining by leaps and bounds; Rossi was also speeding up. Crutchlow had passed him on lap seven and left him a couple of places behind, as he vaulted past the Monster Yamahas of Smith and Espargaro in one lap, and two laps later also Petrucci and Vinales. Next, he pounced on Aleix Espargaro, the Suzuki soon to expire in a cloud of smoke, and then Marquez.

By lap 12, he was fourth and closing rapidly on the leaders. Both Barbera and Redding succumbed on lap 14; now he started working on Iannone.

He took the lead on lap 16, and two laps later was almost two seconds ahead. His pit signals told him to slow down, team owner Lucio Cecchinello unable to watch the final laps, but later he said, "I was already cruising."

As he speeded up, the others were running into trouble; and when Rossi took second on lap 18, the Ducatis were fading fast. Redding had already lost touch, and Marquez took Barbera and Iannone in one sweep with two laps left, moving away for third,

Baz was doing the same thing, with Laverty a couple of seconds behind.

By the end, the podium was quite spaced out – Crutchlow almost 7.3 seconds clear, and Marquez more than two behind Rossi, whose canny race moved him past Lorenzo to second overall. Marquez's lead had stretched nonetheless.

Baz took fourth another three seconds away, team-mate Barbera still close and Laverty on his heels.

Iannone's front tyre was now visibly shedding chunks, and he had succumbed to Petrucci and Vinales, though he managed to get back ahead of the Suzuki by a tenth of a second on the final lap.

Rabat claimed a steady tenth, comfortably clear of Hernandez; Pedrosa a lacklustre 12th, troubled with his now-familiar difficulty in getting his tyres up to temperature, and bemoaning the reversal of his usual wet strength.

Espargaro, Bradl and a deeply troubled Redding took the rest of the points; Lorenzo was 17th, behind Bautista's Aprilia and one lap down, after his tyres betrayed him. He'd pitted on lap 16. Crew chief Ramon Forcada had tried to stop him from swapping to a slick-shod bike, but he had no choice. His tyres were ruined, the slicks no good, and he called in again one lap later.

Smith had gambled on slicks the lap before, but retired directly from his last race for a long spell.

MOTO2 RACE – 20 laps

It was an austere and difficult race for the middle class, with a minimum of overtaking and the top three settled after just four laps. The interest came from the twist in the championship, with pole starter Johann Zarco quite out of sorts in the wet, finishing 11th, and his main rival, Rins, claiming 20 points to close the gap to just 19.

And a frisson also from Australian wild-card Anthony West, riding the only Suter on the grid. He had qualified last, but used his legendary wet-weather skill to push through from 29th to tenth, one place up on Zarco.

Victory went to another good man in the wet, Jonas Folger.

Zarco led into the first corner, but by the exit, Folger had ridden around his outside, and he would never be headed. Rins put the pressure on for the early laps, but by the tenth, the gap was more than one second, and his challenge spent.

Nakagami had been third, but Sam Lowes was on the charge, passing first Syahrin – a fast starter from the fifth row – then also getting past the Japanese rider into third on lap four. He held that to the finish, in a staunch if lonely ride that secured a full house of British podiums.

Nakagami would continue to lose ground, and was ninth when a collision with the ever-eager Corsi knocked him down and out of the race. Corsi, a serial offender, was immediately sanctioned with a ride-through penalty.

Meanwhile, Marquez had managed to get ahead of Syahrin; then also veteran Mattia Pasini got past the Malaysian, with Luca Marini and soon afterwards Cortese joining a somewhat loose-knit group at half-distance.

By the finish, fourth was between Cortese and Pasini, and the former seemed to have made the crucial move last time at the top of the hill into the penultimate corner. But he left a little gap, Pasini came through, they touched, and Cortese fell off.

That left fifth place to Marquez, as his season continued to improve.

Syahrin was a distant sixth; less than two seconds down there came a lively trio, with Danny Kent finally taking control, team-mate Oliveira ninth, Morbidelli sandwiched between them.

Almost ten seconds away, West had revelled in the conditions, gaining four places on the first lap and continuing to pick his way through, passing Zarco on lap five to get into the points, and staying ahead of the Frenchman at the finish to an eventual tenth.

The defending champion had his hands full in a close battle, but narrowly retained 11th, with Tech 3 rider Xavi Vierge scrambling to 12th on the last lap, passing Simon, Vinales and Simeon, tenth to 15th covered by less than 1.4 seconds. It included an unusual variety of bikes: West, Suter; Zarco, Kalex; Vierge and Vinales, Tech 3; Simon and Simeon, Speed Up.

Marini crashed out, as did Wilairot and Axel Pons (on the first lap).

This marked the start of an interesting reversal in the championship trend, which would continue to develop, injecting considerable tension in the coming races.

MOTO3 RACE – 19 laps

The smallest class was as lively as Moto2 was dull, and equally drenched. And with a surprise winner – John McPhee became the first Scotsman to win a GP since Bob McIntyre in 1962.

A little bit of history also for Mahindra, makers of the re-badged Peugeot, with Jorge Martin finishing second – a one-two for the MGP30.

It was all at the expense of runaway title leader Brad Binder, who made his only mistake so far in the season. He'd claimed pole in the dry, but took a couple of laps to get going on the streaming track, assuming the lead from Martin on lap six. McPhee came with him and continued to stalk him as they opened up a little gap.

Canet was now harrying Martin, while fellow rookie Khairul Idham Pawi was barrelling through from 28th on the grid. The double wet winner was up to third by lap ten, now three seconds adrift of the leading pair, but would last only four more laps before slithering off.

By then, Canet had also crashed out, leaving Di Giannantonio to take over on Martin's back wheel.

Up front, Binder now had a little gap on McPhee. Then it was all over, as he lost the rear when he touched the throttle exiting the first corner on lap 15. That left McPhee in control, though he said later he was planning to attack. Martin managed to hang on to second.

Less than a second behind at the end, Bastianini had fought his way back to the front of the pursuit group for fourth, a second clear of Antonelli. On a third Honda, Kornfeil led a close group for sixth.

Binder's team-mate, Bendsneyder, was the first KTM finisher, from fellow rookies Mir and Bulega, then Navarro.

Binder still left with a 61-point lead over Navarro; Bastianini moved into third; Bagnaia dropped to fifth after crashing out.

HJC HELMETS
GRAND PRIX CESKE REPUBLIKY
19–21 AUGUST, 2016

AUTOMOTODROM BRNO
22 laps
Length: 5.403 km / 3.357 miles
Width: 15m

Key
96/60 kph/mph
⚙ Gear

Turn 5 115/71
Turn 9 95/59
Kevin Schwantz 105/65
Turn 4 115/71
Turn 8 95/59
Stadion 95/59
Turn 3 115/71
Turn 11 95/59
Turn 12 120/75
Frantisěk Štasny 130/81
Horizont 105/65
Turn 14 135/84
280/174

MotoGP

RACE DISTANCE: 22 laps, 73.860 miles/118.866km · **RACE WEATHER:** Wet (air 17°C, humidity 100%, track 18°C)

Pos.	Rider	Nat.	No.	Entrant	Machine	Tyres	Race tyre choice	Laps	Time & speed
1	**Cal Crutchlow**	GBR	35	LCR Honda	Honda RC213V	M	F: Hard Wet/R: Hard Wet	22	47m 44.290s 92.8mph/ 149.3km/h
2	**Valentino Rossi**	ITA	46	Movistar Yamaha MotoGP	Yamaha YZR-M1	M	F: Soft Wet/R: Hard Wet	22	47m 51.588s
3	**Marc Marquez**	SPA	93	Repsol Honda Team	Honda RC213V	M	F: Hard Wet/R: Soft Wet	22	47m 53.877s
4	**Loris Baz**	FRA	76	Avintia Racing	Ducati Desmosedici	M	F: Hard Wet/R: Hard Wet	22	47m 56.848s
5	**Hector Barbera**	SPA	8	Avintia Racing	Ducati Desmosedici	M	F: Soft Wet/R: Soft Wet	22	47m 57.383s
6	**Eugene Laverty**	IRL	50	Pull & Bear Aspar Team	Ducati Desmosedici	M	F: Soft Wet/R: Hard Wet	22	47m 58.102s
7	**Danilo Petrucci**	ITA	9	OCTO Pramac Yakhnich	Ducati Desmosedici	M	F: Soft Wet/R: Soft Wet	22	48m 07.704s
8	**Andrea Iannone**	ITA	29	Ducati Team	Ducati Desmosedici	M	F: Soft Wet/R: Soft Wet	22	48m 08.852s
9	**Maverick Vinales**	SPA	25	Team SUZUKI ECSTAR	Suzuki GSX-RR	M	F: Soft Wet/R: Soft Wet	22	48m 08.871s
10	**Tito Rabat**	SPA	53	Estrella Galicia 0,0 Marc VDS	Honda RC213V	M	F: Hard Wet/R: Hard Wet	22	48m 21.421s
11	**Yonny Hernandez**	COL	68	Pull & Bear Aspar Team	Ducati Desmosedici	M	F: Soft Wet/R: Soft Wet	22	48m 24.201s
12	**Dani Pedrosa**	SPA	26	Repsol Honda Team	Honda RC213V	M	F: Soft Wet/R: Soft Wet	22	48m 25.387s
13	**Pol Espargaro**	SPA	44	Monster Yamaha Tech 3	Yamaha YZR-M1	M	F: Soft Wet/R: Soft Wet	22	48m 27.492s
14	**Stefan Bradl**	GER	6	Aprilia Racing Team Gresini	Aprilia RS-GP	M	F: Soft Wet/R: Soft Wet	22	48m 29.977s
15	**Scott Redding**	GBR	45	OCTO Pramac Yakhnich	Ducati Desmosedici	M	F: Soft Wet/R: Soft Wet	22	48m 46.491s
16	Alvaro Bautista	SPA	19	Aprilia Racing Team Gresini	Aprilia RS-GP	M	F: Soft Wet/R: Soft Wet	22	49m 03.131s
17	Jorge Lorenzo	SPA	99	Movistar Yamaha MotoGP	Yamaha YZR-M1	M	F: Soft Wet/R: Hard Wet	21	47m 49.179s
	Andrea Dovizioso	ITA	4	Ducati Team	Ducati Desmosedici	M	F: Soft Wet/R: Soft Wet	15	DNF-technical
	Bradley Smith	GBR	38	Monster Yamaha Tech 3	Yamaha YZR-M1	M	F: Soft Wet/R: Soft Wet	14	DNF-technical
	Aleix Espargaro	SPA	41	Team SUZUKI ECSTAR	Suzuki GSX-RR	M	F: Soft Wet/R: Soft Wet	13	DNF-technical

Fastest lap: Cal Crutchlow, on lap 9, 2m 8.216s, 94.3mph/151.7km/h.
Lap record: Dani Pedrosa, SPA (Honda), 1m 56.027s, 104.1mph/167.6km/h (2014).
Event best maximum speed: Andrea Iannone, 194.1mph/312.4km/h (qualifying).

Qualifying

Weather: Dry
Air Temp: 26° **Track Temp:** 40°
Humidity: 56%

1	Marquez	1m 54.596s
2	Lorenzo	1m 54.849s
3	Iannone	1m 55.227s
4	A. Espargaro	1m 55.324s
5	Barbera	1m 55.437s
6	Rossi	1m 55.509s
7	Dovizioso	1m 55.748s
8	Vinales	1m 55.787s
9	Pedrosa	1m 55.841s
10	Crutchlow	1m 55.930s
11	Smith	1m 56.115s
12	P. Espargaro	1m 56.522s
13	Petrucci	1m 56.148s
14	Redding	1m 56.263s
15	Laverty	1m 56.535s
16	Bradl	1m 56.718s
17	Baz	1m 56.797s
18	Hernandez	1m 56.805s
19	Bautista	1m 57.062s
20	Rabat	1m 57.606s

Fastest race laps

1	Crutchlow	2m 08.216s
2	Lorenzo	2m 08.507s
3	Rossi	2m 08.867s
4	Barbera	2m 09.090s
5	Baz	2m 09.166s
6	Iannone	2m 09.203s
7	Laverty	2m 09.304s
8	Redding	2m 09.418s
9	Marquez	2m 09.507s
10	Pedrosa	2m 09.513s
11	Bautista	2m 09.555s
12	Petrucci	2m 09.829s
13	A. Espargaro	2m 09.850s
14	Dovizioso	2m 09.904s
15	Vinales	2m 09.958s
16	Hernandez	2m 09.958s
17	Smith	2m 10.277s
18	Rabat	2m 10.297s
19	P. Espargaro	2m 10.707s
20	Bradl	2m 10.713s

Championship Points

1	Marquez	197
2	Rossi	144
3	Lorenzo	138
4	Pedrosa	109
5	Vinales	100
6	Iannone	96
7	P. Espargaro	81
8	Dovizioso	79
9	Barbera	76
10	Crutchlow	66
11	Laverty	63
12	Redding	54
13	A. Espargaro	51
14	Miller	42
15	Smith	42
16	Bradl	39
17	Petrucci	38
18	Bautista	35
19	Rabat	26
20	Baz	24
21	Pirro	23
22	Hernandez	8

Constructor Points

1	Yamaha	222
2	Honda	221
3	Ducati	162
4	Suzuki	106
5	Aprilia	53

Grid order		1	2	3	4	5	6	7	8	9	10	11	12	13	14	15	16	17	18	19	20	21	22	
93	MARQUEZ	93	4	4	29	29	29	29	29	29	29	29	29	29	29	29	35	35	35	35	35	35	35	1
99	LORENZO	4	93	29	4	45	45	45	45	45	45	45	45	45	35	35	29	29	46	46	46	46	46	2
29	IANNONE	29	29	45	45	4	4	4	4	4	8	8	8	8	8	8	8	8	29	29	93	93	93	3
41	A. ESPARGARO	41	45	93	93	93	93	8	8	8	93	93	35	35	45	45	46	46	8	8	29	76	76	4
8	BARBERA	25	41	41	41	41	8	93	93	93	41	35	93	93	93	93	93	93	93	8	8			5
46	ROSSI	45	25	25	25	25	41	41	41	41	35	41	41	41	46	46	45	45	45	45	76	50	50	6
4	DOVIZIOSO	44	44	8	8	8	25	25	25	25	25	25	46	25	25	25	76	76	76	50	29	9		7
25	VINALES	8	8	44	44	44	9	9	9	9	9	9	46	25	9	9	76	25	50	50	25	25	29	8
26	PEDROSA	38	38	38	9	9	44	44	35	35	46	46	9	9	76	76	9	9	25	25	9	9	25	9
35	CRUTCHLOW	99	9	9	38	38	38	38	44	44	38	76	76	76	99	50	50	50	9	9	45	53	53	10
38	SMITH	9	46	26	26	26	26	26	38	38	76	38	38	99	50	99	26	26	53	53	53	68	68	11
44	P. ESPARGARO	46	26	46	46	46	46	35	46	44	44	99	99	50	44	26	53	53	26	68	26	26		12
45	REDDING	26	99	99	6	35	35	46	26	76	99	50	44	44	44	44	44	68	26	44	44			13
50	LAVERTY	6	6	6	35	6	76	76	76	26	26	50	44	26	6	53	6	68	44	44	6	6		14
6	BRADL	35	35	35	76	76	6	6	99	99	50	26	26	6	53	6	68	68	6	6	45	45		15
9	PETRUCCI	19	19	76	99	99	99	99	50	50	6	6	6	53	68	68	19	19	19	19	19	19	19	
76	BAZ	76	76	19	19	50	50	50	6	6	19	53	53	68	19	19	99	99	99	99	99	99		
68	HERNANDEZ	50	50	50	50	19	19	19	19	19	53	68	68	19	38	4								
19	BAUTISTA	68	68	68	53	53	53	53	53	53	68	19	19	38	4									
53	RABAT	53	53	53	68	68	68	68	68	68	4	4	4	4										

4 Pit stop   99 Lapped rider

Moto2 — RACE DISTANCE: 20 laps, 67.145 miles/108.060km · RACE WEATHER: Wet (air 16°C, humidity 100%, track 17°C)

Pos.	Rider	Nat.	No.	Entrant	Machine	Laps	Time & Speed
1	**Jonas Folger**	GER	94	Dynavolt Intact GP	Kalex	20	45m 30.342s 88.5mph/ 142.4km/h
2	**Alex Rins**	SPA	40	Paginas Amarillas HP 40	Kalex	20	45m 35.517s
3	**Sam Lowes**	GBR	22	Federal Oil Gresini Moto2	Kalex	20	45m 39.363s
4	**Mattia Pasini**	ITA	54	Italtrans Racing Team	Kalex	20	45m 45.105s
5	**Alex Marquez**	SPA	73	Estrella Galicia 0,0 Marc VDS	Kalex	20	45m 48.301s
6	**Hafizh Syahrin**	MAL	55	Petronas Raceline Malaysia	Kalex	20	45m 54.589s
7	**Danny Kent**	GBR	52	Leopard Racing	Kalex	20	45m 56.038s
8	**Franco Morbidelli**	ITA	21	Estrella Galicia 0,0 Marc VDS	Kalex	20	45m 56.258s
9	**Miguel Oliveira**	POR	44	Leopard Racing	Kalex	20	45m 57.541s
10	**Anthony West**	AUS	95	Montaze Broz Racing Team	Suter	20	46m 06.682s
11	**Johann Zarco**	FRA	5	Ajo Motorsport	Kalex	20	46m 07.096s
12	**Xavi Vierge**	SPA	97	Tech 3 Racing	Tech 3	20	46m 07.719s
13	**Julian Simon**	SPA	60	QMMF Racing Team	Speed Up	20	46m 07.798s
14	**Isaac Vinales**	SPA	32	Tech 3 Racing	Tech 3	20	46m 07.921s
15	**Xavier Simeon**	BEL	19	QMMF Racing Team	Speed Up	20	46m 08.118s
16	Lorenzo Baldassarri	ITA	7	Forward Team	Kalex	20	46m 19.353s
17	Dominique Aegerter	SWI	77	CarXpert Interwetten	Kalex	20	46m 32.109s
18	Marcel Schrotter	GER	23	AGR Team	Kalex	20	46m 39.145s
19	Simone Corsi	ITA	24	Speed Up Racing	Speed Up	20	46m 39.877s
20	Edgar Pons	SPA	57	Paginas Amarillas HP 40	Kalex	20	46m 39.896s
21	Remy Gardner	AUS	87	Tasca Racing Scuderia Moto2	Kalex	20	46m 47.036s
22	Robin Mulhauser	SWI	70	CarXpert Interwetten	Kalex	20	46m 47.193s
23	Sandro Cortese	GER	11	Dynavolt Intact GP	Kalex	20	46m 47.577s
24	Jesko Raffin	SWI	2	Sports-Millions-EMWE-SAG	Kalex	20	47m 14.050s
25	Ratthapark Wilairot	THA	14	IDEMITSU Honda Team Asia	Kalex	19	46m 24.941s
	Takaaki Nakagami	JPN	30	IDEMITSU Honda Team Asia	Kalex	11	DNF
	Luca Marini	ITA	10	Forward Team	Kalex	10	DNF
	Axel Pons	SPA	49	AGR Team	Kalex	0	DNF

Fastest lap: Jonas Folger, on lap 11, 2m 14.528s, 89.8mph/144.5km/h.
Lap record: Tito Rabat, SPA (Kalex), 2m 2.383s, 98.7mph/158.9km/h (2014).
Event best maximum speed: Hafizh Syahrin, 162.4mph/261.4km/h (qualifying).

Qualifying

Weather: Dry
Air Temp: 26° **Track Temp:** 40°
Humidity: 52%

1	Zarco	2m 01.581s
2	Lowes	2m 01.614s
3	Marquez	2m 01.831s
4	Nakagami	2m 02.046s
5	Luthi	2m 02.049s
6	Morbidelli	2m 02.099s
7	Rins	2m 02.139s
8	Folger	2m 02.293s
9	Corsi	2m 02.315s
10	Oliveira	2m 02.372s
11	Schrotter	2m 02.380s
12	Cortese	2m 02.413s
13	Aegerter	2m 02.462s
14	Syahrin	2m 02.528s
15	A. Pons	2m 02.577s
16	Kent	2m 02.667s
17	Pasini	2m 02.669s
18	Marini	2m 02.780s
19	Simon	2m 02.985s
20	Baldassarri	2m 03.024s
21	Gardner	2m 03.316s
22	Wilairot	2m 03.352s
23	E. Pons	2m 03.431s
24	Vierge	2m 03.570s
25	Simeon	2m 03.601s
26	Mulhauser	2m 03.968s
27	Vinales	2m 04.306s
28	Raffin	2m 04.376s
29	West	2m 04.943s

Fastest race laps

1	Folger	2m 14.528s
2	Rins	2m 15.002s
3	Cortese	2m 15.017s
4	Vierge	2m 15.149s
5	Kent	2m 15.203s
6	Lowes	2m 15.233s
7	Marquez	2m 15.288s
8	Pasini	2m 15.297s
9	Morbidelli	2m 15.426s
10	Oliveira	2m 15.570s
11	Simeon	2m 15.822s
12	Zarco	2m 15.910s
13	Vinales	2m 15.942s
14	Simon	2m 15.942s
15	Syahrin	2m 16.061s
16	West	2m 16.106s
17	Baldassarri	2m 16.178s
18	Marini	2m 17.078s
19	Schrotter	2m 17.090s
20	Corsi	2m 17.107s
21	E. Pons	2m 17.265s
22	Wilairot	2m 17.480s
23	Aegerter	2m 17.502s
24	Nakagami	2m 17.587s
25	Mulhauser	2m 17.706s
26	Gardner	2m 17.884s
27	Raffin	2m 18.041s

Championship Points

1	Zarco	181
2	Rins	162
3	Lowes	137
4	Folger	108
5	Luthi	106
6	Morbidelli	94
7	Nakagami	92
8	Syahrin	79
9	Aegerter	71
10	Corsi	59
11	Baldassarri	55
12	Pasini	43
13	A. Pons	41
14	Salom	37
15	Marquez	34
16	Schrotter	33
17	Oliveira	33
18	Simon	30
19	Simeon	29
20	Kent	27
21	Marini	20
22	Cortese	20
23	Vinales	12
24	Raffin	10
25	Vierge	7
26	West	6
27	Gardner	5
28	Mulhauser	4
29	Wilairot	3
30	E. Pons	2

Constructor Points

1	Kalex	275
2	Speed Up	92
3	Tech 3	17
4	Suter	6

Moto3 — RACE DISTANCE: 19 laps, 63.788 miles/102.657km · RACE WEATHER: Wet (air 16°C, humidity 100%, track 17°C)

Pos.	Rider	Nat.	No.	Entrant	Machine	Laps	Time & Speed
1	**John McPhee**	GBR	17	Peugeot MC Saxoprint	Peugeot	19	45m 36.087s 83.9mph/ 135.0km/h
2	**Jorge Martin**	SPA	88	Pull & Bear ASPAR Mahindra Team	Mahindra	19	45m 44.893s
3	**Fabio Di Giannantonio**	ITA	4	Gresini Racing Moto3	Honda	19	45m 45.864s
4	**Enea Bastianini**	ITA	33	Gresini Racing Moto3	Honda	19	45m 46.741s
5	**Niccolo Antonelli**	ITA	23	Ongetta-Rivacold	Honda	19	45m 49.959s
6	**Jakub Kornfeil**	CZE	84	Drive M7 SIC Racing Team	Honda	19	45m 51.620s
7	**Bo Bendsneyder**	NED	64	Red Bull KTM Ajo	KTM	19	45m 51.906s
8	**Joan Mir**	SPA	36	Leopard Racing	KTM	19	45m 52.376s
9	**Nicolo Bulega**	ITA	8	SKY Racing Team VR46	KTM	19	45m 52.560s
10	**Jorge Navarro**	SPA	9	Estrella Galicia 0,0	Honda	19	45m 52.768s
11	**Jules Danilo**	FRA	95	Ongetta-Rivacold	Honda	19	45m 54.285s
12	**Andrea Migno**	ITA	16	SKY Racing Team VR46	KTM	19	45m 57.727s
13	**Tatsuki Suzuki**	JPN	24	CIP-Unicom Starker	Mahindra	19	46m 07.094s
14	**Livio Loi**	BEL	11	RW Racing GP BV	Honda	19	46m 12.982s
15	**Philipp Oettl**	GER	65	Schedl GP Racing	KTM	19	46m 19.738s
16	Karel Hanika	CZE	98	Freundenberg Racing Team	KTM	19	46m 33.901s
17	Gabriel Rodrigo	ARG	19	RBA Racing Team	KTM	19	46m 37.515s
18	Marcos Ramirez	SPA	42	Platinum Bay Real Estate	Mahindra	19	46m 40.221s
19	Maria Herrera	SPA	6	MH6 Team	KTM	19	47m 03.672s
20	Hiroki Ono	JPN	76	Honda Team Asia	Honda	19	47m 04.084s
21	Fabio Quartararo	FRA	20	Leopard Racing	KTM	19	47m 10.029s
22	Fabio Spiranelli	ITA	3	CIP-Unicom Starker	Mahindra	19	47m 10.697s
23	Juanfran Guevara	SPA	58	RBA Racing Team	KTM	19	47m 11.029s
24	Lorenzo Petrarca	ITA	77	3570 Team Italia	Mahindra	19	47m 44.406s
	Andrea Locatelli	ITA	55	Leopard Racing	KTM	16	DNF
	Brad Binder	RSA	41	Red Bull KTM Ajo	KTM	14	DNF
	Khairul Idham Pawi	MAL	89	Honda Team Asia	Honda	14	DNF
	Stefano Valtulini	ITA	40	3570 Team Italia	Mahindra	14	DNF
	Darryn Binder	RSA	40	Platinum Bay Real Estate	Mahindra	13	DNF
	Francesco Bagnaia	ITA	21	Pull & Bear ASPAR Mahindra Team	Mahindra	12	DNF
	Albert Arenas	SPA	12	Peugeot MC Saxoprint	Peugeot	11	DNF
	Adam Norrodin	MAL	7	Drive M7 SIC Racing Team	Honda	9	DNF
	Aron Canet	SPA	44	Estrella Galicia 0,0	Honda	8	DNF

Fastest lap: Brad Binder, on lap 11, 2m 21.567s, 85.3mph/137.3km/h.
Lap record: Romano Fenati, ITA (KTM), 2m 8.064s, 94.3mph/151.8km/h (2014).
Event best maximum speed: Nicolo Bulega, 139.9mph/225.1km/h (qualifying).

Qualifying

Weather: Dry
Air Temp: 21° **Track Temp:** 29°
Humidity: 74%

1	B. Binder	2m 07.785s
2	Migno	2m 07.943s
3	Bastianini	2m 08.042s
4	Martin	2m 08.138s
5	Di Giannantonio	2m 08.257s
6	Bulega	2m 08.333s
7	Antonelli	2m 08.337s
8	Oettl	2m 08.452s
9	Canet	2m 08.495s
10	Kornfeil	2m 08.496s
11	McPhee	2m 08.559s
12	Navarro	2m 08.581s
13	Hanika	2m 08.602s
14	Mir	2m 08.613s
15	Guevara	2m 08.764s
16	Quartararo	2m 08.789s
17	Bagnaia	2m 08.808s
18	Ono	2m 08.936s
19	Locatelli	2m 08.995s
20	Loi	2m 09.012s
21	Norrodin	2m 09.064s
22	Rodrigo	2m 09.121s
23	D. Binder	2m 09.131s
24	Danilo	2m 09.250s
25	Bendsneyder	2m 09.258s
26	Suzuki	2m 09.287s
27	Arenas	2m 09.551s
28	Herrera	2m 09.651s
29	Pawi	2m 09.739s
30	Ramirez	2m 09.941s
31	Valtulini	2m 10.604s
32	Petrarca	2m 11.190s
33	Spiranelli	2m 11.333s

Fastest race laps

1	B. Binder	2m 21.567s
2	McPhee	2m 22.178s
3	Di Giannantonio	2m 22.211s
4	Pawi	2m 22.359s
5	Bendsneyder	2m 22.361s
6	Mir	2m 22.401s
7	Bastianini	2m 22.408s
8	Antonelli	2m 22.517s
9	Navarro	2m 22.677s
10	Kornfeil	2m 22.724s
11	Canet	2m 22.793s
12	Locatelli	2m 22.795s
13	Norrodin	2m 22.823s
14	Bulega	2m 22.832s
15	Martin	2m 22.835s
16	Loi	2m 22.869s
17	Suzuki	2m 22.905s
18	Rodrigo	2m 22.995s
19	Bagnaia	2m 23.071s
20	Migno	2m 23.132s
21	Danilo	2m 23.197s
22	D. Binder	2m 23.240s
23	Valtulini	2m 23.293s
24	Oettl	2m 23.961s
25	Hanika	2m 24.456s
26	Guevara	2m 24.582s
27	Ramirez	2m 24.666s
28	Arenas	2m 24.737s
29	Spiranelli	2m 25.857s
30	Quartararo	2m 25.929s
31	Herrera	2m 26.015s
32	Ono	2m 26.814s
33	Petrarca	2m 28.058s

Championship Points

1	B. Binder	179
2	Navarro	118
3	Bastianini	94
4	Fenati	93
5	Bagnaia	90
6	Bulega	89
7	Mir	83
8	Di Giannantonio	82
9	Antonelli	74
10	Kornfeil	68
11	Pawi	54
12	Locatelli	53
13	Quartararo	52
14	Danilo	46
15	McPhee	45
16	Oettl	44
17	Migno	41
18	Martin	40
19	Bendsneyder	36
20	Canet	34
21	Loi	32
22	Guevara	29
23	Ono	21
24	Suzuki	12
25	Rodrigo	9
26	Dalla Porta	7
27	Herrera	6
28	Norrodin	5
29	D. Binder	4

Constructor Points

1	KTM	226
2	Honda	221
3	Mahindra	127
4	Peugeot	45

BRITISH GRAND PRIX

SILVERSTONE CIRCUIT

OCTO BRITISH
GRAND PR

motoGP

Silverstone

Inset, left: Quiet satisfaction for Vinales, after his first MotoGP win.

Inset, centre left: Crutchlow's great run of form continued with a second at home.
Photos: Gold & Goose

Inset, far left: Even the fans seemed winded as they watched a bruising MotoGP battle.
Photo: Gavan Caldwell Photography

Inset, below left: Gardner, Crafar, Doohan, Hartog and Crosby were just a few of the past heroes in the Barry Sheene tribute parade.

Inset, bottom left: Iannone, up to second, was fending off Crutchlow when he fell.

Main: Vinales secured Suzuki's first win since 2007 in assured style.
Photos: Gold & Goose

Above: With his Suzuki perfectly balanced, Vinales breaks away from Marquez, Crutchlow and the rest.

Above right: Eugene Laverty put in a brave bid for pole.
Photos: Gold & Goose

Right: You put your left leg out... but the battle for second between Marquez, Crutchlow and Rossi was as much about elbows.
Photo: Repsol Honda

FOR a fourth time in five races, weather defined much about the British GP. For a fifth time in five races, there was another different winner. It was an undramatic run on an at-last dry track for first-timer Maverick Vinales, underlining Suzuki's growing strength in its second year back in MotoGP. But a hardy crowd was rewarded for its resilience with an unseemly brawl for second, more fitted to Moto3 than the premier class, but conducted at the highest possible altitude.

Crutchlow, Rossi, Marquez, Pedrosa, Iannone and Dovizioso traded blows in a sustained spectacle, all but Iannone finishing in that order. He had crashed out of a memorable race in a memorable year.

Silverstone acted as a substitute circuit again; the still ephemeral Circuit of Wales holds the contract, but nothing else required to actually run a race. During the weekend, the same stand-in status was confirmed for 2017, with a further option for 2018. With a record crowd of just under 74,000 at the Northamptonshire circuit, swelled by Crutchlow's win a fortnight before, many were hoping the status quo would last longer than that.

Crutchlow made another contribution to jingoism and sentimentality by claiming pole position, the first by a home rider since Barry Sheene at the same circuit in 1977, on a weekend when the 1976 and 1977 champion's legend loomed large. The former airfield circuit rang again to the ring-a-ding of two-strokes when a parade of past heroes ran demonstration laps on contemporary machines, commemorating the 40th anniversary of his first title. An all-star line-up included not only legend Mick Doohan on his equally legendary Honda NSR500, but also Wayne Gardner, Randy Mamola, Sheene's

son Freddie, and many of Sheene's contemporaries, including Graeme Crosby, Paul Smart and Stan Woods. Sadly, Kenny Roberts was absent. Sheene's nemesis was recovering from a recent heart attack, as well as embroiled in a bitter legal battle with his younger son Kurtis.

British fans were denied the chance to cheer on Bradley Smith. The Monster Yamaha rider, 2015's Suzuka 8 Hours winner, had rejoined the factory team in its attempt to win the Endurance title at the Oschersleben 8 Hours, only to suffer serious knee injuries after he was hit by another bike following an otherwise innocuous spill in practice. But there was another local instead: Alex Lowes's test after Brno was converted to a first GP ride in Smith's place, and he acquitted himself very creditably.

So, too, Eugene Laverty (again), whose convincing attempt at claiming pole in the wet was scuppered only at the last when he slipped off. Nonetheless he was on a best ever second row, but was foiled while running with the leaders in the aborted first MotoGP start.

Also, of course, there was Sam Lowes, who claimed pole in Moto2 and was set for a convincing attempt at winning the race when he was skittled by none other than Zarco. He was a furious non-finisher, while Zarco's 30-second penalty was enough at least to rule him out of the points as well, a modicum of justice, and potentially as crucial to his title hopes as the crash was to those of Lowes.

Smith was the worst hurt of a number of injury victims. Jack Miller was back after missing two races, having sustained hairline spine and wrist fractures in Austria, only for more pain in his right hand to indicate another small fracture there. He made it into Q2 for the first time, but fell again on his out-lap. Despite these setbacks, he was able to compete in the race.

Dovizioso was limping and undergoing intensive physiotherapy after a tumble in private Ducati tests at Misano had left him with wrenched knee ligaments.

Petrucci was looking second-hand after a road accident – on his father's scooter as he returned from the barber shop. He had been hit by a car and suffered extensive road rash.

In Moto2, Alex Rins's title hopes took a serious blow when the Spaniard broke his right collarbone in a training fall from a 100cc practice bike. He was at Silverstone, but seriously hampered, after "my mechanics" fitted a plate with six screws. Swiss rider Dominique Aegerter was also out of the British Grand Prix and eventually for the rest of the season, after suffering multiple injuries in a motocross crash, the worst of them to shoulder ligaments. His place was taken by Spanish teenager Iker Lecuona.

Post-Brno tests had born some fruit for Yamaha and Honda riders, but as always it was a matter of pluses and minuses. Yamaha brought a new chassis and swing-arm, and Lorenzo liked the combination, saying it improved his front-end confidence. Rossi was to and fro between old and new chassis in qualifying, but preferred the old swing-arm.

Honda, said Marquez, had focused on their continuing acceleration problem as well as a new chassis. "We made big changes, and some things were positive and we will try them

again, but the best package was as I used in the race," he said. But if the new chassis left the factory riders wondering, HRC pressed it on Crutchlow, reinforcing their growing respect for his abilities. "The feeling is good – better in one way, worse in others. There's always a bit of give and take," he said.

News came that son of a champion Remy Gardner would replace Isaac Vinales in the France-based Tech 3 Moto2 team for 2017, riding the in-house Mistral 610 – one of only a handful of non-Kalex-framed Moto2 bikes. Negotiations had begun at Brno and the signing was confirmed on race day at Silverstone, ending a season of uncertainty when the 20-year-old Australian had only returned mid-season on a race-by-race basis.

Fenati was still out in the cold from Moto3, with talk of him returning with the Ongetta Rivacold Honda team scotched, for 2016 at least, by Honda. Meanwhile, the only woman GP racer, Maria Herrera, was sporting a big question mark on the side of her KTM – a novel request for a sponsor to come forward.

MOTOGP RACE – 19 laps (shortened)

The weather was kind to the top class until qualifying, throwing up some surprises and throwing a number of riders down the road. One was Marquez, with a carbon copy of his first-corner race crash of 2015. He watched trackside as Vinales knocked him off the front row, third behind Crutchlow and Rossi. Then Pedrosa displaced Marquez to fifth, with Laverty sixth. Lorenzo was at the end of row three, behind Redding and Iannone.

The first attempt, on a now-dry track, didn't last for long. Rossi led into the first corner, but Vinales quickly took over, and Laverty, on soft tyres, moved into a brilliant second.

By then, though, Baz and Pol Espargaro had clashed on the way into Maggotts, the second corner. Miraculously, nobody else was involved, as bikes and riders went looping back across the track. They had qualified 13th and 15th respectively, and five or six riders behind them had to take avoiding action.

Espargaro was stretchered away, but the French rider lay ominously still beside the track as medical staff clustered around. Mercifully, within a few minutes, he too was put in the ambulance, waving to the crowd, and later tweeting ironically, "I'm okay. Well, no worse than I already was."

The red flags came out at once, and race distance was cut by one lap. And they were off again, having lost 20 minutes beyond an already unusually late 3.30pm start.

Vinales claimed Suzuki's first since 2007 in dominant style, seizing the lead on lap one at the end of the Hangar Straight, setting fastest lap on the second and continuing to stretch away from an unseemly brawl in his wake. A "base setting change, some electronics" had earned him the front row, which was the key. That and the temperature. "It was cold, so we were fast," he said.

Vinales had also led the first start, from Laverty, before the crash stopped proceedings.

The fight for second was the best race of a good year, with positions changing constantly: Rossi versus Marquez; Crutchlow versus both of them; Iannone getting to the front, only to crash; plus Pedrosa and for a while Dovizioso.

The variety, Rossi opined, was due in large measure to the different tyre choices, which allowed individual approaches to the race. Most went for the soft front, except for Rossi, both Suzuki riders, Crutchlow, Baz and Rabat. For the rear, most went soft, except for Rossi, Crutchlow and both Suzukis again, plus Lorenzo, Marquez, Miller and Rabat. No consensus, and as Crutchlow said later, "Choosing differently wasn't right or wrong," but just what suited different riders, styles and bikes.

Marquez was less sure: "I chose the soft front, but I realised after a few laps it was a mistake. But I made the most of it."

He'd pushed past Crutchlow to take second on lap two,

Above: The race was red-flagged after a frightening crash between Loris Baz and Pol Espargaro. The Frenchman was stretchered away, happily not too seriously injured.

Above right: Bradl emerged unscathed after dropping his Aprilia at the same spot.

Above far right: Redding had a home race to forget, trailing in last after falling twice.

Top: Substituting for the injured Bradley Smith, Alex Lowes brought his Tech 3 Yamaha home in an impressive 13th, after battling with Rabat and Barbera.

Photos: Gold & Goose

and held on as a gang of five built up behind him, Lorenzo dropping off the back of it and Iannone soon past to close up, to tussle with Pedrosa.

The first past Marquez, on lap six, was Rossi. Then came Crutchlow, but as half-distance approached, Iannone cut through the gang in typically bold style, taking second on lap 12. Two laps later, fending off Crutchlow, he fell.

The Briton would hold second from there to the end, with no comfort. Close behind, Rossi and Marquez were battling fiercely, Marquez running off track once without losing position and finally getting ahead, seemingly for good, on lap 16.

Now he set about Crutchlow. He actually got by at the end of the main straight, only to run way out wide, rejoining behind Pedrosa in fifth, with one-and-a-half laps to go. He regained fourth on the last lap.

Dovizioso had dropped away, citing the physical demands of the Ducati for triggering arm-pump problems.

Aleix Espargaro tailed Lorenzo until half-distance, then moved clear for a safe seventh, the defending champion almost five seconds away at the end and blaming his rear tyre. He was still comfortably clear of ninth-placed Petrucci.

Bautista was a lone tenth, having taken it off Hernandez before half-distance. Three seconds away, Laverty had pushed through solidly from a bad second start. Impressive GP debutant Alex Lowes was less than a second behind after prevailing over Barbera; Tito Rabat was a close 15th for the last point, fading team-mate Miller a distant 16th.

Redding was miles down in last, after falling twice and remounting in a nightmare home GP.

The loss of three points to Rossi hardly dented Marquez's overall lead, but Lorenzo's slump continued.

MOTO2 RACE – 18 laps

The rain seemed to have been picking on the middle class, with all but the third free practice session drenched, and also qualifying. With such a limited amount of track time, the often processional class laid on a thriller, rich in drama and surprises, heroism and heartbreak, and complete with a pantomime villain.

That role was taken by Zarco; the heartbreak was for home hero Sam Lowes, fastest in every practice session, who was aiming for the win with four of 18 laps to go. He'd got past Zarco and had set his sights on long-time leader Luthi when the French defending champion sneaked up inside at a tight left-hander.

Zarco explained later that an initial contact had lifted his brake lever, "impeding me from braking hard." He ran on to the paint on the inside of the track and then wide, taking Lowes out with him. Lowes fell, Zarco stayed on board, recovering to finish sixth. But race direction was not impressed: an instant 30-second penalty dropped him out of the points to 22nd.

Lowes was equally unimpressed, saying, "I think he did

it on purpose," and appreciating the justice of at least a matching score of zero points.

Luthi's lead was now fully secure for a second win of the season – two weeks after a heavy crash at Brno had left him unconscious.

A fierce scrap behind brought a strong second for Morbidelli, after he had finally prevailed over Nakagami; Syahrin was still right with them.

The race was a minor triumph for Rins. The Paginas Amarillas Kalex rider was in pain after surgery to repair a collarbone and had struggled through practice, ending up 19th on the grid. Come the race, however, he moved steadily forward, eventually passing Corsi for a fine eighth – promoted to seventh by Zarco's penalty. Nine points moved him to within ten of no-score Zarco, reigniting his title hopes.

Lowes, Zarco and Folger were on the front row, and Folger made the best start. Lowes had taken over by the end of the lap, with Zarco third and soon to take second.

Marquez had qualified on row two and followed team-mate Morbidelli past Folger on lap four, only to slip off yet again.

All the while, Luthi was moving forwards in chunks from eighth on lap one, taking third off Morbidelli on lap seven; and when Lowes slowed for a spell, it was Luthi who took the lead, with Zarco second.

Lowes dropped to fourth, but was back past Morbidelli after two laps, and by the 14th was again part of a close lead trio. He'd moved to second and was aiming for Luthi when Zarco knocked him off.

Folger was a close fifth; then there was a gap until Zarco, who had got ahead of Baldassari with two laps to go.

A couple of seconds adrift, Rins took Corsi on the last lap. Mattia Pasini had followed him through, leaving Axel Pons to complete the top ten, and the rest of the points to Schrotter, Cortese, Vierge, Simon and Kent.

Vinales also crashed out early on; Oliveira retired from a good position in the points.

After two off-colour races, Zarco's lead over Rins was now just ten points. Lowes was the big loser, 44 points adrift.

MOTO3 RACE – 17 laps

The longest track gave no chance to escape in a hectic Moto3 race, with the lead pack at one point 15 strong, and the remaining 11 across the line in 1.6 seconds. Keeping a cool head counted for everything, as Binder took his fourth win to further extend his massive points lead.

His position was helped by fresh misfortune for his 'closest' rival, Jorge Navarro. He had come steadily through from 18th on the grid to join battle with the leaders, only to be knocked flying by a headstrong wild-card with two laps to go. Zero points.

The wild-card was Stefano Manzi, on a Mahindra for his 19th start and through from 34th on the grid, in a dazzling ride. He would finish fourth.

Binder and first-time pole qualifier Bagnaia did most of the leading, with Navarro taking a couple of goes, and also Bastianini. But that was only over the line.

Rookie Red Bull champion Bendsneyder was another major star, starting from row three and in front as they began the last lap. He decided to defer to team-mate Binder in the interests of the championship, then got zapped by Bagnaia for second.

The astonishing Manzi, as well as rookie Bulega, suddenly through from the back of the gang, consigned fellow rookie Di Giannantonio to sixth by inches on the last lap. Antonelli came back to seventh, after losing ground early on when his glove caught in the throttle, jamming it open. He led Bastianini over the line, with Canet ninth, promoted ahead of Mir, who had exceeded track limits on the final lap.

After the race, however, Antonelli was disqualified for failing to make the minimum weight limit.

Migno was knocked down along with Navarro; rookie Valtulini was the only other faller.

Above: Thomas Luthi kept control of a lively Moto2 race, from Morbidelli and Nakagami.
Photo: Gold & Goose

Left: Radiating anger and despair, Sam Lowes cruises in after being robbed of a potential home win.
Photo: Gavan Caldwell Photography

Below: Bagnaia on the Mahindra managed to split the Red Bull KTMs of winner Binder and rostrum rookie Bendsneyder.
Photo: Gold & Goose

Left: Stefano Manzi put the wild into 'wild card' on his way to fourth.

Below left: Binder tightened his grip on the Moto3 title battle, whilst team-mate Bendsneyder rode shotgun to third.
Photos: Gold & Goose

OCTO BRITISH GRAND PRIX

2-4 SEPTEMBER, 2016

SILVERSTONE GRAND PRIX CIRCUIT

19 laps
Length: 5.900km / 3.666 miles
Width: 17m

Key: 96/60 kph/mph · Gear

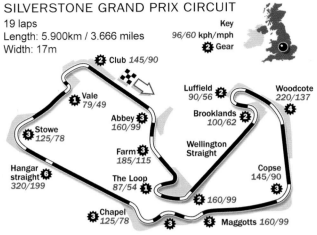

Club 145/90 · Vale 79/49 · Luffield 90/56 · Woodcote 220/137 · Abbey 160/99 · Brooklands 100/62 · Stowe 125/78 · Farm 185/115 · Wellington Straight · Copse 145/90 · Hangar straight 320/199 · The Loop 87/54 · 160/99 · Chapel 125/78 · Maggotts 160/99

MotoGP

RACE DISTANCE: 19 laps, 69.656 miles/112.100km · RACE WEATHER: Dry (air 18°C, humidity 72%, track 18°C)

Pos.	Rider	Nat.	No.	Entrant	Machine	Tyres	Race tyre choice	Laps	Time & speed
1	Maverick Vinales	SPA	25	Team SUZUKI ECSTAR	Suzuki GSX-RR	M	F: Hard/R: Medium	19	39m 03.559s 106.9mph/ 172.1km/h
2	Cal Crutchlow	GBR	35	LCR Honda	Honda RC213V	M	F: Hard/R: Medium	19	39m 07.039s
3	Valentino Rossi	ITA	46	Movistar Yamaha MotoGP	Yamaha YZR-M1	M	F: Hard/R: Medium	19	39m 07.622s
4	Marc Marquez	SPA	93	Repsol Honda Team	Honda RC213V	M	F: Soft/R: Medium	19	39m 09.551s
5	Dani Pedrosa	SPA	26	Repsol Honda Team	Honda RC213V	M	F: Soft/R: Soft	19	39m 09.940s
6	Andrea Dovizioso	ITA	4	Ducati Team	Ducati Desmosedici	M	F: Soft/R: Soft	19	39m 15.862s
7	Aleix Espargaro	SPA	41	Team SUZUKI ECSTAR	Suzuki GSX-RR	M	F: Hard/R: Medium	19	39m 20.231s
8	Jorge Lorenzo	SPA	99	Movistar Yamaha MotoGP	Yamaha YZR-M1	M	F: Soft/R: Medium	19	39m 22.991s
9	Danilo Petrucci	ITA	9	OCTO Pramac Yakhnich	Ducati Desmosedici	M	F: Soft/R: Soft	19	39m 29.177s
10	Alvaro Bautista	SPA	19	Aprilia Racing Team Gresini	Aprilia RS-GP	M	F: Soft/R: Soft	19	39m 35.643s
11	Yonny Hernandez	COL	68	Pull & Bear Aspar Team	Ducati Desmosedici	M	F: Soft/R: Soft	19	39m 39.690s
12	Eugene Laverty	IRL	50	Pull & Bear Aspar Team	Ducati Desmosedici	M	F: Soft/R: Soft	19	39m 42.689s
13	Alex Lowes	GBR	22	Monster Yamaha Tech 3	Yamaha YZR-M1	M	F: Soft/R: Soft	19	39m 43.702s
14	Hector Barbera	SPA	8	Avintia Racing	Ducati Desmosedici	M	F: Soft/R: Soft	19	39m 44.915s
15	Tito Rabat	SPA	53	Estrella Galicia 0,0 Marc VDS	Honda RC213V	M	F: Hard/R: Medium	19	39m 45.502s
16	Jack Miller	AUS	43	Estrella Galicia 0,0 Marc VDS	Honda RC213V	M	F: Soft/R: Medium	19	39m 51.169s
17	Scott Redding	GBR	45	OCTO Pramac Yakhnich	Ducati Desmosedici	M	F: Soft/R: Soft	19	40m 59.736s
	Andrea Iannone	ITA	29	Ducati Team	Ducati Desmosedici	M	F: Soft/R: Soft	13	DNF-crash
	Stefan Bradl	GER	6	Aprilia Racing Team Gresini	Aprilia RS-GP	M	F: Hard/R: Soft	2	DNF-crash
	Loris Baz	FRA	76	Avintia Racing	Ducati Desmosedici	M	F: Hard/R: Soft	0	DNS
	Pol Espargaro	SPA	44	Monster Yamaha Tech 3	Yamaha YZR-M1	M	F: Soft/R: Soft	0	DNS

Fastest lap: Maverick Vinales, on lap 2, 2m 2.339s, 107.9mph/173.6km/h.

Lap record: Dani Pedrosa, SPA (Honda), 2m 1.941s, 108.2mph/174.1km/h (2013).

Event best maximum speed: Andrea Iannone, 202.8mph/326.4km/h (race).

Qualifying

Weather: Wet
Air Temp: 16° **Track Temp:** 17°
Humidity: 94%

1	Crutchlow	2m 19.265s
2	Rossi	2m 20.263s
3	Vinales	2m 20.514s
4	Pedrosa	2m 20.742s
5	Marquez	2m 20.779s
6	Laverty	2m 20.821s
7	Redding	2m 21.074s
8	Iannone	2m 21.446s
9	Lorenzo	2m 21.687s
10	Dovizioso	2m 22.420s
11	A. Espargaro	2m 25.285s
12	Miller	No Time
13	Baz	2m 18.552s
14	Petrucci	2m 18.657s
15	P. Espargaro	2m 18.871s
16	Lowes	2m 18.900s
17	Bradl	2m 19.115s
18	Barbera	2m 19.125s
19	Bautista	2m 20.299s
20	Hernandez	2m 21.255s
21	Rabat	2m 21.774s

Fastest race laps

1	Vinales	2m 02.339s
2	Crutchlow	2m 02.659s
3	A. Espargaro	2m 02.680s
4	Pedrosa	2m 02.721s
5	Rossi	2m 02.745s
6	Iannone	2m 02.790s
7	Marquez	2m 02.815s
8	Dovizioso	2m 02.837s
9	Lorenzo	2m 03.171s
10	Miller	2m 03.720s
11	Petrucci	2m 03.883s
12	Redding	2m 03.939s
13	Bautista	2m 04.061s
14	Hernandez	2m 04.244s
15	Barbera	2m 04.384s
16	Lowes	2m 04.429s
17	Laverty	2m 04.457s
18	Rabat	2m 04.500s
19	Bradl	2m 04.849s

Championship Points

1	Marquez	210
2	Rossi	160
3	Lorenzo	146
4	Vinales	125
5	Pedrosa	120
6	Iannone	96
7	Dovizioso	89
8	Crutchlow	86
9	P. Espargaro	81
10	Barbera	78
11	Laverty	67
12	A. Espargaro	60
13	Redding	54
14	Petrucci	45
15	Miller	42
16	Smith	42
17	Bautista	41
18	Bradl	39
19	Rabat	27
20	Baz	24
21	Pirro	23
22	Hernandez	13
23	Lowes	3

Constructor Points

1	Honda	241
2	Yamaha	238
3	Ducati	172
4	Suzuki	131
5	Aprilia	59

Grid order / Lap chart

Grid order	1	2	3	4	5	6	7	8	9	10	11	12	13	14	15	16	17	18	19
35 CRUTCHLOW	25	25	25	25	25	25	25	25	25	25	25	25	25	25	25	25	25	25	25
46 ROSSI	35	93	93	93	93	46	46	46	46	46	46	46	29	35	35	35	93	35	35
25 VINALES	93	35	35	35	46	93	93	93	93	35	29	29	46	46	93	93	35	46	46
26 PEDROSA	46	46	46	46	35	35	35	35	35	93	35	35	35	93	46	46	46	93	93
93 MARQUEZ	29	29	29	29	29	26	26	26	26	29	93	93	93	26	26	26	26	93	26
50 LAVERTY	26	26	26	26	26	29	29	29	29	26	26	26	26	4	4	4	4	4	4
45 REDDING	45	99	99	99	4	4	4	4	4	4	4	4	4	41	41	41	41	41	41
29 IANNONE	99	4	4	4	99	99	99	99	99	41	41	41	41	99	99	99	99	99	99
99 LORENZO	4	45	41	41	41	41	41	41	41	99	99	99	99	9	9	9	9	9	9
4 DOVIZIOSO	41	41	43	43	9	9	9	9	9	9	9	9	9	19	19	19	19	19	19
41 A. ESPARGARO	43	43	9	9	43	43	43	43	43	19	19	19	19	68	68	68	68	68	68
43 MILLER	50	9	68	68	68	68	68	68	68	68	68	68	68	8	8	8	8	50	50
76 BAZ	9	50	19	19	19	19	19	19	19	43	43	43	8	43	22	22	22	22	22
9 PETRUCCI	6	6	22	22	22	8	8	8	8	8	8	8	43	22	43	50	50	8	8
44 P. ESPARGARO	19	68	8	8	8	22	22	22	22	22	22	22	22	50	50	43	53	53	53
22 LOWES	68	19	53	53	53	53	53	53	50	50	50	50	50	53	53	53	43	43	43
6 BRADL	22	22	50	50	50	50	50	50	53	53	53	53	53	45	45	45	45	45	45
8 BARBERA	53	53	45	45	45	45	45	45	45	45	45	45	45						
19 BAUTISTA	8	8																	
68 HERNANDEZ																			
53 RABAT																			

Moto2 — RACE DISTANCE: 18 laps, 65.990 miles/106.200km · RACE WEATHER: Dry (air 18°C, humidity 74%, track 18°C)

Pos.	Rider	Nat.	No.	Entrant	Machine	Laps	Time & Speed
1	**Thomas Luthi**	SWI	12	Garage Plus Interwetten	Kalex	18	38m 49.473s 102.0mph/ 164.1km/h
2	**Franco Morbidelli**	ITA	21	Estrella Galicia 0,0 Marc VDS	Kalex	18	38m 50.329s
3	**Takaaki Nakagami**	JPN	30	IDEMITSU Honda Team Asia	Kalex	18	38m 50.652s
4	**Hafizh Syahrin**	MAL	55	Petronas Raceline Malaysia	Kalex	18	38m 50.832s
5	**Jonas Folger**	GER	94	Dynavolt Intact GP	Kalex	18	38m 51.443s
6	**Lorenzo Baldassarri**	ITA	7	Forward Team	Kalex	18	38m 54.735s
7	**Alex Rins**	SPA	40	Paginas Amarillas HP 40	Kalex	18	38m 57.435s
8	**Simone Corsi**	ITA	24	Speed Up Racing	Speed Up	18	38m 57.894s
9	**Mattia Pasini**	ITA	54	Italtrans Racing Team	Kalex	18	38m 58.029s
10	**Axel Pons**	SPA	49	AGR Team	Kalex	18	39m 03.213s
11	**Marcel Schrotter**	GER	23	AGR Team	Kalex	18	39m 04.854s
12	**Sandro Cortese**	GER	11	Dynavolt Intact GP	Kalex	18	39m 05.562s
13	**Xavi Vierge**	SPA	97	Tech 3 Racing	Tech 3	18	39m 06.037s
14	**Julian Simon**	SPA	60	QMMF Racing Team	Speed Up	18	39m 11.628s
15	**Danny Kent**	GBR	52	Leopard Racing	Kalex	18	39m 11.663s
16	Xavier Simeon	BEL	19	QMMF Racing Team	Speed Up	18	39m 17.365s
17	Jesko Raffin	SWI	2	Sports-Millions-EMWE-SAG	Kalex	18	39m 18.518s
18	Ratthapark Wilairot	THA	14	IDEMITSU Honda Team Asia	Kalex	18	39m 18.668s
19	Iker Lecuona	SPA	27	CarXpert Interwetten	Kalex	18	39m 21.038s
20	Remy Gardner	AUS	87	Tasca Racing Scuderia Moto2	Kalex	18	39m 21.195s
21	Sam Lowes	GBR	22	Federal Oil Gresini Moto2	Kalex	18	39m 22.174s
22	Johann Zarco	FRA	5	Ajo Motorsport	Kalex	18	39m 24.705s
23	Edgar Pons	SPA	57	Paginas Amarillas HP 40	Kalex	18	39m 27.769s
24	Robin Mulhauser	SWI	70	CarXpert Interwetten	Kalex	18	39m 28.189s
25	Alex Marquez	SPA	73	Estrella Galicia 0,0 Marc VDS	Kalex	18	39m 33.619s
	Luca Marini	ITA	10	Forward Team	Kalex	17	DNF
	Miguel Oliveira	POR	44	Leopard Racing	Kalex	11	DNF
	Isaac Vinales	SPA	32	Tech 3 Racing	Tech 3	0	DNF

Fastest lap: Thomas Luthi, on lap 6, 2m 8.365s, 102.8mph/165.4km/h.

Lap record: Tito Rabat, SPA (Kalex), 2m 7.186s, 103.7mph/166.9km/h (2013).

Event best maximum speed: Thomas Luthi, 168.8mph/271.6km/h (race).

Qualifying

Weather: Wet
Air Temp: 16° **Track Temp:** 16°
Humidity: 93%

1	Lowes	2m 26.740s
2	Zarco	2m 27.139s
3	Folger	2m 27.502s
4	Marquez	2m 27.506s
5	Syahrin	2m 27.963s
6	Morbidelli	2m 28.047s
7	Vinales	2m 28.064s
8	Baldassarri	2m 28.331s
9	Corsi	2m 28.654s
10	Luthi	2m 28.711s
11	Nakagami	2m 28.926s
12	Kent	2m 28.930s
13	Simon	2m 29.052s
14	Cortese	2m 29.073s
15	Oliveira	2m 29.173s
16	Marini	2m 29.187s
17	Vierge	2m 29.741s
18	Raffin	2m 30.614s
19	Rins	2m 31.189s
20	E. Pons	2m 31.311s
21	Gardner	2m 31.373s
22	Simeon	2m 31.391s
23	Schrotter	2m 31.546s
24	Mulhauser	2m 32.336s
25	A. Pons	2m 32.824s
26	Lecuona	2m 33.777s
27	Pasini	2m 34.084s
28	Wilairot	2m 34.352s

Fastest race laps

1	Luthi	2m 08.365s
2	Zarco	2m 08.536s
3	Nakagami	2m 08.559s
4	Lowes	2m 08.581s
5	Morbidelli	2m 08.681s
6	Rins	2m 08.691s
7	Syahrin	2m 08.757s
8	Pasini	2m 08.821s
9	Folger	2m 08.845s
10	A. Pons	2m 08.911s
11	Baldassarri	2m 08.963s
12	Corsi	2m 09.101s
13	Marquez	2m 09.283s
14	Cortese	2m 09.314s
15	Marini	2m 09.487s
16	Wilairot	2m 09.495s
17	Simon	2m 09.501s
18	Schrotter	2m 09.510s
19	Vierge	2m 09.548s
20	Kent	2m 09.581s
21	Oliveira	2m 09.832s
22	Raffin	2m 09.990s
23	Simeon	2m 10.001s
24	Gardner	2m 10.017s
25	Lecuona	2m 10.066s
26	Mulhauser	2m 10.170s
27	E. Pons	2m 10.230s

Championship Points

1	Zarco	181
2	Rins	171
3	Lowes	137
4	Luthi	131
5	Folger	119
6	Morbidelli	114
7	Nakagami	108
8	Syahrin	92
9	Aegerter	71
10	Corsi	67
11	Baldassarri	65
12	Pasini	50
13	A. Pons	47
14	Schrotter	38
15	Salom	37
16	Marquez	34
17	Oliveira	33
18	Simon	32
19	Simeon	29
20	Kent	28
21	Cortese	24
22	Marini	20
23	Vinales	12
24	Raffin	10
25	Vierge	10
26	West	6
27	Gardner	5
28	Mulhauser	4
29	Wilairot	3
30	E. Pons	2

Constructor Points

1	Kalex	300
2	Speed Up	100
3	Tech 3	20
4	Suter	6

Moto3 — RACE DISTANCE: 17 laps, 62.320 miles/100.300km · RACE WEATHER: Dry (air 18°C, humidity 76%, track 16°C)

Pos.	Rider	Nat.	No.	Entrant	Machine	Laps	Time & Speed
1	**Brad Binder**	RSA	41	Red Bull KTM Ajo	KTM	19	38m 39.142s 96.7mph/ 155.6km/h
2	**Francesco Bagnaia**	ITA	21	Northgate Mahindra ASPAR	Mahindra	19	38m 39.325s
3	**Bo Bendsneyder**	NED	64	Red Bull KTM Ajo	KTM	19	38m 39.478s
4	**Stefano Manzi**	ITA	62	Mahindra Racing	Mahindra	19	38m 39.929s
5	**Nicolo Bulega**	ITA	8	SKY Racing Team VR46	KTM	19	38m 39.944s
6	**Fabio Di Giannantonio**	ITA	4	Gresini Racing Moto3	Honda	19	38m 40.025s
7	**Enea Bastianini**	ITA	33	Gresini Racing Moto3	Honda	19	38m 40.158s
8	**Aron Canet**	SPA	44	Estrella Galicia 0,0	Honda	19	38m 40.551s
9	**Joan Mir**	SPA	36	Leopard Racing	KTM	19	38m 40.335s
10	**Jorge Martin**	SPA	88	Northgate Mahindra ASPAR	Mahindra	19	38m 40.766s
11	**Gabriel Rodrigo**	ARG	19	RBA Racing Team	KTM	19	38m 41.542s
12	**Philipp Oettl**	GER	65	Schedl GP Racing	KTM	19	38m 47.727s
13	**Jules Danilo**	FRA	95	Ongetta-Rivacold	Honda	19	38m 51.949s
14	**Andrea Locatelli**	ITA	55	Leopard Racing	KTM	19	38m 51.981s
15	**Jakub Kornfeil**	CZE	84	Drive M7 SIC Racing Team	Honda	19	38m 52.027s
16	Juanfran Guevara	SPA	58	RBA Racing Team	KTM	19	38m 52.316s
17	John McPhee	GBR	17	Peugeot MC Saxoprint	Peugeot	19	38m 52.358s
18	Lorenzo dalla Porta	ITA	48	SKY Racing Team VR46	KTM	19	38m 52.468s
19	Hiroki Ono	JPN	76	Honda Team Asia	Honda	19	38m 56.105s
20	Livio Loi	BEL	11	RW Racing GP BV	Honda	19	39m 11.539s
21	Darryn Binder	RSA	40	Platinum Bay Real Estate	Mahindra	19	39m 18.267s
22	Khairul Idham Pawi	MAL	89	Honda Team Asia	Honda	19	39m 18.282s
23	Adam Norrodin	MAL	7	Drive M7 SIC Racing Team	Honda	19	39m 18.399s
24	Marco Bezzecchi	ITA	53	Mahindra Racing	Mahindra	19	39m 18.556s
25	Tatsuki Suzuki	JPN	24	CIP-Unicom Starker	Mahindra	16	39m 18.658s
26	Maria Herrera	SPA	6	MH6 Team	KTM	14	39m 18.856s
27	Fabio Spiranelli	ITA	3	CIP-Unicom Starker	Mahindra	14	39m 30.821s
28	Lorenzo Petrarca	ITA	77	3570 Team Italia	Mahindra	14	39m 49.012s
29	Andrea Migno	ITA	16	SKY Racing Team VR46	KTM	13	40m 11.882s
	Jorge Navarro	SPA	9	Estrella Galicia 0,0	Honda	17	DNF
	Stefano Valtulini	ITA	43	3570 Team Italia	Mahindra	16	DNF
	Marcos Ramirez	SPA	42	Platinum Bay Real Estate	Mahindra	7	DNF
	Fabio Quartararo	FRA	20	Leopard Racing	KTM	0	DNF
	Albert Arenas	SPA	12	Peugeot MC Saxoprint	Peugeot	0	DNF
	Niccolo Antonelli	ITA	23	Ongetta-Rivacold	Honda	–	DSQ

Fastest lap: Nicolo Bulega, on lap 17, 2m 15.336s, 97.5mph/156.9km/h.

Lap record: Jakub Kornfeil, CZE (KTM), 2m 13.664s, 98.7mph/158.9km/h (2014).

Event best maximum speed: Gabriel Rodrigo, 142.4mph/229.2km/h (race).

Qualifying

Weather: Wet
Air Temp: 16° **Track Temp:** 17°
Humidity: 90%

1	Bagnaia	2m 33.642s
2	Bastianini	2m 33.748s
3	Bendsneyder	2m 33.994s
4	Antonelli	2m 34.383s
5	B. Binder	2m 34.386s
6	Mir	2m 34.479s
7	Danilo	2m 34.604s
8	Martin	2m 34.647s
9	Bulega	2m 34.669s
10	Dalla Porta	2m 34.753s
11	Locatelli	2m 34.815s
12	Canet	2m 34.920s
13	Herrera	2m 35.094s
14	Rodrigo	2m 35.136s
15	Kornfeil	2m 35.169s
16	Pawi	2m 35.266s
17	McPhee	2m 35.336s
18	Navarro	2m 35.588s
19	Ono	2m 35.651s
20	Migno	2m 35.821s
21	Quartararo	2m 35.822s
22	Loi	2m 36.165s
23	Oettl	2m 36.254s
24	Norrodin	2m 36.664s
25	Di Giannantonio	2m 36.842s
26	Ramirez	2m 36.931s
27	D. Binder	2m 37.036s
28	Guevara	2m 37.142s
29	Suzuki	2m 37.567s
30	Petrarca	2m 37.865s
31	Valtulini	2m 38.209s
32	Arenas	2m 38.705s
33	Spiranelli	2m 38.749s
34	Manzi	2m 41.666s
35	Bezzecchi	2m 42.423s

Fastest race laps

1	Bulega	2m 15.336s
2	Mir	2m 15.370s
3	Di Giannantonio	2m 15.377s
4	Navarro	2m 15.397s
5	Migno	2m 15.404s
6	Antonelli	2m 15.456s
7	Canet	2m 15.462s
8	Martin	2m 15.487s
9	Manzi	2m 15.500s
10	Guevara	2m 15.586s
11	B. Binder	2m 15.596s
12	Bastianini	2m 15.606s
13	Bagnaia	2m 15.657s
14	Bendsneyder	2m 15.660s
15	Rodrigo	2m 15.748s
16	Oettl	2m 15.768s
17	Ono	2m 15.830s
18	McPhee	2m 15.938s
19	Danilo	2m 16.145s
20	Dalla Porta	2m 16.189s
21	Locatelli	2m 16.273s
22	Kornfeil	2m 16.468s
23	Bezzecchi	2m 16.922s
24	D. Binder	2m 17.023s
25	Ramirez	2m 17.055s
26	Pawi	2m 17.083s
27	Quartararo	2m 17.224s
28	Loi	2m 17.394s
29	Valtulini	2m 17.415s
30	Norrodin	2m 17.424s
31	Herrera	2m 17.426s
32	Suzuki	2m 17.468s
33	Spiranelli	2m 17.794s
34	Petrarca	2m 19.152s

Championship Points

1	B. Binder	204
2	Navarro	118
3	Bagnaia	110
4	Bastianini	103
5	Bulega	100
6	Fenati	93
7	Di Giannantonio	92
8	Mir	90
9	Antonelli	74
10	Kornfeil	69
11	Locatelli	55
12	Pawi	54
13	Bendsneyder	52
14	Quartararo	52
15	Danilo	49
16	Oettl	48
17	Martin	46
18	McPhee	45
19	Canet	42
20	Migno	41
21	Loi	32
22	Guevara	29
23	Ono	21
24	Rodrigo	14
25	Manzi	13
26	Suzuki	12
27	Dalla Porta	7
28	Herrera	6
29	Norrodin	5
30	D. Binder	4

Constructor Points

1	KTM	251
2	Honda	231
3	Mahindra	147
4	Peugeot	45

SAN MARINO GRAND PRIX

MISANO WORLD CIRCUIT MARCO SIMONCELLI

Inset, left: Pedrosa and his crew celebrate their long-awaited first win of 2016.
Photo: Repsol Honda

Inset, below far left: Blues Brother Rossi copied Miller's Assen boot-sipping routine.

Inset, below left: Lorenzo was back on form, but still beaten.
Photos: Gold & Goose

Main: Pedrosa's tyre gamble preserved a 15-year win record.
Photo: Gold & Goose

Above: Hard but fair. Pedrosa pushes Rossi aside to take the lead.

Opposite page, clockwise from top left: Vinales leads Pirro and Marquez in the battle for fourth; Carmelo Ezpeleta with Paulo Simoncelli; Mahindra celebrated their 100th GP with Stefano Manzi sporting an Indian-flag colour scheme; Alex Lowes put on a fine performance in qualifying, but slipped off in the race.

Right: Valentino Rossi sports his Blues Brothers helmet.

Below right: Javier Fores substituted for the injured Baz at Avintia, but failed to finish.

Photos: Gold & Goose

SOMETIMES it is hard, from grandstand or sofa, to understand just how small the margins are in world-class racing, and that the difference between success or failure is not measured only by the stopwatch, although of course it is the ultimate arbiter.

Psychology is involved, as are personal confidence and momentum; but there is also a changeable technical plethora. Things that until now had prevented Pedrosa from preserving an enviable grand prix record, of winning at least one race per season, not only in his 11 years in MotoGP, but also since 2002, his second year in the 125 class.

There is a simple explanation: in this case, round and black, in Hailwood's deathless phrase. Again simply, at just 51kg, Dani took longer than the other riders to work the new Michelins up to temperature. By the time he had done so, the others had already gone. Yet Marquez didn't have the same trouble, only 8kg heavier and (at 168cm) 8cm taller.

Pedrosa had been addressing this difficulty, working on settings to give more weight transfer without abandoning the stability his smooth style requires; refining electronic responses to achieve better overall throttle control. Clearly, a run of cold and/or wet races had masked his progress, though he'd been strong at Silverstone.

Come good weather, high track temperatures, a new tyre construction and a tyre gamble of his own on the hardworking tight corners at Misano, and he was able to make things clear – becoming the eighth winner in eight races.

Lorenzo had been another victim of combinations of circumstances, but he too bounced back, though not quite as high as he had threatened on Saturday, smashing his own circuit best record as the first under 1m 32s. It was his first pole since Le Mans, and the 64th of his career, taking him one ahead of both Rossi and Marquez in an otherwise irrelevant battle for the record books.

He was back on form in another way, criticising others for dangerous riding. This time, it was Rossi after the race, citing an early overtake at the tightest of the circuit's series of slowing right-handers after the back straight. (At a circuit where passing is notoriously difficult.) He'd had to lift to avoid colliding as his team-mate cut inside him, yet from the outside he'd left the door open, and it looked as though he had had plenty of time to see him coming.

The public spat was at the post-race press conference. It was "too aggressive … he didn't need to make this overtake, but it is his style. Other riders overtake more clean."

Rossi was both amused and aggrieved: "I don't know what I have to say to him [Dani Pedrosa, who had cut past him for the lead]. What must I say to Marc at Silverstone? He overtake me ten times like this. You overtake always aggressive. Why you say me?"

The exchange continued, Rossi playing the crowd for sympathy, and Lorenzo concluding, "Don't laugh. It's my opinion. Race direction will have another opinion."

Michelin's latest upgrade was to the oft-criticised front: a stiffer carcase, intended for better stability in braking and corner entry. It was generally well received, but in blazing hot conditions, some riders – including hard braker Marc Marquez, to his cost – elected to use the hard option with the older casing in qualifying and in the race. Praise for Michelin's efforts to progress faded somewhat after qualifying, however, when many riders had problems with inconsistent rear tyres, including all three on the front row, and were full of apprehension in case they might get a dud one for the race. Pole-setter Lorenzo said, "It sometimes used to happen also with Bridgestone, but this weekend I had one or two tyres with a big gap in performance." He'd had similar problems at Silverstone at the previous round, then in the race a tyre that turned on the rim.

Talking of stopping power, Brembo reprised their 'Last of the Late Brakers' statistics, with more or less the same top five (Iannone absent), but reshuffled. Here, the list comprised Vinales, Rossi, Marquez, Lorenzo and Dovizioso; at

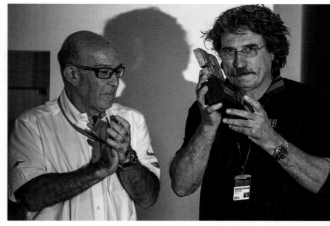

Mugello, the order had been Rossi, Marquez, Iannone, Vinales and Lorenzo.

Iannone was out because his second home race had gone badly wrong in the first free practice, with a heavy crash. He walked away, but was sent to hospital, where a vertebral fracture (T3) was found. He came back on Friday, but was ruled unfit, and he would miss the next two races as well, after a brave attempt at an Aragon comeback.

His absence promoted official Ducati test rider Michele Pirro from wild-card to factory rider, which meant his test mule was put away for the weekend, and with it Ducati's latest aerodynamic experiment for 2017's post-wing era – a rear wheel wearing a speedway-style shroud over the spokes.

Miller missed the race, fresh pain and further tests having revealed undiscovered fractures in his right hand.

Baz was also out once more, his Silverstone crash having caused two new fractures in his much-battered right leg, in spite of his cheerful comments on social media. Fellow crasher Pol Espargaro was back, with Alex Lowes again alongside in the Monster Yamaha pit, and again impressing, making a strong challenge to join the top ten in Q2.

The most interesting contract news concerned runaway Moto3 leader Brad Binder, who would stay with the same Ajo team to replace the departing Zarco in Moto2.

The most flippant reference came from Rossi, who adopted a Blues Brothers motif for his special helmet, featuring himself and best pal Uccio as the two US actors. It also sported the words 'Sweet Home Misano'. He lives nearby.

The most congratulatory ceremony was held to admit 1982 World Champion and now FIM safety delegate Franco Uncini to the MotoGP Hall of Fame as the latest 'legend'.

And the most solemn marked the retirement of the late Marco Simoncelli's number '58' from the MotoGP class. At the same time, Dorna's Ezpeleta announced in the presence of Simoncelli's father, Paolo, that his Moto3 team, named Sic 58, would be admitted to the series in 2017.

MOTOGP RACE – 28 laps

Lorenzo led away from pole, tailed by second qualifier Rossi. On the second lap, the latter triggered a cheer from the 100,000-strong crowd, mostly wearing yellow, with that forceful, controversial (and successful) overtake.

For the next 20 laps, it looked as though the fans' dreams of a Rossi win would come true. He thought so, too. He couldn't escape, "but I had a gap of about a second from Lorenzo, and I could manage that."

The lap times told a different story. Pedrosa had got away from row two in sixth. On lap 11, he broke the lap record for the first time (he would lower it again on lap 13 and finally lap 15).

With better braking and corner speed, and the Honda's acceleration problem at last having submitted to constant development, he was picking up places all the time. By lap six, he was fourth, past Vinales, and then Dovizioso. Now he gradually closed a gap of almost 1.5 seconds to Marquez.

By lap 13, he was on him, one lap later ahead and starting on Lorenzo. He was unstoppable, and on lap 17 he was in second, 1.2 seconds behind Rossi and closing.

"I was worried on the grid because I was almost the only rider with that [soft] front tyre, and I had never used it in hot conditions," he said. His fears soon disappeared. "I knew I could do a good pace, and I knew the key was not to make any mistakes, and not fight too much. Then I saw I was catching, and I decided to take the chance to win."

His own move on Rossi, pushing inside at the slow Turn Four, was also uncharacteristically aggressive. He started the last lap 1.6 seconds clear, and finished it 2.8 seconds in front. It was a massive turnaround.

Rossi had no answer. "I was looking at Marquez and Lorenzo, and I thought my pace was good enough to win. But Dani was just too fast." The day before, he'd warned of Pedrosa's pace, saying, "it is lucky he is on the third row".

And for Lorenzo, "I can't be happy. I had no problems, but they were faster than me. But I am happy for Dani, after a very hard period."

An absorbing front battle overshadowed an otherwise somewhat processional race at a circuit where overtaking is difficult.

Marquez had pushed hard in the early stages, but for a second race his choice of front tyre (this time hard, the previous soft) proved wrong. He'd closed on the Yamahas, but "when Dani passed me, I tried to follow him, but I saw that it was more likely I would crash than finish on the podium."

Dovizioso had got the better of Vinales in the early stages, but succumbed again just before half-distance, and by the end the Suzuki had escaped by four seconds. Dovizioso explained: "We are still struggling to get the bike to turn, and as the laps go by, this difference increases. I have to use a lot of energy, push hard on the handlebars, and my riding style becomes more ragged."

Crutchlow had a difficult race, see-sawing behind this pair, several times almost close enough to challenge. By the end, though, he had dropped away to come under attack from Pirro, the only other rider to choose the soft front; he passed Crutchlow for seventh with two laps to go. Crutchlow successfully appealed against a penalty for exceeding track limits, able to prove that he had not taken advantage. The reason for the run-offs was odd: his sweatband had slipped and his vision was spoiled by a sweat-spattered visor.

Three seconds adrift, Pol Espargaro had got past brother Aleix by lap seven, and the pair tussled it out for the next ten laps, with Petrucci closing up. He had dropped away again when Aleix crashed out on lap 18.

A little way behind were the two Aprilias, at their home test track, with Bautista slow away and taking until after half-distance to get past team-mate Bradl. The pair caught Petrucci, but only Bautista got ahead, the Ducati's stronger acceleration thwarting Brad by three-tenths over the line.

Three seconds away, Barbera prevailed in a three-way fight, eventually leaving Laverty and Redding trailing, the bulky Englishman having familiar grip problems in hot conditions. Hernandez was a distant 16th; Rabat had crashed on the first lap, but had rejoined for the practice to finish five laps down.

Replacement riders Alex Lowes (Monster Yamaha) and Javier Fores (Avintia Ducati) didn't make the finish. The former slipped off unhurt early on, while Fores retired with arm-pump with 13 laps to go.

MOTO2 RACE – 26 laps

The twisty circuit laid on a Moto2 race of unusual variety, with two heroes. One was first-time winner Lorenzo Baldassari. The other was second-placed Rins, still suffering from injury, who led until the penultimate lap. He came within three points of taking over the title lead from an again off-form Zarco.

The big loser was Sam Lowes, with zero points for the fourth time in five races, after he'd crashed out of the group chasing the leader.

Zarco started from pole and led the first two laps. But it was tough at the front, with Morbidelli, Luthi, Lowes, Baldassari and Nakagami trading blows through the tight twists of the compact circuit.

A little way behind, Rins, full of painkillers and adrenalin, was charging through.

He took the lead on lap six and simply cleared off, with Baldassari heading the brawling pursuit, Zarco and Nakagami now fifth and sixth. Four laps later, he was almost two seconds clear as the others scrapped and rubbed. But now Baldassari had finally seen off a persistent Morbidelli and started to close, quite rapidly at first.

Rins responded bravely, saying later, "It was a hard race for me and my shoulder, with a lot of pain."

But with five laps to go, the Italian teenager was on his back wheel; he took the lead with two left. Rins carried on attacking, until on the last lap his rival braked abruptly in front of him into the tricky right-handers near the end of the lap. "We almost touched," said Rins, who was forced to swerve wide, and concede the victory.

Baldassari was naturally overjoyed by his first win. "I was second at Mugello, and now I wanted to be first. Rins was riding very well, but I pushed to the limit."

Nakagami had quickly got ahead of Zarco, leaving him in the thick of it as he moved through to take third at half-distance, as one victim, Lowes, crashed after hitting a bump. The Japanese moved clear at once; Zarco took a little longer and was condemned to fourth.

Morbidelli was fifth, from Luthi; Syahrin had caught the group and passed Folger for seventh as the German ran wide. His team-mate, Sandro Cortese, had also come through, and was a second adrift.

Alex Marquez had dropped away and at the end was in danger of being caught for tenth by Schrotter. Vierge, Marini, Wilairot and Raffin wrapped up the rest of the points.

Zarco's earlier points lead had melted away over the previous three races, and his chances of becoming the first successful Moto2 title defender were now under serious threat from Rins, in spite of his injuries. But Lowes's challenge seemed over, as he dropped to fourth overall behind Luthi.

MOTO3 RACE – 23 laps

It was an atypical Moto3 race, with the usual dozen-strong leading pack breaking up before half-distance. But it was a typical result for champion-elect Brad Binder, whose last-lap tactical masterstroke gave the Red Bull KTM rider his fifth win of the year, extending his championship lead to a massive 106 points.

The battle was with 2015 winner Enea Bastianini, who had led laps one and three, then dogged Binder's wheel tracks, the pair better than a second clear after nine laps.

With five laps to go, the Italian's Honda went ahead, but the move turned out to have been at Binder's invitation, and the South African was relieved to note that the lap times immediately stretched. That left the way open for his last-lap attack, and a win by a quarter of a second.

Battle had raged behind them, with finally another pair breaking clear. Hot rookie Bulega had earlier been stronger, but fellow new boy Mir was faster at the finish, and had even closed to within a second of the leaders as Bastianini took over – only to be penalised for exceeding track limits once too often. He had to drop behind Bulega, then pass him again, to lead him over the line by less than a tenth. But for that, he might have interfered with the front pair.

A couple of seconds behind, fifth to ninth were over the line within two seconds. Kornfeil was at the front. Then Locatelli, Canet, Oettl and Ono. Oettl had caught the pack and come through impressively; Di Giannantonio had slipped off the back of it for tenth, with Antonelli 11th.

Erstwhile challenger Navarro's nightmare continued, with another crash from the leading group. Mahindra's hundredth GP was equally fruitless, with Martin out of the race after a qualifying crash; Bagnaia off form and out of the points; and Silverstone wild-card hero Manzi (his bike in Indian-flag colours), 16th, one place out of the points.

GP TIM DI SAN MARINO E DELLA RIVIERA DI RIMINI

9-11 SEPTEMBER, 2016

MISANO WORLD CIRCUIT MARCO SIMONCELLI

28 laps
Length: 4.226 km / 2.626 miles
Width: 14m

Key 96/60 kph/mph
Gear

Tramonto 75/47
Turn 9
Rio 75/47
Turn 5
Rimini 265/165
Quercia 80/50
Curvone 260/162
Turn 12
Turn 6 120/75
Turn 2
Misano 105/65
Turn 15 135/84
Variante del Parco 155/96
Turn 1 115/71
Carro 65/40
Turn 13 169/105

MotoGP

RACE DISTANCE: 28 laps, 73.526 miles/118.328km · **RACE WEATHER:** Dry (air 28°C, humidity 59%, track 43°C)

Pos.	Rider	Nat.	No.	Entrant	Machine	Tyres	Race tyre choice	Laps	Time & speed
1	Dani Pedrosa	SPA	26	Repsol Honda Team	Honda RC213V	M	F: Soft/R: Medium	28	43m 43.524s 100.8mph/ 162.3km/h
2	Valentino Rossi	ITA	46	Movistar Yamaha MotoGP	Yamaha YZR-M1	M	F: Medium/R: Medium	28	43m 46.361s
3	Jorge Lorenzo	SPA	99	Movistar Yamaha MotoGP	Yamaha YZR-M1	M	F: Medium/R: Medium	28	43m 47.883s
4	Marc Marquez	SPA	93	Repsol Honda Team	Honda RC213V	M	F: Hard/R: Medium	28	43m 53.093s
5	Maverick Vinales	SPA	25	Team SUZUKI ECSTAR	Suzuki GSX-RR	M	F: Hard/R: Medium	28	43m 58.991s
6	Andrea Dovizioso	ITA	4	Ducati Team	Ducati Desmosedici	M	F: Medium/R: Medium	28	44m 03.200s
7	Michele Pirro	ITA	51	Ducati Team	Ducati Desmosedici	M	F: Soft/R: Medium	28	44m 06.460s
9	Cal Crutchlow	GBR	35	LCR Honda	Honda RC213V	M	F: Medium/R: Medium	28	44m 09.226s
8	Pol Espargaro	SPA	44	Monster Yamaha Tech 3	Yamaha YZR-M1	M	F: Medium/R: Medium	28	44m 10.679s
10	Alvaro Bautista	SPA	19	Aprilia Racing Team Gresini	Aprilia RS-GP	M	F: Medium/R: Medium	28	44m 17.492s
11	Danilo Petrucci	ITA	9	OCTO Pramac Yakhnich	Ducati Desmosedici	M	F: Medium/R: Medium	28	44m 22.730s
12	Stefan Bradl	GER	6	Aprilia Racing Team Gresini	Aprilia RS-GP	M	F: Medium/R: Medium	28	44m 23.491s
13	Hector Barbera	SPA	8	Avintia Racing	Ducati Desmosedici	M	F: Medium/R: Medium	28	44m 26.521s
14	Eugene Laverty	IRL	50	Pull & Bear Aspar Team	Ducati Desmosedici	M	F: Medium/R: Medium	28	44m 32.974s
15	Scott Redding	GBR	45	OCTO Pramac Yakhnich	Ducati Desmosedici	M	F: Medium/R: Medium	28	44m 38.403s
16	Yonny Hernandez	COL	68	Pull & Bear Aspar Team	Ducati Desmosedici	M	F: Medium/R: Medium	28	44m 48.596s
17	Tito Rabat	SPA	53	Estrella Galicia 0,0 Marc VDS	Honda RC213V	M	F: Medium/R: Medium	23	44m 23.911s
	Aleix Espargaro	SPA	41	Team SUZUKI ECSTAR	Suzuki GSX-RR	M	F: Hard/R: Medium	17	DNF-crash
	Javier Fores	SPA	12	Avintia Racing	Ducati Desmosedici	M	F: Medium/R: Medium	15	DNF-arm pump
	Alex Lowes	GBR	22	Monster Yamaha Tech 3	Yamaha YZR-M1	M	F: Medium/R: Medium	7	DNF-crash
	Jack Miller	AUS	43	Estrella Galicia 0,0 Marc VDS	Honda RC213V	M	-	-	DNS-injured
	Andrea Iannone	ITA	29	Ducati Team	Ducati Desmosedici	M	-	-	DNS-injured

Fastest lap: Dani Pedrosa, on lap 15, 1m 32.979s, 101.7mph/163.6km/h (record).

Previous lap record: Jorge Lorenzo, SPA (Yamaha), 1m 33.273s, 101.3mph/163.1km/h (2015).

Event best maximum speed: Andrea Dovizioso, 184.6mph/297.1km/h (free practice).

Qualifying

Weather: Dry
Air Temp: 27° **Track Temp:** 43°
Humidity: 57%

1	Lorenzo	1m 31.868s
2	Rossi	32.216s
3	Vinales	32.381s
4	Marquez	32.443s
5	Pirro	32.467s
6	Dovizioso	32.677s
7	Crutchlow	32.743s
8	Pedrosa	32.859s
9	A. Espargaro	32.918s
10	P. Espargaro	1m 33.002s
11	Barbera	33.301s
12	Bautista	33.929s
13	Bradl	33.399s
14	Lowes	33.635s
15	Petrucci	33.716s
16	Laverty	33.772s
17	Miller	33.847s
18	Redding	33.989s
19	Rabat	34.302s
20	Hernandez	34.465s
21	Fores	35.161s

Fastest race laps

1	Pedrosa	1m 32.979s
2	Rossi	1m 33.025s
3	Lorenzo	1m 33.260s
4	Marquez	1m 33.319s
5	Vinales	1m 33.493s
6	Crutchlow	1m 33.689s
7	Dovizioso	1m 33.696s
8	Pirro	1m 33.822s
9	P. Espargaro	1m 33.911s
10	Bautista	1m 34.008s
11	Petrucci	1m 34.090s
12	A. Espargaro	1m 34.094s
13	Bradl	1m 34.286s
14	Barbera	1m 34.437s
15	Redding	1m 34.604s
16	Lowes	1m 34.706s
17	Laverty	1m 34.733s
18	Rabat	1m 34.896s
19	Hernandez	1m 35.200s
20	Fores	1m 36.455s

Championship Points

1	Marquez	223
2	Rossi	180
3	Lorenzo	162
4	Pedrosa	145
5	Vinales	136
6	Dovizioso	99
7	Iannone	96
8	Crutchlow	94
9	P. Espargaro	88
10	Barbera	81
11	Laverty	69
12	A. Espargaro	60
13	Redding	55
14	Petrucci	50
15	Bautista	47
16	Bradl	43
17	Miller	42
18	Smith	42
19	Pirro	32
20	Rabat	27
21	Baz	24
22	Hernandez	13
23	Lowes	3

Constructor Points

	Constructor	Points
1	Honda	266
2	Yamaha	258
3	Ducati	182
4	Suzuki	142
5	Aprilia	65

Grid order

Grid order	1	2	3	4	5	6	7	8	9	10	11	12	13	14	15	16	17	18	19	20	21	22	23	24	25	26	27	28
99 LORENZO	99	46	46	46	46	46	46	46	46	46	46	46	46	46	46	46	46	46	46	46	26	26	26	26	26	26	26	
46 ROSSI	46	99	99	99	99	99	99	99	99	99	99	99	99	99	99	26	26	26	26	46	46	46	46	46	46	46		
25 VINALES	25	25	25	93	93	93	93	93	93	93	93	93	93	26	26	99	99	99	99	99	99	99	99	99	99			
93 MARQUEZ	4	93	93	4	4	4	26	26	26	26	26	26	93	93	93	93	93	93	93	93	93	93	93	93	93			
51 PIRRO	93	4	4	26	26	26	4	4	4	25	25	25	25	25	25	25	25	25	25	25	25	25	25	25	25			
4 DOVIZIOSO	26	26	26	26	25	25	25	25	25	25	4	4	4	4	4	4	4	4	4	4	4	4	4	4	4			
35 CRUTCHLOW	35	35	35	35	35	35	35	35	35	35	35	35	35	35	35	35	35	35	35	51	51	51	51	51	51	51		
26 PEDROSA	41	41	41	51	51	51	51	51	51	51	51	51	51	51	51	51	51	51	51	35	35	35	35	35	35			
41 A. ESPARGARO	51	51	51	41	41	41	41	44	44	44	44	44	44	44	44	44	44	44	44	44	44	44	44	44	44			
44 P. ESPARGARO	44	44	44	44	44	44	44	41	41	41	41	41	41	41	41	41	19	19	19	19	19	19	19	19	19	19		
8 BARBERA	9	9	9	9	9	9	9	9	9	9	9	9	9	9	19	9	9	9	9	9	9	9	9	9	9			
19 BAUTISTA	6	6	6	6	6	6	6	6	6	6	6	6	19	19	19	19	9	6	6	6	6	6	6	6	6			
6 BRADL	19	19	19	19	19	19	19	19	19	19	19	6	6	6	6	6	8	8	8	8	8	8	8	8	8			
22 LOWES	45	45	45	45	45	45	45	50	50	50	50	50	50	50	50	8	8											
9 PETRUCCI	50	50	50	50	50	50	50	45	45	45	8	8	8	8	8	45	45	45	45	45	45	45	45	45	45			
50 LAVERTY	53	22	22	22	22	22	22	8	8	45	45	45	45	45	45	68	68	68	68	68	68	68	68	68				
45 REDDING	22	8	8	8	8	8	8	68	68	68	68	68	68	68	68	68	53	53	53	53	53	53						
53 RABAT	8	68	68	68	68	68	68	12	12	12	12	12	12	12	53	53												
68 HERNANDEZ	68	12	12	12	12	12	12	53	53	53	53	53	53	53														
12 FORES	12	53	53	53	53	53	53																					

53 Pit stop   53 Lapped rider

Moto2

RACE DISTANCE: 26 laps, 68.274 miles/109.876km · RACE WEATHER: Dry (air 27°C, humidity 58%, track 34°C)

Pos.	Rider	Nat.	No.	Entrant	Machine	Laps	Time & Speed
1	**Lorenzo Baldassarri**	ITA	7	Forward Team	Kalex	26	42m 45.885s
							95.8mph/
							154.1km/h
2	**Alex Rins**	SPA	40	Paginas Amarillas HP 40	Kalex	26	42m 48.408s
3	**Takaaki Nakagami**	JPN	30	IDEMITSU Honda Team Asia	Kalex	26	42m 52.084s
4	**Johann Zarco**	FRA	5	Ajo Motorsport	Kalex	26	42m 54.827s
5	**Franco Morbidelli**	ITA	21	Estrella Galicia 0,0 Marc VDS	Kalex	26	42m 55.901s
6	**Thomas Luthi**	SWI	12	Garage Plus Interwetten	Kalex	26	42m 56.980s
7	**Hafizh Syahrin**	MAL	55	Petronas Raceline Malaysia	Kalex	26	42m 58.933s
8	**Jonas Folger**	GER	94	Dynavolt Intact GP	Kalex	26	43m 00.489s
9	**Sandro Cortese**	GER	11	Dynavolt Intact GP	Kalex	26	43m 01.532s
10	**Alex Marquez**	SPA	73	Estrella Galicia 0,0 Marc VDS	Kalex	26	43m 06.605s
11	**Marcel Schrotter**	GER	23	AGR Team	Kalex	26	43m 08.080s
12	**Xavi Vierge**	SPA	97	Tech 3 Racing	Tech 3	26	43m 19.512s
13	**Luca Marini**	ITA	10	Forward Team	Kalex	26	43m 26.021s
14	**Ratthapark Wilairot**	THA	14	IDEMITSU Honda Team Asia	Kalex	26	43m 27.637s
15	**Jesko Raffin**	SWI	2	Sports-Millions-EMWE-SAG	Kalex	26	43m 28.387s
16	Mattia Pasini	ITA	54	Italtrans Racing Team	Kalex	26	43m 35.630s
17	Miguel Oliveira	POR	44	Leopard Racing	Kalex	26	43m 47.907s
18	Federico Fuligni	ITA	42	Team Ciatti	Kalex	26	43m 49.816s
19	Remy Gardner	AUS	87	Tasca Racing Scuderia Moto2	Kalex	26	43m 49.895s
20	Robin Mulhauser	SWI	70	CarXpert Interwetten	Kalex	26	43m 53.268s
21	Iker Lecuona	SPA	27	CarXpert Interwetten	Kalex	26	44m 05.931s
	Edgar Pons	SPA	57	Paginas Amarillas HP 40	Kalex	23	DNF
	Julian Simon	SPA	60	QMMF Racing Team	Speed Up	21	DNF
	Sam Lowes	GBR	22	Federal Oil Gresini Moto2	Kalex	12	DNF
	Danny Kent	GBR	52	Leopard Racing	Kalex	7	DNF
	Isaac Vinales	SPA	32	Tech 3 Racing	Tech 3	3	DNF
	Simone Corsi	ITA	24	Speed Up Racing	Speed Up	1	DNF
	Axel Pons	SPA	49	AGR Team	Kalex	0	DNF
	Xavier Simeon	BEL	19	QMMF Racing Team	Speed Up	0	DNF

Fastest lap: Alex Rins, on lap 9, 1m 37.892s, 96.6mph/155.4km/h.
Lap record: Jonas Folger, GER (Kalex), 1m 37.422s, 97.0mph/156.1km/h (2015).
Event best maximum speed: Jonas Folger, 152.1mph/244.8km/h (warm-up).

Qualifying

Weather: Dry
Air Temp: 28° Track Temp: 39°
Humidity: 57%

1	Zarco	1m 37.436s
2	Nakagami	1m 37.509s
3	Baldassarri	1m 37.550s
4	Lowes	1m 37.777s
5	Morbidelli	1m 37.861s
6	Luthi	1m 37.916s
7	Cortese	1m 37.933s
8	Rins	1m 37.935s
9	Pasini	1m 37.990s
10	Syahrin	1m 38.035s
11	Folger	1m 38.044s
12	Marquez	1m 38.051s
13	Schrotter	1m 38.105s
14	Simon	1m 38.243s
15	Kent	1m 38.308s
16	A. Pons	1m 38.339s
17	Corsi	1m 38.345s
18	Wilairot	1m 38.655s
19	Simeon	1m 38.706s
20	E. Pons	1m 38.808s
21	Marini	1m 38.857s
22	Oliveira	1m 38.885s
23	Raffin	1m 38.912s
24	Lecuona	1m 38.983s
25	Vierge	1m 39.006s
26	Vinales	1m 39.160s
27	Fuligni	1m 39.240s
28	Gardner	1m 39.257s
29	Mulhauser	1m 39.555s

Fastest race laps

1	Rins	1m 37.892s
2	Nakagami	1m 37.927s
3	Baldassarri	1m 37.991s
4	Zarco	1m 38.235s
5	Morbidelli	1m 38.370s
6	Folger	1m 38.372s
7	Lowes	1m 38.385s
8	Cortese	1m 38.447s
9	Syahrin	1m 38.479s
10	Luthi	1m 38.480s
11	Oliveira	1m 38.531s
12	Schrotter	1m 38.670s
13	Marquez	1m 38.724s
14	Lecuona	1m 38.855s
15	Pasini	1m 38.896s
16	E. Pons	1m 38.994s
17	Simon	1m 39.010s
18	Vierge	1m 39.055s
19	Wilairot	1m 39.171s
20	Gardner	1m 39.250s
21	Marini	1m 39.272s
22	Kent	1m 39.409s
23	Raffin	1m 39.477s
24	Fuligni	1m 39.767s
25	Vinales	1m 40.222s
26	Mulhauser	1m 40.488s

Championship Points

1	Zarco	194
2	Rins	191
3	Luthi	141
4	Lowes	137
5	Folger	127
6	Morbidelli	125
7	Nakagami	124
8	Syahrin	101
9	Baldassarri	90
10	Aegerter	71
11	Corsi	67
12	Pasini	50
13	A. Pons	47
14	Schrotter	43
15	Marquez	40
16	Salom	37
17	Oliveira	33
18	Simon	32
19	Cortese	31
20	Simeon	29
21	Kent	28
22	Marini	23
23	Vierge	14
24	Vinales	12
25	Raffin	11
26	West	6
27	Gardner	5
28	Wilairot	5
29	Mulhauser	4
30	E. Pons	2

Constructor Points

1	Kalex	325
2	Speed Up	100
3	Tech 3	24
4	Suter	6

Moto3

RACE DISTANCE: 23 laps, 60.396 miles/97.198km · RACE WEATHER: Dry (air 25°C, humidity 64%, track 29°C)

Pos.	Rider	Nat.	No.	Entrant	Machine	Laps	Time & Speed
1	**Brad Binder**	RSA	41	Red Bull KTM Ajo	KTM	23	39m 37.556s
							91.4mph/
							147.1km/h
2	**Enea Bastianini**	ITA	33	Gresini Racing Moto3	Honda	23	39m 37.818s
3	**Joan Mir**	SPA	36	Leopard Racing	KTM	23	39m 38.972s
4	**Nicolo Bulega**	ITA	8	SKY Racing Team VR46	KTM	23	39m 39.090s
5	**Jakub Kornfeil**	CZE	84	Drive M7 SIC Racing Team	Honda	23	39m 41.834s
6	**Andrea Locatelli**	ITA	55	Leopard Racing	KTM	23	39m 41.943s
7	**Aron Canet**	SPA	44	Estrella Galicia 0,0	Honda	23	39m 42.367s
8	**Philipp Oettl**	GER	65	Schedl GP Racing	KTM	23	39m 43.138s
9	**Hiroki Ono**	JPN	76	Honda Team Asia	Honda	23	39m 43.815s
10	**Fabio Di Giannantonio**	ITA	4	Gresini Racing Moto3	Honda	23	39m 48.452s
11	**Niccolo Antonelli**	ITA	23	Ongetta-Rivacold	Honda	23	39m 51.495s
12	**Juanfran Guevara**	SPA	58	RBA Racing Team	KTM	23	39m 51.647s
13	**Livio Loi**	BEL	11	RW Racing GP BV	Honda	23	39m 51.659s
14	**Jules Danilo**	FRA	95	Ongetta-Rivacold	Honda	23	39m 52.366s
15	**Andrea Migno**	ITA	16	SKY Racing Team VR46	KTM	23	39m 52.424s
16	Stefano Manzi	ITA	62	Mahindra Racing	Mahindra	23	40m 00.848s
17	Lorenzo dalla Porta	ITA	48	SKY Racing Team VR46	KTM	23	40m 00.905s
18	Fabio Quartararo	FRA	20	Leopard Racing	KTM	23	40m 01.079s
19	Albert Arenas	SPA	12	Peugeot MC Saxoprint	Peugeot	23	40m 08.696s
20	John McPhee	GBR	17	Peugeot MC Saxoprint	Peugeot	23	40m 12.701s
21	Francesco Bagnaia	ITA	21	Gaviota Mahindra ASPAR	Mahindra	23	40m 12.726s
22	Khairul Idham Pawi	MAL	89	Honda Team Asia	Honda	23	40m 12.965s
23	Adam Norrodin	MAL	7	Drive M7 SIC Racing Team	Honda	23	40m 13.023s
24	Lorenzo Petrarca	ITA	77	3570 Team Italia	Mahindra	23	40m 25.841s
25	Fabio Spiranelli	ITA	3	CIP-Unicorn Starker	Mahindra	23	40m 34.007s
26	Stefano Valtulini	ITA	43	3570 Team Italia	Mahindra	23	40m 34.042s
	Darryn Binder	RSA	40	Platinum Bay Real Estate	Mahindra	19	DNF
	Tatsuki Suzuki	JPN	24	CIP-Unicorn Starker	Mahindra	15	DNF
	Marcos Ramirez	SPA	42	Platinum Bay Real Estate	Mahindra	13	DNF
	Jorge Navarro	SPA	9	Estrella Galicia 0,0	Honda	7	DNF
	Gabriel Rodrigo	ARG	19	RBA Racing Team	KTM	6	DNF
	Maria Herrera	SPA	6	MH6 Team	KTM	1	DNF
	Bo Bendsneyder	NED	64	Red Bull KTM Ajo	KTM	0	DNF
	Alex Fabbri	RSM	71	Minimoto Portomaggiore	Mahindra	0	DNF

Fastest lap: Andrea Locatelli, on lap 4, 1m 42.627s, 92.1mph/148.2km/h (record).
Previous lap record: Niccolo Antonelli, ITA (Honda), 1m 42.841s, 91.9mph/147.9km/h (2015).
Event best maximum speed: Livio Loi, 130.7mph/210.3km/h (free practice).

Qualifying

Weather: Dry
Air Temp: 27° Track Temp: 40°
Humidity: 59%

1	B. Binder	1m 42.398s
2	Bastianini	1m 42.548s
3	Bulega	1m 42.631s
4	Kornfeil	1m 42.659s
5	Navarro	1m 42.710s
6	Canet	1m 42.842s
7	Oettl	1m 42.955s
8	Ono	1m 42.962s
9	Guevara	1m 42.985s
10	Di Giannantonio	1m 43.033s
11	Rodrigo	1m 43.080s
12	Martin	1m 43.112s
13	Locatelli	1m 43.120s
14	Antonelli	1m 43.133s
15	Danilo	1m 43.222s
16	Mir	1m 43.291s
17	Dalla Porta	1m 43.345s
18	Loi	1m 43.348s
19	Quartararo	1m 43.490s
20	Manzi	1m 43.684s
21	Bendsneyder	1m 43.761s
22	Migno	1m 43.768s
23	Herrera	1m 43.793s
24	Norrodin	1m 43.981s
25	Bagnaia	1m 43.991s
26	Arenas	1m 44.020s
27	Pawi	1m 44.205s
28	Ramirez	1m 44.211s
29	McPhee	1m 44.292s
30	Suzuki	1m 44.314s
31	Valtulini	1m 44.713s
32	Petrarca	1m 44.740s
33	D. Binder	1m 44.901s
34	Spiranelli	1m 45.687s
35	Fabbri	1m 46.133s

Fastest race laps

1	Locatelli	1m 42.627s
2	Mir	1m 42.657s
3	B. Binder	1m 42.778s
4	Bastianini	1m 42.790s
5	Canet	1m 42.819s
6	Bulega	1m 42.832s
7	Kornfeil	1m 42.878s
8	Oettl	1m 42.888s
9	Ono	1m 42.916s
10	Di Giannantonio	1m 42.976s
11	Loi	1m 42.993s
12	Danilo	1m 43.019s
13	Arenas	1m 43.022s
14	Migno	1m 43.023s
15	Antonelli	1m 43.034s
16	Navarro	1m 43.060s
17	D. Binder	1m 43.098s
18	Manzi	1m 43.125s
19	Guevara	1m 43.150s
20	Bagnaia	1m 43.165s
21	Rodrigo	1m 43.209s
22	Quartararo	1m 43.342s
23	Dalla Porta	1m 43.574s
24	Norrodin	1m 43.811s
25	Petrarca	1m 43.812s
26	Ramirez	1m 43.923s
27	Pawi	1m 43.982s
28	Suzuki	1m 44.054s
29	McPhee	1m 44.079s
30	Valtulini	1m 44.128s
31	Spiranelli	1m 44.262s

Championship Points

1	B. Binder	229
2	Bastianini	123
3	Navarro	118
4	Bulega	113
5	Bagnaia	110
6	Mir	106
7	Di Giannantonio	98
8	Fenati	93
9	Kornfeil	80
10	Antonelli	79
11	Locatelli	65
12	Oettl	56
13	Pawi	54
14	Bendsneyder	52
15	Quartararo	52
16	Canet	51
17	Danilo	51
18	Martin	46
19	McPhee	45
20	Migno	42
21	Loi	35
22	Guevara	33
23	Ono	28
24	Rodrigo	14
25	Manzi	13
26	Suzuki	12
27	Dalla Porta	7
28	Herrera	6
29	Norrodin	5
30	D. Binder	4

Constructor Points

1	KTM	276
2	Honda	251
3	Mahindra	147
4	Peugeot	45

ARAGON GRAND PRIX

ARAGON CIRCUIT

GRAN PREMIO
MOVISTAR
DE ARAGÓN

MotorLand Aragón 2016

Inset left: Marquez wheelies over the line to celebrate his first win since Germany.

Inset, below left: Fausto Gresini and Sam Lowes share the spoils of Moto2 victory.

Inset, below: Marquez, sprays the cava after reversing the title trend.

Inset, far left: Moto3 domination for Brad Binder, who wrapped up the crown with four races to spare.

Main: Sam Lowes was out on his own in Moto2.

Photos: Gold & Goose

Above: No more tyre-choice woes: Marquez chose the right Michelins for win number four.

Photo: Repsol Honda

Right: Popular 2006 champion Nicky Hayden was back for one race, with his trade-mark number 69. He earned a point on Miller's Honda.

Photos: Gold & Goose

BRAD BINDER came within three-tenths of making history with a win. As it turned out, Jorge Navarro sneaked back ahead through the final corner as the Red Bull KTM rider ran a little wide. It mattered not. With four races to go, the 21-year-old South African had done enough to make himself unbeatable.

The first championship of 2016 was decided in emphatic style, after an almost flawless campaign in the closest racing of all. Binder was the first South African champion since legendary privateer Jon Ekerold in 1980.

The other classes still had business to pursue, however, and a quirk of tyre allocation and a cool track caused a worrying number of crashes in Saturday morning's FP3, mercifully with no serious injuries.

Michelin had garnered praise for its range of choices, but for this race there were only two each front and rear, classified 'medium' and 'hard'. The medium was much more popular, with race choice running at 12:8 in its favour for the rear, and a significant 17:3 for the front (the exceptions being Marquez, Vinales and Crutchlow).

The medium was the obvious choice for qualifying, however, and with the necessity of saving tyres for that and for the race, riders were more or less forced to use the harder compound in the important FP3, in spite of much lower track temperatures: 24°C, compared with 42 in qualifying, 36 in the race. It led to a spate of front-end washaways.

The first victim was Alex Lowes, who suffered foot injuries that put him out for the weekend. Then Rossi, cruising on his first out-lap – in his case, the rear let go. A little later, Bautista's Aprilia front folded.

It would become more spectacular, in two incidents in-volving Pol Espargaro, the first at the notorious right-hand Turn Two. Pol lost it in an otherwise innocuous low-sider, but his Yamaha slid across the pit-lane exit, directly under the wheels of Petrucci as he was accelerating to join the track. The Italian went looping over the handlebars, his bike cartwheeling to destruction.

Soon afterwards, it was one-race returnee Nicky Hayden's turn to lose the front on the 'Reverse Corkscrew', bike and rider sliding a long way down the escape road. Yellow caution flags came out, but Marquez was already approaching at speed. He saw them at the last minute, grabbed too much front brake and slid off – and it was Pol's turn to be skittled. Hayden and the marshals attending to his bike had to leap for safety as both Yamaha and Honda followed the same route down the tarmac. Marquez ran to Espargaro to apologise and later was called to Race Direction to explain. But video footage revealed that the flags had not yet been out at the previous corner as he went through.

The earlier incident left a questionable aftertaste, for two reasons. Firstly, the track design and the frequency of falls at Turn Two meant that it was an accident waiting to happen. The pit exit needs a serious rethink. Secondly, although Petrucci ran straight back to get on his second bike, he revealed later that he had no memory of the accident or the preceding laps, and even after the race he still felt dizzy. Under questioning, FIM medical officer Giancarlo Di Filippo was defensive: "The situation is under control. It is important to make a big difference between loss of consciousness and not remembering. Danilo never lost consciousness." He had undergone full neurological and SCAt3 concussion assessment tests before the race, but had this been rugby, it is

probable that he would not have been allowed to play. As it was, he knocked team-mate Redding down on the first lap and received a ride-through penalty in consequence.

This was particularly piquant because of the situation in the Pramac squad, where the old adage 'the first person you must beat is your team-mate' already meant more than usual. Both riders had been signed for 2017, but there would be only one factory Ducati. It would go to the rider who scored more points in the run from Brno to the end, earlier races ignored because Petrucci had been injured, while Redding had endured a slew of mechanical problems.

Iannone returned and rode through FP1, placing a creditable sixth, but he withdrew thereafter, citing pain and physical weakness. Miller did not get that far, having withdrawn before the event to give his right hand injuries a chance finally to heal fully before the flyaway rounds. Baz was back, but far from full strength.

In Miller's place, a welcome return for popular 2006 champion Hayden, in a break from Superbike duties. With his breadth of experience, he was able to give an interesting assessment of the 2016 iteration of the RCV. He praised both the smooth power and electronics, but most especially the seamless-shift gearbox. "Acceleration is incredible … bang, bang, bang, going through the gears." He also confirmed the common response to the Michelins. The rear was good, but the front uncommunicative, and indeed that was the cause of his FP3 crash. He made up for it by earning a single point.

Rossi's single-finger gesture to Aleix Espargaro when the Suzuki rider baulked him in practice at Misano had an unexpected repercussion: a round-robin letter to riders from the FIM, threatening a 300-euro fine for similar behaviour. This occasioned great hilarity, with Crutchlow quipping, "If I'm fined for every gesture, I'll soon be bankrupt." There was a slightly puzzled response from other officials. IRTA's Mike Trimby said, "Some of the FIM stewards at Misano suggested rude signals should be penalised, but we said that's nonsense." Race director Mike Webb said, "I think we've got more important things to worry about." And FIM permanent Chief Steward, American Bill Cumbow: "A fist shake is okay, but we have to draw the line somewhere." Accordingly, when

Bulega showed his middle finger to Martin in practice, he was fined.

Livio Loi was put to the back of the grid for a technical gearbox infringement, and there were more penalties in Moto3, for loitering, several for repeat offences; while Folger was fined 300 euros for riding down the front straight with his hands off the handlebars, "causing danger to other competitors".

Most notable was one penalty point and one grid position for Moto2's Morbidelli, after he'd knocked Oliveira off on the first full lap of FP1. The Portuguese rider had braked unexpectedly into Turn Three, he said, clearly with some merit, given the leniency. But Oliveira paid the price, with his right collarbone broken in four places, and his weekend well and truly over.

The 2017 provisional calendar was announced, and Aragon was confirmed (as had been Valencia shortly before) until 2021.

MOTOGP RACE – 23 laps

Marc Marquez broke the spell at Aragon after eight races with different winners, after a dominant weekend, and after the narrowest of escapes. Starting from pole, he'd emerged in front of a furious scramble in the opening two laps, but on the third he came so close to crashing that he needed another of his miraculous recoveries.

"I was on the ground. I don't know how I saved it," he said, adding that he had told himself to calm down after that, to let his hard/asymmetric front tyre get up to temperature.

In fine conditions in front of almost 70,000 fans, it was another race where tyre choice proved crucial, and showed much variety.

Marquez chose hard front and rear; Lorenzo changed on the grid from the medium rear to the hard, going against his dislike of the tyre during practice, after a fall in morning warm-up had obliged him to try both bikes. "Sometimes a positive thing can come from a negative thing," he said. The benefit came later in the race, in a big battle with team-mate/deadly rival Rossi.

Valentino was on the same tyre combination and had led mid-race, but now he was suffering from wheelspin and lost

second to Lorenzo with five of the 23 laps left. He didn't give up, but finally ceded on the penultimate lap, when a lunge into the right-left Aragon Corkscrew put him briefly ahead, only to run wide. "If not, we might have touched, and … disaster," he said.

But construction problems, which caused the medium front to chunk, struck both Pedrosa and Dovizioso.

Marquez had been dominant in qualifying, with a six-tenths advantage over Vinales, but it was the latter who led through the first corners as Marquez and Lorenzo clashed; Rossi was up to third on lap three after Marquez's near crash.

It took three laps for him to get ahead of Lorenzo, and then he rapidly closed on Vinales, taking the lead on lap nine. At the same time, Marquez had regained confidence and speed, and consigned Vinales to third next time around. The Suzuki rider fought back, but ran wide, dropping behind Lorenzo, now almost 1.5 seconds adrift.

Could Rossi fend off Marquez?

No. The Spaniard sliced past on lap 12 and took half a second a lap out of his rival to move rapidly out of reach. "This was an important race, because step by step Valentino had been gaining points on me. I had to stop that, otherwise his mentality would go up," he said.

Lorenzo, too, was picking up pace even as Rossi was losing it. Within four laps, the gap had been halved, and on the 17th Jorge was poised to pass. He cut underneath Rossi after he had braked deep into the first corner, spoiling his exit speed up the hill.

They remained locked in combat until Rossi's error on lap 22. Lorenzo was delighted with second, only three seconds from the winner. "Yesterday, I expected to be sixth or seventh, but this season many unexpected things have happened."

Vinales was a safe, but ultimately distant fourth.

The battle for fifth had been absorbing, with second Suzuki rider Aleix Espargaro hanging on grimly until half-distance, while fast starter Dovizioso fell back into his reach. Dovi would continue to fade, his medium/medium tyre choice not only becoming worse and worse, but a suspect front tyre vibrating with increasing intensity.

Now Espargaro's attackers were Pedrosa and Crutchlow, and both were ahead on lap 11. But Pedrosa's medium front tyre was beginning to come to bits, and he was forced to slow down.

Crutchlow passed him with six laps left and pulled comfortably clear, once again top independent rider, and moving past Dovizioso to fifth overall.

Pedrosa regained sixth on the last lap from Espargaro, who lost two seconds with an error and was all but overtaken by younger brother Pol.

Bautista was ninth, having overtaken tenth-placed Aprilia team-mate Bradl before half-distance and given Pol Espargaro a hard time for a spell.

Dovizioso found little consolation as top Ducati in 11th, two seconds ahead of Iannone stand-in Pirro, describing his afternoon as "a disaster".

Barbera eventually won a lively battle for the last points, outpacing Laverty and Hayden, who said, "I wish it was like Superbikes and there was another race … but I guess everybody thinks that."

The trio had outpaced Hernandez; miles behind, Petrucci was 17th after his ride-through. An angry Redding had crashed and remounted for 19th behind Baz. Rabat had battled past Hayden, but crashed out.

Marquez's 54th career win put him equal fifth overall with Mick Doohan, behind Agostini, Rossi, Nieto and Hailwood; it extended his points lead to more than two races.

MOTO2 RACE – 21 laps

The championship was given another injection of tension at Aragon, as Lowes regained a lot of lost ground with a dominant win, his second of the season, while defending champion Zarco lost another crucial couple of points to the strengthening challenge from Rins.

While Lowes was simply unbeatable all weekend, the other pair were left behind in the middle of a top-ten brawl. Rins was battling illness and a poor 13th-place qualifying position, and Zarco had another off-form weekend.

Rins came out on top, pushing through early on, then narrowly clinging on to head the quartet disputing sixth. Zarco had started from row two, but dropped back as far as tenth, only moving forward gradually as he (as usual) gained strength on used tyres, finishing eighth, just four-tenths behind Rins, with Misano winner Lorenzo Baldassari sandwiched between them.

They finished the European season with Zarco just one point clear, having been 34 ahead just four races before.

There was joy also for Alex Marquez, when he reversed a last-corner attack by team-mate Morbidelli to retain second, and his first podium in Moto2.

Marquez led into the first corner, but Lowes blasted past before the lap was half done, and stretched away without pause to win by better than three seconds.

Baldassari finished lap one third, but Luthi was charging through from the back of a tight pursuit pack and was third by lap three. All the while, Zarco was being shuffled backward, while Rins – tenth on lap one – was edging forward, and already ahead of the Frenchman on lap two.

Nakagami and Morbidelli had closed up to Luthi by half-distance, and the Italian took over third on lap 14. At that point, he was 2.2 seconds adrift of his team-mate in second, but he closed remorselessly. If the race had been one lap longer, he might have taken the position. As it was, his attack into the last pair of corners was "like shooting from a long way away", and though he did get ahead, he ran wide and Marquez exited alongside him, and was half a length in front past the flag.

Luthi saved fourth, with Nakagami dropping away, but the main interest was on a pack of four going for sixth. As Baldassari and Rins disputed the front of it, Zarco picked his way past Folger and with six laps to go also Simone Corsi's Speed Up. But try as he might, he could get no further.

Simon, Pasini, Cortese and Syahrin finished in a close pack; Schrotter led the next to wrap up the final point.

With four races left, Lowes's win cut his deficit to 40 points, giving him "a little bit of hope"; Zarco's lead over Rins dropped to just one point. The fight was closing up ominously for the Frenchman's hope of becoming the first double Moto2 champion.

MOTO3 RACE – 20 laps

Navarro's triumph followed a typically fierce Moto3 race, with four leaders only breaking free from a pack of 11 in the final couple of laps.

Bastianini led an all-Honda front row, and it was another Honda – Navarro's EG machine – that took the lead from him on lap one, and the pair disputed the position at the head of the usual brawl. Binder was constantly near the front, but it was Oettl who took over for two laps before Binder led over the line for the first time on lap nine.

By then, super-rookie Mir had joined the front battle, from 24th on the grid, while another, Bulega, had been the innocent victim of a three-bike crash (with Herrera and Kornfeil) on lap one.

Also prominent up front were Martin and two more hot rookies, Canet and Di Giannantonio, who took the lead on lap 14.

In the last four laps, Navarro, Binder, Bastianini and Di Giannantonio broke free, still exchanging paint and places to the end, crossing the line in that order, within 0.162 of a second.

Mir led the pursuit, 1.5 seconds behind, from Martin (suffering painful foot injuries), team-mates Rodrigo and Guevara, Oettl and Migno, fifth to eleventh within 1.3 seconds.

Quartararo was a lone 12th, while McPhee won a four-bike battle for the last points, from Antonelli, Bendsneyder and the luckless Bagnaia, out of the points by mere inches.

With Binder unassailable, the championship battle was for second, between Navarro, Bastianini and potentially also rookies Mir and Bulega.

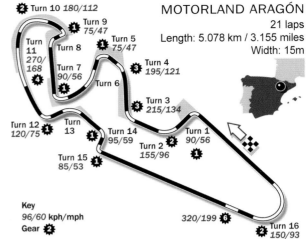

GRAN PREMIO MOVISTAR DE ARAGÓN

23-25 SEPTEMBER, 2016

MOTORLAND ARAGÓN
21 laps
Length: 5.078 km / 3.155 miles
Width: 15m

Turn 10 180/112
Turn 9 75/47
Turn 5 75/47
Turn 11 270/168
Turn 8
Turn 7 90/56
Turn 6
Turn 4 195/121
Turn 3 215/134
Turn 12 120/75
Turn 13
Turn 14 95/59
Turn 2 155/96
Turn 1 90/56
Turn 15 85/53
Turn 16 150/93

Key
96/60 kph/mph
320/199
Gear ⚙

MotoGP — RACE DISTANCE: 23 laps, 72.572 miles/116.794km · RACE WEATHER: Dry (air 22°C, humidity 58%, track 36°C)

Pos.	Rider	Nat.	No.	Entrant	Machine	Tyres	Race tyre choice	Laps	Time & speed
1	**Marc Marquez**	SPA	93	Repsol Honda Team	Honda RC213V	M	F: Hard/R: Hard	23	41m 57.678s
									103.8mph/
									167.0km/h
2	**Jorge Lorenzo**	SPA	99	Movistar Yamaha MotoGP	Yamaha YZR-M1	M	F: Medium/R: Hard	23	42m 00.418s
3	**Valentino Rossi**	ITA	46	Movistar Yamaha MotoGP	Yamaha YZR-M1	M	F: Medium/R: Hard	23	42m 03.661s
4	**Maverick Vinales**	SPA	25	Team SUZUKI ECSTAR	Suzuki GSX-RR	M	F: Hard/R: Hard	23	42m 05.916s
5	**Cal Crutchlow**	GBR	35	LCR Honda	Honda RC213V	M	F: Hard/R: Hard	23	42m 10.899s
6	**Dani Pedrosa**	SPA	26	Repsol Honda Team	Honda RC213V	M	F: Medium/R: Hard	23	42m 14.750s
7	**Aleix Espargaro**	SPA	41	Team SUZUKI ECSTAR	Suzuki GSX-RR	M	F: Medium/R: Hard	23	42m 16.200s
8	**Pol Espargaro**	SPA	44	Monster Yamaha Tech 3	Yamaha YZR-M1	M	F: Medium/R: Hard	23	42m 17.110s
9	**Alvaro Bautista**	SPA	19	Aprilia Racing Team Gresini	Aprilia RS-GP	M	F: Medium/R: Medium	23	42m 20.749s
10	**Stefan Bradl**	GER	6	Aprilia Racing Team Gresini	Aprilia RS-GP	M	F: Medium/R: Medium	23	42m 25.576s
11	**Andrea Dovizioso**	ITA	4	Ducati Team	Ducati Desmosedici	M	F: Medium/R: Medium	23	42m 30.126s
12	**Michele Pirro**	ITA	51	Ducati Team	Ducati Desmosedici	M	F: Medium/R: Medium	23	42m 32.711s
13	**Hector Barbera**	SPA	8	Avintia Racing	Ducati Desmosedici	M	F: Medium/R: Medium	23	42m 33.902s
14	**Eugene Laverty**	IRL	50	Pull & Bear Aspar Team	Ducati Desmosedici	M	F: Medium/R: Medium	23	42m 35.299s
15	**Nicky Hayden**	USA	69	Estrella Galicia 0,0 Marc VDS	Honda RC213V	M	F: Medium/R: Medium	23	42m 38.187s
16	**Yonny Hernandez**	COL	68	Pull & Bear Aspar Team	Ducati Desmosedici	M	F: Medium/R: Medium	23	42m 41.584s
17	Danilo Petrucci	ITA	9	OCTO Pramac Yakhnich	Ducati Desmosedici	M	F: Medium/R: Medium	23	42m 54.418s
18	Loris Baz	FRA	76	Avintia Racing	Ducati Desmosedici	M	F: Medium/R: Medium	23	42m 57.359s
19	Scott Redding	GBR	45	OCTO Pramac Yakhnich	Ducati Desmosedici	M	F: Medium/R: Medium	23	43m 31.804s
	Tito Rabat	SPA	53	Estrella Galicia 0,0 Marc VDS	Honda RC213V	M	F: Medium/R: Medium	16	DNF-crash
	Alex Lowes	GBR	22	Monster Yamaha Tech 3	Yamaha YZR-M1	M	-	-	DNS-injured
	Andrea Iannone	ITA	29	Ducati Team	Ducati Desmosedici	M	-	-	DNS-injured

Fastest lap: Marc Marquez, on lap 15, 1m 48.694s, 104.5mph/168.1km/h.

Lap record: Jorge Lorenzo, SPA (Yamaha), 1m 48.120s, 105.0mph/169.0km/h (2015).

Event best maximum speed: Andrea Dovizioso, 213.5mph/343.6km/h (race).

Qualifying

Weather: Dry
Air Temp: 26° **Track Temp:** 42°
Humidity: 41%

1	Marquez	1m 47.117s
2	Vinales	1m 47.748s
3	Lorenzo	1m 47.778s
4	Dovizioso	1m 47.819s
5	Crutchlow	1m 47.843s
6	Rossi	1m 47.951s
7	Pedrosa	1m 48.017s
8	A. Espargaro	1m 48.230s
9	Petrucci	1m 48.236s
10	Redding	1m 48.242s
11	P Espargaro	1m 48.448s
12	Bradl	1m 49.083s
13	Barbera	1m 48.699s
14	Bautista	1m 48.904s
15	Hernandez	1m 48.954s
16	Laverty	1m 49.052s
17	Pirro	1m 49.139s
18	Rabat	1m 49.319s
19	Hayden	1m 49.490s
20	Baz	1m 49.841s
	Lowes	No Time

Fastest race laps

1	Marquez	1m 48.694s
2	Rossi	1m 48.729s
3	Lorenzo	1m 49.050s
4	Vinales	1m 49.064s
5	Crutchlow	1m 49.309s
6	A. Espargaro	1m 49.318s
7	Dovizioso	1m 49.422s
8	Pedrosa	1m 49.509s
9	P. Espargaro	1m 49.580s
10	Bautista	1m 49.626s
11	Bradl	1m 49.752s
12	Barbera	1m 49.955s
13	Hernandez	1m 50.114s
14	Petrucci	1m 50.121s
15	Pirro	1m 50.155s
16	Rabat	1m 50.227s
17	Laverty	1m 50.236s
18	Hayden	1m 50.362s
19	Redding	1m 50.853s
20	Baz	1m 51.007s

Championship Points

1	Marquez	248
2	Rossi	196
3	Lorenzo	182
4	Pedrosa	155
5	Vinales	149
6	Crutchlow	105
7	Dovizioso	104
8	Iannone	96
9	P. Espargaro	96
10	Barbera	84
11	Laverty	71
12	A. Espargaro	69
13	Redding	55
14	Bautista	54
15	Petrucci	50
16	Bradl	49
17	Miller	42
18	Smith	42
19	Pirro	36
20	Rabat	27
21	Baz	24
22	Hernandez	13
23	Lowes	3
24	Hayden	1

Grid order / lap chart

Grid order	1	2	3	4	5	6	7	8	9	10	11	12	13	14	15	16	17	18	19	20	21	22	23	
93 MARQUEZ	25	93	25	25	25	25	25	25	46	46	46	93	93	93	93	93	93	93	93	93	93	93	93	1
25 VINALES	93	25	99	99	99	46	46	46	25	93	93	46	46	46	46	46	46	46	99	99	99	99	99	2
99 LORENZO	99	99	46	46	46	99	93	93	93	99	99	99	99	99	99	99	99	99	46	46	46	46	46	3
4 DOVIZIOSO	46	46	4	4	93	93	99	99	99	25	25	25	25	25	25	25	25	25	25	25	25	25	25	4
35 CRUTCHLOW	4	4	93	93	4	41	41	41	41	41	26	26	26	26	26	35	35	35	35	35	35	35	35	5
46 ROSSI	41	41	41	41	41	4	4	4	26	26	35	35	35	35	35	35	26	26	41	41	41	41	26	6
26 PEDROSA	26	26	26	26	26	26	26	26	35	35	41	41	41	41	41	41	41	41	26	26	26	26	41	7
41 A. ESPARGARO	35	35	35	35	35	35	35	35	4	4	4	4	4	4	4	44	44	44	44	44	44	44	44	8
9 PETRUCCI	9	9	6	44	44	44	44	44	44	44	44	44	44	44	44	4	4	19	19	19	19	19	19	9
45 REDDING	6	6	44	6	6	6	6	19	19	19	19	19	19	19	19	19	19	4	4	4	4	6	6	10
44 P. ESPARGARO	68	68	9	19	19	19	19	6	6	6	6	6	6	6	6	6	6	6	6	6	4	4		11
6 BRADL	44	44	19	9	68	68	68	68	68	68	68	51	50	50	50	51	51	51	51	51	51	51		12
8 BARBERA	19	19	68	68	9	50	50	50	51	51	51	68	68	68	51	50	50	50	50	50	50	8		13
19 BAUTISTA	69	69	50	50	50	9	51	51	50	50	50	50	51	51	68	68	68	8	8	8	8	50		14
68 HERNANDEZ	51	50	69	69	51	51	9	69	69	69	8	8	8	8	8	8	69	69	69	69	69	69		15
50 LAVERTY	50	51	51	51	69	69	69	9	8	8	69	69	69	53	69	68	68	68	68	68	68			
51 PIRRO	76	76	8	8	8	8	8	8	9	53	53	53	53	53	69	76	76	76	76	9	9			
53 RABAT	53	53	53	53	53	53	53	53	53	76	76	76	76	76	76	9	9	9	9	76	76			
69 HAYDEN	8	8	76	76	76	76	76	76	76	9	9	9	9	9	45	45	45	45	45	45	45			
76 BAZ	45	45	45	45	45	45	45	45	45	45	45	45	45	45										

9 Ride-through penalty

Constructor Points

1	Honda	291
2	Yamaha	278
3	Ducati	187
4	Suzuki	155
5	Aprilia	72

Moto2

RACE DISTANCE: 21 laps, 66.262 miles/106.638km · RACE WEATHER: Dry (air 22°C, humidity 62%, track 32°C)

Pos.	Rider	Nat.	No.	Entrant	Machine	Laps	Time & Speed
1	**Sam Lowes**	GBR	22	Federal Oil Gresini Moto2	Kalex	21	40m 00.885s 99.3mph/ 159.8km/h
2	**Alex Marquez**	SPA	73	Estrella Galicia 0,0 Marc VDS	Kalex	21	40m 04.174s
3	**Franco Morbidelli**	ITA	21	Estrella Galicia 0,0 Marc VDS	Kalex	21	40m 04.206s
4	**Thomas Luthi**	SWI	12	Garage Plus Interwetten	Kalex	21	40m 06.066s
5	**Takaaki Nakagami**	JPN	30	IDEMITSU Honda Team Asia	Kalex	21	40m 11.607s
6	**Alex Rins**	SPA	40	Paginas Amarillas HP 40	Kalex	21	40m 13.049s
7	**Lorenzo Baldassarri**	ITA	7	Forward Team	Kalex	21	40m 13.270s
8	**Johann Zarco**	FRA	5	Ajo Motorsport	Kalex	21	40m 13.497s
9	**Simone Corsi**	ITA	24	Speed Up Racing	Speed Up	21	40m 14.889s
10	**Jonas Folger**	GER	94	Dynavolt Intact GP	Kalex	21	40m 19.049s
11	**Xavier Simeon**	BEL	19	QMMF Racing Team	Speed Up	21	40m 23.298s
12	**Mattia Pasini**	ITA	54	Italtrans Racing Team	Kalex	21	40m 23.556s
13	**Sandro Cortese**	GER	11	Dynavolt Intact GP	Kalex	21	40m 23.794s
14	**Hafizh Syahrin**	MAL	55	Petronas Raceline Malaysia	Kalex	21	40m 24.322s
15	**Marcel Schrotter**	GER	23	AGR Team	Kalex	21	40m 26.178s
16	Axel Pons	SPA	49	AGR Team	Kalex	21	40m 26.713s
17	Xavi Vierge	SPA	97	Tech 3 Racing	Tech 3	21	40m 27.289s
18	Steven Odendaal	RSA	4	AGR Team	Kalex	21	40m 27.410s
19	Remy Gardner	AUS	87	Tasca Racing Scuderia Moto2	Kalex	21	40m 31.226s
20	Jesko Raffin	SWI	2	Sports-Millions-EMWE-SAG	Kalex	21	40m 31.323s
21	Julian Simon	SPA	60	QMMF Racing Team	Speed Up	21	40m 31.390s
22	Dominique Aegerter	SWI	77	CarXpert Interwetten	Kalex	21	40m 42.652s
23	Tetsuta Nagashima	JPN	45	Ajo Motorsport Academy	Kalex	21	40m 42.904s
24	Edgar Pons	SPA	57	Paginas Amarillas HP 40	Kalex	21	40m 42.943s
25	Luca Marini	ITA	10	Forward Team	Kalex	21	40m 46.329s
26	Ratthapark Wilairot	THA	14	IDEMITSU Honda Team Asia	Kalex	21	40m 46.514s
27	Robin Mulhauser	SWI	70	CarXpert Interwetten	Kalex	21	40m 56.771s
28	Isaac Vinales	SPA	32	Tech 3 Racing	Tech 3	21	40m 56.774s
29	Danny Kent	GBR	52	Leopard Racing	Kalex	20	40m 46.807s
	Alan Techer	FRA	89	NTS T Pro Project	NTS	7	DNF

Fastest lap: Franco Morbidelli, on lap 4, 1m 53.672s, 99.9mph/160.8km/h.

Lap record: Alex Rins, SPA (Kalex), 1m 52.767s, 100.7mph/162.1km/h (2015).

Event best maximum speed: Thomas Luthi, 175.6mph/282.6km/h (warm-up).

Qualifying

Weather: Dry

Air Temp: 27° **Track Temp:** 43°

Humidity: 38%

1	Lowes	1m 53.207s
2	Marquez	1m 53.261s
3	Nakagami	1m 53.491s
4	Folger	1m 53.501s
5	Zarco	1m 53.659s
6	Baldassarri	1m 53.750s
7	Morbidelli	1m 53.844s
8	Luthi	1m 53.998s
9	A. Pons	1m 54.001s
10	Pasini	1m 54.027s
11	Corsi	1m 54.075s
12	Syahrin	1m 54.154s
13	Rins	1m 54.163s
14	Cortese	1m 54.199s
15	Simon	1m 54.240s
16	Schrotter	1m 54.312s
17	Simeon	1m 54.350s
18	Odendaal	1m 54.761s
19	Aegerter	1m 54.764s
20	Vierge	1m 54.775s
21	Nagashima	1m 54.830s
22	Raffin	1m 54.959s
23	E. Pons	1m 54.984s
24	Mulhauser	1m 54.998s
25	Gardner	1m 55.068s
26	Techer	1m 55.088s
27	Marini	1m 55.096s
28	Kent	1m 55.245s
29	Wilairot	1m 55.548s
30	Vinales	1m 56.363s
	Oliveira	No Time

Fastest race laps

1	Morbidelli	1m 53.672s
2	Lowes	1m 53.746s
3	Luthi	1m 53.765s
4	Rins	1m 53.875s
5	Marquez	1m 53.913s
6	Nakagami	1m 54.092s
7	Corsi	1m 54.113s
8	Baldassarri	1m 54.248s
9	Folger	1m 54.263s
10	Pasini	1m 54.398s
11	Zarco	1m 54.426s
12	Schrotter	1m 54.498s
13	Cortese	1m 54.604s
14	Simeon	1m 54.665s
15	Syahrin	1m 54.765s
16	Vierge	1m 54.815s
17	Odendaal	1m 54.876s
18	A. Pons	1m 54.961s
19	Raffin	1m 54.974s
20	Simon	1m 55.006s
21	Kent	1m 55.073s
22	Gardner	1m 55.088s
23	Aegerter	1m 55.174s
24	E. Pons	1m 55.273s
25	Nagashima	1m 55.278s
26	Mulhauser	1m 55.383s
27	Wilairot	1m 55.463s
28	Techer	1m 55.493s
29	Marini	1m 55.565s
30	Vinales	1m 55.858s

Championship Points

1	Zarco	202
2	Rins	201
3	Lowes	162
4	Luthi	154
5	Morbidelli	141
6	Nakagami	135
7	Folger	133
8	Syahrin	103
9	Baldassarri	99
10	Corsi	74
11	Aegerter	71
12	Marquez	60
13	Pasini	54
14	A. Pons	47
15	Schrotter	44
16	Salom	37
17	Simeon	34
18	Cortese	34
19	Oliveira	33
20	Simon	32
21	Kent	28
22	Marini	23
23	Vierge	14
24	Vinales	12
25	Raffin	11
26	West	6
27	Gardner	5
28	Wilairot	5
29	Mulhauser	4
30	E. Pons	2

Constructor Points

1	Kalex	350
2	Speed Up	107
3	Tech 3	24
4	Suter	6

Moto3

RACE DISTANCE: 20 laps, 63.106 miles/101.560km · RACE WEATHER: Dry (air 21°C, humidity 67%, track 27°C)

Pos.	Rider	Nat.	No.	Entrant	Machine	Laps	Time & Speed
1	**Jorge Navarro**	SPA	9	Estrella Galicia 0,0	Honda	20	39m 56.973s 94.8mph/ 152.5km/h
2	**Brad Binder**	RSA	41	Red Bull KTM Ajo	KTM	20	39m 57.003s
3	**Enea Bastianini**	ITA	33	Gresini Racing Moto3	Honda	20	39m 57.080s
4	**Fabio Di Giannantonio**	ITA	4	Gresini Racing Moto3	Honda	20	39m 57.135s
5	**Joan Mir**	SPA	36	Leopard Racing	KTM	20	39m 58.697s
6	**Jorge Martin**	SPA	88	Gaviota Mahindra ASPAR	Mahindra	20	39m 58.876s
7	**Aron Canet**	SPA	44	Estrella Galicia 0,0	Honda	20	39m 58.952s
8	**Gabriel Rodrigo**	ARG	19	RBA Racing Team	KTM	20	39m 59.981s
9	**Juanfran Guevara**	SPA	58	RBA Racing Team	KTM	20	40m 00.074s
10	**Philipp Oettl**	GER	65	Schedl GP Racing	KTM	20	40m 00.532s
11	**Andrea Migno**	ITA	16	SKY Racing Team VR46	KTM	20	40m 00.567s
12	**Fabio Quartararo**	FRA	20	Leopard Racing	KTM	20	40m 03.856s
13	**John McPhee**	GBR	17	Peugeot MC Saxoprint	Peugeot	20	40m 06.715s
14	**Niccolo Antonelli**	ITA	23	Ongetta-Rivacold	Honda	20	40m 06.731s
15	**Bo Bendsneyder**	NED	64	Red Bull KTM Ajo	KTM	20	40m 06.749s
16	Francesco Bagnaia	ITA	21	Gaviota Mahindra ASPAR	Mahindra	20	40m 06.904s
17	Andrea Locatelli	ITA	55	Leopard Racing	KTM	20	40m 10.331s
18	Livio Loi	BEL	11	RW Racing GP BV	Honda	20	40m 10.618s
19	Jules Danilo	FRA	95	Ongetta-Rivacold	Honda	20	40m 15.749s
20	Hiroki Ono	JPN	76	Honda Team Asia	Honda	20	40m 19.166s
21	Tatsuki Suzuki	JPN	24	CIP-Unicom Starker	Mahindra	20	40m 19.773s
22	Khairul Idham Pawi	MAL	89	Honda Team Asia	Honda	20	40m 27.432s
23	Adam Norrodin	MAL	7	Drive M7 SIC Racing Team	Honda	20	40m 27.722s
24	Albert Arenas	SPA	12	Peugeot MC Saxoprint	Peugeot	20	40m 33.483s
25	Lorenzo dalla Porta	ITA	48	SKY Racing Team VR46	KTM	20	40m 40.001s
26	Darryn Binder	RSA	40	Platinum Bay Real Estate	Mahindra	20	40m 40.414s
27	Marcos Ramirez	SPA	42	Platinum Bay Real Estate	Mahindra	20	40m 40.451s
28	Maria Herrera	SPA	6	MH6 Team	KTM	20	41m 07.597s
29	Lorenzo Petrarca	ITA	77	3570 Team Italia	Mahindra	20	41m 11.171s
30	Gabriel Martinez-Abrego	MEX	18	Motomex Team Worldwide Race	Mahindra	20	41m 42.908s
	Stefano Valtulini	ITA	43	3570 Team Italia	Mahindra	9	DNF
	Nicolo Bulega	ITA	8	SKY Racing Team VR46	KTM	0	DNF
	Jakub Kornfeil	CZE	84	Drive M7 SIC Racing Team	Honda	0	DNF
	Fabio Spiranelli	ITA	3	CIP-Unicom Starker	Mahindra	0	DNF

Fastest lap: Juanfran Guevara, on lap 5, 1m 58.858s, 95.6mph/153.8km/h.

Lap record: Niccolo Antonelli, ITA (Honda), 1m 58.726s, 95.6mph/153.9km/h (2015).

Event best maximum speed: Khairul Idham Pawi, 148.9mph/239.7km/h (race).

Qualifying

Weather: Dry

Air Temp: 25° **Track Temp:** 35°

Humidity: 46%

1	Bastianini	1m 58.293s
2	Navarro	1m 58.506s
3	Loi	1m 58.521s
4	Rodrigo	1m 58.592s
5	Canet	1m 58.758s
6	Oettl	1m 58.787s
7	B. Binder	1m 58.841s
8	Quartararo	1m 58.929s
9	Ono	1m 58.943s
10	Bendsneyder	1m 58.978s
11	Martin	1m 59.032s
12	Dalla Porta	1m 59.046s
13	Di Giannantonio	1m 59.083s
14	Migno	1m 59.087s
15	Guevara	1m 59.126s
16	Locatelli	1m 59.152s
17	McPhee	1m 59.189s
18	Bulega	1m 59.264s
19	Antonelli	1m 59.326s
20	Danilo	1m 59.348s
21	Bagnaia	1m 59.371s
22	Arenas	1m 59.395s
23	Pawi	1m 59.406s
24	Herrera	1m 59.564s
25	Suzuki	1m 59.674s
26	Kornfeil	1m 59.705s
27	Mir	1m 59.795s
28	D. Binder	1m 59.848s
29	Ramirez	2m 00.047s
30	Norrodin	2m 00.606s
31	Spiranelli	2m 00.950s
32	Valtulini	2m 01.125s
33	Petrarca	2m 01.668s
34	Martinez-Abrego	2m 03.628s

Fastest race laps

1	Guevara	1m 58.858s
2	Mir	1m 58.922s
3	Martin	1m 58.953s
4	Di Giannantonio	1m 58.997s
5	Migno	1m 58.998s
6	Bastianini	1m 59.075s
7	Oettl	1m 59.132s
8	Canet	1m 59.138s
9	Antonelli	1m 59.156s
10	Loi	1m 59.164s
11	Quartararo	1m 59.195s
12	B. Binder	1m 59.238s
13	Navarro	1m 59.239s
14	Rodrigo	1m 59.270s
15	McPhee	1m 59.306s
16	Bagnaia	1m 59.378s
17	Locatelli	1m 59.500s
18	Danilo	1m 59.567s
19	Bendsneyder	1m 59.609s
20	Ono	1m 59.673s
21	D. Binder	1m 59.813s
22	Suzuki	1m 59.889s
23	Pawi	2m 00.057s
24	Arenas	2m 00.080s
25	Norrodin	2m 00.098s
26	Ramirez	2m 00.099s
27	Dalla Porta	2m 00.188s
28	Herrera	2m 01.164s
29	Petrarca	2m 02.275s
30	Valtulini	2m 03.027s
31	Martinez-Abrego	2m 04.042s

Championship Points

1	B. Binder	249
2	Navarro	143
3	Bastianini	139
4	Mir	117
5	Bulega	113
6	Di Giannantonio	111
7	Bagnaia	110
8	Fenati	93
9	Antonelli	81
10	Kornfeil	80
11	Locatelli	65
12	Oettl	62
13	Canet	60
14	Martin	56
15	Quartararo	56
16	Pawi	54
17	Bendsneyder	53
18	Danilo	51
19	McPhee	48
20	Migno	47
21	Guevara	40
22	Loi	35
23	Ono	28
24	Rodrigo	22
25	Manzi	13
26	Suzuki	12
27	Dalla Porta	7
28	Herrera	6
29	Norrodin	5
30	D. Binder	4

Constructor Points

1	KTM	296
2	Honda	276
3	Mahindra	157
4	Peugeot	48

JAPANESE GRAND PRIX

TWIN RING MOTEGI

Marquez was in total command, and
the fruitless pursuit by the Yamaha
pair ended in the gravel.
Photo: Gold & Goose

Above: High fives for Marquez and his Repsol Honda crew.

Top right: Petrucci just held off Redding in their battle for the single 2017 Ducati factory bike.

Centre, clockwise from top left: Hiroki Ono took pole, but was given a grid penalty. Worse was to come – disqualification from the podium; Australian Superbiker Mike Jones acquitted himself well in his first GP; Dani Pedrosa tries the 1966 RC181 Honda for size; Hiroshi Aoyama took over Pedrosa's factory Honda after he was injured in practice.

Below right: Vinales delighted Suzuki big-wigs with a podium, the factory's first at Honda's track since 2000.

Photos: Gold & Goose and HRC

MOTEGI gave meaning to the phrase 'Always expect the unexpected'. The mathematical possibilities were clear – to become unassailable, Marquez needed to win, for Lorenzo to finish lower than fourth and Rossi no higher than 15th. But, as Marquez himself said on race eve, "It's almost impossible."

"Almost" proved good enough. His Honda's weaknesses finally under control, thanks partly to 120 laps of post-race testing at Aragon, Marquez won in dominant style.

Both Yamaha riders paid the price of pushing too hard. Rossi was the first to go, after only six laps. He didn't feel he'd been too wide or too fast at the hairpin, but his front Michelin felt differently.

Lorenzo lasted longer, but suffered the same fate. By then, he was under steady pressure from Dovizioso. It was a familiar tale: no warning, no feedback – and no front grip.

Marquez may not have expected the unexpected, but his team was ready anyway, with T-shirts – 'Give Me Five' for his fifth title – and a special gold-liveried helmet. "They believed in me," said the gratified Spaniard, who credited much of his calm and measured approach to the season to his team's friendship and support, meaning that "I didn't think about the other riders".

It was a gratifying climax to a generally punishing weekend, with many crashes, some crucial. One victim was Alex Rins, on day one, reawakening his shoulder injuries. He qualified 22nd, made a blazing start, but crashed again on only the third corner. Zarco wasn't able to win Moto2, thanks to a splendid weekend for Thomas Luthi. But he regained a measure of control in the points, stretching his advantage from one to 21. With Sam Lowes also crashing out again, and with two consecutive weekends to come, Rins's problems were unlikely to go away.

The worst hurt was Pedrosa, whose propensity for injury meant another broken collarbone after a vicious high-sider at the notorious 90-Degree Corner. He flew home directly for screws and plates. As it happened, 250 champion Hiroshi Aoyama was at the track, and he was pressed into service on the factory bike from Saturday.

Miraculously, Lorenzo suffered no fractures from an equally spectacular high-side during Friday morning's FP3. "I flew many metres," he said. He was stretchered off and later taken in a wheelchair to hospital for a CT scan. But although beaten up, he was relatively unscathed, and back for FP4 and to qualify third.

Eugene Laverty had a similarly brutal crash, and he too was helicoptered to hospital, where the CT scan cleared him to return, only to fall again in the race.

There were many others in the gravel traps, notably the returned Jack Miller – three times in practice and again in the race. At least he understood why his fourth front-wheel washout had occurred. "I braked a little too late in Turn One, tried to stay on line, but I was a little too fast."

Iannone might have been glad he'd stayed away, on his own doctor's advice to avoid risk to his still not fully healed spinal injury. It was all rather last minute: he had informed Ducati only the previous Sunday, promising a Phillip Island return and occasioning a frantic reshuffle. With Pirro engaged testing 2017's bike, Barbera was drafted in from the Avintia team alongside Dovi. His factory-liveried leathers arrived only in time for race day.

His replacement was another scramble, 2015 Australian Superbike Champion Michael Jones. He arrived on Thursday night and climbed on to a MotoGP bike for the first time for FP1 on Friday. He acquitted himself creditably, gaining speed steadily to qualify ahead of Aoyama, who fell in Q1, and fulfilling his ambition of finishing the race. Last, but a finish.

Bradley Smith was back for his own brave showing: his difficulty was not pain, but limited movement in his right knee. He qualified a solid 15th and finished 13th. "No physiotherapy can replicate what a MotoGP bike does to you," he said.

Brembo statistics illustrated the physical punishment of the stop-and-go circuit: with a best lap of 1m 40s, 33 seconds – almost a third of that time – were spent on the brakes. Now the relative weakness of Michelin's front paid some dividends, said Rossi. "You braked much harder with the Bridgestones," he explained.

Aprilia had another engine upgrade, and almost got both

bikes through to Q2, but Bradl crashed at the end of a final lap that would have given him top spot ahead of team-mate Bautista. The latter went on to record the marque's best finish, seventh, aided by both Yamahas crashing, but well-earned.

Yamaha Racing chief Lin Jarvis felt obliged to call a special conference to try to quash rumours of a feud within Yamaha. This related to the fact that while they had "played the game", allowing Lorenzo to test his 2017 Ducati at the official two-day IRTA sessions at Valencia, in the same way that Vinales would test his Yamaha and Iannone his Suzuki, they had refused permission for him to join Ducati's private sessions later in November at Jerez. It was normal business practice, said Jarvis, adding that since Ducati was a major rival, there was no reason for Yamaha to give them extra help. "It would be like giving your hand and someone takes your whole arm".

More stringent, even draconian, new penalties were announced in the effort to stop Moto3 riders from dawdling on track, waiting to pick up a tow in qualifying. A rider going slower than 110 per cent of his best time in any three sectors was previously dropped three grid places, more for repeat offenders. Now it would be 12 places plus one point; do so again at the same event, and it would be back of the grid and two points; again, and it would be a pit-lane start and four points; a fourth time would lead to disqualification.

Japan's top Moto3 rider, Hiroki Ono, fell foul for other reasons, and heartbreakingly. First he was robbed of a home-race pole because of dangerous riding on the first day of practice – down three places. Then he lost a hard-earned podium, his first, when he was found to be below the minimum bike/rider weight limit after the race; he was disqualified.

Dominique Aegerter was out of Moto2, after being "released" by his CarXpert team for having signed to join Leopard in 2017, where he would welcome a return to a Suter chassis. This broke a verbal agreement, said the team.

Oliveira pulled out of the Moto3 race after essaying five laps in FP1, the hard braking punishing his still-fresh collarbone injury from Aragon.

Finally, Honda celebrated the 50th anniversary of its entry into the premier class in 1966 with a display of the seminal four-cylinder RC181 racer, which had won its first race with Jim Redman on board. Not even Mike Hailwood, however, could wrest the title from Agostini and the MV Agusta, and after 1967 Honda pulled out until returning in 1979 with the unsuccessful oval-piston NR500.

MOTOGP RACE – 24 laps

Marquez was strong through practice (along with a flying Aleix Espargaro and Dovizioso) and appeared set for pole, until Rossi managed to pick on Vinales as a target ahead of him and set the first lap inside 1m 44s. Marquez might have topped that, but muffed a couple of laps, then lost his last to yellow flags after Crutchlow fell, very mindful (he said) of having crashed and been censured, as well as injured, under yellows at Silverstone in 2014.

Lorenzo was third; Dovi, Crutchlow and Aleix filled row two; Vinales led the third from Barbera and the other Espargaro.

Marquez led away, but Lorenzo took over aggressively at Turn Two. He was able to stretch a small, but clear advantage as the Honda rider and Rossi traded blows in his wake.

Marquez observed later that while Rossi's strategy – to try to win – had been correct, "he was riding a bit strangely – braking late and going wide. I thought he was a bit nervous, and I didn't want that battle, so I pushed to get away."

On lap four, he was ahead also of Lorenzo and soon moving firmly clear, setting fastest lap on the sixth, just short of the record. Rossi also passed his team-mate in pursuit and was just less than a second adrift when he started lap seven. He wouldn't finish it, ending up in the gravel outside the hairpin, looking nonplussed, one leg trapped under his

Yamaha. "Sincerely, I felt nothing like I was going into the corner too wide or too deep. But I lost the front, so logically I made a mistake."

Marquez was untouchable: two seconds clear of Lorenzo by lap nine and better than three on the 12th. Now his strategy changed and he focused on controlling the gap.

So too Lorenzo, who knew he couldn't catch him – but now Dovizioso was closing and he had to press on to try to preserve second. On lap 20, it was his turn to push harder into Turn Nine than before, "and the front tyre didn't give me any support or feedback, and I crashed." Had he chosen the soft front, he thought, he might have been able to challenge for victory.

Instead, like most, he was on the medium front. Only Crutchlow and Baz had a hard front. Aoyama, Barbera, Hernandez, Smith and Jones took the soft option. There was less variety in rear choice, all going for the soft, except for Hernandez (medium).

Thus Dovizioso inherited second. He'd spent the first five laps stuck behind on-form Aleix Espargaro. Once he'd got by, the Ducati rider set to work on catching Lorenzo, around a second ahead. It was a remorseless, but gradual process, finally resolved only when Lorenzo crashed in front of him.

Espargaro had lost touch after lap 16 and fell back into the clutches of team-mate Vinales, who'd been saving his tyres after a poor start. Espargaro resisted manfully, and it took a couple of laps to make a pass stick. By the 19th, Vinales was ahead and going away for a safe and satisfying Suzuki rostrum.

Crutchlow had been hounding Vinales, confident that his hard front tyre would pay dividends later in the race, but a run-off on lap 12 cost him more than five seconds. He finished fifth, behind the second Suzuki. "But for that mistake, I think I could have fought for the podium," he said.

Pol Espargaro was a lonely sixth, the Monster rider nonetheless the top Yamaha.

There had been a lively battle behind him, with Bautista emerging from it just before half-distance to secure seventh, his and Aprilia's best so far.

He left the uneasy Pramac Ducati team-mates locked together, with second Aprilia rider Bradl losing touch in the closing stages for tenth.

Battling to earn 2017's single factory bike, Petrucci and Redding had plenty at stake. The Italian claimed eighth, Redding three-hundredths behind him, as he had been pretty much all race long, at least over the line.

Factory Yamaha wild-card Katsuyuki Nakasuga was an undramatic 11th, comfortably clear of Hernandez, who in turn was kept honest by brave Bradley Smith.

Rabat was a close 14th; Aoyama took the last point, five seconds clear of Baz.

Barbera, on the factory Ducati, had been chasing Pol Espargaro when he slipped off. He remounted in last and eventually got back ahead of his own replacement, Jones, who piloted the independent Ducati to a steady 18th.

Miller fell shortly after losing touch with the Petrucci/Redding gang; Laverty was an early faller.

MOTO2 RACE – 23 laps

Crashes defined the Moto2 race. The championship had been closing up. On the first lap, that changed, when Rins crashed on only the third corner. And again next time around, when more distant challenger Sam Lowes slipped off, having just got ahead of points leader and deadly rival Zarco.

They did not define the victory. Zarco may have denied pole to a hitherto dominant Luthi, but he couldn't stop the Swiss rider from leading start to finish, try as he might.

The first laps were lively, with Morbidelli in close pursuit of first-away Luthi, while Lowes had pushed past Zarco to third when he fell at Turn Ten, the far hairpin, unable to understand why. After his win at Aragon, this finally annulled his slim, but growing title hopes.

Now Nakagami had also got ahead of Zarco; but there would be no further threat, with Axel Pons a little way back in fifth, and then a gang led by Cortese. His Dynavolt team-mate, Folger, was four places behind, but he too crashed out on lap five.

Above: Enea Bastianini snatched the Moto3 race win from Binder at the last gasp.

Right: On a weekend of many crashes, luckless Jorge Navarro dislocated his shoulder on the first corner in Moto3.

Photos: Gold & Goose

By half-distance, Morbidelli's close pursuit of Luthi was over and he was falling back into the hands of Nakagami. A couple of laps later, Zarco got ahead of the pair of them in one lap. He was less than two seconds down on Luthi, and the chase was on.

It looked like he might do it, and he even started the last lap less than half a second adrift. But Luthi had got the message and had matters under control. The former 125 champion took his third win of the season by less than four-tenths, but it was enough.

"I really expected I could catch him, and that he would get tired, because I am always strong when the tyres are used," said the Frenchman. "But he won."

And Luthi: "Even before the race, I remembered how Zarco took my lead on the last lap in Malaysia last year, but this time I was ready."

Nakagami and Morbidelli had a battle royal on the last lap for third, changing places four times – but it went to the Italian over the line.

Pons had crashed after losing fifth to Cortese on lap 11, leaving the German alone.

A four-strong battle behind raged until close to the end, with Simone Corsi snatching sixth from Pasini on the last lap; Simon was inches behind, and Marcel Schrotter off the back of it by the end.

Xavier Simeon was a safe tenth after passing Vierge's Tech 3 six laps from the end; a couple of seconds behind, Marini took 12th off Syahrin on the last lap. The last points went to Nagashima and Vinales, who had also swapped on the final lap.

Baldassari and Alex Marquez crashed out; Kent retired with a broken gear lever.

Misfortune for his rivals reversed Zarco's dwindling title fortunes and put Luthi in a position of faint hope.

Above: Luthi in control: Zarco attacked, but had to take second, extending his title lead.

Left: The plucky Rins crashed again on lap one. He remounted, but scored no points.

Far left: Podium-bound: Dovizioso had a job getting past an on-form Espargaro.

Photos: Gold & Goose

MOTO3 RACE – 20 laps

A first-corner crash took some of the sting out of the first race of the day, but a thrilling battle through the last corners of the final lap made up for it.

The big victim was the ever-luckless Navarro, who also skittled McPhee and Rodrigo, and dislocated his shoulder.

Ono had topped qualifying, but his penalty had put him on row two and handed a first pole start to Migno, from Binder and Bastianini.

Migno got the jump off the line, but before the end of the lap, Binder was in front, and he would stay there almost all the way.

Bastianini and Mahindra's Bagnaia, from 12th on the grid, were with him, along with Migno, Ono and, after five laps, also Bulega, in a breakaway sextet. Bastianini was the strongest, Bagnaia ultimately the weakest, dropping away with six laps to go.

By the end, Binder had tried to escape, but Bastianini had closed the gap for a final duel. The Italian waited until 90-Degree Corner, outbraked Binder and took his first win of the year by 0.017 of a second. He also took over second in the championship.

Third appeared to have been settled earlier in the lap. Ono had led at the start, under severe pressure from Bulega; then Migno forced past his compatriot, only to touch Ono's back wheel. Migno crashed, Bulega lost crucial yards and Ono took a home podium, his career-best result. Then came heartbreak when the Japanese rider was disqualified because his bike/rider combined weight was found to be below the specified minimum.

Behind them, Oettl had fought through a midfield gang after early problems for an eventual fourth, his last victim Di Giannantonio; while a fading Bagnaia only narrowly clung on to sixth from Loi, with Quartararo, Mir and Antonelli close.

Dalla Porta, Norrodin, a distant Kornfeil, first-timer Arenas and Suzuki wrapped up the points; Canet, Locatelli and Valtulini crashed out; Martin retired with leg injuries.

MOTUL GRAND PRIX OF JAPAN

14-16 OCTOBER, 2016

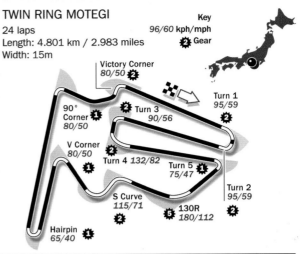

TWIN RING MOTEGI
24 laps
Length: 4.801 km / 2.983 miles
Width: 15m

Key
96/60 kph/mph
Gear

Victory Corner 80/50
Turn 1 95/59
90° Corner 80/50
Turn 3 90/56
V Corner 80/50
Turn 4 132/82
Turn 5 75/47
Turn 2 95/59
S Curve 115/71
130R 180/112
Hairpin 65/40

MotoGP

RACE DISTANCE: 24 laps, 71.597 miles/115.224km · RACE WEATHER: Dry (air 25°C, humidity 37%, track 36°C)

Pos.Rider	Nat.	No.	Entrant	Machine	Tyres	Race tyre choice	Laps	Time & speed
1 Marc Marquez	SPA	93	Repsol Honda Team	Honda RC213V	M	F: Medium/R: Soft	24	42m 34.610s
								100.8mph/
								162.3km/h
2 Andrea Dovizioso	ITA	4	Ducati Team	Ducati Desmosedici	M	F: Medium/R: Soft	24	42m 37.602s
3 Maverick Vinales	SPA	25	Team SUZUKI ECSTAR	Suzuki GSX-RR	M	F: Medium/R: Soft	24	42m 38.714s
4 Aleix Espargaro	SPA	41	Team SUZUKI ECSTAR	Suzuki GSX-RR	M	F: Medium/R: Soft	24	42m 39.336s
5 Cal Crutchlow	GBR	35	LCR Honda	Honda RC213V	M	F: Hard/R: Soft	24	42m 49.659s
6 Pol Espargaro	SPA	44	Monster Yamaha Tech 3	Yamaha YZR-M1	M	F: Medium/R: Soft	24	42m 54.264s
7 Alvaro Bautista	SPA	19	Aprilia Racing Team Gresini	Aprilia RS-GP	M	F: Medium/R: Soft	24	42m 57.642s
8 Danilo Petrucci	ITA	9	OCTO Pramac Yakhnich	Ducati Desmosedici	M	F: Medium/R: Soft	24	43m 03.165s
9 Scott Redding	GBR	45	OCTO Pramac Yakhnich	Ducati Desmosedici	M	F: Medium/R: Soft	24	43m 03.412s
10 Stefan Bradl	GER	6	Aprilia Racing Team Gresini	Aprilia RS-GP	M	F: Medium/R: Soft	24	43m 06.940s
11 Katsuyuki Nakasuga	JPN	21	Yamalube Yamaha Factory Racing	Yamaha YZR-M1	M	F: Medium/R: Soft	24	43m 17.455s
12 Yonny Hernandez	COL	68	Pull & Bear Aspar Team	Ducati Desmosedici	M	F: Soft/R: Medium	24	43m 26.829s
13 Bradley Smith	GBR	38	Monster Yamaha Tech 3	Yamaha YZR-M1	M	F: Soft/R: Soft	24	43m 28.393s
14 Tito Rabat	SPA	53	Estrella Galicia 0,0 Marc VDS	Honda RC213V	M	F: Medium/R: Soft	24	43m 29.370s
15 Hiroshi Aoyama	JPN	73	Repsol Honda Team	Honda RC213V	M	F: Soft/R: Soft	24	43m 34.765s
16 Loris Baz	FRA	76	Avintia Racing	Ducati Desmosedici	M	F: Hard/R: Soft	24	43m 39.050s
17 Hector Barbera	SPA	8	Ducati Team	Ducati Desmosedici	M	F: Soft/R: Soft	24	44m 17.576s
18 Mike Jones	AUS	7	Avintia Racing	Ducati Desmosedici	M	F: Soft/R: Soft	23	42m 51.865s
Jorge Lorenzo	SPA	99	Movistar Yamaha MotoGP	Yamaha YZR-M1	M	F: Medium/R: Soft	19	DNF-crash
Valentino Rossi	ITA	46	Movistar Yamaha MotoGP	Yamaha YZR-M1	M	F: Medium/R: Soft	6	DNF-crash
Jack Miller	AUS	43	Estrella Galicia 0,0 Marc VDS	Honda RC213V	M	F: Medium/R: Soft	6	DNF-crash
Eugene Laverty	IRL	50	Pull & Bear Aspar Team	Ducati Desmosedici	M	F: Medium/R: Soft	2	DNF-crash
Dani Pedrosa	SPA	26	Repsol Honda Team	Honda RC213V	M	–	–	DNS-injured

Fastest lap: Marc Marquez, on lap 6, 1m 45.576s, 101.7mph/163.7km/h.
Lap record: Jorge Lorenzo, SPA (Yamaha), 1m 45.350s, 101.9mph/164.0km/h (2014).
Event best maximum speed: Hector Barbera, 192.6mph/309.9km/h (qualifying).

Qualifying

Weather: Dry
Air Temp: 25° **Track Temp:** 34°
Humidity: 30%

1	Rossi	1m 43.954s
2	Marquez	1m 44.134s
3	Lorenzo	1m 44.221s
4	Dovizioso	1m 44.294s
5	Crutchlow	1m 44.402s
6	A. Espargaro	1m 44.494s
7	Vinales	1m 44.539s
8	Barbera	1m 44.980s
9	P. Espargaro	1m 45.232s
10	Petrucci	1m 45.782s
11	Redding	1m 45.827s
12	Bautista	No Time
13	Bradl	1m 45.823s
14	Miller	1m 46.347s
15	Smith	1m 46.593s
16	Nakasuga	1m 46.627s
17	Hernandez	1m 46.705s
18	Rabat	1m 46.753s
19	Laverty	1m 47.060s
20	Baz	1m 47.501s
21	Jones	1m 47.631s
22	Aoyama	1m 47.788s

Fastest race laps

1	Marquez	1m 45.576s
2	Rossi	1m 45.722s
3	Vinales	1m 45.791s
4	Crutchlow	1m 45.792s
5	Lorenzo	1m 45.819s
6	Dovizioso	1m 45.847s
7	A. Espargaro	1m 45.861s
8	P. Espargaro	1m 46.522s
9	Bradl	1m 46.568s
10	Barbera	1m 46.593s
11	Bautista	1m 46.741s
12	Redding	1m 46.752s
13	Petrucci	1m 46.865s
14	Miller	1m 47.099s
15	Nakasuga	1m 47.512s
16	Hernandez	1m 47.851s
17	Smith	1m 47.881s
18	Baz	1m 47.915s
19	Aoyama	1m 47.954s
20	Rabat	1m 47.966s
21	Laverty	1m 48.688s
22	Jones	1m 50.023s

Championship Points

1	Marquez	273
2	Rossi	196
3	Lorenzo	182
4	Vinales	165
5	Pedrosa	155
6	Dovizioso	124
7	Crutchlow	116
8	P. Espargaro	106
9	Iannone	96
10	Barbera	84
11	A. Espargaro	82
12	Laverty	71
13	Bautista	63
14	Redding	62
15	Petrucci	58
16	Bradl	55
17	Smith	45
18	Miller	42
19	Pirro	36
20	Rabat	29
21	Baz	24
22	Hernandez	17
23	Nakasuga	5
24	Lowes	3
25	Aoyama	1
26	Hayden	1

Constructor Points

1	Honda	316
2	Yamaha	288
3	Ducati	207
4	Suzuki	171
5	Aprilia	81

Grid order

Grid order		1	2	3	4	5	6	7	8	9	10	11	12	13	14	15	16	17	18	19	20	21	22	23	24	
46	ROSSI	99	99	99	93	93	93	93	93	93	93	93	93	93	93	93	93	93	93	93	93	93	93	93	93	1
93	MARQUEZ	93	93	93	99	99	46	99	99	99	99	99	99	99	99	99	99	99	99	99	4	4	4	4	4	2
99	LORENZO	46	46	46	46	46	99	4	4	4	4	4	4	4	4	4	4	4	4	4	25	25	25	25	25	3
4	DOVIZIOSO	41	41	41	41	41	4	41	41	41	41	41	41	41	41	41	41	41	41	41	41	41	41	41	41	4
35	CRUTCHLOW	4	4	4	4	4	41	25	25	25	25	25	25	25	25	25	25	25	25	41	35	35	35	35	35	5
41	A. ESPARGARO	35	25	25	25	25	25	35	35	35	35	35	35	35	35	35	35	35	35	35	44	44	44	44	44	6
25	VINALES	25	35	35	35	35	35	44	44	44	44	44	44	44	44	44	44	44	44	19	19	19	19	19		7
8	BARBERA	44	44	44	44	44	44	8	8	9	19	19	19	19	19	19	19	19	19	9	9	9	9	9		8
44	P. ESPARGARO	9	8	8	8	8	8	9	9	19	9	9	9	9	9	9	9	9	9	45	45	45	45	45		9
9	PETRUCCI	8	9	9	9	9	9	19	19	45	45	45	45	45	45	45	45	45	45	6	6	6	6	6		10
45	REDDING	19	19	19	19	19	19	45	45	6	6	6	6	6	6	6	6	6	6	21	21	21	21	21		11
19	BAUTISTA	43	45	45	45	45	45	6	6	21	21	21	21	21	21	21	21	21	21	68	68	68	68	68		12
6	BRADL	45	43	43	43	43	43	21	21	68	68	68	68	68	68	68	68	68	68	38	38	38	38	38		13
43	MILLER	50	6	6	6	6	6	68	68	38	38	38	38	38	38	38	38	38	38	53	53	53	53	53		14
38	SMITH	21	21	21	21	21	21	38	38	53	53	53	53	53	53	53	53	53	53	73	73	73	73	73		15
21	NAKASUGA	6	50	68	68	68	68	53	53	73	73	73	73	73	73	73	73	73	73	76	76	76	76	76		
68	HERNANDEZ	68	68	38	38	38	38	73	73	76	76	76	76	76	76	76	76	76	76	8	8	8	8	8		
53	RABAT	38	38	53	53	53	53	76	76	7	7	7	7	7	7	7	8	8	8	7	7	7	7			
50	LAVERTY	73	53	73	73	73	73	7	7	8	8	8	8	8	8	8	7	7	7							
76	BAZ	53	73	76	76	76	76																			
7	JONES	76	76	7	7	7	7																			
73	AOYAMA	7	7																							

7 Lapped rider

Moto2

RACE DISTANCE: 23 laps, 68.614 miles/110.423km · RACE WEATHER: Dry (air 23°C, humidity 30%, track 36°C)

Pos.	Rider	Nat.	No.	Entrant	Machine	Laps	Time & Speed
1	Thomas Luthi	SWI	12	Garage Plus Interwetten	Kalex	23	42m 45.854s / 96.3mph / 154.9km/h
2	Johann Zarco	FRA	5	Ajo Motorsport	Kalex	23	42m 46.240s
3	Franco Morbidelli	ITA	21	Estrella Galicia 0,0 Marc VDS	Kalex	23	42m 51.717s
4	Takaaki Nakagami	JPN	30	IDEMITSU Honda Team Asia	Kalex	23	42m 51.944s
5	Sandro Cortese	GER	11	Dynavolt Intact GP	Kalex	23	43m 02.100s
6	Simone Corsi	ITA	24	Speed Up Racing	Speed Up	23	43m 06.258s
7	Mattia Pasini	ITA	54	Italtrans Racing Team	Kalex	23	43m 06.537s
8	Julian Simon	SPA	60	QMMF Racing Team	Speed Up	23	43m 06.614s
9	Marcel Schrotter	GER	23	AGR Team	Kalex	23	43m 10.248s
10	Xavier Simeon	BEL	19	QMMF Racing Team	Speed Up	23	43m 12.967s
11	Xavi Vierge	SPA	97	Tech 3 Racing	Tech 3	23	43m 16.012s
12	Luca Marini	ITA	10	Forward Team	Kalex	23	43m 18.137s
13	Hafizh Syahrin	MAL	55	Petronas Raceline Malaysia	Kalex	23	43m 18.245s
14	Tetsuta Nagashima	JPN	45	Ajo Motorsport Academy	Kalex	23	43m 21.202s
15	Isaac Vinales	SPA	32	Tech 3 Racing	Tech 3	23	43m 21.340s
16	Edgar Pons	SPA	57	Paginas Amarillas HP 40	Kalex	23	43m 25.412s
17	Jesko Raffin	SWI	2	Sports-Millions-EMWE-SAG	Kalex	23	43m 25.544s
18	Ratthapark Wilairot	THA	14	IDEMITSU Honda Team Asia	Kalex	23	43m 31.112s
19	Remy Gardner	AUS	87	Tasca Racing Scuderia Moto2	Kalex	23	43m 33.764s
20	Alex Rins	SPA	40	Paginas Amarillas HP 40	Kalex	23	43m 50.577s
21	Naomichi Uramoto	JPN	63	Japan-GP2	Kalex	23	43m 51.770s
22	Taro Sekiguchi	JPN	84	Team Taro Plus One	TSR	23	44m 12.490s
	Iker Lecuona	SPA	27	Technomag Racing Interwetten	Kalex	14	DNF
	Axel Pons	SPA	49	AGR Team	Kalex	13	DNF
	Lorenzo Baldassarri	ITA	7	Forward Team	Kalex	10	DNF
	Alex Marquez	SPA	73	Estrella Galicia 0,0 Marc VDS	Kalex	7	DNF
	Danny Kent	GBR	52	Leopard Racing	Kalex	7	DNF
	Jonas Folger	GER	94	Dynavolt Intact GP	Kalex	4	DNF
	Sam Lowes	GBR	22	Federal Oil Gresini Moto2	Kalex	1	DNF
	Robin Mulhauser	SWI	70	CarXpert Interwetten	Kalex	1	DNF

Fastest lap: Franco Morbidelli, on lap 3, 1m 50.788s, 96.9mph/156.0km/h (record).
Previous lap record: Maverick Vinales, SPA (Kalex), 1m 50.866s, 96.8mph/155.8km/h (2014).
Event best maximum speed: Thomas Luthi, 161.5mph/259.9km/h (free practice).

Qualifying

Weather: Dry
Air Temp: 23° Track Temp: 28°
Humidity: 34%

1	Zarco	1m 49.961s
2	Luthi	1m 50.028s
3	Morbidelli	1m 50.317s
4	Lowes	1m 50.333s
5	Cortese	1m 50.380s
6	A. Pons	1m 50.501s
7	Nakagami	1m 50.522s
8	Marquez	1m 50.563s
9	Folger	1m 50.743s
10	Pasini	1m 50.822s
11	Schrotter	1m 50.894s
12	Syahrin	1m 50.898s
13	Corsi	1m 50.917s
14	Baldassarri	1m 50.969s
15	Kent	1m 51.035s
16	Simon	1m 51.048s
17	Simeon	1m 51.123s
18	Vierge	1m 51.281s
19	Raffin	1m 51.311s
20	Vinales	1m 51.451s
21	E. Pons	1m 51.490s
22	Rins	1m 51.594s
23	Gardner	1m 51.621s
24	Nagashima	1m 51.739s
25	Wilairot	1m 51.844s
26	Marini	1m 51.925s
27	Mulhauser	1m 51.975s
28	Lecuona	1m 52.233s
29	Uramoto	1m 52.966s
30	Sekiguchi	1m 54.397s

Fastest race laps

1	Morbidelli	1m 50.788s
2	Luthi	1m 50.919s
3	Zarco	1m 50.936s
4	Nakagami	1m 50.993s
5	A. Pons	1m 51.332s
6	Simon	1m 51.421s
7	Marquez	1m 51.446s
8	Corsi	1m 51.454s
9	Folger	1m 51.484s
10	Baldassarri	1m 51.567s
11	Pasini	1m 51.570s
12	Cortese	1m 51.572s
13	Schrotter	1m 51.629s
14	Vierge	1m 51.842s
15	Simeon	1m 51.921s
16	E. Pons	1m 51.954s
17	Vinales	1m 52.108s
18	Marini	1m 52.127s
19	Nagashima	1m 52.154s
20	Syahrin	1m 52.162s
21	Kent	1m 52.185s
22	Gardner	1m 52.224s
23	Raffin	1m 52.254s
24	Rins	1m 52.343s
25	Wilairot	1m 52.497s
26	Lecuona	1m 53.364s
27	Uramoto	1m 53.390s
28	Sekiguchi	1m 54.379s

Championship Points

1	Zarco	222
2	Rins	201
3	Luthi	179
4	Lowes	162
5	Morbidelli	157
6	Nakagami	148
7	Folger	133
8	Syahrin	106
9	Baldassarri	99
10	Corsi	84
11	Aegerter	71
12	Pasini	63
13	Marquez	60
14	Schrotter	51
15	A. Pons	47
16	Cortese	45
17	Simon	40
18	Simeon	40
19	Salom	37
20	Oliveira	33
21	Kent	28
22	Marini	27
23	Vierge	19
24	Vinales	13
25	Raffin	11
26	West	6
27	Gardner	5
28	Wilairot	5
29	Mulhauser	4
30	E. Pons	2
31	Nagashima	2

Constructor Points

1	Kalex	375
2	Speed Up	117
3	Tech 3	29
4	Suter	6

Moto3

RACE DISTANCE: 20 laps, 59.664 miles/96.020km · RACE WEATHER: Dry (air 23°C, humidity 34%, track 35°C)

Pos.	Rider	Nat.	No.	Entrant	Machine	Laps	Time & Speed
1	Enea Bastianini	ITA	33	Gresini Racing Moto3	Honda	20	39m 24.273s / 90.8mph / 146.2km/h
2	Brad Binder	RSA	41	Red Bull KTM Ajo	KTM	20	39m 24.290s
3	Nicolo Bulega	ITA	8	SKY Racing Team VR46	KTM	20	39m 28.275s
4	Philipp Oettl	GER	65	Schedl GP Racing	KTM	20	39m 29.392s
5	Fabio Di Giannantonio	ITA	4	Gresini Racing Moto3	Honda	20	39m 30.561s
6	Francesco Bagnaia	ITA	21	Pull & Bear Aspar Mahindra Team	Mahindra	20	39m 32.012s
7	Livio Loi	BEL	11	RW Racing GP BV	Honda	20	39m 32.022s
8	Fabio Quartararo	FRA	20	Leopard Racing	KTM	20	39m 32.617s
9	Joan Mir	SPA	36	Leopard Racing	KTM	20	39m 33.153s
10	Niccolo Antonelli	ITA	23	Ongetta-Rivacold	Honda	20	39m 33.310s
11	Lorenzo dalla Porta	ITA	48	SKY Racing Team VR46	KTM	20	39m 36.605s
12	Adam Norrodin	MAL	7	Drive M7 SIC Racing Team	Honda	20	39m 37.798s
13	Jakub Kornfeil	CZE	84	Drive M7 SIC Racing Team	Honda	20	39m 43.091s
14	Albert Arenas	SPA	12	Peugeot MC Saxoprint	Peugeot	20	39m 45.536s
15	Tatsuki Suzuki	JPN	24	CIP-Unicom Starker	Mahindra	20	39m 45.564s
16	Jules Danilo	FRA	95	Ongetta-Rivacold	Honda	20	39m 46.000s
17	Marcos Ramirez	SPA	42	Platinum Bay Real Estate	Mahindra	20	39m 58.748s
18	Bo Bendsneyder	NED	64	Red Bull KTM Ajo	KTM	20	40m 04.223s
19	Khairul Idham Pawi	MAL	89	Honda Team Asia	Honda	20	40m 04.450s
20	Fabio Spiranelli	ITA	3	CIP-Unicom Starker	Mahindra	20	40m 11.077s
21	Lorenzo Petrarca	ITA	77	3570 Team Italia	Mahindra	20	40m 13.358s
22	Darryn Binder	RSA	40	Platinum Bay Real Estate	Mahindra	20	40m 16.843s
23	Maria Herrera	SPA	6	MH6 Team	KTM	20	40m 16.955s
24	Andrea Migno	ITA	16	SKY Racing Team VR46	KTM	20	40m 41.047s
25	Juanfran Guevara	SPA	58	RBA Racing Team	KTM	20	40m 46.375s
26	Shizuka Okazaki	JPN	13	UQ & TELURU KOHARA RT	Honda	20	41m 15.896s
	Jorge Martin	SPA	88	Pull & Bear Aspar Mahindra Team	Mahindra	10	DNF
	Aron Canet	SPA	44	Estrella Galicia 0,0	Honda	9	DNF
	Andrea Locatelli	ITA	55	Leopard Racing	KTM	4	DNF
	Stefano Valtulini	ITA	43	3570 Team Italia	Mahindra	3	DNF
	Jorge Navarro	SPA	9	Estrella Galicia 0,0	Honda	0	DNF
	John McPhee	GBR	17	Peugeot MC Saxoprint	Peugeot	0	DNF
	Gabriel Rodrigo	ARG	19	RBA Racing Team	KTM	0	DNF
	Hiroki Ono	JPN	76	Honda Team Asia	Honda	-	DSQ

Fastest lap: Nicolo Bulega, on lap 5, 1m 57.218s, 91.6mph/147.4km/h.
Lap record: Alex Marquez, SPA (Honda), 1m 57.112s, 91.7mph/147.5km/h (2014).
Event best maximum speed: Gabriel Rodrigo, 137.1mph/220.6km/h (free practice).

Qualifying

Weather: Dry
Air Temp: 22° Track Temp: 35°
Humidity: 31%

1	Ono	1m 56.443s
2	Migno	1m 56.529s
3	B. Binder	1m 56.659s
4	Bastianini	1m 56.664s
5	Bulega	1m 56.673s
6	Dalla Porta	1m 56.682s
7	Antonelli	1m 56.740s
8	Quartararo	1m 56.836s
9	Norrodin	1m 56.873s
10	Oettl	1m 56.899s
11	Navarro	1m 56.951s
12	Bagnaia	1m 57.001s
13	Arenas	1m 57.061s
14	Mir	1m 57.062s
15	Loi	1m 57.082s
16	McPhee	1m 57.087s
17	Canet	1m 57.153s
18	Di Giannantonio	1m 57.187s
19	Rodrigo	1m 57.220s
20	Guevara	1m 57.224s
21	Kornfeil	1m 57.236s
22	Pawi	1m 57.395s
23	Martin	1m 57.397s
24	Danilo	1m 57.509s
25	Suzuki	1m 57.552s
26	Ramirez	1m 57.681s
27	Bendsneyder	1m 57.722s
28	D. Binder	1m 57.844s
29	Locatelli	1m 58.506s
30	Herrera	1m 59.243s
31	Petrarca	1m 59.369s
32	Spiranelli	1m 59.380s
33	Valtulini	2m 00.081s
34	Okazaki	2m 02.753s
35	Sato	2m 03.505s

Fastest race laps

1	Bulega	1m 57.218s
2	Di Giannantonio	1m 57.321s
3	Oettl	1m 57.363s
4	D. Binder	1m 57.378s
5	Migno	1m 57.445s
6	Bastianini	1m 57.503s
7	B. Binder	1m 57.509s
8	Loi	1m 57.517s
9	Ono	1m 57.538s
10	Bagnaia	1m 57.568s
11	Martin	1m 57.652s
12	Guevara	1m 57.654s
13	Dalla Porta	1m 57.732s
14	Norrodin	1m 57.735s
15	Antonelli	1m 57.776s
16	Mir	1m 57.784s
17	Canet	1m 57.786s
18	Quartararo	1m 57.829s
19	Suzuki	1m 57.857s
20	Arenas	1m 57.946s
21	Danilo	1m 58.011s
22	Kornfeil	1m 58.014s
23	Ramirez	1m 58.318s
24	Bendsneyder	1m 58.336s
25	Herrera	1m 58.512s
26	Pawi	1m 58.711s
27	Locatelli	1m 58.957s
28	Petrarca	1m 59.101s
29	Spiranelli	1m 59.223s
30	Valtulini	1m 59.797s
31	Okazaki	2m 02.619s

Championship Points

1	B. Binder	269
2	Bastianini	164
3	Navarro	143
4	Bulega	129
5	Mir	124
6	Di Giannantonio	122
7	Bagnaia	120
8	Fenati	93
9	Antonelli	87
10	Kornfeil	83
11	Oettl	75
12	Locatelli	65
13	Quartararo	64
14	Canet	60
15	Martin	56
16	Pawi	54
17	Bendsneyder	53
18	Danilo	51
19	McPhee	48
20	Migno	47
21	Loi	44
22	Guevara	40
23	Ono	28
24	Rodrigo	22
25	Manzi	13
26	Suzuki	13
27	Dalla Porta	12
28	Norrodin	9
29	Herrera	6
30	D. Binder	4
31	Arenas	2

Constructor Points

1	KTM	316
2	Honda	301
3	Mahindra	167
4	Peugeot	50

AUSTRALIAN GRAND PRIX

PHILLIP ISLAND CIRCUIT

Inset, left: Cock-a-hoop Crutchlow threatens to throw Rossi's helmet to the crowd.

Inset, far left: A hardy handful: spectators braved Phillip Island's worst weather.

Inset, centre left: Track temperatures were a critical factor in tyre choice.

Main: Out on his own. Crutchlow heads towards his second win, this one in the dry.

Photos: Gold & Goose

Top and above, left and right: The old Marquez returned. And crashed. He was unscathed; his bike was destroyed.

Photos: John Morris – Mpix Photography

Top right: A fine fight. Aleix Espargaro leads team-mate Vinales and Dovizioso on the plunge down to MG corner.

Above right: South African world champions past and present, Brad Binder and Kork Ballington.

Above far right: Rossi bounced back from his miserable qualifying for a brilliant second.

Right: Nicky Hayden brought his '69' plate back to the Repsol Honda.

Photos: Gold & Goose

WITH its stunning location and rhythmic layout, Phillip Island is a highlight of the year, for riders and fans alike. The downside is the weather. Late Australian resident Barry Sheene liked to describe it as "the world capital of hypothermia".

Frequent freezing squalls, which blow in without warning from the adjacent icy Bass Strait, reliably add to the challenge, again for both riders and fans, and did so again in 2016. Thursday was balmy, but Friday and Saturday floody and miserable, with Friday afternoon's FP2 cut very short for MotoGP and cancelled altogether for Moto2. Saturday wasn't a great deal better, but it all changed for Sunday. Still chilly, but dry and even sunny from time to time.

In a way, this was a gift for Cal Crutchlow. It enabled him not only to take another successful gamble on a hard front tyre, causing him race-long trepidation, but also to prove something that meant a lot to him. The man who succeeded Sheene as Briton's next GP winner showed he could win in the dry as well as the wet.

Crutchlow's second victory of the season should not be overshadowed by the abrupt departure of the erstwhile dominant Marquez. After a season of playing the percentages, the new champion had promised a return to his more familiar swashbuckling approach. It cost him the race, however, when he lost the front at the Turn Four hairpin. He too had risked the harder front, but blamed "my own mistake" rather than the tyre.

Crutchlow, only a couple of seconds behind, couldn't have known that and was on tenterhooks, having lost a secure podium on the Ducati in exactly the same way two years before. As in 2016, that race had started at the late hour of 4pm,

and on that occasion rapidly dropping temperatures had also caught out Marquez while leading.

Crutchlow described afterwards how he had sought a balance between pushing hard enough to keep his Michelin warm and pushing too hard into the crash zone. "When the sun was out, I eased up a bit, then pushed again when it went in."

There was good reason to be nervous. The day before, Moto2 qualifying had run some half an hour later in cold, but dry conditions, and there had been no fewer than 20 crashes, several riders (including Zarco and Lowes) going down twice.

In a crash-heavy weekend, the most frightening was in the Moto3 race, a class where it is usually remarkable that there are so few multiple crashes with such close racing. There was a five-bike tangle on only the second corner: Bulega had been pushed off to crash soon afterwards, then Bagnaia and Di Giannantonio were also knocked flying by Rodrigo.

The real mayhem came soon afterwards, when John McPhee, lying second on the Peugeot-badged Mahindra, lost the front over the crest of Lukey Heights. He fell under the wheels of Migno's KTM and was run over. Bastianini was also brought down and, along with his bike, slid back across the track at the exit of the MG hairpin. He'd been clipped once, but scrambled to his feet to escape, only to be clobbered hard by Jorge Navarro.

By some miracle, both escaped serious injury. McPhee was concussed and had a thumb fracture; Bastianini had a fractured T9 vertebra and a cracked rib. It looked as though it should have been a lot worse.

Weather disruption caused some novelties in MotoGP

qualifying. FP3 was run in drying conditions, and Marquez called in on his out-lap to risk slicks and set a blazing fastest time. Other big names were caught out, and not only Crutchlow had to go into Q1, but also Vinales, Lorenzo and Rossi, with only two of them able to make it through to Q2. Crutchlow nailed that, almost two seconds quicker than Lorenzo; but the other two were in all sorts of trouble.

For Rossi, it was his first time in Q1 since Aragon in 2015, the first time not to run in Q2 since the system had been introduced in 2013; 15th his worst qualifying position since he had been 16th on the grid in Germany in 2011 on the Ducati. His weekend had started badly when his FP1 practice times had been cancelled, because he had run more than the decreed ten-lap maximum on the special super-soft wet front tyre Michelin had brought for cold morning sessions (his team hadn't realised that out- and in-laps would be counted). In true Rossi style, however, he made up for the setback in spades in the race.

Pedrosa's vacant Repsol Honda led to the return of a respected alumnus. Nicky Hayden had won the 2006 title for the team, and he explained how the call-up had instantly reversed his decision never again to let MotoGP or the Suzuka 8 Hours interfere with his new Superbike career. "I'm a softy," he said. "But I love racing motorbikes, and it was pretty good to see my number back on the factory Honda."

Iannone had been expected back, but wasn't, giving Barbera another run on the factory Ducati and Australian Mike Jones an unexpected home GP on the Avintia Ducati. Once again, he performed with restraint and skill, and was rewarded by one point.

Ant West had been on standby to take over Remy Gardner's Moto2 bike, after he had been detained in Japan in connection with his father Wayne's arrest over an alleged road-rage incident at Motegi. Remy was released in time, but the 1987 world champion was still languishing in a cell in the small town of Shimotsuke.

Anyone doubting the force exerted by small fairing-flank winglets thought again when the wind ripped the right-hand wing off Petrucci's fairing in practice. The wings were only pop-riveted in place to avoid inflicting injury; the team was advised to use bigger washers.

Another downbeat performance in Moto2 by Zarco and a career-first back-to-back win for Luthi injected an unexpected new tension in the only remaining unresolved title; but Rins fell again, reducing his own threat and dropping to third overall.

Another raft of penalties in Moto3 for offences other than dawdling included three-place/one-point sanctions for six riders who ignored the red flag at the end of qualifying, after Guevara had crashed and lay doggo: Bastianini, McPhee, Norrodin, Oettl, Valtulini and wild-card Matt Barton. Bagnaia received the same punishment for slowing on the racing line, causing Bulega to fall. And Quartararo was dismayed when his front-row position was cancelled because his team had used unhomologated software. And even more so when, in the restarted Moto3 race, he found he would have to serve the same back-row penalty for a second time.

MOTOGP RACE – 27 laps

MotoGP had looked as though it belonged to Marquez. Unleashed from the responsibility of counting the points, he dominated qualifying and took off convincingly. His control deserted him, though, on lap ten. He locked the front into the first hairpin, and was down and out.

Crutchlow was only a couple of seconds down and thought he might be able to challenge. There was no need, but by now the other star of the race, Rossi, was not much further behind, after carving through from 15th on the grid. He'd been second (to Marquez) in the extended dry morning warm-up, the first real chance for riders to find dry tyres and settings. He couldn't catch the leader, but it had given him the confidence to hold firm against the advancing Vinales,

Above: The Pramac battle went to Redding this time; and brave Bradley Smith would push past Petrucci as well.

Top right: Luthi leads Pasini and Morbidelli in a torrid three-way battle for the lead.

Above right: Andrea Locatelli was a career-best second in Moto3.

Above far right: Back-to-back winner Luthi welcomes Sandro Cortese to his first podium of 2016.

Right: An off-form Zarco was trapped in a midfield battle. The championship leader tails Simeon, Vierge and Schrotter.

Below right: Argy-bargy between Kornfeil (84) and Bendsneyder (44). Dalla Porta (48) and Norrodin (7) hold a watching brief.

Photos: Gold & Goose

through from a 12th-place start. As importantly, with Lorenzo a lacklustre sixth, it moved him 24 points clear in their fight for second overall.

Tyre choice showed little variety. All opted for the same softer 'medium' rear Michelin and most the soft front. Marquez and Crutchlow were joined in a hard-front gamble by both Suzuki riders Vinales and Espargaro, and local hero Jack Miller.

Pol Espargaro was on the front row of the grid for the first time in the season, with Crutchlow and Marquez, and led around the Southern Loop. Marquez was firmly past at the Turn Four hairpin, and it looked like an easy cruise to a third successive win, sixth of the year. Until it ended abruptly at the same corner on lap ten. With the bike barrel-rolling to destruction, it was his first non-finish of the year.

That left Crutchlow by now comfortably clear of Espargaro.

Less comfortably, Rossi was past the Spaniard next time around. He'd set fastest lap on the fifth, but that had been eclipsed on lap six and again on lap eight by Crutchlow. But he was just 1.8 seconds behind. The scene was set for him to pull off a remarkable feat, his seventh Phillip Island win, but from a row-five start.

He thought it possible, but Crutchlow stretched steadily away, 2.4 seconds clear two laps later, and better than three by lap 15. Now all the Englishman had to do was stay on.

"When I saw on my pit board it was Rossi behind, I thought, 'Oh no, from 15th.'" Then he saw the gap growing and concentrated on keeping his front tyre warm enough without taking risks: "The whole weekend has been about keeping your head, often in dangerous conditions."

By now, fast starter Petrucci had dropped back into a huge gang disputing seventh; while Espargaro was behind elder brother Aleix and Dovizioso (Ducati), the pair closely engaged following Rossi.

Vinales had spent the early laps learning to trust in his hard front, which he hadn't tried before, but now he was on the move. He passed the still-tentative Lorenzo on lap six and Pol Espargaro six laps later, then closed quickly on the pair ahead for a skirmish that spanned several laps. Aleix Espargaro foiled every overtaking move, while Dovizioso's Ducati kept reversing any Suzuki passes as he powered down the straight, setting (at 340.5km/h) the fastest top speed of the weekend.

It was resolved when Espargaro became another victim of a Turn Four front-wheel wash-out, by which time Vinales was ahead of Dovizioso and soon clear. He was closing on Rossi

at the finish, but it was too late for better than third, which was better than he had expected.

Behind the lone Lorenzo, who blamed continuing problems on low-grip tracks, six riders were furiously engaged – Miller, Hayden, Petrucci and team-mate Redding, plus Bradl and Barbera. The last would crash out, while Smith would join from behind. Then Hayden was pushed off and down after a touch from an over-eager Miller.

They finished in the order Redding, Smith, Petrucci and Miller, all over the line inside half a second, Bradl still close for 11th.

Second Aprilia rider Bautista narrowly held off Hernandez for 12th after a long battle. The Colombian's team-mate, Laverty, was a distant 14th, while close behind Australian Mike Jones was 15th, after a second solid weekend as a complete GP novice. He'd left Rabat well adrift, while a remounted Hayden was last.

Baz retired early after a pit-lane start, suffering mechanical woes.

Marquez had nothing to worry about; Rossi was now 24 points clear of Lorenzo, who was coming under threat from Vinales, 11 points away. He was seriously looking forward to warm conditions on the next weekend.

MOTO2 RACE – 25 laps

Another race of upset for the championship leaders gave a glimmer of hope for first-time back-to-back winner Luthi. "Somebody asked me on the grid why that had never happened before. I told him, 'That's the reason I am still here'," said the Swiss former 125 champion.

Luthi had claimed pole in another (often all too literally) topsy-turvy qualifying session, from veteran Mattia Pasini and triple session crasher Lowes. Zarco was only tenth after also crashing twice in a session with 20 tumbles.

Alex Marquez was worst off, in great pain, having been crushed up against his fuel tank after a collision with Simon's Speed Up, and out of the race.

Zarco had been only 12th in dry morning warm-up, headed by Franco Morbidelli (another double faller in qualifying), while title challenger Rins, qualified 15th, placed an encouraging fourth.

Luthi shot off in the lead, pursued by Pasini, who was soon displaced by Morbidelli, this trio still in control up front at half-distance.

Lowes was closing on the leaders when he crashed out on

lap three, his third fall in the previous four races, though he won the other.

Rins lasted five more laps, up to sixth when he tumbled after missing a gear at the Southern Loop.

Folger had been losing ground in fourth, and the first past him was Baldassarri, followed soon after by Nakagami and his own team-mate, Cortese. Folger was soon out of touch, but Cortese was picking up speed, and closing on Baldassarri as the Italian tagged on to the leading trio.

Soon he was ahead of Baldassarri and leaning hard on Pasini, now in a close third place. Too hard, and Pasini became another victim of Turn Four.

That gave Luthi and Morbidelli a little breathing space, and as they started the penultimate lap, Morbidelli made a typically brave move around the outside at the Southern Loop. He led as they started the last lap and appeared to have done enough to win his first GP. But Luthi is a wily veteran, and he used all his guile for the perfect slipstream on the run down the straight, claiming victory by a mere hundredth of a second.

"It's a good result for me anyway," said a philosophical Morbidelli, "and for my team, after I did so much damage on Friday and Saturday."

Cortese was half a second behind and delighted with his first podium of the season. Three seconds down, Baldassarri held off a closing Nakagami; Folger was out of touch in sixth.

Corsi was a lone seventh on his Speed Up, first non-Kalex. Three seconds away, Axel Pons retained control of a five-strong group; team-mate Schrotter passed Xavi Vierge's Tech 3 on the last lap.

A surprisingly lacklustre Zarco was at the back of it, close behind Simeon's Speed Up, but bereft of his usual late-race speed and tactics.

Syahrin crashed out on lap one; others to fall were Simon, Lecuona and Kent, plus home hero Remy Gardner, who retired after his second crash.

Luthi's second win made him a distant, but worthy threat, 22 points adrift of Zarco and displacing Rins to third.

MOTO3 RACE – 10 laps (shortened)

Moto3 often surprises by how few crashes there are in such close racing. The opposite was true on this occasion. Pawi, Mir, Loi, Darryn Binder and Martin tangled at Turn Two, the last three able to restart. Soon afterwards, Canet slipped off, but remounted; then front-runner Bulega fell after a brush with Quartararo, through from the back. Next Guevara fell; shortly afterward, Rodrigo tapped Di Giannantonio in the front pack, putting the Honda rider and erstwhile second-placed Bagnaia down and out.

The big crash came on lap six, eliminating McPhee, Bastianini and Migno.

Champion Brad Binder had been leading and was on pole for the restart for a ten-lap sprint.

He led away, soon easily outpacing his only close pursuer, Locatelli; the other 22 surviving riders (out of an original 34) scrambled in a huge gang behind them.

Martin led the group at the mid-point, but younger brother Darryn Binder was on inspired form, and he managed to get to the head of it on the final lap and out of the last corner – only to be denied a double Binder family rostrum when Canet pulled out of draft to take third by five-hundredths.

Third to 12th places were covered by less than a second, the rest not much further adrift. Those in the points were in this order behind Loi in fifth: Martin and Ramirez (both Mahindra), Ono and Danilo (both Honda), Bendsneyder (KTM), Norrodin (Honda), Quartararo (KTM), Suzuki (Mahindra), Oettl and Herrera (both KTM) – a fine mix of machinery, experience and talent.

Antonelli (Gresini Honda) crashed on the first lap, Navarro and Rodrigo with one lap to go.

The championship was little altered, with Binder the only scorer in the top nine.

MICHELIN AUSTRALIAN MOTORCYCLE GRAND·PRIX
21–23 OCTOBER, 2016

PHILLIP ISLAND
27 laps
Length: 4.448 km / 2.764 miles
Width: 13m

Key
96/60 kph/mph
Gear

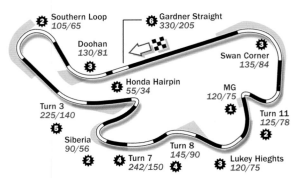

Southern Loop 105/65
Gardner Straight 330/205
Doohan 130/81
Swan Corner 135/84
Honda Hairpin 55/34
MG 120/75
Turn 3 225/140
Turn 11 125/78
Siberia 90/56
Turn 8 145/90
Lukey Hieghts 120/75
Turn 7 242/150

MotoGP
RACE DISTANCE: 27 laps, 74.624 miles/120.096km · **RACE WEATHER:** Dry (air 12°C, humidity 62%, track 33°C)

Pos.	Rider	Nat.	No.	Entrant	Machine	Tyres	Race tyre choice	Laps	Time & speed
1	**Cal Crutchlow**	GBR	35	LCR Honda	Honda RC213V	M	F: Hard/R: Medium	27	40m 48.543s 109.7mph/ 176.5km/h
2	**Valentino Rossi**	ITA	46	Movistar Yamaha MotoGP	Yamaha YZR-M1	M	F: Soft/R: Medium	27	40m 52.761s
3	**Maverick Vinales**	SPA	25	Team SUZUKI ECSTAR	Suzuki GSX-RR	M	F: Hard/R: Medium	27	40m 53.852s
4	**Andrea Dovizioso**	ITA	4	Ducati Team	Ducati Desmosedici	M	F: Soft/R: Medium	27	40m 57.700s
5	**Pol Espargaro**	SPA	44	Monster Yamaha Tech 3	Yamaha YZR-M1	M	F: Soft/R: Medium	27	41m 02.842s
6	**Jorge Lorenzo**	SPA	99	Movistar Yamaha MotoGP	Yamaha YZR-M1	M	F: Soft/R: Medium	27	41m 08.668s
7	**Scott Redding**	GBR	45	OCTO Pramac Yakhnich	Ducati Desmosedici	M	F: Soft/R: Medium	27	41m 16.912s
8	**Bradley Smith**	GBR	38	Monster Yamaha Tech 3	Yamaha YZR-M1	M	F: Soft/R: Medium	27	41m 17.324s
9	**Danilo Petrucci**	ITA	9	OCTO Pramac Yakhnich	Ducati Desmosedici	M	F: Soft/R: Medium	27	41m 17.335s
10	**Jack Miller**	AUS	43	Estrella Galicia 0,0 Marc VDS	Honda RC213V	M	F: Hard/R: Medium	27	41m 17.358s
11	**Stefan Bradl**	GER	6	Aprilia Racing Team Gresini	Aprilia RS-GP	M	F: Soft/R: Medium	27	41m 20.352s
12	**Alvaro Bautista**	SPA	19	Aprilia Racing Team Gresini	Aprilia RS-GP	M	F: Soft/R: Medium	27	41m 36.277s
13	**Yonny Hernandez**	COL	68	Pull & Bear Aspar Team	Ducati Desmosedici	M	F: Soft/R: Medium	27	41m 36.292s
14	**Eugene Laverty**	IRL	50	Pull & Bear Aspar Team	Ducati Desmosedici	M	F: Soft/R: Medium	27	41m 42.854s
15	**Mike Jones**	AUS	7	Avintia Racing	Ducati Desmosedici	M	F: Soft/R: Medium	27	41m 44.418s
16	Tito Rabat	SPA	53	Estrella Galicia 0,0 Marc VDS	Honda RC213V	M	F: Soft/R: Medium	27	41m 54.938s
17	Nicky Hayden	USA	69	Repsol Honda Team	Honda RC213V	M	F: Soft/R: Medium	27	42m 11.147s
	Hector Barbera	SPA	8	Ducati Team	Ducati Desmosedici	M	F: Soft/R: Medium	24	DNF-crash
	Aleix Espargaro	SPA	41	Team SUZUKI ECSTAR	Suzuki GSX-RR	M	F: Hard/R: Medium	22	DNF-crash
	Marc Marquez	SPA	93	Repsol Honda Team	Honda RC213V	M	F: Hard/R: Medium	9	DNF-crash
	Loris Baz	FRA	76	Avintia Racing	Ducati Desmosedici	M	F: Soft/R: Medium	0	DNF-technical

Fastest lap: Cal Crutchlow, on lap 8, 1m 29.494s, 111.2mph/178.9km/h.
Lap record: Marc Marquez, SPA (Honda), 1m 28.108s, 112.9mph/181.7km/h (2013).
Event best maximum speed: Andrea Dovizioso, 211.6mph/340.5km/h (race).

Qualifying
Weather: Dry
Air Temp: 12° **Humidity:** 73%
Track Temp: 19°

1	Marquez	1m 30.189s
2	Crutchlow	1m 30.981s
3	P. Espargaro	1m 31.107s
4	A. Espargaro	1m 31.673s
5	Miller	1m 31.754s
6	Petrucci	1m 32.420s
7	Hayden	1m 32.944s
8	Bradl	1m 33.015s
9	Dovizioso	1m 33.090s
10	Barbera	1m 33.914s
11	Redding	1m 34.682s
12	Lorenzo	1m 36.840s
13	Vinales	1m 40.744s
14	Smith	1m 41.129s
15	Rossi	1m 41.368s
16	Laverty	1m 41.532s
17	Hernandez	1m 41.766s
18	Bautista	1m 41.850s
19	Jones	1m 42.261s
20	Baz	1m 43.128s
21	Rabat	1m 44.096s

Fastest race laps
1	Crutchlow	1m 29.494s
2	Marquez	1m 29.583s
3	Rossi	1m 29.726s
4	Vinales	1m 29.964s
5	A. Espargaro	1m 30.011s
6	Dovizioso	1m 30.131s
7	P. Espargaro	1m 30.264s
8	Redding	1m 30.428s
9	Lorenzo	1m 30.446s
10	Hayden	1m 30.684s
11	Barbera	1m 30.746s
12	Smith	1m 30.834s
13	Miller	1m 30.836s
14	Bradl	1m 30.855s
15	Petrucci	1m 30.909s
16	Bautista	1m 31.573s
17	Jones	1m 31.663s
18	Hernandez	1m 31.749s
19	Laverty	1m 32.114s
20	Rabat	1m 32.416s

Championship Points
1	Marquez	273
2	Rossi	216
3	Lorenzo	192
4	Vinales	181
5	Pedrosa	155
6	Crutchlow	141
7	Dovizioso	137
8	P. Espargaro	117
9	Iannone	96
10	Barbera	84
11	A. Espargaro	82
12	Laverty	73
13	Redding	71
14	Bautista	67
15	Petrucci	65
16	Bradl	60
17	Smith	53
18	Miller	48
19	Pirro	36
20	Rabat	29
21	Baz	24
22	Hernandez	20
23	Nakasuga	5
24	Lowes	3
25	Hayden	1
26	Jones	1
27	Aoyama	1

Grid order	1	2	3	4	5	6	7	8	9	10	11	12	13	14	15	16	17	18	19	20	21	22	23	24	25	26	27	
93 MARQUEZ	93	93	93	93	93	93	93	93	93	35	35	35	35	35	35	35	35	35	35	35	35	35	35	35	35	35	35	1
35 CRUTCHLOW	44	44	44	44	41	35	35	35	35	46	46	46	46	46	46	46	46	46	46	46	46	46	46	46	46	46	46	2
44 P. ESPARGARO	41	35	35	35	35	41	41	41	41	41	41	41	41	41	41	41	41	41	4	41	41	41	25	25	25	25	25	3
41 A. ESPARGARO	35	41	41	41	44	44	4	46	46	4	4	4	4	4	4	4	4	41	4	4	25	4	4	4	4	4	4	4
43 MILLER	9	9	4	4	4	4	46	4	44	44	25	25	25	25	25	25	25	25	25	4	44	44	44	44	44			5
9 PETRUCCI	43	4	9	9	46	46	44	44	44	25	44	44	44	44	44	44	44	44	44	99	99	99	99	99				6
69 HAYDEN	4	43	99	46	99	25	25	25	25	99	99	99	99	99	99	99	99	99	99	45	45	45	45	45				7
6 BRADL	99	99	43	99	25	99	99	99	99	45	45	45	43	9	43	9	69	45	9	45	9	9	9	43	38			8
4 DOVIZIOSO	69	69	46	43	9	9	43	43	45	43	43	43	9	43	9	69	45	69	45	45	9	43	69	69	9	9		9
8 BARBERA	6	25	25	25	43	43	9	45	43	69	9	9	69	69	69	69	9	9	69	43	69	69	43	43	38	43		10
45 REDDING	25	46	69	69	69	69	69	9	69	9	69	69	45	45	45	45	6	43	43	69	43	6	8	38	6	6		11
99 LORENZO	45	6	6	6	6	6	45	69	9	6	8	8	8	8	6	43	43	6	6	6	6	8	6	6	19	19		12
25 VINALES	46	45	45	45	45	45	6	6	8	8	6	6	6	6	8	8	8	8	8	8	8	38	38	19	68	68		13
38 SMITH	8	8	8	8	8	8	8	38	38	38	38	38	38	38	38	38	38	38	38	19	19	68	68	50	50			14
46 ROSSI	50	50	50	50	50	38	38	38	38	50	50	50	68	68	68	68	19	68	68	68	19	68	68	50	7	7		15
50 LAVERTY	19	19	38	38	38	50	50	50	50	68	68	68	50	19	19	19	68	19	19	68	50	50	7	53	53			
68 HERNANDEZ	68	19	19	19	19	68	68	68	68	19	19	19	19	50	50	50	50	50	50	50	7	7	53	69	69			
19 BAUTISTA	38	38	68	68	68	19	19	19	19	7	7	7	7	7	7	7	7	7	7	7	53	53						
7 JONES	7	7	7	7	7	7	7	7	7	53	53	53	53	53	53	53	53	53										
76 BAZ	53	53	53	53	53	53	53	53	53																			
53 RABAT																												

Constructor Points
1	Honda	341
2	Yamaha	308
3	Ducati	220
4	Suzuki	187
5	Aprilia	86

Moto2 — RACE DISTANCE: 25 laps, 69.096 miles/111.200km · RACE WEATHER: Dry (air 12°C, humidity 62%, track 34°C)

Pos.	Rider	Nat.	No.	Entrant	Machine	Laps	Time & Speed
1	**Thomas Luthi**	SWI	12	Garage Plus Interwetten	Kalex	25	39m 15.891s / 105.6mph/ 169.9km/h
2	**Franco Morbidelli**	ITA	21	Estrella Galicia 0,0 Marc VDS	Kalex	25	39m 15.901s
3	**Sandro Cortese**	GER	11	Dynavolt Intact GP	Kalex	25	39m 16.421s
4	**Lorenzo Baldassarri**	ITA	7	Forward Team	Kalex	25	39m 18.972s
5	**Takaaki Nakagami**	JPN	30	IDEMITSU Honda Team Asia	Kalex	25	39m 19.706s
6	**Jonas Folger**	GER	94	Dynavolt Intact GP	Kalex	25	39m 26.978s
7	**Simone Corsi**	ITA	24	Speed Up Racing	Speed Up	25	39m 29.182s
8	**Axel Pons**	SPA	49	AGR Team	Kalex	25	39m 32.302s
9	**Marcel Schrotter**	GER	23	AGR Team	Kalex	25	39m 33.541s
10	**Xavi Vierge**	SPA	97	Tech 3 Racing	Tech 3	25	39m 33.556s
11	**Xavier Simeon**	BEL	19	QMMF Racing Team	Speed Up	25	39m 33.653s
12	**Johann Zarco**	FRA	5	Ajo Motorsport	Kalex	25	39m 33.687s
13	**Jesko Raffin**	SWI	2	Sports-Millions-EMWE-SAG	Kalex	25	39m 47.466s
14	**Edgar Pons**	SPA	57	Paginas Amarillas HP 40	Kalex	25	39m 50.561s
15	**Ratthapark Wilairot**	THA	14	IDEMITSU Honda Team Asia	Kalex	25	39m 56.345s
16	Luca Marini	ITA	10	Forward Team	Kalex	25	40m 03.598s
17	Robin Mulhauser	SWI	70	CarXpert Interwetten	Kalex	25	40m 50.361s
18	Ramdan Rosli	MAL	93	Petronas AHM Malaysia	Kalex	24	39m 26.190s
	Alessandro Nocco	ITA	20	Leopard Racing	Kalex	23	DNF
	Mattia Pasini	ITA	54	Italtrans Racing Team	Kalex	22	DNF
	Danny Kent	GBR	52	Leopard Racing	Kalex	22	DNF
	Remy Gardner	AUS	87	Tasca Racing Scuderia Moto2	Kalex	13	DNF
	Julian Simon	SPA	60	QMMF Racing Team	Speed Up	9	DNF
	Iker Lecuona	SPA	27	CarXpert Interwetten	Kalex	9	DNF
	Alex Rins	SPA	40	Paginas Amarillas HP 40	Kalex	6	DNF
	Sam Lowes	GBR	22	Federal Oil Gresini Moto2	Kalex	2	DNF
	Hafizh Syahrin	MAL	55	Petronas Raceline Malaysia	Kalex	0	DNF

Fastest lap: Franco Morbidelli, on lap 2, 1m 33.414s, 106.5mph/171.4km/h.
Lap record: Alex de Angelis, RSM (Speed Up), 1m 32.814s, 107.2mph/172.5km/h (2013).
Event best maximum speed: Lorenzo Baldassarri, 177.5mph/285.7km/h (race).

Qualifying
Weather: Dry
Air: 10° Track: 14°
Humidity: 79%

1	Luthi	1m 33.992s
2	Pasini	1m 34.051s
3	Lowes	1m 34.057s
4	Cortese	1m 34.094s
5	Raffin	1m 34.217s
6	Folger	1m 34.245s
7	Vierge	1m 34.267s
8	Baldassarri	1m 34.284s
9	Morbidelli	1m 34.410s
10	Zarco	1m 34.470s
11	Schrotter	1m 34.529s
12	Nakagami	1m 34.615s
13	Corsi	1m 34.659s
14	Marquez	1m 34.695s
15	Simon	1m 34.835s
16	Rins	1m 34.893s
17	Wilairot	1m 34.920s
18	Marini	1m 35.094s
19	A. Pons	1m 35.115s
20	Syahrin	1m 35.194s
21	Simeon	1m 35.216s
22	Kent	1m 35.789s
23	Gardner	1m 35.804s
24	E. Pons	1m 36.089s
25	Lecuona	1m 36.236s
26	Vinales	1m 37.913s
27	Rosli	1m 38.803s
28	Mulhauser	1m 39.002s
29	Nocco	1m 39.340s

Fastest race laps

1	Morbidelli	1m 33.414s
2	Cortese	1m 33.451s
3	Luthi	1m 33.600s
4	Baldassarri	1m 33.665s
5	Pasini	1m 33.680s
6	Nakagami	1m 33.715s
7	Rins	1m 33.933s
8	Corsi	1m 33.980s
9	Folger	1m 33.999s
10	Zarco	1m 34.033s
11	A. Pons	1m 34.063s
12	Vierge	1m 34.128s
13	Simeon	1m 34.177s
14	Simeon	1m 34.229s
15	Simon	1m 34.263s
16	E. Pons	1m 34.312s
17	Lowes	1m 34.325s
18	Raffin	1m 34.384s
19	Kent	1m 34.478s
20	Wilairot	1m 34.693s
21	Marini	1m 34.848s
22	Gardner	1m 35.346s
23	Lecuona	1m 35.731s
24	Mulhauser	1m 37.037s
25	Rosli	1m 37.422s
26	Nocco	1m 37.550s

Championship Points

1	Zarco	226
2	Luthi	204
3	Rins	201
4	Morbidelli	177
5	Lowes	162
6	Nakagami	159
7	Folger	143
8	Baldassarri	112
9	Syahrin	106
10	Corsi	93
11	Aegerter	71
12	Pasini	63
13	Cortese	61
14	Marquez	60
15	Schrotter	58
16	A. Pons	55
17	Simeon	45
18	Simon	40
19	Salom	37
20	Oliveira	33
21	Kent	28
22	Marini	27
23	Vierge	25
24	Raffin	14
25	Vinales	13
26	West	6
27	Wilairot	6
28	Gardner	5
29	Mulhauser	4
30	E. Pons	4
31	Nagashima	2

Constructor Points

1	Kalex	400
2	Speed Up	126
3	Tech 3	35
4	Suter	6

Moto3 — RACE DISTANCE: 10 laps, 27.639 miles/44.480km · RACE WEATHER: Dry (air 12°C, humidity 59%, track 34°C)

Pos.	Rider	Nat.	No.	Entrant	Machine	Laps	Time & Speed
1	**Brad Binder**	RSA	41	Red Bull KTM Ajo	KTM	10	16m 22.009s / 101.3mph/ 163.0km/h
2	**Andrea Locatelli**	ITA	55	Leopard Racing	KTM	10	16m 27.946s
3	**Aron Canet**	SPA	44	Estrella Galicia 0,0	Honda	10	16m 31.603s
4	**Darryn Binder**	RSA	40	Platinum Bay Real Estate	Mahindra	10	16m 31.651s
5	**Livio Loi**	BEL	11	RW Racing GP BV	Honda	10	16m 31.689s
6	**Jorge Martin**	SPA	88	Pull & Bear Aspar Mahindra Team	Mahindra	10	16m 31.759s
7	**Marcos Ramirez**	SPA	42	Platinum Bay Real Estate	Mahindra	10	16m 32.005s
8	**Hiroki Ono**	JPN	76	Honda Team Asia	Honda	10	16m 32.124s
9	**Jules Danilo**	FRA	95	Ongetta-Rivacold	Honda	10	16m 32.151s
10	**Bo Bendsneyder**	NED	64	Red Bull KTM Ajo	KTM	10	16m 32.367s
11	**Adam Norrodin**	MAL	7	Drive M7 SIC Racing Team	Honda	10	16m 32.456s
12	**Fabio Quartararo**	FRA	20	Leopard Racing	KTM	10	16m 32.578s
13	**Tatsuki Suzuki**	JPN	24	CIP-Unicom Starker	Mahindra	10	16m 32.691s
14	**Philipp Oettl**	GER	65	Schedl GP Racing	KTM	10	16m 32.988s
15	**Maria Herrera**	SPA	6	MH6 Team	KTM	10	16m 35.772s
16	Albert Arenas	SPA	12	Peugeot MC Saxoprint	Peugeot	10	16m 35.830s
17	Lorenzo Petrarca	ITA	77	3570 Team Italia	Mahindra	10	16m 50.306s
18	Fabio Spiranelli	ITA	3	CIP-Unicom Starker	Mahindra	10	17m 04.045s
19	Lorenzo dalla Porta	ITA	48	SKY Racing Team VR46	KTM	10	17m 12.463s
20	Matt Barton	AUS	14	Suus Honda	FTR Honda	10	17m 45.455s
	Gabriel Rodrigo	ARG	19	RBA Racing Team	KTM	9	DNF
	Jorge Navarro	SPA	9	Estrella Galicia 0,0	Honda	9	DNF
	Stefano Valtulini	ITA	43	3570 Team Italia	Mahindra	8	DNF
	Niccolo Antonelli	ITA	23	Ongetta-Rivacold	Honda	0	DNF
	Nicolo Bulega	ITA	8	SKY Racing Team VR46	KTM	-	DNS
	Andrea Migno	ITA	16	SKY Racing Team VR46	KTM	-	DNS
	John McPhee	GBR	17	Peugeot MC Saxoprint	Peugeot	-	DNS
	Joan Mir	SPA	36	Leopard Racing	KTM	-	DNS
	Francesco Bagnaia	ITA	21	Pull & Bear Aspar Mahindra Team	Mahindra	-	DNS
	Khairul Idham Pawi	MAL	89	Honda Team Asia	Honda	-	DNS
	Enea Bastianini	ITA	33	Gresini Racing Moto3	Honda	-	DNS
	Fabio Di Giannantonio	ITA	4	Gresini Racing Moto3	Honda	-	DNS
	Juanfran Guevara	SPA	58	RBA Racing Team	KTM	-	DNS
	Jakub Kornfeil	CZE	84	Drive M7 SIC Racing Team	Honda	-	DNS

Fastest lap: Andrea Locatelli, on lap 5, 1m 37.335s, 102.2mph/164.5km/h (race part 1).
Lap record: Jack Miller, AUS (KTM), 1m 36.302s, 103.3mph/166.2km/h (2014).
Event best maximum speed: Gabriel Rodrigo, 148.7mph/239.3km/h (warm-up).

Qualifying:
Weather: Dry
Air: 13° Track: 24°
Humidity: 74%

1	B. Binder	1m 37.696s
2	Bulega	1m 38.487s
3	Rodrigo	1m 38.570s
4	McPhee	1m 38.661s
5	Loi	1m 38.776s
6	Migno	1m 38.981s
7	D. Binder	1m 39.195s
8	Martin	1m 39.272s
9	Bagnaia	1m 39.347s
10	Mir	1m 39.353s
11	Bendsneyder	1m 39.439s
12	Navarro	1m 39.448s
13	Herrera	1m 39.472s
14	Locatelli	1m 39.485s
15	Bastianini	1m 39.513s
16	Danilo	1m 39.551s
17	Pawi	1m 39.589s
18	Antonelli	1m 39.624s
19	Oettl	1m 39.630s
20	Di Giannantonio	1m 39.675s
21	Canet	1m 39.740s
22	Norrodin	1m 39.828s
23	Guevara	1m 39.890s
24	Kornfeil	1m 40.110s
25	Suzuki	1m 40.159s
26	Arenas	1m 40.236s
27	Dalla Porta	1m 40.412s
28	Ono	1m 40.537s
29	Valtulini	1m 40.969s
30	Ramirez	1m 40.996s
31	Spiranelli	1m 41.198s
32	Petrarca	1m 41.410s
33	Barton	1m 45.537s
	Quartararo	DSQ

Fastest race laps

1	Locatelli	1m 37.430s
2	B. Binder	1m 37.442s
3	Quartararo	1m 37.466s
4	D. Binder	1m 37.588s
5	Norrodin	1m 37.641s
6	Ono	1m 37.678s
7	Rodrigo	1m 37.683s
8	Oettl	1m 37.697s
9	Canet	1m 37.766s
10	Martin	1m 37.804s
11	Bendsneyder	1m 37.815s
12	Suzuki	1m 37.830s
13	Loi	1m 37.842s
14	Arenas	1m 37.962s
15	Dalla Porta	1m 37.964s
16	Ramirez	1m 38.142s
17	Danilo	1m 38.251s
18	Navarro	1m 38.253s
19	Herrera	1m 38.319s
20	Spiranelli	1m 38.764s
21	Valtulini	1m 38.946s
22	Petrarca	1m 39.036s
23	Barton	1m 44.749s

Championship Points

1	B. Binder	294
2	Bastianini	164
3	Navarro	143
4	Bulega	129
5	Mir	124
6	Di Giannantonio	122
7	Bagnaia	120
8	Fenati	93
9	Antonelli	87
10	Locatelli	85
11	Kornfeil	83
12	Oettl	77
13	Canet	76
14	Quartararo	68
15	Martin	66
16	Bendsneyder	59
17	Danilo	58
18	Loi	55
19	Pawi	54
20	McPhee	48
21	Migno	47
22	Guevara	40
23	Ono	36
24	Rodrigo	22
25	D. Binder	17
26	Suzuki	16
27	Norrodin	14
28	Manzi	13
29	Dalla Porta	12
30	Ramirez	9
31	Herrera	7
32	Arenas	2

Constructor Points

1	KTM	341
2	Honda	317
3	Mahindra	180
4	Peugeot	50

MALAYSIAN GRAND PRIX

SEPANG CIRCUIT

Inset: Dovi lovingly cuddles the winner's trophy; Lorenzo just felt lucky to be with him.

Main: Winner number nine. Dovizioso had to wait a long time for the moment.

Photos: Gold & Goose

Above: Rossi blamed his tyres; Dovi credited his persistence. Once past, he pulled away firmly.

Top right: Jorge Lorenzo rode within his limits, and inherited a podium for his caution.

Above right: Crutchlow pushed the limits, and paid with his third crash of the weekend.

Centre right: Red Bull Rookies champion Ayumu Sasaki took over Bastianini's Gresini Honda, but was knocked down at the second corner.

Right: Iannone was back from injury after missing four races, but crashed out for the sixth time of the year.

Photos: Gold & Goose

RACE by race, Dovizioso's patience had been tested by the same question. Over and over. Could he become the ninth winner of this exceptional season?

At Sepang, finally, he put it to bed, with what looked like a calm and assured victory in difficult drying conditions – a typically well-measured race. Not so, he insisted: "It may have looked from the outside as if I was in control. It was not like this in reality. What allowed me to win was that in the beginning, when the pace was very fast and there was a lot of water, I didn't make a mistake, and I didn't give up."

His first win since a wet Donington Park in 2009 was by three seconds. With Marquez and Crutchlow both crashing, and Rossi securing not just second place, but also second in the championship, it was a popular result.

Also popular, Johann Zarco's celebration of finally becoming the first back-to-back Moto2 champion with a sixth win of the year. Of course, he performed his trademark back-flip off the tyre wall, but with a difference. His brother, dressed in identical leathers and helmet, joined him, and the pair executed the gymnastic feat in perfect unison.

For yet another race, the weather was awkward – sudden showers, some very heavy, disrupted both qualifying and race schedules. The differences from the previous weekend were significant. Firstly, it was warm. Secondly, the resurfaced Sepang circuit, although curiously very slow to dry, had excellent grip even when soaking wet.

Along with the resurface had come several changes, instituted by Dromo, the designers of the Argentinian Termas de Rio Hondo circuit. Major drainage improvements apart, most were minor – a paved run-off here, adjusted kerbing there. Except for the final hairpin. Here, the surface level of the inside of the U-turn had been *raised* by a metre, a counter-intuitive 'improvement' that gave the left-hander an adverse camber. The reasons, said Dromo, were two-fold.

Firstly, for safety – a slower exit speed should also mean a slower arrival at the ensuing Turn One at the end of the pit straight, where run-off is limited by the adjacent highway. This was debatable for MotoGP, with bikes accelerating faster than F1 cars up to 200km/h: in Catalunya, slowing the corner before the front straight had led to higher top speeds, because of a cleaner full-throttle exit.

Secondly, with the worst of the adverse camber right at the clipping point, the corner now offered a variety of lines, thought to give more overtaking opportunities. Again, a moot point for the bikes. The old corner was already a favourite overtaking spot.

Many fears were expressed after the usual Thursday riders' track inspection by scooter, some even calling the modification "dangerous". In the event, it made little difference.

Not so the scooter ride, which became a thing of the past after Moto3 team-mates Fabio Spiranelli and passenger Tatsuki Suzuki fell off, and were both roughed up. IRTA acted promptly: from henceforth, no scooters on track. Future pre-race exploration must be done by bicycle or on foot. This was a blow to all, especially Rossi, in the habit of taking his many young Italian protégés around one by one on a scooter to give them tips.

This was not the only sign of scratchy tempers after more than three gruelling weeks on the road, with Rossi firmly refusing to discuss the notorious 'Did he, didn't he?' kicking incident with Marquez in 2015.

Then there were the penalties slapped on three factories by the FIM stewards for failing to get riders to official autograph sessions on Saturday morning. Repsol Honda escaped with an "Official Warning", after failing to notify Dorna or IRTA that Marquez would be unavailable, due to illness; Ecstar Suzuki paid 500 euros because Aleix Espargaro failed to attend; while Ducati got away with 250 euros, after Dovizioso and Iannone were 15 minutes late.

Marquez was indeed ill, suffering from a stomach bug that meant he also missed Friday afternoon's practice, though he had recovered by race day; and Iannone was indeed back,

crowd of 95,300; and a new contract for five more years was signed on race eve. With Indonesia and Thailand jostling to join the calendar, MotoGP is thriving in South East Asia. In sharp contrast to Formula 1, Sepang seeking to end its contract with that series.

MOTOGP RACE – 19 laps (shortened)

Yet another cloudburst struck while riders were out on their sighting laps, prompting a 20-minute delay to the start and one lap being cut off the race distance. The track was still streaming when they did get under way, and it dried very gradually throughout.

Dovizioso was on pole, from Rossi and Lorenzo; Marquez led Crutchlow and Iannone on row two. Vinales was eighth, behind team-mate Espargaro. Vinales had been fastest in the dry, but was at sea on the wet track.

Lorenzo led into the first corner; Marquez got ahead briefly, but it was Rossi leading lap one, with Iannone breathing down his neck, and ahead of him before lap two was done.

By the end of lap one, Dovizioso was third, ahead of Marquez, who had made the unusual choice of a carbon front brake in spite of the wet – something he had found to be effective in practice on the high-grip wet surface. Fast starter Aleix Espargaro was fourth, while behind him Crutchlow was closing on Lorenzo.

The action up front was furious. Rossi had several goes at getting ahead of Iannone. Every time, Iannone would get directly back ahead. "It was a great battle," said Rossi. "I wanted to be in front because my gloves were completely wet and I couldn't keep [hold of] the throttle. But every time I passed, he passed me back."

It was not until lap 12 that he managed to make it stick. One lap later, Dovi was also in front of his team-mate, and one lap after that Iannone crashed out.

By then, also on lap 12, two other front-runners had left the party.

Crutchlow, nursing painful hand injuries, had passed Marquez and threatened to join the leading trio. On lap nine, Marquez got back ahead. Neither would last much longer.

The Briton was first to go, on the tight Turn Two left-hander – another painful experience as he face-planted the track after a throttle-off high-side. He was out. A bit further around, it was Marquez's turn to lose the front, at Turn 11. He managed to scramble back on board in 15th and set about moving back up the points through the backmarkers. "It was nothing to do with the carbon brakes – they were the right choice," he said.

Now it was just Rossi and Dovi, the Ducati keeping the Yamaha very close company. As the track dried, however, Rossi was in trouble: "I started to suffer a lot with my tyres, especially the front on the right." A couple of moments caused him to slacken his pace, and when he ran wide at the first turn at the start of lap 14, Dovi was through. He immediately opened a gap of two seconds.

The first three were now settled. Lorenzo was some ten seconds adrift, but free from threat. He later admitted, "I was lucky to be on the podium, because of others crashing. But I had a reasonable pace in the wet."

The action behind was lively.

While Aleix Espargaro had run on at Turn One on lap three, dropping to 12th, team-mate Vinales had been losing ground, although promoted to fourth by three crashes. "We still struggle in the wet, with the electronics," he said. Before one-third distance, both Avintia Ducatis had caught him, Baz leading Barbera, and both were ahead on lap eight.

The team-mates battled until Barbera finally found his way past with four laps to go – fourth his career-best finish; Baz was out of touch by the end in fifth. Vinales was a lone sixth.

Behind them, Miller had fallen back into another group, and Bautista had escaped to secure seventh before half-distance, equalling his best finish on the improving Aprilia.

and qualified on the second row. "I expected to struggle a lot more," he said. And he was back to his old tricks when he crashed unhurt in the race.

The injury list had grown, with two of the Moto3 victims at Phillip Island joining Pedrosa and Oliveira on the roster of absentees. McPhee's injuries had turned out to be worse than initially diagnosed. Both lungs had collapsed and he had been forbidden to fly, so was stuck in Australia for several weeks. His SaxoPrint Peugeot seat went to 19-year-old Malaysian Hafiq Azmi, who had two past seasons' experience.

Bastianini was present, but not riding, and the Gresini Honda seat went to new Red Bull Rookies Champion Ayuma Sasaki (16). The Japanese bright hope's grand prix debut didn't last long, however, as he was taken down on only the second corner.

Australian GP winner Crutchlow also had a torrid time, crashing in FP3 and suffering fractures to his left hand. He still headed Q1 to get into Q2, only to crash again early on. Picking up his battered Honda, the handlebar bent and "the brake lever pointing to the ground", he forced through to fifth in the dying moments. "It was a little dangerous, but I couldn't start from 12th," he said.

Pedrosa, meanwhile, was present on social media, furiously denying rumours that he had decided to retire. With Hayden engaged at Losail in the World Superbike final, Aoyama was on the factory Honda once again.

Brembo's pre-race statistics revealed, rather surprisingly, that Sepang rivals Motegi for intensity of braking, with 30 per cent of the lap time spent on the brakes. Choosing some colourful zoological references, they revealed that braking for Turn One took six seconds and covered 289 metres, "equivalent to the length of 120 Malayan tigers placed end to end"; while over race distance, riders would exert a total force of almost 1.1 metric tonnes on the brake levers, equalling the weight of "about 100 macaque monkeys".

With several Malaysian riders, the race drew a record

Top: Barbera trails Avintia team-mate Baz. Both riders excelled in the wet, but Barbera would get ahead at the flag.

Above: Barbera's career-best fourth place made him top independent rider again.

Top left: Patience rewarded, Dovizioso crosses the line for his first victory since 2009 at Donington Park.

Photos: Gold & Goose

Miller was left to battle to and fro with Pol Espargaro and a closing Petrucci. They crossed the line in that order, covered by 1.5 seconds.

Eighth put Miller top Honda finisher. Another couple of seconds down, Marquez was 11th, having passed both Laverty (himself gaining ground at the end) and Espargaro's fading Suzuki on the last lap.

A distant Smith and a lone Redding completed the points, with Aoyama and Rabat well out of touch, Bradl sandwiched between them after falling and remounting. Second Aspar Ducati rider Yonny Hernandez retired.

Thus Rossi made himself impregnable in second overall, while Lorenzo regained ground on the formerly threatening Vinales. And just one race left.

MOTO2 RACE – 19 laps

Zarco needed to win in Malaysia, if his closest rivals Luthi and Rins were to follow him home. He didn't want that, however, and laid down a marker in a damp, drying qualifying, claiming pole on well-worn wet tyres by a massive two seconds.

The same conditions prevailed in the race, which produced the same result.

While Luthi was stuck in a fight and finished sixth, and Rins was bafflingly mired at the far end of the points, the Frenchman returned to his finest form. He followed early leader Morbidelli until there were six laps left, then passed him cleanly and deployed his near-legendary ability on end-of-life tyres to pull clear. He won the race by better than three seconds and became the first back-to-back (indeed, the first double) Moto2 champion with one race to spare.

Qualifying had been chancy, the track wet but drying, with a couple of riders risking slicks. Zarco just stayed out on his wets for an astonishing *tour de force*, going one second faster to secure pole position, then promptly shaving off another second.

Long-time leader Morbidelli stayed second, Axel Pons third at the end, with a rear slick, knocking Folger to head row two from Luthi. Rins was a distant 23rd, almost six seconds off.

With rain falling for the early laps, Morbidelli took off in the lead, with Zarco quickly manoeuvring himself into second

Above: This way up! The Flying Zarco Brothers execute a near-perfect synchronised back-flip after Johann's title win.

Left: Morbidelli and Folger chased Zarco home in Moto2.

Below: Bagnaia survived mayhem for a clear second Moto3 win.

Bottom: After numerous crashes had thinned the field, the 3570 Team Italia riders, Valtulini (43) and Petrarca (77), scored their first points of the year.

Photos: Gold & Goose

past Folger. The three of them soon pulled clear of Simeon's Speed Up.

Lowes and Axel Pons were soon down and out in difficult conditions, as was Pasini; it was a fourth crash in five races for Lowes.

The front three held station, each surviving the occasional slither, Folger fading then closing again after half-distance. Now it was Zarco's time to stamp his authority. He cut firmly into the lead at Turn Four, and two laps later was already 1.7 seconds clear, and still stretching.

For him, the rest was a formality.

There was unfinished business behind, with Folger claiming second on lap 16. Morbidelli fought back, and two laps later the German ran wide, handing a second successive second place to Morbidelli, less than half a second clear.

There was a lively battle behind as four riders closed on and swamped Simeon.

The strongest was Baldassarri, who had broken free for a safe fourth by half-distance.

The remainder exchanged blows and places to the end, with local star Hafizh Syahrin prevailing at the finish, while Luthi finally got the better of Alex Marquez for sixth.

The latter was under threat at the flag by an inspired Xavi Vierge on the Tech3, who had picked his way impressively through another big gang and was closing at the finish.

In his tracks came rookie Marini, in a strong ride, who was narrowly ahead of second Tech 3 rider Vinales. Simone Corsi held on to 11th place, ahead of wild-card Ramdan Rosli and Remy Gardner, seventh to 13th being covered by just over two seconds.

Rins was 14th, having dropped off the back of the gang at the end; Simeon took the last point, after surviving a mid-race tumble. An off-colour Nakagami was 21st.

MOTO3 RACE – 13 laps (shortened)

Moto3 qualifying was interrupted by a cloudburst, but a drying track at the end of the restart saw major shuffling, Binder snatching his sixth pole from latecomer Navarro, who in turn denied an on-form Bagnaia at a track that clearly favoured his Mahindra.

For a second race, there were multiple crashes – out of 31 starters, there were only 17 finishers. And with one of those crashes cutting the lead group from four to one, the survivor – Bagnaia – had a lonely ride to his second win of the year, by a yawning seven seconds.

The pile-ups started at the second corner, when Migno, Guevara and Sasaki all tangled up. A little further around, Martin high-sided in the middle of the pack, taking Bulega, Norrodin, Canet and Oettl with him, and getting run over in the process, luckily not badly hurt.

Bulega and Migno remounted to return to the pits, and oil or water dropped by one of these might have triggered the next crucial multi-crash.

Binder, Bagnaia, Rodrigo, Mir and dalla Porta were all starting to break clear when, at Turn Seven, three of them went down in close formation, to be followed seconds later by Di Giannantonio. Clearly something had been spilled, but Bagnaia survived without losing pace, and he would be alone from there to the premature ending.

Rodrigo recovered, although he dropped back into the pursuit group. This was led by Kornfeil and included Navarro, Quartararo, Antonelli and Bendsneyder.

Navarro and Antonelli would fall, the latter remounting to salvage 12th. Bendsneyder moved to the front to take second on lap 14, only for the race to be red-flagged. It had started to rain again, and he was dropped to third, his second podium.

Quartararo was fourth; Locatelli came through from the next gang for fifth. Jammed up behind were Ramirez, Rodrigo, Pawi, with Loi off the back for ninth. Darryn Binder was a lone tenth.

SHELL MALAYSIA MOTORCYCLE GRAND PRIX

28–30 OCTOBER, 2016

SEPANG INTERNATIONAL CIRCUIT

20 laps
Length: 5.543 km / 3.781 miles
Width: 25m

Key
96/60 kph/mph
Gear ⚙

- Langkawi curve 90/56
- Genting Curve 145/90
- Turn 2 75/47
- Turn 3 175/109
- Turn 5 155/96
- Hairpin 75/47
- Turn 7 130/81
- KLIA Curve 130/81
- Pangkor Laut Chicane 75/47
- Berjaya Tioman Corner 65/40
- Sunway Lagoon Corner 90/56
- Turn 12 155/96
- Kenyir Lake 105/65

MotoGP

RACE DISTANCE: 19 laps, 65.441 miles/105.317km · **RACE WEATHER:** Wet (air 25°C, humidity 97%, track 28°C)

Pos.	Rider	Nat.	No.	Entrant	Machine	Tyres	Race tyre choice	Laps	Time & speed
1	**Andrea Dovizioso**	ITA	4	Ducati Team	Ducati Desmosedici	M	F: Med Wet/R: Med Wet	19	42m 27.333s 92.5mph/ 148.8km/h
2	**Valentino Rossi**	ITA	46	Movistar Yamaha MotoGP	Yamaha YZR-M1	M	F: Med Wet/R: Med Wet	19	42m 30.448s
3	**Jorge Lorenzo**	SPA	99	Movistar Yamaha MotoGP	Yamaha YZR-M1	M	F: Med Wet/R: Med Wet	19	42m 39.257s
4	**Hector Barbera**	SPA	8	Avintia Racing	Ducati Desmosedici	M	F: Med Wet/R: Med Wet	19	42m 47.249s
5	**Loris Baz**	FRA	76	Avintia Racing	Ducati Desmosedici	M	F: Med Wet/R: Med Wet	19	42m 48.686s
6	**Maverick Vinales**	SPA	25	Team SUZUKI ECSTAR	Suzuki GSX-RR	M	F: Med Wet/R: Med Wet	19	42m 50.265s
7	**Alvaro Bautista**	SPA	19	Aprilia Racing Team Gresini	Aprilia RS-GP	M	F: Med Wet/R: Med Wet	19	42m 53.162s
8	**Jack Miller**	AUS	43	Estrella Galicia 0,0 Marc VDS	Honda RC213V	M	F: Med Wet/R: Med Wet	19	43m 00.079s
9	**Pol Espargaro**	SPA	44	Monster Yamaha Tech 3	Yamaha YZR-M1	M	F: Med Wet/R: Med Wet	19	43m 01.037s
10	**Danilo Petrucci**	ITA	9	OCTO Pramac Yakhnich	Ducati Desmosedici	M	F: Med Wet/R: Med Wet	19	43m 01.613s
11	**Marc Marquez**	SPA	93	Repsol Honda Team	Honda RC213V	M	F: Med Wet/R: Med Wet	19	43m 03.813s
12	**Eugene Laverty**	IRL	50	Pull & Bear Aspar Team	Ducati Desmosedici	M	F: Med Wet/R: Med Wet	19	43m 03.971s
13	**Aleix Espargaro**	SPA	41	Team SUZUKI ECSTAR	Suzuki GSX-RR	M	F: Med Wet/R: Soft Wet	19	43m 04.230s
14	**Bradley Smith**	GBR	38	Monster Yamaha Tech 3	Yamaha YZR-M1	M	F: Med Wet/R: Med Wet	19	43m 12.942s
15	**Scott Redding**	GBR	45	OCTO Pramac Yakhnich	Ducati Desmosedici	M	F: Med Wet/R: Med Wet	19	43m 17.112s
16	Hiroshi Aoyama	JPN	7	Repsol Honda Team	Honda RC213V	M	F: Med Wet/R: Soft Wet	19	43m 19.998s
17	Stefan Bradl	GER	6	Aprilia Racing Team Gresini	Aprilia RS-GP	M	F: Med Wet/R: Med Wet	19	43m 20.117s
18	Tito Rabat	SPA	53	Estrella Galicia 0,0 Marc VDS	Honda RC213V	M	F: Med Wet/R: Med Wet	19	43m 22.224s
	Andrea Iannone	ITA	29	Ducati Team	Ducati Desmosedici	M	F: Med Wet/R: Med Wet	12	DNF-crash
	Cal Crutchlow	GBR	35	LCR Honda	Honda RC213V	M	F: Med Wet/R: Med Wet	11	DNF-crash
	Yonny Hernandez	COL	68	Pull & Bear Aspar Team	Ducati Desmosedici	M	F: Soft Wet/R: Med Wet	11	DNF-technical

Fastest lap: Andrea Dovizioso, on lap 12, 2m 11.950s, 94.0mph/151.2km/h.
Lap record: Jorge Lorenzo, SPA (Yamaha), 2m 0.606s, 102.8mph/165.4km/h (2015).
Event best maximum speed: Andrea Iannone, 201.7mph/324.6km/h (free practice).

Qualifying

Weather: Wet
Air Temp: 26° **Track Temp:** 28°
Humidity: 100%

1	Dovizioso	2m 11.485s
2	Rossi	2m 11.731s
3	Lorenzo	2m 11.787s
4	Marquez	2m 11.874s
5	Crutchlow	2m 12.558s
6	Iannone	2m 12.598s
7	A. Espargaro	2m 12.869s
8	Vinales	2m 12.981s
9	Bautista	2m 13.325s
10	Baz	2m 13.452s
11	P. Espargaro	2m 13.707s
12	Barbera	2m 13.973s
13	Smith	2m 12.898s
14	Miller	2m 12.907s
15	Petrucci	2m 13.776s
16	Bradl	2m 13.850s
17	Aoyama	2m 14.179s
18	Redding	2m 14.433s
19	Laverty	2m 14.769s
20	Hernandez	2m 14.786s
21	Rabat	2m 15.894s

Fastest race laps

1	Dovizioso	2m 11.950s
2	Rossi	2m 12.107s
3	Marquez	2m 12.407s
4	Iannone	2m 12.696s
5	Crutchlow	2m 12.830s
6	Barbera	2m 13.065s
7	Lorenzo	2m 13.449s
8	Laverty	2m 13.551s
9	Vinales	2m 13.579s
10	Baz	2m 13.711s
11	Bautista	2m 13.790s
12	Miller	2m 14.081s
13	P. Espargaro	2m 14.129s
14	Petrucci	2m 14.147s
15	A. Espargaro	2m 14.196s
16	Bradl	2m 14.355s
17	Smith	2m 14.560s
18	Rabat	2m 14.598s
19	Aoyama	2m 14.608s
20	Redding	2m 14.954s
21	Hernandez	2m 15.598s

Championship Points

1	Marquez	278
2	Rossi	236
3	Lorenzo	208
4	Vinales	191
5	Dovizioso	162
6	Pedrosa	155
7	Crutchlow	141
8	P. Espargaro	124
9	Barbera	97
10	Iannone	96
11	A. Espargaro	85
12	Laverty	77
13	Bautista	76
14	Redding	72
15	Petrucci	71
16	Bradl	60
17	Miller	56
18	Smith	55
19	Pirro	36
20	Baz	35
21	Rabat	29
22	Hernandez	20
23	Nakasuga	5
24	Lowes	3
25	Aoyama	1
26	Hayden	1
27	Jones	1

Constructor Points

1	Honda	349
2	Yamaha	328
3	Ducati	245
4	Suzuki	197
5	Aprilia	95

Grid order		1	2	3	4	5	6	7	8	9	10	11	12	13	14	15	16	17	18	19	
4	DOVIZIOSO	46	29	29	29	29	29	29	29	29	29	46	46	46	46	4	4	4	4	4	1
46	ROSSI	29	46	46	46	46	46	46	46	46	46	29	4	4	4	46	46	46	46	46	2
99	LORENZO	4	4	4	4	4	4	4	4	4	4	4	29	99	99	99	99	99	99	99	3
93	MARQUEZ	93	93	93	93	35	35	35	35	93	93	93	99	76	76	76	8	8	8	8	4
35	CRUTCHLOW	41	41	99	35	93	93	93	93	35	35	35	76	8	8	8	76	76	76	76	5
29	IANNONE	99	99	35	99	99	99	99	99	99	99	99	8	25	25	25	25	25	25	25	6
41	A. ESPARGARO	35	35	25	25	25	25	25	76	76	76	76	25	19	19	19	19	19	19	19	7
25	VINALES	25	25	43	8	76	76	76	8	8	8	8	19	41	41	41	43	43	43	43	8
19	BAUTISTA	44	43	8	76	8	8	8	25	25	25	25	43	43	43	43	44	44	44	44	9
76	BAZ	43	44	76	43	43	43	43	43	19	19	19	41	44	44	44	9	9	9	9	10
44	P. ESPARGARO	38	8	44	41	41	41	19	19	43	43	43	44	9	9	9	41	41	41	93	11
8	BARBERA	76	76	41	19	19	19	41	41	41	41	41	9	50	50	50	50	50	50	50	12
38	SMITH	8	38	19	44	44	44	44	44	44	44	44	38	38	38	38	93	93	93	41	13
43	MILLER	19	19	38	38	38	9	9	9	9	9	50	45	93	93	93	38	38	38	38	14
9	PETRUCCI	9	9	9	9	9	6	6	6	6	38	38	93	93	45	45	45	45	45	45	15
6	BRADL	6	6	6	6	6	38	38	38	38	45	45	45	7	7	7	7	7	7	7	
7	JONES	68	68	68	45	45	45	45	45	45	50	50	7	6	6	6	6	6	6		
45	REDDING	45	45	45	68	68	68	68	68	50	68	68	6	53	53	53	53	53	53	53	
50	LAVERTY	53	53	53	53	53	53	50	50	68	7	7	53								
68	HERNANDEZ	50	50	50	7	50	50	53	53	7	53	53									
53	RABAT	7	7	7	50	7	7	7	7	53	6	6									

Moto2

RACE DISTANCE: 19 laps, 65.441 miles/105.317km · RACE WEATHER: Wet (air 31°C, humidity 82%, track 35°C)

Pos.	Rider	Nat.	No.	Entrant	Machine	Laps	Time & Speed
1	**Johann Zarco**	FRA	5	Ajo Motorsport	Kalex	19	45m 51.036s 85.6mph/ 137.8km/h
2	**Franco Morbidelli**	ITA	21	Estrella Galicia, 0,0 Marc VDS	Kalex	19	45m 54.292s
3	**Jonas Folger**	GER	94	Dynavolt Intact GP	Kalex	19	45m 54.725s
4	**Lorenzo Baldassarri**	ITA	7	Forward Team	Kalex	19	46m 12.464s
5	**Hafizh Syahrin**	MAL	55	Petronas Raceline Malaysia	Kalex	19	46m 15.736s
6	**Thomas Luthi**	SWI	12	Garage Plus Interwetten	Kalex	19	46m 17.220s
7	**Alex Marquez**	SPA	73	Estrella Galicia 0,0 Marc VDS	Kalex	19	46m 19.213s
8	**Xavi Vierge**	SPA	97	Tech 3 Racing	Tech 3	19	46m 19.891s
9	**Luca Marini**	ITA	10	Forward Team	Kalex	19	46m 20.283s
10	**Isaac Vinales**	SPA	32	Tech 3 Racing	Tech 3	19	46m 21.005s
11	**Simone Corsi**	ITA	24	Speed Up Racing	Speed Up	19	46m 21.902s
12	**Ramdan Rosli**	MAL	93	Petronas AHM Malaysia	Kalex	19	46m 22.296s
13	**Remy Gardner**	AUS	87	Tasca Racing Scuderia Moto2	Kalex	19	46m 22.829s
14	**Alex Rins**	SPA	40	Paginas Amarillas HP 40	Kalex	19	46m 25.733s
15	**Xavier Simeon**	BEL	19	QMMF Racing Team	Speed Up	19	46m 37.705s
16	Jesko Raffin	SWI	2	Sports-Millions-EMWE-SAG	Kalex	19	46m 40.162s
17	Sandro Cortese	GER	11	Dynavolt Intact GP	Kalex	19	46m 40.329s
18	Danny Kent	GBR	52	Leopard Racing	Kalex	19	46m 42.646s
19	Edgar Pons	SPA	57	Paginas Amarillas HP 40	Kalex	19	46m 45.985s
20	Marcel Schrotter	GER	23	AGR Team	Kalex	19	46m 46.497s
21	Takaaki Nakagami	JPN	30	IDEMITSU Honda Team Asia	Kalex	19	46m 59.649s
22	Iker Lecuona	SPA	27	CarXpert Interwetten	Kalex	19	47m 07.610s
23	Mattia Pasini	ITA	54	Italtrans Racing Team	Kalex	19	47m 16.874s
24	Ratthapark Wilairot	THA	14	IDEMITSU Honda Team Asia	Kalex	19	47m 52.671s
	Alessandro Nocco	ITA	20	Leopard Racing	Kalex	12	DNF
	Robin Mulhauser	SWI	70	CarXpert Interwetten	Kalex	5	DNF
	Axel Pons	SPA	49	AGR Team	Kalex	1	DNF
	Sam Lowes	GBR	22	Federal Oil Gresini Moto2	Kalex	1	DNF

Fastest lap: Luca Marini, on lap 19, 2m 21.475s, 87.6mph/141km/h.
Lap record: Thomas Luthi, SWI (Kalex), 2m 7.321s, 97.4mph/156.7km/h (2015).
Event best maximum speed: Alex Rins, 167.5mph/269.6km/h (free practice).

Qualifying

Weather: Wet
Air Temp: 26° **Track Temp:** 27°
Humidity: 100%

1	Zarco	2m 18.621s
2	Morbidelli	2m 20.755s
3	A. Pons	2m 21.383s
4	Folger	2m 21.559s
5	Luthi	2m 21.775s
6	Baldassarri	2m 21.836s
7	Simeon	2m 21.941s
8	Pasini	2m 22.029s
9	Gardner	2m 22.070s
10	Corsi	2m 22.107s
11	Marini	2m 22.556s
12	Rosli	2m 22.697s
13	Lowes	2m 23.187s
14	Syahrin	2m 23.213s
15	Cortese	2m 23.387s
16	Nocco	2m 23.629s
17	Lecuona	2m 23.677s
18	E. Pons	2m 23.785s
19	Vinales	2m 23.913s
20	Nakagami	2m 23.935s
21	Marquez	2m 24.145s
22	Schrotter	2m 24.274s
23	Rins	2m 24.370s
24	Kent	2m 24.542s
25	Vierge	2m 24.639s
26	Wilairot	2m 24.793s
27	Raffin	2m 25.030s
28	Mulhauser	2m 25.611s

Fastest race laps

1	Marini	2m 21.475s
2	Zarco	2m 21.484s
3	Morbidelli	2m 21.532s
4	Folger	2m 21.563s
5	Gardner	2m 21.605s
6	Vinales	2m 21.741s
7	Rosli	2m 21.757s
8	Vierge	2m 22.132s
9	Corsi	2m 22.133s
10	Luthi	2m 22.341s
11	Cortese	2m 22.381s
12	Baldassarri	2m 22.450s
13	Syahrin	2m 22.576s
14	Raffin	2m 23.151s
15	Rins	2m 23.259s
16	Schrotter	2m 23.333s
17	Marquez	2m 23.350s
18	Simeon	2m 23.414s
19	E. Pons	2m 23.748s
20	Kent	2m 23.765s
21	Nakagami	2m 25.443s
22	Pasini	2m 26.016s
23	Lecuona	2m 26.309s
24	Wilairot	2m 27.528s
25	Nocco	2m 27.657s
26	Mulhauser	2m 28.910s

Championship Points

1	Zarco	251
2	Luthi	214
3	Rins	203
4	Morbidelli	197
5	Lowes	162
6	Folger	159
7	Nakagami	159
8	Baldassarri	125
9	Syahrin	117
10	Corsi	98
11	Aegerter	71
12	Marquez	69
13	Pasini	63
14	Cortese	61
15	Schrotter	58
16	A. Pons	55
17	Simeon	46
18	Simon	40
19	Salom	37
20	Marini	34
21	Oliveira	33
22	Vierge	33
23	Kent	28
24	Vinales	19
25	Raffin	14
26	Gardner	8
27	West	6
28	Wilairot	6
29	Rosli	4
30	Mulhauser	4
31	E. Pons	4
32	Nagashima	2

Constructor Points

1	Kalex	425
2	Speed Up	131
3	Tech 3	43
4	Suter	6

Moto3

RACE DISTANCE: 13 laps, 44.775 miles/72.059km · RACE WEATHER: Dry (air 32°C, humidity 60%, track 40°C)

Pos.	Rider	Nat.	No.	Entrant	Machine	Laps	Time & Speed
1	**Francesco Bagnaia**	ITA	21	Pull & Bear Aspar Mahindra Team	Mahindra	13	29m 29.351s 91.1mph/ 146.6km/h
2	**Jakub Kornfeil**	CZE	84	Drive M7 SIC Racing Team	Honda	13	29m 36.459s
3	**Bo Bendsneyder**	NED	64	Red Bull KTM Ajo	KTM	13	29m 36.604s
4	**Fabio Quartararo**	FRA	20	Leopard Racing	KTM	13	29m 37.820s
5	**Andrea Locatelli**	ITA	55	Leopard Racing	KTM	13	29m 41.765s
6	**Marcos Ramirez**	SPA	42	Platinum Bay Real Estate	Mahindra	13	29m 42.057s
7	**Gabriel Rodrigo**	ARG	19	RBA Racing Team	KTM	13	29m 42.738s
8	**Khairul Idham Pawi**	MAL	89	Honda Team Asia	Honda	13	29m 42.857s
9	**Livio Loi**	BEL	11	RW Racing GP BV	Honda	13	29m 43.796s
10	**Darryn Binder**	RSA	40	Platinum Bay Real Estate	Mahindra	13	30m 08.128s
11	**Hafiq Azmi**	MAL	38	Peugeot MC Saxoprint	Peugeot	13	30m 15.178s
12	**Niccolo Antonelli**	ITA	23	Ongetta-Rivacold	Honda	13	30m 18.250s
13	**Stefano Valtulini**	ITA	43	3570 Team Italia	Mahindra	13	30m 18.999s
14	**Lorenzo Petrarca**	ITA	77	3570 Team Italia	Mahindra	13	30m 19.193s
15	**Fabio Di Giannantonio**	ITA	4	Gresini Racing Moto3	Honda	13	30m 44.514s
16	Lorenzo dalla Porta	ITA	48	SKY Racing Team VR46	KTM	13	29m 35.775s
17	Brad Binder	RSA	41	Red Bull KTM Ajo	KTM	10	29m 36.999s
	Maria Herrera	SPA	6	MH6 Team	KTM	–	NC
	Jules Danilo	FRA	95	Ongetta-Rivacold	Honda	6	DNF
	Jorge Navarro	SPA	9	Estrella Galicia 0,0	Honda	5	DNF
	Albert Arenas	SPA	12	Peugeot MC Saxoprint	Peugeot	3	DNF
	Joan Mir	SPA	36	Leopard Racing	KTM	2	DNF
	Tatsuki Suzuki	JPN	24	CIP-Unicom Starker	Mahindra	2	DNF
	Andrea Migno	ITA	16	SKY Racing Team VR46	KTM	2	DNF
	Nicolo Bulega	ITA	8	SKY Racing Team VR46	KTM	1	DNF
	Jorge Martin	SPA	88	Pull & Bear Aspar Mahindra Team	Mahindra	0	DNF
	Aron Canet	SPA	44	Estrella Galicia 0,0	Honda	0	DNF
	Philipp Oettl	GER	65	Schedl GP Racing	KTM	0	DNF
	Juanfran Guevara	SPA	58	RBA Racing Team	KTM	0	DNF
	Adam Norrodin	MAL	7	Drive M7 SIC Racing Team	Honda	0	DNF
	Ayumu Sasaki	JPN	71	Gresini Racing Moto3	Honda	0	DNF

Fastest lap: Joan Mir, on lap 2, 2m 14.201s, 92.3mph/148.6km/h.
Lap record: Brad Binder, RSA (KTM), 2m 13.571s, 92.8mph/149.3km/h (2015).
Event best maximum speed: Gabriel Rodrigo, 141.9mph/228.3km/h (free practice).

Qualifying

Weather: Wet
Air Temp: 25° **Track Temp:** 28°
Humidity: 98%

1	B. Binder	2m 26.268s
2	Navarro	2m 26.361s
3	Bagnaia	2m 26.395s
4	Dalla Porta	2m 27.078s
5	Rodrigo	2m 27.307s
6	Antonelli	2m 27.355s
7	Bendsneyder	2m 27.604s
8	Martin	2m 27.642s
9	Quartararo	2m 27.661s
10	Canet	2m 27.924s
11	Locatelli	2m 27.987s
12	Oettl	2m 28.062s
13	Bulega	2m 28.069s
14	Mir	2m 28.193s
15	Kornfeil	2m 28.215s
16	Suzuki	2m 28.553s
17	Guevara	2m 28.718s
18	Norrodin	2m 28.965s
19	Di Giannantonio	2m 28.982s
20	Pawi	2m 28.989s
21	Sasaki	2m 29.267s
22	Azmi	2m 29.334s
23	Loi	2m 29.380s
24	Danilo	2m 29.595s
25	Ono	2m 30.248s
26	Migno	2m 30.747s
27	Arenas	2m 30.872s
28	Ramirez	2m 30.961s
29	Petrarca	2m 32.151s
30	Valtulini	2m 32.346s

Fastest race laps

1	Mir	2m 14.201s
2	Quartararo	2m 14.646s
3	Kornfeil	2m 14.680s
4	Navarro	2m 14.860s
5	Bagnaia	2m 14.958s
6	Dalla Porta	2m 15.084s
7	Di Giannantonio	2m 15.117s
8	Antonelli	2m 15.221s
9	Bendsneyder	2m 15.300s
10	Rodrigo	2m 15.399s
11	B. Binder	2m 15.453s
12	Ramirez	2m 15.510s
13	Herrera	2m 15.739s
14	Locatelli	2m 15.767s
15	Danilo	2m 15.772s
16	Pawi	2m 15.779s
17	Loi	2m 15.784s
18	Arenas	2m 16.166s
19	D. Binder	2m 16.621s
20	Suzuki	2m 16.670s
21	Petrarca	2m 17.741s
22	Azmi	2m 17.889s
23	Valtulini	2m 18.303s

Championship Points

1	B. Binder	294
2	Bastianini	164
3	Bagnaia	145
4	Navarro	143
5	Bulega	129
6	Mir	124
7	Di Giannantonio	123
8	Kornfeil	103
9	Locatelli	96
10	Fenati	93
11	Antonelli	91
12	Quartararo	81
13	Oettl	77
14	Canet	76
15	Bendsneyder	75
16	Martin	66
17	Pawi	62
18	Loi	62
19	Danilo	58
20	McPhee	48
21	Migno	47
22	Guevara	40
23	Ono	36
24	Rodrigo	31
25	D. Binder	23
26	Ramirez	19
27	Suzuki	16
28	Norrodin	14
29	Manzi	13
30	Dalla Porta	12
31	Herrera	7
32	Azmi	5
33	Valtulini	3
34	Arenas	2
35	Petrarca	2

Constructor Points

1	KTM	357
2	Honda	337
3	Mahindra	205
4	Peugeot	55

Main: Man alone. Lorenzo returned to familiar form for the final round.
Photo: Gold & Goose

Inset, far left: "Now I can sleep deep." Lorenzo looked spent after reaching the "perfect end" of an era with Yamaha.
Photo: Whit Bazemore Photography

Inset, left: Marquez was beaten, but still had plenty to celebrate.

Inset, below: Lorenzo leads Iannone, Vinales, Rossi, Marquez and Pedrosa early on. He was never headed.
Photos: Gold & Goose

FIM WORLD CHAMPIONSHIP · ROUND 18

VALENCIA GRAND PRIX

VALENCIA CIRCUIT

Above: A fierce five-way battle for second – Rossi, Iannone, Marquez, Vinales and Dovizioso.

Top right: Kallio on the all-new KTM fought with Rabat, until he retired.

Above right: Brad Binder took control of Moto3 – twice. He heads Mir, Migno and Bastianini on the final lap.

Centre right: Marquez and doyen Sammy Miller swapped bikes for a photoshoot, but the AJS was too leaky to go out on track.

Centre far right: Loris Capirossi's number '65' was formally retired from the MotoGP class.

Below right: The unlucky Bagnaia bites the dust, victim for a second time of Rodrigo.

Photos: Gold & Goose

THE 2016 season came to an end at Valencia on a day when all three champions excelled. Although not all three of them won.

Binder took his last Moto3 race in heroic style, after a rare error early on had dropped him from second to 22nd. He forged through as at Jerez, only to run wide with just four laps to go, dropping to fourth. It was just the challenge he needed to underline his spectacular championship year. He came through once more to win his seventh race.

Zarco likewise took his seventh victory in his final Moto2 race, which exploded any criticisms that the class is often processional with as much power as the traditional Valencia post-race fireworks. Thanks to Morbidelli, with a bit of help from Rins and Luthi, the number of overtaking moves soon became uncountable. By one assessment (if you count pulling alongside), Morbidelli and Zarco changed places seven times in one lap alone. In the end, and fittingly, the Frenchman stamped his authority again.

Marquez also produced a signal performance, although he didn't win. After a year of 442 racing laps, he needed just two more to have been able to do that. A bad start had left him mired on a one-line track. But once he got to second, more than five seconds adrift of an imperious pole-to-chequer Lorenzo, he rode with trademark abandon and skill to slice half a second or more out of his lead every time around the tortuous 4.005km pocket-handkerchief track. He was just over a second adrift at the flag.

It was a typical high-risk strategy; he said afterwards, "I had nothing to lose." A view not shared by HRC and its retiring figurehead, Shuhei Nakamoto. Had it gone wrong, with team-mate Pedrosa and Crutchlow both having already crashed out, Honda would have lost the constructors' title to Yamaha.

Moto3 produced a couple of real hard-luck stories. Mahindra's Pecco Bagnaia had won Sepang, lucky to escape an oil spill that had taken out the rest of the leading group. That had moved him to third overall, underlining the Indian company's best season. The position might have been stronger had he not been knocked off the weekend before by the increasingly notorious Argentinean, Gabriel Rodrigo. This time, Rodrigo knocked Bagnaia off on the first lap. He finished fourth overall.

And how about Valencian teenager Aron Canet, giggling with delight after claiming his first pole position? His Honda stalled on the grid and he had to start from the pit lane.

KTM's racing debut was respectable. Kallio cut his time by almost two seconds to qualify 20th, ahead of Rabat and Hernandez. But the steel-tube-framed bike did not make the chequered flag, circulating last before pitting with a failed wheel-speed sensor. He'd complained of poor rear grip on corner entry and exit.

The KTM sounded somewhat like the Honda, with so-called 'screamer' firing intervals, but sports director Pit Beirer confirmed that other formats were possible. And may soon emerge, it seems, with Honda expected to switch to closer firing order ('long bang') for their 90-degree V4. A gruffer exhaust note had been heard in tests at Misano earlier in the year and was back for post-Valencia tests. This would bring Honda in line with Ducati, Yamaha and Suzuki.

Eugene Laverty's last MotoGP ride before joining Aprilia's Superbike team was exceptional, in that he failed to score points. This was only the third time, and the first that he had actually been beaten out of the top 15. He'd been knocked down in Austria and crashed at Motegi. His talent may not be completely lost to MotoGP, however, with Aprilia boss Romano Albesiano saying that he will have a testing role, and will be first choice as a substitute.

This news had been given at a second manufacturers' press conference, with Aprilia this time having been invited to join Honda, Yamaha, Suzuki and Ducati (at Brno, they had been left out). It came after generally favourable comments from all about the effect of the new rules, more competitive

racing and the expansion to six factories. Yamaha's Lin Jarvis raised a negative, however. "In general, it pumps up the price of riders. There were six factory seats, and now there are 12. This makes it hard for satellite teams to capture and keep top talent."

Michelin also called a conference to review the season, with Nicolas Goubert taking the opportunity to point out that, in spite of riders' complaints about front tyres, the number of actual race crashes in the first 16 rounds, at 67, was only one up on Bridgestone in 2015. He spoke with pride of the speed of response to problems – such as new-construction rears flown to Texas one week after Redding's rear failure in Argentina; and he promised the same level of resources for 2017. "All in all, we learned a lot," he said. One lesson had been a front tyre with a different profile, more V-shaped, to give a bigger footprint at full lean. It had been part of the allocation for this race and was a popular choice on Sunday.

On the question of intermediates, he said that they had been made at the request of Dorna, to avoid empty tracks in practice, but "we found that riders could use our medium rain tyres on a dry track, and there were some times with riders out using slick, intermediate and rain tyres at the same time. I will not say there won't be intermediates, but maybe there is no need."

Dorna's Ezpeleta caused a flutter when he announced that Loris Capirossi's number '65' was to be retired in all classes – on the same day that new entry lists showed that Philipp Oettl would continue with that number in Moto3 in 2017. Turned out to be a slip of the tongue: it will apply only to MotoGP.

Max Biaggi was in the paddock and in cheerful mood to announce his new small-scale co-operation with Mahindra, supporting two young Italian riders through the national championship with a view towards GPs in 2018. He was putting in his own money, he said, adding, "This is not a competition with the VR46 Academy. We are not focused on big things, but two riders, two chances, two possibilities."

The last race of Dorna's first 25 years was to have been marked by a special celebration: motorcycling doyen Sammy Miller had brought his AJS Porcupine – the bike on which Les Graham had won the first world championship in 1949 – to run a lap alongside Marquez on the latest winning RC213V before the first race on Sunday. It had to be cancelled, however, because one of the bikes was leaking too much oil. It wasn't the Honda.

MOTOGP RACE – 30 laps

Valencia belonged to Lorenzo, back to trademark style. He led into the first corner from a record-breaking pole, then set a new record on lap five to secure a commanding lead. By lap 20, it was better than 5.4 seconds, a breathtaking five-bike battle for second almost out of sight behind.

He seemed set for a third pole-to-chequer victory, a fine farewell to Yamaha after nine years. Then things changed.

The battle behind had been furious, with Iannone disputing second with Rossi; Marquez, Vinales and Dovizioso glued on behind.

By lap 20, Rossi and Iannone were still taking chunks out of one another, the Ducati's speed and its rider's daring trumping Rossi's finesse time and again. Dovi, however, had faded off the back, blaming a poor feeling and difficulty braking; Vinales would soon also lose touch.

Marquez, though, was on the march. His position had been set, on a tortuous one-line track, after "my worst start of the season". A recalcitrant clutch had dropped him from second on the grid to seventh into the first corner. On the other hand, he was one of only four (with Crutchlow, Miller and Laverty) who had chosen the hard front tyre (the new spec). Now was the time for it to pay dividends.

His first pass on Iannone was promptly reversed down the straight, but he made it stick on lap 20 and now fulfilled his promise of a return to full risk after securing the title.

Over the last ten laps, he was slicing half a second a lap

out of Lorenzo's lead. As they started the last lap, he was behind by 1.784 of a second, and his quarry was in sight. By the end of it, 1.185. "If there had been another two laps…" he said.

Was Lorenzo playing it cool, under control?

Far from it, he said. He'd been worried about his rear tyre's grip, especially on the crucial last two left-handers. The worry was doubled when his pit board told him his lead had dropped to 4.5 seconds, "and it was Marquez behind."

He hadn't expected to win, he added, "because already Marquez was strong. But now I can sleep deep, because I had a perfect end with Yamaha."

No less remarkable was the battle for third. Iannone, in only his second race back, was suffering pain and exhaustion. It didn't show. Every time Rossi passed him, he would attack him back directly, and if that failed there was always the surge of Ducati power on the straight.

On the third-last lap, the fight was resolved. Rossi shoved past in the twists over the hill; Iannone pushed straight back, and they touched, forcing Rossi wide over the kerb and finally out of touch.

"I put all of me into this race," said Iannone. Rossi blamed tyre degradation and "not being fast enough" for his fourth place; but with Lorenzo's win, it was enough to secure the teams' title for Movistar Yamaha, ahead of Repsol Honda.

Outpaced, Vinales was three seconds away at the end, comfortably clear of a fierce final battle for sixth.

Dovizioso had been left trailing from half-distance, and by lap 20 he was almost five seconds behind Vinales, blaming poor feel. At that stage, he was the same distance clear of the Espargaro brothers, Monster Yamaha-mounted Pol ahead of Aleix's Suzuki, the pair locked together pretty much all race long.

Steadily they closed the gap on the slowing Ducati, and on the second-last lap the Yamaha was ahead. Dovi used his horsepower to pull alongside over the line, but the Yamaha took sixth by four-hundredths of a second, with the Suzuki three-tenths behind.

Crutchlow had been chasing the pair until just after half-distance, when he slipped off. By then, he had seen off Smith's challenge, the Yamaha rider inheriting a lone ninth.

Another lively battle behind was resolved when Bautista managed to escape from a pressing Barbera, who in turn had passed and dropped off Petrucci.

Bradl took 13th off Redding in the closing laps. Three seconds behind, Jack Miller took the last point, having finally escaped from Laverty and Rabat, with Baz last.

Hernandez was an early faller; Pedrosa a few laps later, not knowing afterwards whether to blame himself or his bike: "The rear stepped out and at the same time I lost the front. I don't know why, because I wasn't at the limit."

Kallio had been circulating the KTM at the back, until he pitted with 11 laps remaining, blaming a sensor problem.

There were no significant changes in the championship standings. Crutchlow hung on to seventh as top Independent Team rider, seven points clear of Pol Espargaro.

MOTO2 RACE – 27 laps

In the end, it was business as usual, but the early laps of Moto2 were a feast of close racing and overtaking up front, more reminiscent of Moto3.

The main contenders were the front-row qualifiers, Zarco, Luthi and Morbidelli, joined by Rins from row two. And the main action came from Morbidelli, who lived up to his reputation for hard passing and dangerous living.

Zarco did most of the leading over the line, but it was different around the back, as Morbidelli pushed and probed, diving inside or swooping around the outside. Zarco fought straight back every time, with an aggression seldom seen.

Luthi was with them all the way, and Rins up to second for a couple of early laps.

On the 12th, Morbidelli led over the line for the first time, as he would for the next three laps. But it would last no longer. Zarco, as usual, had taken better care of his tyres (not that his riding style showed it), while Morbidelli had squeezed the best out of his rear and was sliding badly.

When Zarco passed again to lead lap 16, it was the end of the battle, and he gradually drew clear to win by better than three seconds. "I was happy with pole, but I could see Morbidelli and Luthi had a good pace, so I decided not to let them escape and to fight from the beginning to feel better. Everything worked out exactly as we wanted."

Morbidelli looked safe in second, and Luthi in third, the race assuming the usual processional format as the laps counted down. This was deceptive.

By now, Lowes – gaining pace towards the end – had tagged on to the leading group, and also Julian Simon on

the only Speed Up chassis up front. Simon would crash, but Lowes was ever more threatening.

It came down to the last lap, and by then Morbidelli's rear tyre, in his own words, "was destroyed". He had no answer as Luthi closed to attack, claiming second by a comfortable margin. This was an important result, since it dropped Morbidelli from third overall to fourth, one point adrift of Rins.

This was in spite of Lowes snitching fourth from Rins on the final lap, by just two-tenths.

Six seconds behind, Nakagami had been promoted to sixth by the departure of Simon, after picking his way through a trio from mid-distance.

The trio had become a quartet by the finish, all still close, with veteran Pasini managing to keep control, while Folger picked through to eighth in his wake. Kent had caught up and taken ninth from Schrotter with four laps to go.

Simone Corsi was 11th on the best Speed Up, having fended off a persistent Xavi Vierge's Tech 3; Oliveira, Baldassarri and Syahrin were still close for the last points. Vierge took Rookie of the Year, one point ahead of Oliveira.

Cortese and Axel Pons joined the crash list; Alex Marquez retired with arm-pump.

MOTO3 RACE – 24 laps

It was a day for the champion in the smaller class, too, with a doubly heroic comeback by Brad Binder – first after a second-lap slip had dropped him 20 places, to 22nd; then again, when he ran wide with four laps to go, dropping from first to fourth.

The South African defied the odds again, seizing the lead at the start of the final lap to claim his seventh win of the year by 0.056 of a second.

With pole first-timer Canet starting from the pit lane, Bastianini led the first lap from Binder. By now, Bagnaia was already down and out after Rodrigo had crashed right under his front wheel in the final corner, miraculously with no other riders involved. Rodrigo was able to remount, to escape the wrath of Rossi protégé Bagnaia.

While the lead pack was as close and furious as ever, rookie Joan Mir was able not only to lead for six laps, but also to gain a gap of almost one second – at least partly because Binder was now way back. But Mir had overtaken under a yellow flag and was penalised, having to drop back one position.

This closed up the leading group, and for a spell Migno was at the front, before Mir took over once more. All the while, Binder was picking through rapidly, in front again on lap 21, only to run wide with a second mistake of the race, which dropped him back to fourth. In another precision display, however, he took the lead into the first corner on the final lap.

Mir was second; then came Migno, Bastianini, his rookie team-mate Fabio Di Giannantonio and Juanfran Guevara.

Kornfeil, Oettl, Navarro and Martin completed the top ten.

Binder's winning points margin over Bastianini was 142, just five short of the record margin set in MotoGP in 2005, Rossi over Melandri. Navarro's ninth gave him third over no-score Bagnaia; Mir took top rookie spot ahead of Di Giannantonio by ten points.

GP MOTUL DE LA COMUNITAT VALENCIANA

11–13 NOVEMBER, 2016

CIRCUITO DE LA COMUNITAT VALENCIANA

30 laps
Length: 4.005 km / 2.489 miles
Width: 12m

Key
96/60 kph/mph
⚙ Gear

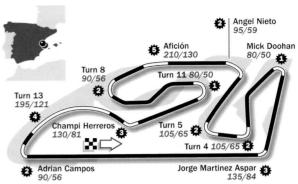

Angel Nieto 95/59
Afición 210/130
Mick Doohan 80/50
Turn 8 90/56
Turn 11 80/50
Turn 13 195/121
Champi Herreros 130/81
Turn 5 105/65
Turn 4 105/65
Adrian Campos 90/56
Jorge Martinez Aspar 135/84

MotoGP — RACE DISTANCE: 30 laps, 74.658 miles/120.150km · RACE WEATHER: Dry (air 22°C, humidity 42%, track 25°C)

Pos.	Rider	Nat.	No.	Entrant	Machine	Tyres	Race tyre choice	Laps	Time & speed
1	**Jorge Lorenzo**	SPA	99	Movistar Yamaha MotoGP	Yamaha YZR-M1	M	F: '17 Medium/R: Soft	30	45m 54.228s 97.6mph/ 157.0km/h
2	**Marc Marquez**	SPA	93	Repsol Honda Team	Honda RC213V	M	F: '17 Hard/R: Soft	30	45m 55.413s
3	**Andrea Iannone**	ITA	29	Ducati Team	Ducati Desmosedici	M	F: '17 Medium/R: Soft	30	46m 00.831s
4	**Valentino Rossi**	ITA	46	Movistar Yamaha MotoGP	Yamaha YZR-M1	M	F: '17 Medium/R: Soft	30	46m 01.896s
5	**Maverick Vinales**	SPA	25	Team SUZUKI ECSTAR	Suzuki GSX-RR	M	F: '17 Medium/R: Soft	30	46m 04.838s
6	**Pol Espargaro**	SPA	44	Monster Yamaha Tech 3	Yamaha YZR-M1	M	F: Medium/R: Soft	30	46m 12.606s
7	**Andrea Dovizioso**	ITA	4	Ducati Team	Ducati Desmosedici	M	F: '17 Medium/R: Soft	30	46m 12.645s
8	**Aleix Espargaro**	SPA	41	Team SUZUKI ECSTAR	Suzuki GSX-RR	M	F: '17 Medium/R: Soft	30	46m 12.906s
9	**Bradley Smith**	GBR	38	Monster Yamaha Tech 3	Yamaha YZR-M1	M	F: Medium/R: Soft	30	46m 20.221s
10	**Alvaro Bautista**	SPA	19	Aprilia Racing Team Gresini	Aprilia RS-GP	M	F: '17 Medium/R: Soft	30	46m 29.293s
11	**Hector Barbera**	SPA	8	Avintia Racing	Ducati Desmosedici	M	F: '17 Medium/R: Soft	30	46m 30.653s
12	**Danilo Petrucci**	ITA	9	OCTO Pramac Yakhnich	Ducati Desmosedici	M	F: '17 Medium/R: Soft	30	46m 36.643s
13	**Stefan Bradl**	GER	6	Aprilia Racing Team Gresini	Aprilia RS-GP	M	F: Medium/R: Soft	30	46m 44.051s
14	**Scott Redding**	GBR	45	OCTO Pramac Yakhnich	Ducati Desmosedici	M	F: Medium/R: Soft	30	46m 46.263s
15	**Jack Miller**	AUS	43	Estrella Galicia 0,0 Marc VDS	Honda RC213V	M	F: '17 Hard/R: Soft	30	46m 49.853s
16	Eugene Laverty	IRL	50	Pull & Bear Aspar Team	Ducati Desmosedici	M	F: Hard/R: Soft	30	46m 52.482s
17	Tito Rabat	SPA	53	Estrella Galicia 0,0 Marc VDS	Honda RC213V	M	F: '17 Medium/R: Soft	30	46m 52.783s
18	Loris Baz	FRA	76	Avintia Racing	Ducati Desmosedici	M	F: '17 Medium/R: Soft	30	47m 00.392s
	Mika Kallio	FIN	36	Red Bull KTM Factory Racing	KTM RC16	M	F: '17 Medium/R: Soft	19	DNF-technical
	Cal Crutchlow	GBR	35	LCR Honda	Honda RC213V	M	F: '17 Hard/R: Soft	16	DNF-crash
	Dani Pedrosa	SPA	26	Repsol Honda Team	Honda RC213V	M	F: Medium/R: Soft	6	DNF-crash
	Yonny Hernandez	COL	68	Pull & Bear Aspar Team	Ducati Desmosedici	M	F: Medium/R: Soft	4	DNF-crash

Fastest lap: Jorge Lorenzo, on lap 5, 1m 31.171s, 98.2mph/158.1km/h (record).
Previous lap record: Jorge Lorenzo, SPA (Yamaha), 1m 31.367s, 98.1mph/157.8km/h (2015).
Event best maximum speed: Andrea Iannone, 200.6mph/322.9km/h (race).

Qualifying

Weather: Dry
Air Temp: 21° **Track Temp:** 26°
Humidity: 39%

1	Lorenzo	1m 29.401s
2	Marquez	1m 29.741s
3	Rossi	1m 30.128s
4	Vinales	1m 30.276s
5	Dovizioso	1m 30.338s
6	P. Espargaro	1m 30.392s
7	Iannone	1m 30.420s
8	Pedrosa	1m 30.574s
9	A. Espargaro	1m 30.885s
10	Smith	1m 30.949s
11	Crutchlow	1m 31.030s
12	Petrucci	1m 31.203s
13	Barbera	1m 30.894s
14	Redding	1m 31.406s
15	Miller	1m 31.686s
16	Baz	1m 31.749s
17	Bradl	1m 31.813s
18	Bautista	1m 31.847s
19	Laverty	1m 31.956s
20	Kallio	1m 32.092s
21	Rabat	1m 32.181s
22	Hernandez	1m 32.240s

Fastest race laps

1	Lorenzo	1m 31.171s
2	Iannone	1m 31.196s
3	Rossi	1m 31.276s
4	Marquez	1m 31.299s
5	Vinales	1m 31.313s
6	Dovizioso	1m 31.317s
7	P. Espargaro	1m 31.744s
8	Pedrosa	1m 31.811s
9	A. Espargaro	1m 31.867s
10	Crutchlow	1m 31.912s
11	Smith	1m 32.050s
12	Barbera	1m 32.334s
13	Bautista	1m 32.387s
14	Petrucci	1m 32.452s
15	Redding	1m 32.577s
16	Laverty	1m 32.659s
17	Miller	1m 32.811s
18	Bradl	1m 32.875s
19	Baz	1m 32.938s
20	Rabat	1m 33.030s
21	Hernandez	1m 33.188s
22	Kallio	1m 33.208s

Championship Points

1	Marquez	298
2	Rossi	249
3	Lorenzo	233
4	Vinales	202
5	Dovizioso	171
6	Pedrosa	155
7	Crutchlow	141
8	P. Espargaro	134
9	Iannone	112
10	Barbera	102
11	A. Espargaro	93
12	Bautista	82
13	Laverty	77
14	Petrucci	75
15	Redding	74
16	Bradl	63
17	Smith	62
18	Miller	57
19	Pirro	36
20	Baz	35
21	Rabat	29
22	Hernandez	20
23	Nakasuga	5
24	Lowes	3
25	Aoyama	1
26	Hayden	1
27	Jones	1

Constructor Points

1	Honda	369
2	Yamaha	353
3	Ducati	261
4	Suzuki	208
5	Aprilia	101

Grid Order / Lap chart

Grid Order	1	2	3	4	5	6	7	8	9	10	11	12	13	14	15	16	17	18	19	20	21	22	23	24	25	26	27	28	29	30	
99 LORENZO	99	99	99	99	99	99	99	99	99	99	99	99	99	99	99	99	99	99	99	99	99	99	99	99	99	99	99	99	99	99	1
93 MARQUEZ	29	29	29	29	29	29	46	29	46	46	46	46	46	46	46	46	29	29	29	93	93	93	93	93	93	93	93	93	93	93	2
46 ROSSI	25	25	25	25	46	46	29	46	29	29	29	29	29	29	29	29	46	46	93	29	29	46	46	29	29	29	29	29	29	29	3
25 VINALES	46	46	46	46	25	93	93	93	93	93	93	93	93	93	93	93	93	93	46	46	46	29	29	46	46	46	46	46	46	46	4
4 DOVIZIOSO	93	93	93	93	93	25	25	25	25	25	25	25	25	25	25	25	25	25	25	25	25	25	25	25	25	25	25	25	25	25	5
44 P. ESPARGARO	26	4	4	4	4	4	4	4	4	4	4	4	4	4	4	4	4	4	4	4	4	4	4	4	4	4	4	4	44	44	6
29 IANNONE	4	26	26	26	26	26	44	44	44	44	44	44	44	44	44	44	44	44	44	44	44	44	44	44	44	44	44	44	4	4	7
26 PEDROSA	44	44	44	44	44	44	41	41	41	41	41	41	41	41	41	41	41	41	41	41	41	41	41	41	41	41	41	41	41	41	8
41 A. ESPARGARO	35	41	41	41	41	41	35	35	35	35	35	35	35	35	35	38	38	38	38	38	38	38	38	38	38	38	38	38	38	38	9
38 SMITH	41	35	35	35	35	35	38	38	38	38	38	38	38	38	38	19	19	19	19	19	19	19	19	19	19	19	19	19	19	19	10
35 CRUTCHLOW	38	38	38	38	38	38	45	45	45	9	9	9	19	19	19	9	9	9	9	9	8	8	8	8	8	8	8	8	8	8	11
9 PETRUCCI	45	45	45	45	45	45	9	9	19	19	19	19	9	9	9	8	8	8	8	9	9	9	9	9	9	9	9	9	9	9	12
8 BARBERA	43	43	19	19	19	19	19	19	19	8	8	8	8	8	8	45	45	45	45	45	45	45	45	45	45	6	6	6	6	6	13
45 REDDING	19	19	9	9	9	9	50	50	8	45	45	45	45	45	45	43	6	6	6	6	6	6	6	6	6	45	45	45	14
43 MILLER	50	50	43	50	50	50	8	8	50	50	50	50	43	43	43	6	43	43	43	43	43	43	43	43	43	43	43	43	15
76 BAZ	9	9	50	43	8	8	43	43	43	43	43	43	50	50	50	6	50	50	50	50	50	50	50	50	50	50	50	50	
6 BRADL	8	8	8	8	43	43	6	6	6	6	6	6	6	6	6	50	50	76	76	76	76	76	76	53	53	53	53	53	53	53	
19 BAUTISTA	6	6	6	6	6	6	76	76	76	76	76	76	76	76	76	53	53	53	53	53	76	76	76	76	76	76	76	76		
50 LAVERTY	76	76	76	76	76	76	53	53	53	53	53	53	53	53	53	36	36	36													
36 KALLIO	36	36	36	36	36	36	36	36	36	36	36	36	36	36	36																
53 RABAT	53	68	68	68	53	53																									
68 HERNANDEZ	68	53	53	53																											

36 Pit stop

Moto2

RACE DISTANCE: 27 laps, 67.192 miles/108.135km · RACE WEATHER: Dry (air 20°C, humidity 45%, track 25°C)

Pos.	Rider	Nat.	No.	Entrant	Machine	Laps	Time & Speed
1	**Johann Zarco**	FRA	5	Ajo Motorsport	Kalex	27	43m 17.626s 93.1mph/ 149.8km/h
2	**Thomas Luthi**	SWI	12	Garage Plus Interwetten	Kalex	27	43m 20.907s
3	**Franco Morbidelli**	ITA	21	Estrella Galicia 0,0 Marc VDS	Kalex	27	43m 22.607s
4	**Sam Lowes**	GBR	22	Federal Oil Gresini Moto2	Kalex	27	43m 23.262s
5	**Alex Rins**	SPA	40	Paginas Amarillas HP 40	Kalex	27	43m 23.476s
6	**Takaaki Nakagami**	JPN	30	IDEMITSU Honda Team Asia	Kalex	27	43m 29.231s
7	**Mattia Pasini**	ITA	54	Italtrans Racing Team	Kalex	27	43m 34.017s
8	**Jonas Folger**	GER	94	Dynavolt Intact GP	Kalex	27	43m 34.590s
9	**Danny Kent**	GBR	52	Leopard Racing	Kalex	27	43m 35.077s
10	**Marcel Schrotter**	GER	23	AGR Team	Kalex	27	43m 35.294s
11	**Simone Corsi**	ITA	24	Speed Up Racing	Speed Up	27	43m 38.081s
12	**Xavi Vierge**	SPA	97	Tech 3 Racing	Tech 3	27	43m 38.537s
13	**Miguel Oliveira**	POR	44	Leopard Racing	Kalex	27	43m 39.276s
14	**Lorenzo Baldassarri**	ITA	7	Forward Team	Kalex	27	43m 40.207s
15	**Hafizh Syahrin**	MAL	55	Petronas Raceline Malaysia	Kalex	27	43m 41.360s
16	Xavier Simeon	BEL	19	QMMF Racing Team	Speed Up	27	43m 43.954s
17	Jesko Raffin	SWI	2	Sports-Millions-EMWE-SAG	Kalex	27	43m 47.047s
18	Remy Gardner	AUS	87	Tasca Racing Scuderia Moto2	Kalex	27	43m 47.293s
19	Edgar Pons	SPA	57	Paginas Amarillas HP 40	Kalex	27	43m 47.375s
20	Ratthapark Wilairot	THA	14	IDEMITSU Honda Team Asia	Kalex	27	43m 56.915s
21	Robin Mulhauser	SWI	70	CarXpert Interwetten	Kalex	27	44m 00.731s
22	Luca Marini	ITA	10	Forward Team	Kalex	27	44m 01.158s
23	Julian Simon	SPA	60	QMMF Racing Team	Speed Up	27	44m 08.897s
24	Iker Lecuona	SPA	27	CarXpert Interwetten	Kalex	27	44m 14.243s
	Alex Marquez	SPA	73	Estrella Galicia 0,0 Marc VDS	Kalex	17	DNF
	Isaac Vinales	SPA	32	Tech 3 Racing	Tech 3	10	DNF
	Federico Fuligni	ITA	42	Team Ciatti	Kalex	5	DNF
	Sandro Cortese	GER	11	Dynavolt Intact GP	Kalex	4	DNF
	Axel Pons	SPA	49	AGR Team	Kalex	4	DNF
	Hugo Clere	FRA	16	Promoto Sport	Transfiormers	4	DNF

Fastest lap: Johann Zarco, on lap 20, 1m 35.521s, 93.8mph/150.9km/h.

Lap record: Thomas Luthi, SWI (Suter), 1m 35.312s, 94.0mph/151.2km/h (2014).

Event best maximum speed: Sandro Cortese, 166.3mph/267.6km/h (race).

Qualifying

Weather: Dry

Air Temp: 21° **Track Temp:** 26°

Humidity: 39%

1	Zarco	1m 34.879s
2	Luthi	1m 34.885s
3	Morbidelli	1m 34.933s
4	Pasini	1m 35.152s
5	Rins	1m 35.184s
6	Simon	1m 35.222s
7	Lowes	1m 35.237s
8	Kent	1m 35.345s
9	Nakagami	1m 35.365s
10	Marquez	1m 35.368s
11	Folger	1m 35.403s
12	Schrotter	1m 35.495s
13	Simeon	1m 35.517s
14	Cortese	1m 35.607s
15	Oliveira	1m 35.650s
16	A. Pons	1m 35.682s
17	Gardner	1m 35.747s
18	Marini	1m 35.756s
19	Vierge	1m 35.797s
20	E. Pons	1m 35.863s
21	Raffin	1m 35.923s
22	Corsi	1m 35.993s
23	Baldassarri	1m 35.995s
24	Syahrin	1m 36.012s
25	Wilairot	1m 36.045s
26	Lecuona	1m 36.278s
27	Mulhauser	1m 36.309s
28	Fuligni	1m 36.728s
29	Vinales	1m 36.787s
30	Clere	1m 40.531s

Fastest race laps

1	Zarco	1m 35.521s
2	Morbidelli	1m 35.601s
3	Lowes	1m 35.634s
4	Luthi	1m 35.673s
5	Rins	1m 35.690s
6	Simon	1m 35.863s
7	Nakagami	1m 35.942s
8	Schrotter	1m 35.944s
9	Folger	1m 35.989s
10	Pasini	1m 36.057s
11	Kent	1m 36.058s
12	Marquez	1m 36.074s
13	Cortese	1m 36.237s
14	E. Pons	1m 36.267s
15	Corsi	1m 36.279s
16	Oliveira	1m 36.333s
17	Syahrin	1m 36.360s
18	Vierge	1m 36.375s
19	Simeon	1m 36.400s
20	Baldassarri	1m 36.407s
21	Gardner	1m 36.465s
22	Raffin	1m 36.509s
23	Wilairot	1m 36.516s
24	A. Pons	1m 36.641s
25	Marini	1m 36.643s
26	Mulhauser	1m 36.734s
27	Lecuona	1m 36.890s
28	Vinales	1m 37.526s
29	Fuligni	1m 37.568s
30	Clere	1m 41.224s

Championship Points

1	Zarco	276
2	Luthi	234
3	Rins	214
4	Morbidelli	213
5	Lowes	175
6	Nakagami	169
7	Folger	167
8	Baldassarri	127
9	Syahrin	118
10	Corsi	103
11	Pasini	72
12	Aegerter	71
13	Marquez	69
14	Schrotter	64
15	Cortese	61
16	A. Pons	55
17	Simeon	46
18	Simon	40
19	Salom	37
20	Vierge	37
21	Oliveira	36
22	Kent	35
23	Marini	34
24	Vinales	19
25	Raffin	14
26	Gardner	8
27	West	6
28	Wilairot	6
29	Rosli	4
30	Mulhauser	4
31	E. Pons	4
32	Nagashima	2

Constructor Points

1	Kalex	450
2	Speed Up	136
3	Tech 3	47
4	Suter	6

Moto3

RACE DISTANCE: 24 laps, 59.726 miles/96.120km · RACE WEATHER: Dry (air 21°C, humidity 43%, track 22°C)

Pos.	Rider	Nat.	No.	Entrant	Machine	Laps	Time & Speed
1	**Brad Binder**	RSA	41	Red Bull KTM Ajo	KTM	24	40m 13.777s 89.0mph/ 143.3km/h
2	**Joan Mir**	SPA	36	Leopard Racing	KTM	24	40m 13.833s
3	**Andrea Migno**	ITA	16	SKY Racing Team VR46	KTM	24	40m 13.858s
4	**Enea Bastianini**	ITA	33	Gresini Racing Moto3	Honda	24	40m 13.924s
5	**Fabio Di Giannantonio**	ITA	4	Gresini Racing Moto3	Honda	24	40m 14.490s
6	**Juanfran Guevara**	SPA	58	RBA Racing Team	KTM	24	40m 14.676s
7	**Jakub Kornfeil**	CZE	84	Drive M7 SIC Racing Team	Honda	24	40m 16.460s
8	**Philipp Oettl**	GER	65	Schedl GP Racing	KTM	24	40m 16.922s
9	**Jorge Navarro**	SPA	9	Estrella Galicia 0,0	Honda	24	40m 19.040s
10	**Jorge Martin**	SPA	88	Pull & Bear Aspar Mahindra Team	Mahindra	24	40m 21.698s
11	**Raul Fernandez**	SPA	31	MH6 Team	KTM	24	40m 21.858s
12	**Darryn Binder**	RSA	40	Platinum Bay Real Estate	Mahindra	24	40m 22.027s
13	**Bo Bendsneyder**	NED	64	Red Bull KTM Ajo	KTM	24	40m 22.380s
14	**Fabio Quartararo**	FRA	20	Leopard Racing	KTM	24	40m 23.060s
15	**Livio Loi**	BEL	11	RW Racing GP BV	Honda	24	40m 23.135s
16	Niccolo Antonelli	ITA	23	Ongetta-Rivacold	Honda	24	40m 23.304s
17	Nicolo Bulega	ITA	8	SKY Racing Team VR46	KTM	24	40m 23.429s
18	Tatsuki Suzuki	JPN	24	CIP-Unicom Starker	Mahindra	24	40m 23.727s
19	Aron Canet	SPA	44	Estrella Galicia 0,0	Honda	24	40m 30.615s
20	Andrea Locatelli	ITA	55	Leopard Racing	KTM	24	40m 32.489s
21	Hiroki Ono	JPN	76	Honda Team Asia	Honda	24	40m 32.514s
22	Karel Hanika	CZE	98	Freundenberg Racing Team	KTM	24	40m 32.753s
23	Vicente Perez	SPA	63	Peugeot MC Saxoprint	Peugeot	24	40m 32.816s
24	Albert Arenas	SPA	12	Peugeot MC Saxoprint	Peugeot	24	40m 38.074s
25	Khairul Idham Pawi	MAL	89	Honda Team Asia	Honda	24	40m 38.303s
26	Jules Danilo	FRA	95	Ongetta-Rivacold	Honda	24	40m 39.108s
27	Adam Norrodin	MAL	7	Drive M7 SIC Racing Team	Honda	24	40m 39.147s
28	Lorenzo Petrarca	ITA	77	3570 Team Italia	Mahindra	24	41m 02.606s
29	Daniel Saez	SPA	26	GA Competicion	KTM	24	41m 02.638s
30	Enzo Boulom	FRA	99	CIP-Unicom Starker	Mahindra	24	41m 03.059s
31	Stefano Valtulini	ITA	43	3570 Team Italia	Mahindra	24	41m 26.186s
	Marcos Ramirez	SPA	42	Platinum Bay Real Estate	Mahindra	7	DNF
	Lorenzo dalla Porta	ITA	48	SKY Racing Team VR46	KTM	3	DNF
	Gabriel Rodrigo	ARG	19	RBA Racing Team	KTM	0	DNF
	Francesco Bagnaia	ITA	21	Pull & Bear Aspar Mahindra Team	Mahindra	0	DNF

Fastest lap: Brad Binder, on lap 10, 1m 39.684s, 89.9mph/144.6km/h.

Lap record: Efren Vazquez, SPA (Honda), 1m 39.400s, 90.1mph/145.0km/h (2014).

Event best maximum speed: Livio Loi, 140.4mph/226.0km/h (warm-up).

Qualifying

Weather: Dry

Air Temp: 17° **Track Temp:** 22°

Humidity: 46%

1	Canet	1m 39.261s
2	B. Binder	1m 39.279s
3	Ono	1m 39.383s
4	Bulega	1m 39.420s
5	Guevara	1m 39.463s
6	Antonelli	1m 39.524s
7	Oettl	1m 39.552s
8	Bendsneyder	1m 39.553s
9	Bastianini	1m 39.559s
10	Mir	1m 39.577s
11	Dalla Porta	1m 39.606s
12	Di Giannantonio	1m 39.616s
13	Hanika	1m 39.660s
14	Rodrigo	1m 39.662s
15	Martin	1m 39.662s
16	Bagnaia	1m 39.736s
17	Navarro	1m 39.793s
18	Migno	1m 39.794s
19	Fernandez	1m 39.835s
20	Loi	1m 39.838s
21	Perez	1m 39.911s
22	Suzuki	1m 39.925s
23	Quartararo	1m 39.927s
24	Kornfeil	1m 39.997s
25	Pawi	1m 40.163s
26	Arenas	1m 40.236s
27	Locatelli	1m 40.261s
28	Danilo	1m 40.300s
29	D. Binder	1m 40.349s
30	Norrodin	1m 40.957s
31	Saez	1m 41.659s
32	Boulom	1m 41.789s
33	Petrarca	1m 42.444s
34	Valtulini	1m 42.637s
35	Ramirez	1m 43.466s

Fastest race laps

1	B. Binder	1m 39.684s
2	Di Giannantonio	1m 39.759s
3	Canet	1m 39.784s
4	D. Binder	1m 39.792s
5	Navarro	1m 39.793s
6	Oettl	1m 39.808s
7	Fernandez	1m 39.817s
8	Bastianini	1m 39.827s
9	Mir	1m 39.831s
10	Kornfeil	1m 39.900s
11	Bulega	1m 39.918s
12	Migno	1m 39.921s
13	Bendsneyder	1m 39.936s
14	Guevara	1m 39.975s
15	Quartararo	1m 40.069s
16	Martin	1m 40.096s
17	Antonelli	1m 40.146s
18	Loi	1m 40.161s
19	Suzuki	1m 40.188s
20	Locatelli	1m 40.300s
21	Hanika	1m 40.378s
22	Pawi	1m 40.452s
23	Perez	1m 40.462s
24	Arenas	1m 40.514s
25	Ono	1m 40.573s
26	Danilo	1m 40.665s
27	Norrodin	1m 40.667s
28	Dalla Porta	1m 40.728s
29	Petrarca	1m 41.030s
30	Boulom	1m 41.051s
31	Saez	1m 41.163s
32	Ramirez	1m 41.283s
33	Valtulini	1m 42.263s

Championship Points

1	B. Binder	319
2	Bastianini	177
3	Navarro	150
4	Bagnaia	145
5	Mir	144
6	Di Giannantonio	134
7	Bulega	129
8	Kornfeil	112
9	Locatelli	96
10	Fenati	93
11	Antonelli	91
12	Oettl	85
13	Quartararo	83
14	Bendsneyder	78
15	Canet	76
16	Martin	72
17	Migno	63
18	Loi	63
19	Pawi	62
20	Danilo	58
21	Guevara	50
22	McPhee	48
23	Ono	36
24	Rodrigo	31
25	D. Binder	27
26	Ramirez	19
27	Suzuki	16
28	Norrodin	14
29	Manzi	13
30	Dalla Porta	12
31	Herrera	7
32	Fernandez	5
33	Azmi	5
34	Valtulini	3
35	Arenas	2
36	Petrarca	2

Constructor Points

1	KTM	382
2	Honda	350
3	Mahindra	211
4	Peugeot	55

WORLD CHAMPIONSHIP POINTS 2016

Compiled by PETER McLAREN

Photos: Gold & Goose

MotoGP – Riders

Position	Rider	Nationality	Machine	Qatar	Argentina	United States	Spain	France	Italy	Catalunya	Netherlands	Germany	Austria	Czech Republic	Great Britain	San Marino	Aragon	Japan	Australia	Malaysia	Valencia	Points total
1	Marc Marquez	SPA	Honda	16	25	25	16	3	20	20	20	25	11	16	13	13	25	25	–	5	20	**298**
2	Valentino Rossi	ITA	Yamaha	13	20	–	25	20	–	25	–	8	13	20	16	20	16	–	20	20	13	**249**
3	Jorge Lorenzo	SPA	Yamaha	25	–	20	20	25	25	–	6	1	16	0	8	16	20	–	10	16	25	**233**
4	Maverick Vinales	SPA	Suzuki	10	–	13	10	16	10	13	7	4	10	7	25	11	13	16	16	10	11	**202**
5	Andrea Dovizioso	ITA	Ducati	20	3	–	–	–	11	9	–	16	20	–	10	10	5	20	13	25	9	**171**
6	Dani Pedrosa	SPA	Honda	11	16	–	13	13	13	16	4	10	9	4	11	25	10	–	–	–	–	**155**
7	Cal Crutchlow	GBR	Honda	–	–	0	5	–	5	10	–	20	1	25	20	8	11	11	25	–	–	**141**
8	Pol Espargaro	SPA	Yamaha	9	10	9	8	11	1	11	13	–	6	3	–	7	8	10	11	7	10	**134**
9	Andrea Iannone	ITA	Ducati	–	–	16	9	–	16	–	11	11	25	8	–	–	–	–	–	–	16	**112**
10	Hector Barbera	SPA	Ducati	7	11	7	6	8	4	5	10	7	–	11	2	3	3	0	–	13	5	**102**
11	Aleix Espargaro	SPA	Suzuki	5	5	11	11	10	7	–	–	2	–	–	9	–	9	13	–	3	8	**93**
12	Alvaro Bautista	SPA	Aprilia	3	6	5	–	7	–	8	–	6	0	0	6	6	7	9	4	9	6	**82**
13	Eugene Laverty	IRL	Ducati	4	13	4	7	5	3	3	9	5	0	10	4	2	2	–	2	4	0	**77**
14	Danilo Petrucci	ITA	Ducati	–	–	–	–	9	8	7	–	–	5	9	7	5	0	8	7	6	4	**75**
15	Scott Redding	GBR	Ducati	6	–	10	0	–	–	0	16	13	8	1	0	1	0	7	9	1	2	**74**
16	Stefan Bradl	GER	Aprilia	–	9	6	2	6	2	4	8	–	0	2	–	4	6	6	5	0	3	**63**
17	Bradley Smith	GBR	Yamaha	8	8	0	4	–	9	–	3	3	7	–	–	–	3	8	2	7	–	**62**
18	Jack Miller	AUS	Honda	2	–	–	0	–	–	6	25	9	–	–	0	–	–	6	8	1		**57**
19	Michele Pirro	ITA	Ducati	–	4	8	0	–	6	1	–	–	4	–	–	9	4	–	–	–	–	**36**
20	Loris Baz	FRA	Ducati	–	–	1	3	4	–	–	–	0	3	13	–	–	0	0	–	11	0	**35**
21	Tito Rabat	SPA	Honda	1	7	3	0	–	–	2	5	0	2	6	1	0	–	2	0	0	0	**29**
22	Yonny Hernandez	COL	Ducati	–	–	2	1	–	0	0	–	0	0	5	5	0	0	4	3	–	–	**20**
23	Katsuyuki Nakasuga	JPN	Yamaha	–	–	–	–	–	–	–	–	–	–	–	–	–	–	5	–	–	–	**5**
24	Alex Lowes	GBR	Yamaha	–	–	–	–	–	–	–	–	–	–	–	3	–	–	–	–	–	–	**3**
25	Hiroshi Aoyama	JPN	Honda	–	–	–	–	–	–	–	–	–	–	–	–	–	–	1	–	0	–	**1**
26	Nicky Hayden	USA	Honda	–	–	–	–	–	–	–	–	–	–	–	–	–	–	1	–	0	–	**1**
27	Mike Jones	AUS	Ducati	–	–	–	–	–	–	–	–	–	–	–	–	–	–	–	0	1	–	**1**
28	Mika Kallio	FIN	KTM	–	–	–	–	–	–	–	–	–	–	–	–	–	–	–	–	–	0	**0**

MotoGP - Teams

Position	Team	Qatar	Argentina	United States	Spain	France	Italy	Catalunya	Netherlands	Germany	Austria	Czech Republic	Great Britain	San Marino	Aragon	Japan	Australia	Malaysia	Valencia	Points total
1	Movistar Yamaha MotoGP	38	20	20	45	45	25	25	6	9	29	20	24	36	36	–	30	36	38	**482**
2	Repsol Honda Team	27	41	25	29	16	33	36	24	35	20	20	24	38	35	26	–	5	20	**454**
3	Ducati Team	20	3	16	9	–	27	9	11	27	45	8	10	19	9	20	13	25	25	**296**
4	Team SUZUKI ECSTAR	15	5	24	21	26	17	13	7	6	10	7	34	11	22	29	16	13	19	**295**
5	Monster Yamaha Tech 3	17	18	9	12	11	10	11	16	3	13	3	7	8	13	19	9		17	**199**
6	OCTO Pramac Yakhnich	6	4	18	–	9	8	7	16	13	13	10	7	6	–	15	16	7	6	**161**
7	Aprilia Racing Team Gresini	3	15	11	2	13	2	12	8	6	–	2	6	10	13	15	9	9	9	**145**
8	LCR Honda	–	–	–	5	–	5	10	–	20	1	25	20	8	11	11	25	–	–	**141**
9	Avintia Racing	7	11	8	9	12	4	6	10	7	3	24	2	3	3	–	1	24	5	**139**
10	Pull & Bear Aspar Team	4	13	6	8	5	3	3	9	5	–	15	9	2	2	4	5	4	–	**97**
11	Estrella Galicia 0,0 Marc VDS	3	7	3	–	–	–	8	30	9	2	6	1	–	1	2	6	8	1	**87**

Moto2

Position	Rider	Nationality	Machine	Qatar	Argentina	United States	Spain	France	Italy	Catalunya	Netherlands	Germany	Austria	Czech Republic	Great Britain	San Marino	Aragon	Japan	Australia	Malaysia	Valencia	Points total
1	Johann Zarco	FRA	Kalex	4	25	16	11	0	25	25	20	25	25	5	0	13	8	20	4	25	25	276
2	Thomas Luthi	SWI	Kalex	25	9	9	10	16	13	11	–	–	13	–	25	10	13	25	25	10	20	234
3	Alex Rins	SPA	Kalex	8	13	25	16	25	9	20	10	–	16	20	9	20	10	0	–	2	11	214
4	Franco Morbidelli	ITA	Kalex	9	0	2	13	13	8	5	16	–	20	8	20	11	16	16	20	20	16	213
5	Sam Lowes	GBR	Kalex	7	20	20	25	10	16	10	13	–	–	16	0	–	25	–	–	–	13	175
6	Takaaki Nakagami	JPN	Kalex	2	7	1	9	11	7	16	25	5	9	–	16	16	11	13	11	0	10	169
7	Jonas Folger	GER	Kalex	–	16	11	20	–	1	9	6	20	0	25	11	8	6	–	10	16	8	167
8	Lorenzo Baldassarri	ITA	Kalex	–	3	0	0	0	20	2	11	11	8	0	10	25	9	–	13	13	2	127
9	Hafizh Syahrin	MAL	Kalex	13	10	0	5	8	11	13	–	9	0	10	13	9	2	3	–	11	1	118
10	Simone Corsi	ITA	Speed Up	16	0	10	–	20	4	–	9	–	–	0	8	–	7	10	9	5	5	103
11	Mattia Pasini	ITA	Kalex	0	6	0	4	0	–	4	0	13	3	13	7	0	4	9	–	0	9	72
12	Dominique Aegerter	SWI	Kalex	11	11	13	8	3	6	–	7	6	6	0	–	0	–	–	–	–	–	71
13	Alex Marquez	SPA	Kalex	–	–	5	–	–	0	0	8	–	10	11	0	6	20	–	–	9	–	69
14	Marcel Schrotter	GER	Kalex	0	5	6	–	2	0	6	3	–	11	0	5	5	1	7	7	0	6	64
15	Sandro Cortese	GER	Kalex	1	–	4	–	–	5	–	4	1	5	0	4	7	3	11	16	–	–	61
16	Axel Pons	SPA	Kalex	–	8	0	–	9	10	7	–	–	7	–	6	–	0	–	8	–	–	55
17	Xavier Simeon	BEL	Speed Up	–	4	8	6	5	–	–	5	–	0	1	0	–	5	6	5	1	0	46
18	Julian Simon	SPA	Speed Up	–	0	7	–	–	0	3	0	16	1	3	2	–	0	8	–	–	0	40
19	Luis Salom	SPA	Kalex	20	1	3	7	6	–	–	–	–	–	–	–	–	–	–	–	–	–	37
20	Xavi Vierge	SPA	Tech 3	–	2	0	–	1	–	0	–	0	0	4	3	4	0	5	6	8	4	37
21	Miguel Oliveira	POR	Kalex	5	0	–	–	7	3	8	1	–	2	7	–	0	–	–	–	–	3	36
22	Danny Kent	GBR	Kalex	10	0	–	–	0	2	–	2	–	4	9	1	–	0	–	–	0	7	35
23	Luca Marini	ITA	Kalex	6	0	–	0	4	–	–	–	10	0	0	–	3	0	4	0	7	0	34
24	Isaac Vinales	SPA	Tech 3	0	0	0	3	0	0	0	0	7	0	2	–	–	0	1	–	6	–	19
25	Jesko Raffin	SWI	Kalex	0	0	0	2	0	0	–	0	8	0	0	0	1	0	3	0	0	0	14
26	Remy Gardner	AUS	Kalex	–	–	–	–	–	–	1	4	0	0	0	0	0	0	0	–	3	0	8
27	Anthony West	AUS	Suter	–	–	–	–	–	–	–	–	–	–	6	–	–	–	–	–	–	–	6
28	Ratthapark Wilairot	THA	Kalex	3	0	0	–	0	0	–	–	0	0	0	2	0	–	1	0	0	0	6
29	Ramdan Rosli	MAL	Kalex	–	–	–	–	–	–	0	–	–	–	–	–	–	–	–	0	4	–	4
30	Robin Mulhauser	SWI	Kalex	0	0	–	1	0	0	0	0	3	0	0	0	–	0	0	0	0	0	4
31	Edgar Pons	SPA	Kalex	–	–	–	–	0	0	0	2	0	0	0	0	–	0	0	2	0	0	4
32	Tetsuta Nagashima	JPN	Kalex	–	–	–	–	–	–	–	–	–	–	–	–	–	0	2	–	–	–	2

Moto3

Position	Rider	Nationality	Machine	Qatar	Argentina	United States	Spain	France	Italy	Catalunya	Netherlands	Germany	Austria	Czech Republic	Great Britain	San Marino	Aragon	Japan	Australia	Malaysia	Valencia	Points total
1	Brad Binder	RSA	KTM	20	16	16	25	25	25	20	4	8	20	–	25	25	20	20	25	0	25	319
2	Enea Bastianini	ITA	Honda	11	0	10	8	–	4	16	–	16	16	13	9	20	16	25	–	–	13	177
3	Jorge Navarro	SPA	Honda	9	20	20	13	16	–	25	–	9	–	6	–	–	25	–	–	–	7	150
4	Francesco Bagnaia	ITA	Mahindra	16	0	2	16	4	16	–	25	6	5	–	20	0	0	10	–	25	–	145
5	Joan Mir	SPA	KTM	4	11	–	10	0	9	8	8	–	25	8	7	16	11	7	–	–	20	144
6	Fabio Di Giannantonio	ITA	Honda	0	0	0	–	0	20	7	20	11	8	16	10	6	13	11	–	1	11	134
7	Nicolo Bulega	ITA	KTM	10	0	6	20	11	8	11	9	–	7	7	11	13	–	16	–	–	0	129
8	Jakub Kornfeil	CZE	Honda	6	7	5	11	7	0	6	3	13	0	10	1	11	–	3	–	20	9	112
9	Andrea Locatelli	ITA	KTM	0	13	11	–	6	–	0	–	20	3	–	2	10	0	–	20	11	0	96
10	Romano Fenati	ITA	KTM	13	0	25	9	20	–	13	13	0	–	–	–	–	–	–	–	–	–	93
11	Niccolo Antonelli	ITA	Honda	25	6	–	–	8	13	0	11	–	0	11	–	5	2	6	–	4	0	91
12	Philipp Oettl	GER	KTM	7	1	13	6	–	0	5	0	11	1	4	8	6	13	2	–	8	–	85
13	Fabio Quartararo	FRA	KTM	3	3	3	–	10	11	9	–	0	13	0	–	4	8	4	13	2	–	83
14	Bo Bendsneyder	NED	KTM	2	0	0	0	0	0	5	7	4	9	9	16	–	1	0	6	16	3	78
15	Aron Canet	SPA	Honda	1	–	9	–	13	–	10	–	1	0	–	8	9	9	–	16	–	0	76
16	Jorge Martin	SPA	Mahindra	–	8	–	–	0	2	–	–	–	10	20	6	–	10	–	10	–	6	72
17	Andrea Migno	ITA	KTM	0	0	1	5	9	6	0	16	–	0	4	0	1	5	0	–	–	16	63
18	Livio Loi	BEL	Honda	8	0	8	0	0	5	0	0	1	2	6	2	0	3	0	9	11	7	63
19	Khairul Idham Pawi	MAL	Honda	0	25	0	2	2	–	–	–	25	0	0	0	0	0	0	–	8	0	62
20	Jules Danilo	FRA	Honda	5	0	7	7	–	5	0	–	10	7	0	5	3	2	0	7	–	0	58
21	Juanfran Guevara	SPA	KTM	0	4	4	4	3	7	3	–	4	0	0	4	7	0	–	–	–	10	50
22	John McPhee	GBR	Peugeot	0	9	0	–	0	0	1	0	10	0	25	0	0	3	–	–	–	–	48
23	Hiroki Ono	JPN	Honda	0	10	0	–	0	10	–	–	1	0	0	7	0	–	8	–	0	–	36
24	Gabriel Rodrigo	ARG	KTM	0	–	–	0	3	–	3	–	–	3	–	0	5	–	8	–	9	–	31
25	Darryn Binder	RSA	Mahindra	0	0	–	–	–	–	–	4	0	–	–	–	–	0	–	13	6	4	27
26	Marcos Ramirez	SPA	Mahindra	–	–	–	–	–	–	–	–	–	0	0	–	0	0	9	10	–	–	19
27	Tatsuki Suzuki	JPN	Mahindra	0	0	0	1	1	0	2	–	5	–	3	0	0	–	1	3	–	0	16
28	Adam Norrodin	MAL	Honda	0	5	–	0	–	–	0	–	–	0	–	–	0	0	4	5	–	0	14
29	Stefano Manzi	ITA	Honda	–	–	–	–	–	–	–	–	–	0	–	13	0	–	–	–	–	–	13
30	Lorenzo dalla Porta	ITA	Honda/KTM	–	–	–	–	–	1	–	6	–	–	–	–	–	5	0	–	–	–	12
31	Maria Herrera	SPA	KTM	0	2	0	0	0	0	–	2	–	2	0	0	–	0	0	1	–	–	7
32	Raul Fernandez	SPA	KTM	–	–	–	–	–	–	–	–	–	–	–	–	–	–	–	–	–	5	5
33	Hafiq Azmi	MAL	Peugeot	–	–	–	–	–	–	–	–	–	–	–	–	–	–	–	–	5	–	5
34	Stefano Valtulini	ITA	Mahindra	0	0	–	–	0	–	0	–	–	–	–	0	–	–	0	–	3	0	3
35	Albert Arenas	SPA	Mahindra/Peugeot	–	–	–	0	–	0	–	–	–	–	–	0	–	0	2	–	–	0	2
36	Lorenzo Petrarca	ITA	Mahindra	0	0	0	–	0	0	0	–	–	0	–	0	0	0	0	0	2	0	2

SASAKI SUPREME

RED BULL ROOKIES CUP REVIEW by PETER CLIFFORD

Above: Close company. Aleix Viu (81), Kaito Toba (67) and Ayumu Sasaki (71), racing three abreast at Aragon.

Top right: The ever-consistent Sasaki celebrates his championship win at Aragon with Fernandez (left) and Rufino Florido.

Above right: Marc Garcia (23) signals his double victory at Brno.

Centre right: The unlucky Aleix Viu was a sporting runner-up.

Centre far right: KTM CEO Stefan Pierer and sporting director Pit Beirer at the Red Bull Rookies Cup Tenth Anniversary celebration at the Austrian GP.

Below right: Aleix Viu wheelies after his second place in race two at the Sachsenring.

Photos: Red Bull/Gold & Goose

THE tenth Red Bull MotoGP Rookies Cup was won by Ayumu Sasaki with a season-long intelligence that overcame flashes and longer spells of genius from the opposition. The 15-year-old Japanese was steadfastly consistent all year, winning four times and finishing every race, never lower than fourth.

The second-year Rookie was not totally dominant, but rather ever present. That might have taken the shine off his success but for the final scene, which he played superbly. Only needing two points from the 13th and final race in Aragon, he escaped even that necessity when arch rival Aleix Viu was brought down on the first lap.

Sasaki used the freedom of having the title in hand to push on and win the race with a fine piece of last-lap trickery. He had been locked in a race-long battle with Spaniards Raul Fernandez and Rufino Florido. Fernandez, 15, had been a title threat after a double victory in Assen and was determined to end the year on a high, while 16-year-old Florido was seeking his first victory.

There was nothing in it between the trio. No one could break free; the slipstream is too important at Motorland. It would all come down to the last lap. Leading down the back straight on the lap gives the opposition the perfect slipstream and the opportunity to lead into the final corner.

Sasaki watched from third, plotted and then, late on, practised a run down the extreme left of the back straight, opposite to the normal racing line. When he did take the lead for the final lap, Fernandez and Florido thought he was handing them the slipstream and the win.

When he pulled across to the left, though, they weren't expecting it. They followed, however, and slipstreamed, but they were wrong-footed when he swung back across to the right to brake for the last long looping left-hander. They passed him, but he had practised braking from his special line. While the others went wide, scratching to hold the turn, Sasaki was on line and accelerating out of the final corner, making it to the line first.

His fourth victory of the season did not make for record-breaking domination, but clearly his was a superior season. He had only been off the podium twice, with fourth places in both first races at the Sachsenring and Aragon. That kind of consistency is almost impossible to beat.

Viu still took second in the title chase, after a very fine performance. The 15-year-old Spaniard had left the first round in Jerez tied on points with Sasaki, as they had shared a win and a second each. The second weekend in Assen was his undoing, however. A fall in the treacherously wet race one, where only 12 finished from the field of 24, then a cautious ride to tenth in race two left him with a points deficit of 27 for the weekend.

It was a deficit from which he never recovered, and without which he would have gone into the final race in Aragon three points ahead of Sasaki. Ifs, buts and maybes are a waste of time, of course, and Viu lost other points. Crucially, he crossed the finish line first on four occasions, but was only credited with two wins, as he was demoted twice for exceeding track limits.

Viu could well look back on the 2016 Rookies Cup season with thoughts of what might have been. He was clipped from behind on lap one of that final race and had to pick up the bike from the gravel, restart and rejoin in last place, half a lap behind. It was so typical of the young man's sportsmanship that he finished the race, though he couldn't close the gap, as the bike was damaged. As he wrote in his blog, "I managed to finish the race, my dear friends, for you, for the championship, for my pride, for knowing how to lose..."

He displayed that attitude and a wonderful smile all through the year, after the disastrous Assen, after having wins taken away at the Red Bull Ring and Misano, and at the end of the season in Aragon as he congratulated Sasaki on winning the Cup.

More than just a great sportsman, Viu proved himself a great rider. Bouncing back after Assen, he was in fabulous form, and at the following races he was a podium fixture.

The Cup battle involved more than just Sasaki and Viu, of course, and the way Fernandez dominated the Dutch round in such difficult conditions, taking a superb double, made him a favourite, as well as putting him second in the championship points table.

In the opening weekend in Jerez, he had finished third in race one, then slid off at the final corner in race two while battling for the lead; he remounted to finish 13th. So he had grabbed useful points, and buoyed by his Assen haul he should have mounted a strong Cup challenge.

With second and fourth at the Sachsenring, he started doing just that. But then it was fifth and seventh at the Red Bull Ring, and he was losing ground to Sasaki and Viu. Fourth and second at Brno was good, but he needed a decisive Misano. He was determined, but while battling Viu for the win on the last lap, they touched, and Fernandez lost out, finishing fifth.

So he went to Aragon with only a mathematical chance of taking the title, and in the event he could not quite steal second from Viu either. Both are very strong, capable of stepping up to the Moto3 World Championship after two seasons as Rookies, as is Sasaki.

There should have been a third Spaniard in the battle for the Cup, but as always in racing you need a touch of good fortune, and that simply escaped 16-year-old Marc Garcia.

The quiet rider had progressed steadily through his first two seasons in the series, ending 2015 with a win in Aragon. He was one of the favourites for 2016, but a coming-together with another rider on the sighting lap for the first race of the season left him watching instead of racing. Fifth in Jerez race two, second in the soaking Assen race one, but ninth in race two was not the consistency he needed.

He looked for it at the Sachsenring and found it in Austria, where he scored first and third. A double victory at Brno put him back in the Cup chase, and he was very much the man of form and one of four who would fight all the way through Aragon for glory. Then he was involved in a multi-bike accident at a non-Cup event, sustaining a badly broken finger that needed surgery. So he missed Misano and wasn't quite at his best in Aragon, managing a pair of sixth places.

For some, it is not so much a question of missing good fortune, but of the difficulty in making the perfect connection with the machine. This is where Kaito Toba struggled at times. The 16-year-old Japanese had demonstrated his talent in his first season in 2015, when he was already fast in pre-season testing and on the podium at the Sachsenring.

Errors marred his points score in that first year, however, and it was the same in 2016, when he crashed out of the first three races. He also won twice, though: the second race at the Sachsenring and then race one in Aragon. Then he fell in race two. He concluded his Rookies Cup career of ups and downs with the frank admission that he and the bike were not always the best of friends.

Before the last Rookies Cup race of the season was under way at Aragon, Brad Binder was already celebrating his Moto3 World Championship, the second ex-Rookie to take the title in two years.

The Rookies all see Moto3 as their next step, of course, and some stride very rapidly in that direction. Fabio Di Giannantonio, who finished second in the 2015 Cup, had already scored a Moto3 World Championship second place in Mugello in May, in only his sixth grand prix. The 2015 champion, Bo Bendsneyder, Binder's team-mate in the Red Bull KTM Ajo squad, did not make the podium quite as quickly or frequently, but he was third in the British Grand Prix and working his way towards a second year in the factory team.

So the first ten years of the Red Bull MotoGP Rookies Cup ended, and in that time 144 riders from 30 different countries have chased their dreams, producing 41 different winners in 119 races. With alumni so far going on to win four world championships and 54 grands prix, a lot of those dreams have been realised.

He also had the ability to qualify fast and was happy to lead races, for lap after lap. Usually he would lead by far the most laps, even if ultimately he didn't take the victory.

The issue of exceeding track limits came to a head in the penultimate round at Misano. There is only ever a single race in Italy, as the track invasion by Rossi fans prohibits a post-MotoGP race on Sunday. In Saturday's race, six KTM RC 250 Rs battled fiercely for the lead, and not everyone was sticking to the delineated track area.

This was after Viu had lost his race-two victory at the Red Bull Ring for exceeding track limits, so the idea of penalties was not new. In Italy, it was Viu, Kaito Toba and Florido who flashed across the line, chased by Sasaki, but the first three were all judged to have exceeded track limits on several occasions. Sasaki had not and, in accordance with the rules, the trio were all docked one place.

This group demotion vaulted Sasaki to first, which so boosted his points score that he had one hand on the Cup with just the Aragon races remaining. It seemed a disproportionate gain, but then he'd stuck to the rules. He didn't appreciate the manner of his winning, however; it was the glummest podium in Rookies history. But it was correct.

SUPERBIKE WORLD CHAMPIONSHIP REVIEW OF 2016

By GORDON RITCHIE

65

JONATHAN-REA.COM

THANK YOU
AGAIN

WORLD

CHAMPION

ENHANCED PRODUCTION VALUES

By GORDON RITCHIE

Above: Jonathan Rea's Kawasaki leads the way over Phillip Island's Lukey Heights in the season opener. He was fast and consistent, nine wins among 23 podiums earning him a second straight title.

Right: Kawasaki and Ducati dominated, but Yamaha and Honda (here at Assen) hope to challenge in 2017.

Photos: Gold & Goose

IT was another year of on- and off-track sizzle for the FIM Superbike World Championship. A 13-round, 26-race global contest that went to the final weekend somehow was deemed less competitive overall than the biggest one of all, although MotoGP ended as a contest three races and three rounds early..

Once again, the external perceptions of WorldSBK were at odds with the reality on the ground, looking at the health of the whole paddock at least. The crowds, however, still proved too small all over the calendar, even at Donington, where British victory on a tough world stage is almost guaranteed. Some said that when the success of indigenous riders is almost a foregone conclusion, there are fewer reasons to go and watch. That is logic viewed through a hall of mirrors.

Donington was one of the few tracks that took advantage of Dorna's Saturday and Sunday race meeting initiative to make it a kind of mini-festival, to use the extra fan opportunities in the most open world championship of all.

Ironically, MotoGP being so unpredictable in its many race winners, having so much global focus, and still having Rossi around and winning, actually allows Dorna to remove the shackles from WorldSBK like never before. It is really no threat to GPs, so it could be grown consistently each year. But still the overweening atmosphere and 'feel' from the upper echelons is of how many issues and situations are still problematic in WorldSBK.

Politics was everywhere in 2016 – real stuff in governments and unreal stuff in championship governance. As with any 'new' government, there comes a time when responsibility for the perception of the state has to be taken over from the previous administration, and that time is overdue in WorldSBK. Unremitting positivity and endless self-promotion is required. Otherwise, how can the potential on-site fans and TV viewers be persuaded to vote for WorldSBK with their feet and remote controls when there is so little optimism radiating out?

Of course, there are real issues in WorldSBK that do need addressing. A nine-weekend summer break was inexplicable. A wander into the wilderness after Laguna, just as things were becoming interesting at the top of the table. A 'reserve track' initiative turned farcical when Monza's return became the phantom of the soap opera and Vallelunga proved a bluff in the reserve stakes.

WorldSBK's immediate future is looking good. The 2017 championship will have a healthy quality of new and existing packages taking to the tracks, from Aprilia, BMW, Ducati, Honda, Kawasaki, MV Agusta and Yamaha. Riders Melandri (Italian), Laverty (Irish) and Bradl (German) will all try to break up the Union Jack's hijacking of the podiums. On a new Fireblade, Hayden (USA) could be a true contender.

There will also be a 300 Supersport class to get young riders into the paddock on suitable bikes of real variety.

The biggest boost WorldSBK can give itself, however, is to continually tell the world how great it is, always has been and always will be. Because that's how it grew to prominence first time around.

Left: Ducati's Chaz Davies had an outstanding season with no less than seven wins.

Below: Superbike and Supersport achievers receive their gongs after the last round in Qatar. *From left:* Jules Cluzel, Chaz Davies, Jonathan Rea, Kenan Sofuoglu, Tom Sykes, Kyle Smith and Randy Krummenacher.
Photos: Gold & Goose

CHAMPION PROFILE: JONATHAN REA

DOUBLE FIRST GRADUATE

By GORDON RITCHIE

The feat of securing back-to-back wins in the FIM Superbike World Championship is one that should not be underestimated. It had not been done since that all time great of the class, Carl Fogarty, bridged the trophy gap directly between the 1998 and '99 seasons.

It is so momentous a thing that, to view it from a proper perspective, you have to recognise that what Jonathan Rea and his official Kawasaki Racing Team collective have just achieved had last been done in the previous millennium.

After leaving BSB for WorldSSP in 2008, then WorldSBK in 2009, career-Honda rider Rea took a very long time to find himself on a bike that was truly and objectively able to win the championship itself, and not just a few brilliant races each year.

In joining the only Japanese factory team left in the championship at that stage – Kawasaki Heavy Industries - on a Ninja ZX-10R nearing the end of its five-year development life, Rea knew he was a possible champion from his very first winter test in 2014. The missing X-factor had now come his way with a Z in front of it.

The outwardly conventional in-line four Kawasaki suited his rounded and almost relaxed riding style down to the ground all year. But for a technical issue at the very last round he would have won the 2015 championship with a record points score. He still got within a very few points of it despite losing up to 25 to the fates. He and his bike were just best mates on track and he made the business of winning look the opposite of what it ever is. Easy.

In 2016 he actually lost his 2015 bike completely. A new model Ninja ZX-10R had a much lighter engine inertia and from the off he and his crew were searching to find his ideal base set-up. When you consider that he changed to a 2015 rear swingarm at the penultimate round in Jerez overnight - between race one and two and before he had even quite won the championship – they maybe never did.

And yet Rea won nine races and took 23 of 26 possible podiums. It would have been more but for two DNFs: a crash due to gear changing problem and a technical failure.

In many ways everything was working against Rea winning the big prize again in 2016. His new machine, as a base for racing, was much more suited to his teammate's hard braking, hard accelerating style, having had Tom Sykes' development input applied for years. Ducati had also made the Panigale, in the hands of Chaz Davies, as red hot as its paint scheme. And even his alma mater Honda resorted to more radical tuning and an ex-MotoGP champion to try and keep up with the Joneses, Reas, Sykes' and Davies'.

Then there was the curse of the number one plate, which nobody had been able to keep since 1998-9.

The unspoken question was had the 2015 title been a peak for Rea, with a motivational-hangover waiting on the down slope after the desire to possess the number one plate had finally been sated?

With Tom Sykes not suddenly rocketing forward on the Kawasaki early season either, had they all gone backwards in their efforts to go forward?

The jury is out on the 2016 bike maybe still but the answer to the question of did Rea have what it took to win again was answered by the rider, team and KHI with his second title.

His wet weather attack at the bumpy, slippery and downright iffy Lausitzring surface in race two, after his crash in race one due to his latest issues with finding neutral, was beyond brave and committed. A true champion's display. It was 'all in' as they say in poker. And 25 points out just when he really needed them.

There is no question that Rea simply had to give more of himself in 2016 than 2015.

He had to watch, impotently it seemed at times, as Davies racked up wins near the end. A younger rider, a less intelligent rider, a less mature champion may have lost it at least once in frustration at missing out on the adrenaline buzz that comes with race victories and nothing else. Rea, behind his leading points barricade, showed that if the long game was required he had it in his armoury too.

Being pushed to the final round demonstrates, in a practical sense, how much more difficult 2016 was than 2015 had been. In essence, Rea had to give much more of himself to make the matter certain this time.

SUPERBIKE WORLD CHAMPIONSHIP
2016 TEAMS &RIDERS

By GORDON RITCHIE

APRILIA

IodaRacing Team
A late inclusion for the legendary Giampiero Sacchi's IodaRacing squad, who found no more room at the MotoGP inn. On 2015's official bikes, they fielded injured, but recovering, GP star Alex de Angelis (32) and 2015 Superstock 1000 FIM Cup winner (also on an RSV-4) Lorenzo Savadori (23). As it transpired, this was much more of a top-five thriller than backmarker filler.

BMW

Milwaukee SMR BMW
The reigning BSB champions, with champion Josh Brookes (33) partnered by MotoGP refugee Karel Abraham (26). With customer-supported S1000RR engines and electronics, they all toiled, as predictably as the old paddock hands had expected. Shaun Muir's squad had revised their plans for 2017 long before the 2016 season was complete, in a necessarily profound fashion. A potentially top team, in almost all aspects, with a strong sponsorship base.

Althea Racing BMW
Twice IDM champion, young Markus Reiterberger (22) made the jump to a full WorldSBK squad, which was part his previous German team, but mostly the same Althea squad that had won the world championship in 2011 with Carlos Checa. BMWs were a new departure for them and proved tricky, but this was another strong entry capable of more than middling in the midfield.

Add the prowess of eventual top BMW rider of the year Jordi Torres (29), and this was a decent template of how to go privateer racing at world level.

It was not all plain sailing, of course. Jan Witteveen was tech chief, but left at the halfway point. Eventual Superstock champion Raffaele de Rosa (29) had the occasional ride, too, to cover for the injured 'Reiti', and in his own right at Losail.

Team ASPI BMW
Matthieu Lussiana (28) was a wild-card and scored a point at Assen, but no points at home in France.

DUCATI

Aruba.it Racing – Ducati World Superbike Team
It was something of a groundhog year for the official Ducati squad, what with Chaz Davies (29) winning races, but not being able to make a final title challenge, while Davide Giugliano (26) scored podiums like a veteran, and sometimes crashed like a rookie. Ernesto Marinelli had reformatted the shape of the crew behind Giugliano, but Davies was the man who did the winning.

Barni Racing Ducati
Javier 'Xavi' Fores (31) had earned glory in Spain and Germany, but his leap to the full world championship came with good support from Ducati and the second-year Barni squad. He rewarded them with some great rides, including a podium.

VFT Racing Ducati
Up from World Supersport, the VFT team was a family affair. An early-season injury for Fabio Menghi (30) sidelined him until Misano. He had to pull out again, however, despite travelling to America in an attempt to continue his comeback.

Matteo Baiocco (32) in the first half, and Luca Scassa (33) in the second half, substituted for Menghi for almost the whole rookie year of the team at this level.

Desmo Sport Ducati
Aussie wildcard Mike Jones (22) turned up at round one and scored points for 14th in race one.

HONDA

Honda World Superbike Team
Nicky Hayden (35) sprinkled stardust around the 2016 paddock without even trying, such was his pull with most fans. He eclipsed team-mate Michael van der Mark (23) at times, but the weekend-by-weekend fight for Honda supremacy was compelling all the way.

Honda Europe made some investments that were largely met by improved performance. The Honda was no old dog, but it sure learned cool new tricks in the cost-capped/lower-tuning era, all under the care of Ten Kate Racing.

KAWASAKI

Kawasaki Racing Team
Once again, Jonathan Rea (29) and Tom Sykes (31) teamed up in a little changed squad. Provec Racing managed the race effort day to day, while KHI, Akira and Showa were important partners in performance.

Ichiro Yoda oversaw the tech side for KHI. Manufacturer and rider champions, plus team award winners – despite the other strong entries – this is how to win and keep on winning.

Pedercini Racing Kawasaki
Lucio Pedercini took a sideways step from the old family firm in his self-managed full Superbike team. Qatari rider Saeed al Sulaiti (31) learned his new international craft at a decent rate of improvement, but Sylvain Barrier (28) was again desperately unlucky with an injury early in the season.

Barrier was replaced from Assen onwards, first by man-for-all-classes Lucas Mahias (27), then the potent Anthony West (35) for a few rounds in succession, then Mathieu Lagrive (36), West again in Jerez, and finally the early Christmas present of Leon Haslam (33) at Qatar.

Team GoEleven Kawasaki
Roman Ramos (25) came back for a second season and again was a strong midfield runner. In some ways, it was a hard year to be a privateer, but injury for Ramos was the main problem for the Italian-based team, run by former Stock and World Supersport rider Denis Sacchetti. Gianluca Vizziello (36) replaced him at a few rounds, before joining another team to see out the season.

Grillini SBK Team Kawasaki
Dominic Schmitter (22) was a full-season runner for the Grillini squad, but original signing Josh Hook (23) was injured, missed a few races, competed for a while and then was let go by the team in acrimonious circumstances.

This precipitated a rash of new riders on the second bike. The 2015 Superstock 600 champion, Toprak Razgatlioglu (20), rode in round one in Australia, but had to withdraw with injury. Sahustchai Kaewjaturaporn (31) rode as a wild-card at his home venue in Thailand. Sheridan Morais (31) was supposed to ride from Donington onwards, but crashed and hurt his shoulder, and was unable to start either race. Gianluca Vizziello (36) saw out the year.

MV AGUSTA

MV Agusta Reparto Corse
Leon Camier (30) returned for MV, in the official team. This time around, it was operated as a separate entity from the factory itself. Andrea Quadranti was the team principal, Claudio Quintarelli the team manager. Camier, a lone rider, liked the status and liked the bike as well, particularly how the team made it better all year.

YAMAHA

Pata Yamaha Official WorldSBK Team
Alex Lowes (26) and Sylvain Guintoli (34) were a perfect pre-season pairing to take Yamaha's new official era of WorldSBK competition forward. The paddock had missed them, but the first year back was a tough one. A major injury for Guintoli at Imola spoiled most of his year. Lots of injuries for Lowes prevented him from realising his own and his machine's true potential.

Had Cameron Beaubier (23) not turned up at Donington, they would have had no riders due to Lowes's latest injury, while Niccolo Canepa (28) rode all kinds of Yamahas in 2016, including Guintoli's factory bike at Misano and Laguna.

Team Toth Yamaha
Swapping their 2015 BMW for 2016 Yamahas did nothing for the prospects of the Toth squad. Imre Toth (31) started the season, but was lapped frequently, so regular pick Peter Sebestyen (22) was joined by the vastly experienced Pawel Szkopek (41). He left before the end of the year, and Karel Pesek (24) raced in his stead at Jerez.

Yamaha Thailand Racing Team
Anucha Nakcharoensri (32) was a wild-card at his home race in Thailand, scoring no points and recording a best of 18th in race two.

3ART Yamaha Team
Alex Plancassagne (30) was a wild-card at Magny-Cours on his French R1.

JONATHAN REA

CHAZ DAVIES

TOM SYKES

ROMAN RAMOS

ALEX DE ANGELIS

MARCUS REITERBERGER

JOSH BROOKES

NICKY HAYDEN

MICHAEL VAN DER MARK

DAVIDE GIUGLIANO

XAVI FORES

LORENZO SAVADORI

JORDI TORRES

DAVID SALOM

MATTEO BAIOCCO

KAREL ABRAHAM

NICCOLO CANEPA

ANTHONY WEST

ALEX LOWES

SYLVAIN GUINTOLI

LEON CAMIER

THE SUPERBIKES OF 2016

By GORDON RITCHIE

BMW S1000RR

APRILIA RSV4

DUCATI 1199R

APRILIA RSV4 FACTORY

The original 65-degree DOHC V4 RSV-4 was such a gem of a race package that the 78 x 52.3mm bore-and-stroke engine has only been developed, hardly massively improved upon, in all these years. Plainly, it was still nearly good enough to win races in 2016.

The list of changes from the 2015 model was not long, with the IodaRacing team stating that they had tried a new link after a mid-season test session. Other than that, the bikes were basically as they had been in 2015, older Öhlins suspension units and all.

The development was all in the pit box, as Aprilia had no official involvement in WorldSBK, but the data and advice were all there after so many years and three riders' world championships.

The RSV-4 had been fully adjustable, in terms of chassis geometry. The damage had been done by regulatory limitations, according to Max Biaggi's wild-card rides in 2015, as the engine was fixed in its original position then – by regulation.

Cassette gearbox? Surplus to real-world requirements, as each rider had one declared set of internal ratios per season.

As fast as they come, as race-ready and alterable as anything ever produced, 2016's now private Aprilia RSV-4 was, bizarrely, the epitome of run-what-they-brung racing.

BMW S1000RR

A slightly upgraded road bike, the S1000RR had the most radical engine in the paddock, despite being a conventionally across-the-frame four, with a 999cc displacement. The seriously oversquare bore and stroke of 80 x 49.7mm, and the finger-style cam followers, always marked this power plant as a rev-monster. With split throttles for 2016, it was a bike that needed as much management of power as pure power itself.

Akrapovic support helped smooth the delivery and feedback. For some reason, there was no exhaust valve on the Althea team's pipes.

Once again under BMW's customer support programme, the German manufacturer went about the business of supplying tuned engines and electronics packages – their own electronics of course – and power was not often lacking from the engines. Improving delivery was a constant job, but finding the sweet spot apparently was not the easiest task.

For 2016, when the BMW teams pleased themselves with their choice of chassis parts and suppliers, the Althea squad opted for the newest Öhlins RVP 42mm forks, despite starting out in the winter with the previous items, with reservoirs on the fork bottoms.

DUCATI 1199R

Largely unchanged, but completely developed in every area, as well as external advances like the latest Öhlins forks and shocks, and a modified stock swing-arm of different stiffness, the 2016 Ducati benefited from advances in power and power delivery.

Despite some obvious engine mods, the Panigale appeared to be almost all about the chassis. Chaz Davies did not know that he had found the optimum range of front suspension and geometry settings early on in the season. On these, he could brake hard and still get around corners quickly.

The monocoque chassis, which also formed the headstock tube holder, airbox and top engine mount, was complicated and certainly unusual. Davies came to know the feel to look for each time and was confident in his Panigale's race-long pace.

The exposed and horizontal rear shock absorber, on the left side, was operated by a single-sided swing-arm via a triangulated rear link. The rear end was complicated, but worked well. The engine was a stressed member, indeed was part of the chassis itself.

Up front, there were 42mm Öhlins forks with top-mounted adjusters; the rear featured a 40mm internal damper.

T-type Brembo brakes, with graceful Evo calipers, operated a variety of disc sizes, but the larger ones were used most often.

The 112 x 60.8mm motor never suffered the indignity of having to run any of the air restrictors allowed for by the balancing rules. Being a vee, the Panigale breathed via separate throttle bodies and therefore had a split throttle set-up by design default.

The ECU was the almost ubiquitous Magneti Marelli MLE cost-capped unit, with software developed by Ducati and passed out to the other Ducati teams.

The astoundingly noisy 115db silencers developed for Ducati by Akrapovic boosted power by their convoluted big-bore design and balanced one cylinder against the other by having different diameters of final exit orifices.

HONDA CBR1000RR SP

The only valid complaint about the Honda CBR1000RR SP's combined engine and chassis design was that it was just a bit older than the rest. As a result, little could be done about the slightly out of mode 76 x 55.1mm bore and stroke.

For 2016, the top end was much improved, after positive reinvestment of time and resources by Honda and Ten Kate Honda's tuning partners, Cosworth.

There had been a degree of conservatism in 2015, but for the new season limits were pushed in the engine, and some reliability issues surfaced. But so did more power and competitiveness.

Allied to Cosworth's own-brand MQ12 ECU electronic hardware – and self-coded custom software – real gains were made in 2016, enough to ensure that Hayden and van der Mark would be the biggest threat to the Ducati and Kawasaki combined hegemony. That was an achievement that was unexpected, but well noted by the paddock techies.

A split throttle body system was used again, with obvious actuators and tellbacks.

Once again, Nissin was the technical partner of Honda for brakes, mated with Yutaka discs. Hayden, a heavy user of the rear brake, had a special four-pot caliper.

The front suspension featured the latest Öhlins 42mm units, originally developed for Moto2 and saving

HONDA CBR1000RR SP

MV AGUSTA F4 RR

KAWASAKI NINJA ZX-10R

YAMAHA YZF-R1

well over a kilo for the forks alone. The rear shock was relocated a tad, for one obvious reason. The swing-arm was a backward step to go forward, as Ten Kate dug out the 2014 adjustable version. Top plates of different stiffness allowed the rigidity to be 'tuned'.

The Honda was a bit too heavy at 173kg, quite a bit over the 168kg lower limit for the class.

KAWASAKI NINJA ZX-10R

Kawasaki had a new model for 2016, with many changes aimed at racing and some not. The 76 x 55mm bore-and-stroke engine was hardly class-leadingly oversquare, but the main change was a 20-per cent lighter stock crankshaft. This would help the engine really spin in race mode, especially as only five per cent of crank weight could be lost during tuning under the latest rules.

Rea did not take to the reduced crank inertia and ran with the full stock alternator assembly in place. Sykes, by contrast, wanted it even lighter.

With stock pistons a requirement in 2016, lots of preparatory combustion-chamber work had to be done at the production stage, as no machining of the piston was permitted. The race exhaust pipe from Akrapovic ran a power valve to help control engine braking and corner exit.

The Marelli MLE ECU and ignition unit ran split throttles, despite the road machine only having four linked butterflies, of 47mm diameter, with two injectors per cylinder. Larger-diameter exhaust valves, in titanium, were featured on the new stock bike.

Cost-capped Showa suspension was updated, lightened and generally improved in 2016, and the forks featured some changes. The Horizontal Back Link rear suspension layout was retained, with the rear shock just off-centre in relation to the machine itself, and almost laid down.

With the chassis geometry allowed to be changed a bit more in 2016, via inserts and (limited) alterable pivot points, Kawasaki did just that, making the bike more nimble. The biggest Brembo T-type disc rotors were used, with Brembo Evo calipers.

Unlike MotoGP, brakes were steel, rather than carbon, and Sykes used his rear brake so hard at times under acceleration (to control wheelies or spin) that they overheated twice. The quick fix was more frequent renewal of the calipers.

MV AGUSTA F4 RR

The latest iteration of the MV Agusta F4 had all the good stuff from previous years. The variable inlet tracts were 'open' or 'closed', not gradual in operation, although the point of transition was adjustable.

The engine was well oversquare, at 70 x 50.9mm, and had split throttle bodies. The radial layout of the four-valve heads meant that work on the cams was necessarily complicated, since the valves were at different angles.

More power – some 10bhp up on 2015 – was evident, but still not at the level of the very best.

An SC exhaust was used, and three steps of development in its layout helped the power figures each time.

Titanium inlet and exhaust valves in stock form had become even more important additions to the armoury, since all the stock parts needed to be retained.

The Magneti Marelli MLE ECU was well known to the electronics staff, who made some great inroads into making the bike rideable; it reacted well under braking and acceleration.

Despite still being much heavier than most of the opposition, the new fuel tank, which played a structural role for the chassis, produced a 2kg saving, and was slimmer and neater.

The unique MV Agusta mix of an alloy rear swing-arm plate and rear suspension mounting, bolted to a lattice of steel tubes ending in the headstock, was said by the tech staff to be the bike's biggest advantage in race situations. It was easy on tyres, and many times Camier made great lap times and gains in the second half of a race.

The big box-section, single-sided swing-arm was designed to offer some flex in some planes, but be more rigid in others – and to be lighter than the original. The

bellcrank rear suspension was retained, but not quite in the same way as on the road bike, given the different swing-arm.

Yamaha YZF-R1

Around for a year or so in many other forms of Superbike racing, the outwardly sane, but actually slightly barking M1-replica YZF-R1 was very far from just another four-cylinder. Almost as radical in its engine architecture as the screamadelic BMW, the Yamaha's 79 x 50.9 mm bore-and-stroke figures ensured it would have the potential for revs.

Its quirky, but well-proven, cross-plane crankshaft design, making it a kind of virtual V4, also imbued it with some handy grunt and, theoretically, gentle tyre wear characteristics.

There are lots of limits on what can be tuned in a modern WorldSBK machine, and even on what parts have to be stock or replaced by ones of the same material and weight. Yamaha could not simply tear out the street stuff and start again with M1 parts. This showed in the R1 not having the same corner exit push as most of its rivals. They claimed 220bhp, and once it was singing that may have been true, but by then the very best of the others were a bit further down the track.

A Magneti Marelli MLE ECU controlled the engine management duties and drove the split throttles that fed the engine's eight inlet valves.

Akrapovic looked after the exhaust, and a new pipe near the end of the season was an improvement. The Yamaha did not make full use of the 115db limit in 2016, even though it had been relatively noisy in early winter testing.

With brakes and suspension components cost-capped again in 2016, the new-design 42mm Öhlins front forks were the same for all, but Yamaha used the longer version. Both riders had the larger 336mm Brembo front brakes.

Remarkably, the aluminium deltabox chassis itself needed no bracing or gusseting, so good was it out of the crate, according to the team.

PHILLIP ISLAND

ROUND 1 · AUSTRALIA

Above: The opening race of the season began with a titanic battle between Rea, Giugliano, Davies and van der Mark.

Right: Shaun Muir headed the Milwaukee BMW team on its debut in WorldSBK.

Centre right: MotoGP refugee Karel Abraham prepares for his global Superbike debut.

Below right: Michael van der Mark leads Rea, Davies and Hayden in race two.

Opposite page, from top: Lowes crashes out of race one; Rea was doubly unbeatable; comeback kid Giugliano raced his Ducati to fourth- and third-place finishes; Michael van der Mark was endlessly combative, taking second place in race two.

Opposite page, bottom right: Josh Brookes was back in WorldSBK action on home soil on his Milwaukee BMW. The BSB champion leads Ramos and Savadori in race one.

Photos: Gold & Goose

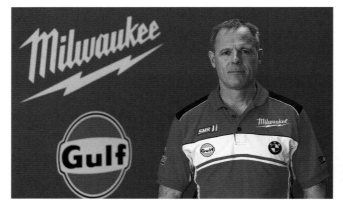

A NEW oil sponsor for the FIM Superbike World Championship, in the form of Motul, ensured a smooth beginning to the 29th consecutive year of global Superbike competition. Once again, it all started well away from the usual base of European operations, at the magnificent Phillip Island circuit in Australia.

Enticingly rapid and commensurately risky for the unwary, the tyre-melting layout always ensures close competition, some slipstreaming on the main straight, and sometimes weird and wonderful results.

The top riders, desperate to get going for real after a two-day pre-race test, ensured that there was competition right to the end of each 22-lap race – one on Saturday and one on Sunday for 2016.

There were two long hours of 'free' practice on Friday – a bizarre misnomer, as they were important qualifying sessions. They were the only two that counted when it came to making it into Superpole 2 directly (for first ten) or initially passing through Superpole 1 (everybody else on the grid in 2016, rather than just the 11th to 20th fastest).

After a 15-minute FP3 run out on Saturday, Superpole 1 led to Superpole 2, for the final grid places for the front four rows. Tom Sykes (KRT) scooped his 31st Superpole qualifying 'win', despite pushing too hard on his out-lap to get away from two following riders. His lap of 1m 30.020s was a new best for the 4.445km circuit.

There was no rest for the field as the burst of Superpole adrenaline grew to a full-blown hit of point-scoring addiction in race one.

Ninth on the grid for potential title challenger Chaz Davies made his start far from easy. Jonathan Rea (KRT) led early on, was passed by Sykes, but pushed ahead again. Then both Ducati riders – Davies and Davide Giugliano – simply barged past Sykes, followed soon after by both Honda World Superbike riders, Michael van der Mark and Nicky Hayden.

On the entry to the final lap, the leading four were Rea, Davies, van der Mark and Giugliano.

A brave and effective pass from Davies into the MG hairpin looked perfect until Rea scored a higher final mark from his flick-and-squirt manoeuvre, cutting off Davies's nose as he leaned into the next left. Rea would win the high-lean-angle drag race all the way to upright again, and thereafter a more conventional sprint to the line.

His success came with a very small winning margin of 0.063 second.

Behind, two riders still looking for their first wins in the class battled it out for third, with van der Mark mounting the bronze podium step and Giugliano earning 13 points for fourth place.

With the top four covered by just 0.647 second, it was a loud and brash round-one wake-up call, worth the effort for those watching it live in Europe. Trackside, it was even more visceral.

In fifth, Sykes was a fading 3.429 seconds from his victorious team-mate, while his 2014 nemesis, Sylvain Guintoli, was just behind on the all-new official Pata Yamaha.

The second race, a whole day later, was a very slightly more clear-cut winning display by Rea, if only right at the end. Davies had fallen as he attacked Rea into Turn Four, clambering back on to finish tenth.

The lead Ducati man's misfortune left van der Mark second by 0.831s and Giugliano on the podium after all in his comeback weekend, 1.472s back from Rea.

New-start WorldSBK rider and old MotoGP superstar Hayden was right on Giugliano's tail in fourth, 1.511 seconds from his first Superbike win. He was on for a top-three, but could not quite prevent Giugliano's audacious inside pass between the two superfast final left-handers.

Guintoli was fifth, Sykes sixth, just over three seconds off the winners again.

BURIRAM

ROUND 2 · THAILAND

Above: Rea and Sykes lead the field at the start of race one.

Top right: New kid on the block. Markus Reiterberger took an impressive fifth for BMW in race one.

Above right: Sykes finally got the upper hand over Rea in race two. Chaz Davies was a whisker behind in third at the finish.

Opposite, clockwise from top left: Van der Mark scored his first Superpole win and then a podium; Alex Lowes took a promising sixth for Yamaha in race one; local wildcard entry Anucha Nakcharoensri appeared on a Yamaha; Sylvain Guintoli confers with his Pata Yamaha crew.

Photos: Gold & Goose

IT is appropriate that the stadium-style Chang International Circuit is so close to the stadium of local football team Buriram United, because the races in Thailand proved to be a game of two halves, played out over two days.

Superpole, part of a busy Saturday, was mildly historic. Michael van der Mark took the first pole for a Dutch rider, on what was clearly a rejuvenated Honda. Lots of winter work to maximise engine tuning and chassis modifications proved to be well conceived and executed.

After a great first WorldSBK year for the geometric, but intense Thai circuit in 2015, track modifications in the form of recently resurfaced tarmac made certain sections almost impossibly slippery, resulting in some bizarre lines in places (particularly Turn Three).

There was embarrassment all round because this situation had been allowed to develop so close to a race weekend. With vast areas of asphalt off limits on the inside of Turn Three, the lap proved to be longer than the official 4.554km of the time sheets. Partly for that reason, no Superpole or race lap record was broken, but they got pretty close all the same.

In the first 20-lap race, KRT riders Rea and Sykes won the start-line drag, van der Mark going away with them. He ran off track and lost the tow, however, subsequently finishing almost ten seconds from the win.

Sykes led from lap two to lap 15, but Rea took over when it mattered most to record his third straight win of the year, this time by 0.222 second from his team-mate.

With van der Mark third, Chaz Davies won the battle of the Ducatis, but finished 17 seconds away in fourth. Giugliano crashed and restarted to finish out of the points.

Markus Reiterberger (Althea Racing BMW) deserves honourable mention, having gone from ninth on the grid to fifth on his S1000RR; ex-GP tech legend Jan Witteveen was in overall engineering control of the effort.

In race two, the fans in the crowded grandstand were treated to some even more aggressive moves, with van der Mark and Davies clanging at Chang on lap one. Halfway through, Davies dispatched the Honda and began closing on the leading Kawasakis.

At the front, Rea probed for weaknesses, but this time Sykes was so determined to win that he responded when Rea passed. Then he ran wide with some weird rear-end locking that put him third behind Davies at one stage.

The scrap between the leading three sent the crowd into vocal mode, and Sykes's reputation for not relishing a fight was soon demolished. Rea thought he would be able to make his last-lap passes stick, but after running wide, rival Sykes got back in front, defending with blocks and manoeuvres that brought grudging admiration from Rea – tempered with some less evident unhappiness at how tough some of it had been in certain corners.

Sykes won by 0.190 second – his first victory since September, 2015.

Davies was just adrift of the battling KRT riders, by 0.314 second. The Welshman had mitigated his horrible Saturday at a track he considered the worst for his bike. A top-three finish was some kind of redemption.

Van der Mark finished fourth in race two; team-mate Hayden was fifth, another five seconds back.

Guintoli scored a creditable sixth on his Pata Yamaha, but the big story of the weekend was that Rea left Thailand having been beaten for the first time in 2016. Even so, he was still only five championship points from early-season perfection.

With the first four races having gone to Kawasaki riders, the all-new and full-factory Kawasaki appeared to be headed towards virtual domination.

Above: Sykes (66) and the Pata Yamahas of Guintoli (50) and Lowes (22) lead away in race two, with Rea (1), Davies (7) and Giugliano (34) in hot pursuit.

Right: Xavi Fores took fourth in both races for the Barni Racing Team.

Below right: In race one, Savadori won a tight Aprilia battle for tenth place with de Angelis.

Centre: Davies jumps for joy on the podium after breaking the Kawasaki winning streak.

Far right: Davies left the green machines trailing in a victorious double-header for Ducati.

Photos: Gold & Goose

I N the rights holders' home territory of Spain, Dorna would have their first look at a new style of race weekend in its new normal European format, with races starting at 13.00 on Saturday and Sunday.

Pre-race, this was the best chance for Chaz Davies to get on to the winning scoreboard in 2016, but he missed the front row in Superpole, which was dominated by that man Sykes again, from the encouragingly fast Pata Yamahas of Guintoli and Lowes, in second and third respectively.

In race one, under the early spring sunshine, Sykes and Guintoli headed off into a stretching lead. But Davies, his Ducati Panigale sporting a new and spectacularly noisy asymmetric, double-exit, high-level exhaust – part of a major redevelopment – worked his way forward to pass Guintoli on lap four; van der Mark crashed out on the same lap. The Welshman had set a new lap record of 1m 50.421s on lap three as he chased the top two.

Then the No. 7 rider passed Sykes for the lead, before easing away at will to take the win in confident fashion by just over four seconds. It was Davies's tenth career win and the beginning of a red weekend.

Rea had passed Sykes with nine laps to go to secure second. Sykes was close behind, but unable to challenge at the end.

Privateer progress had been a factor following the technical changes in the championship, aimed at limiting cost and increasing availability of top-level parts and software. Thus it was not much of a surprise that Spain's Xavi Fores (Barni Racing Ducati) got past the works bike of Giugliano after a tense battle, finally 13 seconds behind the win.

This was Fores's best result in WorldSBK, but fifth was an obvious disappointment for Giugliano.

American Hayden was sixth, and another Spanish rider, Jordi Torres (Althea Racing BMW), seventh.

The 18-lap second race was the 700th in WorldSBK's near 30-year history.

Sykes took an early lead, but had to work hard to keep Davies behind. Once Chaz was away, however, he was gone to the power of two.

Once again, Rea had worked on his bike's bugs and intricacies before the race, and his great start to the year continued, despite his unsettled approach to the new machine's set-up. Closing in on Sykes, he passed and eased away for a while, only for Sykes to make up some ground. Then came drama as Rea ran on into Turn One with four laps to go. He had been experiencing some vibration from the rear during this race, which led to what at first looked like simple rider errors.

Sykes seized the opportunity for second, but nobody had anything for Davies, who moved to within 26 points of Rea with his milestone victory in race No. 700. Even the Welshman felt it was special, saying that Ducati had turned a corner in their 2016 campaign as they came within 25 points of the previously unstoppable Kawasaki effort.

Behind the podium finishers, Fores took his second fourth place of the weekend for Barni Racing, while fifth went to fellow Spaniard Jordi Torres, who was ahead of the struggling Giugliano in sixth.

Hayden recorded a no-score following a technical problem, his second non-finish in only six races.

Sylvain Barrier (Pedercini Racing Kawasaki) crashed early in race two, spoiling his season and opening up opportunities for others in the new-look Pedercini squad.

Not as combative as Phillip Island or Thailand, Aragon at least was a whole new ball game, with those in red shirts walking a few centimetres taller towards the exit gates.

SUPERBIKE WORLD CHAMPIONSHIP
ASSEN
ROUND 4 · NETHERLANDS

Above: Savadori and Lowes battle in race one.

Above right: Settling in. Former MotoGP champ Hayden took his first WorldSBK podium for Honda.

Top: Rea took the honours in both races. The Northern Irishman leads KRT team-mate Sykes at the fateful final chicane.

Right: Before crashing out, Josh Brookes was one of many leaders in the rain-affected race two – three times in all.

Photos: Gold & Goose

A WET Friday, a dry Superpole and a sunny first race – it was all looking good for a top-class contest at Assen, despite the lack of dry track time. Or perhaps because of it…

To the surprise of few, Sykes won Superpole, with Guintoli and Giugliano just behind him. That made for a Kawasaki/Yamaha/Ducati front-row colour palette of green, blue and red.

As it transpired, and despite the dry track, none of the top three finished the race. Guintoli crashed on lap four; Giugliano dropped back and finally retired at half-distance. And Sykes? At least it started well for him.

Sykes and Rea led them all off yet again, until Davies passed them both to lead outright on lap four. Meanwhile, Nicky Hayden had started to close in on the leading group from his tenth-place grid position.

Van der Mark would go second, but as Rea got past Sykes, the English rider tried to get into position to pass again into the final chicane, only to run off line, go out too far to the left and then fall under braking as he tried to regain track position to turn right.

That left a top four. With five laps remaining, Rea passed van der Mark and then Davies.

With the partisan home crowd cheering him on, van der Mark took the lead for a time, pushing hard enough to draw black lines from the rear and work his front tyre hard. Too hard, it transpired, after Rea made a late pass and executed a successful escape plan.

Desperate to stay in contention for what would be his first WorldSBK race win, and in front of his home fans, van der Mark simply asked too much of his front tyre and crashed at speed, totalling his bike.

With Davies not quite able to apply his tractor beam of torque to Rea's Kawasaki in the final lap, he finished 1.662 seconds down in second.

Rea's eventually classy and peerless race win was overshadowed, however, by a first podium for the other superstar Honda rider on this particular week-end, Nicky Hayden. Five seconds back from Rea, he was calmer than anyone about his first WorldSBK podium, saying he was happy, but not getting carried away, as it was a podium, not a win.

The second race started wet, and most riders set off on wet tyres. As the track dried, however, the grip from the tyres and track waxed and waned.

Sykes was the early leader, but as the laps progressed and the rain re-gressed, the race was led, in turn, by Josh Brookes (Milwaukee BMW), Rea, van der Mark, Brookes again, Alex Lowes, Brookes again, Lukas Mahias (Pedercini Racing Kawasaki, substituting for the injured Sylvain Barrier) and finally race winner Rea, from lap 14 to the 21st and last.

Amazingly, only three riders did not finish, among them the luckless Brookes, who slid off just after changing to the required slick tyre set-up.

Rea and Sykes had stopped for slicks at the right time, but Sykes's muffled request for a rear slick, not an intermediate, went unheard by his team, and he left with a less-than-ideal inter fitted. Considering this, his second-place performance was a ride to be proud of after Saturday's disappointment. Rea took the win by 2.442 seconds.

After the desperate late fail by van der Mark on Saturday, Sunday's devo-tions from the local Dutch racing congregation lifted him to third place, albeit 15 seconds down.

Regardless of the weather conditions, fourth from the Ioda Racing Project and their star-in-the-making, Lorenzo Savadori, was a top ride; he was even ahead of Chaz Davies, who was fifth. Hayden finished the second race sixth.

Above: Sykes slides out in race one.

Left: Van der Mark on the grid before race two.

Top: A happy race-one podium for Davies, Rea and Hayden.

Below left: Spaniard Ramos scored good points for Team GoEleven in both races.

Below: Mahias leads Lussiana (94) and Ramos in race two.

Photos: Gold & Goose

Above: The field blasts off the grid in front of a decent Saturday crowd – it was Italy after all.

Right: Giugliano was second in Superpole, but ended up out of the podium places in both races.

Below right: Pure local joy for Davies and his Bolognese crew after his race-one win.

Centre right: Davies was in complete command and his Panigale's pace too hot for the competition.

Far right, top: Alex Lowes manages sixth for Yamaha in race two.

Far right, bottom: Jordi Torres grabbed a fine fourth for BMW in race one, albeit ten seconds from the podium.

Photos: Gold & Goose

NOT the most obviously modern or run-off-heavy circuit in the world, Imola has a certain something that makes it stand out, justifying its status as a classic circuit of the old school. Modern chicanes may have slowed it, but they add to the overtaking dramas, while steel barriers and mini-Coliseum walls ring it, adding to the risk. The track follows nature's contours, and the town of Imola lovingly enfolds it, in Europe's most motorsport-junkie-friendly country.

No doubt inspired by being so close to the point of origin of the Ducati Panigale, Chaz Davies came out on top in Superpole, while Ducati's favoured deities ensured that Davide Giugliano would line up alongside him on the grid each time.

Saturday was dry and temperate, but Davies's front-running pace was unstoppably hot for his opponents.

In front of most of Ducati's main players, and no small number of *Ducatisti* from Bologna and beyond, Davies was rampant, wiping out memories of 2015's double trouble at the same venue with what would be the first of two race wins. He led every lap, heading off Rea as the 18-lap race progressed.

Rea ran wide at Turn Seven, reducing the gap back to Sykes in third. Davies probably did not need the help of Rea's recurring braking and corner-entry problems, and his extravagant gestures across the line showed just how happy he was to take a much-needed victory.

Rea, finally second, beat team-mate Sykes by just over 0.3 second, keeping his 100-per cent podium finishing record intact.

Fourth was taken by the flowing figure of Jordi Torres, who secured his best finish of the year to date. He had to relegate front-row starter and local man Davide Giugliano

to fifth to put his score on the board and was an eventual ten seconds behind any potential podium.

Leon Camier (MV Agusta Reparto Corse) was well over a second a lap off the best rider. Given that he was mounted on the relatively heavy, still not powerful enough and plain cash-strapped lone official F4RR, a top-six finish was well received by the crowd – and a credit to rider and team.

In race two, Davies launched well once more, and he was away and clear before the chasing pack realised he had gone. The Welshman's eventual margin of victory was 4.262 seconds.

Behind, the Kawasakis were at it again, but this time Sykes nearly got a second place, after Rea's rear tyre hit the trackside Astroturf on the exit of the tricky final chicane and started a rear-end tank-slapper fit to loosen his fillings. Even so, he was 0.4 second or so ahead of Sykes across the line.

With his team-mate out front, being 13 seconds back was poor reward for Giugliano, who was fourth behind the Kawasakis.

This time, Camier was 16.2 seconds from the winning time, and in fifth place, his best MV result in the dry.

Relatively speaking, Alex Lowes was having a better weekend than some, sixth, and well in the top points.

Torres was seventh, but the wheels had clearly come off the recently successful Honda effort again, with Hayden eighth and van der Mark ninth. The latter had been seventh in race one, Hayden ninth, so it was no race-two flash-in-the-pan to be put down to freak circumstances.

The Honda was hot or cold, it appeared, but nothing in between.

STEAM power has long been out of favour in most countries, but it certainly seems alive and well in the jungles of Malaysia. Hot enough to singe body hair, as it sometimes seems in Sepang, and steamy enough to poach the average northern European after spending half an hour in what is effectively an open-air sauna, the heat and humidity can make Malaysian races incredible ordeals.

So race-day temperatures of 32°C (dry on Saturday) and 26°C (wet on Sunday) were almost a welcome relief compared to what might have been.

The news that Sepang had been resurfaced over the winter was met with near panic after the Chang debacle. And while water still bubbled up from some parts of the track long after the rains had come and gone during practice, the surface grew better all weekend, and in most regards it was a big improvement.

There was also the spectacle of the 'humpback whale' final left corner. Track designers Dromo had deliberately raised the inside pavement way up high, so any rider who dived inside too tightly would have to roll off a bit or risk a front-end wipe-out over a ridge. Remarkably, this drastic (if not outright dastardly) initiative actually made sense.

Sykes was a lone meteor out front in race one, in the dry, and on new-lap-record pace. He crossed the line fully 5.6 seconds ahead of team-mate Rea, who in turn was well clear of third-placed Davies.

Behind the strung-out podium trio, there was a bit more in the way of action and adventure, although it was misadventure for young German Markus Reiterberger (Althea Racing BMW). He had been on course for fourth, but his bike quit and he no-scored close to the end.

His team-mate, Jordi Torres, inherited the first off-podium place instead, his best ride so far in 2016. Ditto for Alex Lowes and Yamaha, in fifth and just a second from fourth, despite running wide early on. Lowes had been second in Superpole, behind the inevitability of Sykes taking the best grid spot.

Race two was soaking wet at the start, but had dried out a bit by the finish.

Hayden, fourth on the grid, got going well, passing first Sykes and then Rea to take the lead before the end of lap one. Despite the rapidly advancing Giugliano causing him some moments of concern in the final laps, the American hung on to win his first full WorldSBK race after only 12 attempts as a full-time top runner.

Just 1.254 seconds ahead of Giugliano, Hayden headed a podium that was completed by ever present top runner Jonathan Rea. Six rounds and 12 races in, he was still podium-perfect. He had to fight at times to maintain positions, passing Davies and then hauling himself into clean air, 3.6 from the win.

Davies was fourth, 5.720 seconds behind Hayden.

This time, the American did allow himself some emotion in the post-race interviews. He had used his vast experience to keep the throttle cable hot and his head cool enough to win.

A brilliant fifth for new WorldSBK rider Anthony West was the perfect way to announce his new status as replacement for the still injured Barrier at the Pedercini Racing Team.

Michael van der Mark held off a forceful Alex de Angelis (IodaRacing Team Aprilia) for sixth. In a world of wet-set-up pain, Sykes was eighth, hardly the outcome he had in mind after winning on Saturday.

A weekend of two halves was so much more than the sum of its parts, with the rain adding drama on track to contrast with what had been a slightly processional first race.

Left: The wet conditions in race two allowed Nicky Hayden to move smoothly through the field to take victory in race two.

Below far left: Giugliano leads Davies and Rea in their pursuit of Hayden.

Below left: Jordi Torres sits and sweats on the steamy grid.

Bottom far left: Hayden celebrates his first WorldSBK win – as popular with the fans as it was with the Honda camp.

Bottom left: New boy Anthony West shone in the wet conditions to take fifth in race two.

Below: Tom Sykes holds the lead from Rea, Davies and van der Mark on his way to winning race one.
Photos: Gold & Goose

Above: Rea takes to the grass at Goddards during race one. Gremlins at work.
Photo: Clive Challinor Motorsport Photography

Above left: Sykes leads the field as they sweep through Craner Curves.

Right: Cameron Beaubier, a substitute for Guintoli, became Yamaha's lone rider following Lowes's withdrawal through injury.
Photos: Gold & Goose

Top: Chaz Davies hangs it all out during his pursuit of the Kawasakis in race two.
Photo: Clive Challinor Motorsport Photography

Left, clockwise from far left: Davies, Sykes and Savadori are joined by four-times champion Carl Fogarty for the Superpole presentation; Savadori shone on the Ioda Aprilia; Davide Giugliano prepares for his run to second in race one; Davies falls in front of Brookes in race one.
Photos: Gold & Goose

Right: Sykes won the battle of KRT's Britons from Rea in race two.
Photo: Gold & Goose

BRITAIN may no longer be considered as 'Superbike Island', even by UK fans, but as always at least there were a couple of British riders front and centre in the WorldSBK results.

Donington has been very much Tom Sykes's territory as far as recent seasons have been concerned, and in 2016 it was more of the same, putting him into the record books as the most successful rider in WorldSBK history at the circuit.

Saturday had elicited a predictable Superpole win for Sykes, but it was a remarkable and record-breaking 1m 26.712s lap all the same.

Davies and Savadori joined Sykes on the front row. The Kawasaki/Ducati/Aprilia line-up had a pleasing visual and aural variety.

There was an additional star-spangled banner being waved this weekend, in the official Yamaha garage, as MotoAmerica star Cameron Beaubier was riding as the replacement for the injured Sylvain Guintoli. He was the only factory R1 man on track at Donington, Alex Lowes having succumbed to recent injury and been ruled out of both 23-lap hometown adventures.

The first truly was an adventure for some, but a misadventure for Beaubier, who fell and retired on the very first lap.

Davies, outgunned of late, despite his early-season competitiveness, was too intimate with his home asphalt not once, but twice. The second fall was a fast one, at Coppice, as he tried to get back into contention. That ended his interest in race one. It was something of a difficult weekend for him, as his bike had caught fire on Friday, causing the loss of vital track time on what is the only real day of practice under the new schedule.

Davide Giugliano, on the other works Ducati, led race one for 11 of the 23 laps.

Jonathan Rea also had an eventful first contest, running off track at the final hairpin of Goddards (twice, no less), and having to use all of his skill to stay on and get back to third at the flag. He had hit false neutrals five times in all.

The Saturday win went to Sykes, after some combative action with Giugliano, who finally finished second by just over two seconds.

With Rea third, Leon Camier and the remarkably resilient MV Agusta Reparto Corse team took fourth. Any result inside the top ten was some kind of achievement for such a cash-strapped squad and its lone British rider. Fifth was Sepang race winner Nicky Hayden, with Savadori sixth, in a close-fought off-podium battle.

The second race on Sunday was run in slightly cooler conditions than the opener, but the same rider came out on top – Sykes. His eighth straight race win at Donington was a remarkable feat by any standards. Fast enough down the flowing sections, superfast in some of the sweepers and best in the stop-start Melbourne Loop section, Sykes has a special relationship with Donington. Perhaps it should be renamed DoningTom Park!

With a night to work out what was wrong, Rea and his crew came back strong to finish second in race two, after yet another run-on just as he had taken the lead from Sykes. For Rea, it was a weekend of gaining on Davies, but losing advantage to Sykes, who had moved to second in the title chase.

Third was a decent comeback for Davies, but his bike just did not allow him to fight all the way with the warring Kawasaki pairing.

Savadori placed fourth in another strong weekend, with Camier fifth and even closer to the win in terms of overall race time than on Saturday.

Hayden was sixth, while seventh-placed Giugliano was a whopping 24 seconds behind the win. Beaubier showed well and placed tenth, just one back from 2015 British champion Josh Brookes.

SUPERBIKE WORLD CHAMPIONSHIP
MISANO
ROUND 8 · ITALY

Above: Rea beats Sykes over the line to win race two by 0.090s.

Right: Rea sports the Northern Ireland flag to show his support for the over-performing team in the Euro 2016 football tournament.

Centre right: Double champ Max Biaggi turned up with interesting hair colouring!

Below right: Sykes and Rea also battled hard for supremacy for a period in race two.

Opposite page, from top: After his first-race tumble, Savadori salvaged fifth place in race two; with Guintoli still unfit to race, Niccolo Canepa was drafted in to handle the Pata Yamaha; Davide Giugliano, sporting a helmet in tribute to Fabrizio Pirovano, took a fine third in race two; pit-lane tribute to the recently departed Pirovano and Luis Salom.

Photos: Gold & Goose

ISANO World Circuit Marco Simoncelli would host the second and last Italian round of the season, after the planned Monza round in July was cancelled and the first alternate circuit of Vallelunga could not take its place.

As layouts go, Misano has never been the most interesting venue. It is unique, however. The ever slower series of corners entering the tight Curva del Carro section is a result of the switch from a counterclockwise to clockwise layout ten years ago. It is also as flat as Imola is undulating.

The Riviera di Rimini round took place after something of a spring break in the calendar after Donington. It was business as usual for the top two riders in the championship, however, from early in the race weekend, with Sykes winning Superpole and almost into the 1m 33s with his new record of 1m 34.037s. Rea was confidently second on the grid. At his Barni Racing Team's home track, Spaniard Javier Fores put his private Ducati third in Superpole. Giugliano was seventh and Davies ninth on the official Panigales.

In the early laps of race one, Aprilia hotshot Lorenzo Savadori slid off and could not restart. His fall sent Chaz Davies wide and relegated down the order to ninth for a time. Also off, and properly in this case, was Giugliano, who restarted to finish 14th. Nicky Hayden was a terminal faller on lap two as he pursued the leaders.

As Davies set about his chase back to the top, which would result in a fourth-place finish, leaders Rea and Sykes raced on with less than half a second between them.

It would be much closer on the final lap as Sykes dodged and weaved in Rea's slipstream, having a real go out of the final corner and coming to within 0.090 second of taking the win. Rea had defended as well as he had led, however, to return to winning ways.

Behind the Kawasakis, just over three seconds from the win, Michael van der Mark regained his podium prowess, enjoying almost three seconds of a cushion ahead of the determined Davies. Althea BMW's Jordi Torres was fifth, team-mate Markus Reiterberger sixth. This time around, Pata Yamaha had Niccolo Canepa substituting for Guintoli, and he finished seventh.

Very early in race two, a high-altitude high-side terminated in a heavy impact that resulted in Reiterberger sustaining vertebrae injuries, but thankfully no nerve damage.

On lap three, Davies crashed – again – as he chased Fores, his front-end slip-off collecting Michael van der Mark while exiting the last right-hander at Del Carro. Both were lucky to escape with no significant injury, despite the relatively low speed of the impact. Van der Mark got going again for tenth.

Sykes led all the way beyond lap 16, but Rea passed him at the start of the next and pulled away strongly to win by almost three seconds.

Rea's tenth career double win was masterful in the timing and execution of his final pass, a fitting result for a rider who once again was pulling away from his peers.

Some 6.356 seconds from the win, Giugliano took a popular third place. An Italian rider on the podium was a fitting local tribute to early-era WorldSBK legend Fabrizio Pirovano, who had passed away after a long illness shortly before the Misano round.

Slipping into fourth place, Fores eventually had a lonely ride, while in the warring pack behind, Savadori overcame the pressure from Hayden and Torres. Alex Lowes missed out on a potential top five late in the race, dropping several places in one lap.

What could have been another strong weekend for the MV Agusta team proved disappointing on home soil, with Leon Camier eighth in race one and out of race two with a technical issue.

Above: Winner Sykes and Giugliano were almost inseparable during race two.

Left: Fores shone once more on the Barni Ducati.

Below left: Van der Mark just missed the podium in race one.

Below: Milwaukee BMW riders Brookes (25) and Abraham continued to struggle.

Far left: The Kawasakis of Sykes and Rea lead the Ducatis of Giugliano and Davies over the scary Turn One rise.

Photos: Gold & Goose

Far left, top: American Nicky Hayden proudly flew the Stars and Stripes on the race-two podium.

Far left, bottom: Giugliano crashes out of race one.

Centre left: Super-sub Raffaele de Rosa leads West and Ramos through the infamous Corkscrew.

Left: During the pre-race track walk, a clowning Torres mimics a ride down the Corkscrew.

Right: Alex Lowes shelters from the heat on the grid.

Photos: Gold & Goose

THE storm before the long becalming summer interval broke in the almost desert conditions of Laguna Seca. The old dry lake provides a popular and unique round for the visiting teams, but the co-headlining MotoAmerica round, on Dunlops, ensures we see no more Wild-West wild-cards in the global corral.

With Davies starting out almost 100 points off Rea's championship lead, the 2015 Laguna double winner needed two good results. He got one.

In Superpole, Sykes was top man once again, with Rea and Giugliano alongside him on the front row. Nicky Hayden, back on home ground, was best Honda rider, sixth on the grid. With the first race just a couple of hours after Superpole, anticipation was hot.

Markus Reiterberger having been sidelined by injury, the Althea Racing BMW team fielded Superstocker Raffaele de Rosa. Canepa again subbed for the missing Guintoli.

Rea ate into Sykes's early advantage, but it was Davies who went into the lead, pushing into Sykes's line. Then only a few corners later, the Ducati rider crashed out at Turn Five, with fully 21 laps to go.

Rea had got by Sykes as Davies hit the lead and then the deck, but Sykes got back ahead for a time after Rea ran wide at the Corkscrew. The latter made it stick to the end of lap 25, however. The margin of victory was just 0.819s, but Sykes simply could not get past his team-mate and championship rival.

It was Rea's first Laguna Seca win.

Behind the leading two, Giugliano had fallen at half-distance at the same turn as Davies.

A dark day in the sunshine for Ducati, then, but a Saturday that was immeasurably brightened for the local fans by a third place for their hero, Hayden, albeit 12.296s down. His charging team-mate, van der Mark, had been closing in and finished uncomfortably near, while Lowes and Savadori were not far off the podium places either.

It took two goes to get the entire ninth round boxed off on Sunday.

The first start was heralded by a crash by midfielder van der Mark at the entrance to the Corkscrew, while Giugliano practised front-seat driving for a while. A heavier crash by Team Toth Yamaha rider Pawel Szkopek broke his foot and brought out the red flags as he lay trackside, eliciting a 21-lap re-start, with van der Mark back in the mix.

With 18 laps to go, Rea cut the gap to Giugliano and Sykes to nothing, then passed both of them in one audacious move inside at the Corkscrew. He was determined to lead, but it lasted for a few seconds only, as he ran off on to the red earth and suffered his first non-finish of the year. The cause was an unspecified internal technical issue.

Opportunity had knocked Sykes's championship door back on to its hinges, but there was the small matter of keeping both factory Ducati riders behind him to cut into Rea's 71-point championship lead.

The three-rider fight ended with a scintillating final three laps, during which Davies and Giugliano almost punted each other off at one stage, after heeling into the scary Turn One together.

In the end, it was Sykes from Giugliano and Davies, the trio covered by only 0.786s. Sykes had cut Rea's lead to just 46 points.

Xavi Fores was fourth, Hayden fifth and Torres sixth.

After the duel in the dust, we had to wait nine straight weekends before WorldSBK racing resumed.

Above: Dwarfed by the huge grand-stand, Davies leads the field at the start of race two.

Right: Chaz was in complete control in the dry race.

Centre right: Leon Camier excelled on the MV once again, taking fourth in race one.

Below: Sylvain Guintoli tiptoes on his Yamaha as the pack negotiates the tricky conditions at the start of race two.

Photos: Gold & Goose

Facing page, from top: Riders head for a meeting with the stewards over safety concerns on such a wet track; in a welcome race return, the rain afforded Alex de Angelis the chance to claim a brilliant second; third-placed – and a priva-teer – Xavi Fores was Ducati's top finisher in race two.

Right: In taking third in race one, just behind Tom Sykes, Nicky Hayden was pleasantly surprised by the pace of his Honda.

Far right: Race-two winner Jonathan Rea flanked by unexpected compan-ions de Angelis and Fores.

Photos: Gold & Goose

FOR Round Ten at the Lausitzring, WorldSBK made a racing return to asphalt not visited since 2007, although many had tested there. During Friday's two-hour session, KRT's Rea and Sykes were obviously missing pure pace. Having only 'tested' road-bike-spec machines at Lausitz during the long summer break, the track's bumps, data-vacuum (and the avaricious efforts of their peers) meant that even Rea initially had to get out of Superpole 1 before going for a final grid placing in Superpole 2. He recovered to the last place on row two.

Davies won a portentous pole. It heralded a Saturday race win in the dry that blew the minds of rival and spectator alike.

Chaz led across the line on each of the 21 laps. On lap two, he set a new record of 1m 37.357s that would also be the new track best. Off the boil before the summer break, his victory over a chasing Sykes was 10.561 seconds. He set a 1m 37s lap 15 times; his rivals were lucky to do one or two.

Finally, with some data to work with, Sykes made a strong recovery from his first-day doldrums to score second place, although he had to work hard to keep his advantage over Honda-mounted Nicky Hayden, who took third. That must have come as a surprise for the American rider who, before the race, had said that the limit of his package was fifth or sixth in dry conditions.

Once again nearly on the podium, Althea BMW rider Torres was fourth. The same could be said of the small-scale MV Agusta effort of Leon Camier and Reparto Corse, in fifth. Second to fifth was covered by only 2.5 seconds.

What of Rea, the points leader? Another DNF?

A false neutral had intervened, and when the gear eventually engaged, just as he was running off track, he was tipped off completely and his bike damaged. It was his second non-finish in a row, his points lead trimmed back to just about one race's worth – it was all unravelling rapidly.

Until the rain and initial mess of race two.

The very nature of the Lausitzring's surface ensured that when the rain arrived on Sunday, just before the second race, even the switch to wet tyres did not allow a start. There was too much standing water, which led to too much spray. The ruts and ripples and horrid bumps retained water in their troughs. After a meeting of the safety commission, an easing of the rain and complete wet set-ups for the whole field, the race started late, to be run over only 16 laps and – ironically – in rainy conditions.

Less than one lap in, Sykes fell under braking, but he got going again to finish 12th.

Davies was unable to find the right settings to compete this time, but Rea put it all on the never-drying line to win by an eventual 9.396 seconds.

Everyone was lifted by the return to the podium of former GP racer Alex de Angelis – still battling left-arm nerve damage after his big 2015 crash at Motegi. It gave a rookie-season podium to IodaRacing Aprilia, gave Alex his first top three in WorldSBK and put privateers on the podium – finally. What could be better?

Another novelty podium, that's what. Xavi Fores (Barni Racing Team) was third on his high-spec private Panigale to put another group of first-timers in the victory circle.

With Camier fourth for MV, and returning former champion Sylvain Guintoli (Pata Yamaha) fifth, it was a big mixed bag compared to any previous 2016 race. Except for Rea, who had danced on the outer limits of his wet tyres' event horizon.

MAGNY-COURS

ROUND 11 · FRANCE

Above: A double celebration for Davies and his official Ducati crew.

Right: The clever use of intermediate tyres brought Davies the victory in race one.

Top: Chaz overcame a stern challenge from the Kawasakis to double up at Magny-Cours.

Photos: Gold & Goose

Above left: Savadori eventually claimed fifth place in the wet/dry race one.

Left: Guintoli, Torres and Hayden scrap for seventh in race two.

Below left: Star stand-in Matthieu Lagrive used his tyre combination to great effect in race one.

Below: Michael van der Mark and Leon Camier battle for fourth place in race two, in front of the usual good crowd.

Below right: Sykes slides his Kawasaki ahead of Rea in race one.

Photos: Gold & Goose

AT the 11th round of the season, Chaz Davies doubled Ducati's profits with his latest pair of wins. This was his third double of the year, and his best.

Kawasaki's monopoly of the full-points market, which had gathered pace after Ducati's mid-season slump, had been subverted somewhat by two successful summer tests for Davies compared to KRT's 'not quite' single outing on road bikes and neo-road bikes at Lausitz.

The KRT guys knew that Davies would have won both races in Germany if it had remained dry each day, but this time around even a contrast in weather between races in France could not stop the red storm rising. Not even after Rea had won Superpole (only the seventh of his career) in damp conditions.

Davies secured race one by the clever use of intermediate tyres – a real racer's choice, for two reasons. He had never used them before, but trusted that they would work on what he expected to be a wet then drying track surface. He knew that he would lose time initially, but thought he could get it all back again as the track dried, because he would not have to make a pit stop.

He was right on both counts.

He even realised that he would win early in the race, despite dropping to over 20 seconds behind the lead at one stage.

Those on full wets led at first, before their almost inevitable tyre changes, and there were four different leaders – Sykes, Camier, Savadori and the only one who mattered, Davies. He was almost ten seconds ahead over the line and slowed to celebrate.

In a race during which 16 riders pitted to change tyres, van der Mark finished on slicks in second place for Honda, although Sykes almost took it from him with a late charge on slicks after a relatively late change of tyres. Rea, who had been holding station with his only realistic championship rival, Sykes, throughout – even pitting at exactly the same time – took on a rear intermediate at his change, but he still came home fourth, minimising his points damage.

Savadori played a V4 tune in fifth, but one of the sensations of the race was stand-in Pedercini Racing Kawasaki rider Matthieu Lagrive. The Bol d'Or veteran used his front wet/rear intermediate combo for a start-to-finish sixth.

Had the weather stayed a bit wetter for longer, Leon Camier would have won the race for MV, as he had passed both Kawasaki leaders fair and square on the wet track.

Surely race two would not be so complex. Not quite...

Davies's race-two win was not a foregone conclusion, as the two Kawasaki riders fought an increasingly profound needle match up front.

Sykes, who brakes late, flicks it on and then gets hard on the gas on the way out, is always difficult to pass. Rea, sitting just behind and frustrated that a closing Davies would surely get by, made a tough overtake at the hairpin, but only succeeded in running Sykes and himself a little wide.

Wide enough for Davies to negate his 0.7s deficit and take the lead.

With Sykes coming out of the corner ahead of Rea, after both had lost drive, Davies powered away. Rea had to wait for another chance to pass and eventually took it for second, but by then Davies was gone, winning by a margin of 2.091 seconds.

Fourth place went to Camier and the MV. Being competitive in the wet was one thing, being nearly competitive on his spare bike after a technical mishap during Sunday morning warm-up was quite remarkable. He beat van der Mark (fifth) and Savadori (sixth). Torres just pipped local hero Guintoli for seventh.

JEREZ
ROUND 12 · SPAIN

Above: Davies shows a clean pair of heels in race two.

Left: The paddock was awash with bodies in the autumn sun.

Below left: Fores and Giugliano took themselves out of race one.

Right: Hayden just pips team-mate van der Mark for fourth in race one.

Facing page:
Left, from top: Super-sub Anthony West scored points for Pedercini in both races; Team Toth's Peter Sebestyen took his only point of the year; Chaz Davies celebrates another double victory with his Ducati crew.

Top right: Despite missing out on wins, Sykes and Rea secured the manufacturers' championship for Kawasaki for a second year.

Photos: Gold & Goose

IT must have been a strange feeling for Jerez double race winner Chaz Davies. Not only did he lose his last chance of taking the championship title, but also he proved to be unbeatably fast again.

Two race days in the dry were a welcome change of pace, yet they were two days with evidently different track conditions, simply because of the strange surface at Jerez. No matter the relative grip, Davies had both races covered and both Kawasaki riders beaten – straight up – yet again.

But for Rea's quite extraordinary dance on the edge of reason in the rain at Lausitzring, Davies almost certainly would have taken six victories in a row. He equalled Rea's tally of nine wins through the season with his pair of victories at Jerez.

Tissot Superpole superstar Sykes – eight poles from 12 rounds – was the early leader in race one, but on lap four Davies went past and went away, winning by 3.290 seconds.

Sykes got the better of Rea and cut the championship lead by four points, taking second place from his team-mate. The latter just could not get his bike into a happy enough place and would make some major set-up changes for race two.

The 2015 champion was unhappily 7.151 seconds adrift of Davies, but paradoxically satisfied to have scored his first ever podium place at Jerez.

Behind the top three, the two Honda riders eventually became locked in a last-lap scrap for fourth place. Nicky Hayden proved the most effective on the final lap, keeping van der Mark just a short shadow behind.

Hayden knew the top Ducati out front was as much of an alien creation this weekend as the famous Jerez 'flying saucer' over the start/finish, but he really felt he could catch the little green men.

With some machine adjustments, and a different front tyre, he very nearly did that a day later.

Sylvain Guintoli was sixth in the opener, having returned to one of the places he first tested the YZF-R1. His season had been largely ruined by injury, but he was showing class and quality by doing as much as could be expected on a bike that was proving surprisingly tricky and underpowered.

Race two: same result as race one for Davies, but this time he flipped on the afterburners early and rocketed away out front for all 20 laps.

He was nearly six seconds ahead this time, with Rea as runner-up. All those big changes in set-up were the latter's solution to beating Sykes to the second flag, but Davies was just riding on his same basic early-season chassis settings, picking off wins like they were berries in a hedgerow.

The second race was almost 12 seconds slower than the first on Saturday, but Davies's margin of victory just grew.

Sykes, like Rea, was still trying to get his bike to suit him completely after it had arrived as a heavily revamped base model for 2016. He was at his limit to finish very close behind his team-mate, but was still over six seconds from the win.

Sykes's thoughts had been partly occupied by an impression that he had been slowed by his team-mate after Rea's pass at the halfway point.

Rea's tactic had appeared to be to allow Hayden to catch up and maybe pass Sykes for third. Had the American been able to do so, with Rea second, the championship would have been decided in Spain, not Qatar.

Hayden himself was just hoping to get past Sykes to beat a Kawasaki fair and square in the dry. The extent to which the whole Honda project had moved on in the final year of the current Fireblade genus was evident from the fact that he was so close to doing it, just over 0.7 seconds away.

Guintoli was fifth, van der Mark sixth as the eventual championship celebrations went to the final round after all.

Left: A podium at last for Guintoli and Yamaha.

Below left: Fores took a pair of seventh places.

Below centre left: Sykes congratulates Rea on clinching the title at the end of race one.

Far left: Lights out and floodlights on for the start of race two.

Centre, from left: Guintoli slips past Sykes to claim third place in race one; substitute Leon Haslam claimed an impressive fifth; Supersport champion Raffaele de Rosa brought a decent haul of points to Althea BMW.

Bottom left: Chaz Davies heads for victory in race two.

Bottom: Another double for Davies, but he still ended third overall.

Bottom right: Jonathan Rea – the first successive World Superbike champion in 17 years.

Photos: Gold & Goose

Afterthe 2015's Rea-fest, the fact that the Superbike World Championship went all the way to the final round was a true indicator of the season's change in top-end rider power.

As it stood in the run-up to race weekend, Rea had a 48-point cushion. That meant that only the two best possible results for Sykes and two impossibly low scores, or no-scores, from Rea would be enough for Sykes to win it.

In fact, Sykes was more preoccupied with not losing second in the championship to Davies, given the form he had been showing of late. Indeed, but for the late race-two intervention of his team-mate, Rea, Sykes would have lost his runner-up spot.

Saturday night, at the Kubrick-esque floodlit Losail circuit, and Rea was starting from pole, having taken his second top grid spot of the season. But in a clean first race of 17 laps, Davies led, and then led some more, going on to win confidently.

Behind came Rea, almost four seconds back, but now the new world champion as well as the old. That back-to-back effort from 2015 to 2016 made him the first since Carl Fogarty to garner consecutive championships. The 17-year gap demonstrated how hard that was to do.

Sykes had only been fourth in the race, but it did not matter to Rea, who had all the points he needed and more.

Sylvain Guintoli scurried across the desert sands at Losail fast enough to give the Pata Yamaha team, and the full WorldSBK-spec R1, their first modern-era podium finish.

Nicky Hayden had toiled to third in the race for seven laps, but could not keep Guintoli back. As the American's motor started to fail slowly – his last available engine from his allocation of seven – he would fall prey to Sykes on the final lap. He would have to start from the pit lane in race two, on his regulation-busting eighth engine.

Sykes would need the points in his battle to finish second and give Kawasaki a historic 1-2 in the championship.

After some dark Shakespearean-like tragedies involving Sykes and team-mates/team orders in the past, he was the one who would benefit in race two – once the mess it had become was reordered.

Sykes was well on in the first race start, behind Davies, but comfortably so, enough to be second overall by two points. Rea had run on after his gear-change load-cell sensor had failed, and he was working hard in the midfield with an electronics suite not designed to handle no-load inputs and endless clutch action.

Then came a red flag. The reason was an oil spill from Saeed al Sulaiti's Pedercini Kawasaki, which resulted in the bike in flames as Sulaiti hurtled across the gravel run-off. A restart was ordered, with full points awarded and only ten laps in which to get them.

For this, the real race two, Rea's crew had executed repairs and the champion started moving forward, picking off riders and then getting past Sykes. He posted a new lap record, but could not quite get to Davies.

In second place, Rea was preventing Sykes from being second in the championship, so on the final lap, he slowed, popping wheelies out of corners, and Sykes finally got a rub of the green from a team-mate, securing second and relegating race winner Davies to third overall.

As professional racers, Davies, Rea and Sykes knew the score and were on gracious terms with each other as the twitter-sphere lit up about the rights and wrongs of team tactics.

Behind the top three, Guintoli was fourth, and stand-in rider for Pedercini, Leon Haslam, a brilliant dry-weather fifth after a brutally truncated Friday practice session.

Some amazing Losail results all round as the season floodlights finally went out, with fireworks, scandal and talking points enough for three regular races.

2016 WORLD SUPERBIKE CHAMPIONSHIP RESULTS

Compiled by Peter McLaren

Round 1	PHILLIP ISLAND, Australia · 27–28 February, 2016 · 2.762-mile/4.445km circuit · WEATHER: Race 1 · Dry · Track 36°C · Air 22°C; Race 2 · Dry · Track 41°C · Air 22°C

Race 1: 22 laps, 60.764 miles/97.790km

Time of race: 33m 47.823s · **Average speed:** 107.874mph/173.607km/h

Pos.	Rider	Nat.	No.	Entrant	Machine	Tyres	Time & Gap	Laps
1	Jonathan Rea	GBR	1	Kawasaki Racing Team	Kawasaki ZX-10R	P		22
2	Chaz Davies	GBR	7	Aruba.it Racing – Ducati	Ducati 1199 Panigale R	P	0.063s	22
3	Michael van der Mark	NED	60	Honda World Superbike Team	Honda CBR1000RR SP	P	0.487s	22
4	Davide Giugliano	ITA	34	Aruba.it Racing – Ducati	Ducati 1199 Panigale R	P	0.647s	22
5	Tom Sykes	GBR	66	Kawasaki Racing Team	Kawasaki ZX-10R	P	3.429s	22
6	Sylvain Guintoli	FRA	50	Pata Yamaha Official WorldSBK Team	Yamaha YZF R1	P	3.510s	22
7	Leon Camier	GBR	2	MV Agusta Reparto Corse	MV Agusta 1000 F4	P	10.721s	22
8	Jordi Torres	ESP	81	Althea BMW Racing Team	BMW S1000 RR	P	11.539s	22
9	Nicky Hayden	USA	69	Honda World Superbike Team	Honda CBR1000RR SP	P	15.534s	22
10	Joshua Brookes	AUS	25	Milwaukee BMW	BMW S1000 RR	P	23.239s	22
11	Roman Ramos	ESP	40	Team GoEleven	Kawasaki ZX-10R	P	23.411s	22
12	Lorenzo Savadori	ITA	32	IodaRacing Team	Aprilia RSV4 RF	P	24.012s	22
13	Karel Abraham	CZE	17	Milwaukee BMW	BMW S1000 RR	P	37.281s	22
14	Mike Jones	AUS	46	Desmo Sport Ducati	Ducati 1199 Panigale R	P	44.720s	22
15	Sylvain Barrier	FRA	20	Pedercini Racing	Kawasaki ZX-10R	P	46.357s	22
16	Dominic Schmitter	SUI	9	Grillini Racing Team	Kawasaki ZX-10R	P	1m 08.238s	22
17	Saeed al Sulaiti	QAT	11	Pedercini Racing	Kawasaki ZX-10R	P	1m 08.299s	22
18	Peter Sebestyen	HUN	56	Team Toth	Yamaha YZF R1	P	1m 30.771s	22
19	Imre Toth	HUN	10	Team Toth	Yamaha YZF R1	P	1 Lap	21
	Markus Reiterberger	GER	21	Althea BMW Racing Team	BMW S1000 RR	P	DNF	21
	Alex Lowes	GBR	22	Pata Yamaha Official WorldSBK Team	Yamaha YZF R1	P	DNF	16
	Xavi Fores	ESP	12	Barni Racing Team	Ducati 1199 Panigale R	P	DNF	11
	Alex de Angelis	RSM	15	IodaRacing Team	Aprilia RSV4 RF	P	DNF	3

Fastest race lap: Davide Giugliano on lap 22, 1m 31.445s, 108.734mph/174.990km/h.

Race 2: 22 laps, 60.764 miles/97.790km

Time of race: 33m 48.377s · **Average speed:** 107.845mph/173.559km/h

Pos.	Rider	Time & Gap	Laps
1	Jonathan Rea		22
2	Michael van der Mark	0.831s	22
3	Davide Giugliano	1.472s	22
4	Nicky Hayden	1.511s	22
5	Sylvain Guintoli	2.439s	22
6	Tom Sykes	3.320s	22
7	Jordi Torres	13.744s	22
8	Markus Reiterberger	15.084s	22
9	Joshua Brookes	15.106s	22
10	Chaz Davies	16.276s	22
11	Karel Abraham	30.147s	22
12	Roman Ramos	30.251s	22
13	Alex de Angelis	30.437s	22
14	Alex Lowes	39.946s	22
15	Sylvain Barrier	53.515s	22
16	Dominic Schmitter	58.450s	22
17	Saeed al Sulaiti	1m 01.836s	22
18	Peter Sebestyen	1m 30.672s	22
19	Imre Toth	1 Lap	21
	Mike Jones	DNF	11
	Leon Camier	DNF	7
	Lorenzo Savadori	DNF	2

Fastest race lap: Chaz Davies on lap 4, 1m 31.321s, 108.882mph/175.228km/h.

Lap record: Chaz Davies, GBR (Ducati), 1m 30.949s, 109.327mph/ 175.945km/h (2014).

	Superpole	
1	Sykes	1m 30.020s
2	Giugliano	1m 30.098s
3	Rea	1m 30.170s
4	Guintoli	1m 30.281s
5	Lowes	1m 30.354s
6	Van der Mark	1m 30.468s
7	Hayden	1m 30.479s
8	Savadori	1m 30.609s
9	Davies	1m 30.717s
10	Camier	1m 30.795s
11	Reiterberger	1m 31.031s
12	Torres	1m 31.207s
13	Fores	1m 31.871s
14	Brookes	1m 31.927s
15	Barrier	1m 32.077s
16	Abraham	1m 32.117s
17	Ramos	1m 32.194s
18	De Angelis	1m 33.507s
19	Schmitter	1m 33.664s
20	Al Sulaiti	1m 33.690s
21	Jones	1m 33.722s
22	Sebestyen	1m 34.346s
23	Toth	1m 36.272s
24	Razgatlioglu	No Time

Points

1, Rea 50; 2, Van der Mark 36; 3, Giugliano 29; 4, Davies 26; 5, Guintoli 21; 6, Sykes 21; 7, Hayden 20; 8, Torres 17; 9, Brookes 13; 10, Camier 9; 11, Ramos 9; 12, Reiterberger 8; 13, Abraham 8; 14, Savadori 4; 15, De Angelis 3; 16, Lowes 2; 17, Jones 2; 18, Barrier 2.

WORLD SUPERBIKE CHAMPIONSHIP · 2016

Race 1: 20 laps, 56.594 miles/91.080km

Time of race: 31m 32.311s · **Average speed:** 107.667mph/173.274km/h

Pos.	Rider	Nat.	No.	Entrant	Machine	Tyres	Time & Gap	Laps
1	**Jonathan Rea**	GBR	1	Kawasaki Racing Team	Kawasaki ZX-10R	P		20
2	**Tom Sykes**	GBR	66	Kawasaki Racing Team	Kawasaki ZX-10R	P	0.222s	20
3	**Michael van der Mark**	NED	60	Honda World Superbike Team	Honda CBR1000RR SP	P	9.623s	20
4	**Chaz Davies**	GBR	7	Aruba.it Racing – Ducati	Ducati 1199 Panigale R	P	17.167s	20
5	**Markus Reiterberger**	GER	21	Althea BMW Racing Team	BMW S1000 RR	P	18.894s	20
6	**Alex Lowes**	GBR	22	Pata Yamaha Official WorldSBK Team	Yamaha YZF R1	P	20.754s	20
7	**Sylvain Guintoli**	FRA	50	Pata Yamaha Official WorldSBK Team	Yamaha YZF R1	P	24.221s	20
8	**Jordi Torres**	ESP	81	Althea BMW Racing Team	BMW S1000 RR	P	31.064s	20
9	**Alex de Angelis**	RSM	15	IodaRacing Team	Aprilia RSV4 RF	P	34.348s	20
10	**Lorenzo Savadori**	ITA	32	IodaRacing Team	Aprilia RSV4 RF	P	34.479s	20
11	**Leon Camier**	GBR	2	MV Agusta Reparto Corse	MV Agusta 1000 F4	P	37.013s	20
12	**Roman Ramos**	ESP	40	Team GoEleven	Kawasaki ZX-10R	P	41.113s	20
13	**Matteo Baiocco**	ITA	151	VFT Racing	Ducati 1199 Panigale R	P	44.369s	20
14	**Xavi Fores**	ESP	12	Barni Racing Team	Ducati 1199 Panigale R	P	45.053s	20
15	**Joshua Brookes**	AUS	25	Milwaukee BMW	BMW S1000 RR	P	51.939s	20
16	Sylvain Barrier	FRA	20	Pedercini Racing	Kawasaki ZX-10R	P	54.314s	20
17	Saeed al Sulaiti	QAT	11	Pedercini Racing	Kawasaki ZX-10R	P	1m 06.541s	20
18	Davide Giugliano	ITA	34	Aruba.it Racing – Ducati	Ducati 1199 Panigale R	P	1m 09.530s	20
19	Dominic Schmitter	SUI	9	Grillini Racing Team	Kawasaki ZX-10R	P	1m 40.904s	20
20	Peter Sebestyen	HUN	56	Team Toth	Yamaha YZF R1	P	1 Lap	19
21	Sahustcha Kaewjaturaporn	THA	19	Grillini Racing Team	Kawasaki ZX-10R	P	1 Lap	19
22	Imre Toth	HUN	10	Team Toth	Yamaha YZF R1	P	1 Lap	19
23	Anucha Nakcharoensri	THA	14	Yamaha Thailand Racing Team	Yamaha YZF R1	P	3 Laps	17
	Karel Abraham	CZE	17	Milwaukee BMW	BMW S1000 RR	P	DNF	19
	Nicky Hayden	USA	69	Honda World Superbike Team	Honda CBR1000RR SP	P	DNF	9

Fastest race lap: Jonathan Rea on lap 14, 1m 33.936s, 108.446mph/174.527km/h.

Race 2: 20 laps, 56.594 miles/91.080km

Time of race: 31m 33.493s · **Average speed:** 107.600mph/173.166km/h

Pos.	Rider	Time & Gap	Laps
1	**Tom Sykes**		20
2	**Jonathan Rea**	0.190s	20
3	**Chaz Davies**	0.314s	20
4	**Michael van der Mark**	5.199s	20
5	**Nicky Hayden**	10.643s	20
6	**Sylvain Guintoli**	13.068s	20
7	**Markus Reiterberger**	14.481s	20
8	**Jordi Torres**	14.504s	20
9	**Lorenzo Savadori**	21.694s	20
10	**Davide Giugliano**	23.794s	20
11	**Leon Camier**	27.205s	20
12	**Roman Ramos**	32.309s	20
13	**Matteo Baiocco**	36.672s	20
14	**Alex de Angelis**	38.761s	20
15	**Karel Abraham**	39.789s	20
16	Joshua Brookes	42.840s	20
17	Sylvain Barrier	46.158s	20
18	Anucha Nakcharoensri	1m 04.628s	20
19	Dominic Schmitter	1m 21.675s	20
20	Peter Sebestyen	1m 21.687s	20
21	Imre Toth	1 Lap	19
22	Sahustcha Kaewjaturaporn	1 Lap	19
	Alex Lowes	DNF	9
	Xavi Fores	DNF	9
	Saeed al Sulaiti	DNF	7

Superpole		
1	Van der Mark	1m 33.452s
2	Sykes	1m 33.671s
3	Rea	1m 33.671s
4	Davies	1m 33.844s
5	Guintoli	1m 33.866s
6	Giugliano	1m 33.983s
7	Lowes	1m 34.371s
8	Hayden	1m 34.416s
9	Reiterberger	1m 34.796s
10	Torres	1m 34.859s
11	Abraham	1m 34.958s
12	Baiocco	1m 35.513s
13	Brookes	1m 35.207s
14	Camier	1m 35.288s
15	Ramos	1m 35.605s
16	Fores	1m 35.686s
17	Barrier	1m 35.699s
18	Savadori	1m 35.771s
19	De Angelis	1m 35.794s
20	Al Sulaiti	1m 37.179s
21	Nakcharoensri	1m 37.416s
22	Sebestyen	1m 37.757s
23	Schmitter	1m 38.150s
24	Toth	1m 39.091s
25	Kaewjaturaporn	1m 41.373s

Fastest race lap: Jonathan Rea on lap 5, 1m 33.997s, 108.376mph/174.414km/h.

Lap record: Jonathan Rea, GBR (Kawasaki), 1m 33.817s, 108.584mph/ 174.749km/h (2015).

Points

1, Rea 95; 2, Sykes 66; 3, Van der Mark 65; 4, Davies 55; 5, Guintoli 40; 6, Giugliano 35; 7, Torres 33; 8, Hayden 31; 9, Reiterberger 28; 10, Camier 19; 11, Savadori 17; 12, Ramos 17; 13, Brookes 14; 14, Lowes 12; 15, De Angelis 12; 16, Abraham 9; 17, Baiocco 6; 18, Fores 2; 19, Jones 2; 20, Barrier 2.

Race 1: 18 laps, 56.785 miles/91.386km

Time of race: 33m 31.464s · **Average speed:** 101.630mph/163.557km/h

Pos.	Rider	Nat.	No.	Entrant	Machine	Tyres	Time & Gap	Laps
1	**Chaz Davies**	GBR	7	Aruba.it Racing – Ducati	Ducati 1199 Panigale R	P		18
2	**Jonathan Rea**	GBR	1	Kawasaki Racing Team	Kawasaki ZX-10R	P	4.168s	18
3	**Tom Sykes**	GBR	66	Kawasaki Racing Team	Kawasaki ZX-10R	P	4.948s	18
4	**Xavi Fores**	ESP	12	Barni Racing Team	Ducati 1199 Panigale R	P	12.723s	18
5	**Davide Giugliano**	ITA	34	Aruba.it Racing – Ducati	Ducati 1199 Panigale R	P	13.151s	18
6	**Nicky Hayden**	USA	69	Honda World Superbike Team	Honda CBR1000RR SP	P	21.117s	18
7	**Jordi Torres**	ESP	81	Althea BMW Racing Team	BMW S1000 RR	P	22.112s	18
8	**Alex Lowes**	GBR	22	Pata Yamaha Official WorldSBK Team	Yamaha YZF R1	P	25.575s	18
9	**Sylvain Guintoli**	FRA	50	Pata Yamaha Official WorldSBK Team	Yamaha YZF R1	P	28.941s	18
10	**Lorenzo Savadori**	ITA	32	IodaRacing Team	Aprilia RSV4 RF	P	34.956s	18
11	**Alex de Angelis**	RSM	15	IodaRacing Team	Aprilia RSV4 RF	P	35.075s	18
12	**Roman Ramos**	ESP	40	Team GoEleven	Kawasaki ZX-10R	P	37.310s	18
13	**Joshua Brookes**	AUS	25	Milwaukee BMW	BMW S1000 RR	P	37.442s	18
14	**Markus Reiterberger**	GER	21	Althea BMW Racing Team	BMW S1000 RR	P	37.731s	18
15	**Karel Abraham**	CZE	17	Milwaukee BMW	BMW S1000 RR	P	52.270s	18
16	Sylvain Barrier	FRA	20	Pedercini Racing	Kawasaki ZX-10R	P	56.295s	18
17	Matthieu Lussiana	FRA	94	Team ASPI	BMW S1000 RR	P	1m 07.602s	18
18	Dominic Schmitter	SUI	9	Grillini Racing Team	Kawasaki ZX-10R	P	1m 35.691s	18
19	Peter Sebestyen	HUN	56	Team Toth	Yamaha YZF R1	P	1m 35.746s	18
20	Imre Toth	HUN	10	Team Toth	Yamaha YZF R1	P	1 Lap	17
	Saeed al Sulaiti	QAT	11	Pedercini Racing	Kawasaki ZX-10R	P	DNF	16
	Matteo Baiocco	ITA	151	VFT Racing	Ducati 1199 Panigale R	P	DNF	13
	Josh Hook	AUS	16	Grillini Racing Team	Kawasaki ZX-10R	P	DNF	13
	Leon Camier	GBR	2	MV Agusta Reparto Corse	MV Agusta 1000 F4	P	DNF	9
	Michael van der Mark	NED	60	Honda World Superbike Team	Honda CBR1000RR SP	P	DNF	3

Fastest race lap: Chaz Davies on lap 3, 1m 50.421s, 102.851mph/165.523km/h (record).

Race 2: 18 laps, 56.785 miles/91.386km

Time of race: 33m 36.606s · **Average speed:** 101.370mph/163.140km/h

Pos.	Rider	Time & Gap	Laps
1	**Chaz Davies**		18
2	**Tom Sykes**	6.471s	18
3	**Jonathan Rea**	9.161s	18
4	**Xavi Fores**	11.436s	18
5	**Jordi Torres**	15.969s	18
6	**Davide Giugliano**	18.278s	18
7	**Michael van der Mark**	20.931s	18
8	**Alex de Angelis**	24.790s	18
9	**Alex Lowes**	25.246s	18
10	**Sylvain Guintoli**	25.548s	18
11	**Lorenzo Savadori**	27.675s	18
12	**Roman Ramos**	29.364s	18
13	**Joshua Brookes**	31.749s	18
14	**Karel Abraham**	34.314s	18
15	**Markus Reiterberger**	34.333s	18
16	Leon Camier	34.777s	18
17	Matteo Baiocco	41.449s	18
18	Matthieu Lussiana	1m 16.542s	18
19	Dominic Schmitter	1m 22.960s	18
20	Peter Sebestyen	1m 25.830s	18
21	Saeed al Sulaiti	1m 28.363s	18
22	Imre Toth	1 Lap	17
	Nicky Hayden	DNF	15
	Josh Hook	DNF	12
	Sylvain Barrier	DNF	1

Superpole		
1	Sykes	1m 49.374s
2	Guintoli	1m 49.583s
3	Lowes	1m 49.708s
4	Davies	1m 49.909s
5	Rea	1m 50.003s
6	Giugliano	1m 50.316s
7	Camier	1m 50.360s
8	Torres	1m 50.390s
9	Fores	1m 50.538s
10	Hayden	1m 50.551s
11	Van der Mark	1m 50.744s
12	Savadori	1m 50.958s
13	Reiterberger	1m 50.938s
14	Ramos	1m 51.560s
15	Abraham	1m 52.052s
16	De Angelis	1m 52.173s
17	Baiocco	1m 52.246s
18	Brookes	1m 52.443s
19	Barrier	1m 53.169s
20	Lussiana	1m 54.042s
21	Schmitter	1m 54.569s
22	Al Sulaiti	1m 54.719s
23	Sebestyen	1m 55.444s
24	Hook	1m 56.023s
25	Toth	1m 57.217s

Fastest race lap: Chaz Davies on lap 4, 1m 51.053s, 102.266mph/164.581km/h.

Previous lap record: Tom Sykes, GBR (Kawasaki), 1m 50.890s, 102.416mph/ 164.823km/h (2015).

Points

1, Rea 131; 2, Davies 105; 3, Sykes 102; 4, Van der Mark 74; 5, Giugliano 56; 6, Guintoli 53; 7, Torres 53; 8, Hayden 41; 9, Reiterberger 31; 10, Fores 28; 11, Savadori 28; 12, Lowes 27; 13, De Angelis 25; 14, Ramos 25; 15, Brookes 20; 16, Camier 19; 17, Abraham 12; 18, Baiocco 6; 19, Jones 2; 20, Barrier 2.

WORLD SUPERBIKE CHAMPIONSHIP · 2016

Race 1: 21 laps, 59.268 miles/95.382km

Time of race: 34m 12.542s · **Average speed:** 103.951mph/167.293km/h

Pos.	Rider	Nat.	No.	Entrant	Machine	Tyres	Time & Gap	Laps
1	Jonathan Rea	GBR	1	Kawasaki Racing Team	Kawasaki ZX-10R	P		21
2	Chaz Davies	GBR	7	Aruba.it Racing – Ducati	Ducati Panigale R	P	1.662s	21
3	Nicky Hayden	USA	69	Honda World Superbike Team	Honda CBR1000RR SP	P	5.365s	21
4	Leon Camier	GBR	2	MV Agusta Reparto Corse	MV Agusta 1000 F4	P	15.542s	21
5	Jordi Torres	ESP	81	Althea BMW Racing Tea	BMW S1000 RR	P	16.922s	21
6	Lorenzo Savadori	ITA	32	IodaRacing Team	Aprilia RSV4 RF	P	22.460s	21
7	Markus Reiterberger	GER	21	Althea BMW Racing Team	BMW S1000 RR	P	23.909s	21
8	Alex Lowes	GBR	22	Pata Yamaha Official WorldSBK Team	Yamaha YZF R1	P	29.893s	21
9	Roman Ramos	ESP	40	Team GoEleven	Kawasaki ZX-10R	P	41.910s	21
10	Lucas Mahias	FRA	44	Pedercini Racing	Kawasaki ZX-10R	P	48.323s	21
11	Joshua Brookes	AUS	25	Milwaukee BMW	BMW S1000 RR	P	53.638s	21
12	Alex de Angelis	RSM	15	IodaRacing Team	Aprilia RSV4 RF	P	56.322s	21
13	Xavi Fores	ESP	12	Barni Racing Team	Ducati Panigale R	P	1m 03.741s	21
14	Matteo Baiocco	ITA	151	VFT Racing	Ducati Panigale R	P	1m 14.792s	21
15	Matthieu Lussiana	FRA	94	Team ASPI	BMW S1000 RR	P	1m 38.485s	21
16	Josh Hook	AUS	16	Grillini Racing Team	Kawasaki ZX-10R	P	1 Lap	20
17	Pawel Szkopek	POL	119	Team Toth	Yamaha YZF R1	P	1 Lap	20
	Michael van der Mark	NED	60	Honda World Superbike Team	Honda CBR1000RR SP	P	DNF	19
	Karel Abraham	CZE	17	Milwaukee BMW	BMW S1000 RR	P	DNF	12
	Davide Giugliano	ITA	34	Aruba.it Racing – Ducati	Ducati Panigale R	P	DNF	11
	Tom Sykes	GBR	66	Kawasaki Racing Team	Kawasaki ZX-10R	P	DNF	8
	Sylvain Guintoli	FRA	50	Pata Yamaha Official WorldSBK Team	Yamaha YZF R1	P	DNF	4

Race 2: 21 laps, 59.268 miles/95.382km

Time of race: 38m 2.779s · **Average speed:** 93.467mph/150.420km/h

Pos.	Rider	Time & Gap	Laps
1	Jonathan Rea		21
2	Tom Sykes	2.442s	21
3	Michael van der Mark	15.189s	21
4	Lorenzo Savadori	25.507s	21
5	Chaz Davies	30.853s	21
6	Nicky Hayden	36.458s	21
7	Alex Lowes	39.263s	21
8	Davide Giugliano	46.789s	21
9	Leon Camier	1m 05.023s	21
10	Xavi Fores	1m 05.468s	21
11	Sylvain Guintoli	1m 24.948s	21
12	Roman Ramos	1m 35.035s	21
13	Lucas Mahias	1 Lap	20
14	Karel Abraham	1 Lap	20
15	Jordi Torres	1 Lap	20
16	Markus Reiterberger	1 Lap	20
17	Matthieu Lussiana	1 Lap	20
18	Pawel Szkopek	1 Lap	20
19	Peter Sebestyen	2 Laps	19
20	Dominic Schmitter	2 Laps	19
	Joshua Brookes	DNF	12
	Matteo Baiocco	DNF	10
	Josh Hook	DNS	0

Superpole		
1	Sykes	1m 35.440s
2	Guintoli	1m 36.073s
3	Giugliano	1m 36.391s
4	Rea	1m 36.401s
5	Van der Mark	1m 36.643s
6	Davies	1m 36.940s
7	Reiterberger	1m 37.300s
8	Fores	1m 37.351s
9	Torres	1m 37.413s
10	Hayden	1m 37.449s
11	Savadori	1m 37.587s
12	Lowes	1m 38.214s
13	Camier	1m 38.375s
14	Brookes	1m 38.754s
15	Baiocco	1m 39.305s
16	De Angelis	1m 39.327s
17	Mahias	1m 39.459s
18	Ramos	1m 41.339s
19	Lussiana	1m 41.743s
20	Szkopek	1m 42.443s
21	Hook	1m 43.957s
22	Abraham	No Time
	Sebestyen	DNQ
	Schmitter	DNQ
	Al Sulaiti	DNQ

Fastest race lap: Chaz Davies on lap 2, 1m 36.486s, 105.302mph/169.467km/h.

Fastest race lap: Jonathan Rea on lap 20, 1m 37.706s, 103.987mph/167.351km/h.
Lap record: Jonathan Rea, GBR (Kawasaki), 1m 35.889s, 105.957mph/170.522km/h (2015).

Points

1, Rea 181; 2, Davies 136; 3, Sykes 122; 4, Van der Mark 90; 5, Hayden 67; 6, Torres 65; 7, Giugliano 64; 8, Guintoli 58; 9, Savadori 51; 10, Lowes 44; 11, Reiterberger 40; 12, Camier 39; 13, Fores 37; 14, Ramos 36; 15, De Angelis 29; 16, Brookes 25; 17, Abraham 14; 18, Mahias 9; 19, Baiocco 8; 20, Jones 2; 21, Barrier 2; 22, Lussiana 1.

Race 1: 18 laps, 55.208mi/88.848km

Time of race: 32m 15.999s · **Average speed:** 102.659mph/165.213km/h

Pos.	Rider	Nat.	No.	Entrant	Machine	Tyres	Time & Gap	Laps
1	Chaz Davies	GBR	7	Aruba.it Racing – Ducati	Ducati Panigale R	P		18
2	Jonathan Rea	GBR	1	Kawasaki Racing Team	Kawasaki ZX-10R	P	3.406s	18
3	Tom Sykes	GBR	66	Kawasaki Racing Team	Kawasaki ZX-10R	P	3.729s	18
4	Jordi Torres	ESP	81	Althea BMW Racing Team	BMW S1000 RR	P	13.631s	18
5	Davide Giugliano	ITA	34	Aruba.it Racing – Ducati	Ducati Panigale R	P	19.948s	18
6	Leon Camier	GBR	2	MV Agusta Reparto Corse	MV Agusta 1000 F4	P	25.586s	18
7	Michael van der Mark	NED	60	Honda World Superbike Team	Honda CBR1000RR SP	P	27.262s	18
8	Lorenzo Savadori	ITA	32	IodaRacing Team	Aprilia RSV4 RF	P	28.300s	18
9	Nicky Hayden	USA	69	Honda World Superbike Team	Honda CBR1000RR SP	P	29.263s	18
10	Xavi Fores	ESP	12	Barni Racing Team	Ducati Panigale R	P	29.426s	18
11	Alex Lowes	GBR	22	Pata Yamaha Official WorldSBK Team	Yamaha YZF R1	P	29.622s	18
12	Matteo Baiocco	ITA	151	VFT Racing	Ducati Panigale R	P	30.005s	18
13	Markus Reiterberger	GER	21	Althea BMW Racing Team	BMW S1000 RR	P	34.667s	18
14	Joshua Brookes	AUS	25	Milwaukee BMW	BMW S1000 RR	P	57.050s	18
15	Alex de Angelis	RSM	15	IodaRacing Team	Aprilia RSV4 RF	P	1m 03.267s	18
16	Karel Abraham	CZE	17	Milwaukee BMW	BMW S1000 RR	P	1m 14.668s	18
17	Josh Hook	AUS	16	Grillini Racing Team	Kawasaki ZX-10R	P	1m 50.796s	18
18	Pawel Szkopek	POL	119	Team Toth	Yamaha YZF R1	P	2 Laps	16
	Saeed al Sulaiti	QAT	11	Pedercini Racing	Kawasaki ZX-10R	P	DNF	7
	Dominic Schmitter	SUI	9	Grillini Racing Team	Kawasaki ZX-10R	P	DNF	0
	Peter Sebestyen	HUN	56	Team Toth	Yamaha YZF R1	P	DNF	0

Race 2: 19 laps, 58.275 miles/93.784km

Time of race: 34m 7.278s · **Average speed:** 102.472mph/164.913km/h

Pos.	Rider	Time & Gap	Laps
1	Chaz Davies		19
2	Jonathan Rea	4.262s	19
3	Tom Sykes	4.604s	19
4	Davide Giugliano	13.093s	19
5	Leon Camier	16.250s	19
6	Alex Lowes	20.078s	19
7	Jordi Torres	23.622s	19
8	Nicky Hayden	26.803s	19
9	Michael van der Mark	28.577s	19
10	Xavi Fores	32.630s	19
11	Lorenzo Savadori	34.669s	19
12	Markus Reiterberger	38.244s	19
13	Joshua Brookes	41.100s	19
14	Alex de Angelis	12.823s	19
15	Dominic Schmitter	55.258s	19
16	Saeed al Sulaiti	1 Lap	18
17	Pawel Szkopek	1 Lap	18
	Matteo Baiocco	DNF	11
	Karel Abraham	DNF	1
	Gianluca Vizziello	DNF	1
	Josh Hook	DNF	1

Superpole		
1	Davies	1m 45.598s
2	Giugliano	1m 46.055s
3	Rea	1m 46.328s
4	Sykes	1m 46.331s
5	Savadori	1m 46.531s
6	Torres	1m 46.867s
7	Camier	1m 46.911s
8	Reiterberger	1m 46.952s
9	Hayden	1m 47.429s
10	Baiocco	1m 47.471s
11	Van der Mark	1m 47.563s
12	Guintoli	1m 48.677s
13	Fores	1m 47.811s
14	Lowes	1m 48.001s
15	Brookes	1m 48.046s
16	Abraham	1m 49.167s
17	De Angelis	1m 49.321s
18	Schmitter	1m 49.857s
19	Sebestyen	1m 49.916s
20	Szkopek	1m 51.020s
21	Hook	1m 51.827s
22	Al Sulaiti	1m 52.108s
23	Mahias	No Time

Fastest race lap: Chaz Davies on lap 3, 1m 46.700s, 103.482mph/166.538km/h (record).

Fastest race lap: Chaz Davies on lap 6, 1m 47.240s, 102.961mph/165.699km/h.
Previous lap record: Tom Sykes, GBR (Kawasaki), 1m 46.707s, 103.475mph/166.527km/h (2015).

Points

1, Rea 221; 2, Davies 186; 3, Sykes 154; 4, Van der Mark 106; 5, Giugliano 88; 6, Torres 87; 7, Hayden 82; 8, Savadori 64; 9, Camier 60; 10, Lowes 59; 11, Guintoli 58; 12, Fores 49; 13, Reiterberger 47; 14, Ramos 36; 15, De Angelis 32; 16, Brookes 30; 17, Abraham 14; 18, Baiocco 12; 19, Mahias 9; 20, Jones 2; 21, Barrier 2; 22, Schmitter 1; 23, Lussiana 1.

WORLD SUPERBIKE CHAMPIONSHIP · 2016

Round 6   SEPANG, Malaysia · 14-15 May, 2016 · 3.447-mile/5.543km circuit · WEATHER: Race 1 · Dry · Track 46°C · Air 32°C; Race 2 · Wet · Track 30°C · Air 26°C

Race 1: 16 laps, 55.108 miles/88.688km

Time of race: 33m 30.487s · **Average speed:** 98.677mph/158.806km/h

Pos.	Rider	Nat.	No.	Entrant	Machine	Tyres	Time & Gap	Laps
1	**Tom Sykes**	GBR	66	Kawasaki Racing Team	Kawasaki ZX-10R	P		16
2	**Jonathan Rea**	GBR	1	Kawasaki Racing Team	Kawasaki ZX-10R	P	5.600s	16
3	**Chaz Davies**	GBR	7	Aruba.it Racing – Ducati	Ducati Panigale R	P	8.039s	16
4	**Jordi Torres**	ESP	81	Althea BMW Racing Team	BMW S1000 RR	P	17.666s	16
5	**Alex Lowes**	GBR	22	Pata Yamaha Official WorldSBK Team	Yamaha YZF R1	P	18.613s	16
6	**Davide Giugliano**	ITA	34	Aruba.it Racing – Ducati	Ducati Panigale R	P	19.871s	16
7	**Michael van der Mark**	NED	60	Honda World Superbike Team	Honda CBR1000RR SP	P	24.120s	16
8	**Nicky Hayden**	USA	69	Honda World Superbike Team	Honda CBR1000RR SP	P	25.461s	16
9	**Anthony West**	AUS	13	Pedercini Racing	Kawasaki ZX-10R	P	32.989s	16
10	**Leon Camier**	GBR	2	MV Agusta Reparto Corse	MV Agusta 1000 F4	P	35.464s	16
11	**Joshua Brookes**	AUS	25	Milwaukee BMW	BMW S1000 RR	P	39.437s	16
12	**Karel Abraham**	CZE	17	Milwaukee BMW	BMW S1000 RR	P	39.860s	16
13	**Luca Scassa**	ITA	99	VFT Racing	Ducati Panigale R	P	46.721s	16
14	**Xavi Fores**	ESP	12	Barni Racing Team	Ducati Panigale R	P	52.634s	16
15	**Josh Hook**	AUS	16	Grillini Racing Team	Kawasaki ZX-10R	P	1m 10.599s	16
16	Dominic Schmitter	SUI	9	Grillini Racing Team	Kawasaki ZX-10R	P	1m 19.352s	16
17	Saeed al Sulaiti	QAT	11	Pedercini Racing	Kawasaki ZX-10R	P	1m 21.034s	16
18	Gianluca Vizziello	ITA	4	Team GoEleven	Kawasaki ZX-10R	P	1m 51.315s	16
19	Imre Toth	HUN	10	Team Toth	Yamaha YZF R1	P	1 Lap	15
	Markus Reiterberger	GER	21	Althea BMW Racing Team	BMW S1000 RR	P	DNF	12
	Lorenzo Savadori	ITA	32	IodaRacing Team	Aprilia RSV4 RF	P	DNF	9
	Alex de Angelis	RSM	15	IodaRacing Team	Aprilia RSV4 RF	P	DNF	7
	Pawel Szkopek	POL	119	Team Toth	Yamaha YZF R1	P	DNF	6

Fastest race lap: Tom Sykes on lap 2, 2m 3.637s, 100.288mph/161.398km/h (record).

Race 2: 16 laps, 55.108 miles/88.688km

Time of race: 37m 4.047s · **Average speed:** 89.202mph/143.557km/h

Pos.	Rider	Time & Gap	Laps
1	**Nicky Hayden**		16
2	**Davide Giugliano**	1.254s	16
3	**Jonathan Rea**	3.684s	16
4	**Chaz Davies**	5.720s	16
5	**Anthony West**	15.989s	16
6	**Michael van der Mark**	19.979s	16
7	**Alex de Angelis**	20.028s	16
8	**Tom Sykes**	23.011s	16
9	**Leon Camier**	24.045s	16
10	**Markus Reiterberger**	25.139s	16
11	**Xavi Fores**	25.208s	16
12	**Joshua Brookes**	25.835s	16
13	**Jordi Torres**	26.757s	16
14	**Lorenzo Savadori**	30.729s	16
15	**Josh Hook**	1m 05.347s	16
16	Gianluca Vizziello	1m 17.761s	16
17	Luca Scassa	1m 18.121s	16
18	Pawel Szkopek	1m 31.412s	16
19	Dominic Schmitter	2m 07.000s	16
20	Saeed al Sulaiti	2m 08.836s	16
21	Imre Toth	1 Lap	15
	Alex Lowes	DNF	12
	Karel Abraham	DNF	0

Superpole		
1	Sykes	2m 02.246s
2	Lowes	2m 03.002s
3	Rea	2m 03.021s
4	Hayden	2m 03.435s
5	Davies	2m 03.485s
6	Reiterberger	2m 03.549s
7	Savadori	2m 03.612s
8	Torres	2m 03.855s
9	Giugliano	2m 04.052s
10	Van der Mark	2m 04.183s
11	West	2m 04.440s
12	Camier	2m 05.399s
13	De Angelis	2m 06.691s
14	Brookes	2m 06.699s
15	Fores	2m 06.787s
16	Abraham	2m 07.192s
17	Scassa	2m 07.628s
18	Hook	2m 11.197s
19	Al Sulaiti	2m 11.320s
20	Toth	2m 11.720s
21	Schmitter	2m 11.881s
22	Szkopek	2m 12.277s
23	Vizziello	2m 16.701s

Fastest race lap: Davide Giugliano on lap 13, 2m 16.716s, 90.694mph/145.958km/h.

Previous lap record: Tom Sykes, GBR (Kawasaki), 2m 3.654s, 100.274mph/ 161.376km/h (2015).

Points

1, Rea 257; 2, Davies 215; 3, Sykes 187; 4, Van der Mark 125; 5, Giugliano 118; 6, Hayden 115; 7, Torres 103; 8, Camier 73; 9, Lowes 70; 10, Savadori 66; 11, Guintoli 58; 12, Fores 56; 13, Reiterberger 53; 14, De Angelis 41; 15, Brookes 39; 16, Ramos 36; 17, West 18; 18, Abraham 18; 19, Baiocco 12; 20, Mahias 9; 21, Scassa 3; 22, Jones 2; 23, Hook 2; 24, Barrier 2; 25, Schmitter 1; 26, Lussiana 1.

Round 7   DONNINGTON PARK, Great Britain · 28-29 May, 2016 · 2.500-mile/4.023km circuit · WEATHER: Race 1 · Dry · Track 33°C · Air 17°C; Race 2 · Dry · Track 27°C · Air 15°C

Race 1: 23 laps, 57.495 miles/92.529km

Time of race: 34m 4.276s · **Average speed:** 101.249mph/162.945km/h

Pos.	Rider	Nat.	No.	Entrant	Machine	Tyres	Time & Gap	Laps
1	**Tom Sykes**	GBR	66	Kawasaki Racing Team	Kawasaki ZX-10R	P		23
2	**Davide Giugliano**	ITA	34	Aruba.it Racing – Ducati	Ducati Panigale R	P	2.869s	23
3	**Jonathan Rea**	GBR	1	Kawasaki Racing Team	Kawasaki ZX-10R	P	9.808s	23
4	**Leon Camier**	GBR	2	MV Agusta Reparto Corse	MV Agusta 1000 F4	P	13.747s	23
5	**Nicky Hayden**	USA	69	Honda World Superbike Team	Honda CBR1000RR SP	P	14.007s	23
6	**Lorenzo Savadori**	ITA	32	IodaRacing Team	Aprilia RSV4 RF	P	14.640s	23
7	**Jordi Torres**	ESP	81	Althea BMW Racing Team	BMW S1000 RR	P	16.337s	23
8	**Michael van der Mark**	NED	60	Honda World Superbike Team	Honda CBR1000RR SP	P	16.535s	23
9	**Karel Abraham**	CZE	17	Milwaukee BMW	BMW S1000 RR	P	36.874s	23
10	**Anthony West**	AUS	13	Pedercini Racing	Kawasaki ZX-10R	P	39.074s	23
11	**Markus Reiterberger**	GER	21	Althea BMW Racing Team	BMW S1000 RR	P	41.144s	23
12	**Xavi Fores**	ESP	12	Barni Racing Team	Ducati Panigale R	P	41.275s	23
13	**Roman Ramos**	ESP	40	Team GoEleven	Kawasaki ZX-10R	P	48.094s	23
14	**Joshua Brookes**	AUS	25	Milwaukee BMW	BMW S1000 RR	P	50.125s	23
15	**Dominic Schmitter**	SUI	9	Grillini Racing Team	Kawasaki ZX-10R	P	1m 18.008s	23
16	Pawel Szkopek	POL	119	Team Toth	Yamaha YZF R1	P	1m 29.605s	23
17	Saeed al Sulaiti	QAT	11	Pedercini Racing	Kawasaki ZX-10R	P	1 Lap	22
18	Imre Toth	HUN	10	Team Toth	Yamaha YZF R1	P	2 Laps	21
	Luca Scassa	ITA	99	VFT Racing	Ducati Panigale R	P	DNF	16
	Chaz Davies	GBR	7	Aruba.it Racing – Ducati	Ducati Panigale R	P	DNF	14
	Alex de Angelis	RSM	15	IodaRacing Team	Aprilia RSV4 RF	P	DNF	13
	Matthieu Lussiana	FRA	94	Team ASPI	BMW S1000 RR	P	DNF	9
	Cameron Beaubier	USA	6	Pata Yamaha Official WorldSBK Team	Yamaha YZF R1	P	DNF	0
	Alex Lowes	GBR	22	Pata Yamaha Official WorldSBK Team	Yamaha YZF R1	P	DNS	0

Fastest race lap: Jonathan Rea on lap 5, 1m 27.988s, 102.278mph/164.600km/h.

Race 2: 23 laps, 57.495 miles/92.529km

Time of race: 33m 55.601s · **Average speed:** 101.681mph/163.639km/h

Pos.	Rider	Time & Gap	Laps
1	**Tom Sykes**		23
2	**Jonathan Rea**	2.017s	23
3	**Chaz Davies**	4.437s	23
4	**Lorenzo Savadori**	6.423s	23
5	**Leon Camier**	11.808s	23
6	**Nicky Hayden**	12.455s	23
7	**Davide Giugliano**	24.212s	23
8	**Michael van der Mark**	25.931s	23
9	**Joshua Brookes**	26.512s	23
10	**Cameron Beaubier**	26.955s	23
11	**Jordi Torres**	29.684s	23
12	**Anthony West**	35.433s	23
13	**Roman Ramos**	35.862s	23
14	**Xavi Fores**	39.240s	23
15	**Alex de Angelis**	45.790s	23
16	Markus Reiterberger	46.252s	23
17	Luca Scassa	56.488s	23
18	Dominic Schmitter	1m 18.282s	23
19	Pawel Szkopek	1m 23.479s	23
	Saeed al Sulaiti	DNF	11
	Imre Toth	DNF	6
	Matthieu Lussiana	DNF	5
	Karel Abraham	DNF	0
	Alex Lowes	DNS	0

Superpole		
1	Sykes	1m 26.712s
2	Davies	1m 27.572s
3	Savadori	1m 27.591s
4	Rea	1m 27.601s
5	Giugliano	1m 27.602s
6	Torres	1m 28.046s
7	Hayden	1m 28.127s
8	Camier	1m 28.409s
9	Beaubier	1m 28.617s
10	Fores	1m 28.663s
11	Abraham	1m 30.345s
	Lowes	No Time
13	Van der Mark	1m 28.806s
14	De Angelis	1m 28.866s
15	Brookes	1m 29.029s
16	Ramos	1m 29.289s
17	Scassa	1m 29.377s
18	West	1m 29.377s
19	Reiterberger	1m 29.406s
20	Schmitter	1m 30.275s
21	Lussiana	1m 30.635s
22	Al Sulaiti	1m 31.378s
23	Szkopek	1m 31.742s
24	Toth	1m 34.549s

Fastest race lap: Jonathan Rea on lap 2, 1m 27.605s, 102.724mph/165.319km/h (record).

Previous lap record: Tom Sykes, GBR (Kawasaki), 1m 27.640s, 102.683mph/ 165.253km/h (2015).

Points

1, Rea 293; 2, Sykes 237; 3, Davies 231; 4, Giugliano 147; 5, Van der Mark 141; 6, Hayden 136; 7, Torres 117; 8, Camier 97; 9, Savadori 89; 10, Lowes 70; 11, Fores 62; 12, Guintoli 58; 13, Reiterberger 58; 14, Brookes 48; 15, De Angelis 42; 16, Ramos 42; 17, West 28; 18, Abraham 25; 19, Baiocco 12; 20, Mahias 9; 21, Beaubier 6; 22, Scassa 3; 23, Jones 2; 24, Schmitter 2; 25, Hook 2; 26, Barrier 2; 27, Lussiana 1.

WORLD SUPERBIKE CHAMPIONSHIP · 2016

Race 1: 21 laps, 55.144 miles/88.746km

Time of race: 33m 44.254s · **Average speed:** 98.070mph/157.829km/h

Pos.	Rider	Nat.	No.	Entrant	Machine	Tyres	Time & Gap	Laps
1	Jonathan Rea	GBR	1	Kawasaki Racing Team	Kawasaki ZX-10R	P		21
2	Tom Sykes	GBR	66	Kawasaki Racing Team	Kawasaki ZX-10R	P	0.090s	21
3	Michael van der Mark	NED	60	Honda World Superbike Team	Honda CBR1000RR SP	P	3.093s	21
4	Chaz Davies	GBR	7	Aruba.it Racing – Ducati	Ducati Panigale R	P	5.878s	21
5	Jordi Torres	ESP	81	Althea BMW Racing Team	BMW S1000 RR	P	15.955s	21
6	Markus Reiterberger	GER	21	Althea BMW Racing Team	BMW S1000 RR	P	18.200s	21
7	Niccolo Canepa	ITA	59	Pata Yamaha Official WorldSBK Team	Yamaha YZF R1	P	19.385s	21
8	Leon Camier	GBR	2	MV Agusta Reparto Corse	MV Agusta 1000 F4	P	19.918s	21
9	Roman Ramos	ESP	40	Team GoEleven	Kawasaki ZX-10R	P	26.272s	21
10	Anthony West	AUS	13	Pedercini Racing	Kawasaki ZX-10R	P	32.593s	21
11	Joshua Brookes	AUS	25	Milwaukee BMW	BMW S1000 RR	P	36.825s	21
12	Alex de Angelis	RSM	15	IodaRacing Team	Aprilia RSV4 RF	P	37.084s	21
13	Alex Lowes	GBR	22	Pata Yamaha Official WorldSBK Team	Yamaha YZF R1	P	38.181s	21
14	Davide Giugliano	ITA	34	Aruba.it Racing – Ducati	Ducati Panigale R	P	41.201s	21
15	Pawel Szkopek	POL	119	Team Toth	Yamaha YZF R1	P	1m 20.992s	21
16	Peter Sebestyen	HUN	56	Team Toth	Yamaha YZF R1	P	1m 21.783s	21
17	Dominic Schmitter	SUI	9	Grillini Racing Team	Kawasaki ZX-10R	P	1m 24.623s	21
18	Fabio Menghi	ITA	61	VFT Racing	Ducati Panigale R	P	1m 25.068s	21
19	Saeed al Sulaiti	QAT	11	Pedercini Racing	Kawasaki ZX-10R	P	1m 31.041s	21
20	Gianluca Vizziello	ITA	4	Grillini Racing Team	Kawasaki ZX-10R	P	1 Lap	20
	Xavi Fores	ESP	12	Barni Racing Team	Ducati Panigale R	P	DNF	17
	Karel Abraham	CZE	17	Milwaukee BMW	BMW S1000 RR	P	DNF	9
	Nicky Hayden	USA	69	Honda World Superbike Team	Honda CBR1000RR SP	P	DNF	1
	Lorenzo Savadori	ITA	32	IodaRacing Team	Aprilia RSV4 RF	P	DNF	0

Fastest race lap: Tom Sykes on lap 6, 1m 35.507s, 98.980mph/159.293km/h.

Race 2: 21 laps, 55.144 miles/88.746km

Time of race: 33m 38.497s · **Average speed:** 98.350mph/158.279km/h

Pos.	Rider	Time & Gap	Laps
1	Jonathan Rea		21
2	Tom Sykes	2.963s	21
3	Davide Giugliano	6.356s	21
4	Xavi Fores	11.691s	21
5	Lorenzo Savadori	15.164s	21
6	Nicky Hayden	15.248s	21
7	Jordi Torres	15.587s	21
8	Alex Lowes	17.276s	21
9	Niccolo Canepa	20.082s	21
10	Michael van der Mark	23.832s	21
11	Anthony West	25.004s	21
12	Roman Ramos	28.020s	21
13	Alex de Angelis	29.703s	21
14	Joshua Brookes	40.695s	21
15	Karel Abraham	56.679s	21
16	Dominic Schmitter	1m 03.741s	21
17	Fabio Menghi	1m 10.624s	21
18	Peter Sebestyen	1m 13.063s	21
19	Saeed al Sulaiti	1m 22.765s	21
20	Pawel Szkopek	1m 59.149s	21
	Gianluca Vizziello	DNF	14
	Leon Camier	DNF	11
	Chaz Davies	DNF	2
	Markus Reiterberger	DNF	0

Superpole		
1	Sykes	1m 34.037s
2	Rea	1m 34.257s
3	Fores	1m 34.623s
4	Lowes	1m 34.641s
5	Savadori	1m 34.694s
6	Hayden	1m 34.707s
7	Giugliano	1m 34.826s
8	Camier	1m 35.047s
9	Davies	1m 35.097s
10	Van der Mark	1m 35.108s
11	Reiterberger	1m 35.115s
12	Torres	1m 36.014s
13	West	1m 35.765s
14	Ramos	1m 36.328s
15	Canepa	1m 36.335s
16	Brookes	1m 37.314s
17	Menghi	1m 38.143s
18	Schmitter	1m 38.238s
19	Abraham	1m 38.380s
20	Sebestyen	1m 38.446s
21	Al Sulaiti	1m 38.813s
22	Szkopek	1m 38.975s
23	Vizziello	1m 39.171s
24	De Angelis	1m 42.023s

Fastest race lap: Alex Lowes on lap 2, 1m 35.165s, 99.336mph/159.865km/h.

Lap record: Jonathan Rea, GBR (Kawasaki), 1m 34.720s, 99.803mph/ 160.617km/h (2015).

Points

1, Rea 343; 2, Sykes 277; 3, Davies 244; 4, Giugliano 165; 5, Van der Mark 163; 6 Hayden 146; 7, Torres 137; 8, Camier 105; 9, Savadori 100; 10, Lowes 81; 11, Fores 75; 12, Reiterberger 68; 13, Guintoli 58; 14, Brookes 55; 15, Ramos 53; 16, De Angelis 49; 17, West 39; 18, Abraham 26; 19, Canepa 16; 20, Baiocco 12; 21, Mahias 9; 22, Beaubier 6; 23, Scassa 3; 24, Jones 2; 25, Schmitter 2; 26, Hook 2; 27, Barrier 2; 28, Szkopek 1; 29, Lussiana 1.

Race 1: 25 laps, 56.079 miles/90.250km

Time of race: 35m 18.180s · **Average speed:** 95.310mph/153.386km/h

Pos.	Rider	Nat.	No.	Entrant	Machine	Tyres	Time & Gap	Laps
1	Jonathan Rea	GBR	1	Kawasaki Racing Team	Kawasaki ZX-10R	P		25
2	Tom Sykes	GBR	66	Kawasaki Racing Team	Kawasaki ZX-10R	P	0.819s	25
3	Nicky Hayden	USA	69	Honda World Superbike Team	Honda CBR1000RR SP	P	12.296s	25
4	Michael van der Mark	NED	60	Honda World Superbike Team	Honda CBR1000RR SP	P	13.067s	25
5	Alex Lowes	GBR	22	Pata Yamaha Official WorldSBK Team	Yamaha YZF R1	P	13.335s	25
6	Lorenzo Savadori	ITA	32	IodaRacing Team	Aprilia RSV4 RF	P	13.816s	25
7	Xavi Fores	ESP	12	Barni Racing Team	Ducati Panigale R	P	15.541s	25
8	Jordi Torres	ESP	81	Althea BMW Racing Team	BMW S1000 RR	P	15.838s	25
9	Alex de Angelis	RSM	15	IodaRacing Team	Aprilia RSV4 RF	P	19.999s	25
10	Niccolo Canepa	ITA	59	Pata Yamaha Official WorldSBK Team	Yamaha YZF R1	P	22.832s	25
11	Leon Camier	GBR	2	MV Agusta Reparto Corse	MV Agusta 1000 F4	P	24.065s	25
12	Anthony West	AUS	13	Pedercini Racing	Kawasaki ZX-10R	P	28.902s	25
13	Joshua Brookes	AUS	25	Milwaukee BMW	BMW S1000 RR	P	39.957s	25
14	Karel Abraham	CZE	17	Milwaukee BMW	BMW S1000 RR	P	46.552s	25
15	Roman Ramos	ESP	40	Team GoEleven	Kawasaki ZX-10R	P	55.791s	25
16	Dominic Schmitter	SUI	9	Grillini Racing Team	Kawasaki ZX-10R	P	59.021s	25
17	Peter Sebestyen	HUN	56	Team Toth	Yamaha YZF R1	P	1 Lap	24
18	Pawel Szkopek	POL	119	Team Toth	Yamaha YZF R1	P	1 Lap	24
	Gianluca Vizziello	ITA	4	Grillini Racing Team	Kawasaki ZX-10R	P	DNF	16
	Saeed al Sulaiti	QAT	11	Pedercini Racing	Kawasaki ZX-10R	P	DNF	16
	Davide Giugliano	ITA	34	Aruba.it Racing – Ducati	Ducati Panigale R	P	DNF	12
	Raffaele de Rosa	ITA	35	Althea BMW Racing Team	BMW S1000 RR	P	DNF	12
	Chaz Davies	GBR	7	Aruba.it Racing – Ducati	Ducati Panigale R	P	DNF	4

Fastest race lap: Chaz Davies on lap 4, 1m 23.443s, 96.777mph/155.747km/h.

Race 2: 21 laps, 47.106 miles/75.810km

Time of race: 29m 35.285s · **Average speed:** 95.524mph/153.731km/h

Pos.	Rider	Time & Gap	Laps
1	Tom Sykes		21
2	Davide Giugliano	0.209s	21
3	Chaz Davies	0.786s	21
4	Xavi Fores	11.379s	21
5	Nicky Hayden	12.219s	21
6	Jordi Torres	12.465s	21
7	Michael van der Mark	13.705s	21
8	Niccolo Canepa	20.449s	21
9	Anthony West	29.153s	21
10	Roman Ramos	33.013s	21
11	Raffaele de Rosa	39.910s	21
12	Karel Abraham	40.059s	21
13	Dominic Schmitter	49.211s	21
14	Alex Lowes	51.347s	21
15	Saeed al Sulaiti	54.783s	21
16	Peter Sebestyen	1m 03.249s	21
17	Gianluca Vizziello	1m 25.191s	21
	Jonathan Rea	DNF	5
	Lorenzo Savadori	DNF	2
	Alex de Angelis	DNS	-
	Joshua Brookes	DNS	-
	Leon Camier	DNS	-
	Pawel Szkopek	DNS	-

Superpole		
1	Sykes	1m 22.155s
2	Rea	1m 22.210s
3	Giugliano	1m 22.479s
4	Davies	1m 22.696s
5	Fores	1m 22.979s
6	Hayden	1m 22.988s
7	Torres	1m 23.085s
8	Savadori	1m 23.096s
9	Canepa	1m 23.098s
10	Lowes	1m 23.116s
11	Van der Mark	1m 23.455s
12	Camier	1m 23.459s
13	De Angelis	1m 23.661s
14	West	1m 24.128s
15	Brookes	1m 24.598s
16	Ramos	1m 24.788s
17	Abraham	1m 24.811s
18	De Rosa	1m 24.867s
19	Schmitter	1m 25.354s
20	Al Sulaiti	1m 25.589s
21	Szkopek	1m 25.970s
22	Sebestyen	1m 26.859s
23	Vizziello	1m 27.240s

Fastest race lap: Tom Sykes on lap 2, 1m 23.552s, 96.651mph/155.544km/h.

Lap record: Davide Giugliano, ITA (Ducati), 1m 23.403s, 96.823mph/155.822km/h (2014).

Points

1, Rea 368; 2, Sykes 322; 3, Davies 260; 4, Giugliano 185; 5, Van der Mark 185; 6, Hayden 173; 7, Torres 155; 8, Camier 110; 9, Savadori 110; 10, Fores 97; 11, Lowes 94; 12, Reiterberger 68; 13, Ramos 60; 14, Guintoli 58; 15, Brookes 58; 16, De Angelis 56; 17, West 50; 18, Abraham 32; 19, Canepa 30; 20, Baiocco 12; 21, Mahias 9; 22, Beaubier 6; 23, De Rosa 5; 24, Schmitter 5; 25, Scassa 3; 26, Jones 2; 27, Hook 2; 28, Barrier 2; 29, Al Sulaiti 1; 30, Szkopek 1; 31, Lussiana 1.

WORLD SUPERBIKE CHAMPIONSHIP · 2016

Race 1: 21 laps, 55.653 miles/89.565km

Time of race: 34m 20.100s · **Average speed:** 97.253mph/156.514km/h

Pos.	Rider	Nat.	No.	Entrant	Machine	Tyres	Time & Gap	Laps
1	Chaz Davies	GBR	7	Aruba.it Racing – Ducati	Ducati Panigale R	P		21
2	Tom Sykes	GBR	66	Kawasaki Racing Team	Kawasaki ZX-10R	P	10.561s	21
3	Nicky Hayden	USA	69	Honda World Superbike Team	Honda CBR1000RR SP	P	11.536s	21
4	Jordi Torres	ESP	81	Althea BMW Racing Team	BMW S1000 RR	P	12.493s	21
5	Leon Camier	GBR	2	MV Agusta Reparto Corse	MV Agusta 1000 F4	P	12.965s	21
6	Michael van der Mark	NED	60	Honda World Superbike Team	Honda CBR1000RR SP	P	18.863s	21
7	Davide Giugliano	ITA	34	Aruba.it Racing – Ducati	Ducati Panigale R	P	18.970s	21
8	Alex Lowes	GBR	22	Pata Yamaha Official WorldSBK Team	Yamaha YZF R1	P	27.395s	21
9	Sylvain Guintoli	FRA	50	Pata Yamaha Official WorldSBK Team	Yamaha YZF R1	P	33.221s	21
10	Xavi Fores	ESP	12	Barni Racing Team	Ducati Panigale R	P	33.459s	21
11	Anthony West	AUS	13	Pedercini Racing	Kawasaki ZX-10R	P	46.665s	21
12	Alex de Angelis	RSM	15	IodaRacing Team	Aprilia RSV4 RF	P	1m 02.000s	21
13	Roman Ramos	ESP	40	Team GoEleven	Kawasaki ZX-10R	P	1m 05.734s	21
14	Joshua Brookes	AUS	25	Milwaukee BMW	BMW S1000 RR	P	1m 05.890s	21
15	Luca Scassa	ITA	99	VFT Racing	Ducati Panigale R	P	1m 14.908s	21
16	Dominic Schmitter	SUI	9	Grillini Racing Team	Kawasaki ZX-10R	P	1m 24.523s	21
17	Pawel Szkopek	POL	119	Team Toth	Yamaha YZF R1	P	1m 33.495s	21
18	Peter Sebestyen	HUN	56	Team Toth	Yamaha YZF R1	P	1 Lap	20
19	Gianluca Vizziello	ITA	4	Grillini Racing Team	Kawasaki ZX-10R	P	1 Lap	20
	Saeed al Sulaiti	QAT	11	Pedercini Racing	Kawasaki ZX-10R	P	DNF	17
	Markus Reiterberger	GER	21	Althea BMW Racing Team	BMW S1000 RR	P	DNF	8
	Lorenzo Savadori	ITA	32	IodaRacing Team	Aprilia RSV4 RF	P	DNF	7
	Jonathan Rea	GBR	1	Kawasaki Racing Team	Kawasaki ZX-10R	P	DNF	7
	Karel Abraham	CZE	17	Milwaukee BMW	BMW S1000 RR	P	DNF	1

Fastest race lap: Chaz Davies on lap 2, 1m 37.357s, 97.995mph/157.708km/h (record).

Race 2: : 16 laps, 42.402 miles/68.240km

Time of race: 31m 39.737s · **Average speed:** 80.353mph/129.315km/h

Pos.	Rider	Time & Gap	Laps
1	Jonathan Rea		16
2	Alex de Angelis	9.396s	16
3	Xavi Fores	13.041s	16
4	Leon Camier	15.728s	16
5	Sylvain Guintoli	17.100s	16
6	Chaz Davies	19.780s	16
7	Joshua Brookes	32.208s	16
8	Michael van der Mark	54.373s	16
9	Roman Ramos	57.271s	16
10	Nicky Hayden	59.671s	16
11	Luca Scassa	1m 01.938s	16
12	Tom Sykes	1m 14.028s	16
13	Gianluca Vizziello	1m 14.038s	16
14	Pawel Szkopek	1m 46.309s	16
15	Karel Abraham	1m 51.775s	16
16	Peter Sebestyen	1 Lap	15
	Dominic Schmitter	DNF	12
	Saeed al Sulaiti	DNF	10
	Alex Lowes	DNF	9
	Markus Reiterberger	DNF	8
	Lorenzo Savadori	DNF	6
	Anthony West	DNF	6
	Jordi Torres	DNF	6
	Davide Giugliano	DNF	3

	Superpole	
1	Davies	1m 37.883s
2	Sykes	1m 38.008s
3	Hayden	1m 38.875s
4	Savadori	1m 39.208s
5	Torres	1m 39.220s
6	Rea	1m 39.421s
7	Camier	1m 39.525s
8	Giugliano	1m 39.729s
9	Guintoli	1m 39.786s
10	Van der Mark	1m 40.399s
11	Reiterberger	1m 41.583s
12	Lowes	No Time
13	Fores	1m 46.973s
14	Schmitter	1m 47.040s
15	Ramos	1m 47.776s
16	West	1m 48.448s
17	Brookes	1m 48.616s
18	De Angelis	1m 49.945s
19	Scassa	1m 50.132s
20	Vizziello	1m 51.418s
21	Szkopek	1m 51.870s
22	Abraham	1m 52.074s
23	Sebestyen	1m 52.356s
24	Al Sulaiti	1m 54.203s

Fastest race lap: Xavi Fores on lap 13, 1m 56.386s, 81.973mph/131.923km/h.

Previous lap record: Noriyuki Haga, JPN (Yamaha), 1m 38.622s, 96.741mph/ 155.690km/h (2007).

Points

1, Rea 393; 2, Sykes 346; 3, Davies 295; 4, Van der Mark 203; 5, Hayden 195; 6, Giugliano 194; 7, Torres 168; 8, Camier 134; 9, Fores 119; 10, Savadori 110; 11, Lowes 102; 12 De Angelis 80; 13, Guintoli 76; 14, Ramos 70; 15, Brookes 69; 16, Reiterberger 68; 17, West 55; 18, Abraham 33; 19, Canepa 30; 20, Baiocco 12; 21, Mahias 9; 22, Scassa 9; 23, Beaubier 6; 24, De Rosa 5; 25, Schmitter 5; 26, Vizziello 3; 27, Szkopek 3; 28, Jones 2; 29, Hook 2; 30, Barrier 2; 31, Al Sulaiti 1; 32, Lussiana 1.

Race 1: 21 laps, 57.558 miles/92.631km

Time of race: 38m 51.932s · **Average speed:** 88.857mph/143.002km/h

Pos.	Rider	Nat.	No.	Entrant	Machine	Tyres	Time & Gap	Laps
1	Chaz Davies	GBR	7	Aruba.it Racing – Ducati	Ducati Panigale R	P		21
2	Michael van der Mark	NED	60	Honda World Superbike Team	Honda CBR1000RR SP	P	9.871s	21
3	Tom Sykes	GBR	66	Kawasaki Racing Team	Kawasaki ZX-10R	P	10.218s	21
4	Jonathan Rea	GBR	1	Kawasaki Racing Team	Kawasaki ZX-10R	P	18.031s	21
5	Lorenzo Savadori	ITA	32	IodaRacing Team	Aprilia RSV4 RF	P	19.974s	21
6	Matthieu Lagrive	FRA	76	Pedercini Racing	Kawasaki ZX-10R	P	24.661s	21
7	Leon Camier	GBR	2	MV Agusta Reparto Corse	MV Agusta 1000 F4	P	25.743s	21
8	Xavi Fores	ESP	12	Barni Racing Team	Ducati Panigale R	P	27.409s	21
9	Sylvain Guintoli	FRA	50	Pata Yamaha Official WorldSBK Team	Yamaha YZF R1	P	49.455s	21
10	Alex de Angelis	RSM	15	IodaRacing Team	Aprilia RSV4 RF	P	52.570s	21
11	Alex Lowes	GBR	22	Pata Yamaha Official WorldSBK Team	Yamaha YZF R1	P	52.788s	21
12	Joshua Brookes	AUS	25	Milwaukee BMW	BMW S1000 RR	P	53.947s	21
13	Roman Ramos	ESP	40	Team GoEleven	Kawasaki ZX-10R	P	54.929s	21
14	Jordi Torres	ESP	81	Althea BMW Racing Team	BMW S1000 RR	P	1m 22.280s	21
15	Luca Scassa	ITA	99	VFT Racing	Ducati Panigale R	P	1m 27.383s	21
16	Karel Abraham	CZE	17	Milwaukee BMW	BMW S1000 RR	P	1 Lap	20
17	Markus Reiterberger	GER	21	Althea BMW Racing Team	BMW S1000 RR	P	1 Lap	20
18	Saeed al Sulaiti	QAT	11	Pedercini Racing	Kawasaki ZX-10R	P	1 Lap	20
19	Peter Sebestyen	HUN	56	Team Toth	Yamaha YZF R1	P	1 Lap	20
20	Matthieu Lussiana	FRA	94	Team ASPI	BMW S1000 RR	P	1 Lap	20
21	Gianluca Vizziello	ITA	4	Grillini Racing Team	Kawasaki ZX-10R	P	1 Lap	20
22	Alex Plancassagne	FRA	57	3ART	Yamaha YZF R1	P	2 Laps	19
	Imre Toth	HUN	10	Team Toth	Yamaha YZF R1	P	DNF	9
	Nicky Hayden	USA	69	Honda World Superbike Team	Honda CBR1000RR SP	P	DNF	9
	Dominic Schmitter	SUI	9	Grillini Racing Team	Kawasaki ZX-10R	P	DNF	8
	Davide Giugliano	ITA	34	Aruba.it Racing – Ducati	Ducati Panigale R	P	DNS	–

Fastest race lap: Tom Sykes on lap 21, 1m 40.491s, 98.189mph/158.020km/h.

Race 2: 21 laps, 57.558 miles/92.631km

Time of race: 34m 29.197s · **Average speed:** 100.140mph/161.160km/h

Pos.	Rider	Time & Gap	Laps
1	Chaz Davies		21
2	Jonathan Rea	2.091s	21
3	Tom Sykes	2.586s	21
4	Leon Camier	9.154s	21
5	Michael van der Mark	11.020s	21
6	Lorenzo Savadori	16.062s	21
7	Jordi Torres	18.242s	21
8	Sylvain Guintoli	18.951s	21
9	Nicky Hayden	19.099s	21
10	Xavi Fores	24.627s	21
11	Joshua Brookes	31.514s	21
12	Markus Reiterberger	35.665s	21
13	Roman Ramos	51.053s	21
14	Alex de Angelis	54.239s	21
15	Matthieu Lagrive	59.954s	21
16	Karel Abraham	1m 12.959s	21
17	Gianluca Vizziello	1m 18.008s	21
18	Peter Sebestyen	1m 19.245s	21
19	Alex Lowes	1m 27.462s	21
20	Alex Plancassagne	1 Lap	20
21	Imre Toth	1 Lap	20
	Saeed al Sulaiti	DNF	13
	Matthieu Lussiana	DNF	10
	Luca Scassa	DNF	0
	Dominic Schmitter	DNS	–
	Davide Giugliano	DNS	–

	Superpole	
1	Rea	1m 52.881s
2	Sykes	1m 53.593s
3	Davies	1m 54.087s
4	Guintoli	1m 54.574s
5	Camier	1m 55.303s
6	Van der Mark	1m 55.334s
7	Hayden	1m 55.529s
8	Savadori	1m 55.811s
9	Lagrive	1m 56.744s
10	Fores	1m 56.878s
11	Lowes	1m 57.547s
12	Torres	1m 58.353s
13	Giugliano	1m 56.494s
14	Brookes	1m 57.312s
15	De Angelis	1m 57.355s
16	Scassa	1m 57.475s
17	Ramos	1m 58.421s
18	Abraham	1m 58.765s
19	Lussiana	1m 59.363s
20	Reiterberger	1m 59.800s
21	Sebestyen	2m 00.463s
22	Plancassagne	2m 01.140s
23	Vizziello	2m 02.231s
24	Toth	2m 02.495s
25	Schmitter	2m 06.811s
26	Al Sulaiti	2m 07.317s

Fastest race lap: Tom Sykes on lap 3, 1m 37.864s, 100.825mph/162.262km/h (record).

Previous lap record: Tom Sykes, GBR (Kawasaki), 1m 37.932s, 100.755mph/ 162.149km/h (2013).

Points

1, Rea 426; 2, Sykes 378; 3, Davies 345; 4, Van der Mark 234; 5, Hayden 202; 6, Giugliano 194; 7, Torres 179; 8. Camier 156; 9, Fores 133; 10, Savadori 131; 11, Lowes 107; 12, Guintoli 91; 13, De Angelis 88; 14, Brookes 78; 15 Ramos 76; 16, Reiterberger 72; 17, West 55; 18, Abraham 33; 19, Canepa 30; 20, Baiocco 12; 21, Lagrive 11; 22, Scassa 10; 23, Mahias 9; 24, Beaubier 6; 25, De Rosa 5; 26, Schmitter 5; 27, Vizziello 3; 28, Szkopek 3; 29, Jones 2; 30, Hook 2; 31, Barrier 2; 32, Al Sulaiti 1; 33, Lussiana 1.

Round 12 JEREZ, Spain · 15–16 October, 2016 · 2.748-mile/4.423km circuit · WEATHER: Race 1 · Dry · Track 35°C · Air 21°C; Race 2 · Dry · Track 37°C · Air 24°C

Race 1: 20 laps, 54.966mi/88.460km

Time of race: 34m 8.161s · **Average speed:** 96.613mph/155.484km/h

Pos.	Rider	Nat.	No.	Entrant	Machine	Tyres	Time & Gap	Laps
1	Chaz Davies	GBR	7	Aruba.it Racing – Ducati	Ducati Panigale R	P		20
2	Tom Sykes	GBR	66	Kawasaki Racing Team	Kawasaki ZX-10R	P	3.290s	20
3	Jonathan Rea	GBR	1	Kawasaki Racing Team	Kawasaki ZX-10R	P	7.151s	20
4	Nicky Hayden	USA	69	Honda World Superbike Team	Honda CBR1000RR SP	P	13.212s	20
5	Michael van der Mark	NED	60	Honda World Superbike Team	Honda CBR1000RR SP	P	13.251s	20
6	Sylvain Guintoli	FRA	50	Pata Yamaha Official WorldSBK Team	Yamaha YZF R1	P	17.834s	20
7	Leon Camier	GBR	2	MV Agusta Reparto Corse	MV Agusta 1000 F4	P	20.911s	20
8	Jordi Torres	ESP	81	Althea BMW Racing Team	BMW S1000 RR	P	26.182s	20
9	Markus Reiterberger	GER	21	Althea BMW Racing Team	BMW S1000 RR	P	29.837s	20
10	Joshua Brookes	AUS	25	Milwaukee BMW	BMW S1000 RR	P	31.246s	20
11	Alex de Angelis	RSM	15	IodaRacing Team	Aprilia RSV4 RF	P	32.399s	20
12	Roman Ramos	ESP	40	Team GoEleven	Kawasaki ZX-10R	P	33.007s	20
13	Lorenzo Savadori	ITA	32	IodaRacing Team	Aprilia RSV4 RF	P	36.266s	20
14	Anthony West	AUS	13	Pedercini Racing	Kawasaki ZX-10R	P	1m 01.064s	20
15	Peter Sebestyen	HUN	56	Team Toth	Yamaha YZF R1	P	1m 07.941s	20
16	Gianluca Vizziello	ITA	4	Grillini Racing Team	Kawasaki ZX-10R	P	1m 08.160s	20
17	Dominic Schmitter	SUI	9	Grillini Racing Team	Kawasaki ZX-10R	P	1m 08.260s	20
18	Karel Pesek	CZE	82	Team Toth	Yamaha YZF R1	P	1m 38.143s	20
	Matthieu Lussiana	FRA	94	Team ASPI	BMW S1000 RR	P	DNF	6
	Alex Lowes	GBR	22	Pata Yamaha Official WorldSBK Team	Yamaha YZF R1	P	DNF	2
	Xavi Fores	ESP	12	Barni Racing Team	Ducati Panigale R	P	DNF	1
	Davide Giugliano	ITA	34	Aruba.it Racing – Ducati	Ducati Panigale R	P	DNF	1
	Luca Scassa	ITA	99	VFT Racing	Ducati Panigale R	P	DNF	0
	Saeed al Sulaiti	QAT	11	Pedercini Racing	Kawasaki ZX-10R	P	DNF	0

Fastest race lap: Tom Sykes on lap 3, 1m 41.467s, 97.509mph/156.926km/h.

Race 2: 20 laps, 54.966mi/88.460km

Time of race: 34m 20.026s · **Average speed:** 96.057mph/154.588km/h

Pos.	Rider	Time & Gap	Laps
1	Chaz Davies		20
2	Jonathan Rea	5.893s	20
3	Tom Sykes	6.030s	20
4	Nicky Hayden	6.750s	20
5	Sylvain Guintoli	10.762s	20
6	Michael van der Mark	11.310s	20
7	Alex Lowes	16.413s	20
8	Jordi Torres	19.232s	20
9	Anthony West	24.095s	20
10	Lorenzo Savadori	25.379s	20
11	Roman Ramos	26.036s	20
12	Joshua Brookes	29.230s	20
13	Davide Giugliano	34.879s	20
14	Markus Reiterberger	49.708s	20
15	Gianluca Vizziello	1m 02.245s	20
16	Luca Scassa	1m 08.295s	20
17	Matthieu Lussiana	1m 20.252s	20
18	Dominic Schmitter	1m 33.859s	20
19	Karel Pesek	1m 33.965s	20
	Xavi Fores	DNF	8
	Saeed al Sulaiti	DNF	8
	Alex de Angelis	DNF	3
	Leon Camier	DNF	2
	Peter Sebestyen	DNF	0

Superpole

1	Sykes	1m 39.190s
2	Rea	1m 39.602s
3	Giugliano	1m 39.977s
4	Lowes	1m 39.980s
5	Hayden	1m 40.103s
6	Davies	1m 40.111s
7	Torres	1m 40.111s
8	Fores	1m 40.170s
9	Guintoli	1m 40.239s
10	Camier	1m 40.276s
11	Van der Mark	1m 40.291s
12	West	1m 41.188s
13	Reiterberger	1m 41.528s
14	Savadori	1m 41.622s
15	Ramos	1m 41.838s
16	De Angelis	1m 41.876s
17	Brookes	1m 41.978s
18	Scassa	1m 42.710s
19	Sebestyen	1m 43.238s
20	Vizziello	1m 43.364s
21	Schmitter	1m 44.011s
22	Al Sulaiti	1m 44.436s
23	Pesek	1m 45.262s
24	Lussiana	1m 45.373s

Fastest race lap: Chaz Davies on lap 2, 1m 41.492s, 97.485mph/156.887km/h.

Lap record: Jonathan Rea, GBR (Kawasaki), 1m 41.136s, 97.828mph/157.439km/h (2015).

Points

1, Rea 462; 2, Sykes 414; 3, Davies 395; 4, Van der Mark 255; 5, Hayden 228; 6, Giugliano 197; 7, Torres 195; 8, Camier 165; 9, Savadori 140; 10, Fores 133; 11, Lowes 116; 12, Guintoli 112; 13, De Angelis 93; 14, Brookes 88; 15, Ramos 85; 16, Reiterberger 81; 17, West 64; 18, Abraham 33; 19, Canepa 30; 20, Baiocco 12; 21, Lagrive 11; 22, Scassa 10; 23, Mahias 9; 24, Beaubier 6; 25, De Rosa 5; 26, Schmitter 5; 27, Vizziello 4; 28, Szkopek 3; 29, Jones 2; 30, Hook 2; 31, Barrier 2; 32, Sebestyen 1; 33, Al Sulaiti 1; 34, Lussiana 1.

Round 13 LOSAIL, Qatar · 29–30 October, 2016 · 3.343-mile/5.380km circuit · WEATHER: Race 1 · Dry · Track 28°C · Air 27°C; Race 2 · Dry · Track 27°C · Air 26°C

Race 1: 17 laps, 56.831 miles/91.460km

Time of race: 33m 32.214s · **Average speed:** 101.674mph/163.629km/h

Pos.	Rider	Nat.	No.	Entrant	Machine	Tyres	Time & Gap	Laps
1	Chaz Davies	GBR	7	Aruba.it Racing – Ducati	Ducati Panigale R	P		17
2	Jonathan Rea	GBR	1	Kawasaki Racing Team	Kawasaki ZX-10R	P	3.904s	17
3	Sylvain Guintoli	FRA	50	Pata Yamaha Official WorldSBK Team	Yamaha YZF R1	P	10.498s	17
4	Tom Sykes	GBR	66	Kawasaki Racing Team	Kawasaki ZX-10R	P	12.606s	17
5	Nicky Hayden	USA	69	Honda World Superbike Team	Honda CBR1000RR SP	P	12.766s	17
6	Xavi Fores	ESP	12	Barni Racing Team	Ducati Panigale R	P	17.879s	17
7	Alex Lowes	GBR	22	Pata Yamaha Official WorldSBK Team	Yamaha YZF R1	P	18.461s	17
8	Jordi Torres	ESP	81	Althea BMW Racing Team	BMW S1000 RR	P	19.045s	17
9	Michael van der Mark	NED	60	Honda World Superbike Team	Honda CBR1000RR SP	P	20.882s	17
10	Lorenzo Savadori	ITA	32	IodaRacing Team	Aprilia RSV4 RF	P	30.057s	17
11	Leon Haslam	GBR	91	Pedercini Racing	Kawasaki ZX-10R	P	34.270s	17
12	Raffaele de Rosa	ITA	35	Althea BMW Racing Team	BMW S1000 RR	P	34.420s	17
13	Alex de Angelis	RSM	15	IodaRacing Team	Aprilia RSV4 RF	P	34.936s	17
14	Roman Ramos	ESP	40	Team GoEleven	Kawasaki ZX-10R	P	37.786s	17
15	Joshua Brookes	AUS	25	Milwaukee BMW	BMW S1000 RR	P	37.834s	17
16	Luca Scassa	ITA	99	VFT Racing	Ducati Panigale R	P	55.890s	17
17	Saeed al Sulaiti	QAT	11	Pedercini Racing	Kawasaki ZX-10R	P	1m 09.075s	17
18	Leon Camier	GBR	2	MV Agusta Reparto Corse	MV Agusta 1000 F4	P	1m 19.301s	17
19	Dominic Schmitter	SUI	9	Grillini Racing Team	Kawasaki ZX-10R	P	1m 25.103s	17
20	Peter Sebestyen	HUN	56	Team Toth	Yamaha YZF R1	P	1m 47.707s	17
21	Gianluca Vizziello	ITA	4	Grillini Racing Team	Kawasaki ZX-10R	P	4 Laps	13
	Karel Abraham	CZE		Milwaukee BMW	BMW S1000 RR	P	DNF	14
	Davide Giugliano	ITA	34	Aruba.it Racing – Ducati	Ducati Panigale R	P	DNF	10
	Markus Reiterberger	GER	21	Althea BMW Racing Team	BMW S1000 RR	P	DNF	7
	Pawel Szkopek	POL	119	Team Toth	Yamaha YZF R1	P	DNS	-

Fastest race lap: Chaz Davies on lap 2, 1m 57.371s, 102.536mph/165.015km/h.

Race 2: 10 laps, 33.430 miles/53.800km

Time of race: 19m 38.203s · **Average speed:** 102.145mph/164.386km/h

Pos.	Rider	Time & Gap	Laps
1	Chaz Davies		10
2	Tom Sykes	5.855s	10
3	Jonathan Rea	6.376s	10
4	Sylvain Guintoli	8.493s	10
5	Leon Haslam	11.862s	10
6	Jordi Torres	12.232s	10
7	Nicky Hayden	13.599s	10
8	Xavi Fores	14.210s	10
9	Raffaele de Rosa	14.282s	10
10	Alex Lowes	14.414s	10
11	Michael van der Mark	15.169s	10
12	Lorenzo Savadori	19.401s	10
13	Leon Camier	22.236s	10
14	Roman Ramos	25.995s	10
15	Markus Reiterberger	29.701s	10
16	Luca Scassa	33.205s	10
17	Gianluca Vizziello	44.627s	10
18	Dominic Schmitter	44.753s	10
19	Peter Sebestyen	45.186s	10
20	Pawel Szkopek	1m 00.135s	10
	Karel Abraham	DNF	9
	Alex de Angelis	DNF	0
	Saeed al Sulaiti	DNS	-
	Joshua Brookes	DNS	-
	Davide Giugliano	DNS	-

Superpole

1	Rea	1m 56.356s
2	Hayden	1m 56.561s
3	Davies	1m 56.602s
4	Guintoli	1m 56.866s
5	Sykes	1m 56.935s
6	Lowes	1m 57.014s
7	Fores	1m 57.018s
8	Savadori	1m 57.094s
9	Van der Mark	1m 57.126s
10	Torres	1m 57.485s
11	Giugliano	1m 57.956s
12	Camier	1m 58.480s
13	De Rosa	1m 58.289s
14	Brookes	1m 58.437s
15	De Angelis	1m 58.518s
16	Haslam	1m 58.622s
17	Reiterberger	1m 58.633s
18	Abraham	1m 58.934s
19	Ramos	1m 58.958s
20	Al Sulaiti	1m 59.734s
21	Scassa	1m 59.792s
22	Vizziello	1m 59.968s
23	Szkopek	2m 00.876s
24	Schmitter	2m 01.624s
25	Sebestyen	2m 01.667s

Fastest race lap: Jonathan Rea on lap 3, 1m 56.974s, 102.884mph/165.575km/h (record).

Previous lap record: Tom Sykes, GBR (Kawasaki), 1m 57.317s, 102.583mph/ 165.091km/h (2015).

Points

1, Rea 498; 2, Sykes 447; 3, Davies 445; 4, Van der Mark 267; 5, Hayden 248; 6, Torres 213; 7, Giugliano 197; 8, Camier 168; 9, Forres 151; 10, Savadori 150; 11, Guintoli 141; 12, Lowes 131; 13, De Angelis 96; 14, Brookes 89; 15, Ramos 89; 16, Reiterberger 82; 17, West 64; 18, Abraham 33; 19, Canepa 30; 20, Haslam 16; 21, De Rosa 16; 22, Baiocco 12; 23, Lagrive 11; 24, Scassa 10; 25, Mahias 9; 26, Beaubier 6; 27, Schmitter 5; 28, Vizziello 4; 29, Szkopek 3; 30, Jones 2; 31, Hook 2; 32, Barrier 2; 33, Sebestyen 1; 34, Al Sulaiti 1; 35, Lussiana 1.

Photo: Gold & Goose

Position	Rider	Nationality	Machine	Phillip Island/1	Phillip Island/2	Buriram/1	Buriram/2	Aragon/1	Aragon/2	Assen/1	Assen/2	Imola/1	Imola/2	Sepang/1	Sepang/2	Donington/1	Donington/2	Misano/1	Misano/2	Lausitzring/1	Lausitzring/2	Laguna Seca/1	Laguna Seca/2	Magny-Cours/1	Magny-Cours/2	Jerez/1	Jerez/2	Losail/1	Losail/2	Total Points
1	**Jonathan Rea**	GBR	Kawasaki	25	25	25	20	20	16	25	25	20	20	20	16	16	20	25	25	25	–	–	25	13	20	16	20	20	16	**498**
2	**Tom Sykes**	GBR	Kawasaki	11	10	20	25	16	20	–	20	16	16	25	8	25	25	20	20	20	25	20	4	16	16	20	16	13	20	**447**
3	**Chaz Davies**	GBR	Ducati	20	6	13	16	25	25	20	11	25	25	16	13	–	16	13	–	–	16	25	10	25	25	25	25	25	25	**445**
4	**Michael van der Mark**	NED	Honda	16	20	16	13	–	9	–	16	9	7	9	10	8	8	16	6	13	9	10	8	20	11	11	10	7	5	**267**
5	**Nicky Hayden**	USA	Honda	7	13	–	11	10	–	16	10	7	8	8	25	11	10	–	10	16	11	16	6	–	7	13	13	11	9	**248**
6	**Jordi Torres**	ESP	BMW	8	9	8	8	9	11	11	1	13	9	13	3	9	5	11	9	8	10	13	–	2	9	8	8	8	10	**213**
7	**Davide Giugliano**	ITA	Ducati	13	16	–	6	11	10	–	8	11	13	10	20	20	9	2	16	–	20	9	–	–	–	–	3	–	–	**197**
8	**Leon Camier**	GBR	MV Agusta	9	–	5	5	–	–	13	7	10	11	6	7	13	11	8	–	5	–	11	13	9	13	9	–	–	3	**168**
9	**Xavi Fores**	ESP	Ducati	–	–	2	–	13	13	3	6	6	6	2	5	4	2	–	13	9	13	6	16	8	6	–	–	10	8	**151**
10	**Lorenzo Savadori**	ITA	Aprilia	4	–	6	7	6	5	10	13	8	5	–	2	10	13	–	11	10	–	–	–	11	10	3	6	6	4	**150**
11	**Sylvain Guintoli**	FRA	Yamaha	10	11	9	10	7	6	–	5	–	–	–	–	–	–	–	–	7	11	7	8	10	11	–	–	16	13	**141**
12	**Alex Lowes**	GBR	Yamaha	–	2	10	–	8	7	8	9	5	10	11	–	–	–	3	8	11	2	8	–	5	–	–	9	9	6	**131**
13	**Alex de Angelis**	RSM	Aprilia	–	3	7	2	5	8	4	–	1	2	–	9	–	1	4	3	7	–	4	20	6	2	5	–	3	–	**96**
14	**Joshua Brookes**	AUS	BMW	6	7	1	–	3	3	5	–	2	3	5	4	2	7	5	2	3	–	2	9	4	5	6	4	1	–	**89**
15	**Roman Ramos**	ESP	Kawasaki	5	4	4	4	4	4	7	4	–	–	3	3	7	4	1	6	3	7	3	3	4	5	2	2	–	–	**89**
16	**Markus Reiterberger**	GER	BMW	–	8	11	9	2	1	9	–	3	4	6	5	–	10	–	–	–	–	–	4	7	2	–	1	–	–	**82**
17	**Anthony West**	AUS	Kawasaki	–	–	–	–	–	–	–	–	–	–	7	11	6	4	6	5	4	7	5	–	–	–	2	7	–	–	**64**
18	**Karel Abraham**	CZE	BMW	3	5	–	1	1	2	–	2	–	–	–	–	4	7	–	–	–	1	2	4	–	–	–	1	–	–	**33**
19	**Niccolo Canepa**	ITA	Yamaha	–	–	–	–	–	–	–	–	–	–	–	–	–	–	9	7	6	8	–	–	–	–	–	–	–	–	**30**
20	**Leon Haslam**	GBR	Kawasaki	–	–	–	–	–	–	–	–	–	–	–	–	–	–	–	–	–	–	–	–	–	–	–	–	5	11	**16**
21	**Raffaele de Rosa**	ITA	BMW	–	–	–	–	–	–	–	–	–	–	–	–	–	–	–	–	–	–	–	5	–	–	–	–	4	7	**16**
22	**Matteo Baiocco**	ITA	Ducati	–	–	3	3	–	–	2	–	4	–	–	–	–	–	–	–	–	–	–	–	–	–	–	–	–	–	**12**
23	**Matthieu Lagrive**	FRA	Kawasaki	–	–	–	–	–	–	–	–	–	–	–	–	–	–	–	–	–	–	–	–	10	1	–	–	–	–	**11**
24	**Luca Scassa**	ITA	Ducati	–	–	–	–	–	–	–	–	–	–	3	–	–	–	–	–	–	–	1	5	1	–	–	–	–	–	**10**
25	**Lucas Mahias**	FRA	Kawasaki	–	–	–	–	–	–	6	3	–	–	–	–	–	–	–	–	–	–	–	–	–	–	–	–	–	–	**9**
26	**Cameron Beaubier**	USA	Yamaha	–	–	–	–	–	–	–	–	–	–	–	–	–	6	–	–	–	–	–	–	–	–	–	–	–	–	**6**
27	**Dominic Schmitter**	SUI	Kawasaki	–	–	–	–	–	–	–	–	–	1	–	1	–	–	–	–	–	3	–	–	–	–	–	–	–	–	**5**
28	**Gianluca Vizziello**	ITA	Kawasaki	–	–	–	–	–	–	–	–	–	–	–	–	–	–	–	–	–	–	3	–	–	–	–	1	–	–	**4**
29	**Pawel Szkopek**	POL	Yamaha	–	–	–	–	–	–	–	–	–	–	–	–	–	–	1	–	–	–	2	–	–	–	–	–	–	–	**3**
30	**Mike Jones**	AUS	Ducati	2	–	–	–	–	–	–	–	–	–	–	–	–	–	–	–	–	–	–	–	–	–	–	–	–	–	**2**
31	**Josh Hook**	AUS	Kawasaki	–	–	–	–	–	–	–	–	–	–	1	1	–	–	–	–	–	–	–	–	–	–	–	–	–	–	**2**
32	**Sylvain Barrier**	FRA	Kawasaki	1	1	–	–	–	–	–	–	–	–	–	–	–	–	–	–	–	–	–	–	–	–	–	–	–	–	**2**
33	**Peter Sebestyen**	HUN	Yamaha	–	–	–	–	–	–	–	–	–	–	–	–	–	–	–	–	–	–	–	–	–	–	1	–	–	–	**1**
34	**Saeed al Sulaiti**	QAT	Kawasaki	–	–	–	–	–	–	–	–	–	–	–	–	–	–	–	–	1	–	–	–	–	–	–	–	–	–	**1**
35	**Matthieu Lussiana**	FRA	BMW	–	–	–	–	–	–	1	–	–	–	–	–	–	–	–	–	–	–	–	–	–	–	–	–	–	–	**1**

WORLD SUPERSPORT REVIEW
FIVE SPICE TRAIL
By GORDON RITCHIE

Above: Donington Park take-off for Kenan Sofuoglu. He won six of 12 races, and his fifth Supersport title.

Top right: Consistent American PJ Jacobsen lays black rubber at Jerez. He claimed four podiums on his Honda, was fourth overall.

Above right: Sofuoglu's dominance enshrined his status as the most successful World Supersport rider.

Right: Randy Krummenacher won the first race, but his title challenge ran out of steam.

Photos: Gold & Goose

THE FIM Supersport World Championship came with a nice slice of history on the side in 2016. All-time records were extended in most areas.

After WorldSBK had had its tech package overhauled following Dorna's take-over a few years ago, WorldSSP came under more scrutiny for 2016. Free electronics were curtailed with the banning of launch and traction control, etc, but teams could still use homologated ECU kits.

On the sporting side, there was also a two-part Superpole, just like Superbike. And, just like WorldSBK, everybody who had not earned the right to get into Superpole 2 in free practice was eligible. In 2015, only the next best ten had the chance.

There were other limits and tweaks, and lots of small, but significant, things to keep everybody as close as they could be. But this is bike racing and what material they had, who was looking after it, and how much they could test and play with it were all hugely important still, despite any changes on the periphery of the regulations.

Hence the championship winning Kawasaki Puccetti Racing squad from 2015, and their champion rider, Kenan Sofuoglu, again looked like the target to aim for. They had tested their new WP suspension, insisted on by Sofuoglu, and had gone with it for 2016.

Their own target was the championship again, to make Sofuoglu even more of an all-time legend. Winning a fifth title would indelibly enshrine his status as an all-time great.

Competition was everywhere, however, at least on paper.

Jules Cluzel (MV Agusta Reparto Corse) was back and motivated after injury. There was no "Core" Motorsport team in 2016, but a late reprieve for Patrick 'PJ' Jacobsen (Honda World Supersport) kept him in the class, too, inside the Ten Kate garages.

Recent Moto2 runner Randy Krummenacher joined Sofuoglu as an official Kawasaki rider at Puccetti. Arguably, the most coveted seat of all.

Kyle Smith (CIA Landlord Insurance Honda) was back in the fold, while Gino Rea (GRT MV Agusta) played a three-pistoned tune in 2016, as one of many MV runners in a large field. Lorenzo Zanetti was alongside Cluzel, and even former 125GP Champion Nico Terol (Schmidt Racing MV Agusta) was on a middleweight and production-derived machine.

As it played out, over 12 rounds alongside the WorldSBK riders everywhere except America, Sofuoglu once again was masterful in his approach, execution and sheer will to win. Having done so much of it, and knowing how to win a title more than once, could only help any subsequent campaign.

At the first round in Australia, the Turk – the pole man – appeared to have it all under control, but a crash after a rear tyre failure – at a circuit that is harder on tyres than any other – sent him into a rage and opened the door for some new Supersport names.

The race was finally won by rookie Krummenacher, who could not believe his good fortune so early in his new career. One WorldSSP race and one win. Easy for an old Moto2 man like him...

For a while at least, maybe.

Second, 2.7 seconds back, was young Italian charger Federico Caricasulo (Bardahl Evan Bros. Honda). And in third, right in Caricasulo's shadow, was Anthony West (Tribeca Rac-

274 WORLD SUPERSPORT REVIEW

ing Yamaha). Now that was a podium no one would have predicted, not in that or any other order. With Sofuoglu out, Cluzel was also in the gravel. He got going again to finish 17th – no points.

West had been on a private Yamaha, funded from a number of sources, as he began an itinerant year, racing to earn money one week to ensure a better ride the next.

For round two, the series headed to Thailand, and Cluzel headed back upwards to a win in the heat. His MV was fragile at times, however, and there would be technical issues through the F3 ranks all season as the supply of spare parts dried up, but at Chang he beat Sofuoglu and Jacobsen, all three within a second.

When the series moved on to Motorland Aragon, there was a podium surprise in store. Sofuoglu had won from Krummenacher, but in third was the MV Agusta of former World 125 Champion Nico Terol. Cluzel, still limping from his old injury, was fourth.

Another race – Assen – another surprise. For a class that sometimes is ignored for being staid and samey, 2016 brought plenty of variety to the podium.

In the wet of a six-lap restarted race, both winner Smith and runner-up Rea beat up Sofuoglu in the final laps, the Turk appearing to play a kind of long game after his first-round no-score. Krummenacher was fourth, and still the points leader.

There was drama at Imola, where Krummenacher rode on with a fluid leak, but did not notice. He was prevented from restarting in a shortened 11-lap race. Sofuoglu won, Cluzel was second, Jacobsen third. The Swiss rider's main rivals were massing as the Turk took the championship lead.

At Sepang, there was more madness of a unique kind. On a resurfaced circuit, and in the wet, stand-in rider Ayrton Badovini, former Ducati factory WorldSBK rider, scored the win. On a Lorini Honda Gemar Ballons CBR that he had only been riding since Assen, the wet specialist from Italy held off Malaysian Zulfahmi Khairuddin by just 0.050 of a second, as the local crowd had something to cheer. Rea was less than a second away in third. Krummenacher was eighth and 20 seconds off.

Donington Park marked the cross-over point between the first half of the season and the second. Sofuoglu celebrated with the first of three race victories on the bounce. Jacobsen took his best result with a second place, and Krummenacher slid into the third spot. Cluzel was only eighth, having been ninth in Malaysia.

Sofuoglu won Misano, from Jacobsen and Rea. Those two riders, one from America and one from England, were enjoying their last podiums of the year, had they but known it. In fact, it would be Rea's last point score.

A gigantic and simply useless summer break ensued, from Misano on 19th June to Lausitzring on 18th September. Three months...

Those who could remember what their bikes looked like reconvened at the old WorldSBK venue of Lausitzring in Germany. It was sub-standard in surface and kerbing, and had too many walls that were too close, but it is an impressively proportioned speed bowl, complete with oversize US-style grandstand.

Sofuoglu won, but only just, as a young Finn, Niki Tuuli (Kallio Racing Yamaha) had come to pay his respects as a one-off rider, and then paid reputations no heed. Cluzel was third, and Krummenacher's chances of the title were receding fast. He was sixth and had no answer to rival Sofuoglu.

The Turkish rider had a bad answer to the question of whether he could win the title in France, because he fell from the lead and no-scored.

Krummenacher did not take the maximum benefit of this good fortune, finishing fifth, in a race that local man Cluzel won, his second of the year. In second place, again, was the pugilistic and fast Finn, Tuuli. Third place was grabbed by Badovini.

Looking to win or bust in Jerez, to ensure that Sofuog-

lu could not win the title in Spain with a whole round to go, Krummenacher ran out front, but he fell, and his rival scooped up another win – his sixth of 2016. And in the process, he took his fifth title. This was the first time that he had won a title by winning a race.

Tuuli was second again, fearless and fast, and bringing it home like a metronome. That made it three runner-up places in three races.

Third, after a last-lap fight with Jacobsen, was the British-born, but Spanish-raised, Kyle Smith. On one of his local circuits, he had found a strong podium prowess and carried it on to the next and last race under floodlights in Qatar.

He had won that race the year before, and he even managed to do it again in 2016.

Coming through the pack and locked in a fight with Sofuoglu, Smith repassed the Kawasaki rider on the final corner and won the sprint down the long Losail main straight. By 0.006 of a second.

Sofuoglu, who bizarrely had worn red leathers and ridden a red official Kawasaki in practice and Superpole, went green again for the race and came so close to win number seven of the season.

The fight after Jerez was for second overall.

After his late-season drop in confidence or form, or both, Krummenacher was only fifth in Losail. Not enough to prevent third-placed rider Cluzel from jumping over his final points tally to take second.

Five different race winners, three different winning bikes and 12 different riders on the podium – it was busy in WorldSSP during 2016.

The biggest story, however, was Sofuoglu.

The Turkish rider's achievements include 116 starts in the class, five championships (two for Honda, three for Kawasaki), 38 race wins, 78 podium places, 30 pole positions, 94 front-row starts, 27 fastest laps and 1,885 points. All are record scores in the class, except for the number of starts – Fabien Foret has 151.

In a similar fashion to Jonathan Rea in Superbike, this official Kawasaki rider also scored back-to-back wins in 2016, and was the first person to have done so for many years. Sebastien Charpentier had scored two in a row between 2005 and 2006, for Honda.

As well as the regular WorldSSP competition in 2016, there was an initiative designed to replace the old Superstock 600 European Championship. The European Supersport Cup ran to the same tech rules as WorldSSP, but was a championship within a championship for teams and riders who only competed at the European rounds.

Axel Bassani (San Carlo Team Italia Kawasaki) was the eventual winner, with 55 points to the 39 of Illia Mikhalchik (DS Junior Team Kawasaki). On occasion, Alessandro Zaccone (San Carlo Team Italia Kawasaki) was the top rider of the three, but in the final analysis he was third in ESS on 31 points.

The points in the class were allocated in relation to the number of points that were scored in the full WorldSSP class. In that ranking, Bassani was eventually 12th.

The numbers of ESS riders in the WorldSSP class were small, but they added much to the European rounds. The best individual finish was by Bassani, who was fourth in the full class results in France.

Superstock 1000 FIM Cup

A thriller all the way, the Superstock 1000 FIM Cup featured some updated models in 2016. It is well supported by manufacturers – as an effective showplace for their flagship products – and is valued by almost all of them.

The 2016 season became a man-to-man fight between eventual champion Raffaele de Rosa (Althea Racing BMW) and Leandro Mercado (Aruba.it Racing Junior Team).

The advantage waxed and waned between them, but Mercado was the stronger for the most part, until he fell and then had his bike quit on the sighting lap of the final round in Spain. He could not prevent de Rosa from collecting enough points at Jerez to seize the crown for himself. And for BMW, not Ducati.

Kevin Calia (Nuova M2 Racing Aprilia) placed third overall, but had won no races. Lucas Mahias (Pata Yamaha) started without a permanent ride, but still won two races as an injury replacement. He was fourth in the final points. The only other race winner was Spanish-based Chilean Maximilian Scheib, who took his BMW to victory in the final round at Jerez.

Above and above left: Raffaele de Rosa (35, BMW) just shaded Leandro Mercado's Ducati in the Superstock 1000 FIM Cup.

Above centre: Another fast Finn: Niki Tuuli came late to Supersport, and was at once second. Three times. Here, he leads Sofuoglu.

Top: Ayrton Badovini (86) just beat home hero Zulfhami Khairrudin (63) and Gino Rea (4) at a wet Sepang.

Top left: Kyle Smith ended the season with a win at Losail.

Left: Splitting the Kawasakis in the points, MV-mounted Jules Cluzel was second overall.

Photos: Gold & Goose

PROVING A POINT

By MICHAEL GUY

Above: Out of the shadows. Michael Dunlop bounced back from his 2015 travails to win the Superbike and Senior TTs on his BMW.
Photo: Gavan Caldwell

Right: Padgetts entered a MotoGP replica Honda RC213-VS, but Bruce Anstey's challenge was blunted by a crash in practice.
Photos: Bernd Fischer

Far right: Honda-mounted John McGuinness couldn't match the pace of BMW riders Michael Dunlop and Ian Hutchinson.
Photo: David Collister/photocycles.com

IN previous years, singling out the men most likely to do the winning at the Isle of Man TT had been reasonably straightforward, but in 2016 the event had an air of genuine unpredictability.

John McGuinness, the 23-times TT winner and the man who ultimately stole the show in 2015 with his stunning Senior TT win and lap record, was clearly a banker. Despite having turned 44 earlier in the year, he was free from injury, riding regularly and still a member of the formidable official Honda squad, which has made winning habitual on the Island since 1961, two years after its arrival in 1959.

But while McGuinness seemed a shoo-in to increase his tally of TT victories, in a bid to match his all-time hero Joey Dunlop's tally of 26 wins, the competition for top honours was intense.

Ian Hutchinson had already demonstrated just how deep his desire and passion runs by coming back from a life-threatening leg injury and close to 30 operations, to win the two Supersport races on the 37.733-mile mountain course 12 months earlier. But rather than leaving the 2015 race overjoyed at his return to the winners' enclosure, he was infuriated at being denied victory in both the Superbike and Senior races.

For 2016, the Bingley rider had switched from the PBM Kawasaki squad to the renowned Tyco BMW team. This move meant that in addition to his road racing commitments, he would also compete in the tough British Superstock championship, run alongside British Superbike events. As a result, Hutchy arrived on the Island with the confidence that only track time and race victories can bring.

In pre-TT interviews, he had no qualms in making his inten-

tions clear. His aim was simple – to repeat his incredible feat of 2010 and win five TTs in a week. And with the proven Tyco BMW Superbike and Superstock machines at his disposal, along with the immaculate Team Traction Control Yamaha R6 on which he had won both Supersport races in 2015, he was certainly well placed to turn his goals into reality.

But while Hutchinson oozed pre-race confidence, he had to contend with another rider with a point to prove – the irrepressible Michael Dunlop. Staying with the Hawk Racing BMW team for 2016, Dunlop was under no illusion of what was at stake. The 12-times TT winner had won four races in a week in 2014, and like Marc Marquez in MotoGP at that time, it was difficult to see past him as the man who would be dominating the sport for the considerable future. But in 2015, with the world at his feet, it all came crashing down – he failed to win a single TT. The man who had appeared indestructible left the Island with his tail between his legs and his one-time soaring stock value on the slide. As a result, he arrived on the Island in 2016, where the Dunlop name is synonymous with success, quietly and under the radar.

But while he wasn't in the mood for making any bold predictions of whether he could win again, his 1000-yard stare, trademark intensity and bullish nature remained intact.

Bruce Anstey is another who historically makes an unheralded arrival on the Island, but in 2016 that simply was not possible. The 2015 Superbike TT winner and his Padgett's Honda Racing squad sent shockwaves throughout the paddock after revealing that they would be parking their proven, race-winning Honda Fireblade and running a Honda RC213V-S in both the Superbike and Senior races. The

£138,000 road-going replica of the factory Repsol Honda RC213V used by Marc Marquez and Dani Pedrosa hadn't turned a wheel before reaching the Island, but it had been meticulously prepared by Clive Padgett, who'd spent hours with it on the dyno, with input from Repsol Honda's MotoGP engineers.

Signs that the rest of the paddock were rattled by the arrival of such an exotic and potentially rapid machine soon surfaced, with rumours that protests about its legality as a production bike had been raised. Nipping the problem in the bud, TT organisers made it clear that the bike was legal to race, leaving Anstey's rivals sweating on just how fast the flying Kiwi would be on the opening night of practice.

Speculation was also widespread about the first ever 133mph lap. Having set a new lap record of 132.701mph in the 2015 Senior, McGuinness remained realistic about going even faster, citing an improvement in both his Dunlop tyres and the power characteristics of his Honda Superbike. But not before reminding everyone just how hard he'd ridden to win the 2015 Senior and set the lap record.

But while McGuinness remained humble and avoided predictions, rivals Ian Hutchinson and Michael Dunlop had a glint in their eye whenever anyone mentioned breaking into the uncharted territory in a bid to become members of a new 133mph club.

Conspicuous by his absence was road-racer-turned-TV-celebrity Guy Martin. The former Tyco BMW man remains the most successful rider never to have won a TT, with 16 podiums to his name, but following his spectacular Ulster Grand Prix crash in 2015 and subsequent injuries, along with his ever increasing outside interests and TV commitments, he elected not to race. So instead of drawing the crowds and consolidating his position as one of the fastest ever riders around the TT course, instead he headed to America to compete in a tortuous 2,500-mile mountain bike race called the Tour Divide.

The first night of practice is generally a session of familiarisation, but clearly nobody told the top men. Fastest off the blocks was Tyco BMW rider Hutchinson. It wasn't that long ago that 130mph was the benchmark and the pace needed to win the Senior, but at the end of the first night, Hutchinson

had topped the time sheets with a lap nudging the magic 130 – 129.964mph.

Not to be outgunned, Michael Dunlop blasted his Hawk Racing BMW to 129.670, while traditionally measured starter John McGuinness was in third, having ridden his Honda to a lap of 128.871mph.

Anstey's RCV debut occurred under the gaze of massed fans and journalists – everyone desperate to hear the V4-powered MotoGP replica rumble along the pit lane and accelerate down Bray Hill for the first time. Despite having never ridden the bike, Anstey had unconditional faith in his long-time team boss, Clive Padgett – essentially adopting the philosophy that if Clive said it was alright, then it would be.

From a standing start, he posted an incredible 122mph lap, before upping his pace to 127mph at the end of his third lap. To the dismay of his rivals, he also set the fastest speed through the trap at 193.4mph. His lap time was good enough for fifth fastest, slotting in behind official Honda Racing rider and Manxman Connor Cummings.

If the opening night of practice had set a high bar, on the second night Hutchinson pushed the boundaries once again. His 130.626mph best put him comfortably atop the time sheets, ahead of McGuinness, after Michael Dunlop had broken down while on schedule to post a 130mph lap.

While everything appeared to be going exactly to plan for Hutchinson, on the third night of practice, his early domination came to an abrupt end. Despite going even faster and setting a 130.691mph lap, it was nowhere near enough. Dunlop laid down a stunning 131.574mph best, before announcing to the assembled media that there was "more where that came from".

Anstey suffered a high-speed crash after losing control of his Valvoline Padgetts RC213V-S at Keppel Gate. He was airlifted to Nobles Hospital, but although badly battered and bruised, he was given the all-clear to continue racing.

On the fourth evening of practice, Dunlop backed up his claim in unequivocal fashion by topping the time sheets with a lap of 132.365mph. In near-perfect conditions, both Hutchinson and McGuinness at least were able to keep the Ulsterman honest with 131mph laps.

The final night of practice felt more like the race itself in

terms of intensity, with both Hutchinson and Dunlop desperate to gain the upper hand in preparation for the opening Superbike race. In near-ideal conditions, the two went head to head, with Hutchy posting the fastest ever lap of the TT circuit at an average speed of 132.803mph. But incredibly the new benchmark was set on his Tyco BMW Superstock machine – not his Superbike. His close-to-perfect lap highlighted just how good real-world stock machines have become, and also the tyre technology, with his time set on treaded Metzeler rubber.

Hutchinson's best Superbike lap of 131.521mph was only good enough for second spot, Dunlop taking top honours with a blistering 132.754mph.

And with that, the scene was set, with the mouthwatering prospect of lap records being smashed and intense rivalry – race week was upon us. All played out in front of a record number of sun-baked spectators, who'd made their annual pilgrimage to the small, but significant island in the middle of the Irish Sea.

SUPERBIKE

After such an intense week of practice, utterly dominated by the BMWs of Dunlop and Hutchinson, it was difficult to look beyond these two men for the likely winner. Starting first, John McGuinness got the six-lap race under way, but within the opening minutes, it became about one man – Michael Dunlop.

Setting a pace that none of his rivals could come close to matching, from the moment he got the tap on the shoulder and headed down Bray Hill, Dunlop set two new sector records on his opening lap. By the time he had completed that lap, McGuinness's 2015 lap record had become a thing of the past, Dunlop claiming the accolade of the fastest ever and first sub-17-minute lap with a 133.256mph average from a standing start.

Hutchinson slotted into second. He had haemorrhaged 16 seconds to Dunlop in one lap, unable to match his rival's unfathomable commitment to push the limits with new tyres and a full tank of fuel. Then his unprecedented pace was taken to another level when, on his second lap, he posted another new lap record at 133.393mph, despite having to slow for his first pit stop.

And, unlike in 2015, when Dunlop had lost valuable time in the pits, in 2016 his team, made up of the same personnel, delivered faultless pit stops to keep his lead intact.

Having started behind Hutchinson, Dunlop caught and passed his main rival, although Hutchy returned the favour on the final lap to post his fastest ever race lap of the TT at 132.767mph. But it wasn't enough, and Dunlop won the six-lap race by a comfortable 19.064s.

Speaking about the opening lap, Dunlop said, "It was a good standing-start lap, which was a bit stronger than I thought, because I had a few issues with the front. Everyone here has got pace. I just went into it with what I've got, and if it's good enough, then that's all well and good."

Clearly disappointed at being beaten by such a big margin, Hutchinson remained philosophical, saying that he was pleased with his early pace and happy to get his first race on the BMW under his belt, but he cited the need for improvement in the pits, where he had lost valuable seconds.

John McGuinness secured third place, having benefited from a tow from Hutchinson, which allowed him to drag himself out of the grasp of Dean Harrison and Peter Hickman. "My bike was brilliant. I thought I rode pretty good, but I had no answer for Michael and Ian," he said.

Peter Hickman, competing in only his second year at the TT and racing a full-blown JG Speedfit Kawasaki Superbike for the first time, secured fourth place thanks to a stunning 132.465mph final lap. He finished ahead of Kawasaki-mounted Dean Harrison in fifth, with BMW's Michael Rutter in sixth.

SUPERSPORT – Race One

If the opening Superbike race had been all about Michael Dunlop, Ian Hutchinson hit back with a vengeance with an emphatic victory in the opening Supersport race. Riding the Team Traction Control Yamaha R6 on which he'd won in 2015, he showed his clear affinity with the smaller machine by dominating the four-lap race.

After a blistering start, the 36-year-old was leading Dunlop by a second at Glen Helen, but by the end of the opening lap, he enjoyed a six-second advantage. From there, the smooth-riding Yamaha man controlled proceedings, eventually winning by over 15 seconds.

With the podium celebrations over and attention already turning to the opening Superstock race, the TT paddock was hit by controversy when Dunlop was excluded from the Supersport results, following an inspection of his MD Racing Yamaha. TT technical inspectors excluded him for having an illegal coating on the cam buckets of his R6. The coating had been legal two years before, when the engine had been built by Mar-Train Racing, but that was no longer the case under the new-for-2016 Supersport technical regulations.

The disqualification increased the already intense rivalry between Dunlop and Hutchinson. It also meant that Dean Harrison (RC Express Racing Kawasaki) inherited the second step on the podium, while James Hillier secured another TT podium to add to his tally in third. Local man Conor Cummins was fourth, ahead of fellow Honda rider John McGuinness and Lee Johnston (Triumph).

SUPERSTOCK

Having set an almost unbelievable 132.803mph lap in the final night of practice, aboard his Superstock-spec Tyco BMW on Metzeler treaded tyres, Ian Hutchinson appeared to be the man to beat in Superstock. Fresh from his dominant Supersport race win earlier in the day, and desperate to beat main rival Dunlop in a big-bike race, he started as he meant to go on, posting an incredible 133.098mph lap from a standing start in the four-lap race.

The expected challenge from Dunlop was short lived, the Northern Irishman retiring at the end of the opening lap with a broken gear lever. He was already 16 seconds adrift of Hutchinson when he retired, giving the Tyco BMW rider a healthy early lead, which he managed comfortably to the chequered flag.

While the victory was hugely significant for Hutchinson, it also marked a huge step for his Northern Irish TAS Racing Tyco BMW team. Their previous victory at the TT had been way back in 2008, when Australian Cameron Donald had won the Superstock race on the Relentless Suzuki.

Speaking after the victory and his incredible 133mph opening lap on treaded tyres, Hutchinson said, "It's astonishing, but I did expect it. The conditions have just been getting better and better, but the problem now is that the tarmac is starting to melt. At the start, having just got off the 600, I was running a bit wide in places, and it took me until Glen Helen to get back into Superstock mode. The BMW road bike is so good as standard, and our race bike is so close, so it's unbelievable what it can do."

On the final lap, Hutchinson had broken two absolute sector records, raising the prospect of what might be possible in the Senior TT race at the end of the week, if the near-perfect weather conditions held.

Second place went to RC Express Racing's Dean Harrison, who finished 27.644s adrift of Hutchinson, while Quattro Plant Kawasaki's James Hillier was third, just 1.905 seconds behind. Their results marked a repeat of their Supersport podium achievements and established them as clearly the best of the rest in another fiercely contested race.

Michael Rutter continued his incredible racing career by finishing fourth, ahead of TT winners Gary Johnson and John McGuinness.

SUPERSPORT – Race Two

After perfect racing conditions all week, the second Supersport race was delayed due to mist on the mountain, following heavy overnight rain. A lot of the rubber had been washed off the circuit, and riders commented on the comparative lack of grip, but it was not enough to slow Ian Hutchinson, whose Supersport rampage continued.

Riding the Team Traction Control Yamaha R6, Hutchinson dominated proceedings once again to win the four-lap encounter by 17.547 seconds ahead of Dunlop. The slower track conditions showed in the lap times, with Hutchinson still the fastest man at 127.736mph, but slower than Dunlop's 128.666mph lap record.

Hutchinson's victory brought his 2016 race win tally to three. It was also his fourth consecutive Supersport TT win and eighth of his career, making him the most successful Supersport rider in history. It was another step towards cementing his name among the all-time TT greats, his tally of TT wins climbing to 14, to match the late, great Mike Hailwood.

Hutchinson said, "To be spoken about alongside Mike Hailwood is astonishing for me. I was on 13 wins and didn't want to be there too long, so I was keen to get through that race and get another win. I'm just having fun; it feels like it did in 2010, and when it's like that, it's a great place to ride around.

"Compared to the Superstock bike, it's a lot easier to ride, but you have to be so precise, pinpoint accurate with your apexes and hold massive corner speed. As a result, I get a lot of satisfaction from riding it. When you get it right, there is such a sweet spot on the 600."

Following his disqualification in the opening Supersport race for an illegal engine, Dunlop and his MD Racing team faced a battle against the clock to be ready for the second Supersport race. With no spare race engine, former racer and now team manager Robin Appleyard lent Dunlop a newly-race-prepared R6 engine, which had to be flown to the Island by private jet the night before the race. After fitting the engine, the team then worked into the daylight hours on the dyno, with Dunlop telling a packed press conference after the race that he'd been working on the bike until 4.30am, and his team had finished at 5.30am. The huge effort was rewarded with a second place, ahead of the ever improving and effervescent Dean Harrison. The podium was the RC Express Kawasaki rider's third of the week.

Fourth place went to another Kawasaki man, James Hillier, with the injured Bruce Anstey in fifth aboard his Honda, and Triumph-mounted Lee Johnston in sixth.

TT ZERO

The TT Zero race has struggled for credibility since its inauguration in 2010, and the 2016 event did little to improve the situation. With only 11 bikes entered, some of which did not even make it off the start line, there were just five finishers in the one-lapper.

But while the appetite to race in the class appears to be dwindling, Mugen – the Japanese manufacturer that has won the last three TT Zeros – appear to be taking it more seriously than ever. For 2016, they brought an all-new bike. Not content with their previous success, the stunning 2-16 model was complete with carbon chassis and an all-new billet motor, along with ever improving battery technology.

Riding the most expensive and technologically advanced bike in the TT paddock, John McGuinness was expected to be the man to beat and was bidding to increase his TT win tally to 24. Before the race, the team spoke of wanting to improve their previous best lap time of 119.279mph, with a target in the region of 122mph. But on the day, neither aim was realised, after McGuinness accidentally hit the cut-out switch with his backside on landing from a jump at Ballacrye. The race was won by his team-mate, Bruce Anstey, with a lap of 118.416mph.

A NEW NORTON AND TWO-STROKE RETURN

IT was not only the Padgetts Racing Honda RCV of Bruce Anstey that attracted the crowds at the 2016 TT. There was a new bike from Norton, ridden by Australian Dave Johnson (*right*), and the stunning Suter two-stroke campaigned by ten-times TT winner Ian Lougher.

After a number of years when they simply could not compete with their Japanese rivals, Norton took a huge step with their V4-powered SG5, Johnson setting a best lap of 130.872 in the Superbike race to finish seventh. That represented a huge increase in pace compared to Cameron Donald's fastest lap of 2015, when he set a 124.81mph best.

Lougher failed to finish the Superbike race, but claimed 34th in the Senior aboard the 576cc Suter V4 two-stroke.

LIGHTWEIGHT

The Lightweight TT was won by Ivan Lintin aboard his RC Express Kawasaki, after he fended off an early challenge from former winner James Hillier. It was Lintin's second consecutive win in the Lightweight race and the third for his team, who had won with Dean Harrison in 2014.

At the end of the opening lap, 31-year-old Lintin trailed Hillier by two seconds, but after fighting back on lap two, and benefiting from a faultless pit stop while Hillier had problems, he opened up an advantage that he never relinquished. By the end of the four-lap race, he had secured his second TT victory by 9.472 seconds.

He said, "I was in the mix from the start, which was what I wanted. Before the race, I thought it was going to be between myself, James [Hillier] and Michael [Rutter]. My guys did a great job in the pits; we knew exactly how much fuel to take on and that was where I got my gap. Coming over the mountain for the last time was a really nice ride. It was a bit midge-infested, but all good, and the bike was mint."

While Hillier was unable to repeat his Lightweight victory of 2013, he remained philosophical about finishing in second place, especially given that he was still riding the same 2012-spec bike.

"Yes, you always want to win, but second isn't too bad. That's four seconds and a win for that old girl [Kawasaki ER6], and I'm retiring her now. She's done enough.

"I've learnt a few things this week, and I wanted to try them out in the race. I honestly thought we were going faster than last year, but the times say we weren't. It was tough; Ivan picked away at me, and on the last lap he had plus ten or eleven, and you're never going to get that time back on one of these bikes round here."

The race was a TT breakthrough for Riders Kawasaki man Martin Jessopp, who took third to claim his first ever TT podium. He finished 2.384 seconds ahead of Gary Johnson, while Stefano Bonnetti aboard the Paton was fifth. Michael Rutter retired from the race on the opening lap.

SIDECAR – Races One & Two

Watching a sidecar lap the TT course is a sight to behold, and in recent years the competition between teams has led to the two races garnering ever increasing kudos and popularity.

The opening race appeared set to be another classic, but it was dealt a blow before it even started when TT legend Dave Molyneux didn't make it to the start line following a technical problem. This was compounded when 2014 winner Conrad Harrison failed to start after his passenger, Dean Kilkenny, pulled out.

That left 2015 double winners Ben and Tom Birchall to make the running, which they did in style by posting a new lap record of 116.798mph. With the win seemingly in the bag, the brothers started the final lap, only to break down at Sulby crossroads, leaving 59-year-old John Holden and passenger Andrew Winkle to win aboard their Silicone Engineering Honda. Holden's victory made him the oldest ever TT winner.

Out to make amends in the second race of the week, the Birchall brothers fought off an early challenge from Molyneux to win their fourth TT by 38.7 seconds, ahead of Holden and Winkle. Third place went to former sidecar TT winner Tim Reeves and Patrick Farrance.

SENIOR

In the days leading up to the blue-riband Senior race, tension between Hutchinson and Dunlop reached fever pitch. Not only had their on-track rivalry been intense during both practice and race week, but also it had spilled over into the paddock when they weren't even on their bikes.

Dunlop's exclusion from the opening Supersport race had

Above: After disappointment in race one, the Birchall brothers took a fighting win in the second of the sidecar races.
Photo: David Collister/photocycles.com

Left: Ivan Lintin won the Lightweight for the second year in succession.

Top left: Dave Johnson took seventh in Superbike on the improved Aprilia-based Norton.

Far left: At 59, John Holden (with passenger Andrew Winkle) became the oldest TT winner.
Photos: Bernd Fischer

Below left: Bruce Anstey won the all-electric TT Zero one-lapper after team-mate McGuinness hit the wrong button.

Below: A poignant tableau in tribute to the fallen Paul Shoesmith.
Photos: Gavan Caldwell

OBITUARIES

Rider and team manager Paul Shoesmith was killed when he crashed his Ice Valley BMW during practice. The 50-year-old had set his fastest ever lap in the Superbike race earlier in the day with a speed of 125.896mph.

Sidecar driver Dwight Beare lost his life during the opening Sidecar race. The 27-year-old crashed at Rhencullen.

Ian Bell, 2003 Sidecar race winner, died after crashing at Ballaspur in the second Sidecar race. He was 58 years old.

Andrew Soar was killed in the Senior TT when he crashed at Keppel Gate. The 32-year-old had won the Manx Grand Prix in 2014.

stunned the paddock, but it was the post-race scrutineering following the second Supersport race that became the catalyst for the real bad blood between the two riders and their teams. Hutchinson had won that race and Dunlop had been second, but a question was raised about the legality of the pistons in Hutchinson's Team Traction Control Yamaha R6, which started to spiral out of control.

The TT organisers issued a statement to confirm that no discrepancies had been identified in any of the motorcycles checked, and TT boss Paul Phillips later explained that a problem had arisen following "an inappropriate comment from a race official", which had "set something running". Although no official protest was lodged against Hutchinson, there were some very disgruntled people in the Dunlop camp, with rumours even emerging that the rider was going to boycott the Senior race in protest.

Instead, Dunlop not only showed up on the grid to race, but also brought his A-game. In the most prestigious road race there is, he stormed to his second victory of the week with an emphatic win and outright lap record.

In a repeat of his Superbike win earlier in the week, the Hawk Racing BMW rider crushed the competition from the moment he started off down Bray Hill, setting a pace on new tyres and with a full tank of fuel that his rivals simply were unable to match.

Dunlop's opening lap of 133.256mph from a standing start was enough to produce a commanding lead over his nemesis, Hutchinson. But if his first lap had set the bar high, his second of 133.962mph, while slowing down for the pits, put the result beyond doubt. At the same time, he made history with the fastest ever lap of the 37.733-mile circuit.

With two solid pit stops and unrelenting pace over the remaining four laps, Dunlop remained in control of the race, winning by 31.521 seconds.

His incredible performance slashed a massive 1m 24.256s off John McGuinness's 2013 Senior race record, and a full 18 seconds off his own record set in the Superbike race earlier in the week.

"To do a 133.9mph on the second lap slowing into the pits, I'm happy. The bike worked really well and I can't thank the team enough. Steve and Stuart Hicken put a great bike underneath me, and that made it easy for me. It's a real family effort, so it's a privilege to win for them."

Hutchinson finished second, having set his best race lap of 132.892mph. He revealed that he had run his Superstock engine in his Superbike. "I did six laps the best I could do, but at the end of the day we've been beaten."

Third place went to Honda-mounted John McGuinness,

who had nothing but admiration for his younger, and this time significantly faster, rivals.

"This is my 20th year of racing at the TT. I can remember setting off down Bray Hill on my little 250 Honda, and I never thought I'd be here at 44 years old with my 46th podium. It's been unbelievable.

"This time last year, I won the Senior, but this year it's been about Michael and Hutchy. I know how hard it is and how hard I rode out there, so for them to take 30 or 40 seconds out of me – they've done an amazing job. Michael did a 133.9 lap; no one had an answer to that. The best man won on the day."

Dean Harrison secured fourth place to add to his hat trick of podiums, albeit close to a minute behind McGuinness; Bruce Anstey was fifth aboard the RCV, and Conor Cummins was sixth.

As the final press conference of the 2016 TT drew to a close and the controversies of Wednesday's Supersport race appeared to be forgotten, Hutchinson launched into a scathing attack on Dunlop, saying, "I've done my best to congratulate Michael all week, but on Wednesday I was pretty disgusted with his behaviour. The scrutineers were suspect about something that there was nothing wrong with, and Michael's team protested us, and then he's tried to spread a rumour that we had oversized pistons."

The 14-times TT winner also went on to suggest that Dunlop had been given access to a higher-spec engine by BMW.

"The engine we had in practice week had all top end and no bottom end, so it's quite difficult to ride. The latest-spec engine that Michael has, has got both bottom end and top end. The Superstock engine has got bottom end and not top end, so I knew we'd be a little bit down on speed, but I'd be able to ride the bike how I wanted to."

But it was a claim Dunlop refused to accept, saying, "If he wants to bitch at me, that's no problem. We bought factory engines and I'd like to thank the boys in Munich. Even though BMW got rid of me, I've still got friends there and they put a good engine together. Everyone can buy my engine, the exact same thing."

Despite the bad feelings, Dunlop and Hutchinson had ruled TT 2016. Their unprecedented ability to treat the wall-lined, 37.733-mile circuit as if it were a short circuit separated them from the rest of the pack. Lap records were broken and boundaries pushed as the dream of doing a 133mph lap became a reality, and almost commonplace. Hutchy left with three more TT wins; Dunlop left with two – but those two just happened to be the Superbike and Senior, the two biggest prizes in road racing.

Above: Michael Dunlop flies his BME to his record-smashing Senior TT win.
Photo: David Collister/photocycles.com

Left: Ian Hutchinson could do nothing against his deadly rival on his Tyco BMW.
Photo: Gavan Caldwell

Right: Hutchinson was a sore loser, opining that Dunlop had been provided with superior power by BMW.
Photo: Bernd Fischer

Far right: Third in the Senior, John McGuinness lives up to his 'McPint' nickname in the beer tent.
Photo: Gavan Caldwell

OLD KING SHAKEY RULES AGAIN

By OLLIE BARSTOW

Above: Shane Byrne celebrates his fifth British Superbike title after the Brands Hatch triple-header in October.
Photo Clive Challinor Motorsport Photography

Main: 'Shakey' flies high at Cadwell, on the at-last-competitive Ducati Panigale.
Photo: Gavan Caldwell

I T had been 13 years since Shane Byrne had clinched his first British Superbike Championship title, an accolade he had replicated on more than one occasion during the intervening period, and there was a definite tinge of nostalgia to complement his record-breaking fifth trophy in 2016.

In 2003, the then 26-year-old Byrne had swept to the first of his BSB titles aboard the Paul Bird Motorsport-prepared MonsterMob Ducati 998. So it was fitting that his 'high five', again masterminded by Paul Bird's team and aboard the latest generation of Ducati's venerable twin-cylinder Superbike, the Panigale R, bore all the hallmarks of his maiden victory

While the path forged over those 13 years produced plenty of bumps, detours and hurdles along the way, with titles in 2003, 2008, 2012 and 2014, in addition to his latest success, and 77 race wins to his name, 'Shakey' is now comfortably established as the most decorated rider in British Superbike history.

At the beginning of the 2016 season, however, there was still a crown to be taken, and 2015 winner Josh Brookes had marked his long-awaited maiden BSB title by stepping up to World Superbike and taking the Milwaukee-backed Shaun Muir Racing with him.

While that might have signalled the end of an era for one of BSB's spikiest conflicts, a bevy of fresh and familiar faces was ready to forge new rivalries, headed by returnee Leon Haslam. Runner-up to Byrne in 2008, before joining him in the switch to World Superbikes, Haslam may have outlasted his countryman on the international stage, but he returned to BSB in 2016 with JG Speedfit Kawasaki to reignite a fiery battle against an old foe.

While the rider/team combination may have been familiar as PBM and Byrne entered a fifth consecutive season together, 2016 still represented a fresh challenge for both, following the switch from Kawasaki to Ducati. Indeed, past results notwithstanding, the decision to collaborate with the Italian manufacturer was not without its risks. While Byrne had swept the board in 2008 aboard the all-dominant 1098R, its successor, the Panigale R, had struggled to make a similar impression on the Superbike racing world since its modest debut in 2013. Even so, with the Be Wiser-backed team receiving full factory support, few regarded Byrne and rookie team-mate Glenn Irwin – who had stepped up from the Supersport class – as anything less than contenders.

Filling the void left by PBM's move to Ducati, GBmoto – competing under the JG Speedfit banner – stepped up to become Kawasaki's factory-backed representative in BSB. This lofty status was complemented by a formidable three-man line-up, headlined by former WorldSBK runner-up Haslam, together with experienced race winner James Ellison and fans' favourite Peter Hickman. Meanwhile, Quattro Plant, WD-40 and newcomers FS-3 Racing reinforced the healthy ZX-10R contingent with bikes for Luke Mossey, Jack Kennedy and Billy McConnell.

With its title-winning collaborators SMR having defected to World Superbikes, Yamaha's factory effort found an intriguing new home with ex-champion-turned-team owner Tommy Hill and his burgeoning TH Motorsport ePayMe outfit. Four years on from their iconic title showdown, Hill had enlisted former on-track sparring partner John Hopkins to lead Yamaha's defence, alongside experienced race winner Stuart Easton.

Above: Leon Haslam was back in the series on the JG Speedfit Kawasaki; he ran Byrne close to the end.
Photo: Clive Challinor Motorsport Photography

Top left: Michael Laverty is shadowed by Tyco BMW team-mate Christian Iddon at Assen.
Photo: BMW Press Club

Above left: Peter Hickman scored two wins on the PBM Kawasaki, and took the Superbike Riders' Cup for riders outside the Showdown top six.
Photo: Clive Challinor Motorsport Photography

Right: Former champion Ryuichi Kyonari started the year on the Halsall/ Bennetts Suzuki, but he did not see it through.
Photo: BMW Press Club

Anvil Hire TAG Racing bolstered the R1 ranks with entries for James Rispoli and Shaun Winfield.

Still seeking its first BSB title, BMW came into 2016 boasting an impressive blend of quality and quantity, Tyco having signed 2015 Suzuki standout Christian Iddon to join Michael Laverty, while Buildbase – runner-up in 2014 – entrusted its efforts to Richard Cooper and Lee Jackson. Elsewhere, RAF Reserves welcomed former Showdown contender Alistair Seeley back to BSB, while Smiths Racing began its campaign with Jakub Smrz and Howie Mainwaring-Smart.

Honda, meanwhile, retained its line-up of Dan Linfoot and Jason O'Halloran, the Australian back to full fitness after his 2015 campaign had been scuppered by injury, while Suzuki had lured three-times champion Ryuichi Kiyonari and race winner Tommy Bridewell for its Bennetts-backed bid on the GSX-R1000.

With 26 races over 12 rounds once more outlining the twists and turns of a path towards title glory, Silverstone raised the curtain on the 2016 season, the 'home of British motorsport' playing host to a 26-strong grid brimming with potential race winners. Seven of those riders would go on to taste the winner's champagne over the course of the year, while 13 would take a trip to the podium.

The season began exactly where it had finished in 2015, Laverty marking the start of his title bid with a dominant lights-to-flag victory in race one.

Peter Hickman was a popular winner on his JG Speedfit debut in race two, having prevailed in an entertaining dice with Byrne that had gone all the way to the line, the Kawasaki rider nudging ahead at the flag to win by 0.099s.

Above: Jason O'Halloran took a maiden win on the ageing Honda Fireblade and made the Showdown.

Top right: Christian Iddon jumps for joy after taking his first podium at Silverstone.
Photos: Clive Challinor Motorsport Photography

Above right: Buildbase BMW rider Richard Cooper took a fine wet win at the Oulton Park season opener.
Photo: BMW Press Club

Right: Luke Mossey leads the pack at Brands Hatch. The Quattro Plant Tec-care Kawasaki rider impressed all year, and secured a Showdown place ahead of more fancied runners.
Photo: Clive Challinor Motorsport Photography

Regardless, a brace of second-place finishes marked an encouraging return for Byrne and Be Wiser PBM on its first weekend with the Panigale R, while Iddon completed the podium in both races, his first ever trips to the rostrum.

That was a milestone the Tyco BMW rider built on during round two at Cheshire's Oulton Park, where he went one better each time with a pair of seconds.

It could have been a pair of wins, but Iddon had fallen just short of relieving Haslam of a grandstand BSB victory in race one, the Superbike veteran rolling back the years by succeeding in only his third race back. It had looked to be heading the way of Honda's Linfoot after he had clawed his way to the front in tricky damp-to-dry conditions. With a potential maiden BSB win little more than two laps away, however, a high-side exiting the Hislop chicane had put him out of the race, opening the door for Haslam to lead Iddon and Ellison to the chequered flag.

Similarly greasy conditions greeted the riders for race two, which came down to an all-BMW battle between Richard Cooper and Iddon. Buildbase man Cooper took control of the race in the early stages, but he was reeled in and passed during the latter drying laps. Then, Iddon's leery exit from the final Old Hall bend allowed Cooper to snatch his first ever BSB win at the line.

Nevertheless, Iddon still left round two with a surprise early lead in the championship standings, from Byrne, Laverty and Haslam. The last named had completed the podium in the second race to begin his push towards the top end of the leaderboard.

Round three and the short sprint around the Brands Hatch Indy Circuit presented a clearer narrative of the season's script. Haslam and Byrne topped the podium, a sight that

would become all too familiar over the coming rounds ahead of the Title Showdown.

Haslam's victory in race one had all the hallmarks of his racing experience as he went from third to first on the final lap, passing Bridewell at Paddock Hill Bend, before mugging team-mate Ellison out of the final corner and on the drag to the finish line, inching ahead by 0.057s.

Byrne's race-two win proved similarly hard fought. He had steadily picked his way through the order to snatch the lead off Cooper – eyeing his second win in three races – on the penultimate lap. It was Ducati's first BSB win since 2010.

With a win apiece, Haslam and Byrne headed the standings, a position they would lock out to the end of the season in what was fast becoming a two-horse race for the title.

The journey northwards for round four at Knockhill offered more of the same. Haslam and Byrne took a victory apiece to eke out their advantage still further.

Haslam's win came after an entertaining duel with a gutsy Linfoot, the pair swapping the lead several times before the more experienced rider prevailed with some canny defence in the closing laps. By contrast, a rare fall for Byrne at the hairpin, after his first pole position of the year, consigned him to an unusual DNF, but the 39-year-old simply turned it around with a superb charge from 11th to first in a torrid race two, scything through the leaders before seeing off the threat from fellow podium finishers Ellison and Linfoot.

Round five, at Snetterton, produced the second maiden race winner of the season in O'Halloran, the Australian breaking his duck a year on from stepping on the podium for the first time at the same event. It was a red-letter day for Honda, as O'Halloran and Linfoot notched up the Japanese firm's first BSB 1-2 since 2011. It could just as easily have

gone the other way, after Linfoot scuppered his hopes of a first win by getting out of shape exiting the final corner, allowing his team-mate to pounce on the run to the finish line.

Nevertheless, with Linfoot and O'Halloran complementing their race-one success with top-five results in race two, they left Norfolk in the Title Showdown reckoning.

Byrne, meanwhile, fought back to third after an off while disputing the lead with Linfoot and O'Halloran in race one had sent him across the grass at Brundle. He made amends in the truncated second race by being in the right place at the right time when red flags were deployed following a crash by Jenny Tinmouth, which resulted in an oil spill. Linfoot and Laverty completed the podium.

Haslam, riding at Snetterton for the first time since it had been reconfigured in 2011, was down the order with a fifth and sixth, and Byrne edged ahead of his main rival. Indeed, they had put enough daylight between themselves and their rivals at the top of the table to all but certify their claims to two of the Showdown spots, so attention turned towards the increasingly competitive battle for the remaining four.

O'Halloran's first win and Linfoot's four straight podiums had helped them stake their claims, while Iddon and Cooper held on to the final two positions, albeit with race winners Hickman and Laverty, as well as the painstakingly consistent Ellison, still very much in contention.

It was on to the fast, open stretches of Thruxton for round six, where Laverty would find his form again on the S1000RR, his podium at Snetterton presaging an almost perfect weekend, as he notched up a second place and a win around the fearsome Hampshire 'speedway'.

The former MotoGP rider took the fight to pole-sitter Byrne in the first race, helped in part by a red flag that allowed him a renewed shot at challenging his Ducati rival, though it would be the multiple champion who would come out on top. Race two, however, was Laverty's to lose, after Byrne dropped out with technical issues, which helped the BMW man to clinch a second win of the year from the on-form O'Halloran and rookie Irwin, making up for his team-mate's exit on the sister Panigale R.

Irwin was just the latest in a line of 'new' names that caught the eye amid more experienced rivals during the first half of the season, with race winner O'Halloran, the consistent Jackson and Mossey – a two-times pole-sitter and podium winner at Brands Hatch and Thruxton – among the standouts from the competitive opening six events.

By contrast, the 2016 season had been something of a reality check for some of the more seasoned contenders

Far from picking up where it had left off from its 2015 title exploits, Yamaha, in its new collaboration with Tommy Hill's team, struggled for both pace and reliability. Though Hopkins managed an against-form fourth at Knockhill, injury – an all too familiar tale for the risk-taking American –hampered development even before Easton quit the team altogether after Thruxton, to be replaced by ex-WorldSBK rider Broc Parkes.

Elsewhere, just two years on from very nearly clinching the title in 2014, Kiyonari once more was struggling to find his form on the Bennetts Suzuki. The Japanese rider – a three-times champion and 50-times race winner at BSB level – notched up a few anonymous top-ten results before leaving the Halsall Racing team after Thruxton.

With just two rounds and seven races remaining until the shift towards the all-important Title Showdown, there would be no let-up in the increasingly intense battle between Byrne and Haslam. Now only fate could intervene to prevent them from making it through the three-event shootout, but with scant margins between them, the focus for the duo was on accumulating podium credits.

With this in mind, Byrne thus far had gained the edge with his four race wins to Haslam's three, accumulating 27 podium credits compared to his rival's 17. It was a margin that he would widen further upon the return to Brands Hatch with a comprehensive double win, which affirmed his status as the colloquially titled 'King of Brands'. They were hard-fought successes, too, with poor starts from the front row in each race sucking him into the pack before he made his meticulous progress back into contention. Haslam had to make do with a brace of seconds.

Joining them on the podium was Mossey in race one,

the Quattro Plant Kawasaki rider having demonstrated his own affinity with Brands Hatch, not to mention his burgeoning Title Showdown credentials, by starting both races from pole position, as he had done earlier in the year. O'Halloran inched closer to his top-six spot with a third podium in three rounds in race two.

With a win and a second place apiece keeping honours and margins even between Byrne and Haslam at Cadwell Park, the Kawasaki rider hit back at his main rival in spectacular style at Oulton Park, clinching a rare trio of wins at the pivotal triple-header.

By contrast, Byrne suffered an unusually error-strewn weekend, failing to reach the podium. It meant that, once podium credits had been taken into account, Haslam led into the Title Showdown, by a meagre three points.

However, the remaining Showdown positions proved the bigger talking point at Oulton Park. While O'Halloran was comfortably clear in third place, with just 27 points covering seven riders and only three spots up for grabs, competition was fierce.

With Iddon – who hadn't managed another top-five result since his round-two peak – and the more inconsistent Cooper and Hickman fading out of contention, podiums for Ellison and Linfoot at Oulton Park pushed them past the threshold to book their Showdown places for a second season in a row.

That left Mossey and Laverty to contest the sixth and final spot, and remarkably it was the more experienced rider who cracked under pressure. Laverty's crash in race two and Mossey's hard-fought second place in race three took him past the former MotoGP rider and into the Showdown for the first time.

Donington Park, Assen and Brands Hatch set the stage for the annual run to the British Superbike title, and when the points were equalised and the podium credits tallied, it was Haslam who led from Byrne by 546 points to 543, followed by O'Halloran and Ellison tied on 513, with Linfoot and Mossey starting on 511 and 506 respectively.

Keen to maintain the momentum of his Oulton Park whitewash, Haslam duly took pole at his home circuit, only

Above: Halsall/Bennetts Suzuki rider Tommy Bridewell had to compete with an ageing machine, but scored podium finishes nonetheless.

Top: John Hopkins rode a Yamaha, but a big crash at Knockhill spoiled his season.

Top right: Irishman Glen Irwin had a strong rookie season alongside Ducati team-mate Byrne.

Photos: Clive Challinor Motorsport Photography

to meet stern competition from Byrne and his JG Speedfit team-mate, Ellison. With the trio swapping positions – and occasionally paint, it was Byrne who eventually broke away to deny Haslam and retake the championship lead.

Race two featured more of the same aggressive manoeuvring, the trio almost tripping over one another at one stage. Just as Byrne and Haslam began to break away, however, the latter suffered a major blow to his title hopes amid a shower of gravel, after slipping off at Redgate.

With the pressure off, Byrne kept his nose clean to reel off his ninth win of the year. Thus the Ducati man headed to the penultimate round of the season – at the iconic Assen TT Circuit in the Netherlands – armed with a comfortable 27-point lead.

A venue synonymous with close thrilling competition, the 'Cathedral' lived up to its reputation with two typically breathless races. Nevertheless, for all of the passing manoeuvres and some plucky performances from all six Title Showdown contenders, it was Byrne and Haslam who once again rose to the fore. On this occasion, though, Haslam had the edge, getting the run out of the final corner in race one to win by a remarkable 0.01s!

Race two proved rather more comfortable for the Kawasaki rider, who broke away out front as Byrne battled in the midfield, sealing a crucial double win. Even so, Byrne had clawed his way back to second place to limit the damage to his overall lead, which meant he'd take a 17-point cushion into the triple-header finale at Brands Hatch.

The margin might have appeared comfortable on paper, but with a maximum of 75 points on offer, a single slip was all it would have taken to produce serious consequences. With a dank autumn day adding a curve ball with a wet and shortened 15-lap first race of the weekend, the stakes were even higher.

It was Haslam who literally slipped under the pressure, high-siding out of a slick Druids on the opening lap of the restart, which put him out of the race and all but left his title aspirations in tatters. He had looked well placed to make inroads on Byrne's advantage as the championship leader played it safe in tricky surroundings, but with his main rival out, Shakey settled for taking the chequered flag in sixth.

The modest result meant that Byrne needed a mere handful of points from either of the final two races of the weekend to seal the title. He didn't need asking twice, keeping Haslam directly in sight from start to finish in race two, the pair crossing the line fifth and sixth to ensure title confirmation with a race in hand.

It was a fitting end to a hard-fought, gutsy, yet clean fight between two of BSB's most respected protagonists. Byrne's fifth title marked a welcome return to the top step for Ducati, ten years after the same rider had delivered its last championship trophy.

With neither Byrne nor Haslam topping the podium at Brands Hatch, it was the JG Speedfit team who signed off both the 2016 season and GBmoto's involvement in BSB in style. Hickman won his second race of the season in the damp opening encounter, while Ellison finally cracked his season duck by clinching wins in races two and three.

This late-season charge rewarded Ellison with third in the standings, the Brands Hatch double raising his 2016 podium tally to eight and allowing him to leapfrog Linfoot who, in turn, had showed well in the final three rounds to get the better of Honda Racing team-mate O'Halloran in fifth. Mossey, meanwhile, demonstrated consistency on his Showdown debut to confirm his breakthrough sixth overall for the Quattro Plant team.

Bookending his season with wins, Hickman clinched the BSB Riders' Cup as the highest-scoring non-Showdown contender, compounding a frustrating season for eighth-placed Laverty, who, having been bumped out of the Showdown spots at the very last moment, saw his form dip in the concluding races. By contrast, his team-mate, Iddon, had a better end to the year, returning to the podium at Brands Hatch to secure ninth overall, ahead of race winner Cooper in tenth.

Outside the top ten, Bridewell upheld Suzuki honours in 11th, ahead of the season's top rookie, Irwin, Jackson on the second of the Buildbase BMWs and Hopkins. The American gave the embattled ePayMe Yamaha team something to smile about, heading into the off-season with a pair of podiums from the final round.

MCE BRITISH SUPERBIKES
2017 SEASON LISTINGS

31 MARCH - 2 APRIL	DONINGTON PARK
15 - 17 APRIL	BRANDS HATCH INDY*
29 APRIL - 1 MAY	OULTON PARK*
16 - 18 JUNE	KNOCKHILL
30 JUNE - 2 JULY	SNETTERTON 300
21 - 23 JULY	BRANDS HATCH GP
4 - 6 AUGUST	THRUXTON
18 - 20 AUGUST	CADWELL PARK
8 - 10 SEPTEMBER	SILVERSTONE GP
15 - 17 SEPTEMBER	OULTON PARK
29 SEPT - 1 OCT	ASSEN
13 - 15 OCTOBER	BRANDS HATCH GP

FOR TICKET SALES:

BRITISHSUPERBIKE.COM

 /BRITISHSUPERBIKE  @OFFICIALBSB  @OFFICIALBSB

*DENOTES BANK HOLIDAY WEEKEND
PLEASE NOTE ALL DATES ARE PROVISIONAL AND SUBJECT TO CHANGE

Above: Tarran Mackenzie took the Kawasaki ZX-6R to his first national title.

Top right: James Westmoreland (Yamaha) was a favourite, and Mackenzie's closest rival.

Above right: All in the family: the Mackenzies celebrate Tarran and Taylor's double titles.

Above far right: Andy Reid was a strong contender, with a double at Thruxton, but injury at Oulton Park ended his challenge.

Right: Bradley Ray leads the Supersport pack at Oulton Park. A strong late-season run put him third overall.

Photos: Clive Challinor Motorsport Photography

Dickies British Supersport Championship

TALENTED though he had shown himself to be in the junior categories, it would have taken a bold person to predict Tarran Mackenzie to be 2016's title winner in the hard-fought Dickies British Supersport Championship – except perhaps his former British Superbike Championship-winning father, Niall Mackenzie.

It was a proud year for one of the BSB's most decorated riders and his family. Not only was Tarran a surprise Supersport winner, but also his older brother, Taylor, won the similarly competitive Superstock 1000 class

Riding the Stauff Connect Academy Kawasaki ZX-6R prepared by GR Motorsport, Mackenzie overcame a stuttering start to the year to engineer a marvellous run of mid-season form that took him all the way to the top of the standings, belying the greater experience of his rivals. He sealed the title in style in the final round.

On paper at least, Mackenzie – better known as 'Taz' – might not have been regarded as a standout title challenger, not least because he had progressed to the category with the two riders who had beaten him into third place in 2015's Superstock 600 series, Mason Law and Ben Currie.

The smart money was going towards experienced former British Superbike Title Showdown contender and Supersport race winner James Westmoreland, who had returned to the intermediate series on the Traction Control Racing-prepared CAME BPT Yamaha, as well as 2015 standout Andy Reid on the Quattro Plant Kawasaki.

Reid signalled his intentions early, with victory at Brands Hatch, a feat he would replicate next time out at Oulton Park, establishing an early overall lead; while Westmoreland quickly found his form on 600cc machinery with two trips to the podium before getting back to winning ways in round three at Brands Hatch.

Mackenzie, meanwhile, endured an indifferent start to his campaign: a podium at the season opener followed immediately by three DNFs.

After returning to the podium at Brands Hatch, however, Mackenzie was soon celebrating his first British Supersport win at Knockhill. It was a breakthrough success that triggered a devastating run of form, with three wins and three

podiums from the next seven races, which lifted him all the way to the top of the leaderboard.

Even so, it remained close, with Westmoreland's consistency making up for his relative lack of race-winning silverware. The Yamaha rider even nosed ahead after round 16 (of 24) with a stronger weekend at Cadwell Park; while Reid remained in the hunt thanks to a double victory at Thruxton.

Unfortunately for Reid, a crash at Oulton Park left him nursing a broken wrist, and that truncated his campaign, reducing the title battle to a two-horse race.

With honours almost even, and three events and six races remaining, Mackenzie would edge ahead of Westmoreland over the final rounds. Better finishes in four of five races earned him a comfortable 21-point cushion heading into the final. He concluded his year in style with a fifth win and 15th podium at Brands Hatch. He was crowned British Supersport champion at his first attempt.

With Westmoreland second, Bradley Ray completed the top three, having been spurred on by an incredible run of form in the second half of the season on the FAB Yamaha. The former British Motostar champion had struggled initially on his Supersport debut, but after picking up his first victory at Cadwell Park, he went on to win six of the final ten races, which lifted him into the overall top three.

One of the year's unexpected standouts, EHA Yamaha's David Allingham, was rewarded for his ten top-five results with fourth overall, ahead of two-times race winner Law on the Gearlink Kawasaki. Luke Jones, Joe Francis and Ben Currie each stepped atop the podium in 2016 en route to sixth, seventh and eighth respectively, ahead of the unfortunate Reid and Andrew Irwin in tenth.

Pirelli National Superstock 1000 Championship

Following on from Tarran's success in the Supersport class, big brother Taylor made it double title joy for the Mackenzie family with an impressive run in the hotly-contested Pirelli National Superstock 1000 Championship.

The 23-year-old Mackenzie enjoyed a turnaround in fortune after a difficult rookie campaign in the Superbike class in 2015, having come out fighting aboard the Buildbase BMW S1000RR. He took three wins from the opening four

Above: Superstock 600 Champion
Jordan Weaving beat fellow Kawasaki
rider Carl Phillips by 13 points.

Above right: Eleven wins took Aaron
Wright to top honours in the one-
make KTM Junior Cup.

Right: Fourteen-year-old Charlie Nesbitt (KTM) dominated the Motostar
Championship with 16 wins.

Photos: Clive Challinor Motorsport Photography

races, establishing a championship lead he would retain all the way to the end.

With three more wins from the total of 12 races, Mackenzie ended the season comfortably clear of an accomplished field, not least runner-up Ian Hutchinson. The Isle of Man TT legend supplemented his continued success on the roads with a fine short-circuit performance on the Tyco BMW.

Wins at Snetterton and Cadwell Park were among Hutchinson's nine visits to the podium, and he might have mounted a stronger challenge had he not been forced to miss the season opener due to clashing road-racing commitments, or crashed while dicing with Mackenzie at Oulton Park.

Returning to the class he had won in 2012, Keith Farmer finished third overall, thanks in part to wins at Oulton Park and Knockhill on the Quay Garage Honda. He was only 17 points behind Hutchinson.

Having made his BSB debut in the year title-winner Mackenzie had been born, Michael Rutter nonetheless proved more than capable of keeping up with his younger rivals with a run to fourth overall, topped by a popular victory at the Brands Hatch finale aboard the Bathams BMW.

Looking to achieve the unprecedented by defending his Superstock 1000 title after moving from Morello Kawasaki to the factory Tyco BMW team, 2015 champion Josh Elliot would fall short of matching his dominant performance of a year before. He was still a race winner, at Oulton Park, on his way to fifth overall.

Fraser Rogers, Adam Jenkinson and Hudson Kennaugh followed in sixth, seventh and eighth, the only other riders in the field to step on the podium in 2016.

Above: Supersport Champion Taylor Mackenzie leads veteran Michael Rutter and TT star Ian Hutchinson at Brands Hatch.
Photo: BMW Press Club

Right: Ricky Stevens and Ryan Charlwood narrowly fended off the Tim Reeves/Gregory Cluze pair in the sidecar series.

Below: Leon Morris lifted the Ducati TriOptions Cup from Sam Neary and Rob Guiver at the final round.
Photos: Clive Challinor Motorsport Photography

Pirelli National Superstock 600 Championship

Jordan Weaving was crowned Pirelli National Superstock 600 champion after overhauling Carl Phillips in an exciting two-way fight for the title in the second half of the season.

Two wins and two second places for Sandown Kawasaki's Phillips allowed him to establish an initial advantage early in the year, but Weaving turned it around on the NMT No Limits Kawasaki. Four victories from the final six races assured title success at the final round by just 13 points.

In a 12-race season with six different winners, Keenan Armstrong and Bradley Jones followed up in third and fourth overall, ahead of Lewis Rollo and Davey Todd, each riding Kawasaki's venerable ZX-6R stock bike.

HEL Performance British Motostar Championship

With an extraordinary 16 wins from 22 races, Charlie Nesbitt emerged as the clear champion in the HEL Performance British Motostar Championship, having seen off a sizeable field of upcoming talent to dominate from start to finish.

Nesbitt was spurred on by a mid-season charge of 11 consecutive wins, and only twice did he complete a race behind another rider over the course of the year on the e3 Motorsport/Redline KTM.

Jake Archer clinched the runner-up spot with one win and 12 podiums, ahead of Daniel Saez in third, who had victories at Silverstone and Assen. Edward Rendell, Tom Booth-Amos and Taz Taylor each enjoyed a moment at the top of the podium over the course of the season. Dan Jones was a clear champion in the 'Standard' class, with 16 victories.

Ducati TriOptions Cup

The 2016 Ducati TriOptions Cup came down to a thrilling three-way showdown, with Leon Morris snatching the title from Rob Guiver at the very final round. With eight wins to his name, Guiver came into the concluding round at Brands Hatch with a slim advantage over Morris, whose four wins had been tempered by greater overall consistency; and Sam Neary, who had closed significant ground with an impressive run in the second half of the season.

With Guiver having struggled for form when it mattered, a brace of seconds at Brands Hatch allowed Morris – runner-up in 2015 – to usurp his rival and clinch an elusive title. Neary's pair of wins at Brands Hatch elevated him to second, just five points behind Morris, while Guiver ended the year third, despite claiming more wins than his rivals.

Santander Consumer Finance KTM British Junior Cup

Aaron Wright emerged as a clear winner in the competitive Santander Consumer Finance KTM British Junior Cup for 13–18-year-olds. In 20 races, Wright topped the podium on 11 occasions aboard the standard KTM RC 390 to defeat Taylor Fox Moreton, Scott Swann and Jack Nixon.

Hyundai Heavy Industries British Sidecar Championship

Headlined by the debut of British Superbike legend Chris Walker, the Hyundai Heavy Industries British Sidecar Championship proved a favourite among fans in 2016.

Ricky Stevens and Ryan Charlwood emerged as the 2016 title winners for Quattro Plant Kawasaki, their season-long blend of speed and consistency just enough to resist Tim Reeves and Gregory Cluze, whose six wins in the final six races almost allowed them to snatch the trophy.

Walker, alongside Ashley Hawes, picked up nine podiums en route to fourth overall.

FIVE UP FOR PEKKA

By JOHN McKENZIE

IN the last year of the brutal 1000cc engines in the Sidecar World Championship, there were yet more packed grids and ever-close racing involving three world champions – Pekka Paivarinta, Tim Reeves and Bennie Streuer; five proven race winners, including Seb Delannoy and Markus Schlosser; and three engines (BMW, Suzuki and Yamaha), all disputing the nine-race series at six venues. The fight once again went down to the last round.

For his title defence, 2015 Champion Streuer stuck with Suzuki GSXR power in a new LCR chassis; Paivarinta went into his second season using a BMW S1000RR; while Reeves went for Yamaha, completing the set by having used all four Japanese engines.

Round 1 – Le Mans, France

In a desperately damp weekend in France, home-crowd favourites Seb Delannoy and Kevin Rousseau grabbed pole during the one frustratingly brief dry period, but they couldn't use their advantage in a miserably wet and cold race.

Five times world champion Tim Reeves and passenger Greg Cluze were first away with their Remse Racing Yamaha-powered LCR, and they had the benefit of a clear view ahead. Behind them, the spray thrown up by the field made vision utterly impossible, and the race had to be red-flagged after just two laps.

It was decided to restart for 12 laps, and once again it was Reeves who made the decisive move, followed closely by Swiss veteran Markus Schlosser and passenger Thomas Hofer. Two laps in, and Andy Peach, who'd fought through to second, spun out, flipping his machine, thankfully without injury.

That gave second place to Paivarinta, with Schlosser in third. A lap later, Mike Roscher had had enough and pitted, having decided it was simply too dangerous to continue. Delannoy's hopes of a home win were dashed when he too spun out, but he was able to rejoin.

Reeves, Paivarinta and Schlosser then spread out, allowing plenty of safe space, and raced home without further incident or challenge. All crews were relieved to get through a tough outing, put points on the board and get out of the hideous weather.

Paivarinta's passenger Kirsi Kainulainen's fingers were so numb with cold that she couldn't undo her helmet or take off her gloves. Schlosser, nursing a leg injury, was happy with third after a weekend of engine problems with Hofer Racing.

Visibility problems held defending champions Streuer and Koerts back in eighth.

Round 2 – Rijeka, Croatia

The two-month gap until round two was sufficient for the teams to dry out. It was the first 50-point weekend of the season. Much to be gained, and much possibly to be lost. But it was sunny.

The ten-lap Sprint race was led away by Markus Schlosser, closely attended by Reeves, who was forced to pit at the end of lap two to reattach an exhaust. That left Schlosser to race home alone and record a second world championship win, some nine years after his first. Seb Delannoy and Kevin Rousseau were second with their LCR Suzuki, while Paivarinta took a useful third.

In Sunday's 18-lap Gold race, Schlosser, Reeves and Paivarinta barrelled into the first corner, before Reeves and the Finnish pair got past and tried to open a gap. But four laps in, the red flags stopped the race after Tomas Axelsson crashed.

When the second leg of 14 laps was started, Schlosser shot away, but, challenged hard by Paivarinta, he relinquished the lead.

Behind them, Reeves couldn't prevent John Holden and Stuart Ramsey from taking third.

With seven laps to go, Paivarinta was still in control, but he couldn't shake off Schlosser, who managed to force past for his second win in 24 hours,

with Delannoy taking the final rostrum place. Two wins for the revitalised Swiss veteran, who had cut his racing teeth in the two-stroke era, pushed him to a ten-point lead over Paivarinta. Reeves's weekend-long problems and the meagre haul of 14 points from a possible 50 would cost him dear.

Round 3 – Pannonia-Ring, Hungary

A week on, and the circus moved to Hungary for another double scoring round.

In Saturday's ten-lap opening Sprint race, run in 35-degree heat, the BMW LCR of Pekka Paivarinta was first away, jostled by Reeves and Delannoy (on his first visit to the 4.74km circuit), with Schlosser, buoyed by his Croatian success. Reeves managed to force through to the lead before his airbox came adrift, causing him to slow almost to a stop. A frantic repair was in vain, the motor giving out with two laps remaining.

Meanwhile, Schlosser's hope of a hat trick of wins was foiled by fuelling problems with a lap to go.

At the front, Paivarinta and Kirsi Kainulainen struggled to keep Delannoy at bay, but they managed to do enough to win by 0.277 of a second to ride into the record books. It was the first time ever that a woman had taken a win in a world championship road race.

The 31-year-old former solo racer was ecstatic: "I am so pleased. I wanted to stand on the top spot at least once this year, and it has happened. And maybe I can do it again. Pekka has helped me so much. Let's see what happens tomorrow in the Gold race."

Third place went to Holden.

Streuer's hopes of getting some momentum back into his title defence were dashed by a broken chain while challenging in the leading group.

With temperatures reduced slightly for the 15-lap Gold race on Sunday, Delannoy grabbed the initiative, with Paivarinta, and Reeves hard at them, the last having endured a late-night engine rebuild. Into lap

Above: Markus Schlosser and Thomas Hofer lead Tim Reeves and Gregory Cluze. Schlosser took four wins after nine dry years.

Left: Pekka Paivarinta and Kirsi Kainulainen after their win in Hungary.

Far left: The 2016 champions in action.

Photos: Mark Walters

two, and Reeves and Paivarinta were past Delannoy and pulling a slight lead over the Frenchman. Reeves was setting a hard pace at the front, but with five laps to go, the red flags came out following Holden's unplanned exit, thankfully without serious injury.

That gave Reeves a much-needed win, but he faced an uphill battle in the title race. Paivarinta's second place was enough to lift him a useful 18 points clear at the halfway stage of the season, while Delannoy's consistency gave him third place and second in the rankings.

Kirsi Kainulainen was still on cloud nine: "This weekend was the most emotional one of my whole motor sport career. I can't get this feeling anywhere else than from motor sport."

Fourth place for Markus Schlosser was some consolation for the previous non-finish, and it kept him in third place overall.

Round 4 – Assen, Netherlands

In 2015, Bennie Streuer was the memorable winner at Assen on his way to lifting the title. So far his season had stuttered, with a best of fourth in Croatia, and he was sixth overall. He desperately needed a good showing on his home circuit. However, it was the vastly experienced Reeves who pipped him for pole for the 17-lap race.

The frantic first-corner sprint was won by Schlosser, but Reeves was not having it and scythed through going into the Strubben corner. Paivarinta and Streuer made up the leading quartet.

Reeves had the fast pace under control, and after eight laps he started to gain some space. But with three laps to go, he came under threat. Paivarinta had clawed back the advantage and on the final lap moved alongside Reeves, both outfits hurtling into the chicane. In an incredible finish, Reeves just held the better line and outdragged the Finn to win by 0.054 of a second.

Paivarinta's 20 points extended his title lead to 26 over third-place finisher Markus Schlosser.

Streuer came home a downbeat fourth. "I don't know, our tyre was no good again, our lap times are slower, but the other teams are slower, too, this year. The podium would have been great, but it was not to be," he said.

Round 5 – Oschersleben, Germany

With two races over the weekend at the 3.667km circuit, the championship options for Paivarinta, Schlosser, Delannoy and Reeves would be quite clear come Sunday evening. Streuer's title hopes were long gone, and to further dampen his mood, passenger Geert Koerts had been injured in a domestic race, which put him out for the rest of the season. Gerard Daalhuizen stood in for him.

Schlosser took pole and led away in the 12-lap Sprint race, holding off Reeves and Paivarinta until the race was red-flagged following an incident involving John Smits and Jeffrey Verhagen.

Nine laps were planned to complete the race, and again Schlosser sprinted away. Holding his nerve, he kept Reeves at bay to take the flag and his fourth race win, posting the fastest lap at 1m 31.298s.

Schlosser's win cut third-placed Paivarinta's points lead to just 17.

Sunday dawned dry and even hotter for the Gold race, and once again it was Schlosser who got the jump. Nineteen laps of effort looked like delivering him first to the flag, but cruelly, with one tour remaining, electrical gremlins struck and at a stroke removed any chance they had for the title. To add further insult, the machine restarted after the race and they drove it back to the paddock.

That handed the win to a jubilant Reeves.

Paivarinta's second place left him with a pretty watertight 23-point margin going into the last round. He was on the brink of making yet more history.

Round 6 – Donington Park, Great Britain

With Paivarinta only needing three points even if Reeves were to win, the plan for the fast Finn and passenger Kirsi Kainulainen was obvious – stay out of trouble. Consistency and rostrum places in every outing had put their fate in their own hands.

Schlosser having decided to miss the last round, Reeves knew that only his win and a DNF from Paivarinta could give him the championship. But that had happened before in sidecar racing.

The last round was also the final outing for the 1000cc engines, a rule change for 2017 meaning that it would be 600cc for all. As it had been in 1949–50, in fact.

In true fighting spirit, Reeves used his pole position to lead the charge, and he was never headed on his way to his 50th race win. Having rejected the easy option of touring around, Paivarinta followed Reeves home, albeit at a safe distance, easing the BMW LCR to the line and his fifth world title. It was BMW's first championship since 1974.

But memorably, yet another line was written in the record books, with Kirsi Kainulainen becoming the first woman to win an FIM world championship title. It was a remarkable and emotional achievement.

"This is unbelievable," she said. "I am a world champion! I have to thank everybody who has made this possible, all our sponsors and fans. And I have to thank Pekka too; he has helped me so much.

"It is fun to compete with men, but also extremely hard. They fight with full power and don't give up even a bit. So there is no way of them treating you like a lady on the track!"

Driver Pekka, now five times a world champion, beamed, "Unbelievable! Big, big thanks to Kirsi. She is great; what a passenger. I am so pleased for her being champion now."

For the unassuming 45-year-old Paivarinta, it was yet another landmark result. He had been the first Finn to win a world championship; had had the oldest passenger in Dolf Haenni in 2013; had had the first rostrum and race win with a woman; and now he had the crowning glory, the first world championship for a woman. If nothing else, he could not be accused of not being inclusive.

It was a truly popular win in the close-knit world of sidecar racing, and it underlined the sportsmanship and ultra-competitiveness, but above all, the pervading camaraderie and bonhomie of the last true race-for-fun class.

Paivarinta's points tally was 177, with Reeves on 159 and Delannoy on 139.

THINGS TO COME

WITH the forthcoming switch to 600cc machines in 2017, the second story underlying the championship had been the decision to run the World F2 (600cc) Championship concurrently, with both types of machine on the grid.

That gave 2009 World Champions Ben and Tom Birchall the perfect opportunity to send a clear message for 2017. They took the pole and win in every race, and were always mixing it within the leading groups, despite their 400cc disadvantage.

With two seasons of development, who would bet against them? Reeves has won F2 world championships, too, and no doubt the rivalries will be renewed with considerable intensity in the new season.

TWO-TIMER

By LARRY LAWRENCE

Cameron Beaubier beat Yamaha team-mate Josh Hayes to the MotoAmerica title for the second year running, after a nailbiting series finale...

Above: **The big four. The Graves Motorsports pair of Cameron Beaubier and Josh Hayes lead their main rivals, Roger Hayden and Toni Elias of the Yoshimura Suzuki team, at Road Atlanta.**
Photo: MotoAmerica/Brian J. Nelson

Top right: **Beaubier won his second consecutive Superbike title at the last gasp.**

Above right: **Veteran Josh Hayes finished just six points adrift of his team-mate.**
Photos: Y.E.S./Graves/Yamaha

Right: **Toni Elias leads team-mate Roger Hayden and Hayes in the crucial finale.**
Photo: MotoAmerica/Brian J. Nelson

IT had to be one of the most bizarre ways that a championship was decided. Yamaha's Cameron Beaubier went into the final race of the season at New Jersey Motorsports Park with a solid 22-point lead in the standings. All the defending champ had to do was finish the finale just about anywhere and the No. 1 plate would be his again. Then the unthinkable happened. With eight laps to go, Beaubier's Yamaha quit running and wouldn't re-fire. He rolled to a stop in the far reaches of the circuit and sat on a guardrail. He could not hear the PA, could not see the scoring screens – all he could do was watch team-mate Josh Hayes battling the two Yoshimura Suzuki riders, Toni Elias and Roger Hayden, in the closing stages as they sped by on each lap.

If Hayes managed to win the finale, he would steal the title from Beaubier. That forced him into an unusual position of rooting for the other team.

"I honestly didn't know exactly how many laps were left because I didn't have any live feed or any live timing out there or anything," Beaubier said of his agonising eight-lap wait. "I was just kind of sitting there. Honestly, I was so nervous I didn't even want to watch the race because I was like, 'I can't believe that just happened to me.' I know how strong Josh [Hayes] has been all weekend, along with Roger [Hayden] and Toni [Elias]. Man, I don't ever want to root against my team-mate, but when I saw Toni and Roger ahead of

Josh, I wasn't bummed. I will say that. I love you, Josh, but I'm sorry."

When, on the final lap, Suzuki riders Elias and Hayden crossed the finish in front of Hayes, the championship was Beaubier's again. In the final tally, he won it by a scant six points over his team-mate (311–305). Former Moto2 world champion Elias was very much in contention for the entire season and ended the year a close third with 304 points.

Afterwards, Beaubier described the gamut of feelings he experienced in the final minutes of the 2016 MotoAmerica Superbike season.

"I was pretty speechless up there on the podium. I didn't really know what to say because there were just so many emotions going through my mind," Beaubier said. "I was so pissed off right when it happened, then got upset and then kind of just a big thing of joy. It was just a big emotion swing. No matter what happened with the bike, I think that was just an unlucky thing. I know how good those guys are and how hard they work. I think the bottom line was it was just pretty dramatic. I had so much fun racing all these guys this year. Growing up looking up to all three of these guys and being able to fight with them every weekend and be able to beat them. It's just the best feeling in the world. Like I said, I looked up to these guys coming up racing motocross and racing supermoto and getting my feet wet in road racing. It's the best feeling in the world."

Although Beaubier was the pre-season favourite, his winning of a second consecutive MotoAmerica AMA Superbike Championship was a story of a major comeback. Moreover, it underscored his ability to hold up under the pressure of both his team-mate and the unexpected success of Yoshimura Suzuki's Elias.

Beaubier's 2016 campaign began with no points scored in two of the first three rounds, but then the 23-year-old Californian turned things around in a big way by winning a series-leading eight races. Newcomer Elias won six, while Hayes and Hayden scored two victories each.

Whether or not Beaubier, still America's great hope to break through to world championship level, can parlay his American success into a top-flight World Superbike or MotoGP ride is an open question. For now, he seems content to stay home and rack up more wins, championships and money, as it was announced that he had re-signed with Yamaha to race MotoAmerica again in 2017.

A former 125cc grand prix competitor, Beaubier put a toe on to the world stage again in 2016, contesting the British round of World Superbike at Donington Park as a substitute for the injured Sylvain Guintoli on a Pata Yamaha. Beaubier crashed on the opening lap in race one while running sixth, but bounced back to finish tenth in the second race. Respectable, but not necessarily the kind of performance that would cause team managers to come running, contracts in their hands.

For now, American road racing fans can only hope that Beaubier will follow in the path of Ben Spies, who won three AMA Superbike titles before going to World Superbike and winning that championship in his debut season, then moving on to MotoGP. Their two stories have many similarities, both being young riders who had to figure out a way to beat more experienced team-mates to win championships. If Beaubier can make the leap to world competition after another domestic championship in 2017, his path would be strikingly identical to Spies. He would even be 24 years old when he makes the move, the same age as Spies.

MotoAmerica's goal was to align its rules package to that of World Superbike, and it was announced that the technical spec will be comparable in 2017. This is designed to help other manufacturers participate on a level footing (only Yamaha and Suzuki had factory teams in MotoAmerica in 2016), but also presumably better prepare MotoAmerica riders for world championship competition.

Above: Beaubier leads Roger Hayden and Hayes on his way to the race-one win at Road America in Wisconsin.
Photo: MotoAmerica/Brian J. Nelson

Top right: Texan Garrett Gerloff took the Supersport title, beating team-mate JD Beach.
Photo: Y.E.S./Graves/Yamaha

Above right: Brandon Paasch (15) won six races and the KTM RC title, America's version of Europe's Rookies Cup.

Top far right: Tony Elias was a late replacement at Yoshimura Suzuki, and he challenged for the title. He shares the final podium with champion Beaubier.

Right: Italian Claudio Corti, another former GP racer, won five Superstock races on an Aprilia.
Photos: MotoAmerica/Brian J. Nelson

Circuit of the Americas – 9–10 April

The pre-season injury of Yoshimura Suzuki's Jake Lewis caused the team to call up long-time grand prix and World Superbike veteran Toni Elias to fill in. After a stunning sweep of the opening two MotoAmerica Superbike races at the Circuit of the Americas by the 33-year-old Spaniard, Yoshimura quickly signed him for the rest of the season and shifted Lewis to a satellite Superstock 1000 squad.

"I'm happy and I'm satisfied," Elias said. "At the beginning of the race, I was a little bit worried. I didn't have a great, great feeling, but we start, I try to stay behind Roger [Hayden] and Cameron [Beaubier]. Finally, I found myself again and try to go away, but was impossible. Roger was there all the time. My rhythm was good, the tyres were sliding a lot all the time, but I make one mistake and he passed me again. Finally, I could do what I wanted and take some gap, but only in the last three laps. I was at home [without a ride] and I cannot ask for more. It's amazing. It's perfect."

Road Atlanta – 17 April

Toni Elias proved his victory in Texas the week before had been no fluke. At Road Atlanta, a challenging hilly and technical course he'd never seen before, he scored his third straight victory. Team-mate Hayden was second, while Jake Gagne was third on the independent Roadrace Factory Yamaha R1. The Yoshimura Suzuki squad could hardly believe their luck, having swept the first three rounds after being winless in 2015.

The second race at Road Atlanta stopped the bleeding for the Monster Energy Yamaha squad, defending series champion Beaubier having turned the tables by winning race two over Hayes and Hayden as his terrible luck of the new season finally turned for the better.

"I'm really happy to get on the podium and to get a win after the disaster of a weekend we had in CoTA and in the first race," Beaubier said. "All in all, I felt good, and it was an awesome race. It was pretty fun dicing back and forth with Josh, and I knew Rog was right there behind us, too. It seemed like Josh had his spots, and there were spots where I knew I was better than him. It felt good to actually pass Josh decently on the brakes, too, because I've struggled with that in the past."

New Jersey Motorsports Park 1 – 1 May

The hole Cameron Beaubier had dug for himself at CoTA was practically filled in a single day of amazing racing at a wet New Jersey Motorsports Park. The defending MotoAmerica Superbike champion won both races to vault back into championship contention.

Beaubier, who started the day seventh in the championship, scored a perfect 50 points in trying conditions as rainstorms invaded south New Jersey and wreaked havoc. Josh Hayes finished second in both races, but wasn't able to match the pace displayed by his young team-mate.

"To be honest, at the beginning I was kind of stressed out," Beaubier said after his race-two win. "I felt a lot better than in the first race today, feeling-wise I felt a little bit faster. I came by and I had half a second, and the next lap I was like, 'Oh, man, this is going to be good.' I came back around and it said plus zero. I was like, 'Oh, no.' I put my head down and just kept pushing. I knew Josh was right there, and it seemed like he made a little bobble and I came by, and it said plus two. It just started growing from there, and I just tried to ride as smart as I could and eased my way around the track at the end. And I was able to do the double."

The Yoshimura Suzuki squad suffered a terrible weekend, with Elias finishing out of the points in race one and then 12th in race two. Hayden was ninth in the first race, but crashed in the second.

Virginia International Raceway – 15 May

At VIR, 41-year-old Josh Hayes extended his championship lead to 11 points, after ending his six-race winless streak in race one and then taking second to Cameron Beaubier in race two. Both races were intense battles from start to finish, with Hayes beating Roger Hayden by just 0.307 of a second in race one, before losing out to Beaubier by just 0.151 of a second in race two.

"Definitely relief," Hayes said after winning his first race of the season. "It's been a pretty tough weekend. It's such a busy racetrack, such a physical racetrack, with all the ups and downs and high-speed switchbacks. It's definitely a racetrack that takes its toll on you and doesn't give you any time to take a break."

Beaubier's victory in race two was the 15th of his Superbike career.

Road America – 5 June

Cameron Beaubier established control of the series mid-season with a clean sweep at Road America. The two wins also propelled him into the lead in the championship, 176–169, over team-mate Josh Hayes.

Both races were thrillers from start to finish, with Beaubier beating Hayden to the line by just 0.442 of a second in race one, before leading Yoshimura Suzuki's Elias by 0.684 of a second in race two. Hayes was third in both races, 1.9 seconds adrift in race one and just 0.721 of a second behind in race two.

With his 16th career win at Elkhart Lake, Beaubier moved into a tie with MotoAmerica President and three-times 500cc World Champion Wayne Rainey for tenth on the all-time win list. In race two, his 17th win later in the day, Beaubier pulled even with 2006 MotoGP World Champion Nicky Hayden for ninth on the all-time list.

RETURN OF THE ALIENS

THE American road racing championships had long been a place for foreign riders to race, earn a good living and sometimes win championships. From Troy Corser to Mat Mladin, the AMA always provided ample opportunity for riders of all nationalities. That all ended with America's great recession starting in 2008, which hammered motorcycle sales, especially sports bikes.

In 2016, there were signs that a few opportunities were opening again for international riders. Spaniard Toni Elias, Italian Claudio Corti and Frenchman Valentin Debise were a trio of Europeans who added depth to MotoAmerica grids.

Elias injected an intriguing new storyline to the American series, bursting out of the gates and winning the first two rounds of the Superbike championship, and breathing new life into the Yoshimura Suzuki squad, which had gone winless for the first time in 13 years in 2015.

Corti scored solid results, winning five races in Superstock 1000 for Aprilia HSBK, an independent-rider team based in Houston. He finished third in the series, in spite of breaking his ankle and some ribs in the middle of the season at Barber.

In Supersport, Endurance racing specialist Debise won on the M4 SportbikeTrackGear.com Suzuki GSX-R600, a machine previously thought to be totally outclassed by the Yamaha R6. The Frenchman concluded his remarkable maiden season in the States with 11 podium finishes, including a victory at Road America, and took third in the championship.

The success of Elias, Corti and Debise may serve as a beacon for future GP or World Superbike refugees looking for a way to continue earning a living at racing when world championship opportunities dry up.

MotoAmerica is all too happy to welcome riders from overseas. The hope is that the foreign talent will bolster the series as a whole and force American riders to step up their game.

Above: Josh Herrin, 2015 Supersport runner-up, moved up to win the Superstock 1000 championship. Here he leads Jake Gagne (32), Danny Eslick (69), Claudio Corti (71) and Matthew Scholtz at the Utah Motorsport Campus.
Photo: MotoAmerica/Brian J. Nelson

Far left: JD Beach won eight races in his Supersport championship battle, but came up just four points short of team-mate Gerloff.
Photo: Y.E.S./Graves/Yamaha

Left: Gerloff celebrates his championship at the New Jersey final.
Photo: MotoAmerica/Brian J. Nelson

Barber Motorsports Park – 12 June

Yoshimura Suzuki bounced back solidly in the oppressive heat of Alabama, where Roger Hayden and Toni Elias split the wins. The former scored victory over his team-mate in the first race, before Elias returned the favour in the second. For Hayden, the victory was especially sweet, since it was his first of the season and his first Superbike win since 2014.

"I'm just really happy to get this win, finally," said Hayden, who had last won at New Jersey Motorsports Park in 2014. "It's been a long time. I'm glad my family's here. My dad and my mom and brothers, and a bunch of people from home, so it makes it a little more special. My guys [his crew], they need this win, too. We all want to win. We were all getting tired of getting second all the time, so it's good for them."

Elias dedicated his race-two victory to Luis Salom, the Spanish Moto2 racer who lost his life that weekend at the Catalunya Grand Prix.

The Suzuki wins tightened up the standings between the top four, with just 19 points separating series leader Beaubier from fourth-place Elias, Hayes and Hayden sandwiched in between.

Utah Motorsports Campus – 25 June

With legal issues ongoing, there was some doubt early on that the event at the track formerly known as Miller Motorsports Park would even happen. In the end, the race ran, and Beaubier and Elias both took wins.

Beaubier upped the pace to take over at the front on the 16th lap. From there, he was never headed, winning his seventh race of the season by just 0.171 of a second over Hayes. Yoshimura Suzuki's Roger Hayden was third, 1.1 seconds behind, with Elias a few tenths adrift in fourth and seething with grip issues.

The normally cheerful Elias was irritable, even after a three-hour cooling-off period, as he started the second race. He took out his anger on the field, assuming the lead when Hayes ran off the track on the second lap and leading the majority of the way. Hayes dropped back to 16th, but had recovered by the end of the race and finished fourth.

For race two, Elias had grip, and it made all the difference. "We put new tyres on and the bike was working perfect again," Elias said of race two. "These guys are riding really strong and were pushing a lot, but we could win this race. But today was a day to reduce the gap of the championship, and we lost points. We lost six or seven points. I am happy for the victory and also for my team, but I am not happy."

Laguna Seca Raceway – 10 July

Yamaha team-mates Cameron Beaubier and Josh Hayes both came away with victories on a sunny Sunday at Mazda Raceway Laguna Seca, during the combined World Superbike/MotoAmerica weekend. Hayes reached a milestone by scoring his 60th career Superbike win.

The four-way championship battle was effectively reduced to three (Beaubier, Hayes and Toni Elias) after Laguna Seca. Roger Hayden took himself out of championship contention with a crash in race one and a fourth-place finish in race two.

New Jersey Motorsports Park 2 – 11 September

The MotoAmerica series returned to New Jersey for the season finale, and to say it was filled with drama would be putting it lightly. Cameron Beaubier went into the weekend all but having clinched the championship. Race one went according to plan. It was a thriller, with Roger Hayden topping Josh Hayes by just 0.104 of a second for his second win of the season. Toni Elias was a charging third, after a poor start left him lagging, and Beaubier played it very conservatively, coming home a safe fourth.

Another conservative finish would easily settle the title for

Beaubier, but then his Yamaha quit running with eight laps to go and he was stranded trackside, powerless to do anything. Beaubier suddenly became Elias and Hayden's biggest fan, probably doing all he could not to physically root for them as they passed on each lap.

Fortunately for Beaubier, the Suzuki duo were able to hold his Yamaha team-mate Hayes at bay, and the championship belonged to him for the second year running.

It marked the seventh straight MotoAmerica/AMA Superbike Championship for Yamaha, dating back to 2010. That matched the longest streak by a single manufacturer, tying with Suzuki's run of AMA titles from 2003 to 2009.

Superstock 1000

Josh Herrin found a second life in racing after returning to America, following an ill-fated run in the Moto2 world championship in 2014. He was runner-up in MotoAmerica Supersport in 2015, and in 2016 he moved up to Superstock 1000, riding a McGraw Powersports/Meen Yamaha. He easily clinched that title with two rounds remaining, after winning eight rounds, including a stretch of seven in a row. Herrin won the title over Bobby Fong and Claudio Corti.

MotoAmerica modified the rules somewhat in 2016, incorporating Superstock 1000 into Superbike, much as World Superbike ran the Evo class and MotoGP the Open class. Superbike and Superstock 1000 riders were awarded championship points based solely on their overall finish, irrespective of class

Supersport

Y.E.S. Graves Yamaha's Garrett Gerloff, a 21-year-old Texan, took the 2016 MotoAmerica Supersport title by just four points over team-mate JD Beach after 16 races. Beach did all he could in the final round, winning his eighth race of the season and his seventh in a row, but it wasn't enough. Both riders had incredible seasons, but Gerloff, with 15 podiums and six wins, was able to fulfill a near lifelong dream of winning a professional road racing championship in his fifth season as a pro.

"It feels so good," Gerloff said. "I saw myself with a No. 1 plate back a long time ago when I was, like, 12 years old with my first ever road race bike, and to finally get there and do what I always knew I could do ... it was amazing. This year has been so awesome. I rediscovered my love for motorcycles, which I don't want to say has been missing, but I just needed some time to grow up a little bit. I love racing."

Superstock 600

Bryce Prince won nine of the 15 MotoAmerica Superstock 600 rounds to put that championship away early. The racer from Bakersfield, California had shown flashes of brilliance in the 2015 series, but in 2016 the floodgates opened and Prince was nearly unstoppable.

The only rider to keep Prince in sight for most of the season was Mexican racer Richie Escalante, who came to MotoAmerica with experience in the CEV Series. Escalante missed the first four races due to an off-season injury. Once in the championship, however, he won three races. Travis Wyman, Michael Gilbert and Dakota Mamola, son of former GP star Randy Mamola, also scored wins.

KTM RC Cup

The series that is hoped to prepare American riders for GP racing, in the same manner as Moto3, produced a new champion in 15-year-old Brandon Paasch from New Jersey. Paasch, who has international experience in the Moriwaki 250 Junior Cup, scored six victories en route to the KTM RC Cup Championship over Anthony Mazziotto III and second-generation road racer Ashton Yates.

MAJOR RESULTS

OTHER CHAMPIONSHIP RACING SERIES WORLDWIDE

Compiled by PETER McLAREN

MOTOAMERICA/AMA North American Road Race Championship

8-9 April 2016 (15 laps, 51.400miles/ 82.720km)
Race 1 (9 laps, red flag, oil)
1 Toni Elias (Suzuki); **2** Roger Hayden (Suzuki); **3** Josh Hayes (Yamaha); **4** Jake Gagne (Yamaha); **5** Bobby Fong (Kawasaki); **6** Josh Herrin (Yamaha); **7** Josh Day (Yamaha); **8** Taylor Knapp (Yamaha); **9** Sheridan Morais (Yamaha); **10** Danny Eslick (Yamaha).

Race 2
1 Toni Elias (Suzuki); **2** Roger Hayden (Suzuki); **3** Josh Hayes (Yamaha); **4** Cameron Beaubier (Yamaha); **5** Bobby Fong (Kawasaki); **6** Claudio Corti (Aprilia); **7** Josh Herrin (Yamaha); **8** Danny Eslick (Yamaha); **9** Jake Gagne (Yamaha); **10** Taylor Knapp (Yamaha).

Road Atlanta, Braselton, Georgia, 17 April 2016 (22 laps, 55.880miles/ 89.930km)
Race 1
1 Toni Elias (Suzuki); **2** Roger Hayden (Suzuki); **3** Jake Gagne (Yamaha); **4** Claudio Corti (Aprilia); **5** Josh Herrin (Yamaha); **6** Bobby Fong (Kawasaki); **7** Taylor Knapp (Yamaha); **8** Hayden Gillim (Yamaha); **9** Sheridan Morais (Yamaha); **10** Kyle Wyman (Yamaha).

Race 2
1 Cameron Beaubier (Yamaha); **2** Josh Hayes (Yamaha); **3** Roger Hayden (Suzuki); **4** Josh Herrin (Yamaha); **5** Taylor Knapp (Yamaha); **6** Claudio Corti (Aprilia); **7** Bobby Fong (Kawasaki); **8** Jake Gagne (Yamaha); **9** Hayden Gillim (Suzuki); **10** Sheridan Morais (Yamaha).

New Jersey Motorsports Park 1, Millville, New Jersey, 1 May 2016 (18 laps, 40.500 miles/65.180km)
Race 1
1 Cameron Beaubier (Yamaha); **2** Josh Hayes (Yamaha); **3** Claudio Corti (Aprilia); **4** Larry Pegram (Suzuki); **5** Jake Gagne (Yamaha); **6** Corey Alexander (Ducati); **7** Ryan Jones (Yamaha); **8** Danny Eslick (Yamaha); **9** Roger Hayden (Suzuki); **10** Hayden Gillim (Suzuki).

Race 2 (15 laps, rain)
1 Cameron Beaubier (Yamaha); **2** Josh Hayes (Yamaha); **3** Claudio Corti (Aprilia); **4** Hayden Gillim (Suzuki); **5** Corey Alexander (Ducati); **6** Larry Pegram (Suzuki); **7** Taylor Knapp (Yamaha); **8** Ryan Jones (Yamaha); **9** Danny Eslick (Yamaha); **10** Josh Herrin (Yamaha).

Virginia International Raceway, Danville, Virginia, 15 May 2016 (25 laps, 56.520 miles/90.525km)
Race 1
1 Josh Hayes (Yamaha); **2** Roger Hayden (Suzuki); **3** Toni Elias (Suzuki); **4** Cameron Beaubier (Yamaha); **5** Claudio Corti (Aprilia); **6** Bobby Fong (Kawasaki); **7** Taylor Knapp (Yamaha); **8** Hayden Gillim (Suzuki); **9** Jake Lewis (Suzuki); **10** Kyle Wyman (Yamaha).

Race 2
1 Cameron Beaubier (Yamaha); **2** Josh Hayes (Yamaha); **3** Toni Elias (Suzuki); **4** Roger Hayden (Suzuki); **5** Danny Eslick (Yamaha); **6** Bobby Fong (Kawasaki); **7** Josh Herrin (Yamaha); **8** Hayden Gillim (Suzuki); **9** David Anthony (Kawasaki); **10** Kyle Wyman (Yamaha).

Road America, Elkhart Lake, Wisconsin, 5 June 2016 (14 laps, 56.000 miles/ 90.123km)
Race 1
1 Cameron Beaubier (Yamaha); **2** Roger Hayden (Suzuki); **3** Josh Hayes (Yamaha); **4** Toni Elias (Suzuki); **5** Josh Herrin (Yamaha); **6** Claudio Corti (Aprilia); **7** Matthew Scholtz (Yamaha); **8** Bobby Fong (Kawasaki); **9** Jake Lewis (Suzuki); **10** Kyle Wyman (Yamaha).

Race 2
1 Cameron Beaubier (Yamaha); **2** Toni Elias (Suzuki); **3** Josh Hayes (Yamaha); **4** Roger Hayden (Suzuki); **5** Josh Herrin (Yamaha); **6** Claudio Corti (Aprilia); **7** Hayden Gillim (Yamaha); **8** David Anthony (Kawasaki); **9** Bobby Fong (Kawasaki); **10** Jake Lewis (Suzuki).

Barber Motorsports Park, Birmingham, Alabama, 12 June 2016 (23 laps, 54.740 miles/88.095km)
Race 1
1 Roger Hayden (Suzuki); **2** Toni Elias (Suzuki); **3** Cameron Beaubier (Yamaha); **4** Josh Hayes (Yamaha); **5** Josh Herrin (Yamaha); **6** Bobby Fong (Kawasaki); **7** Matthew Scholtz (Yamaha); **8** Kyle Wyman (Yamaha); **9** Hayden Gillim (Suzuki); **10** Jake Lewis (Suzuki).

Race 2
1 Toni Elias (Suzuki); **2** Roger Hayden (Suzuki); **3** Cameron Beaubier (Yamaha); **4** Josh Hayes (Yamaha); **5** Josh Herrin (Yamaha); **6** Bobby Fong (Kawasaki); **7** Danny Eslick (Yamaha); **8** Claudio Corti (Aprilia); **9** Matthew Scholtz (Yamaha); **10** Kyle Wyman (Yamaha).

Utah Motorsports Campus, Tooele, Utah, 25 June 2016 (18 laps, 54.864 miles/ 88.295km)
Race 1
1 Cameron Beaubier (Yamaha); **2** Josh Hayes (Yamaha); **3** Roger Hayden (Suzuki); **4** Toni Elias (Suzuki); **5** Josh Herrin (Yamaha); **6** Mathew Scholtz (Yamaha); **7** Danny Eslick (Yamaha); **8** Jake Gagne (Yamaha); **9** Bobby Fong (Kawasaki); **10** Claudio Corti (Aprilia).

Race 2
1 Toni Elias (Suzuki); **2** Cameron Beaubier (Yamaha); **3** Roger Hayden (Suzuki); **4** Josh Hayes (Yamaha); **5** Jake Gagne (Yamaha); **6** Josh Herrin (Yamaha); **7** Danny Eslick (Yamaha); **8** Mathew Scholtz (Yamaha); **9** Bobby Fong (Kawasaki); **10** Sheridan Morais (Yamaha).

Laguna Seca Raceway, Monterey, California, 10 July 2016 (23 laps, 51.474 miles/ 82.839km)
Race 1 (20 laps)
1 Cameron Beaubier (Yamaha); **2** Toni Elias (Suzuki); **3** Josh Hayes (Yamaha); **4** Josh Herrin (Yamaha); **5** Mathew Scholtz (Yamaha); **6** Danny Eslick (Yamaha); **7** Claudio Corti (Aprilia); **8** Bobby Fong (Kawasaki); **9** Sheridan Morais (Yamaha); **10** Jake Lewis (Suzuki).

Race 2
1 Josh Hayes (Yamaha); **2** Cameron Beaubier (Yamaha); **3** Toni Elias (Suzuki); **4** Roger Hayden (Suzuki); **5** Claudio Corti (Aprilia); **6** Mathew Scholtz (Yamaha); **7** Sheridan Morias (Yamaha); **8** Josh Herrin (Yamaha); **9** Kyle Wyman (Yamaha); **10** Jake Lewis (Suzuki).

New Jersey Motorsports Park 2, Millville, New Jersey, 11 September 2016 (25 laps, 56.250 miles/90.526km)
Race 1
1 Roger Hayden (Suzuki); **2** Josh Hayes (Yamaha); **3** Toni Elias (Suzuki); **4** Cameron Beaubier (Yamaha); **5** Bobby Fong (Kawasaki); **6** Jake Gagne (Yamaha); **7** Mathew Scholtz (Yamaha); **8** Danny Eslick (Yamaha); **9** Taylor Knapp (Yamaha); **10** Hayden Gillim (Suzuki).

Race 2
1 Toni Elias (Suzuki); **2** Roger Hayden (Suzuki); **3** Josh Hayes (Yamaha); **4** Bobby Fong (Kawasaki); **5** Josh Herrin (Yamaha); **6** Claudio Corti (Aprilia); **7** Kyle Wyman (Yamaha); **8** Danny Eslick (Yamaha); **9** Taylor Knapp (Yamaha); **10** Hayden Gillim (Suzuki).

Final Superbike Championship points:

1	Cameron Beaubier,	311
2	Josh Hayes,	305
3	Toni Elias,	304
4	Roger Hayden,	284
5	Josh Herrin,	163
6	Claudio Corti,	146

7 Bobby Fong, 144; **8** Danny Eslick, 110; **9** Hayden Gillim, 105; **10** Jake Gagne, 84.

Final Superstock 1000 Championship points:

1	Josh Herrin,	335
2	Bobby Fong,	287
3	Claudio Corti,	272
4	Danny Eslick,	214
5	Hayden Gillim,	192
6	Taylor Knapp,	143

7 Mathew Scholtz, 139; **8** Max Flinders, 113; **9** Jake Lewis, 111; **10** Sheridan Morais, 85.

Final Supersport Championship points:

1	Garrett Gerloff,	326
2	JD Beach,	322
3	Valentin Debise,	246
4	Cameron Petersen,	189
5	Benny Solis Jr,	147
6	Joe Roberts,	142

7 Bryce Prince, 141; **8** Dakota Mamola, 94; **9** Travis Wyman, 91; **10** Richie Escalante, 86.

Final Superstock 600 Championship points:

1	Bryce Prince,	332
2	Richie Escalante,	200
3	Travis Wyman,	185
4	Dakota Mamola,	177
5	JC Camacho,	159
6	Conner Blevins,	145

7 Michael Gilbert, 128; **8** Andy DiBrino, 106; **9** Nick McFadden, 98; **10** Deion Campbell, 93.

Final KTM RC Cup points:

1	Brandon Paasch,	311
2	Anthony Mazziotto III,	266
3	Ashton Yates,	239
4	Jody Barry,	195
5	Alejandro Gutierrez,	142
6	Josh Serne,	116

7 Jackson Blackmon, 113; **8** Benjamin Smith, 90; **9** Renzo Ferreira, 79; **10** Brandon Altmeyer, 77.

Endurance World Championship

24 HEURES MOTO, Le Mans Bugatti Circuit, France, 9-10 April 2016.
FIM Endurance World Championship, Round 1.
819 laps of the 2.600-mile/4.185km circuit, 2129.8 miles/3427.5km
1 SRC Kawasaki: 24h 1m 54.080s.
2 Team April Moto Motors Events: 810 laps; **3** F.C.C. TSR Honda: 808 laps; **4** Team R2CL: 804 laps; **5** Suzuki Endurance Racing Team: 802 laps; **6** Team 3ART Yam'avenue: 800 laps; **7** AM Moto Racing Competition: 792 laps; **8** Voelpker NRT48 by Schubert-Motors: 790 laps; **9** Racing Team Sarazin: 789 laps; **10** MACO Racing Team: 786 laps; **11** YART Yamaha Official EWC Team: 785 laps; **12** Starteam PAM-Racing: 785 laps; **13** Cottard Motosport: 784 laps; **14** Space Moto 37: 782 laps; **15** TRT 27/Bazar 2 La Becane: 780 laps.
Fastest lap: Team R2CL, 1m 38.448s, 95.0mph/ 153.0km/h, on lap 148.
Championship points: 1 SRC Kawasaki, 60; **2** Team April Moto Motors Events, 45; **3** F.C.C. TSR Honda, 44; **4** Team R2CL, 36; **5** Team 3ART Yam'avenue, 22; **6** Suzuki Endurance Racing Team, 21.

12 Hours EWC Portimao, Portugal, 11 June 2016.
FIM Endurance World Championship, Round 2.
393 laps of the 2.853-mile/4.592km circuit, 1121.4 miles/1804.7km
1 GMT94 Yamaha: 12h 0m 0.856s.
2 Suzuki Endurance Racing Team: +0.081s; **3** Honda Endurance Racing: 389 laps; **4** YART Yamaha Official EWC Team: 387 laps; **5** Team April Moto Motors Events: 387 laps; **6** Tati Team Beaujolais Racing: 385 laps; **7** Voelpker NRT48 by Schubert-Motors: 385 laps; **8** Junior Team LMS Suzuki: 385 laps; **9** Team 3ART Yam'avenue: 383 laps; **10** Lukoil BMW Motorrad CSEU: 382 laps; **11** Team Louit Moto 33 Traqueur: 381 laps; **12** F.C.C. TSR Honda: 381 laps; **13** AM Moto Racing Competition: 380 laps; **14** Team Bolliger Switzerland: 378 laps; **15** TECMAS Racing Team – BMW: 376 laps.
Fastest lap: Parkalgar Racing Team, 1m 46.067s, 96.81mph/155.8km/h, on lap 261.
Championship points: 1 Team April Moto Motors Events, 66; **2** SRC Kawasaki, 60; **3** Suzuki Endurance Racing Team, 59; **4** F.C.C. TSR Honda, 53; **5** GMT94 Yamaha, 45; **6** Honda Endurance Racing, 43.

SUZUKA 8 HOURS, Suzuka, Japan, 31 July 2016.
FIM Endurance World Championship, Round 3.
218 laps of the 3.617-mile/5.821km circuit, 788.5 miles/1269.0km
1 Yamaha Factory Racing Team: 8h 0m 40.124s.
2 Team Green: +2m 17.883s; **3** Yoshimura Suzuki Shell Advance: 217 laps; **4** YART Yamaha Official EWC Team: 214 laps; **5** Moto Map Supply: 214 laps; **6** Team Kagayama: 213 laps; **7** Eva RT Test Type-01 Trickstar: 213 laps; **8** Satu-Hati Honda Team Asia: 212 laps; **9** Mistresa with ATS: 212 laps; **10** Teluru Kohara RT: 212 laps; **11** Toho Racing: 211 laps; **12** Team R2CL: 210 laps; **13** Honda Endurance Racing: 210 laps; **14** GMT94 Yamaha: 210 laps; **15** Team Bolliger Switzerland: 209 laps.
Fastest lap: Yamaha Factory Racing Team, 2m 8.411s, 101.40mph/163.19km/h, on lap 105.
Championship points: 1 Team April Moto Motors Events, 68; **2** SRC Kawasaki, 60; **3** YART Yamaha Official EWC Team, 60; **4** Suzuki Endurance Racing Team, 59; **5** F.C.C. TSR Honda, 56; **6** GMT94 Yamaha, 52.

OSCHERSLEBEN 8 HOURS, Oschersleben, Germany, 27 August 2016.
FIM Endurance World Championship, Round 4.
309 laps of the 2.279-mile/3.667km circuit, 704.1 miles/1133.1km
1 GMT94 Yamaha: 8h 1m 13.549s.
2 Suzuki Endurance Racing Team: +21.315s; **3** Penz13.com – BMW Motorrad Team: 306 laps; **4** Honda Endurance Racing: 304 laps; **5** MACO Racing Team: 303 laps; **6** Team 3ART Yam'avenue: 302 laps; **7** Lukoil BMW Motorrad CSEU: 302 laps; **8** Starteam PAM-Racing: 301 laps; **9** AM Moto Racing Competition: 301 laps; **10** Tati Team Beaujolais Racing: 300 laps; **11** Team April Moto Motors Events: 299 laps; **12** Junior Team LMS Suzuki: 299 laps; **13** Yamaha Viltaïs Experience: 298 laps; **14** Team Rabid Transit: 297 laps; **15** Ecurie Chrono Sport: 292 laps.
Fastest lap: YART Yamaha Official EWC Team, 1m 27.113s, 94.14mph/151.5km/h, on lap 49.

Final FIM Endurance World Championship points:

1	Suzuki Endurance Racing Team, (Anthony Delhalle/Etienne Masson/ Vincent Philippe)	88
2	GMT94 Yamaha, (Niccolo Canepa/David Checa/ Lucas Mahias/Louis Rossi)	87
3	Team April Moto Motors Events – Suzuki, (Gregg Black/Alex Cudlin/Gregory Fastre)	78
4	Honda Endurance Racing, (Julien da Costa/FreddyForay/ Sebastien Gimbert/ Kyle Smith)	72
5	SRC Kawasaki, (Fabien Foret/Matthieu Lagrive/ Gregory Leblanc)	60
6	YART Yamaha Official EWC Team, (Marvin Fritz/Igor Jerman/ Max Neukirchner/Broc Parkes/Ivan Silva/ Bradley Smith)	60

7 F.C.C. TSR Honda (Damian Cudlin/Patrick Jacobsen/Alan Techer/Arturo Tizon/Kazuma Watanabe), 56; **8** Team 3ART Yam'avenue – Yamaha (Louis Bulle/Alex Plancassagne/Gabriel Pons/ Lukas Trautmann), 50; **9** Team R2CL – Suzuki (Antonio Alarcos/Lucas Mahias/Aaron Morris/ Nicolas Pouhair/Marius Tabaries), 45; **10** AM Moto Racing Competition – Kawasaki (Alexandre Ayer/Kevin Denis/Jonathan Goetschy/Jimmy Maccio), 38; **11** Yamaha Factory Racing Team (Pol Espargaro/Katsuyuki Nakasuga/Alex Lowes), 35; **12** MACO Racing Team – Yamaha (Anthony dos Santos/Marko Jerman/Greg Junod), 35; **13** Voelpker NRT48 by Schubert-Motors – BMW (Stefan Kerschbaumer/Bastien Mackels/Dominik Vincon), 35; **14** Junior Team LMS Suzuki (Robin Camus/Eddy Dupuy/Baptiste Guittet/Romain Maitre), 34; **15** Team Bolliger Switzerland – Kawasaki (Horst Saiger/Michaël Savary/Roman Stamm/Gianluca Vizziello), 34.

Isle of Man Tourist Trophy Races

ISLE OF MAN TOURIST TROPHY COURSE, 4-10 June 2016, 37.73-mile/60.72km circuit.
RST Superbike TT (6 laps, 226.38 miles/ 364.32km)
1 Michael Dunlop (BMW), 1h 44m 14.259s, 130.306mph/209.707km/h.
2 Ian Hutchinson (BMW), 1h 44m 33.323s; **3** John McGuinness (Honda), 1h 45m 27.498s; **4** Peter Hickman (Kawasaki), 1h 45m 44.951s; **5** Dean Harrison (Kawasaki), 1h 46m 9.896s; **6** Michael Rutter (BMW), 1h 46m 40.202s; **7** David Johnson (Norton), 1h 46m 56.430s; **8** Bruce Anstey (Honda), 1h 47m 5.936s; **9** Gary Johnson (BMW), 1h 47m 16.523s; **10** Lee

Johnston (BMW), 1h 47m 16.614s; **11** James Hillier (Kawasaki), 1h 47m 51.985s; **12** Steve Mercer (Honda), 1h 47m 59.875s; **13** Daniel Hegarty (Kawasaki), 1h 48m 43.051s; **14** Ivan Lintin (Kawasaki), 1h 49m 22.224s; **15** Horst Saiger (Kawasaki), 1h 49m 50.755s.
Fastest lap: Michael Dunlop (BMW), 16m 58.254s, 133.393mph/214.675km/h, on lap 2 (record).
Previous Superbike TT lap record: Bruce Anstey (Honda), 17m 6.682s, 132.298mph/212.913km/h (2014).

Sure Sidecar TT Race 1 (3 laps, 113.19 miles/182.16km)
1 John Holden/Andrew Winkle (LCR), 59m 25.609s, 114.282mph/183.919km/h.
2 Peter Founds/Jevan Walmsley (Suzuki), 1h 0m 19.858s; **3** Alan Founds/Aki Aalto (LCR), 1h 1m 0.006s; **4** Steve Ramsden/Matty Ramsden (LCR), 1h 1m 20.447s; **5** Matt Dix/Shaun Parker (Baker), 1h 1m 29.129s; **6** Wayne Lockey/Mark Sayers (Ireson Honda), 1h 1m 51.410s; **7** Gary Bryan/Jamie Winn (Baker), 1h 1m 59.466s; **8** Gary Knight/Daniel Evanson (DrVR), 1h 2m 23.337s; **9** Gordon Shand/Philip Hyde (SHAND F2), 1h 3m 5.111s; **10** Darren Hope/Paul Bumfrey (Honda), 1h 3m 6.754s; **11** Mike Cookson/Alun Thomas (Honda), 1h 3m 33.064s; **12** Mike Roscher/Ben Hughes (Suzuki), 1h 3m 34.341s; **13** Mick Alton/Chrissie Clancy (LCR Suzuki), 1h 3m 38.644s; **14** Lewis Blackstock/Patrick Rosney (Suzuki), 1h 3m 46.201s; **15** John Saunders/Frank Claeys (Shelbourne), 1h 3m 54.090s.
Fastest lap: Ben Birchall/Tom Birchall (LCR), 19m 22.928s, 116.798mph/187.968km/h, on lap 2 (record).
Previous Sidecar lap record: Dave Molyneux/Benjamin Binns (Suzuki), 19m 23.056s, 116.785mph/187.947km/h (2015).

Monster Energy Supersport TT Race 1 (4 laps, 150.92 miles/242.88km)
1 Ian Hutchinson (Yamaha), 1h 11m 36.808s, 126.445mph/203.494km/h.
2 Dean Harrison (Kawasaki), 1h 12m 29.720s; **3** James Hillier (Kawasaki), 1h 12m 47.770s; **4** Conor Cummins (Honda), 1h 12m 48.506s; **5** John McGuinness (Honda), 1h 12m 53.286s; **6** Lee Johnston (Triumph), 1h 13m 32.704s; **7** William Dunlop (Yamaha), 1h 13m 51.684s; **8** Steve Mercer (Honda), 1h 14m 12.890s; **9** Gary Johnson (Triumph), 1h 14m 34.627s; **10** Cameron Donald (Honda), 1h 14m 45.843s; **11** James Cowton (Honda), 1h 14m 48.982s; **12** Jamie Coward (Kawasaki), 1h 14m 54.289s; **13** Ben Wylie (Yamaha), 1h 15m 27.476s; **14** Michal Dokoupil (Yamaha), 1h 15m 28.667s; **15** Robert Wilson (Yamaha), 1h 15m 39.921s.
Fastest lap: Ian Hutchinson (Yamaha), 17m 39.013s, 128.259mph/206.413km/h, on lap 2.
Supersport lap record: Michael Dunlop (Honda), 17m 35.659s, 128.666mph/207.069km/h (2013).

RL360 Quantum Superstock TT (4 laps, 150.92 miles/242.88km)
1 Ian Hutchinson (BMW), 1h 9m 47.543s, 129.745mph/208.804km/h.
2 Dean Harrison (Kawasaki), 1h 10m 15.187s; **3** James Hillier (Kawasaki), 1h 10m 17.092s; **4** Michael Rutter (BMW), 1h 10m 46.047s; **5** Gary Johnson (BMW), 1h 10m 49.292s; **6** John McGuinness (Honda), 1h 10m 58.053s; **7** Conor Cummins (Honda), 1h 11m 26.858s; **8** William Dunlop (Kawasaki), 1h 12m 5.049s; **9** David Johnson (BMW), 1h 12m 11.448s; **10** Steve Mercer (Honda), 1h 12m 27.594s; **11** Daniel Hegarty (Kawasaki), 1h 12m 32.217s; **12** Ivan Lintin (Kawasaki), 1h 12m 47.272s; **13** Horst Saiger (Kawasaki), 1h 13m 19.345s; **14** Jamie Coward (Honda), 1h 13m 55.115s; **15** Sam West (BMW), 1h 13m 59.702s.
Fastest lap: Ian Hutchinson (BMW), 17m 0.510s, 133.098mph/214.200km/h, on lap 1 (record).
Previous Superstock lap record: Michael Dunlop (Honda), 17m 15.114s, 131.220mph/211.178km/h (2013).

Monster Energy Supersport TT Race 2 (4 laps, 150.92 miles/242.88km)
1 Ian Hutchinson (Yamaha), 1h 11m 55.261s, 125.905mph/202.624km/h.
2 Michael Dunlop (Yamaha), 1h 12m 12.808s; **3** Dean Harrison (Kawasaki), 1h 12m 29.452s; **4** James Hillier (Kawasaki), 1h 12m 42.986s; **5** Bruce Anstey (Honda), 1h 12m 44.287s; **6** Lee Johnston (Triumph), 1h 12m 44.950s; **7** Conor Cummins (Honda), 1h 12m 48.719s; **8** Peter Hickman (Kawasaki), 1h 13m 14.311s; **9** Gary Johnson (Triumph), 1h 13m 38.285s; **10** Michael Rutter (Kawasaki), 1h 13m 39.394s; **11** Steve Mercer (Honda), 1h 14m 8.963s; **12** Jamie Coward (Kawasaki), 1h 14m 15.701s; **13** Ivan Lintin (Kawasaki), 1h 14m 36.769s; **14** Martin Jessopp (Triumph), 1h 14m 55.862s; **15** Michal Dokoupil (Yamaha), 1h 15m 10.414s.
Fastest lap: Ian Hutchinson (Yamaha), 17m 43.346s, 127.736mph/205.571km/h, on lap 2.
Supersport lap record: Michael Dunlop (Honda), 17m 35.659s, 128.667mph/207.069km/h (2013).

Bennetts Lightweight TT (4 laps, 150.92 miles/242.88km)
1 Ivan Lintin (Kawasaki), 1h 16m 26.681s, 118.454mph/190.633km/h.
2 James Hillier (Kawasaki), 1h 16m 39.153s; **3** Martin Jessopp (Kawasaki), 1h 18m 23.536s; **4** Gary Johnson (WK Bikes), 1h 18m 25.920s; **5** Stefano Bonetti (Paton), 1h 18m 30.782s; **6** Daniel Cooper (Kawasaki), 1h 19m 6.561s; **7** Jamie Coward (Kawasaki), 1h 19m 37.988s; **8** Colin Stephenson (Kawasaki), 1h 20m 24.695s; **9** Bjorn Gunnarsson (Kawasaki), 1h 20m 25.519s; **10** James Cowton (Kawasaki), 1h 20m 30.711s; **11** Michal Dokoupil (Kawasaki), 1h 21m 12.530s; **12** Maria Costello (Kawasaki), 1h 21m 12.595s; **13** Barry Furber (Suzuki), 1h 21m 15.871s; **14** Dave Moffitt (Suzuki), 1h 21m 27.226s; **15** Adrian Harrison (Kawasaki), 1h 21m 36.358s.
Fastest lap: Ivan Lintin (Kawasaki), 18m 53.731s, 119.806mph/192.809km/h, on lap 2.
Lightweight TT record: James Hillier (Kawasaki), 18m 43.955s, 120.848mph/194.486km/h (2015).

SES TT Zero (1 lap, 37.73 miles/60.72km)
1 Bruce Anstey (Mugen),19m 7.043s, 118.416mph/190.570km/h.
2 William Dunlop (Victory), 19m 32.504s; **3** Daley Mathison (University of Nottingham), 22m 39.864s; **4** John McGuinness (Mugen), 23m 50.538s; **5** Allann Venter (Brunel), 23m 55.383s.
TT Zero lap record: John McGuinness (Mugen), 18m 58.743s, 119.279mph/191.961km/h (2015).

Sure Sidecar TT Race 2 (3 laps, 113.19 miles/182.16km)
1 Ben Birchall/Tom Birchall (LCR), 58m 43.187s, 115.658mph/186.134km/h.
2 John Holden/Andrew Winkle (LCR), 59m 21.971s; **3** Tim Reeves/Patrick Farrance (DMR), 59m 40.371s; **4** Karl Bennett/Lee Cain (Suzuki), 1h 1m 3.336s; **5** Matt Dix/Shaun Parker (Baker), 1h 1m 27.058s; **6** Steve Ramsden/Matty Ramsden (LCR), 1h 1m 37.240s; **7** Alan Founds/Aki Aalto (LCR), 1h 1m 50.291s; **8** Gary Bryan/Jamie Winn (Baker), 1h 1m 53.080s; **9** Tony Baker/Fiona Baker-Milligan (Suzuki), 1h 2m 4.277s; **10** Gordon Shand/Philip Hyde (SHAND F2), 1h 2m 55.143s; **11** Colin Buckley/Robbie Shorter (Suzuki), 1h 3m 0.791s; **12** Gary Knight/Daniel Evanson (DrVR), 1h 3m 1.333s; **13** Michael Grabmuller/Manfred Wechselberger (Yamaha), 1h 3m 35.243s; **14** Lewis Blackstock/Patrick Rosney (Suzuki), 1h 3m 48.118s; **15** John Saunders/Frank Claeys (Shelbourne), 1h 4m 14.475s.
Fastest lap: Ben Birchall/Tom Birchall (LCR), 19m 24.756s, 116.615mph/187.674km/h, on lap 2.
Sidecar lap record: Ben Birchall/Tom Birchall (LCR), 19m 22.928s, 116.798mph/187.968km/h (2016).

PokerStars Senior TT (6 laps, 226.38 miles/364.32km)
1 Michael Dunlop (BMW), 1h 43m 56.129s, 130.685mph/210.317km/h.
2 Ian Hutchinson (BMW), 1h 44m 27.605s; **3** John McGuinness (Honda), 1h 44m 58.651s; **4** Dean Harrison (Kawasaki), 1h 45m 51.385s; **5** Bruce Anstey (Honda), 1h 46m 8.108s; **6** Conor Cummins (Honda), 1h 46m 11.570s; **7** Michael Rutter (BMW), 1h 46m 20.009s; **8** Lee Johnston (BMW), 1h 47m 0.201s; **9** James Hillier (Kawasaki), 1h 47m 3.679s; **10** Ivan Lintin (Kawasaki), 1h 48m 22.931s; **11** Daniel Hegarty (Kawasaki), 1h 48m 32.609s; **12** Martin Jessopp (BMW), 1h 48m 42.225s; **13** Derek Sheils (Suzuki), 1h 49m 19.800s; **14** Shaun Anderson (Suzuki), 1h 49m 32.535s; **15** Horst Saiger (Kawasaki), 1h 49m 41.156s.
Fastest lap: Michael Dunlop (BMW), 16m 53.929s, 133.962mph/215.591km/h, on lap 2 (new Outright TT lap record).
Previous Senior TT lap record: John McGuinness (Honda), 17m 3.567s, 132.701mph/213.562km/h (2015).

British Championships

SILVERSTONE, 10 April 2016, 3.667-mile/5.902km circuit.
MCE British Superbike Championship, Round 1 (2 x 14 laps, 51.338 miles/82.621km)
Race 1
1 Michael Laverty (BMW), 29m 46.292s, 103.47mph/166.52km/h.
2 Shane Byrne (Ducati); **3** Christian Iddon (BMW); **4** Luke Mossey (Kawasaki); **5** Dan Linfoot (Honda); **6** Jason O'Halloran (Honda); **7** Danny Buchan (Ducati); **8** Lee Jackson (BMW); **9** John Hopkins (Yamaha); **10** Tommy Bridewell (Suzuki); **11** Ryuichi Kiyonari (Suzuki); **12** Richard Cooper (BMW); **13** James Ellison (Kawasaki); **14** Glenn Irwin (Ducati); **15** Jakub Smrz (BMW).
Fastest lap: Linfoot, 2m 5.758s, 104.98mph/168.95km/h.

Race 2
1 Peter Hickman (Kawasaki), 29m 43.355s, 103.64mph/166.79km/h.
2 Shane Byrne (Ducati); **3** Christian Iddon (BMW); **4** Jason O'Halloran (Honda); **5** Leon Haslam (Kawasaki); **6** Michael Laverty (BMW); **7** Lee Jackson (BMW); **8** James Ellison (Kawasaki); **9** Dan Linfoot (Honda); **10** Luke Mossey (Kawasaki); **11** Richard Cooper (BMW); **12** Ryuichi Kiyonari (Suzuki); **13** Glenn Irwin (Ducati); **14** Alastair Seeley (BMW); **15** Jakub Smrz (BMW).
Fastest lap: Hickman, 2m 6.403s, 104.44mph/168.09km/h.
Championship points: 1 Shane Byrne, 40; **2** Michael Laverty, 35; **3** Christian Iddon, 32; **4** Peter Hickman, 25; **5** Jason O'Halloran, 23; **6** Luke Mossey, 19.

Dickies British Supersport Championship, Round 1
Race 1 (12 laps 44.004 miles/70.818km)
1 Andy Reid (Kawasaki), 26m 23.696s, 100.03mph/160.98km/h.
2 Tarran Mackenzie (Kawasaki); **3** Mason Law (Kawasaki); **4** Ross Twyman (Yamaha); **5** James Westmoreland (Yamaha); **6** Jamie Perrin (Yamaha); **7** David Allingham (Yamaha); **8** Sam Coventry (Kawasaki); **9** Matthew Paulo (Yamaha); **10** Matt Truelove (Honda); **11** Bjorn Estment (Triumph); **12** Levi Day (Kawasaki); **13** Tommy Philp (Yamaha); **14** Josh Daley (Kawasaki); **15** Ryan Dixon (Yamaha).
Fastest lap: Reid, 2m 10.654s, 101.04mph/162.62km/h.
Championship points: 1 Reid, 25; **2** Mackenzie, 20; **3** Law, 16; **4** Twyman, 13; **5** Westmoreland, 11; **6** Perrin, 10.

HEL British Motostar Championship, Round 1
Race 1 (8 laps 29.336 miles/47.212km)
1 Charlie Nesbitt (KTM), 19m 49.396s, 88.80mph/142.91km/h.
2 Edward Rendell (Honda); **3** Jake Archer (KTM FTR); **4** Jorel Boerboom (Kalex KTM); **5** Josh Owens (Kalex KTM); **6** Tim Georgi (KTM); **7** Vasco van der Valk (Honda); **8** Elliot Lodge (Honda); **9** Mike Brouwers (Husqvarna); **10** Edmund Best (KTM); **11** Philipp Freitag (Honda); **12** Matthias Meggle (Honda); **13** Oliver Konig (Honda); **14** Sam Llewellyn (Honda); **15** Cameron Fraser (Kalex KTM).
Fastest lap: Nesbitt, 2m 26.388s, 90.18mph/145.14km/h.

Race 2 (10 laps 36.670 miles/59.015 km)
1 Dani Saez (Honda), 23m 49.054s, 92.38mph/148.67km/h.
2 Tim Georgi (KTM); **3** Edmund Best (KTM); **4** Elliot Lodge (Honda); **5** Ernst Dubbink (Honda); **6** Brian Slooten (Honda); **7** Richard Kerr (KTM); **8** Max Cook (Repli-Cast Moto3); **9** Oliver Konig (Honda); **10** Matthias Meggle (Honda); **11** Simon Jespersen (Honda); **12** Dirk Geiger (Honda); **13** Cameron Fraser (Kalex KTM); **14** Rick Dunnik (Honda); **15** Tomas de Vries (Honda).
Fastest lap: Saez, 2m 20.736s, 93.80mph/150.97km/h.
Championship points: 1 Best, 27; **2** Nesbitt, 25; **3** Lodge, 25; **4** Saez, 25; **5** Rendell, 20; **6** Archer, 16.

OULTON PARK, 2 May 2016, 2.692-mile/4.332km circuit.
MCE British Superbike Championship, Round 2 (2 x 18 laps, 48.456 miles/77.982km)
Race 1
1 Leon Haslam (Kawasaki), 31m 31.339s, 92.23mph/148.43km/h.
2 Christian Iddon (BMW); **3** James Ellison (Kawasaki); **4** Jason O'Halloran (Honda); **5** Alastair Seeley (BMW); **6** Michael Laverty (BMW); **7** Jack Kennedy (Kawasaki); **8** Shane Byrne (Ducati); **9** Richard Cooper (BMW); **10** Billy McConnell (Kawasaki); **11** John Hopkins (Yamaha); **12** Peter Hickman (Kawasaki); **13** Glenn Irwin (Ducati); **14** Lee Jackson (BMW); **15** Tommy Bridewell (Suzuki).
Fastest lap: Laverty, 1m 42.972s, 94.11mph/151.46km/h.

Race 2
1 Richard Cooper (BMW), 29m 50.563s, 97.42mph/156.78km/h.
2 Christian Iddon (BMW); **3** Leon Haslam (Kawasaki); **4** James Ellison (Kawasaki); **5** Michael Laverty (BMW); **6** Shane Byrne (Ducati); **7** Glenn Irwin (Ducati); **8** Jason O'Halloran (Honda); **9** Jack Kennedy (Kawasaki); **10** Stuart Easton (Yamaha); **11** Howie Mainwaring Smart (BMW); **12** Peter Hickman (Kawasaki); **13** Lee Jackson (BMW); **14** Tommy Bridewell (Suzuki); **15** Jakub Smrz (BMW).
Fastest lap: Ellison, 1m 36.473s, 100.45mph/161.66km/h.
Championship points: 1 Christian Iddon, 72; **2** Shane Byrne, 58; **3** Michael Laverty, 56; **4** Leon Haslam, 52; **5** Jason O'Halloran, 44; **6** Richard Cooper, 41.

Dickies British Supersport Championship, Round 2
Race 1 (10 laps 26.920 miles/43.324km)
1 Benjamin Currie (Yamaha), 18m 27.789s, 87.48mph/140.79km/h.
2 Luke Jones (Triumph); **3** James Westmoreland (Yamaha); **4** Andrew Irwin (Yamaha); **5** Luke Hedger (Kawasaki); **6** Ross Twyman (Yamaha); **7** Andy Reid (Kawasaki); **8** Mason Law (Kawasaki); **9** Bjorn Estment (Triumph); **10** Ben Stafford (Kawasaki); **11** Ryan Dixon (Yamaha); **12** Matt Truelove (Kawasaki); **13** David Allingham (Yamaha); **14** Tommy Philp (Yamaha); **15** Sam Coventry (Kawasaki).
Fastest lap: Jones, 1m 47.982s, 89.74mph/144.43km/h.

Race 2 (10 laps 26.920 miles/43.320km)
1 Andy Reid (Kawasaki), 17m 0.802s, 94.93mph/152.78km/h.
2 Luke Hedger (Kawasaki); **3** James Westmoreland (Yamaha); **4** Jake Dixon (MV Agusta); **5** Luke Jones (Triumph); **6** David Allingham (Yamaha); **7** Jamie Perrin (Yamaha); **8** Sam Coventry (Kawasaki); **9** Ben Stafford (Kawasaki); **10** Bjorn Estment (Triumph); **11** Ian Hutchinson (Yamaha); **12** Matt Truelove (Kawasaki); **13** Josh Daley (Kawasaki); **14** Ryan Dixon (Yamaha); **15** Levi Day (Kawasaki).
Fastest lap: Mackenzie, 1m 38.363s, 98.52mph/158.56km/h.
Championship points: 1 Reid, 59; **2** Westmoreland, 43; **3** Jones, 31; **4** Hedger, 31; **5** Currie, 25; **6** Law, 24.

HEL British Motostar Championship, Round 2
Race 1 (14 laps 37.688 miles/60.653km)
1 Charlie Nesbitt (KTM), 25m 19.135s, 89.31mph/143.73km/h.
2 Josh Owens (Kalex KTM); **3** Jake Archer (KTM FTR); **4** Dani Saez (Honda); **5** Elliot Lodge (Honda); **6** Tom Booth-Amos (Tigcraft); **7** Vasco van der Valk (Honda); **8** Max Cook (Repli-Cast Moto3); **9** Mike Brouwers (Husqvarna); **10** Eugene McManus (KTM); **11** Stephen Campbell (Honda); **12** Asher Durham (Honda); **13** Cameron Horsman (Honda); **14** TJ Toms (Honda); **15** Mark Clayton (Honda).
Fastest lap: Owens, 1m 47.090s, 90.49mph/145.64km/h.
Championship points: 1 Nesbitt, 50; **2** Saez, 38; **3** Lodge, 36; **4** Archer, 32; **5** Owens, 31; **6** Best, 27.

BRANDS HATCH INDY, 22 May 2016, 1.208-mile/1.944km circuit.
MCE British Superbike Championship, Round 3 (2 x 30 laps, 36.240 miles/58.323km)
Race 1
1 Leon Haslam (Kawasaki), 23m 31.105s, 92.45mph/148.78km/h.
2 James Ellison (Kawasaki); **3** Tommy Bridewell (Suzuki); **4** Richard Cooper (BMW); **5** Luke Mossey (Kawasaki); **6** Michael Laverty (BMW); **7** Peter Hickman (Kawasaki); **8** Jason O'Halloran (Honda); **9** Shane Byrne (Ducati); **10** Dan Linfoot (Honda); **11** Christian Iddon (BMW); **12** John Hopkins (Yamaha); **13** Glenn Irwin (Ducati); **14** Stuart Easton (Yamaha); **15** Lee Jackson (BMW).
Fastest lap: Mossey, 45.590s, 95.38mph/153.50km/h.

Race 2
1 Shane Byrne (Ducati), 23m 31.155s, 92.44mph/148.77km/h.
2 Richard Cooper (BMW); **3** Leon Haslam (Kawasaki); **4** Tommy Bridewell (Suzuki); **5** Dan Linfoot (Honda); **6** Jason O'Halloran (Honda); **7** Christian Iddon (BMW); **8** Peter Hickman (Kawasaki); **9** Stuart Easton (Yamaha); **10** Luke Mossey (Kawasaki); **11** John Hopkins (Yamaha); **12** Lee Jackson (BMW); **13** Howie Mainwaring Smart (BMW); **14** Alastair Seeley (BMW); **15** Danny Buchan (Ducati).
Fastest lap: Byrne, 45.590s, 95.38mph/153.50km/h.
Championship points: 1 Leon Haslam, 93; **2** Shane Byrne, 90; **3** Christian Iddon, 86; **4** Richard Cooper, 74; **5** Michael Laverty, 66; **6** Jason O'Halloran, 62.

Dickies British Supersport Championship, Round 3
Race 1 (12 laps 14.496 miles/23.329 km)
1 James Westmoreland (Yamaha), 10m 4.838s, 86.27mph/138.84km/h.
2 Joe Francis (Yamaha); **3** Jake Dixon (MV Agusta); **4** Andy Reid (Kawasaki); **5** Andrew Irwin (Yamaha); **6** Joe Collier (Triumph); **7** Ross Twyman (Yamaha); **8** Jamie Perrin (Yamaha); **9** Luke Hedger (Kawasaki); **10** Bradley Ray (Yamaha); **11** Mark Conlin (Triumph); **12** Sam Lambert (Kawasaki); **13** David Allingham (Yamaha); **14** Joe Thompson (Kawasaki); **15** Tommy Philp (Yamaha).
Fastest lap: Francis, 48.149s, 90.31mph/145.34km/h.

Race 2 (26 laps 31.408 miles/50.546 km)
1 Joe Francis (Yamaha), 20m 33.382s, 91.66mph/147.51km/h.
2 Tarran Mackenzie (Kawasaki); **3** Luke Jones (Triumph); **4** Andy Reid (Kawasaki); **5** James Westmoreland (Yamaha); **6** Luke Hedger (Kawasaki); **7** Jake Dixon (MV Agusta); **8** Andrew Irwin (Yamaha); **9** Joe Collier (Triumph); **10** Jamie

Perrin (Yamaha); **11** Bjorn Estment (Triumph); **12** Bradley Ray (Yamaha); **13** Mason Law (Kawasaki); **14** Ben Stafford (Kawasaki); **15** Sam Coventry (Kawasaki).
Fastest lap: Jones, 46.842s, 92.83mph/149.40km/h.
Championship points: 1 Reid, 85; **2** Westmoreland, 79; **3** Hedger, 48; **4** Jones, 47; **5** Francis, 45; **6** Mackenzie, 40.

HEL British Motostar Championship, Round 3
Race 1 (16 laps 19.328 miles/31.105km)
1 Tom Booth-Amos (Tigcraft), 13m 45.386s, 84.29mph/135.65km/h.
2 Jake Archer (KTM FTR); **3** Elliot Lodge (Honda); **4** Jorel Boerboom (Kalex KTM); **5** Max Cook (Repli-Cast Moto3); **6** Charlie Nesbitt (KTM); **7** Vasco van der Valk (Honda); **8** Josh Owens (Kalex KTM); **9** Edward Rendell (Ten Kate Honda); **10** Richard Kerr (KTM); **11** Lee Hindle (KTM); **12** Mike Brouwers (Husqvarna); **13** Brian Slooten (Honda); **14** Sam Llewellyn (Honda); **15** Eugene McManus (KTM).
Fastest lap: Booth-Amos, 50.510s, 86.09mph/138.55km/h.

Race 2 (22 laps 26.576 miles/42.77km)
1 Charlie Nesbitt (KTM), 18m 49.736s, 84.68mph/136.28km/h.
2 Jake Archer (KTM FTR); **3** Jorel Boerboom (Kalex KTM); **4** Edmund Best (KTM); **5** Vasco van der Valk (Honda); **6** Brian Slooten (Honda); **7** Max Cook (Repli-Cast Moto3); **8** Josh Owens (Kalex KTM); **9** Elliot Lodge (Honda); **10** Mike Brouwers (Husqvarna); **11** Lee Hindle (KTM); **12** Cameron Fraser (Kalex KTM); **13** Eugene McManus (KTM); **14** Dani Saez (Honda); **15** Tomas de Vries (Honda).
Fastest lap: Nesbitt, 49.611s, 87.65mph/141.06km/h.
Championship points: 1 Nesbitt, 85; **2** Archer, 72; **3** Lodge, 59; **4** Owens, 47; **5** Booth-Amos, 44; **6** Cook, 42.

KNOCKHILL, 26 June 2016, 1.267-mile/2.039km circuit.
MCE British Superbike Championship, Round 4 (2 x 30 laps, 38.007 miles/61.166km)
Race 1
1 Leon Haslam (Kawasaki), 25m 32.723s, 89.27mph/143.67km/h.
2 Dan Linfoot (Honda); **3** Luke Mossey (Kawasaki); **4** John Hopkins (Yamaha); **5** Peter Hickman (Kawasaki); **6** Richard Cooper (BMW); **7** James Ellison (Kawasaki); **8** Michael Laverty (BMW); **9** Jason O'Halloran (Honda); **10** Danny Buchan (Ducati); **11** Glenn Irwin (Ducati); **12** Tommy Bridewell (Suzuki); **13** Lee Jackson (BMW); **14** Christian Iddon (BMW); **15** Alastair Seeley (BMW).
Fastest lap: Linfoot, 48.458s, 94.12mph/151.47km/h.

Race 2
1 Shane Byrne (Ducati), 26m 49.388s, 85.02mph/136.83km/h.
2 James Ellison (Kawasaki); **3** Dan Linfoot (Honda); **4** Peter Hickman (Kawasaki); **5** Jason O'Halloran (Honda); **6** Leon Haslam (Kawasaki); **7** Richard Cooper (BMW); **8** Tommy Bridewell (Suzuki); **9** Howie Mainwaring Smart (BMW); **10** Christian Iddon (BMW); **11** Danny Buchan (Ducati); **12** Luke Mossey (Kawasaki); **13** Jake Dixon (BMW); **14** Stuart Easton (Yamaha); **15** Lee Jackson (BMW).
Fastest lap: Ellison, 52.482s, 86.90mph/139.86km/h.
Championship points: 1 Leon Haslam, 128; **2** Shane Byrne, 115; **3** Christian Iddon, 94; **4** Richard Cooper, 93; **5** James Ellison, 89; **6** Jason O'Halloran, 80.

Dickies British Supersport Championship, Round 4
Race 1 (18 laps 22.804 miles/36.699km)
1 Benjamin Currie (Yamaha), 16m 32.546s, 82.71mph/133.11km/h.
2 James Westmoreland (Yamaha); **3** Luke Jones (Triumph); **4** Lee Johnston (Triumph); **5** Joe Francis (Yamaha); **6** Ross Twyman (Yamaha); **7** David Allingham (Yamaha); **8** Tarran Mackenzie (Kawasaki); **9** Matt Truelove (Yamaha); **10** Mason Law (Kawasaki); **11** Andrew Irwin (Yamaha); **12** Joe Collier (Triumph); **13** Bradley Ray (Yamaha); **14** Ben Stafford (Kawasaki); **15** Ryan Dixon (Yamaha).
Fastest lap: Currie, 53.864s, 84.67mph/136.27km/h.

Race 2 (26 laps 32.939 miles/53.01km)
1 Tarran Mackenzie (Kawasaki), 23m 38.465s, 83.60mph/134.54km/h.
2 Luke Jones (Triumph); **3** James Westmoreland (Yamaha); **4** Benjamin Currie (Yamaha); **5** Joe Francis (Yamaha); **6** Luke Hedger (Kawasaki); **7** Andrew Irwin (Yamaha); **8** Andy Reid (Kawasaki); **9** David Allingham (Yamaha); **10** Ben Stafford (Kawasaki); **11** Matt Truelove (Yamaha); **12** Bjorn Estment (Triumph); **13** Bradley Ray (Yamaha); **14** Sam Coventry (Kawasaki); **15** Robert Kennedy (Yamaha).
Fastest lap: Jones, 53.553s, 85.17mph/137.06km/h.
Championship points: 1 Westmoreland, 115; **2** Reid, 93; **3** Jones, 83; **4** Mackenzie, 73; **5** Francis, 67; **6** Currie, 63.

HEL British Motostar Championship, Round 4
Race 1 (16 laps 20.270 miles/32.621km)
1 Charlie Nesbitt (KTM), 14m 16.380s, 85.21mph/137.13km/h.
2 Jake Archer (KTM FTR); **3** Edward Rendell (Ten Kate Honda); **4** Dani Saez (Honda); **5** Elliot Lodge (Honda); **6** Tom Booth-Amos (Tigcraft); **7** Jorel Boerboom (Kalex KTM); **8** Mike Brouwers (Husqvarna); **9** Edmund Best (KTM); **10** Lee Hindle (KTM); **11** Max Cook (Repli-Cast); **12** Joel Marklund (Honda); **13** Sam Llewellyn (Honda); **14** Dan Jones (Honda); **15** Mark Clayton (Honda).
Fastest lap: Nesbitt, 52.841s, 86.31mph/138.91km/h.

Race 2 (22 laps 27.872 miles/44.856km)
1 Edward Rendell (Ten Kate Honda), 21m 33.998s, 77.54mph/124.79km/h.
2 Charlie Nesbitt (KTM); **3** Jorel Boerboom (Kalex KTM); **4** Tom Booth-Amos (Tigcraft); **5** Jake Archer (KTM FTR); **6** Edmund Best (KTM); **7** Mike Brouwers (Husqvarna); **8** Dani Saez (Honda); **9** Mark Clayton (Honda); **10** Dan Jones (Honda); **11** Sam Llewellyn (Honda); **12** Max Cook (Repli-Cast); **13** Stephen Campbell (Honda); **14** Tomas De Vries (Honda); **15** Asher Durham (Honda).
Fastest lap: Nesbitt, 57.201s, 79.73mph/128.32km/h.
Championship points: 1 Nesbitt, 130; **2** Archer, 103; **3** Lodge, 70; **4** Rendell, 68; **5** Booth-Amos, 67; **6** Boerboom, 67.

SNETTERTON, 10 July 2016, 2.969-mile/4.778km circuit.
MCE British Superbike Championship, Round 5
Race 1 (16 laps 47.504 miles/76.450km)
1 Jason O'Halloran (Honda), 29m 20.434s, 97.14mph/156.33km/h.
2 Dan Linfoot (Honda); **3** Shane Byrne (Ducati); **4** Billy McConnell (Kawasaki); **5** Leon Haslam (Kawasaki); **6** Jake Dixon (BMW); **7** Luke Mossey (Kawasaki); **8** Tommy Bridewell (Suzuki); **9** Stuart Easton (Yamaha); **10** Lee Jackson (BMW); **11** Jakub Smrz (BMW); **12** Danny Buchan (Ducati); **13** James Rispoli (Yamaha); **14** Alastair Seeley (BMW); **15** Filip Backlund (Kawasaki).
Fastest lap: Byrne, 1m 47.714s, 99.22mph/159.68km/h.

Race 2 (12 laps 35.628 miles/57.338km)
1 Shane Byrne (Ducati), 21m 52.481s, 97.72mph/157.27km/h.
2 Dan Linfoot (Honda); **3** Michael Laverty (BMW); **4** Leon Haslam (Kawasaki); **5** Jason O'Halloran (Honda); **6** Christian Iddon (BMW); **7** Glenn Irwin (Ducati); **8** Peter Hickman (Kawasaki); **9** Danny Buchan (Ducati); **10** Tommy Bridewell (Suzuki); **11** Richard Cooper (BMW); **12** Jake Dixon (BMW); **13** Luke Mossey (Kawasaki); **14** Billy McConnell (Kawasaki); **15** Lee Jackson (BMW).
Fastest lap: Linfoot, 1m 48.223s, 98.75mph/158.93km/h.
Championship points: 1 Shane Byrne, 156; **2** Leon Haslam, 152; **3** Jason O'Halloran, 116; **4** Dan Linfoot, 111; **5** Christian Iddon, 104; **6** Richard Cooper, 98.

Dickies British Supersport Championship, Round 5
Race 1 (9 laps 26.721 miles/43.003km)
1 Luke Stapleford (Triumph), 18m 8.107s, 88.40mph/142.27km/h.
2 Tarran Mackenzie (Kawasaki); **3** David Allingham (Yamaha); **4** Bradley Ray (Yamaha); **5** Andrew Irwin (Yamaha); **6** Andy Reid (Kawasaki); **7** Ross Twyman (Yamaha); **8** Lee Johnston (Triumph); **9** Joe Francis (Yamaha); **10** Mason Law (Kawasaki); **11** Joe Collier (Triumph); **12** Jamie Perrin (Yamaha); **13** Ben Stafford (Kawasaki); **14** Matt Truelove (Yamaha); **15** Tommy Philp (Yamaha).
Fastest lap: Stapleford, 1m 52.222s, 95.24mph/153.27km/h.

Race 2 (15 laps 44.535 miles/71.672km)
1 Tarran Mackenzie (Kawasaki), 28m 16.042s, 94.52mph/152.12km/h.
2 Luke Stapleford (Triumph); **3** Bradley Ray (Yamaha); **4** Mason Law (Kawasaki); **5** Luke Jones (Triumph); **6** David Allingham (Yamaha); **7** James Westmoreland (Yamaha); **8** Benjamin Currie (Yamaha); **9** Matt Truelove (Yamaha); **10** Andrew Irwin (Yamaha); **11** Luke Hedger (Kawasaki); **12** Joe Collier (Triumph); **13** Jamie Perrin (Yamaha); **14** Sam Coventry (Kawasaki); **15** Joe Francis (Yamaha).
Fastest lap: Stapleford, 1m 51.677s, 95.70mph/154.02km/h.
Championship points: 1 Westmoreland, 124; **2** Mackenzie, 118; **3** Reid, 103; **4** Jones, 94; **5** Francis, 75; **6** Currie, 71.

HEL British Motostar Championship, Round 5
Race 1 (9 laps 26.721 miles/43.003km)
1 Charlie Nesbitt (KTM), 18m 32.749s, 86.44mph/139.11km/h.
2 Josh Owens (Kalex KTM); **3** Richard Kerr (KTM); **4** Edward Rendell (Ten Kate Honda); **5** Brian Slooten (Bakker Honda); **6** Jake Archer (KTM FTR); **7** Mike Brouwers (Husqvarna); **8** Tom Booth-Amos (Tigcraft); **9** Edmund Best (KTM); **10** Jorel Boerboom (Kalex KTM); **11** Elliot Lodge (Honda); **12** Dani Saez (Honda); **13** Max Cook (Repli-Cast Moto3); **14** Dan Jones (Honda); **15** Eugene McManus (KTM).
Fastest lap: Kerr, 2m 2.553s, 87.21mph/140.35km/h.

Race 2 (10 laps 29.690 miles/47.781km)
1 Charlie Nesbitt (KTM), 20m 29.167s, 86.95mph/139.93km/h.
2 Tom Booth-Amos (Tigcraft); **3** Edward Rendell (Ten Kate Honda); **4** Mike Brouwers (Husqvarna); **5** Elliot Lodge (Honda); **6** Jake Archer (KTM FTR); **7** Brian Slooten (Bakker Honda); **8** Richard Kerr (KTM); **9** Eugene McManus (KTM); **10** Jorel Boerboom (Kalex KTM); **11** Dani Saez (Honda); **12** Dan Jones (Honda); **13** Storm Stacey (Honda); **14** Max Cook (Repli-Cast Moto3); **15** Tomas De Vries (Honda).
Fastest lap: Nesbitt, 2m 1.997s, 87.60mph/140.99km/h.
Championship points: 1 Nesbitt, 180; **2** Archer, 123; **3** Rendell, 97; **4** Booth-Amos, 95; **5** Lodge, 86; **6** Boerboom, 79.

THRUXTON, 24 July 2016, 2.356-mile/3.792km circuit.
MCE British Superbike Championship, Round 6
Race 1 (12 laps 28.272 miles/45.499km)
1 Shane Byrne (Ducati), 15m 26.616s, 109.83mph/176.75km/h.
2 Michael Laverty (BMW); **3** Luke Mossey (Kawasaki); **4** Tommy Bridewell (Suzuki); **5** James Ellison (Kawasaki); **6** Jason O'Halloran (Honda); **7** Ryuichi Kiyonari (Suzuki); **8** Richard Cooper (BMW); **9** Jakub Smrz (BMW); **10** Martin Jessopp (BMW); **11** Glenn Irwin (Ducati); **12** Peter Hickman (Kawasaki); **13** Leon Haslam (Kawasaki); **14** Luke Stapleford (BMW); **15** Filip Backlund (Kawasaki).
Fastest lap: Byrne, 1m 15.858s, 111.80mph/179.93km/h.

Race 2 (18 laps 42.408 miles/68.249km)
1 Michael Laverty (BMW), 22m 53.903s, 111.12mph/178.83km/h.
2 Jason O'Halloran (Honda); **3** Glenn Irwin (Ducati); **4** Luke Mossey (Kawasaki); **5** Leon Haslam (Kawasaki); **6** Peter Hickman (Kawasaki); **7** James Ellison (Kawasaki); **8** Tommy Bridewell (Suzuki); **9** Dan Linfoot (Honda); **10** Lee Jackson (BMW); **11** Ryuichi Kiyonari (Suzuki); **12** Jakub Smrz (BMW); **13** Christian Iddon (BMW); **14** Josh Hook (Kawasaki); **15** Martin Jessopp (BMW).
Fastest lap: Linfoot, 1m 15.363s, 112.54mph/181.12km/h.
Championship points: 1 Shane Byrne, 181; **2** Leon Haslam, 166; **3** Jason O'Halloran, 146; **4** Michael Laverty, 135; **5** Dan Linfoot, 118; **6** James Ellison, 109.

Dickies British Supersport Championship, Round 6
Race 1 (12 laps 28.272 miles/45.499km)
1 Andy Reid (Kawasaki), 15m 41.789s, 108.07mph/173.92km/h.
2 Tarran Mackenzie (Kawasaki); **3** James Westmoreland (Yamaha); **4** Bradley Ray (Yamaha); **5** Mason Law (Kawasaki); **6** Luke Jones (Triumph); **7** Benjamin Currie (Yamaha); **8** David Allingham (Yamaha); **9** Andrew Irwin (Kawasaki); **10** Ross Twyman (Yamaha); **11** Matt Truelove (Yamaha); **12** Bjorn Estment (Triumph); **13** Matthew Paulo (Yamaha); **14** Ben Stafford (Kawasaki); **15** Joe Collier (Triumph).
Fastest lap: Ray, 1m 17.228s, 109.82mph/176.74km/h.

Race 2 (16 laps 37.696 miles/60.666km)
1 Andy Reid (Kawasaki), 20m 51.747s, 108.41mph/174.47km/h.
2 Bradley Ray (Yamaha); **3** Tarran Mackenzie (Kawasaki); **4** James Westmoreland (Yamaha); **5** Benjamin Currie (Yamaha); **6** David Allingham (Yamaha); **7** Bjorn Estment (Triumph); **8** Joe Francis (Yamaha); **9** Matt Truelove (Yamaha); **10** Sam Wilford (Yamaha); **11** Ross Twyman (Yamaha); **12** Jamie Perrin (Yamaha); **13** Joe Collier (Triumph); **14** Levi Day (Kawasaki); **15** Sam Coventry (Kawasaki).
Fastest lap: Reid, 1m 17.457s, 109.50mph/176.22km/h.
Championship points: 1 Mackenzie, 154; **2** Reid, 153; **3** Westmoreland, 153; **4** Jones, 104; **5** Currie, 91; **6** Allingham, 85.

HEL British Motostar Championship, Round 6
Race 1 (10 laps 23.560 miles/37.916km)
1 Charlie Nesbitt (KTM), 13m 43.914s, 102.94mph/165.67km/h.
2 Mike Brouwers (Husqvarna); **3** Jake Archer (KTM FTR); **4** Dani Saez (Honda); **5** Jorel Boerboom (Kalex KTM); **6** Josh Owens (Kalex KTM); **7** Edward Rendell (Ten Kate Honda); **8** Eugene McManus (KTM); **9** Edmund Best (KTM); **10** Richard Kerr (KTM); **11** Elliot Lodge (Honda); **12** Dan Jones (Honda); **13** Sam Llewellyn (Honda); **14** Cameron Horsman (Honda); **15** Max Cook (Repli-Cast Moto3).
Fastest lap: Brouwers, 1m 21.376s, 104.22mph/167.73km/h.

Race 2 (12 laps 28.272 miles/45.499km)
1 Charlie Nesbitt (KTM), 16m 26.298s, 103.19mph/166.07km/h.
2 Josh Owens (Kalex KTM); **3** Dani Saez (Honda); **4** Edward Rendell (Ten Kate Honda); **5** Richard Kerr (KTM); **6** Eugene McManus (KTM); **7** Max Cook (Repli-Cast Moto3); **8** Elliot Lodge (Honda); **9** Dan Jones (Honda); **10** Sam Llewellyn (Honda); **11** Tom Booth-Amos (Tigcraft); **12** Mark Clayton (Honda); **13** Liam Delves (Honda); **14** Asher Durham (Honda); **15** Storm Stacey (Honda).
Fastest lap: Brouwers, 1m 21.259s, 104.37mph/167.97km/h.
Championship points: 1 Nesbitt, 230; **2** Archer, 139; **3** Rendell, 119; **4** Booth-Amos, 101; **5** Lodge, 99; **6** Saez, 99.

BRANDS HATCH GP, 7 August 2016, 2.433-mile/3.916km circuit.
MCE British Superbike Championship, Round 7
Race 1 (20 laps 48.660 miles/78.311km)
1 Shane Byrne (Ducati), 29m 19.348s, 99.58mph/160.26km/h.
2 Leon Haslam (Kawasaki); **3** Luke Mossey (Kawasaki); **4** Jason O'Halloran (Honda); **5** Lee Jackson (BMW); **6** Broc Parkes (Yamaha); **7** Dan Linfoot (Honda); **8** Richard Cooper (BMW); **9** Christian Iddon (BMW); **10** James Ellison (Kawasaki); **11** Peter Hickman (Kawasaki); **12** Billy McConnell (Kawasaki); **13** Jake Dixon (BMW); **14** Michael Laverty (BMW); **15** John Hopkins (Yamaha).
Fastest lap: Mossey, 1m 25.753s, 102.15mph/164.39km/h.

Race 2
1 Shane Byrne (Ducati), 32m 16.000s, 99.54mph/160.19km/h.
2 Leon Haslam (Kawasaki); **3** Jason O'Halloran (Honda); **4** Glenn Irwin (Ducati); **5** Richard Cooper (BMW); **6** Lee Jackson (BMW); **7** Luke Mossey (Kawasaki); **8** Dan Linfoot (Honda); **9** James Ellison (Kawasaki); **10** Christian Iddon (BMW); **11** Peter Hickman (Kawasaki); **12** Jake Dixon (BMW); **13** Broc Parkes (Yamaha); **14** Jakub Smrz (BMW); **15** Billy McConnell (Kawasaki).
Fastest lap: Byrne, 1m 25.687s, 102.23mph/164.52km/h.
Championship points: 1 Shane Byrne, 231; **2** Leon Haslam, 206; **3** Jason O'Halloran, 175; **4** Michael Laverty, 137; **5** Dan Linfoot, 135; **6** Richard Cooper, 125.

Dickies British Supersport Championship, Round 7
Race 1 (12 laps 29.196 miles/46.986km)
1 Tarran Mackenzie (Kawasaki), 18m 40.627s, 93.80mph/150.96km/h.
2 Bradley Ray (Yamaha); **3** Luke Jones (Triumph); **4** Mason Law (Kawasaki); **5** David Allingham (Yamaha); **6** Luke Hedger (Yamaha); **7** Andy Reid (Kawasaki); **8** Joe Francis (Yamaha); **9** Matt Truelove (Yamaha); **10** Benjamin Currie (Yamaha); **11** Joe Collier (Triumph); **12** Jamie Perrin (Yamaha); **13** Sam Wilford (Yamaha); **14** Phil Wakefield (Triumph); **15** Tommy Philp (Yamaha).
Fastest lap: Westmoreland, 1m 28.577s, 98.89mph/159.15km/h.

Race 2 (12 laps 29.196 miles/46.986km)
1 Tarran Mackenzie (Kawasaki), 17m 52.740s, 97.99mph/157.7km/h.
2 James Westmoreland (Yamaha); **3** Bradley Ray (Yamaha); **4** David Allingham (Yamaha); **5** Joe Francis (Yamaha); **6** Ross Twyman (Yamaha); **7** Benjamin Currie (Yamaha); **8** Andy Reid (Kawasaki); **9** Sam Wilford (Yamaha); **10** Joe Collier (Triumph); **11** Jamie Perrin (Yamaha); **12** Matthew Paulo (Yamaha); **13** Sam Coventry (Kawasaki); **14** Ryan Dixon (Yamaha); **15** Phil Wakefield (Triumph).
Fastest lap: Westmoreland, 1m 28.378s, 99.11mph/159.51km/h.

Race 3 (14 laps 34.062 miles/54.817km)
1 James Westmoreland (Yamaha), 21m 41.129s, 94.25mph/151.68km/h.
2 Luke Jones (Triumph); **3** Mason Law (Kawasaki); **4** David Allingham (Yamaha); **5** Benjamin Currie (Yamaha); **6** Andy Reid (Kawasaki); **7** Joe Francis (Yamaha); **8** Jamie Perrin (Yamaha); **9** Sam Coventry (Kawasaki); **10** Sam Wilford (Yamaha); **11** Joe Collier (Triumph); **12** Matthew Paulo (Yamaha); **13** Bjorn Estment (Triumph); **14** Tommy Philp (Yamaha); **15** Robert Kennedy (Yamaha).
Fastest lap: Currie, 1m 28.677s, 98.78mph/158.97km/h.
Championship points: 1 Mackenzie, 204; **2** Westmoreland, 198; **3** Reid, 180; **4** Jones, 140; **5** Allingham, 122; **6** Currie, 117.

HEL British Motostar Championship, Round 7
Race 1 (10 laps 24.330 miles/39.155km)
1 Charlie Nesbitt (KTM), 15m 45.054s, 92.69mph/149.17km/h.

2 Josh Owens (Kalex KTM); 3 Jake Archer (KTM FTR); 4 Dani Saez (Honda); 5 Edward Rendell (Ten Kate Honda); 6 Brian Slooten (Bakker Honda); 7 Tom Booth-Amos (Tigcraft); 8 Elliot Lodge (Honda); 9 Jorel Boerboom (Kalex KTM); 10 Edmund Best (KTM); 11 Max Cook (Repli-Cast Moto3); 12 Dan Jones (Honda); 13 Tomas De Vries (Honda); 14 Sam Llewellyn (Honda); 15 TJ Toms (Honda).
Fastest lap: Nesbitt, 1m 33.712s, 93.47mph/150.43km/h.
Race 2 (14 laps 34.062 miles/54.817km)
1 Charlie Nesbitt (KTM), 22m 4.559s, 92.58mph/148.99km/h.
2 Josh Owens (Kalex KTM); 3 Jake Archer (KTM FTR); 4 Richard Kerr (KTM); 5 Dani Saez (Honda); 6 Edward Rendell (Ten Kate Honda); 7 Brian Slooten (Bakker Honda); 8 Elliot Lodge (Honda); 9 Max Cook (Repli-Cast Moto3); 10 Dan Jones (Honda); 11 TJ Toms (Honda); 12 Sam Llewellyn (Honda); 13 Thomas Strudwick (Honda); 14 Lee Hindle (KTM); 15 Mark Clayton (Honda).
Fastest lap: Nesbitt, 1m 33.809s, 93.37mph/150.27km/h.
Championship points: 1 Nesbitt, 280; 2 Archer, 171; 3 Rendell, 140; 4 Owens, 137; 5 Saez, 123; 6 Lodge, 115.

CADWELL PARK, 29 August 2016, 2.180-mile/3.508km circuit.
MCE British Superbike Championship, Round 8 (2 x 18 laps, 39.240 miles/63.151km)
Race 1
1 Shane Byrne (Ducati), 26m 20.366s, 89.38mph/143.84km/h.
2 Leon Haslam (Kawasaki); 3 Jason O'Halloran (Honda); 4 Tommy Bridewell (Suzuki); 5 Glenn Irwin (Ducati); 6 James Ellison (Kawasaki); 7 Peter Hickman (Kawasaki); 8 Richard Cooper (BMW); 9 Jake Dixon (BMW); 10 Michael Laverty (BMW); 11 Danny Buchan (Kawasaki); 12 Luke Mossey (Kawasaki); 13 Billy McConnell (Kawasaki); 14 John Hopkins (Yamaha); 15 Alastair Seeley (BMW).
Fastest lap: Haslam, 1m 26.590s, 90.63mph/145.86km/h.

Race 2
1 Leon Haslam (Kawasaki), 27m 9.544s, 86.68mph/139.5km/h.
2 Jason O'Halloran (Honda); 3 Shane Byrne (Ducati); 4 Peter Hickman (Kawasaki); 5 Tommy Bridewell (Suzuki); 6 Dan Linfoot (Honda); 7 Glenn Irwin (Ducati); 8 James Ellison (Kawasaki); 9 Luke Mossey (Kawasaki); 10 Jake Dixon (BMW); 11 Lee Jackson (BMW); 12 Michael Laverty (BMW); 13 Billy McConnell (Kawasaki); 14 Danny Buchan (Kawasaki); 15 John Hopkins (Yamaha).
Fastest lap: Haslam, 1m 26.849s, 90.36mph/145.42km/h.
Championship points: 1 Shane Byrne, 272; 2 Leon Haslam, 251; 3 Jason O'Halloran, 211; 4 Michael Laverty, 147; 5 Dan Linfoot, 145; 6 James Ellison, 140.

Dickies British Supersport Championship, Round 8
Race 1 (12 laps 26.160 miles/42.100km)
1 Bradley Ray (Yamaha), 18m 0.320s, 87.17mph/140.29km/h.
2 Mason Law (Kawasaki); 3 Luke Jones (Triumph); 4 Andrew Irwin (Kawasaki); 5 James Westmoreland (Yamaha); 6 David Allingham (Yamaha); 7 Ross Twyman (Yamaha); 8 Benjamin Currie (Yamaha); 9 Tarran Mackenzie (Kawasaki); 10 Luke Hedger (Yamaha); 11 Joe Francis (Yamaha); 12 Joe Collier (Triumph); 13 Matthew Paulo (Yamaha); 14 Freddy Pett (Triumph); 15 Sam Wilford (Yamaha).
Fastest lap: Ray, 1m 29.111s, 88.07mph/141.73km/h.

Race 2 (16 laps 34.880 miles/56.134km)
1 Bradley Ray (Yamaha), 24m 3.872s, 86.96mph/139.95km/h.
2 Mason Law (Kawasaki); 3 James Westmoreland (Yamaha); 4 Benjamin Currie (Yamaha); 5 Tarran Mackenzie (Kawasaki); 6 David Allingham (Yamaha); 7 Luke Hedger (Yamaha); 8 Ross Twyman (Yamaha); 9 Joe Collier (Triumph); 10 Sam Coventry (Kawasaki); 11 Freddy Pett (Triumph); 12 Sam Wilford (Yamaha); 13 Bjorn Estment (Triumph); 14 Joey Thompson (Kawasaki); 15 Phil Wakefield (Triumph).
Fastest lap: Ray, 1m 29.606s, 87.58mph/140.95km/h.
Championship points: 1 Westmoreland, 225; 2 Mackenzie, 222; 3 Reid, 180; 4 Ray, 164; 5 Jones, 156; 6 Allingham, 142.

HEL British Motostar Championship, Round 8
Race 1 (10 laps 21.800 miles/35.084km)
1 Charlie Nesbitt (KTM), 15m 45.227s, 83.02mph/133.61km/h.
2 Jake Archer (KTM FTR); 3 Edward Rendell (Ten Kate Honda); 4 Dani Saez (Honda); 5 Tom Booth-Amos (Tigcraft); 6 Edmund Best (KTM); 7 Elliot Lodge (Honda); 8 Jorel Boerboom (Kalex KTM); 9 Brian Slooten (Bakker Honda); 10 Josh Owens (Kalex KTM); 11 Max Cook (Repli-Cast Moto3); 12 Eugene McManus (KTM); 13 Lee Hindle (KTM); 14 Tomas de Vries (Honda); 15 Joel Marklund (Honda).
Fastest lap: Nesbitt, 1m 33.143s, 84.25mph/135.60km/h.

Race 2 (12 laps 26.160 miles/42.100km)
1 Charlie Nesbitt (KTM), 18m 54.601s, 83.00mph/133.58km/h.
2 Dani Saez (Honda); 3 Edward Rendell (Ten Kate Honda); 4 Jake Archer (KTM FTR); 5 Jorel Boerboom (Kalex KTM); 6 Edmund Best (KTM); 7 Elliot Lodge (Honda); 8 Eugene McManus (KTM); 9 Max Cook (Repli-Cast Moto3); 10 Tomas de Vries (Honda); 11 Dan Jones (Honda); 12 Joel Marklund (Honda); 13 Sam Llewellyn (Honda); 14 Asher Durham (Honda); 15 Tasia Rodink (Honda).
Fastest lap: Nesbitt, 1m 33.536s, 83.90mph/135.03km/h.
Championship points: 1 Nesbitt, 330; 2 Archer, 204; 3 Rendell, 172; 4 Saez, 156; 5 Owens, 143; 6 Lodge, 133.

OULTON PARK, 11 September 2016, 2.692-mile/4.332km circuit.
MCE British Superbike Championship, Round 9 (3 x 18 laps, 48.456 miles/77.982km)
Race 1
1 Leon Haslam (Kawasaki), 28m 40.371s, 101.39mph/163.17km/h.
2 James Ellison (Kawasaki); 3 Peter Hickman (Kawasaki); 4 Jason O'Halloran (Honda); 5 Dan Linfoot (Honda); 6 Richard Cooper (BMW); 7 Luke Mossey (Kawasaki); 8 Michael Laverty (BMW); 9 Shane Byrne (Ducati); 10 Lee Jackson (BMW); 11 Jake Dixon (BMW); 12 John Hopkins (Yamaha); 13 Danny Buchan (Kawasaki); 14 Broc Parkes (Yamaha); 15 Stuart Easton (Ducati).
Fastest lap: Haslam, 1m 34.564s, 102.48mph/164.93km/h.

Race 2
1 Leon Haslam (Kawasaki), 28m 45.141s, 101.11mph/162.72km/h.
2 James Ellison (Kawasaki); 3 Dan Linfoot (Honda); 4 Jason O'Halloran (Honda); 5 Luke Mossey (Kawasaki); 6 Tommy Bridewell (Suzuki); 7 Peter Hickman (Kawasaki); 8 Jake Dixon (BMW); 9 Glenn Irwin (Ducati); 10 Ryuichi Kiyonari (BMW); 11 Christian Iddon (BMW); 12 Richard Cooper (BMW); 13 Danny Buchan (Kawasaki); 14 Broc Parkes (Yamaha); 15 Alastair Seeley (BMW).
Fastest lap: O'Halloran, 1m 34.941s, 102.07mph/164.27km/h.

Race 3
1 Leon Haslam (Kawasaki), 30m 17.984s, 95.95mph/154.42km/h.
2 Luke Mossey (Kawasaki); 3 Tommy Bridewell (Suzuki); 4 Michael Laverty (BMW); 5 Shane Byrne (Ducati); 6 Richard Cooper (BMW); 7 Peter Hickman (Kawasaki); 8 Lee Jackson (BMW); 9 Christian Iddon (BMW); 10 Broc Parkes (Yamaha); 11 Glenn Irwin (Ducati); 12 Billy McConnell (Kawasaki); 13 Alastair Seeley (BMW); 14 Danny Buchan (Kawasaki); 15 Ryuichi Kiyonari (BMW).
Fastest lap: Iddon, 1m 35.036s, 101.97mph/164.11km/h.

The top six BSB riders in points after Oulton Park qualified for The Showdown, to decide the championship over the last three rounds. These title fighters had their points equalised at 500 and then podium credits added from their main season results (5 points for each 1st place, 3 points for 2nd, 1 point for 3rd).

Championship points for start of Showdown: 1 Leon Haslam, 546; 2 Shane Byrne, 543; 3 Jason O'Halloran, 513; 4 James Ellison, 513; 5 Dan Linfoot, 511; 6 Luke Mossey, 506.

Dickies British Supersport Championship, Round 9
Race 1 (12 laps 32.304 miles/51.988km)
1 Mason Law (Kawasaki), 19m 46.265s, 98.03mph/157.76km/h.
2 Bradley Ray (Yamaha); 3 Tarran Mackenzie (Kawasaki); 4 James Westmoreland (Yamaha); 5 David Allingham (Yamaha); 6 Andrew Irwin (Kawasaki); 7 Joe Francis (Yamaha); 8 Joe Collier (Triumph); 9 Benjamin Currie (Yamaha); 10 Sam Coventry (Kawasaki); 11 Bjorn Estment (Triumph); 12 Jamie Perrin (Yamaha); 13 Luke Hedger (Yamaha); 14 Freddy Pett (Triumph); 15 Sam Wilford (Yamaha).
Fastest lap: Ray, 1m 37.766s, 99.12mph/159.53km/h.

Race 2 (15 laps 40.380 miles/64.985km)
1 Bradley Ray (Yamaha), 24m 43.789s, 97.97mph/157.67km/h.
2 Mason Law (Kawasaki); 3 James Westmoreland (Yamaha); 4 Tarran Mackenzie (Kawasaki); 5 David Allingham (Yamaha); 6 Joe Francis (Yamaha); 7 Andrew Irwin (Kawasaki); 8 Joe Collier (Triumph); 9 Jamie Perrin (Yamaha); 10 Luke Hedger (Yamaha); 11 Bjorn Estment (Triumph); 12 Sam Wilford (Yamaha); 13 Freddy Pett (Triumph); 14 Sam Coventry (Kawasaki); 15 Dean Harrison (Kawasaki).
Fastest lap: Ray, 1m 38.254s, 98.63mph/158.73km/h.
Championship points: 1 Westmoreland, 254; 2 Mackenzie, 251; 3 Ray, 209; 4 Reid, 180; 5 Law, 177; 6 Allingham, 164.

HEL British Motostar Championship, Round 9 (12 laps 32.304 miles/51.988km)
1 Charlie Nesbitt (KTM), 21m 12.759s, 91.37mph/147.05km/h.
2 Josh Owens (Kalex KTM); 3 Dani Saez (KTM); 4 Edmund Best (KTM); 5 Jake Archer (KTM FTR); 6 Eugene McManus (KTM); 7 Jorel Boerboom (Kalex KTM); 8 Elliot Lodge (Honda); 9 Richard Kerr (KTM); 10 Max Cook (Repli-Cast Moto3); 11 Mike Brouwers (Husqvarna); 12 Lee Hindle (KTM); 13 Mark Clayton (Honda); 14 Dan Jones (Honda); 15 Asher Durham (Honda).
Fastest lap: Saez, 1m 44.611s, 92.64mph/149.09km/h.
Championship points: 1 Nesbitt, 355; 2 Archer, 215; 3 Rendell, 172; 4 Saez, 172; 5 Owens, 163; 6 Lodge, 141.

DONINGTON PARK, 18 September 2016, 2.487-mile/4.002km circuit.
MCE British Superbike Championship, Round 10 (2 x 20 laps, 49.740 miles/80.049km)
Race 1
1 Shane Byrne (Ducati), 29m 52.369s, 99.84mph/160.68km/h.
2 Leon Haslam (Kawasaki); 3 Jason O'Halloran (Honda); 4 James Ellison (Kawasaki); 5 Peter Hickman (Kawasaki); 6 Richard Cooper (BMW); 7 Dan Linfoot (Honda); 8 Christian Iddon (BMW); 9 John Hopkins (Yamaha); 10 Michael Laverty (BMW); 11 Jakub Smrz (BMW); 12 Lee Jackson (BMW); 13 Glenn Irwin (Ducati); 14 Josh Hook (Kawasaki); 15 Vittorio Iannuzzo (Kawasaki).
Fastest lap: Byrne, 1m 29.136s, 100.45mph/161.67km/h.

Race 2
1 Shane Byrne (Ducati), 29m 56.112s, 99.63mph/160.34km/h.
2 Dan Linfoot (Honda); 3 Christian Iddon (BMW); 4 Peter Hickman (Kawasaki); 5 Richard Cooper (BMW); 6 Tommy Bridewell (Suzuki); 7 James Ellison (Kawasaki); 8 Luke Mossey (Kawasaki); 9 Billy McConnell (Kawasaki); 10 Glenn Irwin (Ducati); 11 Lee Jackson (BMW); 12 Jakub Smrz (BMW); 13 Michael Laverty (BMW); 14 Stuart Easton (Ducati); 15 Vittorio Iannuzzo (Kawasaki).
Fastest lap: Byrne, 1m 28.896s, 100.72mph/162.10km/h.
Championship points: 1 Shane Byrne, 593; 2 Leon Haslam, 566; 3 Dan Linfoot, 540; 4 James Ellison, 535; 5 Jason O'Halloran, 529; 6 Luke Mossey, 514.

Dickies British Supersport Championship, Round 10
Race 1 (10 laps 24.870 miles/40.024km)
1 Bradley Ray (Yamaha), 15m 29.110s, 96.22mph/154.85km/h.
2 Tarran Mackenzie (Kawasaki); 3 Mason Law (Kawasaki); 4 James Westmoreland (Yamaha); 5 David Allingham (Yamaha); 6 Andrew Irwin (Kawasaki); 7 Luke Jones (Triumph); 8 Luke Hedger (Yamaha); 9 Joe Collier (Triumph); 10 Sam Coventry (Kawasaki); 11 Freddy Pett (Triumph); 12 Jamie Perrin (Yamaha); 13 Sam Wilford (Yamaha); 14 Tommy Philp (Yamaha); 15 Dean Harrison (Kawasaki).
Fastest lap: Westmoreland, 1m 31.688s, 97.66mph/157.17km/h.

Race 2 (18 laps 44.766 miles/72.044km)
1 Bradley Ray (Yamaha), 27m 50.319s, 96.41mph/155.16km/h.
2 Tarran Mackenzie (Kawasaki); 3 James Westmoreland (Yamaha); 4 David Allingham (Yamaha); 5 Joe Francis (Yamaha); 6 Luke Jones (Triumph); 7 Benjamin Currie (Yamaha); 8 Luke Hedger (Yamaha); 9 Sam Wilford (Yamaha); 10 Freddy Pett (Triumph); 11 Joe Collier (Triumph); 12 Andrew Irwin (Kawasaki); 13 Jamie Perrin (Yamaha); 14 Sam Coventry (Kawasaki); 15 Dean Harrison (Kawasaki).
Fastest lap: Ray, 1m 32.017s, 97.31mph/156.61km/h.
Championship points: 1 Mackenzie, 291; 2 Westmoreland, 283; 3 Ray, 259; 4 Law, 193; 5 Allingham, 188; 6 Reid, 180.

HEL British Motostar Championship, Round 10
Race 1 (10 laps 24.870 miles/40.024km)
1 Charlie Nesbitt (KTM), 16m 50.860s, 88.44mph/142.33km/h.
2 Dani Saez (KTM); 3 Richard Kerr (KTM); 4 Jake Archer (KTM FTR); 5 Jorel Boerboom (Kalex KTM); 6 Lee Hindle (KTM); 7 Tom Booth-Amos (Tigcraft); 8 Edmund Best (KTM); 9 Elliot Lodge (Honda); 10 Josh Owens (Kalex KTM); 11 Dan Jones (Honda); 12 Mark Clayton (Honda); 13 Asher Durham (Honda); 14 Shane Faber (Honda); 15 TJ Toms (Honda).
Fastest lap: Nesbitt, 1m 37.861s, 91.50mph/147.25km/h.

Race 2 (14 laps 34.818 miles/56.034km)
1 Charlie Nesbitt (KTM), 23m 0.278s, 90.72mph/146km/h.
2 Dani Saez (KTM); 3 Jake Archer (KTM FTR); 4 Jorel Boerboom (Kalex KTM); 5 Max Cook (Repli-Cast Moto3); 6 Elliot Lodge (Honda); 7 Dan Jones (Honda); 8 Asher Durham (Honda); 9 Eugene McManus (KTM); 10 Mark Clayton (Honda); 11 Storm Stacey (Honda); 12 TJ Toms (Honda); 13 Tomas de Vries (Honda); 14 Shane Faber (Honda); 15 Thomas Strudwick (Honda).
Fastest lap: Nesbitt, 1m 37.667s, 91.68mph/147.55km/h.
Championship points: 1 Nesbitt, 405; 2 Archer, 244; 3 Saez, 212; 4 Rendell, 172; 5 Owens, 169; 6 Lodge, 158.
ASSEN, 2 October 2016, 2.822-mile/4.452km circuit.
MCE British Superbike Championship, Round 11 (2 x 18 laps, 50.796 miles/81.748km)
Race 1
1 Leon Haslam (Kawasaki), 29m 26.102s, 103.55mph/166.65km/h.
2 Shane Byrne (Ducati); 3 James Ellison (Kawasaki); 4 Dan Linfoot (Honda); 5 Jason O'Halloran (Honda); 6 Michael Laverty (BMW); 7 Luke Mossey (Kawasaki); 8 Richard Cooper (BMW); 9 Broc Parkes (Yamaha); 10 John Hopkins (Yamaha); 11 Glenn Irwin (Ducati); 12 Christian Iddon (BMW); 13 Billy McConnell (Kawasaki); 14 Jakub Smrz (BMW); 15 Lee Jackson (BMW).
Fastest lap: O'Halloran, 1m 37.196s, 104.53mph/168.22km/h.

Race 2
1 Leon Haslam (Kawasaki), 29m 33.696s, 103.10mph/165.92km/h.
2 Shane Byrne (Ducati); 3 Jason O'Halloran (Honda); 4 Dan Linfoot (Honda); 5 Luke Mossey (Kawasaki); 6 Michael Laverty (BMW); 7 James Ellison (Kawasaki); 8 Christian Iddon (BMW); 9 Broc Parkes (Yamaha); 10 Richard Cooper (BMW); 11 Jakub Smrz (BMW); 12 Glenn Irwin (Ducati); 13 Lee Jackson (BMW); 14 Peter Hickman (Kawasaki); 15 John Hopkins (Yamaha).
Fastest lap: Byrne, 1m 37.149s, 104.58mph/168.31km/h.
Championship points: 1 Shane Byrne, 633; 2 Leon Haslam, 616; 3 Dan Linfoot, 566; 4 James Ellison, 560; 5 Jason O'Halloran, 556; 6 Luke Mossey, 534.

Dickies British Supersport Championship, Round 11 (2 x 12 laps, 33.864 miles/54.499km)
Race 1
1 Mason Law (Kawasaki), 20m 16.968s, 100.18mph/161.22km/h.
2 David Allingham (Yamaha); 3 Eemeli Lahti (Suzuki); 4 James Westmoreland (Yamaha); 5 Tarran Mackenzie (Kawasaki); 6 Andrew Irwin (Kawasaki); 7 Bradley Ray (Yamaha); 8 Luke Hedger (Yamaha); 9 Scott Deroue (MV Agusta); 10 Bjorn Estment (Triumph); 11 Joe Collier (Triumph); 12 Ross Twyman (Yamaha); 13 Benjamin Currie (Yamaha); 14 Jamie Perrin (Yamaha); 15 Matt Truelove (Yamaha).
Fastest lap: Westmoreland, 1m 40.537s, 101.05mph/162.63km/h.

Race 2
1 Luke Jones (Triumph), 22m 25.233s, 90.63mph/145.85km/h.
2 Joe Francis (Yamaha); 3 Tarran Mackenzie (Kawasaki); 4 Andrew Irwin (Kawasaki); 5 Benjamin Currie (Yamaha); 6 James Westmoreland (Yamaha); 7 David Allingham (Yamaha); 8 Scott Deroue (MV Agusta); 9 Mason Law (Kawasaki); 10 Bjorn Estment (Triumph); 11 Luke Hedger (Yamaha); 12 Joe Collier (Triumph); 13 Sam Coventry (Kawasaki); 14 Dean Harrison (Kawasaki); 15 Ross Twyman (Yamaha).
Fastest lap: Mackenzie, 1m 48.761s, 93.41mph/150.34km/h.
Championship points: 1 Mackenzie, 318; 2 Westmoreland, 306; 3 Ray, 268; 4 Law, 225; 5 Allingham, 217; 6 Jones, 200.

HEL British Motostar Championship, Round 11
Race 1 (9 laps 25.398 miles/40.874km)
1 Dani Saez (KTM), 17m 59.249s, 84.72mph/136.34km/h.
2 Jorel Boerboom (Kalex KTM); 3 Tom Booth-Amos (Tigcraft); 4 Jake Archer (KTM FTR); 5 Edward Rendell (Ten Kate Honda); 6 Brian Slooten (Bakker Honda); 7 Sasha de Vits (Honda); 8 Richard Kerr (KTM); 9 Dirk Geiger (Honda); 10 Jason Dupasquier (KTM); 11 Toni Erhard (Honda); 12 Ernst Dubbink (Honda); 13 Max Cook (Repli-Cast Moto3); 14 Leon Orgis (Honda); 15 Sam Llewellyn (Honda).
Fastest lap: Boerboom, 1m 57.341s, 86.58mph/139.34km/h.

Race 2 (12 laps 33.864 miles/54.499km)
1 Jake Archer (KTM FTR), 21m 34.268s, 94.20mph/151.6km/h.
2 Dani Saez (KTM); 3 Jorel Boerboom (Kalex KTM); 4 Edward Rendell (Ten Kate Honda); 5 Tom Booth-Amos (Tigcraft); 6 Brian Slooten (Bakker Honda); 7 Eugene McManus (KTM); 8 Elliot Lodge (Honda); 9 Mike Brouwers (Husqvarna); 10 Richard Kerr (KTM); 11 Toni Erhard (Honda); 12 Sander Kroeze (Honda); 13 Kevin Orgis (Honda); 14 Jason Dupasquier (KTM); 15

Edmund Best (KTM).
Fastest lap: Archer, 1m 46.604s, 95.30mph/153.38km/h.
Championship points: 1 Nesbitt, 405; **2** Archer, 282; **3** Saez, 257; **4** Rendell, 196; **5** Boerboom, 186; **6** Lodge, 170.

BRANDS HATCH GP, 16 October 2016, 2.433-mile/3.9126km circuit.
MCE British Superbike Championship, Round 12
Race 1 (15 laps 36.495 miles/58.733km)
1 Peter Hickman (Kawasaki), 25m 51.085s, 84.71mph/136.33km/h.
2 Christian Iddon (BMW); **3** Glenn Irwin (Ducati); **4** Dan Linfoot (Honda); **5** Tommy Bridewell (Suzuki); **6** Shane Byrne (Ducati); **7** John Hopkins (Yamaha); **8** Lee Jackson (BMW); **9** Alastair Seeley (BMW); **10** Jakub Smrz (BMW); **11** Michael Laverty (BMW); **12** Billy McConnell (Kawasaki); **13** Luke Mossey (Kawasaki); **14** Ryuichi Kiyonari (BMW); **15** Vittorio Iannuzzo (Kawasaki).
Fastest lap: Iddon, 1m 38.827s, 88.63mph/142.64km/h.

Race 2 (20 laps 48.660 miles/78.311km)
1 James Ellison (Kawasaki), 29m 22.973s, 99.37mph/159.92km/h.
2 John Hopkins (Yamaha); **3** Peter Hickman (Kawasaki); **4** Dan Linfoot (Honda); **5** Leon Haslam (Kawasaki); **6** Shane Byrne (Ducati); **7** Glenn Irwin (Ducati); **8** Tommy Bridewell (Suzuki); **9** Jason O'Halloran (Honda); **10** Luke Mossey (Kawasaki); **11** Jakub Smrz (BMW); **12** Alastair Seeley (BMW); **13** Lee Jackson (BMW); **14** Broc Parkes (Yamaha); **15** Ryuichi Kiyonari (BMW).
Fastest lap: Ellison, 1m 26.722s, 101.01mph/162.56km/h.

Race 3 (10 laps 24.330 miles/39.155km)
1 James Ellison (Kawasaki), 14m 27.589s, 100.96mph/162.48km/h.
2 John Hopkins (Yamaha); **3** Shane Byrne (Ducati); **4** Leon Haslam (Kawasaki); **5** Christian Iddon (BMW); **6** Dan Linfoot (Honda); **7** Ryuichi Kiyonari (BMW); **8** Tommy Bridewell (Suzuki); **9** Luke Mossey (Kawasaki); **10** Broc Parkes (Yamaha); **11** Jason O'Halloran (Honda); **12** Peter Hickman (Kawasaki); **13** Alastair Seeley (BMW); **14** Billy McConnell (Kawasaki); **15** Richard Cooper (BMW).
Fastest lap: Byrne, 1m 25.516s, 102.43mph/164.85km/h.

Dickies British Supersport Championship, Round 12
Race 1 (10 laps 24.330 miles/39.155km)
1 Bradley Ray (Yamaha), 14m 47.534s, 98.69mph/158.83km/h.
2 Tarran Mackenzie (Kawasaki); **3** Joe Francis (Yamaha); **4** David Allingham (Yamaha); **5** James Westmoreland (Yamaha); **6** Luke Jones (Triumph); **7** Sam Wilford (Yamaha); **8** Luke Hedger (Yamaha); **9** Benjamin Currie (Yamaha); **10** Ross Twyman (Yamaha); **11** Joe Collier (Triumph); **12** Andrew Irwin (Kawasaki); **13** Sam Coventry (Kawasaki); **14** Matt Truelove (Yamaha); **15** Jamie Perrin (Yamaha).
Fastestlap: Mackenzie, 1m27.814s, 99.75mph/160.53km/h.

Race 2 (9 laps 21.897 miles/35.24km)
1 Tarran Mackenzie (Kawasaki), 13m 20.132s, 98.53mph/158.57km/h.
2 Bradley Ray (Yamaha); **3** Joe Francis (Yamaha); **4** Benjamin Currie (Yamaha); **5** Sam Wilford (Yamaha); **6** Andrew Irwin (Kawasaki); **7** Luke Hedger (Yamaha); **8** Joe Collier (Triumph); **9** Matt Truelove (Yamaha); **10** Scott Deroue (MV Agusta); **11** Tommy Philp (Yamaha); **12** Freddy Pett (Triumph); **13** Harry Truelove (Yamaha); **14** Bjorn Estment (Triumph); **15** Ryan Dixon (Yamaha).
Fastestlap: Mackenzie, 1m28.151s, 99.37mph/159.92km/h.

HEL British Motostar Championship, Round 12
Race 1 (10 laps 24.330 miles/39.155km)
1 Charlie Nesbitt (KTM), 15m 47.435s, 92.45mph/148.78km/h.
2 Dani Saez (Honda); **3** Jake Archer (KTM); **4** Jorel Boerboom (Kalex KTM); **5** Richard Kerr (KTM); **6** Josh Owens (Kalex KTM); **7** Edward Rendell (Ten Kate Honda); **8** Max Cook (Repli-Cast Moto3); **9** Tom Booth-Amos (Tigcraft); **10** Eugene McManus (KTM); **11** Edmund Best (KTM); **12** Brian Slooten (Bakker Honda); **13** Dan Jones (Honda); **14** Mark Clayton (Honda); **15** Asher Durham (Honda).
Fastest lap: Taylor, 1m 33.077s, 94.11mph/151.46km/h.

Race 2 (12 laps 29.196 miles/46.986km)
1 Taz Taylor (Kalex KTM), 19m 21.289s, 90.51mph/145.66km/h.
2 Jake Archer (KTM FTR); **3** Jorel Boerboom (Kalex KTM); **4** Josh Owens (Kalex KTM); **5** Edward Rendell (Ten Kate Honda); **6** Eugene McManus (KTM); **7** Elliot Lodge (Honda); **8** Lee Hindle (KTM); **9** Brian Slooten (Bakker Honda); **10** Dan Jones (Honda); **11** Victor Rodriguez (Honda); **12** Liam Delves (Honda); **13** Asher Durham (Honda); **14** TJ Toms (Honda); **15** Tomas de Vries (Honda).
Fastest lap: Taylor, 1m 34.838s, 92.36mph/148.64km/h.

Final British Superbike Championship points:

1	Shane Byrne,	669
2	Leon Haslam,	640
3	James Ellison,	610
4	Dan Linfoot,	602
5	Jason O'Halloran,	568
6	Luke Mossey,	550

7 Peter Hickman, 233; **8** Michael Laverty, 202; **9** Christian Iddon, 199; **10** Richard Cooper, 193; **11** Tommy Bridewell, 172; **12** Glenn Irwin, 143; **13** Lee Jackson, 108; **14** John Hopkins, 105; **15** Billy McConnell, 51.

Final British Supersport Championship points:

1	Tarran Mackenzie,	363
2	James Westmoreland,	317
3	Bradley Ray,	313
4	David Allingham,	230
5	Mason Law,	225
6	Luke Jones,	210

7 Joe Francis, 198; **8** Benjamin Currie, 188; **9** Andy Reid, 180; **10** Andrew Irwin, 153; **11** Luke Hedger, 143; **12** Joe Collier, 111; **13** Ross Twyman, 100; **14** Jamie Perrin, 82; **15** Bjorn Estment, 70.

Final British Motostar Moto3 Championship points:

1	Charlie Nesbitt,	430
2	Jake Archer,	318
3	Dani Saez,	277
4	Edward Rendell,	216
5	Jorel Boerboom,	215
6	Josh Owens,	192

7 Elliot Lodge, 179; **8** Tom Booth-Amos, 164; **9** Max Cook, 129; **10** Edmund Best, 128; **11** Richard Kerr, 120; **12** Brian Slooten, 106; **13** Eugene McManus, 102; **14** Mike Brouwers, 96; **15** Tomas de Vries, 67.

Supersport World Championship

PHILLIP ISLAND, Australia, 28 February 2016, 2.762-mile/4.445km circuit.
Supersport World Championship, Round 1 (18 laps, 49.716 miles/80.010km)
1 Randy Krummenacher, SWI (Kawasaki), 28m 34.745s, 104.375mph/167.976km/h.
2 Federico Caricasulo, ITA (Honda); **3** Anthony West, AUS (Yamaha); **4** Christian Gamarino, ITA (Kawasaki); **5** Patrick Jacobsen, USA (Honda); **6** Alex Baldolini, ITA (MV Agusta); **7** Gino Rea, GBR (MV Agusta); **8** Ondrej Jezek, CZE (Kawasaki); **9** Roberto Rolfo, ITA (MV Agusta); **10** Aiden Wagner, AUS (MV Agusta); **11** Nico Terol, ESP (MV Agusta); **12** Glenn Scott, AUS (Honda); **13** Zulfahmi Khairuddin, MAS (Kawasaki); **14** Alex Phillis, AUS (Honda); **15** Mitch Levy, AUS (Yamaha).
Fastest lap: Lorenzo Zanetti, ITA (MV Agusta), 1m 34.152s, 105.608mph/169.959km/h.
Championship points: 1 Krummenacher, 25; **2** Caricasulo, 20; **3** West, 16; **4** Gamarino, 13; **5** Jacobsen, 11; **6** Baldolini, 10.

BURIRAM, Thailand, 13 March 2016, 2.830-mile/4.554km circuit.
Supersport World Championship, Round 2 (17 laps, 48.105 miles/77.418km)
1 Jules Cluzel, FRA (MV Agusta), 28m 9.359s, 102.512mph/164.977km/h.
2 Kenan Sofuoglu, TUR (Kawasaki); **3** Patrick Jacobsen, USA (Honda); **4** Randy Krummenacher, SWI (Kawasaki); **5** Kyle Smith, GBR (Honda); **6** Alex Baldolini, ITA (MV Agusta); **7** Zulfahmi Khairuddin, MAS (Kawasaki); **8** Lorenzo Zanetti, ITA (MV Agusta); **9** Gino Rea, GBR (MV Agusta); **10** Ondrej Jezek, CZE (Kawasaki); **11** Decha Kraisart, THA (Yamaha); **12** Kevin Wahr, GER (Honda); **13** Glenn Scott, AUS (Honda); **14** Luke Stapleford, GBR (Honda); **15** Aiden Wagner, AUS (MV Agusta).
Fastest lap: Kyle Smith, GBR (Honda), 1m 38.618s, 103.297mph/166.241km/h.
Championship points: 1 Krummenacher, 38; **2** Jacobsen, 27; **3** Cluzel, 25; **4** Sofuoglu, 20; **5** Caricasulo, 20; **6** Baldolini, 20.

ARAGON, Spain, 3 April 2016, 3.155-mile/5.077km circuit.
Supersport World Championship, Round 3 (16 laps, 50.475 miles/81.232km)
1 Kenan Sofuoglu, TUR (Kawasaki), 30m 58.615s, 97.767mph/157.340km/h.
2 Randy Krummenacher, SUI (Kawasaki); **3** Nico Terol, ESP (MV Agusta); **4** Jules Cluzel, FRA (MV Agusta); **5** Alessandro Zaccone, ITA (Kawasaki); **6** Axel Bassani, ITA (Kawasaki); **7** Federico Caricasulo, ITA (Honda); **8** Zulfahmi Khairuddin, MAS (Kawasaki); **9** Kevin Wahr, GER (Honda); **10** Christian Gamarino, ITA (Kawasaki); **11** Kyle Smith, GBR (Honda); **12** Kyle Ryde, GBR (Yamaha); **13** Ilya Mykhalchyk, UKR (Kawasaki); **14** Ondrej Jezek, CZE (Kawasaki); **15** Nacho Calero, ESP (Kawasaki).
Fastest lap: Kenan Sofuoglu, TUR (Kawasaki), 1m 55.344s, 98.461mph/158.458km/h.
Championship points: 1 Krummenacher, 58; **2** Sofuoglu, 45; **3** Cluzel, 38; **4** Caricasulo, 29; **5** Jacobsen, 27; **6** Terol, 21.

ASSEN, Holland, 17 April 2016, 2.822-mile/4.542km circuit.
Supersport World Championship, Round 4 (6 laps, 16.934 miles/27.252km)
1 Kyle Smith, GBR (Honda), 12m 17.543s, 82.654mph/133.019km/h.
2 Gino Rea, GBR (MV Agusta); **3** Kenan Sofuoglu, TUR (Kawasaki); **4** Randy Krummenacher, SUI (Kawasaki); **5** Alex Baldolini, ITA (MV Agusta); **6** Ilya Mykhalchyk, UKR (Kawasaki); **7** Ayrton Badovini, ITA (Honda); **8** Axel Bassani, ITA (Kawasaki); **9** Ondrej Jezek, CZE (Kawasaki); **10** Christian Gamarino, ITA (Kawasaki); **11** Federico Caricasulo, ITA (Honda); **12** Luke Stapleford, GBR (Triumph); **13** Nico Terol, ESP (MV Agusta); **14** Kyle Ryde, GBR (Yamaha); **15** Cedric Tangre, FRA (Suzuki).
Fastest lap: Kyle Smith, GBR (Honda), 1m 58.225s, 85.939mph/138.306km/h.
Championship points: 1 Krummenacher, 71; **2** Sofuoglu, 61; **3** Smith, 41; **4** Cluzel, 38; **5** Rea, 36; **6** Caricasulo, 34.

IMOLA, Italy, 1 May 2016, 3.067-mile/4.936km circuit.
Supersport World Championship, Round 5 (11 laps, 33.738 miles/54.296km)
1 Kenan Sofuoglu, TUR (Kawasaki), 20m 37.091s, 98.179mph/158.004km/h.
2 Jules Cluzel, FRA (MV Agusta); **3** Patrick Jacobsen, USA (Honda); **4** Alex Baldolini, ITA (MV Agusta); **5** Alessandro Zaccone, ITA (Kawasaki); **6** Ondrej Jezek, CZE (Kawasaki); **7** Federico Caricasulo, ITA (Honda); **8** Ayrton Badovini, ITA (Honda); **9** Nico Terol, ESP (MV Agusta); **10** Kyle Smith, GBR (Honda); **11** Kevin Wahr, GER (Honda); **12** Ilya Mykhalchyk, UKR (Kawasaki); **13** Axel Bassani, ITA (Kawasaki); **14** Roberto Rolfo, ITA (MV Agusta); **15** Kyle Ryde, GBR (Yamaha).
Fastest lap: Jules Cluzel, FRA (MV Agusta), 1m 51.966s, 98.615mph/158.705km/h.
Championship points: 1 Sofuoglu, 86; **2** Krummenacher, 71; **3** Cluzel, 58; **4** Smith, 46; **5** Baldolini, 44; **6** Jacobsen, 43.

SEPANG, Malaysia, 15 May 2016, 3.447-mile/5.543km circuit.
Supersport World Championship, Round 6 (14 laps, 48.220 miles/77.602km)
1 Ayrton Badovini, ITA (Honda), 33m 22.944s, 86.668mph/139.478km/h.
2 Zulfahmi Khairuddin, MAS (Kawasaki); **3** Gino Rea, GBR (MV Agusta); **4** Patrick Jacobsen, USA (Honda); **5** Kyle Smith, GBR (Honda); **6** Kenan Sofuoglu, TUR (Kawasaki); **7** Jules Cluzel, FRA (MV Agusta); **8** Randy Krummenacher, SUI (Kawasaki); **9** Alex Baldolini, ITA (MV Agusta); **10** Federico Caricasulo, ITA (Honda); **11** Christian Gamarino, ITA (Kawasaki); **12** Roberto Rolfo, ITA (MV Agusta); **13** Lorenzo Zanetti, ITA (MV Agusta); **14** Luke Stapleford, GBR (Triumph); **15** Hikari Okubo, JPN (Honda).
Fastest lap: Patrick Jacobsen, USA (Honda), 2m 21.142s, 87.850mph/141.381km/h.
Championship points: 1 Sofuoglu, 96; **2** Krummenacher, 79; **3** Cluzel, 67; **4** Smith, 57; **5** Jacobsen, 56; **6** Rea, 52.

DONINGTON PARK, Great Britain, 29 May 2016, 2.500-mile/4.023km circuit.
Supersport World Championship, Round 7 (20 laps, 49.996 miles/80.460km)
1 Kenan Sofuoglu, TUR (Kawasaki), 30m 29.814s, 98.362mph/158.298km/h.
2 Patrick Jacobsen, USA (Honda); **3** Randy Krummenacher, SUI (Kawasaki); **4** Gino Rea, GBR (MV Agusta); **5** Luke Stapleford, GBR (Triumph); **6** Kyle Smith, GBR (Honda); **7** Alex Baldolini, ITA (MV Agusta); **8** Jules Cluzel, FRA (MV Agusta); **9** Ayrton Badovini, ITA (Honda); **10** Lorenzo Zanetti, ITA (MV Agusta); **11** Federico Caricasulo, ITA (Honda); **12** Alessandro Zaccone, ITA (Kawasaki); **13** Ilya Mykhalchyk, UKR (Kawasaki); **14** Roberto Rolfo, ITA (MV Agusta); **15** Hikari Okubo, JPN (Honda).
Fastest lap: Kyle Smith, GBR (Honda), 1m 30.887s, 99.015mph/159.350km/h.
Championship points: 1 Sofuoglu, 121; **2** Krummenacher, 95; **3** Jacobsen, 76; **4** Cluzel, 75; **5** Smith, 68; **6** Rea, 65.

MISANO, Italy, 19 June 2016, 2.626-mile/4.226km circuit.
Supersport World Championship, Round 8 (19 laps, 49.892 miles/80.294km)
1 Kenan Sofuoglu, TUR (Kawasaki), 31m 35.005s, 94.782mph/152.537km/h.
2 Patrick Jacobsen, USA (Honda); **3** Gino Rea, GBR (MV Agusta); **4** Randy Krummenacher, SUI (Kawasaki); **5** Lorenzo Zanetti, ITA (MV Agusta); **6** Alex Baldolini, ITA (MV Agusta); **7** Axel Bassani, ITA (Kawasaki); **8** Luke Stapleford, GBR (Triumph); **9** Christoffer Bergman, SWE (Honda); **10** Davide Stirpe, ITA (Kawasaki); **11** Hikari Okubo, JPN (Honda); **12** Kevin Manfredi, ITA (Suzuki); **13** Luigi Morciano, ITA (Kawasaki); **14** Aiden Wagner, AUS (MV Agusta), **15** Kevin Wahr, GER (Honda).
Fastest lap: Kenan Sofuoglu, TUR (Kawasaki), 1m 39.056s, 95.434mph/153.586km/h.
Championship points: 1 Sofuoglu, 146; **2** Krummenacher, 108; **3** Jacobsen, 96; **4** Rea, 81; **5** Cluzel, 75; **6** Baldolini, 70.

LAUSITZRING, Germany, 18 September 2016, 2.644-mile/4.255km circuit.
Supersport World Championship, Round 9 (19 laps, 50.353 miles/81.035km)
1 Kenan Sofuoglu, TUR (Kawasaki), 32m 18.677s, 93.502mph/150.477km/h.
2 Niki Tuuli, FIN (Yamaha); **3** Jules Cluzel, FRA (MV Agusta); **4** Patrick Jacobsen, USA (Honda); **5** Federico Caricasulo, ITA (Honda); **6** Randy Krummenacher, SUI (Kawasaki); **7** Lorenzo Zanetti, ITA (MV Agusta); **8** Christoffer Bergman, SWE (Honda); **9** Kyle Smith, GBR (Honda); **10** Hikari Okubo, JPN (Honda); **11** Luke Stapleford, GBR (Triumph); **12** Alex Baldolini, ITA (MV Agusta); **13** Ayrton Badovini, ITA (Honda); **14** Ilya Mykhalchyk, UKR (Kawasaki); **15** Axel Bassani, ITA (Kawasaki).
Fastest lap: Niki Tuuli, FIN (Yamaha), 1m 41.035s, 94.428mph/151.967km/h (record).
Championship points: 1 Sofuoglu, 171; **2** Krummenacher, 118; **3** Jacobsen, 109; **4** Cluzel, 91; **5** Rea, 81; **6** Smith, 75.

MAGNY-COURS, France, 2 October 2016, 2.741-mile/4.411km circuit.
Supersport World Championship, Round 10 (19 laps, 52.076 miles/83.809km)
1 Jules Cluzel, FRA (MV Agusta), 32m 31.738s, 96.056mph/154.587km/h.
2 Niki Tuuli, FIN (Yamaha); **3** Ayrton Badovini, ITA (Honda); **4** Axel Bassani, ITA (Kawasaki); **5** Randy Krummenacher, SUI (Kawasaki); **6** Federico Caricasulo, ITA (Honda); **7** Kyle Smith, GBR (Honda); **8** Illia Mykhalchyk, UKR (Kawasaki); **9** Lorenzo Zanetti, ITA (MV Agusta); **10** Zulfahmi Khairuddin, MAS (Kawasaki); **11** Kyle Ryde, GBR (Kawasaki); **12** Hannes Soomer, EST (Yamaha); **13** Ondrej Jezek, CZE (Kawasaki); **14** Xavier Pinsach, ESP (Honda); **15** Luke Stapleford, GBR (Triumph).
Fastest lap: Niki Tuuli, FIN (Yamaha), 1m 42.095s, 96.646mph/155.537km/h.
Championship points: 1 Sofuoglu, 171; **2** Krummenacher, 129; **3** Cluzel, 116; **4** Jacobsen, 109; **5** Smith, 84; **6** Rea, 81.

JEREZ, Spain, 16 October 2016, 2.748-mile/4.423km circuit.
Supersport World Championship, Round 11 (19 laps, 52.218 miles/84.037km)
1 Kenan Sofuoglu, TUR (Kawasaki), 33m 22.362s, 93.882mph/151.088km/h.
2 Niki Tuuli, FIN (Yamaha); **3** Kyle Smith, GBR (Honda); **4** Patrick Jacobsen, USA (Honda); **5** Axel Bassani, ITA (Kawasaki); **6** Jules Cluzel, FRA (MV Agusta); **7** Illia Mykhalchyk, UKR (Kawasaki); **8** Ayrton Badovini, ITA (Honda); **9** Christoffer Bergman, SWE (Honda); **10** Lorenzo Zanetti, ITA (MV Agusta); **11** Alessandro Zaccone, ITA (Kawasaki); **12** Xavier Pinsach, ESP (Honda); **13** Hikari Okubo, JPN (Honda); **14** Luke Stapleford, GBR (Triumph); **15** Zulfahmi Khairuddin, MAS (Kawasaki).
Fastest lap: Niki Tuuli, FIN (Yamaha), 1m 44.355s, 94.811mph/152.583km.
Championship points: 1 Sofuoglu, 196; **2** Krummenacher, 129; **3** Cluzel, 126; **4** Jacobsen, 122; **5** Smith, 100; **6** Rea, 81.

LOSAIL, Qatar, 30 October 2016, 3.343-mile/5.380km circuit.
Supersport World Championship, Round 12 (15 laps, 50.145 miles/80.700km)
1 Kyle Smith, GBR (Honda), 30m 51.533s, 97.498mph/156.908km/h.
2 Kenan Sofuoglu, TUR (Kawasaki); **3** Jules Cluzel, FRA (MV Agusta); **4** Patrick Jacobsen, USA (Honda); **5** Randy Krummenacher, SUI (Kawasaki); **6** Ayrton Badovini, ITA (Honda); **7** Zulfahmi Khairuddin, MAS (Kawasaki); **8** Christoffer Bergman, SWE (Honda); **9** Massimo Roccoli, ITA (MV Agusta); **10** Alex Baldolini, ITA (MV Agusta); **11** Ondrej Jezek, CZE (Kawasaki); **12** Loris Cresson, BEL (Yamaha); **13** Hikari Okubo, JPN (Honda); **14** Kyle Ryde, GBR (Kawasaki); **15** Lachlan Epis, AUS (Kawasaki).
Fastest lap: Kyle Smith, GBR (Honda), 2m 2.443s, 98.288mph/158.180km/h.

Final World Supersport Championship points:

1	Kenan Sofuoglu, TUR,	216
2	Jules Cluzel, FRA,	142
3	Randy Krummenacher, SUI,	140
4	Patrick Jacobsen, USA,	135
5	Kyle Smith, GBR,	125
6	Ayrton Badovini, ITA,	86

7 Gino Rea, GBR, 81; **8** Alex Baldolini, ITA, 80; **9** Federico Caricasulo, ITA, 75; **10** Niki Tuuli, FIN, 60; **11** Zulfahmi Khairuddin, MAS, 56; **12** Axel Bassani, ITA, 55; **13** Lorenzo Zanetti, ITA, 50; **14** Ondrej Jezek, CZE, 41; **15** Illia Mykhalchyk, UKR, 39.